Literacy's Beginnings

Supporting Young Readers and Writers

Lea M. McGee
Boston College

Donald J. Richgels
Northern Illinois University

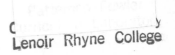
Allyn and Bacon   BOSTON   LONDON   SYDNEY   TORONTO

To Richard and Kristen,
and to Mary, Ted, and Carrie

Copyright © 1990 by Allyn and Bacon
A Division of Simon & Schuster, Inc.
160 Gould Street
Needham Heights, MA 02194

Series Editor: Sean W. Wakely
Manufacturing Buyer: Tamara McCracken
Cover Administrator: Linda K. Dickinson
Cover Designer: Susan Slovinsky
Text Designer: Deborah Schneck
Editorial Production Service: Kathy Smith

Library of Congress Cataloging-in-Publication Data

McGee, Lea M.
    Literacy's beginnings: supporting young readers and writers / Lea
M. McGee, Donald J. Richgels.
        p.   cm.
    Bibliography: p.
    Includes index.
    ISBN 0–205–12045–8
    1. Reading—United States.   2. Language arts—United States.
I. Richgels, Donald J.   II. Title.
LB1050.M378   1989
372.4′0973—dc20   89–6943
                                                         CIP

Printed in the United States of America

10 9 8 7 6 5 4 3 2 1   94 93 92 91 90 89

Contents

Preface

POINT OF VIEW

Literacy's Beginnings: Supporting Young Readers and Writers is intended to help preservice and inservice teachers, parents, and other care givers of young children to be aware of and supportive of children's literacy knowledge as it grows and changes in the years from birth through early elementary school. Our purpose is to provide a guide to the long continuum of literacy growth, from the very beginning years when children's reading and writing efforts are difficult to recognize through the early elementary school years when children begin to receive formal literacy instruction.

We believe that children's literacy learning is developmental, but not in the sense of proceeding in an irreversible, step-by-step progression. No child's discoveries about and experiments with literacy exactly match those of another child. Furthermore, an individual child's literacy behaviors vary in sophistication depending on the task and the situation.

Literacy learning is developmental in a very commonsensical way that makes sense to anyone who has spent time writing and reading with children. Literacy learning is developmental in the sense that what an individual child knows about writing and reading changes dramatically over time. Not only do young children's constructions of literacy differ from those of adults, but children's present constructions also differ from their own former and future constructions.

We believe that teachers have an important role to play in young children's literacy learning. The subtitle of our book emphasizes the supportive nature of that role. We hope that our descriptions of literacy events involving young children and our suggestions for classroom support will help teachers to be aware of the directions in which children's literacy knowledge can move over the period covered by this book. Such awareness can make easier one of the most difficult tasks in teaching: the close observation of many different children. From a basis of careful observation, teachers can respect what children know and support children's continued learning in ways that make sense to the children.

ORGANIZATION OF THE TEXT

We have presented literacy learning in five parts. The first part provides an overview and important background information. Chapter 1 describes *what* it is that children learn as they become literate. Chapter 2 tells *how* children learn written language. Chapter 3 describes ways in which teachers can organize classrooms and plan activities that support children's literacy learning. The ideas introduced in Part 1 are applied throughout the rest of the text.

The next three parts describe literacy learning in terms of first steps (Part 2), transitions (Part 3), and accomplishments (Part 4). Each part describes a cluster of literacy knowledges which is followed by extensive descriptions of classroom supports for children who exhibit those knowledges. We have called children who usually exhibit those clusters of knowledges by four names: *beginners, novices, experimenters,* and *accomplished readers and writers*. We use these names as a shorthand way of referring to complex concepts. These terms and a term even more essential to our topic, *literacy,* have everyday connotations which are not necessarily what we intend when we use those terms.

To us, being *literate* means being able to find meaning in written symbols. This definition includes much territory left out by everyday definitions of literacy; for example, a pretend reading of a favorite storybook qualifies as a literate act by our definition, but does not usually qualify under the everyday definition. Still, our definition does not include everything that very young children do with books and writing materials. We use the two names *beginners* and *novices* in order to distinguish between the general meaning making in literacy events by children we call beginners and the more focused meaning making involving printed symbols by children we call novices.

Because we wanted to begin at the beginning, we include in Chapter 4 what infants do with books and writing materials. Infants have meaningful experiences with books and writing materials, but they do not find meaning in printed symbols themselves, and they do not make written marks with the intentions of communicating particular messages. Chapter 5 explains how children we call novices, though far from being literate by everyday standards, are literate by our definition. Novices do find meaning in the print symbols on signs and in books, and they do intend messages with their writing. Chapter 6 illustrates classroom activities that support novices.

In Part 3, Chapter 7 describes a cluster of knowledges that typify experimenters, and Chapter 8 describes classroom support for experimenters. We use the term *experimenters* to capture the added awareness and intensity of involvement with written language that these children exhibit.

In Part 4, Chapter 9 decribes what accomplished readers and writers know about written language. We use the term *accomplished* only to emphasize that what these children do when they read and write appears more accomplished than the reading and writing behavior of children described in earlier parts. Chapters 10 and 11 describe what teachers in elementary schools can do to support accomplished readers and writers.

Although Parts 2, 3, and 4 use the terms *beginners, novices, experimenters,* and *accomplished readers and writers,* we emphasize our earlier point about development. These descriptive terms are not meant to define rigid, irreversible stages. Indeed, we do not call them stages. A child may exhibit many of the knowledges in the cluster of knowledges we associate with one of those four terms. For example, he or she may usually read or write like a novice, but in some situations and with some tasks, that child will also read or write like an experimenter. The important point is that over time, children will more often resemble the accomplished readers and writers in the Part 4 examples than the beginning readers and writers in the Part 2 examples. Over time they gain a richer developmental repertoire of literacy knowledge and strategies.

Part 5 consists of Chapter 12. It describes the literacy needs of special populations including children with developmental or learning differences, children with language differences, and children with cultural differences. Techniques for supporting these children are described.

Each chapter in *Literacy's Beginnings* ends with three sections designed to help readers consolidate and apply what they have learned. "Applying the Information" presents a case study of children's interactions with written language similar to the many examples given in the chapter. The reader is asked to apply the chapter's concepts to this example. "Going Beyond the Text" suggests ways readers can seek out real-life experiences that will test both the chapter's ideas and readers' understandings. We ask questions and make suggestions to guide readers' planning and reflecting on those experiences. "References" provides a list of all publications that were cited in the chapter.

THE CHILDREN AND TEACHERS IN THIS BOOK

Literacy's Beginnings is based in part on a growing body of research about emerging literacy, and in part on our experiences with young children, including our own children. We include many descriptions of those experiences. We wish to include here two important cautions that we will repeat throughout the text. The first is about children's ages. We usually give the age of the children in our examples in order to fully represent the facts. However, we do not intend for those ages to serve as norms against which to compare other children

Our second caution is about backgrounds. Many, but not all, of the children in our examples have had numerous and varied home experiences with books and writing materials. Their meaningful interactions with written language are often what one would expect of children from such environments. Children with different backgrounds may exhibit different initial orientations toward written language. However, our involvement with teachers whose children come to preschool or elementary school with different backgrounds has shown us that nearly all children can benefit from the informed observation and child-centered, meaning-oriented support described in this book.

The classroom support chapters of this book are based on our own teaching experiences and on our observations of teachers. Just as we have known and observed many literate young children, so also have we known and observed many very sensitive, intelligent, and effective teachers of young children. When our classroom descriptions are composites, we introduce them either by asking the reader to imagine a situation or by telling the reader that we will call the teacher by a fictitious name. All the samples of children's reading and writing in this book are authentic cases from our own research and the research of others cited in the text.

ACKNOWLEDGMENTS

We owe a great deal to the many children whose experiences with written language were the basis for much of this book. We thank them and their parents for cooperating so generously with us—for supporting *us* in the extended "literacy event" of writing this book. We thank the teachers who shared their classroom experiences with us: Mary Jane Everett, Phyllis Horton, Candice Jones, Karen Kurr, Roberta McHardy, Nancy Miller, Terry Morel, Lynn Morrison, Lois Rector, Kathy Tonore, Mike Tunnell, and Kathy Walker.

We owe much to our editors at Allyn and Bacon. We thank Susanne Canavan, who began this project with us, and Sean Wakely, who guided it to its conclusion. We owe special thanks to our copyeditor, Kathy Smith, for her thoughtful suggestions. We also thank many reviewers for their helpful comments and suggestions: Jean Ann Clyde of the University of Louisville, MaryAnne Hall of Georgia State University, Victoria Chou Hare of the University of Illinois, Christine M. L. Roberts of The University of Connecticut, Eileen Tway of Miami University, Oxford, Ohio, and Donna L. Wiseman of Texas A&M University.

We acknowledge the contributions of our many students. We learned from our discussions with them about literacy's beginnings and from the examples they shared of their interactions with young readers and writers. We are particularly grateful to Sue Hernandez, who compiled the literature lists in Chapters 3 and 11.

Understanding Literacy Learning

Part 1 sets the stage for studying young children's literacy learning. We will explore children's reading and writing from the preschool years through the first few years in elementary school. Chapter 1, "What Young Children Learn about Literacy," describes what children in their early childhood years (infancy through eight years old) are learning about literacy. Chapter 2, "How Young Children Learn about Literacy," discusses theories of learning that help explain how children learn language, especially written language. It includes some strategies children seem to use to teach themselves about written language. Chapter 3, "Literacy-Rich Classrooms," describes characteristics and conditions of literate preschool and elementary classroom environments in which children are supported in their reading and writing learning. The three chapters included in Part 1 provide the theoretical foundations for the remainder of the text.

What Young Children Learn about Literacy

Chapter 1 begins with a description of two children, Ted and Carrie, as they play together with their father. They write, read, draw, talk, and use dramatic play. We will pose the question: What do Ted and Carrie know about reading and writing?

This question will be answered from two perspectives. The first perspective used to examine Ted's and Carrie's knowledge of reading and writing might be called the *traditional perspective*. The traditional perspective has been well respected in education for the past several decades. Many of the ideas from the traditional perspective can still be observed in current reading and writing instructional practices in schools; thus it is important to know about it.

Educators and other researchers have more recently begun to look anew at young children and literacy. The next portion of the chapter deals with the second perspective on literacy and young children, which is called the *psycho-sociolinguistic perspective*. We will reexamine what Ted and Carrie know about reading and writing from this new perspective.

The last portion of the chapter uses the psycho-sociolinguistic perspective to examine in more detail what children learn about literacy and written language. We will describe children's knowledge of four aspects of written language. (1) Children learn *meanings* that are communicated in written language. (2) Children learn the *forms* of written language. (3) Children learn *relationships* between meanings that are communicated in written language and the forms of written language. (4) Finally, children learn *functions* that written language serves.

TED'S DELIGHT: TWO CHILDREN READING
AND WRITING

Ted, who is eight years old, and his sister Carrie, who is three years old, were playing in the corner of the living room. They had set up their card table playhouse. Taped on the playhouse was the sign shown in Figure 1.1.

Figure 1.1 *"Ted's Delight" Sign*

Ted and Carrie had collected Carrie's plastic play food and doll dishes and put them behind the playhouse. When their father entered the room, he looked at the sign and said, "Oh, I think I need some lunch." The children asked him to visit their restaurant. He entered the playhouse and Carrie presented him with a menu (Figure 1.2).

Carrie asked, "May I take your order?" Her father read the menu and said, "I'll take pancakes and coffee." Carrie checked off two items on the menu and took it out to Ted, who was behind the playhouse. He pretended to fix pancakes and pour coffee. Ted brought the dishes into the playhouse to his father, who pretended to eat with much relish. When he finished he asked, "May I have my check, please?" Carrie picked up a pad of paper and a pencil and wrote a check (Figure 1.3). Her father pretended to pay the check and left the playhouse.

Later that evening, the family discussed the restaurant play. Ted said he had made the sign so the playhouse could be a restaurant. He had asked Carrie if he could use her toy food and dishes. She had wanted to play, too. Ted said he and Carrie decided to write on the menu the names of the play food they had. In the middle of his writing the menu, Carrie insisted on helping him. "She wrote the letter that looks like a backwards *J* in the middle of the menu," Ted reported. "I had to turn it into the word *Enjoy* to make sense."

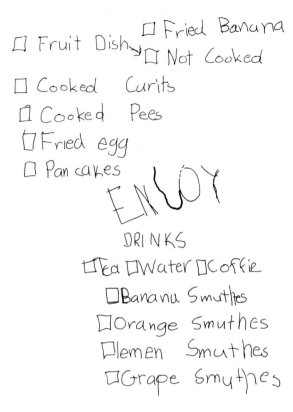

Figure 1.2 *"Ted's Delight" Menu*

Figure 1.3 *Carrie's Check*

EXAMINING LITERACY
FROM TWO PERSPECTIVES

What do Ted and Carrie know about reading and writing? One perspective we use to answer this question is based on a traditional view of children's learning reading and writing. We caution that not all educators have embraced the traditional perspective as we describe it. Our presentation does not include all of the profound changes and controversies that have emerged in the rich history of reading and writing (Smith, 1965; von Bracht Donsky, 1984).

The Traditional Perspective

The traditional perspective usually involves comparing what children do with what adult, mature readers and writers do. It first considers what adult, mature readers and writers know which allows them to read and write and then compares children's literacy knowledge with the adult knowledge base. Within the traditional perspective, mature readers and writers are assumed to know a great deal about reading and writing.

Mature readers recognize printed words quickly. They can instantly identify, pronounce, and discuss the meanings of many words. When mature readers cannot immediately recognize a printed word, it is thought that they "sound it out"; that is, they know sounds associated with letters and use this knowledge to pronounce unknown words. Mature readers understand sentences and texts, and they find or infer themes and main ideas.

Mature writers know alphabet letter forms and can write these forms legibly. They know the spellings of a large number of words. These writers have a substantial knowledge of grammar which they use to write sentences and essays or themes. Their writings contain logical arguments and well-drawn conclusions.

Traditional Assumptions

The traditional perspective included at least four assumptions about children learning literacy: (1) reading and writing were difficult to learn; (2) children were considered knowledgeable about literacy only when their reading and writing approximated adults' reading and writing; (3) reading required readiness; and (4) writing was learned after reading.

Reading and writing were difficult to learn. One belief that formed part of the traditional perspective was the assumption that learning to read and write was difficult. Educators might have come to this conclusion by comparing learning to read and write with learning to talk. Children learn to talk quite early in life without any special efforts on the part of parents. It seems to occur naturally without instruction. In contrast, most children do not learn to read or write at home with seemingly little instruction. Rather, they learn in school with intensive instruction. Therefore, most educators drew the conclusion that learning to read and write was somehow not as natural as learning to talk.

Children were considered knowledgeable about literacy only when their reading and writing approximated adults' reading and writing. A second assumption underlying the traditional perspective of reading and writing involved educators' definitions of who readers and writers were. Children who could identify written words without picture clues were considered readers. Similarly, children who could spell words so that adults could read them were considered writers. These definitions of reading and writing were based on what adults could do. Children who could not read or write according to these definitions were considered nonreaders and nonwriters. Many traditionalist educators assumed that children who could not read and write like adults had little understanding of reading and writing.

Reading required readiness. During the 1920s and 1930s educators became alarmed by the number of children failing the first grade. Many failed because they did not learn to read (Holmes, 1927). In 1931 two well-respected educators published a study concluding that children could not learn to read successfully until they had reached a mental age of 6.5 years (Morphett & Washburne, 1931). This study had an enormous impact; schools began delaying reading instruction for first graders until they were ready (had gained mental maturity).

Educators began to consider how to get children ready to read. They developed new instructional programs and new tests. These programs and tests were called *reading readiness* programs and tests. Readiness programs were used in kindergarten and first grade classrooms. Readiness activities included helping children acquire oral language facility, knowledge of alphabet letter names, ability to detect whether two shapes are alike or different, and ability to identify whether two spoken words have the same beginning sound.

Writing was learned after reading. No formal programs of readiness for writing were developed because most educators assumed that children could not write until they had begun reading. They thought that if children could not read words, they could not spell words. Writing was usually taught only in the second half of the first grade or at least not until children had acquired some proficiency in reading such as learning some letter–sound correspondences (Cramer, 1978). As a result, many teachers spent considerably more time on reading instruction than on writing instruction.

Ted's and Carrie's Knowledge from a Traditional Perspective

We return to our question: What do Ted and Carrie know about reading and writing? Most traditionalists would emphasize what Ted and Carrie do *not* know compared to adults. From a traditional perspective, Carrie is not a reader or a writer. We cannot read the "check" she wrote to her father. The way Carrie wrote suggests that she does not know the letters *E* or *J*. She would probably be given activities where she would trace and copy the letters *E* and *J*. She might be given worksheets where she would be expected to find all the letters that look like the letters *E* or *J*. Traditionalists would be likely to encourage Carrie to participate in oral language activities as preparation for later reading and writing.

Ted is a reader and a writer. We can read his sign and menu. We note that although Ted spelled several words correctly, he misspelled seven words out of the twenty-eight he wrote. Ted uses capital letters and punctuation marks (for possessives) correctly. We assume that Ted knows how to read many words and that he knows much about letter–sound relations, given that he spelled many words correctly. However, he might need to work on identifying words with the letters *ee* and *ea*. He also needs to learn how to spell (and possibly read) *oo* words (he spelled the word *Smoothies* as *Smuthes*). Traditionalists would be likely to give Ted several activities focusing on spelling.

The Psycho-Sociolinguistic Perspective Emerges

In the last decade educators and other researchers have begun to reexamine the traditional assumptions about reading and writing knowledge and learning. New research and theories have emerged that challenged these traditional assumptions. A new perspective on children's literacy began to take shape as researchers realized the importance of observing children in *literacy events*. Literacy events are activities involving people reading and writing for real purposes. ''Ted's Delight'' is an example of the kinds of literacy events that researchers began to observe.

Traditional Assumptions Challenged

Research and thinking regarding three aspects of children's learning were especially important in changing views on children's literacy. Researchers found that some children could read before they entered school. They discovered that sometimes children were writing before they learned how to read. Finally, theorists reexamined reading and writing as language processes.

A few children read before they enter school. The publication of research reports which identified some children who could already read and write before they entered school and before they received any formal reading or writing instruction (Clark, 1976; Durkin, 1966) challenged the notion that learning to read and write was difficult and unnatural. Educators began to wonder how children could have learned to read and write on their own. One hypothesis was that these children were especially bright and were maturationally ahead of their peers, but the research showed that some of these children had average intelligence (Clark, 1976). Another hypothesis was that the parents of these children had deliberately taught them to read and write. However, some of the parents reported that they had not taught their children (Plessas & Oakes, 1964).

Educators began to think that even if only a few children learned to read and write before entering school, then learning to read and write must be easier and might be more natural than they had assumed. They questioned the notion that children had to reach a certain maturational level before learning to read and wondered whether readiness activities were appropriate or necessary.

Writing comes before reading. Another line of research that caused educators to reexamine their assumptions about literacy learning was the discovery that some preschool children could spell words in systematic ways and in ways that could be recognized by adults (Chomsky, 1971; Read, 1971). What was so arresting about the findings of these studies was that the children who were inventing spellings in their writing were not yet readers (according to the traditional definition). Figure 1.4 presents four-year-old Jocelyn's writing. Jocelyn was not a reader when she wrote this note. The words in Jocelyn's writing (a joke that was popular in her preschool class) are not conventionally spelled except for the words *the* and *did,* but the note is readable. Figure 1.5 presents a picture that Melissa drew and a sentence that she wrote about her dog. As Melissa wrote her sentence, she slowly said, "This is Kookoo." Although not a reader, Melissa's writing captures much of her message.

Figure 1.4 *Jocelyn's Chicken Joke*

Figure 1.5 *"This is Kookoo"*

Jocelyn's and Melissa's writings are similar to the writing samples researchers were gathering from young children in literacy events. Their discovery that some children who were not yet reading (as traditionally defined) were writing by inventing spellings made educators question the assumption that children learned to write only after learning to read.

Reading and writing are viewed as language processes. Theorists began to argue that reading and writing are language processes (Goodman, 1967; Smith, 1973). As such, it should be possible for children to use the same language learning capabilities to learn reading and writing that they do to learn spoken language. As with spoken language, children learn written language in order to make use of its many communicative functions, and they learn it in social settings. Although reading and writing are often thought to be solitary activities, their use often involves others, especially when children are learning to read and write.

It is worth noting that this is the opposite of the oral language argument that was made under the traditional perspective. This perspective began with the *observation* that oral language learning is easy, natural, and nearly universal and that written language learning in schools is difficult, unnatural, and frequently unsuccessful. The traditionalists concluded that learning written language was a different process than learning oral language. The new perspective that was emerging began with a *premise* (not an observation) that written language cannot be so very different from spoken language because they are both language. Educators concluded that learning both kinds of language, spoken and written, ought to be natural, easy, and nearly universal. They thought learning to speak and to listen should not be considered a necessary prerequisite for learning to write and to read. Reading, writing, speaking, and listening are all considered similar language processes that emerge simultaneously.

Ted's and Carrie's Knowledge
from a Psycho-Sociolinguistic Perspective

Once educators realized that young children were learning something about reading and writing before they could be traditionally defined as readers and writers, they began to wonder exactly what and how children were learning. They realized that young children live in a world filled with written language and written language users. No longer could adult standards apply to what children were doing. Instead, educators began to carefully observe children in their natural interactions with written language and in their written language use in literacy events. We will reexamine "Ted's Delight" as a literacy event and interpret what Ted and Carrie are learning about literacy from the newly emerging psycho-sociolinguistic perspective.

First we might note, as we did from the traditional perspective, that Ted is a reader and writer. The sign and menu he wrote suggest Ted is learning that written language communicates *meanings*. His sign communicated a message to his father: a restaurant is open for business. Ted also knows that the messages communicated in written language should be meaningful given the written language context. Ted knew that the "backwards *J*" that Carrie wrote somehow had to be incorporated into a message that would be communicated on a menu. Random letters on menus do not communicate meaningful messages. Ted made the random letter meaningful by incorporating it into the word *Enjoy*. Carrie also showed that she knows written language communicates messages. Even though we cannot read her "check," her behavior as she gave it to her father (and her father's reactions to the written check) suggests her writing communicates a message something like "pay some money for your food."

The sign and menu suggest Ted is learning about written language *forms—* what written language looks like. These two writing samples certainly look like a sign and a menu. His menu is written in the form of a list. The content of his menu is organized like a menu is usually organized—drinks and food are grouped and listed separately. Carrie is also learning what at least a few written language forms look like. The writing on her check looks something like the letters *E* and *J*. Even though Carrie's letters are not yet conventional, they suggest she is paying attention to what letters look like. Much of what she notices about letters corresponds with what adults notice about letters. Although Carrie's *E*'s sometimes have too many cross lines, she has obviously noticed that cross lines are included on letters. And, even though Carrie's *J*'s seem to be backwards, she does include a "hook" expected on this letter. There is one exception: Carrie put a circle on her letter *E*. Most letter *E*'s do not include circles. Figure 1.6 (Carrie's name written as her preschool teacher wrote it) suggests why Carrie may have included the circle on her *E*. Carrie obviously noticed that her preschool teacher wrote circles on her letters, so Carrie may have decided to put the same circles on her own letters.

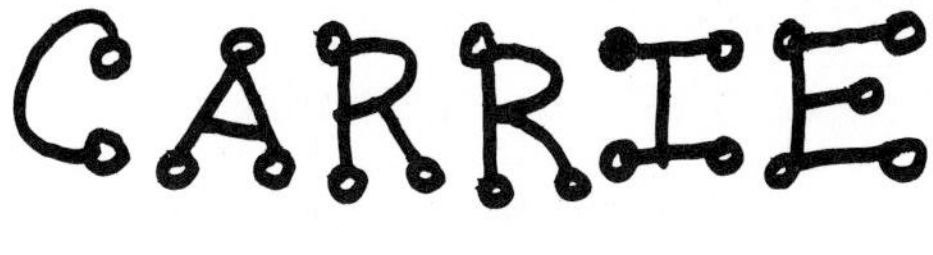

CARRIE

Figure 1.6 "Carrie" as Written by Her Preschool Teacher

Ted's spelling errors on the menu suggest a great deal about his knowledge of how spoken and written language are related. Ted knows that certain letters (written language) are associated with certain sounds (spoken language). Ted wrote *pees* for *peas*. He knows that the letters *ee* often take the sound of long *e*. Ted knows that to communicate the meaning "small, round green vegetable," he must write letters that will correspond with the spoken word *peas*.

Both Ted's and Carrie's behaviors indicate that they understand many ways that written language is used. Carrie knows that a waitress writes something when a customer orders and when he asks for his check. Carrie seems to be learning, just as Ted is, that writing and reading are *functional*. Ted and Carrie used written language to get their customer into their restaurant (they made a sign), to let their customer know what was available to eat (they made a menu), and to let their customer know how much his meal cost (they wrote a check).

The Psycho-Sociolinguistic Perspective

Ted and Carrie have learned a great deal about written language. Their knowledge is not unique. Young children learn many of the same things about written language and literacy that were illustrated in the "Ted's Delight" literacy event. As researchers studied young children in similar literacy events, they discovered that children—even those who were not traditionally considered readers and writers—were learning about the following four aspects of written language:

1. written language's ability to communicate meanings

2. forms of written language

3. relationships of written language to spoken language, and

4. functions of written language

The psycho-sociolinguistic perspective emphasizes more than just *what* children learn about written language and literacy; it emphasizes *how* children learn. Ted and Carrie were learning about written language as they used it as a part of their play. Their written language play reflected written language use in real life. Their father performed an important part in their play. He was willing to enter the dramatic play and participated as a playmate rather than as a parent. Psycho-sociolinguists have discovered that children learn about written language as they engage in written language use and as they interact with other written language users (Cook-Gumperz, 1986; Scollon & Scollon, 1981).

LITERACY KNOWLEDGE FROM A PSYCHO-SOCIOLINGUISTIC PERSPECTIVE

Within the psycho-sociolinguistic perspective children are viewed as learning four aspects of written language: the ability of written language to communicate meanings or messages, the forms of written language, the relation between written language (letters) and spoken language (sounds), and the functions served by written language.

Written Language Meanings

Reading and writing are meaning-making activities (Halliday, 1975). They involve communication of meanings between the reader and the writer. As we read, we build meanings and explore messages that authors communicate through written language. As we write, we build and discover meanings that we communicate to readers through written language. Ted and Carrie demonstrated their meaning making through reading and writing. In order to communicate the message "restaurant," Ted wrote the sign "Ted's Delight."

Reading and writing, of course, are only a few of the ways we can communicate meanings. We communicate meanings through facial expression, gesture, dance, art, conversation, and music. For young children, communicating in spoken language and play are very closely related to communicating in written language. Mary's play with her dolls illustrates how children's talk, actions, and play communicate meanings in ways that are similar to communicating meaning in written language (Wolf, 1984).

Communicating Meaning in Play, Talk, and Written Language

Mary was playing with cardboard boxes and two dolls. One of the dolls was "Mommy" and the other was "baby." Mary stood one of the cardboard boxes up next to the dolls and said, as if she were the "baby," "Mommy, I want to ride the elevator." Then Mary said, as if she were a narrator in a story, "And they talked and talked." As she spoke, the cardboard box began to tip over. Mary said, as if she were "Mommy," "See, it's dangerous, it's tippy, that's why you have to go with grown-ups" (Wolf, 1984, p. 846).

In this literacy event, Mary communicated meaning—a story about a mother and her little girl who were going to ride an elevator—through her actions, talk, and props. The story's meaning is communicated through the talk of "Mommy" and "baby" and through the talk of a "narrator." Although Mary was involved in make-believe play, there are characteristics of her spoken language that make it more like a written language story than an oral conversation. For example, Mary narrated. Having a special person who communicates part of a story is found in written stories, but not in oral conversation. There is one other characteristic of Mary's play that signals her language is more like written language than spoken language. Mary kept the talk of the people in her play ("Mommy" and "baby") related to the meaning of the make-believe story she was developing. She did not allow the real situation of the cardboard box nearly falling over to interfere with the story's meaning. Rather, she incorporated the box falling over as part of the meaning in the story. "Baby" in the make-believe story could not ride the elevator because the *elevator,* not the box, was tippy.

This literacy event illustrates that young children learn to communicate written-language-like meanings in their play and spoken language. It might not seem surprising or special that children use spoken language to practice what they will need to use in written language. As expert readers, we assume that what we write, we can read aloud and say. What we say aloud, we can write. However, as Mary's play demonstrated, written language is not exactly "talk written down." Meanings in written language are communicated in special ways that are different from meanings communicated in spoken language.

Differences between Meanings Communicated through Spoken and Written Language

There are several differences between meanings communicated in spoken and written language that children must learn. These include prosody, sustained language, text-bound language, and written language register.

Prosody.   One difference between meanings communicated through spoken and written language involves the way speakers use stress, intonation, and pauses (Rubin, 1978). These features are called *prosody.* Prosody communicates much meaning. For example, prosody helps signal pronoun referents. Suppose a speaker said the sentence, "Sue hugged Beth and then David hugged her" stressing the word *David.* Spoken in this way, the speaker implies David hugged Beth. In contrast, suppose a speaker said the same sentence stressing the word *her.* Spoken in this way, the speaker implies that David hugged Sue. The meanings communicated in this one sentence differ depending on stress.

In contrast to spoken language, prosody is poorly signaled in written language. Underlining, using italics, and using boldface print are used almost incidentally; periods and commas only give a rough idea of how long to pause; and many pauses are not signaled by punctuation at all. Young children depend on prosody to understand spoken language (Rubin, 1978). Written language's imperfect prosodic cues may make reading difficult for children.

Sustained language.   Another difference between how meanings are communicated in spoken and written language involves differences between the sustained nature of written language and the dialogic or conversational nature of spoken language. Conversations involve people in both listening and speaking roles. They are interactive. Speakers make sure what they have said is understood by asking questions ("you know?") and restating information. They determine what to say, in part, by cues from the listener.

On the other hand, writing is sustained. It is like a monologue. Writers must sustain the flow of words without cues from a listener. Essays composed by young, school-age writers are often short and appear to be like a single turn in a conversation; they are what you would expect if you wrote what one person in a conversation would say before the other speaker entered the conversation (Scardamalia, Bereiter, & Goelman, 1982).

Text-bound language.   The third difference between meanings communicated in spoken and written language involves differences in context. Context refers to real situations. For example, the context of a pair of seven-year-olds playing in a neighborhood park includes setting (the park), people in the setting (the boys and the other people around them in the park), and actions of people in the setting (the boys throwing a ball and other people sitting on benches, walking their dogs, or having a picnic). Spoken language makes much use of situations or context. Because conversation is often face-to-face and speakers and listeners are known to each other, speakers make reference to the physical situation or context in which the conversation is taking place or to previous shared experiences. Gestures such as pointing to things in the setting or looking at the same object in the setting are commonly used to convey meaning in conversations. The boys in the park might make conversation such as, "Boy, look at that" and "I can't believe you did that." The boys would accompany their comments with gestures and shared looks.

Speakers and listeners use context in another way to communicate meaning.

They rely on context to supply the meanings of many commonly used words. Understanding pronouns such as *then, that, next, there,* and *here* depends on the context in which the words are used. Because understanding much of spoken language depends on speakers and listeners sharing the same context, it is called *context-bound* (Olson, 1977).

In contrast, readers do not share the same physical settings as writers. Therefore, more information in written language depends on the words that authors use in their texts. Meaning in written language can only be conveyed through text. Therefore, it is referred to as *text-bound* (Olson, 1977).

Written language register. There are many ways that the language of written texts differs from the spoken language of conversations (Purcell-Gates, 1989). The language in written texts includes use of clarifying phrases (such as open *the door* instead of open *it*), literary vocabulary (such as the words *villager, ogre,* and *alas*), and literary word order (such as *up the hill they went* instead of *they went up the hill*). These special uses of language are called the *written language register.* Young children who are read to begin to use the written language register in their play, like Mary did with her doll. They also use it to tell their own stories (Purcell-Gates, 1988) or pretend read a favorite storybook (Pappas & Brown, 1988).

Written Language Forms

Learning written language forms means knowing what written language looks like. Carrie was learning what one kind of written language form—alphabet letters—looked like. Ted knew what several kinds of written language forms— menus, words, and letters—looked like. There are three aspects of written language forms that children learn. First, they learn that there are different kinds of written language forms such as letters, words, stories, maps, and lists. Each form is called a *written language unit.* Second, they learn the features of written language units. Third, they learn how different written language units such as stories are organized.

Units of Written Language

There are many written language units, some of which are smaller and embedded in other written language units. The sentence "The boy is running down the road" has several different written language units. *T* is an example of the smallest unit we recognize, a letter. The letter *T* is embedded in another unit, the word *The.* The word *The* is embedded in an even larger unit, the sentence *The boy is running down the road.* There are other units of written language that are larger than a sentence—paragraph, chapter, or book.

Because we are readers and writers, we assume that anyone looking at a page of written text would see them. Yet, detecting different units in written language is not so easy. Readers must first learn what units to expect and what the units look like before they are obvious (Smith, 1982). One way to demonstrate this is to try to detect units in a written language we are not familiar with. A poem written in Chinese is presented in Figure 1.7. We suspect that most readers expect that the units in this poem represent letter units. By comparing the English translation to the Chinese symbols, we find that each unit is something like a word. Actually each unit stands for an idea (which might comprise more than one word).

Children begin learning much about the different units of written language as they watch their parents read books aloud to them, as they interact with print on familiar signs and labels, and as their parents react to their writing. We will discuss more about *how* children learn to detect written language units in Chapter 2. In this section we focus on *what* children learn about each of the different written language units. One thing they learn are the features of different written language units.

Features of Written Language Units

Features are attributes of an object. For example, features of a car include wheels, windows, hood, trunk, and doors. Written language units have features. The letter *L* includes the features of a vertical line and a horizontal line. The word *boy* includes the feature of three letters. Children must learn the features of all kinds of different written language units (Gibson & Levin, 1975).

Letter features.   Children learn the features of letters (Lavine, 1977). One way we could find out about children's knowledge of letter features is to ask them whether letters are alike or different (Gibson, Gibson, Pick, & Osser, 1962). We might give children the letter *O* and the letter *U* and ask if they were alike or different. The two letters differ on the feature *closed* versus *open*. We

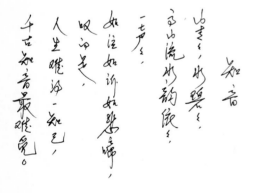

The mountain is green, the water is clean,
The water runs from the mountain to the stream,
The sound it makes so soft and sweet,
Like someone is sobbing and sighing.
For
Life is so long, the world is so big.
Yet
To find an intimate friend is not easy.

Figure 1.7 An Intimate Friend

might show children the letters *V* and *A,* which differ on the feature *rotated* versus *upright.* Three-year-olds know that the letters *U* and *O* are different, but do not know that the letters *V* and *A* are different. They know the feature *closed* versus *open,* but do not know the feature *rotated* versus *upright.* In contrast, seven-year-olds know that both sets of letters are different because they know both features.

Children also demonstrate their knowledge of letter features in their writing. Figure 1.8 presents one preschooler's writing. This writing looks like it might include letters, but a close inspection reveals none of the twenty-six Roman alphabet letters. Clay (1975) called letters such as these *mock letters.*

Figure 1.8 *Mock Letters*

Word features.   Children also learn about the features of words. If we wanted to know about children's knowledge of word features, we might ask them to sort cards into two piles, one pile for ''words'' and one pile for ''not words'' (Pick, Unze, Brownell, Drozdal, & Hopmann, 1978). On the cards we would write single letter words (*a*), short words (*horse* and *obese*), and long words (*dictionary*). We would also write some nonwords on the cards, including single-letter nonwords (*u*), short nonwords (*keald*), and long nonwords (*cdaflcotphm*).

When three-year-olds sort the cards, they will put all the cards into the "word" pile except the cards with single letters. In contrast, first graders are quite proficient in discriminating "words" from "not words." However, they think that short words that they do not know the meaning of (*obese*) are also "not words."

Both three-year-olds and first graders have ideas about word features. The feature of words that three-year-olds know is that words can have no fewer than three different letters (Ferreiro & Teberosky, 1982; Lavine, 1977). The feature of words that first graders know is that words can be single letters, but that they must have meaning known to them. There are three noteworthy aspects in this example. First, three-year-olds and first graders know some features of words. Second, the features three-year-olds and first graders know are not the features of words adults know, although first graders know more features that adults would accept. Third, children's knowledge of word features grows and changes.

Children also demonstrate their knowledge of word features in their writing (Clay, 1975; Sulzby, 1986). Figure 1.9 presents a letter that Michael wrote. His writing indicates a beginning awareness of words as subunits of longer text. Michael wrote his letter in six different colors of magic markers. In the third line of his letter he wrote the word *Michael* in blue, followed by the words *you so* in orange. In the fourth line he wrote the word *swet* in purple, the word *you* in orange, and the words *Dr. McGee* in black. Of importance is the fact that Michael never changed colors in the middle of words; he only changed colors at word boundaries. Michael's use of colors to separate words indicates his growing awareness of words as units of language. Later, Michael will learn to signal words with the conventional feature, a space between words.

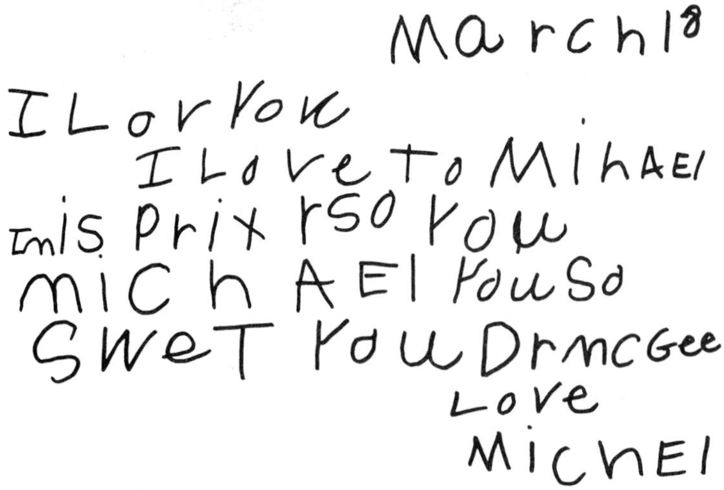

Figure 1.9 Michael's Letter

Sentence features.   Pierre's writing (Figure 1.10) indicates his awareness of sentences. His use of one line for each sentence and his emphatic periods are

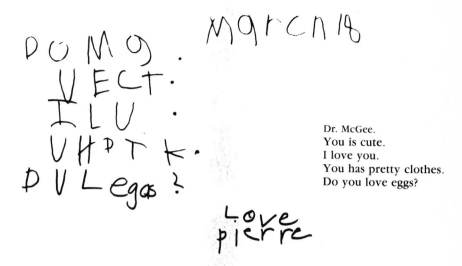

Dr. McGee.
You is cute.
I love you.
You has pretty clothes.
Do you love eggs?

Figure 1.10 *Pierre's Sentences*

undoubtedly related to his kindergarten teacher's writing and to her talk about sentences and periods. However, Pierre only puts periods at the ends of sentences, and all of his lines of writing marked by periods qualify as sentences. Pierre's knowledge of a sentence as a unit in written language marked by punctuation is noteworthy in a kindergartner. Even some second and third graders struggle to identify sentences in their writing; their compositions often consist of one big sentence.

Text features.   Texts are written language units that are larger than sentences and paragraphs. Although technically the word *text* might describe a sentence or even a single word, we generally use it to describe larger written language units. There are many of kinds of texts, including poems, recipes, maps, newspapers, dictionaries, books, magazine articles, *TV Guides,* and directions. One thing young children learn about these different text units is how they look. Figure 1.11 presents a preschooler's story. This writing looks like a story—it fills a page with lines of writing.

An important feature of texts is the kind of content found in them. For example, the content in recipes includes cooking ingredients and directions. The content in stories includes characters and settings. The content in a newspaper article includes who, how, when, where, what, and why information. There are many ways that children display their growing awareness of text content. They tell a story beginning with "Once upon a time." They write "The End" prominently at the end of their stories. When asked to read a grocery list, four-year-olds reply, "green beans, bread, coffee." When dictating a letter five-year-olds say, "I love you." When asked what a traffic sign might say, they reply, "Turn here for McDonald's."

Children's writing also demonstrates their knowledge of the kinds of con-

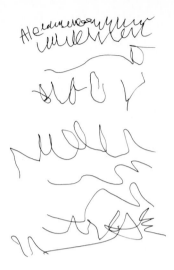

Figure 1.11 *Preschooler's Story*

tent found in specific types of texts. Figure 1.12 presents a second grader's map. It not only looks like a map, but also includes content that is expected on a map—words that describe and label locations. Figure 1.13 presents a nine-year-old's letter to her principal. The letter is an argument for locating a Coke machine on the playground. The content of the letter indicates that Andrea knows argument texts must include logical reasons that will persuade the reader.

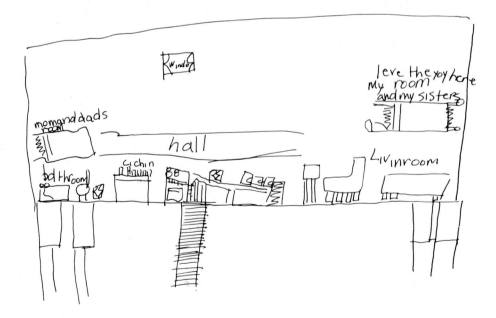

Figure 1.12 *Second-Grader's Map*

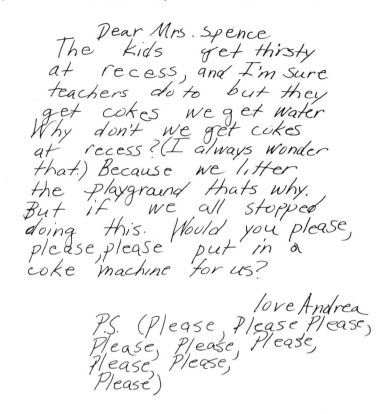

Dear Mrs. Spence
The kids get thirsty at recess, and I'm sure teachers do to but they get cokes we get water Why don't we get cokes at recess? (I always wonder that.) Because we litter the playground thats why. But if we all stopped doing this. Would you please, please, please put in a coke machine for us?

love Andrea

P.S. (Please, Please Please,) Please, Please, Please, Please, Please, Please)

Figure 1.13 *Persuasion Letter*

Written Language Organization

Children learn more than the features of written language. They learn how these features are organized. Units of written language are structured or organized in particular ways. In written English, sentences are organized in horizontal lines from top to bottom on a page. Many preschoolers demonstrate knowledge of linearity; their stories are organized in lines (see Figure 1.11). Left-to-right organization is a related kind of organization.

Left-to-right organization. Some kindergartners know that letters and words are organized from left to right in written English. Many kindergartners will point to the top left line of print when asked where to begin reading (Johns, 1980). They often write mock cursive stories (such as in Figure 1.11) by writing from left to right.

However, learning left-to-right organization is not a simple task. Jane's writing (Figure 1.14) demonstrates difficulties children can experience with left-to-right organization. Prior to writing the story presented in Figure 1.14, Jane frequently wrote mock cursive stories from left to right. But in the writing in Figure 1.14, left-to-right organization is not apparent. Jane began this story by drawing

Figure 1.14 *"Kentucky Fried Chicken"*

From "On Becoming a Writer: Child and Teacher" by J. Newman, 1983, *Language Arts, 60,* p. 864.
Copyright © 1983 by the National Council of Teachers of English. Reprinted with permission.

a picture of a chicken. She decided to write "Kentucky Fried Chicken." She said
to herself, "Tucky, /t/, /t/" and wrote a letter *T* near the outstretched leg of her
chicken. Next she concentrated on the sound of *ck* in her word *tucky.* She wrote
several *C*'s scattered around the page. Then she said, "Fried, /f/, /f/" and wrote
an *F* and an *R.* Finally, she tried to write the word *chicken* and wrote the letters
CK (looks like *CH*) and *N* (looks like *W*) (Newman, 1983, p. 863–864).

Jane listened to the sounds in the words *Kentucky Fried Chicken* in order,
but did not write her letters in order from left to right. In this case, it is not that
Jane did not know left-to-right organization (she demonstrated that knowledge
many times in her previous stories). Rather, it seems as if she abandoned left-to-
right organization in order to concentrate on another aspect of written language,
the relation between sounds and letters.

Text organizations.   All texts have an organization that we can identify.
For example, a fairy tale involves certain types of information organized in a
specific manner. "A hero or heroine encounters a problem, frequently supernat-
ural; several obstacles to solving the problem are met; a solution is found, often
through magical powers; and a happy ending is achieved" (McGee & Tompkins,
1980, p. 428). A recipe includes a list of foods and amounts, followed by a paragraph detailing how the foods are to be mixed and cooked. A theme begins with
a thesis statement, followed by supporting evidence and assertions. Each supporting assertion must be clearly related to the thesis statement.

Children's knowledge of the content and organization of texts is often referred to as their *schema* (Bartlett, 1932). Children have schemas for many different kinds of texts, as the writing examples in Figures 1.13 and 1.14 indicate.

Psychologists believe that children's schemas are particularly important for understanding and producing texts (Rumelhart, 1975). A special schema for stories, called a *story schema,* helps children understand and remember stories (Mandler & Johnson, 1977) and compose stories (Golden, 1984).

Metalinguistic Awareness of Written Language Units

We have been using words such as *letter, word, sentence,* and *story,* which make it easy to describe written language. They constitute *language about language.* Children's understanding of and ability to use language about language is one particular kind of knowledge called *metalinguistic awareness* (Yaden & Templeton, 1986). There are several aspects of metalinguistic awareness that children acquire. One aspect is the ability to examine a written language form apart from the meaning that is associated with the form (Templeton, 1980). For example, the word *dog* can be examined as a written language form—it is composed

of three letters with the graphic shape of . The word *dog* also has meaning—a hairy, four-legged animal. Young children have difficulty examining form apart from meaning. When asked to name a long word, they might reply "bus." They are likely to say "paper clip" when asked to name a short word. Young children use the meaning of a word to determine whether a word is long or short. Older children who have metalinguistic awareness would use the form of the written word to identify and name long and short words such as *encyclopedia* and *I.*

The example of a child's saying that "paper clip" is a short word illustrates another aspect of metalinguistic awareness, *concept of word.* This child did not realize either that the question "What is a short word?" implies that only one word should be given or that *paper clip* is two words. There are several components of concept of word, including the ability to identify a single word in a spoken sentence, the ability to identify a single word from a written sentence, and the ability to answer the question, "What is a word?" (Downing & Oliver, 1973–1974).

Relations between Written and Spoken Language

Ted demonstrated knowlege of the relations between written and spoken language when he spelled the word *peas* as *pees* and spelled the word *coffee* as *coffie.* He demonstrated that he knew at least two letter combinations for capturing the long *e* sound. Ted knew that the letters *ie* (as in the word *Connie*) and *ee* (as in the word *tree*) are related to the long *e* sound. Ted knew that written language (letters) was related to spoken language (sounds).

The correspondence between letters in written words and sounds in spoken words is obvious to experienced readers. This obvious (although not one-to-one) correspondence between written language and spoken language often obscures a more important point about written language and spoken language relations. That is, the relation between spoken language and written language allows readers to capture *meaning* that writers intend and it allows writers to convey *meaning* to readers. It is easy to overlook that Ted's spellings (even when not conventional) convey meaning. When we first saw Ted's menu and read the words *coffie* and *pees,* we had no trouble realizing that Ted was communicating that his restaurant served a hot drink made from coffee beans and a small, round, green vegetable.

The way meaning is conveyed in written English is very complex, as we have already discussed in the section on differences between meanings communicated in written and spoken language. What is significant about the relation between written and spoken language is that this relation *provides the means whereby meaning (the message) is linked to written forms (letters, words, sentences, text).* Most children do not immediately grasp that the link between written forms and meaning is through spoken language.

Because the important concept that children acquire is the notion of how meaning relates to written form, we will abandon our earlier heading "Relations between Written and Spoken Language." Instead, we will use the heading "Meaning-Form Links" to identify the concept of relating messages and forms in written language.

Meaning-Form Links

There are many possible ways of linking meaning with written form, only one of which is the letter–sound correspondence method of our English writing system. Even when children do not use letter–sound correspondences to link meaning with form, they still display knowledge of meaning-form links. One way they link meaning with written forms is to make their written forms look like the meaning they intend with forms like pictures or pictographic writing. Pictographic writing consists of signs or symbols that look like objects and actions (Gelb, 1952).

Pictographic meaning-form links. It is interesting to note that when some young children begin exploring meaning-form links through pictographic writing, they are using the first kind of writing that emerged in history (Gelb, 1952). In the earliest writing systems, written signs looked like the object or action they were used to represent. For example, a writer might have written a sign consisting of a circle with lines radiating out from it to mean "sun."

Dexter is a kindergartner who uses pictures as a link between meaning and written forms. He said that the word "deer" begins with the letter O because "It's [the letter O] shaped like a deer" (Dyson, 1984, p. 23). Dexter even drew an O and turned it into a deer by adding a set of antlers. To children like Dexter, units of written language such as letters directly represent meaning by looking like the meaning. A letter O can convey the meaning of *deer* if a writer makes the letter look like a deer.

Meaning-form links through syllables.   Eventually in the history of writing, writers began representing meaning by making a sign for each syllable in a spoken word. These writing systems were called *syllabaries* (Gelb, 1952). Sometimes children explore a syllable link between spoken language and written language. For example, Heather learned to say the poem *Twinkle, Twinkle Little Star.* Her kindergarten teacher wrote the poem on a chart and asked Heather to read it and "point to each word." Heather performed the task by reading and pointing as follows.

Text:	Twinkle	Twinkle	Little	Star		
Heather:	Twink	le		Twink	le	

Text:	How	I	Wonder	What	You	Are
Heather:	Lit	tle	Star		How	I	Won

Heather hesitated and then pointed back at the beginning of the poem:

Text:	Twinkle	Twinkle	Little	Star	
Heather:	Won	der	What	You	

Text:	How	I	Wonder	What	You	Are
Heather:	Are					

Then Heather stopped, pointed to the remainder of the text, and said, "I don't know what the rest says."

Heather used a strategy of pointing to each written word unit as she said a syllable. Heather was experimenting with the concept of word. She pointed to each written word and tried to match it with each spoken "word." She experimented by using a spoken syllable to match every written word.

Letter–sound correspondences as meaning-form links.   In spite of many changes in the long history of writing systems that have contributed to our not-so-close correspondence between a single letter and a single sound, we still depend on letters (individually or in common patterns) to stand for the important sounds in words. For example, the four important sounds in the word *bank* (the sounds of *b*, æ, ŋ, and *k*) are represented by four letters. Ted demonstrated knowledge of the alphabetic principles of our written language when he wrote the word *pees* for *peas*. Jane demonstrated that knowledge when she listened very carefully to the sounds as she said "Tucky Fried Chicken."

The links that children explore between meaning and written form illustrate reading and writing as symbol-using activities. Because reading and writing are symbol-using activities, they are related to children's other symbol-using activities—talking, drawing, and imaginary play.

Relations among Talking, Drawing, Writing, Reading, and Playing

Talking, drawing, writing, reading, and playing are related because they are symbol-using media (Vygotsky, 1978). A symbol is a representation of something—an object, action, experience, or idea—which exists separately from what it represents. We draw symbols for houses—we do not create real houses on paper. Similarly, we write a symbol for house (the word *house*). In dramatic play children create symbols by tranforming objects and people into different objects and people. For example, a child might say, "I'll be the doctor and you hand me the scalpel" as he points to a plastic knife. In this play, the child uses talking to become a doctor and to transform the knife into a scalpel. The child becomes a symbol for doctor and the knife becomes a symbol for scalpel.

Children often use many symbolic systems interactively to create meaning. They may draw, write, and even act out stories during writing (Fueyo, 1989).

Written Language Functions

Ted and Carrie's restaurant play demonstrated their awareness of purposes for using written language. Ted and Carrie used written language to identify and label; they created a restaurant by making a written sign declaring that their card table playhouse was a restaurant. Ted and Carrie used written language to direct behavior; their written sign directed their father's behavior by prompting him to act like a customer. Their writing also directed their own behavior by prompting them to take on roles of "waitress" and "chef."

Written language is used to meet a variety of needs. Neighborhood store owners want customers to buy their merchandise, so they tell people about their goods through signs and announcements in their windows and through newspaper advertisements or flyers. People want to relax after work, so they read detective novels, best sellers, or magazines. An important part of learning to read and write involves learning more about the functions that written language serves.

Functions of Spoken Language

Children have a head start learning about written language's functions because they already use their spoken language to meet a variety of needs. Children, like the adults around them, use their spoken language in functional ways. The famous linguist, Michael Halliday (1975), argued that spoken language is learned because language does things. Halliday said that long before children acquire their first words, they use *protolanguage* (sounds) to get things done for them. Children point at the milk cup, say "ug, ug" and they mean, "I want you to get the cup so I can have a drink."

Halliday (1975) identified seven functions of spoken language. These functions represent different ways we use language. Table 1.1 summarizes Halliday's seven functions of language. This table gives examples from children's spoken language that illustrate each of the seven language functions (Halliday, 1975).

Table 1.1 *Hallliday's Language Functions*

LANGUAGE	FUNCTION	SPOKEN LANGUAGE EXAMPLES	WRITTEN LANGUAGE EXAMPLES
Instrumental Language	satisfies needs and wants	"I want to watch Big Bird." "I want the colors."	advertisements, bills, reminder notes, sign-up sheet
Regulatory Language	controls others	"Don't use purple." "Andrew, stop."	traffic signs, policy statements, directions
Interactional Language	creates interaction with others	"Let's go in the playroom." "Who wants the rest?"	personal letters, notes, personals in the newspaper
Personal Language	expresses personal thoughts and opinions	"I like Mr. T." "I'm not tired."	editorials, diaries, autobiographies, journals
Heuristic Language	seeks information	"What does this say?" "What is that?"	letters of request and inquiry, application forms, registration forms
Imaginative Language	creates imaginary worlds	"You be Judy and I'm Peewee." "This is a big green haystack."	poetry, drama, stories
Informative Language	communicates information	"Dad's giving a speech tonight." "The flowers opened."	wedding announcements, obituaries, dictionaries, textbooks, reports, telephone books

Adapted from Halliday (1975).

Unique Functions of Written Language

Since children are acquainted with using spoken language for several purposes, it is not surprising that they learn how to use written language to accomplish a variety of goals as well. In fact, many of written language's purposes are the same as spoken language's purposes. Table 1.1 also presents several examples of written language that serve each of Halliday's seven functions.

Much of becoming literate—becoming a capable reader and writer—involves learning uses of language that are unique to reading and writing. There are several benefits to using written language rather than spoken language. We use written language when we want to send information over distances and over time, and when we want to remember something. Written language is also useful for communicating with people we really do not know well. There are three additional unique functions of written language: to establish identity, to record information, and to increase knowledge.

Establishing identity.   Young children quickly recognize written language's ability to establish identity. Ted and Carrie established that the card table was a restaurant by making a sign that declared it to be a restaurant. Another example of children's use of written language to establish identity involves two groups of preschoolers who were arguing about the use of a large refrigerator box. One group insisted that the box become a doll house. The other group wanted it to be a fire station. Two boys in the fire station group went to a mother helper and asked her to write the word *fire station.* They copied her writing on a large sheet of paper and taped it to the box. One child pointed to the sign and said, "This is not a house. This is a fire station" (Cochran-Smith, 1984, p. 90).

Recording information and increasing knowledge.   Researchers have argued that written language serves at least two other functions not served by oral language (Stubbs, 1980). One function is to record information. Writing allows information to become permanent and transportable. Another function of written language is to increase knowledge. Because information can be recorded and reread, facts can be accumulated. These facts can be studied and considered critically, which may lead to new discoveries and theories. This new knowledge is made possible by studying in detail the accumulation of past knowledge.

Both the recording and increasing knowledge functions of written language can be observed in list making. People make lists to help organize what they need to get done. Writers often brainstorm lists of ideas before they begin to write. Sometimes it is through their lists that they discover a new idea—something they want to write about. Children also make lists. It may be through their list making that they first begin to explore the recording and increasing knowledge functions of written language. Taylor (1983) described several young children who used written language in a variety of ways, including making lists as a part of club activities. The children made many lists that negotiated who were to be members and who were not, lists of furnishings they needed for the clubhouse, and lists of jobs to do for the club.

NEW ASSUMPTIONS ABOUT LITERACY LEARNING
FROM A PSYCHO-SOCIOLINGUISTIC PERSPECTIVE

Just as the traditional perspective included notions about what and how children learned about reading and writing, the psycho-sociolinguistic perspective also includes notions about what and how children learn about written language. These assumptions are reflected in the literacy events that we presented in this chapter. We will discuss five assumptions about literacy learning, which are derived from the psycho-sociolinguistic perspective, that we believe underlie literacy learning. The first three assumptions deal with what children learn about written language. The last two assumptions have to do with how children learn about written language.

Even Very Young Children Are Knowledgeable of Written Language

At the time of the literacy event "Ted's Delight," Carrie was only three years old. She already knew a great deal about being literate. She knew when to write an order and a check in a restaurant. Her writing included many features of written language form. Within the restaurant play activity, Carrie was a reader and a writer. We will show later in this book that even infants begin learning about reading as they interact with books or other print items and with their parents or other readers.

Teachers can expect that children will begin their school literacy experiences with important and useful knowledge about reading and writing. They can examine each child's literacy knowledge and insights, with the understanding that the kinds and amounts of knowledge each child has will depend on his or her interactions with reading and writing.

Young Children's Reading and Writing May Be Different from Adults' Reading and Writing, But It Is No Less Important

Young children's notions about written language are often quite different from adults' notions about written language. Carrie's letter *E* (Figure 1.3) was not a conventional letter *E*. Heather's reading was different from an adult's reading of the poem *Twinkle Twinkle Little Star*. Even at school age, children's notions about certain aspects of written language are different from adults' notions. At that stage, children are developing their own ideas about written language, which will eventually come to be more like adult ideas (we examine this further in Chapter 2).

Teachers will not expect children to conform to adult models of correctness. They will expect that children's reading and writing efforts will not always look like what adults consider reading and writing. Teachers will provide many opportunities for children to try out what they know, without making them conform to an adult model.

Reading and Writing Are Similar and Interrelated Activities

Reading and writing are highly interactive and interrelated. In real literacy events it is hard to separate reading from writing. Ted and Carrie wrote and read what they wrote. Their father read their writing. Children learn about reading by writing and learn about writing by reading. This makes sense because both reading and writing have a common element—written language. They are both meaning-making activities. Reading and writing are related to other meaning-making activites including talking, drawing, and playing. Children's knowledge of written language is often displayed in these activities.

Teachers will recognize that children's literacy knowledge and learning is often interwoven with many activities in addition to reading and writing. In the classroom, teachers will encourage children and provide opportunities for them to talk, draw, read, write, and play. Teachers will also look for ways to help children apply their knowledge of written language in literacy events that include several meaning-making activities, such as occurred in Ted and Carrie's restaurant play or Mary's dramatic play.

Young Children Acquire Literacy Knowledge as They Participate in Meaningful Activities

The key to young children's literacy learning is their participation in meaningful activities in which reading and writing are used. Ted and Carrie's restaurant play activity was a highly meaningful one—it was a favorite playtime activity. Michael's writing was part of a letter-writing activity and he sent his letter to a frequent visitor to his classroom. Joni's map was drawn in order to help the tooth fairy locate her room.

Teachers will expect that children are best supported in their literacy learning in meaningful activities in which reading and writing are used to meet everyday needs. Thus they will plan literacy events in their classrooms, knowing that children seem to learn about reading and writing as they use reading and writing.

Young Children Acquire Literacy Knowledge as They Interact with Others

Children's reading and writing efforts are supported by others who respond to their efforts in ways that make them readers and writers. Carrie's father responded to Carrie's writing just as he would respond to a written check in a real restaurant. His response supported Carrie's writing.

In the classroom, children's literacy efforts will be best supported by teachers' interactions with children and by children's interactions with each other. Teachers will want to know effective ways of responding to children's literacy efforts that will extend and challenge children's learning.

Chapter Summary

We have looked at two perspectives for viewing young children's reading and writing: the traditional perspective and the psycho-sociolinguistic perspective. The traditional perspective emphasizes adults' knowledge of reading and writing. There were four assumptions underlying this perspective: (1) reading and writing were difficult and unnatural to learn; (2) children were considered knowledgeable about reading and writing only when their efforts approximated adults' reading and writing; (3) reading required readiness; and (4) writing was learned after reading.

Three areas of research and theory

caused educators to reexamine these traditional assumptions about literacy learning. Researchers found that: (1) some children learned to read and write before having instruction; (2) some children learned to write before they learned to read; and (3) reading and writing were reconsidered as language processes. These findings led to a new perspective for literacy learning called the psycho-sociolinguistic perspective. This perspective emphasizes the cognitive, social, and language factors involved in literacy events, activities involving reading and writing everyday uses.

Within the psycho-sociolinguistic perspective, children are viewed as knowledgeable of four aspects of written language: meanings, forms, meaning-form links, and functions. Children display their knowledge of meaning making in their play and talk. Talk in some imaginative play is more like written language than spoken language. Written language includes special features such as being text-bound and sustained and using clarifying phrases, literary vocabulary, and literary word order. These features are in contrast to conversations that use context-bound language and prosody to signal meaning.

Children display their knowledge of written language forms by learning features that distinguish among written language units such as letters, words, and texts. Children also learn how written language units are organized, such as from left to right. They also acquire mental conceptions of text organizations called schemas. A story schema is a mental conception of story organization. Children learn to talk about the forms of written language. This is part of their metalinguistic ability, which encompasses children's ability to talk

about written language form apart from meaning and their concept of word.

Children explore many ways that meaning and written language forms are linked. Many of the links that children explore reflect links that have been used in early writing systems. Some children use pictures and picture-like symbols in their drawing and writing to represent meaning. Some children use a syllable strategy to link what they know about a memorized story to the written forms of that story. Other children discover letter–sound correspondences and invent spellings. Children's explorations of links between meanings and writing are related to their explorations of symbols in drawing and in imaginary play.

Children learn to use written language to meet a variety of needs. They discover that written language can be used in many of the same ways as spoken language. Like spoken language, written language can be used to control others, to fulfill needs, to interact with others, to seek information, to give information, to express personal ideas, and to explore the imagination. Children also learn when written language is especially powerful: to establish identity, to record information, and to increase knowledge.

Five assumptions about children's literacy learning can be drawn from the psycho-sociolinguistic perspective: (1) even young children are knowledgeable of written language; (2) young children's reading and writing are as important as adults' reading and writing; (3) reading and writing are interrelated and are also related to talking, drawing, and playing; (4) children acquire literacy knowledge by participating in meaningful activities; and (5) children acquire literacy knowledge as they interact with others.

Children simultaneously acquire knowledge of the four domains of written language knowledges. No single aspect of written language knowledge is more important than the others. We have described children learning about these domains separately; however, children do not learn about them sepa-rately, nor do they learn them in the order in which we describe them. The four domains of written language knowledge overlap and interact. It is frequently difficult to categorize arbitrarily children's knowledge into these four domains. We do so only in order to help teachers become careful observers of children so that they are sensitive to children's learning.

Applying the Information

A case study of a literacy event follows. Read this case study carefully and think about the four domains of written language knowledge. Discuss what each of the children in the case study is learning about written language (1) meanings, (2) forms, (3) meaning-form links, and (4) functions. Consider what each of the children shows about the five psycho-sociolinguistic assumptions of literacy learning.

Figure 1.15 *Kristen's Picture*

Four children and their sitter were sitting around the kitchen table. It was a rainy afternoon and the children had become restless. The sitter earlier had decided to read a book to the children to entertain them. She read *George Shrinks* (Joyce, 1985), a story of a little boy's adventures when he shrinks to the size of a mouse. Then the sitter suggested that the children draw a picture about the story.

Kristen, a two-year-old, immediately grabbed a marker and began to draw (see Figure 1.15). Ryan, a three-year-old, selected a marker and said, "I'm going to draw his brother." (George's little brother who has not shrunk is a prominent character in the story.) Ryan's picture is presented in Figure 1.16. Danielle, a four-year-old, complained, "I can't draw a cat." The sitter

Figure 1.16 *Ryan's Picture*

Figure 1.17 Danielle's Picture

said, "Sure you can. A cat has pointed ears and whiskers." Danielle's cat is shown in Figure 1.17. The sitter commented, "Hey, that's a good cat." Then she asked, "Is that George?" as she pointed to the other object in the picture. She continued, "Would you like to write about that?" Danielle said, "No, you write it. Write 'The cat is going to eat him.'"

Kristen joined in the conversation. She gave her drawing to the sitter and said, "I drew, um um, something." Ryan said, "Write on mine, too." The sitter asked, "What shall I write?" Ryan replied, "Um, um, his brother."

Matthew, a six-year-old, had been drawing and writing quietly while the other children talked to the sitter (see Figure 1.18). The sitter noticed his picture and writing. She asked him to read his story. Matthew read, "The cat thought George was a mouse." Then he said, "I can tell the story. George was

sleeping in his bed. After he woke up he shrinked small as a mouse and he was so little than a book . . ."

Ryan interrupted, "I can tell the story, too. There's George. The cat came out to get George. The, but, um, the cat didn't eat him." Meanwhile, Danielle had noticed Matthew's picture and writing. She drew another picture of a cat (Figure 1.19). She asked the sitter, "How do you spell cat?" The sitter said each letter as she wrote them. Then Danielle wrote what looks like a colon. Next she copied the word *George.* She said, "*G,* what's that next letter?" Matthew replied, "An *e.*" Danielle said, "It doesn't look like an *e.*" Matthew responded by adding a mark to his letter *e.* Danielle continued to write words by saying each letter aloud to herself. After she was finished, the sitter asked her to read her writing. Danielle replied, "It says just what Matthew's writing says."

Figure 1.18 *Matthew's Picture and Story*

Figure 1.19 *Danielle's Writing*

Going Beyond the Text

Observe a literacy event with at least two children. One way to initiate a literacy event is to prepare for some dramatic play with children. Plan a dramatic play activity that could include reading and writing. For example, plan a restaurant play activity. Bring dramatic props such as an apron, dishes, and a table cloth, as well as reading and writing materials such as large sheets of paper, small pads of paper, crayons or markers, placemats with puzzles, and menus. Suggest to two or three children that they might want to play "restaurant" and propose that they use the paper and crayons in their play. Observe their actions and talk. Use the observations to find out what the children know about written language meanings, forms, meaning-form links, and functions.

References

APPLEBEE, A. N. (1978). *The child's concept of story.* Chicago, IL: University of Chicago Press.

BARTLETT, F. (1932). *Remembering: A study in experimental and social psychology.* Cambridge: Cambridge University Press.

BRITTAIN, W. L. (1979). *Creativity, art, and the young child.* New York: Macmillian.

CHOMSKY, C. (1971). Write first, read later. *Childhood Education, 47,* 296–299.

CLARK, M. M. (1976). *Young fluent readers.* London: Heinemann Educational Books.

CLAY, M. M. (1975). *What did I write?* Aukland: Heinemann Educational Books.

COCHRAN-SMITH, M. (1984). *The making of a reader.* Norwood, NJ: Ablex Publishing Corporation.

COOK-GUMPERZ, J. (Ed.). (1986). *The social construction of literacy.* Cambridge: Cambridge University Press.

CRAMER, R. (1978). *Children's writing and language growth.* Columbus: Charles E. Merrill Publishing Company.

DOWNING, J., & OLIVER, P. (1973–1974). The child's conception of a word. *Reading Research Quarterly, 9,* 568–582.

DURKIN, D. (1966). *Children who read early.* New York: Teachers College Press.

DYSON, A. H. (1984). Emerging alphabetic literacy in school contexts toward defining the gap between school curriculum and child mind. *Written Communication, 1,* 5–55.

FERREIRO, E. (1978). What is written in a written sentence? *Journal of Education, 160,* 25–39.

FERREIRO, E., & TEBEROSKY, A. (1982). *Literacy before schooling.* Exeter, NH: Heinemann Educational Books.

FUEYO, J. (1989). One child moves into meaning—his way. *Language Arts, 66,* 137–146.

GELB, I. J. (1952). *The study of writing.* Chicago, IL: The University of Chicago Press.

GIBSON, E. J., GIBSON, J. J., PICK, A. D., & OSSER, H. (1962). A developmental study of discrimination of letter-like forms. *Journal of Comparative Physiological Psychology, 55,* 897–906.

GIBSON, E. J., & LEVIN, H. (1975). *The psychology of reading.* Cambridge: The MIT Press.

GOLDEN, J. M. (1984). Children's concept of story in reading and writing. *The Reading Teacher, 37,* 578–584.

GOODMAN, K. S. (1967). Reading: A psycholinguistic guessing game. *Journal of the Reading Specialist, 6,* 126–135.

HALLIDAY, M. A. K. (1975). *Learning how to mean.* New York: Elsevier.

HARSTE, J. C., BURKE, C. L., & WOODWARD, V. A. (1983). *The young child as writer-reader and informant* (Final Report of NIE-G-80-0121). Bloomington, IN: Language Education Department.

HEATH, S. B. (1983). *Ways with words: Language, life, and work in communities and classrooms.* New York: Cambridge University Press.

HOLMES, M. C. (1927). Investigation of reading readiness of first grade entrants. *Child Education, 111,* 215–221.

JOHNS, J. L. (1980). First graders' concepts about print. *Reading Research Quarterly, 15,* 529–549.

JOYCE, W. (1985). *George shrinks.* New York: Harper & Row.

LAVINE, L. O. (1977). Differentiation of letter-like forms in prereading children. *Developmental Psychology, 13,* 89–94.

LOMAX, R. G., & McGEE, L. M. (1987). Interrelationships among young children's concepts about print and reading: Toward a model of word reading acquisition. *Reading Research Quarterly, 22,* 237–256.

MANDLER, L., & JOHNSON, N. (1977). Rememberance of things parsed: Story structure and recall. *Cognitive Psychology, 9,* 11–51.

McGEE, L. M., LOMAX, R. G., & HEAD, M. H. (1988). Young children's written language knowledge: What environmental and functional print reveals. *Journal of Reading Behavior, 20,* 99–118.

McGEE, L. M., & TOMPKINS, G. E. (1980). The video tape answer to independent reading comprehension activities. *The Reading Teacher, 34,* 427–433.

MORPHETT, M. V., & WASHBURNE, C. (1931). When should children begin to read? *Elementary School Journal, 31,* 496–503.

NEWMAN, J. (1983). On becoming a writer: Child and teacher. *Language Arts, 60,* 860–870.

OLSON, D. (1977). From utterance to text: The basis of language in speech and writing. *Harvard Educational Review, 47,* 257–281.

PAPPAS, C. C., & BROWN, E. (1988). The development of children's sense of the written language register: An analysis of the texture of "pretend reading" texts. *Linguistics and Education, 1,* 45–79.

PICK, A. D., UNZE, M. G., BROWNELL, C. A., DROZDAL, J. G., JR., & HOPMANN, M. R. (1978). Young children's knowledge of word structure. *Child Development, 49,* 669–680.

PLESSAS, G. P., & OAKES, C. R. (1964). Prereading experiences of selected early readers. *The Reading Teacher, 17,* 241–245.

PURCELL-GATES, V. (1988). Lexical and syntactic knowledge of well-read-to kindergartners and second graders. *Research in the Teaching of English, 22,* 128–160.

PURCELL-GATES, V. (1989). What oral/written language differences can tell us about beginning reading instruction. *The Reading Teacher, 42,* 290–294.

READ, C. (1971). Pre-school children's knowledge of English phonology. *Harvard Educational Review, 41,* 1–34.

RUBIN, A. D. (1978). *A theoretical taxonomy of the differences between oral and written language* (Technical Report 35). Champaign, IL: Center for the Study of Reading, University of Illinois.

RUMELHART, D. (1975). Notes on a schema for stories. In D. Bobrow & A. Collins (Eds.), *Representation and Understanding* (pp. 211–236). New York: Academic Press.

SCARDAMALIA, M., BEREITER, C., & GOELMAN, H. (1982). The role of production factors in writing ability. In M. Nystrand (Ed.), *What writers know: The language process and structure of written discourse* (pp. 173–210). New York: Academic Press.

SCOLLON, R., & SCOLLON, S. (1981). *Narrative, literacy, and face in inter-ethnic communication.* Norwood, NJ: Ablex.

SMITH, F. (1973). *Psycholinguistics and reading.* New York: Holt Rinehart & Winston.

SMITH, F. (1982). *Understanding reading* (3rd ed.). New York: Holt Rinehart & Winston.

SMITH, N. B. (1965). *American reading instruction.* Newark, DE: International Reading Association.

STUBBS, M. (1980). *The sociolinguistics of reading and writing: Language and literacy,* London: Routledge & Kegan Paul.

SULZBY, E. (1986). Children's elicitation and use of metalinguistic knowledge about word during literacy interactions. In D. B. Yaden, Jr. & S. Templeton (Eds.), *Metalinguistic awareness and beginning literacy* (pp. 219–233). Portsmouth, NH: Heinemann Educational Books.

TAYLOR, D. (1983). *Family literacy.* Exeter, NH: Heinemann Educational Books.

TEMPLE, C. A., NATHAN, R. G., BURRIS, N. A., & TEMPLE, F. (1988). *The beginnings of writing* (2nd ed.). Boston, MA: Allyn and Bacon.

TEMPLETON, S. (1980). Young children invent words: Developing concepts of "word-ness." *The Reading Teacher, 33,* 454–459.

TOMPKINS, G. E., & McGEE, L. M. (1986). Visually impaired and sighted children's concepts about written language. In D. Yaden, Jr. & S. Templeton (Eds.), *Metalinguistic awareness and beginning literacy* (pp. 259–275). Portsmouth, NH: Heinemann Educational Books.

VON BRACHT DONSKY, B. (1984). Trends in elementary writing instruction, 1900–1959. *Language Arts, 61,* 795–803.

VYGOTSKY, L. S. (1978). *Mind in society: The development of higher psychological processes* (Michael Cole, Trans.). Cambridge: Harvard University Press.

WOLF, D. (1984). Research currents: Learning about language skills from narratives. *Language Arts, 61,* 844–850.

YADEN, D. B., JR., & TEMPLETON, S. (1986). Introduction: Metalinguistic awareness—an etymology. In D. B. Yaden, Jr. & S. Templeton (Eds.), *Metalinguistic awareness and beginning literacy* (pp. 3–10). Portsmouth, NH: Heinemann Educational Books.

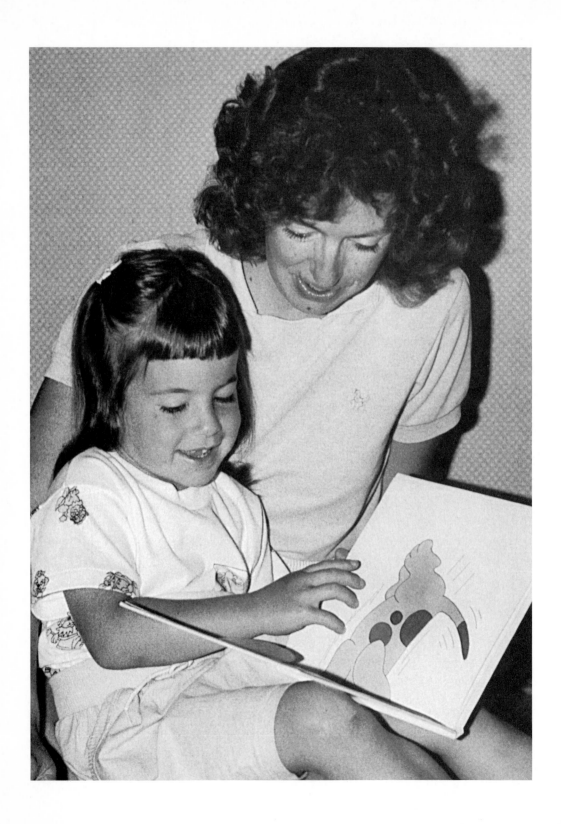

CHAPTER 2

How Young Children Learn about Literacy

Chapter 1 contained examples of what young children seem to be learning about reading, writing, and written language. In this chapter, we will examine *how* this learning about written language takes place. Before we address that question, we will look briefly at why children learn so much about written language. Then we will discuss how children learn in general (children do learn a lot about many things before they enter school!), and how learning in general applies to learning written language. We will show that learning about *written* language is like the learning of *spoken* language. Finally, we will look at specific examples from observational research and case studies that illustrate how young children have directed their own learning and how adults have helped young children to learn about written language.

WHY YOUNG CHILDREN LEARN ABOUT WRITTEN LANGUAGE

Children learn many things about written language. Children discover that written language *is* language, not just a drawing or marks on the page. Then children learn that written language has meaning and structure, or form, which helps convey that meaning. They also learn that written language is used with other people and for the specific purposes, or functions, that arise from the needs of people living together.

It is important to determine why young children bother to learn all these concepts. They have much to learn as it is—about their world, about their place in it, and about spoken language. In comparison, learning about written language may seem unnecessary and almost frivolous. One reason many young children direct their learning abilities toward written language is simply that written language is such a large part of their world. Children are surrounded by written language in use. Young children learn written language, in part, just because they are learning about their world and about their place in it. Written language is part of that world and can help them make their place among other people. Furthermore, young children learn about written language because they are already learning about spoken language. Learning spoken language and learning written language can be mutually supportive; they work in many of the same ways.

Young children learn about reading and writing because they are learning creatures, because they are social creatures, and because they are language-using creatures. They learn when they are given opportunities to engage their problem-solving minds. They learn when their needs and desires to interact with others are tapped. Finally, children learn whenever language is involved; language is a great ongoing learning project of at least their first ten years.

The world of the young child is filled with written-language-related stimuli that meet these criteria. Children see problems to be solved. They ask themselves:

> "What in the book makes Mommy and Daddy say what they say—they can't just say whatever they want?"

> "What are those shapes (letters in a store's logo) that appear on the drug store sign and on the sacks from the drug store?"

Children have social needs. They ask themselves:

> "How can I get more of this close one-to-one attention that goes with being read to?"

> "How can I announce for all time whose room this is? Or whose toy this is?"

Children interact with language. They ask themselves:

> "Could those squiggly lines on paper be doing the same thing that talking seems to be doing?"

> "What better way (better than wanting and hoping or even stamping my feet or crying or pointing) can I use to get attention, to announce, to remind?"

We do not mean that children consciously ask these questions. We do believe, however, that their actions strongly indicate that they are trying to solve the puzzles posed in these questions.

One requirement that must be met if children are to learn written language is that they must receive encouragement and support. Such encouragement and support includes inviting children to solve problems and helping children to put problems and their solutions into words. Parents and teachers provide that encouragement and support when they help write a child's announcement, reminder, or bid for attention. They provide support when they help a child to see that written language works the same wonders as spoken language, and when they encourage a child to explore the mechanics of writing as a way of putting language to work. With such support, children's understanding of written language can expand and grow along with their understanding of the rest of their world. When that happens, it is possible not only to see why children learn written language, but also to begin to see how they learn written language.

HOW YOUNG CHILDREN LEARN
ABOUT WRITTEN LANGUAGE

We have already mentioned that children are learning creatures and natural problem solvers. We talked about young children's having to understand their world and their place in it. We hinted that language plays a big role in accomplishing those major tasks. These notions come from the work of child development experts, people like Piaget and Vygotsky, who devoted their lives to understanding how children learn. In order to answer the question of how children learn language, we will look more closely at theories of child development, theories about how children grow and learn in general, and then apply these notions to children's learning of both spoken and written language.

Learning in General

Part of a child's intellectual or cognitive development involves making sense of early experiences. Language is one of those experiences. Both Piaget (1955) and Vygotsky (1962) examined how children acquire knowledge of the world and knowledge of language, but more importantly, both were interested in the relation between language learning and other learning. They agreed about many aspects of children's intellectual development, but they also had differences. Their most famous difference was in their theories about the relation between the development of intelligence and the development of language in young children. Both theories make important contributions to our understanding of cognitive development and language development, and we will look at important aspects of each theory, especially as they relate to young children's abilities to produce and understand spoken and written language.

Schemas and Learning

An important idea from both Piaget's and Vygotsky's work is the notion that knowledge is stored in mental structures or *schemas.* These schemas allow for easy access to knowledge and allow for it to be changed, added to, or rearranged to emphasize newly discovered relations between old ideas. For example, consider the concept, ''pineapple.'' Just the mention of the word *pineapple* probably brings to most people's minds several *features* of pineapples (that they are fruity, sweet, juicy, hard-to-eat, spiky, fresh or canned) and several *related concepts* (Hawaii, fruit salad, fruit cocktail, sharp knife, pina colada, bananas, mangos, garbage—lots to throw away with fresh pineapples). This is because one's knowledge of pineapples is organized. A mental organization of information (for example, about pineapples) is sometimes called a schema. We all have schemas about many things. Recognition, memory, and other mental processes depend on schemas. The features we use to recognize a pineapple or to remember a pineapple are somehow stored in the schema "pineapple." Similarly, the "pineapple" schema is somehow connected to related concepts or schemas (of Hawaii and fruit salad).

Schemas can grow and change. Suppose for the first time, we see someone save the green, spiky-leafed top of a pineapple, root it, and grow it as a house plant. As a result, we might modify our pineapple schema to include the new feature "decorative," and it may become newly connected to such concepts as "houseplant" and "asexual reproduction" (growing a new plant from a leaf, or root, or stem of an old plant, rather than from a seed).

One way to think about very young children's mental development is to imagine that children begin life with few concepts—or even none. Children's minds may be thought of as vacant structures, or empty schemas. There are only empty slots where features can go. This is the *tabula rasa* or blank slate notion of the young child's mind. One of Piaget's greatest insights was a suggestion of how children acquire the knowledge to begin filling those slots with features and making connections among schemas. He suggested that the infant's mind is actually far from a blank slate. It is true that young children have no (or very little) knowledge of *content* of the *things* (such as pineapples) that will eventually occupy their minds. However, children do have considerable inborn knowledge of *processes*. They seem to know how to go about acquiring content knowledge, or knowledge of things.

Piaget's idea was that young humans learn through action. They are born with special schemas for how to act and how to respond to their world. These action schemas bring children in contact with reality (things) in ways that produce knowledge of the world. More action produces more knowledge. As children acquire knowledge and continue to act, changes result in the things they are in contact with (for example, milk gets spilled) and changes result in previous knowledge (for example, the schema for milk gets changed to include the idea that milk does not behave like a cracker—it doesn't keep a shape). The action schemas themselves change as active, problem-solving children evolve more effective strategies for making their way in the world.

Two very important conclusions can be drawn from Piaget's theory of how children learn. One is that children create their own knowledge by forming and reforming schemas in their minds. The second conclusion is that children's state of knowledge—or view of the world—can be very different from one time to the next, and especially very different from an adult's. Returning to the pineapple example, we can ask what an infant's notion of a pineapple is. An infant is certainly not born with any knowledge of pineapples. In fact, infants do not know that anything or anyone else exists apart from themselves. One of the things infants have to learn early in life is that there is a world separate from them; this notion is called *object separateness*. Another, later notion is that objects in that world exist independently of children's experiencing them, even when children cannot see or hold or taste them; this notion is called *object permanence.* Infants must solve these two problems and acquire these two notions before having anything like an adult's concept of pineapple. Without notions of object separateness and object permanence, even seeing a pineapple every day would do little good. Even when children learn the object separateness concept, their notion of pineapple is incomplete. It will be added to and better connected with other notions as they have more experience with pineapples and eventually as they merely think more about pineapples. Even adults add to and adjust connections among schemas associated with pineapples, as shown in our example of pineapples-as-house-plants.

The point we wish to emphasize is that, because children construct their own knowledge, this knowledge does not come fully developed and is often quite different from that of an adult. Thus, there will be differences between how an adult understands reading and writing and how a child understands reading and writing. It is important for us to remember that such differences are just as real, just as natural (that is, they come from the way children are set up to learn), and just as understandable as differences between an adult's and a child's understandings of what a pineapple is.

The Relation between Language and Learning

Piaget's and Vygotsky's views differ on the role that language plays in the acquisition of schemas. We have already discussed the importance of action to Piaget's idea of learning. Children's actions may physically change objects in the world. A child may pull or stretch a lump of modeling clay, changing its shape. But then that same action may change the child's concept of modeling clay, adding the feature "stretchy," and it may allow the child to see a connection between modeling clay and bread dough (NOVA, 1985).

But can children change their schema for modeling clay to include the notion that it is stretchy without their hearing or using the *word* "stretchy"? Can they pretend that modeling clay is bread dough without hearing someone else say, or being able themselves to say, that both are "stretchy"? Another way to put these questions is to ask: How important is it for the child to have the word *stretchy* available as a label for what is experienced in such a situation? Piaget and Vygotsky would answer this question differently. Vygotsky placed more importance on the child's having language along with action in order to learn. He stressed the importance of having someone with the child who could supply that language. According to Vygotsky, a mother who says to her child, "Look at that *stretchy* clay!" plays a vital role in her child's learning about clay. Vygotsky placed a strong emphasis on the *social* component of cognitive and language development.

Vygotsky believed that children need to be able to talk about a new problem or a new concept in order to understand it and use it. Adults supply language that fits children's needs at a particular stage or in response to a particular problem. Language is part of a routinized situation. It can label the situation or parts of the situation, or it can help pose a problem or structure a problem-solving task.

As the child gradually internalizes the language that was first supplied by an adult, the problem and a routine task that helps in solving the problem become the child's own.

An example of a child's internalizing a routine is how the child learns to use the words *all gone.* The parents of a child who is working on the object permanence problem might repeatedly hide a favorite toy and then say, "All gone!" Then they reveal the toy and say "Here it is!" This becomes a game for the child. Eventually, the child may play the game without the adult, using the same language, "All gone" and "Here it is." Thus, such play—in which the words are an essential part—becomes an important first step in the child's learning object permanence.

Vygotsky spoke of a "zone of proximal development" that is an opportune area for growth, but one in which children are dependent on help from others. An adult or perhaps an older child must give young children advice if they are to succeed within this zone and if eventually, by internalizing that advice, they are to perform independently.

Although he stressed the role of biology, Piaget's theories of development were not without a social component as well. Piaget suggested that the persons most qualified to help children solve a new problem and move to the next stage of intellectual development are those who have just done so themselves. That is, children who are at that next stage, but not any higher, are the best guides to learning. Adults may even confuse children with their explanations. Adults' facility with language is not as valuable as the still very recent experience of children who have just successfully used action to make the changes in their schemas that are now needed by the younger child.

The teacher of young children must resist the temptation to see Vygotsky and Piaget as engaged in a great debate, and instead must look for common ground. It is easy when discussing Piaget and Vygotsky to stress their differences. Piaget is described as saying that thought comes before language and Vygotsky is described as saying the opposite. But, as our "All gone" example may have suggested to you, it is not that simple. Many psychologists are pointing out the merits of a compromise position.

Many children begin using the word *gone* at the same time that they are working on the object permanence problem. *Gone* is a word adults use to talk about that problem (Gopnick & Meltzoff, 1986). In other words, children use words that are related to the problems they are solving. This suggests that language and cognition really emerge at about the same time. Perhaps using the word *gone* helps children to solve the cognitive problem of object permanence, or perhaps *gone* suddenly acquires a fascination for children who have just solved that problem, making it a word they are very likely to use (Meltzoff, 1985).

Effective teachers get what they can from all current theories. They look for "zones of proximal development"; that is, they are aware of what is the next most fruitful area of exploration for the young child. Effective teachers provide opportunities for children to act and interact with each other, and they model new learning strategies and explain them to their students.

In the next section, we will look more closely at language. In answer to the question "How do children learn language?" we will again see that some theories emphasize inborn abilities and others emphasize a social component of language learning.

Learning Language

From numerous observations of young children's language behavior, language development experts have gained a growing understanding of *what* children learn about language (Gleason, 1989; Menyuk, 1988; Owens, 1988). They have even learned when, approximately, children acquire various abilities that are part of producing and comprehending spoken language. *What* children learn is very complex, and involves an elaborate interplay of abilities in the areas of syntax (word order), semantics (meaning), phonology (sound), and pragmatics (use of language). *When* children learn is variable; there are no hard and fast rules about at what age a child ought to be showing specific abilities, but there are agreed-upon sequences of abilities. For example, children use and understand the passive voice later than the active voice (Menyuk, 1969), and their ability to interpret sentences purely on the basis of syntax appears later than their ability to understand rote phrases that are well supported by familiar contexts and by routines (Snow & Goldfield, 1983).

The Nativist Theory of Language Learning

There is less consensus, even among experts, about the more theoretical question of *how* language ability is acquired. The *nativist theory* emphasizes what children are born with, and suggests that to a large extent language learning is an innate process. According to Chomsky (1957, 1983, 1988), some kind of innate "language acquisition device" is necessary to explain how a body of knowledge as complex as language can be acquired by almost all humans. That is, humans are born with an inclination to learn language, and they may even already know what kind of solutions to look for when solving language learning problems.

Some of what we know about how very young infants respond to language supports a notion of inborn language knowledge of some kind. Even four-week-old babies perceive speech sounds categorically. When a repeated "tah" sound is replaced by a repeated "dah" sound, the babies show they notice a change by increasing their sucking on a pacifier. It is important to note that the difference between "tah" and "dah" is very important in English—the *t* sound and the *d* sound are all that distinguish the members of many word pairs, for example, *duck/tuck* and *dime/time*. In other words, infants who are too young to have learned it know which sound differences are going to be important in their learning spoken language (Eimas, 1974).

Researchers have carefully observed such infant–mother exchanges as the baby's cooing, the mother's smiling and talking, and then the baby's smiling back. Some believe that this demonstrates that the babies have a natural, inborn motivation and ability to communicate (Trevarthan, 1985). This belief comes from observing that even this early behavior is very complex (too complex to have been learned so early in life) and that the baby is as active in initiating and directing interaction as the mother (Trevarthan & Marwick, 1986).

There is much controversy about how powerful children's inborn inclination to learn language is. All experts agree that there is some role for a biological component. The question is whether a language acquisition device needs only a minimal triggering from the child's environment or whether it requires adults' supporting it in complex ways.

The Social Interactionist Theory of Language Learning

A theory that puts more emphasis on a social component of language acquisition is the *social interactionist* theory. Proponents of this theory stress not so much the child's desire to communicate as the parents' or other care givers' desires that the child be communicative. Motivated by this desire, parents treat even babies' accidental or random sounds as intentional, communicative acts. An example would be when a baby makes a gurgling sound and her mother responds as if the baby intended something meaningful by that sound. She may say, "Oh really?! And what else is new?" (Snow, 1985).

The assumptions of the social interactionist theory of language development are that children start out not being truly communicative, and that an essential characteristic of language is intentionality. Care givers actively teach children that language is intentional. That is what babies learn from hearing someone answer their nonlanguage sounds (like gurgling) even though the babies did not intend the sounds to be meaningful.

In order to adequately appreciate the importance of intentionality, we must sometimes turn our attention away from what usually attracts it. Often what we notice most easily about young children's language development are the surface features such as new words, long words, new sentence structures, and complex sentence structures.

When four-year-old Carrie is playing in the sandbox and she uses a novel word in an unusual phrase ("I'm going to *nicen it up* with the rake"), adults notice. Likewise, when she uses a complex sentence—with a conditional and a time reference, no less!—("If you don't know about this, then you never made it before"), adults are likely to notice.

As amazing as all this is, however, what is more important for the child is to get things done. We will see this if we focus our attention on intentionality and on the fact that the child speaks *to someone*. A child does not learn the surface features for their own sake, but in order to express intentions, to get things done in the world—things like requesting, indicating, protesting, and asserting. Learning language requires the close, purposeful interaction of *two* human beings, one of whom already knows how to use language and can provide the learner with the desirable outcomes of intending (Bruner, 1984, 1985). It is as if the child is thinking, "If this is what Mommy or Daddy will do when they think I meant something by that sound (or word or words), maybe I'll try it again—

and maybe really mean it next time!'' Those who study these interactions have called them ''language learning routines'' or ''formats'' or ''scaffolds'' (Bruner, 1978, 1983; Gleason, Hay, & Cain, 1989, Snow, 1983).

Routines for language learning. Language learning routines are repeated situations, such as peek-a-boo games, bedtime activities, or storyreading sessions in which adults provide recurring, predictable objects and actions. Within these situations, children are able to test, retest, use with increasing independence, and otherwise explore, the unchanging words and phrases that are just one part of the routine. Adults are able to observe children's developing language abilities and to react appropriately, such as by expecting children to contribute more of the language that is part of the situation (Ninio & Bruner, 1978).

An example of a routine is what often happens at bedtime. In the bedtime routine, a very young child's mother or father may routinely turn on the nightlight, put down the child's crib rail, and say ''It's time for you to go to bed now.'' The child may respond appropriately, putting away a toy or book and coming over to the bed. This is impressive behavior, but at first it probably does not mean that the child understands every word in ''It's time for you to go to bed now,'' nor is it likely that the child knows how the syntax of that sentence works (Gleason, 1985). When the routir is still new, the child is responding to the situation, which is full of clues (pro, nd the parent's own appropriate actions) and has been repeated night after night for a long time.

As the routine gets older and the child learns what behavior is appropriate for the situation, he or she can begin to learn a great deal about the words, which are as much a part of the situation as the props and actions are. The repeated use of those words gives the child time and support so that eventually he or she can do a syntactic analysis of it, and can understand the words and how they work in that sentence structure (Snow, 1985). At some point, the child will even be able to apply this understanding to similarly structured sentences in different contexts.

Bookreading as a routine for language learning. One of the best opportunities for language learning by routines occurs when parents and children read books together. The pictures and text in a book remain the same regardless of how often parents and children return to the book (and children often demand to return to the same book many times!). One of the first comprehensive studies of such a routine was of picture-book reading by a mother and her son from when he was eight months old to when he was eighteen months old (Ninio & Bruner, 1978). Their interaction had the structure of a routinized dialogue. The mother spoke and then the child spoke, at first just with sounds, but later with words. At first, the mother interpreted the child's gestures and babbling as attempts at labeling and responded by giving the label herself as if in confirmation of what the boy had said. Once he began using words, the mother insisted that he say words; if the boy babbled, she would respond, ''What's that?'' Although their respective parts in the routine changed, the routine itself, (that is, the structure of the dialogue) remained the same. Ninio and Bruner stress that first the boy and his mother had to learn this ritualized dialogue; only after that could the boy learn names for the objects shown in the picture books. The interaction of boy and mother is more than mere modeling and imitation; it is social and complex.

Bookreading routines can also involve older children and other kinds of books. When a mother and her three-year-old read *The Cat in the Hat* (Seuss, 1958) together over a four-month period, they too developed a routine (Snow, Dubber, & deBlauw, 1982). After one month and between 10 and 20 readings, the child participated by supplying rhyming words or short phrases that completed a sentence or verse from the book. The mother read "they have come here to play/they will give you some fun on this" and the child finished with "wet wet wet wet day" (p. 65). Three months later, the mother's parts were the smaller ones; they were prompts (for example, "What's that say?") or first words or phrases of sentences. The child was taking the longer turns, providing memorized—but shortened and restructured—chunks of the text. The bookreading routine had begun with the mother doing most of the reading, but ended with just the opposite. The child had acquired the language which had at first been supplied by the mother and which was kept constant for both of them by the book, or more accurately, by the routinized use of the book and by the author's, the mother's, and the child's intentional, social use of written language.

Instructional routines. Routines for both spoken and written language learning can continue to influence children's development well into the elementary school years. Teachers and students can negotiate routines and devise agreed-upon patterns of interaction to be used again and again for learning many different things. The term *instructional scaffolding* refers to this kind of interaction (Applebee & Langer, 1983). For example, a teacher and her class may have worked out a way of talking about books students are reading, papers they are writing, or projects they are working on. In any of these situations, the teacher and the students know that the participants in a teacher-to-student or a student-to-student interaction will talk about purposes, will take turns giving input in a collaborative manner, and will return the task to the student who started it for him or her to internalize and build on what was discussed.

Learning Written Language

Children learn about written language in much the same way that they learn anything else, including spoken language. They acquire and modify schemas for the various aspects of written language knowledge that were presented in Chapter 1. They use inborn abilities, and they depend on interactions with others. There are both Piagetian and Vygotskian perspectives on learning written language; some people who have studied the literacy learning of young children emphasize biology, and others emphasize social interaction.

A Piagetian Approach

Children's written language learning can be explored from a Piagetian perspective. This view of literacy development emphasizes stages of development. From this view we would expect that reading and writing behavior at some stages would be very different from conventional reading and writing because it reflects concepts of, or schemas for, reading and writing *as the child has constructed them.*

Children's concepts of reading and writing are shaped more by what they accomplished in preceding developmental stages than by their simply imitating adults' behavior or following adults' directions. At an early stage, children may use the same two or three letters in a few two- or three-letter combinations (such as CT, OT, CTO, and CC) for any word they want to write. They do so because they happen to know how to form three letters and because they have constructed a notion or schema for a written word that is very different from an adult's. A written word is thought of simply as a combination of letters (Ferreiro & Teberosky, 1982). It does not matter that children see adults using other letters; they may actually resist an adult's telling them to spell certain words in conventional ways. They may be happy for the time being with their own solutions to the problem of "What is a written word?" and want to keep that solution. Adults need not be alarmed, though. Experience eventually forces children to abandon concepts that are very different from those of adults.

Children's understandings about written language parallel their understandings in other areas (Ferreiro, 1985), and the means by which they reach those understandings are the same. For example, at one stage children discover a "principle of syllabication" as a solution to the puzzle of how to make their written words correspond to their talk. They make one mark per syllable in their writing; this idea suits their writing needs well at this stage. This principle is very similar to the principle of one-to-one correspondence in counting. It is learned through problem-solving action; then it is challenged by additional data the child receives from the environment. Children soon begin to encounter many words that do not follow the principle of one mark per syllable. In the face of this difficulty, they act to reach new levels of understanding, and eventually discover the alphabetic principle upon which the English writing system is based. They may at first be happy with an early solution to the written language puzzle, but eventually experience forces them to reconstruct old schemas to account for new discoveries (again, whether it be a schema for the written word or one for pineapple). This literacy learning behavior is very similar to what Piaget describes as children learn about other things such as object permanence. According to this view, there is more involved than simply the social influences of adults and older children (Ferreiro, 1985). In fact, social influences, especially an adult's suggestions based on the conventions of the mature, standard writing system, can sometimes be harmful.

It is true that adults' comments can be positive. That is the case when the comments are easy to assimilate or even when they pose problems that force the child to find new solutions. For example, an adult may notice that a child's writing is governed by the principle of syllabication. Let us suppose that the adult has observed the child writing six marks on the page while saying a six-syllable message about a drawing, "Riding at Fun Fair Park." A supportive adult might say, "Oh, I see how that works," and point to each mark while repeating each word of the child's message. Then, if the child seems ready for the problem that will lead him or her beyond the principle of syllabication, the adult might point to two identical marks for different syllables (for example, *Fair* and *Park*) and ask, "I wonder how you could show that those two are different words?"

However, sometimes adults' comments can be negative—when they simply inhibit the child's going through the steps that necessarily precede attainment of the final, mature principles. This would be the case, for example, if the adult in the above example had said, "No. No. You need more than one letter for each of these words. See—*Riding* is spelled, *R* for 'rrrr,' *I* for 'eye,' *D* for 'duh,' *I–N–G* for 'ing.' And *at* has two letters. And *Fun Fair Park* is spelled like this: F–U–N F–A–I–R P–A–R–K. See?" The child would probably not see—for as we already mentioned, he or she probably does not even know many letters at this stage and may not know what the words *sound* and *letter* mean.

Furthermore, even if the child did know something about sounds and letters (and had written "Riding at Fun Fair Park" as RETFFP), the point is that his or her concept of writing has no room yet for all the rules the adult is giving. Teachers of young children must note at what stage a child is operating and watch how the child receives their actions and suggestions.

A Vygotskian Approach

Children's written language learning can also be explored from a Vygotskian perspective. This view of literacy learning emphasizes social interaction and it places less emphasis on predetermined stages of behavior than a Piagetian view does. There is an emphasis, instead, on the social aspect of young children's literacy behaviors, especially on their intending to communicate with others (Harste, Burke, & Woodward, 1983) and on their using routines to learn about written language (Snow, 1983).

A very young child's drawing and writing do not always look meaningful. When adults cannot understand what a child intended, they often assume that nothing was intended. This is a mistake. It is just as important with written language as with spoken language for adults to show children that they know the children are intending to convey meanings. One of the best ways of insuring that this is done is for the child and adult to have routine ways of interacting during literacy events.

We can illustrate this by returning to our "Fun Fair Park" example. The first (positive) adult in that example recognized the child's intention to communicate by repeating the child's message while reading what the child had written—even though there were only six marks on the page. The adult would not have been able to do this if the adult and the child had not already established a routine of the child's writing labels for pictures, the adult's observing *while the child worked,* and the adult's reading whatever the child wrote.

The following real-life example illustrates the importance of expecting children to communicate and recognizing their intentions to communicate with written language. Figure 2.1 looks like a meaningless conglomeration of random letters, pictures, and scribbles. We know better, however, because one of the authors was present when Cody wrote it. It is actually a very meaningful piece; its composition was not at all haphazard.

Figure 2.1 *Cody's Drawing and Writing*

Four-year-old Cody was staying for a few hours with one of her mother's friends. After they had spent time looking at books together, the friend asked Cody if she wanted to write her own book. Cody said she could write her name. She said, "My name is C–O–D–Y." Her writing is shown in Figure 2.2. Next, Cody wanted to write an S, but said to her friend, "I can't write S. Will you write S for me?" The friend wrote the large S shown in the upper right in Figure 2.1 and then urged her to draw a picture for her book. Cody said she would draw herself and proceeded to draw her face, hair, mouth, nose, and eyes (see

Figure 2.2 *Cody's Signature*

face in upper left in Figure 2.1). When she had finished her drawing, Cody wrote
three wavy lines and identified them: ''I wrote a bedtime story'' (see Figure 2.3).
Next, Cody said ''I need a blanket.'' She scribbled all over the top of her bedtime
story (that is, over her wavy lines—making them look like Figure 2.4) and announced, ''There is my blanket.'' Finally, she asked her friend, ''How do you
spell your name?'' Her friend said, ''L–E–A.'' First Cody said ''A,'' and then ''E''
as she wrote those letters (seen in the bottom right of Figure 2.1). Then she
asked, ''Now how do you write L?'' and wrote the backwards L in her friend's
name shown in Figure 2.1.

Figure 2.3 *Cody's Bedtime Story*

Figure 2.4 *Cody's Picture of a Blanket*

It is probably clear by now that if you superimpose the very meaningful
drawing and writing in Figures 2.2 through 2.4, your result is the seemingly
haphazard piece in Figure 2.1. This haphazard piece has been revealed to be a
bedtime story. Because the three wavy lines were so quickly covered up, Cody's
friend could not ask her to read the bedtime story, and so we may only
guess what it is about. However, this written record of it survives, complete with
Cody's name, her friend's name, and a picture of Cody under a blanket.

It is fascinating to note Cody's sophisticated knowledge about written language. She writes names with real letters. Her story is composed of wavy lines

that simulate the lines of print on a book's page; this shows that she knows a story involves a lot more writing than a name does. She strives for unity—the very opposite of haphazardness; she even connected her self-portrait with her bedtime story by putting it under a blanket. It is important to note that all of this would have gone undetected and unsupported if her adult friend had not treated Cody as a writer, communicating the message to Cody that, like the authors of the books the friend and she had read together, Cody could write a book. This example emphasizes the value of a Vygotskian approach to children's literacy learning efforts. Sensitive parents or teachers will support children like Cody in their writing and reading efforts; they will routinely open "zones of proximal development" by giving them the words to describe their creations. They will say, for example, "That's a great *story*," or "I hope you'll make more *stories* like that for me."

BEYOND THEORY: STRATEGIES CHILDREN AND ADULTS USE FOR WRITTEN LANGUAGE LEARNING

We have looked at theories of development and at how cognitive development, oral language development, and written language development are interrelated. Next we will examine some specific strategies that children use to direct their own learning, as well as strategies adults use to support this learning. The strategies are drawn from observations of children and their parents, teachers, siblings, and friends as they experiment with written language. It is important to apply theory to the strategies as they are presented, and we will examine relations between theory and the observational research and case studies. We begin with children's strategies for learning literacy.

Strategies Children Use to Learn about Written Language

Children use many strategies to learn about literacy. Some of their strategies are for writing, some are for reading, and some encompass both. This is not surprising; the two processes are closely related and children learn about the two at the same time and in some of the same ways.

We use the observations of four groups of researchers who have made it possible for us to begin to see what tools children use to direct and control their own learning about written language. Although there are many possible strategies to describe, we will devote our attention to eight which we believe will help readers appreciate that children are indeed able to write and read long before many adults think they can. Table 2.1 presents a summary of each of these strategies.

Strategy One: Looking for Intended Meanings

Harste, Burke, and Woodward (1983, 1984) are a team of researchers who have studied young children's reading and writing. They describe several principles

Table 2.1 *Strategies Children Use to Learn about Written Language*

NAME OF STRATEGY	EXAMPLE	VERBALIZATION
Looking for intended meanings	Trademark symbol	"I know that there is a meaning here. It would do me good to find it. Each part must make sense in relation to all the other parts."
Using language as an open-ended process	THANK YOU FOR NOT SMOKING	"I know this doesn't have to say just one thing. What does it say to me?"
Taking risks	"You mean pretend to read?"	"How can I take this risk and not end up looking like a fool?"
Repeating elements of written language	Figure 2.6	"I want to write. Much writing that I've seen fills a page. I want to fill a page. I'll make a long statement by making the same symbol again and again and again."
Experimenting with what you know	Figures 2.6 and 2.7	"I know that there are lots of different letters. But I don't know how to make them all. How far can I change the letter forms that I do know? Will I end up with a different Letter? Will I end up with a letter at all?"
Generating a lot from a little	Figure 2.8	"I know how to make only three (or four or five) letters. But I have a lot to say. I can make a long statement by using those letters to make lots of different, 'words,' different combinations of those letters."
Talking and drawing while making written language	"Sister, open up the door."	"I can draw a story. I can say the story while I draw it and write it. And I can read it if I say the same thing again."
Asking an adult questions	"Where's the *puzzled elves*?"	"If I can't find a unified meaning here, I should not just assume there is none. There should be one. So I will ask what it is."

that children use as they make their way toward becoming readers and writers. The first three strategies we describe follow from young writers' acting according to these principles.

One strategy many children use for learning about written language is to concentrate on meaning in written language settings. A simple example has to do with the first reading that many very young children do. They look for words (on a sign in front of a store or the tiny "ON" and "OFF" printed on an electric switch) that might be congruent with the context in which they are found. Children know that the words "ON" and "OFF" on an electric switch must match the meaning of turning lights on and off; they will not be related to eating or going to the store, or anything else. They *must* relate to the setting, to turning lights on and off. Similarly, children read other environmental print by paying attention to the context, to the situation, and to what people are doing. When Ted was two years old, he could read the sign identifying the grocery store where his family always shopped. He knew it said ''Eagle'' because it was located on the front of the grocery store and his mother had told him they were going to get some groceries.

When some children are a little older they use this strategy to read their own writing. In our example of the bedtime story Cody wrote (see Figures 2.1–2.4), we emphasized the importance of adults' treating children's writing as intentional and meaningful even when it appears illegible. One of the benefits of this is that children learn to treat their own writing this way. At first, they may not even remember what they were intending when they created a particular piece of writing. However, if adults frequently ask them to read their pieces, they will come to know that they can retrieve their intended meanings. Along with this comes the understanding that they can retrieve the meanings others intended in many kinds of writing, not just grocery store signs and McDonald's labels.

In other words, children use their understanding that all language is intentional to make discoveries about others' writings. They expect even the writing in books (not just signs and labels) to have something to say to them. They know written language is not just a random occurrence of squiggly lines and shapes. Furthermore, they know that, in the long run, it is not good to ignore or disregard such writing; it is important to know its meanings.

A literacy event involving four-year-old Charles is a particularly appropriate example of a child's looking for intended meaning in environmental print. Charles read ''Jello'' when shown a box of Jello pudding. But even more illustrative of his search for meaning was his adding, ''What's that little mark mean?'' and pointing to the trademark symbol. Later, Charles read ''Band aid'' when shown a Johnson & Johnson's Band-Aid box, but again he tried to understand how that other part of the written mark related to its meaning. Looking at the trademark symbol, he said ''There it is again'' (Harste, Burke, & Woodward, 1983, pp. 112–113.)

In a literacy event involving five-year-old Beth, we have an example of a child's examination of her own writing for intended meanings. Beth was videotaped while writing, drawing, scribbling, and talking to herself. By the time she finished, she had created what looked like a page of scribbles. When she was asked to read what she had written, however, she said that it was a story about herself and her brothers playing rocket at home. When researchers analyzed the videotape, they were able to see when Beth wrote her name, when she wrote her brothers' names, when she drew their house and a rocket, when she wrote numbers for the countdown, and when she obliterated her creation with scribbles that represented the exhaust from the rocket's launch (Harste, Burke, & Woodward, 1983).

We have an example of a child looking for intended meanings in a storybook in a literacy event involving five-year-old Jill. She was asked to read or pretend to read the book, *The Ten Little Bears*. This is a book with pictures and text about ten bears who leave home, one at a time. Although Jill could only read the pictures (and not the text), she was quite able to attend to meaning. At first she thought it was a story about a group of bears who went on various trips. But then she noticed the many pictures showing the bears who were left at home after another bear had set out on its own. She had to make the pictures fit her story and make what she said at each page fit that page's picture. So she counted the bears who were left at one point and decided the caption was "Then five little bears stayed home." The actual text was "Then five little bears were at home" (Harste, Burke, & Woodward, 1983, p. 112).

So the principle of intentionality not only enlightens our observations of children's reading and writing, but it also motivates children to explore written language. They approach written language with a strategy that might be expressed: "I know that there is a meaning here. It would do me good to find it. Each part must make sense in relation to all the other parts."

Strategy Two: Using Language as an Open-Ended Process

A second strategy children use to learn about literacy is to use written language in an open-ended way. Harste, Burke, and Woodward (1983), call this the principle of *generativeness*. "In an open-ended way" means responding to the fact that language is an open system; it can be used to make an infinite number of messages.

One way that language is open is that its symbols—words, clauses, sentences—can be used in an infinite number of combinations. We will address this aspect in Strategy Six. Another way that language is an open-ended system is that users of language interpret a given instance of language in their own ways, depending on their purposes and background experiences.

Most people do not regard a "THANK YOU FOR NOT SMOKING" sign on someone's desk simply as a graphic representation of a prohibition. Nonsmokers might not even notice the message; the sign is just another object on a probably already filled-up desk top. Smokers who acknowledge that others have a right to control the quality of the air that fills their work space may see the sign as a rather polite declaration of that right and so respect it. On the other hand, smokers who think nonsmokers have gone too far in imposing their life style on others may see the sign as an affront or even a challenge; they may resent or ignore the sign, depending both on their status relative to the desk's occupant and on the relationship they would like to establish or maintain with that person.

An anecdote involving three-year-old Nathan provides an example of the open-endedness of written language, even when very young children are involved. Like Charles in our earlier example, Nathan was asked to read a Jello pudding box. He said, "It's got sugar in it" (Harste, Burke, & Woodward, 1983, p. 125). Harste, Burke, and Woodward note that General Foods would probably prefer that language operate in a more closed manner, that their label not mean "sugar product" to anyone. But General Foods has no more control over people's interpretations than the desk's occupant has over the various irrelevant, polite, or confrontational meanings others see in the "THANK YOU FOR NOT SMOKING" sign.

What Nathan is doing that all language users and learners do is approaching this writing sample with a strategy that might be expressed: "I know this doesn't have to say just one thing. What does it say to me?" Although written language depends on conventions (for example, it simplifies matters if we agree on a system for spelling *thank you,* and *for* and *not* and *smoking*), and although one of its greatest advantages is its permanence (you don't have to keep asking people not to smoke—the sign is always there), it is not and cannot be absolutely precise.

Strategy Three: Taking Risks

A third strategy children use to learn about written language is to take risks. All language is social, but written language has the added feature of being permanent (Harste, Burke, & Woodward, 1983). This means that writers leave behind a trail of marks for all to see and readers can be held accountable to the written text. This can be intimidating, especially for beginners.

When four-year-old Benjamin was asked to read *The Ten Little Bears,* he balked. "You mean pretend to read?" he asked. When he was assured "Yes, just do the best you can," he was able to proceed and read (Harste, Burke, & Woodward, p. 144). Benjamin was following a strategy that might be expressed: "How can I take this risk and not end up looking like a fool?" As long as everyone knew he was just pretending to do something that he knew was beyond his powers, everything was all right.

Some children have a hard time learning to take risks. Unfortunately, they give up at the point when they perceive that there are processes involved in reading and writing that they do not know. Adults must help them to acquire the strategy of risk taking. Without being helped to take risks, children may not make the exploratory steps that lead to learning those processes.

Strategy Four: Repeating Elements
of Written Language

Marie Clay is another researcher who has studied young children's reading and writing. She describes several principles that children use as they make their way toward becoming writers (Clay, 1975). We will use three of her principles as sources of strategies that many young writers employ.

The first strategy is that of repeating written elements. This is based on Clay's (1975) *recurring principle.* Clay noticed that children often go through a stage of spontaneously repeating forms—in both their drawing and their writing. Children draw pages full of the same pictures or variations of the same basic form, as Carrie did in Figure 2.5. Similarly, they fill pages with repeated letters or words, as Carrie did in Figure 2.6.

It is as if the child who knows only a few letters is using a strategy that might

Figure 2.5 *Carrie's Repeated Drawings*

Figure 2.6 *Carrie's Repeated Letter Forms*

be expressed: "I want to write. Much writing that I've seen fills a page. I want to fill a page. I'll make a long statement by making the same symbol again and again and again."

It is important to note that when a teacher assigns a repeated copying task, it can be boring for the child and the results can be more and more poorly formed letters. But when children do it because they are spontaneously using the repeating strategy, they can feel a wonderful sense of accomplishment (Clay, 1975). It is also important to remember that although a page full of the same forms may appear meaningless, children do not perform such a language act without intending it to mean something; this accomplishment is an expression of meaning.

Strategy Five: Experimenting with What You Know

The repeating strategy does not hold up for long. Children learn that written language is not really pages full of the same letter or word. They discover the *flexibility principle.* By this Clay (1975) means that children come to realize that some variation is allowed and even appropriate in written forms.

Many children experiment with writing before they know how to make conventional forms. They create forms that are not what adults use, but resemble what adults use. Thus, children growing up surrounded by English will at first make forms that look like English letters, but which are not exactly English letters, and children in other cultures do the same with respect to their culture's writing. Three children's scribblings collected by Harste, Burke, and Woodward (1983) make this point. An American child's scribbling is clearly influenced by English cursive writing; it consists of two rows of humps and loops and peaks. A Saudi Arabian child's scribbling is influenced by Arabic script; it consists of tighter loops and more individual units embellished with dots and accent marks. An Israeli child's scribbling is influenced by Hebrew characters; it consists of several separate block-like forms. In Figure 2.7, a five-year-old Chinese girl has labeled her picture by writing two symbols that resemble Chinese characters, although neither is a real Chinese character.

Figure 2.7 *A Five-Year-Old's Drawing with Mock Chinese Characters*

Children who know a few conventional forms use them as starting points for experimentation; they make variations on those forms. When Carrie made the repeated forms in Figure 2.6, she knew how to form only a few English letters, among them *C, i,* and *H.* A *C* and an *i* are discernable in this sample. Most of the forms she has made, however, are not those known letters, but variations on them. Thus, her flexibility and creativity manifest themselves in creatively formed ''letters.''

The strategy illustrated in these examples might be expressed: ''I know that there are lots of different letters. But I don't know how to make them all. How far can I change the letter forms that I do know? Will I end up with a different letter? Will I end up with a letter at all?''

As children experiment in this way, they come closer and closer to orthodox letter forms (Clay, 1975). It is as if they are learning the limits by testing them, pushing at the boundaries of what is allowed. Eventually the limits will be found to be, in one sense at least, quite restrictive. That is, even very slight variations produce changes in meaning that the writer might not have intended. You cannot, for example, shorten the first stroke in *hot* by very much without its becoming *not*. You may, however, change *hot* to **hot** or to *HOT* without necessarily creating problems.

Strategy Six: Generating a Lot From a Little

Children exploit the characteristic of open-endedness in their strategy of generating a lot from a little. For example, once children learn how to form letters, they can combine them to make a seemingly endless number of words. They can also combine words to make a literally endless number of sentences. This is what Clay (1975) describes as the *generating principle.* As soon as children have even a few symbols at their disposal, they discover that a new kind of variation (different from what was described in Strategy Five) is possible; they can create different patterns from those few symbols. We see this in a drawing/writing Carrie made shortly after she created Figures 2.5 and 2.6. In Figure 2.8 she has generated an entire tableau based on different combinations of forms (both picture and letter forms) that she had perfected earlier.

This strategy for producing written language might be expressed: ''I know how to make only three (or four or five) letters. But I have a lot to say. I can make a long statement by using those letters to make lots of different 'words,' different combinations of those letters.'' It is interesting to notice how much more children have discovered about written language by the time they are using this strategy than they had when they were solving the same problem (wanting to write a long statement but knowing only a few letters) using only the strategy of repeating elements (compare Figures 2.6 and 2.8).

Strategy Seven: Talking and Drawing While Making Written Language

Another observer of young children's writing, Anne Haas Dyson, has noted a relation between drawing development and writing development. Dyson (1985)

Figure 2.8 *Carrie's Drawing with Letter Combinations*

noted that children sometimes talked to themselves as they wrote and drew at writing centers in preschools and kindergarten classrooms. Other times, they talked to Dyson as she sat at the writing table with them. In either case, the talk not only revealed their processes to the observer, but also held the child on a story-making track. This talking strategy was important for the making of the story and for its retrieval because not all of the story was recorded either in pictures or in written symbols, and because the written symbols were seldom ones that the children themselves or anyone else could really read, in the conventional sense of reading. Often all three elements—talking, drawing, and writing—complemented one another; they were consistent with the story and they showed the same orientation or motivation on the part of the child.

An example of a five-year-old named Rachel illustrates this strategy of talking and drawing while writing. Rachel drew a house with people inside and outside and wrote a line of nonconventional print at the top of the paper. Rachel spoke the part of one of the characters in her picture as she drew the picture. She even knocked on the table when that character was to knock on the door of the house she had drawn. Then Rachel said to herself, "That's what it's gonna be saying" and wrote the line of print. When she had finished, Rachel invited Dyson to come to her table and told Dyson that the line of print said, "Open the door, Sister. Open, open, open, else I'm gonna' throw this pumpkin shell right on your head" (Dyson, 1985, p. 99). A grown-up would not have been able to read Rachel's line of print. Rachel, however, read it by using almost exactly the same words she had used when she had spoken her character's part while drawing. It is as if Rachel were using a strategy that might be expressed: "I can draw a story. I can say the story while I draw it and write it. And I can read it if I say the same thing again."

In this example, the motivation for the talk, the drawing, and the writing was Rachel's clear sense of audience. We have described similar interactions in the examples of Cody's and Beth's writing. In all three of these cases, important factors included the child's talking to himself or herself, the child's drawing, and the child's talking with an adult either during or after the writing process. The children's drawing and their talking are as much a part of their encoding process as their writing. The talk and drawing help to reveal the encoding process (putting down on paper) to us; but more importantly *for the child*, they seem to help the child with the later decoding process (saying for someone else what they were thinking and saying as they wrote and drew).

Strategy Eight: Asking an Adult Questions

Another kind of children's talk that helps them to learn about written language is their asking questions about reading and writing and meaning. Many researchers (for example, Durkin, 1966; Price, 1976) have found that young children persistently ask questions about print. Yaden and his colleagues (Yaden & McGee, 1984) studied how young children's talk about illustrations and about the print that accompanies illustrations in children's books helps the children with meaning making (in this case, understanding the meaning the author intended). Yaden analyzed the questions that his two sons asked as he read to them. Jon-Marc was two years and two months old and David was four years and one month old at the start of the sixteen-month period of study. These children asked many kinds of questions. For example, Jon-Marc frequently asked "What's that?" about something in a picture. Often this question interrupted the flow of the oral reading; it had no obvious tie to what his father had just read. A different, more integrated kind of question began to appear in storyreading sessions with David. It was the text-cued question, a question about print rather than about a picture. Actually, David's earliest text-cued questions were about print *in* pictures (speech "balloons," signs, and storefronts within illustrations). Later, however, he asked about the print that constituted the text of the story his father was reading. An example of a later text-cued question is David's asking, "Where's the *puzzled elves?*" when his father had just read a sentence containing that unusual phrase.

During the sixteen months of Yaden's study, both children asked a growing number of text-cued questions. Many of these questions showed a desire for coherence between text and pictures. There is the same search for unity of meaning that we saw in the strategy of looking for intended meanings (Strategy One): Everything has to go together, whether it is the Jello label and the strange trademark symbol that Charles noticed by it, or a storybook illustration and the strange words, "puzzled elves," that David had just heard his father read.

The strategy children use to find that unity when it is not immediately apparent to them is to *ask*. This strategy might be worded: "If I can't find a unified meaning here, I should not just assume there is none. There should be one. So I will ask what it is." Charles did this when his first response to the trademark symbol was to *ask*, "What's that little mark mean?"

Before we move to adults' strategies, we must add three notes of caution. The first is that we have presented only some of the strategies that children use as they attempt to solve the puzzles of how to produce and understand written language. The second is that children do not consciously use the words we have used to illustrate these strategies. However, from what we have observed, children seem to be using means to solve reading and writing puzzles that would follow from thinking or saying the words in our illustrations. The third caution is that, although our examples have used children who are in the early stages of literacy learning, many of the principles and strategies cited last into the elementary school years (and even beyond). In later chapters, we will show how these principles and strategies can operate in the elementary school as well as the nursery school, provided teachers understand them and support them.

Strategies Adults Use to Help Children
Learn about Written Language

In the past, parents were warned not to teach their preschool children to read nor even to encourage them to experiment with reading. It was thought that parents might do more harm than good. One reason this notion has been rejected (see Chapter 1) is that several case studies have shown that parents and other adults *can* do much good in supporting children's literacy learning. We will look at some of these case studies.

First we will review what we have already shown about how important adults are in children's learning. In Chapter 1, Ted and Carrie's father joined in their restaurant play, taking cues from the context, from their talk, and from their writing about how to play their game. He did not criticize Ted's spelling or point out how incomplete Carrie's check was. Similarly, adults encouraged Beth, Rachel, Charles, Cody, Nathan, and Benjamin by asking them questions that carried the message, "I know you can read (or write). Show me what you know." They were respectful of and curious about the stage of each child's literacy learning. Jon-Marc and David's father answered their questions; but he did even more than that by first of all establishing a positive, warm, secure, interactive routine in which they enjoyed storybook reading and felt free to ask questions.

These examples show that adult strategies may be found by looking for counterparts to many of the children's strategies we have already mentioned. Supportive adults look for intended meanings in their children's use of written language; they treat their children's written language behavior in an open-ended manner, that is, they are open to their children's non-literal use of written language; and they make risk taking easier for their children. We will examine some specific examples of adults' using these strategies. As with the children's strategies, most of the adults' strategies are unconscious. The adults *act as if* they were thinking or saying the words we will use to describe the strategies. We present these adult strategies partly with the objective of enabling teachers to use them in preschool and elementary classrooms. Table 2.2 presents a summary of the four strategies for adults that follow.

Table 2.2 *Strategies Adults Use to Help Children Learn about Written Language*

NAME OF STRATEGY	EXAMPLE	VERBALIZATION
Engaging children in dialogue about written language	*In the Night Kitchen*	"I will not be just a performer, but a model and a leader, showing how to build—and getting us cooperatively to build—an interpretation of this story. I will comment on the story, be aware of my listeners' responses, and adjust my further reading and commentary to those responses. I will engage in dialogue with my listeners."
Being a supportive player	"I play golf."	"My child sees reading and writing going on all around her. She will naturally role play reading and writing. I will take the lead from her. She'll show me what she understands and what help she needs by the kinds of questions she asks."
Socializing the young	Bedtime story or no bedtime story in three communities.	"Reading and writing are an important part of our community's culture. Part of my job as a parent is to help my children function in this community. I'm going to let them in on the use of reading and writing just as I let them in on other important pieces of cultural knowledge."
Accepting and encouraging children's own constructions of literacy knowledge	"You write it and I'll be able to read it."	"I know this child has something to say. I also know he does not have the same understanding of our writing system as I do. I will take cues from him about what reading and writing mean to him in this situation. I will accept and encourage his reading and writing in that manner."

Strategy One: Engaging Children in Dialogue about Written Language

Cochran-Smith (1984) studied the literacy learning that occurred in one nursery school. She described the actions, words, and beliefs of the teachers, children, and parents. One of her many insightful observations was of the highly interactive nature of storybook reading in this nursery school. The adult reader did not just read, and the children did not just listen. The storyreader saw her role as doing more than just reading the words of the text and displaying the pictures. She involved the children by asking questions and encouraging their comments.

Together she and the children determined the meaning; they "*interactively* participated in order to build jointly or *negotiate* a meaning for the story" (Cochran-Smith, 1984, p. 126). Cochran-Smith calls this "interactive and listener-participative" storyreading, as opposed to "reader-as-spokesperson-for-the-text" storyreading (p. 156). The storyreader is aware that storyreading can be more than just turning print into sound for nonreaders, but rather a means of showing nonreaders how to interpret a story. It is as if the reader is using a strategy that might be expressed: "I will not be just a performer, but a model and a leader, showing how to build—and getting us cooperatively to build—an interpretation of this story. I will comment on the story, be aware of my listeners' responses, and adjust my further reading and commentary to those responses. I will engage in dialogue with my listeners."

One of Cochran-Smith's many examples is of the teacher reading Maurice Sendak's (1970) *In the Night Kitchen* (pp. 126–144). The teacher invites children to read words (which are familiar from previous readings) from speech bubbles in the illustrations; she invites them to chant with her as she chants certain repetitive, rhythmical parts of the text; she invites them to identify with the main character ("Cause you're all the bakers now. Aren't you?"); she asks questions ("But where's Mickey?"); and she responds to the children's answers ("For real?").

There are many advantages to storyreading with dialogue. It helps children make the move from the spoken language that they know very well to the written language which is still new to them, by combining the two modes. Children are used to dialogue and negotiation of meaning in their everyday use of spoken language in conversation. This strategy uses the features of conversation to help children learn what to do with texts so that eventually they can build sense from reading on their own.

Strategy Two: Being a Supporting Player

Schickedanz (1984) collected information about the kinds of literacy events that occurred in the homes of six preschool girls who were between three and one-half and five years old. These children were identified as being intensely interested in reading and writing. She interviewed their parents, who had been instructed to keep notes to help them remember literacy events they engaged in with their daughters. Using an analogy to a drama, Schickedanz reported that these children played leading roles and their parents were supporting actors in the scripts the children designed for their literacy events. Children initiated activities involving reading and writing, but seldom proceeded alone. Parents helped to set the stage and provided encouragement. The overwhelming majority of instances of their giving instruction were in response to a child's request for help. Seldom did the parents volunteer instruction in the form of correction. Schickedanz borrowed Smith's (1984) notion that the parent interacts with the child like a master with an apprentice. But Schickedanz added that the parents of these six intensely literacy-oriented children seemed to *expect* the children to be apprentices. They believed that children *must* be apprentices and that parents ought to supervise and support them as such.

These parents sound very much like Ted and Carrie's father in the restaurant literacy event described in Chapter 1. It is as if they are using a strategy that might be expressed: "My child sees reading and writing going on all around her. She will naturally role play reading and writing. I will take the lead from her. She'll show me what she understands and what help she needs by the kinds of questions she asks."

A mother's report of an interaction between her daughter and the daughter's grandfather illustrates an adult's use of the supporting player strategy. The daughter, mother, and grandfather were riding in the car. The girl noticed a tablet and a pencil and asked her grandfather if she could use it. Then she began interviewing her grandfather by asking, "What do you do all day?" He said, "I play golf." The girl repeated, "Golf" and asked, "How do you spell that?" He spelled it for her and the interview continued. This grandparent had fallen easily into the role of supporting player (Schickedanz, 1984, p. 17).

Strategy Three: Socializing the Young

Parents' styles of interacting with their children about written language differ, as they would about anything else. Heath (1983) observed children learning to use language in three communities over a five-year period. She found differences in the functions of language, particularly written language, in the three communities.

In a working-class black community, children were included in a stream of adult conversation from birth. They learned to tell entertaining stories early in their lives, but they were not entertained with storyreading. The children were, however, expected to pay attention to print in order to accomplish such errands as buying something at the local store. Print was used primarily as a means of maintaining community life (for example, to learn about community events, to know what bills were due, or to confirm religious beliefs by reading the Bible). Parents supported children's learning those uses of print.

In a white, working-class community, reading and writing were seen as the means of getting an education. Print had an additional educational purpose. Parents read to their children at bedtime both to entertain and to educate. For example, they might use a story as a stimulus for talking about the children's future.

In a professional class community, the purpose of the parents' own reading was to increase their ability to discuss politics, religion, or sociological topics. The parents' talk with their children involved continuous commentary about their actions and about both present and past experiences. In this context, written language had a critical/educational function. Even such literacy events as reading bedtime stories to children served as a beginning point for discussion, and parents would relate past experiences to the story content.

In all three communities, both spoken and written language served the needs and purposes of community members. Parents in each community introduced children at an early age to the kind of written language upon which their community depended. When anthropologists speak of socialization, they mean the process of a society's teaching its young all the ways of acting and believing that they need in order to function in that society. Teaching and learning the place of reading and writing in their lives was just as much a part of the socialization process in these communities as teaching and learning any other aspect of cultural knowledge—from how to talk to how to operate a television, and from how to address your elders to how to choose clothes when you are dressing up.

It is as if parents were using a strategy that might be expressed: "Reading and writing are an important part of our community's culture. Part of my job as a parent is to help my children function in this community. I'm going to let them in on the use of reading and writing just as I let them in on other important pieces of cultural knowledge."

As with the other strategies we have described so far, this strategy is largely unconscious. Parents do not say these words and they do not necessarily intend to act that way; they just do. An aspect that complicates this strategy is the fact that societies have set up schools specifically to help with the socialization of their young. The amount of socialization schools are expected to do varies from culture to culture and from time to time. In the United States, formal instruction in the "how to" of reading and writing is still largely reserved for the elementary schools. But Heath has shown that parents from three very different communities do not put off socializing their children in the "why" of reading and writing. That is, they teach their children the place literacy has in the overall functioning of their community, in their community's accomplishing what it holds dear. Both preschool and elementary school teachers can do better jobs if they are sensitive to the cultural knowledge about literacy that their students have acquired at home. This does not mean stereotyping their students, but rather giving them various opportunities to use written language and observing the aspects with which their students are familiar.

Strategy Four: Accepting and Encouraging
Children's Own Constructions of Literacy Knowledge

The ways in which adults respond to children's reading or writing may not always be helpful to the children. McCully (1982) examined adults' talk with children in several situations. She was particularly interested in the tenor of the talk, that is, whether it was warm or cold, encouraging or controlling. The situations involved parents' or a teacher's inviting children to draw a picture and then to write about it. Parents were found to be accepting and encouraging when their children were drawing, but to be very controlling and directive when their children were writing. Parents' talk was responsive to cues in their children's pictures and to what their children said while drawing. For example, when a child said, "A tree. It's like that one we climb," the parent said, "Oh? Those must be the branches you climb.'' (Hoffman & McCully, 1984, p. 42) But when talking about the writing, parents told their children the correct way to form letters and to spell words. In such exchanges, the children's contributions tended to be statements of what they wanted to write and answers to the adults' questions about whether or not they could spell various words.

The teacher was trained to be warm and encouraging about both writing and drawing. She learned to tell children to write their messages the way they thought they should and to reassure them that she would be able to read their writing. The messages produced with the trained teacher were more meaningful and personal than those produced with the parents (Hoffman & McCully, 1984).

This study shows that parents are sometimes too concerned about the form and correctness of written language. Those who were quite willing to believe in their children's ability to make representational, meaningful pictures lacked a similar willingness with respect to writing. Perhaps parents and teachers must, in this case, *consciously* use a strategy of accepting children's early writing efforts. Such a strategy might be expressed: ''I know this child has something to say. I also know he does not have the same understanding of our writing system as I do. I will take cues from him about what reading and writing mean to him in this situation. I will accept and encourage his reading and writing in that manner.'' One of the purposes of this book is to help teachers to understand differences in children's written language knowledge so that the teachers can respond to the children in ways that are sensitive to each child's understanding of literacy in a given situation.

There are overlaps among the adults' strategies we have presented. They may all be summarized by saying that adults best help children direct their own literacy learning by understanding and encouraging that learning (Baghban, 1989; Taylor & Dorsey-Gaines, 1987; Taylor & Strickland, 1986).

CHILD-TO-CHILD SUPPORT
FOR LITERACY LEARNING

Although the strategies listed in the previous section stress the role of adults, we must not lose sight of the important role other children play. With encouragement and modeling, children easily engage in dialogue with one another about books and about one another's writings. They are natural supportive players for one another and are often more accepting of non-conventional literacy behaviors than adults are.

Recently, there has been a revolution in the way we think about writing processes and about the connection between writing and reading (Calkins, 1986; Graves, 1983; Mason, 1989; Tierney & Pearson, 1983). One of the benefits of that revolution has been the realization that writing and reading are not always the solitary activities of popular stereotypes. We often picture a reader curled up by himself or herself, lost in a book. We imagine a writer hunched over a desk in a private room or in the corner of a room. There is some truth to those images, but it is also true that people love to talk about what they are reading. They even thrust their reading material into the hands of those who will put up with it, saying, "Oh you've got to read this!" It is also true that the best writers depend on editors, and that most writers like to "bounce" their plans for writing or even their early drafts of a piece off the "heads" of others.

This is especially true for children who are just learning how to read and write. Observers in preschool writing centers and in elementary school peer writing conferences have noted the many ways children find to help one another and to serve as audiences for one another (Connell, 1988; Rowe, 1987). This is consistent with the social nature of language learning described in this chapter.

Because children use written language in their play with other children (as Carrie and Ted did in the example in Chapter 1), supporting adults should plan for such play. Teachers can include writing materials in play centers. Teachers can also make the writing center in preschool and kindergarten classrooms a truly social place where teacher-to-child and child-to-child talk is encouraged. Children should be free to drop in and out of the writing center.

Chapter Summary

Young children learn about reading and writing because of their curiosity, their sociability, and their experience with and understanding of spoken language. Because learning involves forming and reforming schemas in their minds, children's state of knowledge about many things, including literacy, can be very different from one time to the next, and can be very different from that of an adult.

There is an inborn component to children's learning; they are born knowing some very basic action schemas and those action schemas produce knowledge schemas. Still, adults—and even other children—can play an important role in all kinds of learning, including language learning. Adults involve young children in language learning routines. These are repeated situations, such as bedtime activities, in which adults provide predictable objects, actions, and words. Parents notice that a child is

learning how the objects, actions, and words in a routine go together, and they expect greater verbal participation from the child. One of the best opportunities for language learning by routines occurs when parents and children read books together.

A Piagetian approach to describing how children learn written language emphasizes the developmental stages that children move through as they solve written language problems. A Vygotskian approach stresses that writing and reading are intentionally communicative and that adults can help children by recognizing their intentionality and talking to them about their early writing and reading efforts.

Children seem to use several strategies for solving reading and writing puzzles. They use and interpret written language by looking for intended meanings, by using written language in an open-ended manner, and by taking risks. In their early writing, they repeat elements, experiment with what they know, and generate a lot from a little. They talk and draw as they produce written language and they ask questions as they are read to.

Adults support young children's literacy learning in several ways. They model how to build sense from text by using dialogue or conversation with their listeners during their storyreading. They provide the support children need by playing along in the literacy events that children often initiate but usually do not want to proceed with by them-selves. They let their children in on the functions of reading and writing in their communities. They must be willing to believe in their children's ability to produce meaningful writing without being too concerned about form and correct-ness. These adults' strategies may be summarized by saying that adults best help children direct their own literacy learning by understanding and encour-aging that learning.

Finally, children are natural support-ive players for one another. They find many ways to help one another and to serve as audiences for one another.

Applying the Information

A case study of a literacy event follows. As you read it, think about how young children learn about literacy. Discuss strategies children use to learn and strategies adults use to support chil-dren's learning. Which are exemplified in this case study?

A mother was awakened on Easter morning by her four-year-old daughter. The girl presented her mother with an Easter card she had made. The mother was very pleased and interested. The card consisted of little notes glued and taped to a paper bunny. The daughter explained what the letters *EST* spelled: "You think it says 'Happy Easter,' but it only says 'Easter.'" The daughter ex-plained that she had run out of room to write all of *Easter*. The mother showed how to spell *Easter*. The daughter was aware that her word was incomplete; she said, "Well, there isn't the rest of the word. It said 'east' not 'Easter.'" But she was not very interested; the mother could not get her to say how to spell the missing part, so she let the matter go.

The mother turned her attention to another of the little attached notes, a piece of paper with scribbles on it that looked like cursive writing. She asked what that was and the daughter re-ported that it was the kind of writing you use to write a letter, but she didn't know what it said (Schickedanz, 1984, p. 18).

Going Beyond the Text

Observe a child, become involved with his or her literacy learning, and then re-flect on your experience. Tape record a literacy event between you and a child, but first observe the child to find out what kind of literacy activity might in-terest him or her. Suggestions for activi-ties include a play activity in which you introduce written language props (like the restaurant play activity suggested in

"Going Beyond the Text" for Chapter 1); a writing activity at a classroom writing center or at a kitchen table in the child's home (begin by writing something yourself and showing the child what you are doing in order to attract his or her attention and motivate participation); or a reading activity in which you and the child share one of his or her favorite books (be sure to interact with the child, and give him or her opportunities to read, comment, or ask questions).

Remember the four strategies adults use to help children learn about written language (Table 2.2). Do not use them as a lesson plan or check list, but involve yourself with the child and be supportive, in the spirit suggested by those strategies. Listen to your tape recording. What strategies did the child use to deal with written language in the event? How did you support his or her learning?

References

APPLEBEE, A. N., & LANGER, J. A. (1983). Instructional scaffolding: Reading and writing as natural language activities. *Language Arts, 60,* 168–175.

BAGHBAN, M. (1989). *You can help your young child with writing.* Newark, DE: The International Reading Association.

BRUNER, J. S. (1978). Learning how to do things with words. In J. S. Bruner and R. A. Garton (Eds.), *Human growth and development* (62–84). Oxford: Oxford University Press.

BRUNER, J. S. (1983). *Child's talk: Learning to use language.* New York: Norton.

BRUNER, J. S. (1984). Interaction, communication, and self. *Journal of the American Academy of Child Psychiatry, 23,* 1–7.

BRUNER, J. S. (1985). In *Baby talk, NOVA transcript #1207.* Boston, MA: WGBH Transcripts.

CALKINS, L. M. (1986). *The art of teaching writing.* Portsmouth, NH: Heinemann.

CHOMSKY, N. (1957). *Syntactic structures.* The Hague: Mouton.

CHOMSKY, N. (1983). Interview with J. Gliedman. *Omni, 6,* pp. 112–118, 171–174.

CHOMSKY, N. (1988). *Language and problems of knowledge.* Cambridge, MA: MIT Press.

CLAY, M. M. (1975). *What did I write? Beginning writing behavior.* Exeter, NH: Heinemann.

COCHRAN-SMITH, M. (1984). *The making of a reader.* Norwood, NJ: Ablex.

CONNELL, J. V. (April 1988). *Conferencing behaviors of first grade authors: An observation study.* Paper presented at the annual meeting of the American Educational Research Association, New Orleans, LA.

DURKIN, D. (1966). *Children who read early.* New York, NY: Teachers College Press.

DYSON, A. H. (1985). Individual differences in emerging writing. In M. Farr (Ed.), *Advances in writing research, Volume one: Children's early writing development* (pp. 59–125). Norwood, NJ: Ablex.

EIMAS, P. D. (1974). Linguistic processing of speech by young infants. In R. L. Schiefelbusch and L. L. Lloyd (Eds.), *Language perspectives: Acquisition, retardation, and intervention* (pp. 55–73). Baltimore, MD: University Park Press.

FERREIRO, E. (1985). Literacy development: A psychogenetic perspective. In D. R. Olson, N. Torrance, and A. Hildyard (Eds.), *Literacy, language, and learning* (217–228). Cambridge: Cambridge University Press.

FERREIRO, E., & TEBEROSKY, A. (1982). *Literacy before schooling.* Exeter, NH: Heinemann.

GLEASON, J. B. (1985). In *Baby talk, NOVA transcript #1207.* Boston, MA: WGBH Transcripts.

GLEASON, J. B. (Ed.). (1989). *The development of language* (2nd ed.). Columbus, OH: Merrill.

GLEASON, J. B., HAY, D., & CAIN, L. (1989). The social and affective determinants of language acquisition. In M. L. Rice & R. L. Schiefelbusch (Eds.), *The teachability of language* (pp. 171–186). Baltimore, MD: P. H. Brookes.

GOPNICK, A., & MELTZOFF, A. Z. (1986). Relations between semantic and cognitive development in the one-word stage: The specificity hypothesis. *Child Development, 57,* 1040–1053.

GRAVES, D. H. (1983). *Writing: Teachers and children at work.* Portsmouth, NH: Heinemann.

HARSTE, J. C., BURKE, C. L., & WOODWARD, V. A. (1983). *The young child as writer-reader, and informant (Final NIE report #NIE-G-80-0121).* Bloomington, IN: Language Education Departments, Indiana University.

HARSTE, J. C., BURKE, C. L. & WOODWARD, V. A. (1984). *Language stories and literacy lessons.* Portsmouth, NH: Heinemann.

HEATH, S. B. (1983). *Ways with words: Language, life, and work in communities and classrooms.* New York, NY: Cambridge University Press.

HOFFMAN, S., & McCULLY B. (1984). Oral language functions in transaction with children's writing. *Language Arts, 61,* 41–50.

MASON, J. M. (Ed.). (1989). *Reading and writing connections.* Boston, MA: Allyn and Bacon.

McCULLY, B. (1982). *A phenomenological investigation of the home learning environment and its influence on the concept of written language of selected prekindergarten children.* Unpublished doctoral dissertation, University of Missouri–Columbia.

MELTZOFF, A. (1985). In *Baby talk, NOVA transcript #1207.* Boston, MA: WGBH Transcripts.

MENYUK, P. (1969). *Sentences children use.* Cambridge, MA: MIT Press.

MENYUK, P. (1988). *Language development: Knowledge and use.* Glenview, IL: Scott, Foresman.

NINIO, A., & BRUNER, J. (1978). The achievement and antecedents of labelling. *Journal of Child Language, 5,* 1–15.

NOVA (1985). *Baby talk, NOVA transcript #1207.* Boston, MA: WGBH Transcripts.

OWENS, R. E., JR. (1988). *Language development.* Columbus, OH: Merrill.

PIAGET, J. (1955). *The language and thought of the child.* Cleveland, OH: World.

PRICE, E. H. (1976). How thirty-seven gifted children learned to read. *The Reading Teacher, 30,* 44–48.

ROWE, D. W. (1987, December). *The classroom as a community of authors: The role of social context in literacy learning.* Paper presented at the annual meeting of the National Reading Conference, St. Petersburg Beach, FL.

SCHICKEDANZ, J. A. (1984). *A study of literacy events in the homes of six preschoolers.* Paper presented at the annual meeting of the National Reading Conference, St. Petersburg Beach, FL.

SENDAK, M. (1970). *In the night kitchen.* New York: Harper and Row.

SEUSS, DR. (THEODORE GEISEL) (1958). *The cat in the hat.* New York: Beginner Books (Random House).

SMITH, F. (1984). The creative achievement of literacy. In H. Goelman, A. Oberg, and F. Smith (Eds.), *Awakening to literacy* (pp. 143–153). Exeter, NH: Heinemann.

SNOW, C. (1983). Literacy and language: Relationships during the preschool years. *Harvard Educational Review, 53,* 165–189.

SNOW, C. (1985). In *Baby talk, NOVA transcript #1207.* Boston, MA: WGBH Transcripts.

SNOW, C., DUBBER, C., & DE BLAUW, A. (1982). Routines in mother-child interaction. In L. Feagans and D. C. Farran (Eds.), *The language of children reared in poverty* (pp. 53–72). New York: NY: Academic Press.

SNOW, C. & GOLDFIELD, B. (1983). Turn the page please: Situation-specific language acquisition. *Journal of Child Language, 10,* 551–569.

TAYLOR, D., & DORSEY-GAINES, C (1987). *Growing up literate: Learning from inner-city families.* Portsmouth, NH: Heinemann.

TAYLOR, D., & STRICKLAND, D. (1986). *Family storybook reading.* Portsmouth, NH: Heinemann.

TIERNEY, R. J., & PEARSON, P. D. (1983). Toward a composing model of reading. *Language Arts, 60,* 568–580.

TREVARTHAN, C. (1985). In *Baby talk, NOVA transcript #1207.* Boston, MA: WGBH Transcripts.

TREVARTHAN, C., & MARWICK, H. (1986). Signs of motivation for speech in infants, and the nature of a mother's support for development of language. In B. Lindblom and R. Zetterstrom (Eds.), *Precursors of early speech* (279– 308). New York: Stockton Press.

VYGOTSKY, L. S. (1962). *Thought and language.* Cambridge, MA: MIT Press.

YADEN, D., & McGEE, L. (1984). Reading as a meaning-seeking activity: What children's questions reveal. In J. A. Niles and L. A. Harris (Eds.), *Changing perspectives on research in reading/language processing and instruction, 33rd yearbook of The National Reading Conference* (pp. 101–109). Rochester, NY: The National Reading Conference.

Literacy-Rich Classrooms

The purpose of Chapter 3 is to apply what we know about children's literacy learning to child care, nursery school, preschool, and elementary school settings. We will explore the conditions and characteristics of literacy-rich environments for children in their early childhood years (infancy through eight years old). This chapter presents the general characteristics that apply to supporting children's literacy learning in classroom situations, whether they are informal preschool settings or more formal third grade classrooms. Other chapters in this book will provide more specific descriptions of classroom settings and activities appropriate for infants, toddlers, and two-year-olds (Chapter 4), preschoolers and kindergartners (Chapter 6), kindergartners and first graders (Chapter 8), and first through third graders (Chapters 10 and 11).

In this chapter, we use three approaches to examine literacy-rich classrooms. First, we describe classroom practices that have been recommended by early childhood, reading, and writing professional organizations. Next, we describe the home environments of children who begin to read and write early, who are successful readers and writers in school, and who like to and choose to read and write frequently. Finally, we list seven characteristics of these literacy-rich homes that we believe contribute strongly to reading and writing learning. It is our belief that literacy-rich classrooms have the same seven characteristics.

The last section of the chapter contains a detailed discussion of the seven characteristics of literacy-rich environments. First, we examine the extent to which researchers have found each of these characteristics in typical classrooms. Next, we present research that shows that when the literacy-rich characteristics are present in classrooms, then children enjoy reading and writing and they are more successful in their efforts. Finally, we draw from this research to describe specific practices and activities that teachers can use to create literacy-rich classrooms.

PROFESSIONAL RECOMMENDATIONS: APPROPRIATE PRACTICE IN EARLY CHILDHOOD CLASSROOMS

The early childhood years, from birth through eight years of age, are crucial for all aspects of children's development: physical, emotional, social, intellectual, and aesthetic. We believe children's preschool and elementary school experiences in literacy are important. However, learning about literacy is only a small part of the learning and development that children accomplish in their early childhood years. Children will best learn about literacy when it is a part of a larger curriculum that focuses on all aspects of child development.

Appropriate Practice in Early Childhood

Early childhood professionals have become increasingly concerned with the rush to prepare young children for cognitive tasks related to schooling. They are concerned that young children are being required to complete tasks that are inappropriate to their level of development and incompatible with their natural avenues of learning.

There is a reason to be concerned. Reading and writing educators must be particularly aware of these issues because many of the inappropriate practices that so concern early childhood experts are centered on the teaching of reading and writing. A large number of educators, who are aware of the importance of early experiences, have prepared reading and writing activities (often called pre-reading or readiness activities) for young children. Unfortunately, many of these activities are not appropriate for young children's developmental levels. Materials intended for first graders or kindergartners (many of which are inappropriate for six- and seven-year-olds) are being used by preschoolers. Recent versions of reading tests require kindergartners to complete the same tasks that previous versions of the test had required of first and second graders.

To combat the unfortunate trend of pushing younger children to learn skills that only a few years ago were reserved for older children, several early childhood organizations have prepared statements about appropriate classroom practice. The Association for Childhood Education International has recommended a child-centered kindergarten (Moyer, Egertson, & Isenberg, 1987) and the National Association for the Education of Young Children has recommended developmentally appropriate practice for children from birth through age eight (Bredekamp, 1987).

Professional recommendations on appropriate practice stress the need to recognize children's age, development, uniqueness, and interests when planning activities and organizing classroom environments. According to these guidelines, teachers should provide activities that help children grow in all areas of development, not just in their cognitive development. These recommendations specify that young children need hands-on experiences with materials they can manipulate in activities they find meaningful. These statements caution educators against overuse of paper-and-pencil activities in which children are required to sit for lengthy time periods; this is especially true for younger children. Rather, recommended practice is to provide a variety of activities from which children can choose, to plan a majority of independent or small group activities, and to encourage play as an important component of learning. During these activities children should be allowed to explore materials and to interact with other children and the teacher. Children should have ample opportunities to select their own activities and to direct their own learning. Teachers should emphasize learning processes rather than finished, adult-like products, understanding that children's early efforts at reading and writing, much like their early efforts at talking, will be unconventional.

Most of the statements on appropriate practice in early childhood classrooms focus on pre-first grade children. However, the statement by the National Association for the Education of Young Children includes recommendations for children through age eight (third grade). According to these recommendations, children at age eight should have learning environments and activities similar to those of children who are three or four years old. While children who are seven or eight years old are increasingly able to reason and deal with symbolic experiences, their understanding is still based on their ability to tie the abstract to the concrete. Hands-on activities are still more appropriate for this age than seatwork (Bredekamp, 1987, p. 6).

Appropriate Literacy Practice

Many organizations involved with young children, reading, and writing have jointly issued a statement of concern about present practices in pre-first grade reading instruction (International Reading Association, 1986). This position statement describes recommendations for improving literacy instruction in preschool and kindergarten; it is presented in this chapter as Appendix A. The concerns expressed in this statement are similar to those expressed in other statements of appropriate practice.

The National Association for the Education of Young Children describes appropriate and inappropriate practice in language and literacy programs for the primary grades (first through third grade) (Bredekamp, 1987, p. 70). This statement is presented in Figure 3.1. We recommend that teachers of young children be familiar with the recommendations for developmentally appropriate literacy practice presented in both Appendix A and Figure 3.1.

Implications from Appropriate
Practice Recommendations

There are many implications that can be drawn from the recommendations on appropriate early childhood practice. One is that whole classrooms of young children will spend little time working on the same required task such as completing a workbook page or copying from the blackboard. Rather, small groups of children will be working at many different learning centers or centers of activities. The activities in these centers will probably be related to a common theme.

Figure 3.1 *Appropriate and Inappropriate Language and Literacy Practices*

APPROPRIATE Practice

The goals of the language and literacy program are for children to expand their ability to communicate orally and through reading and writing, and to enjoy these activities. Technical skills or subskills are taught as needed to accomplish the larger goals, not as the goal itself. Teachers provide generous amounts of time and a variety of interesting activities for children to develop language, writing, spelling, and reading ability, such as: looking through, reading, or being read high quality children's literature and nonfiction for pleasure and information; drawing, dictating, and writing about their activities or fantasies; planning and implementing projects that involve research at suitable levels of difficulty; creating teacher-made or child-written lists of steps to follow to accomplish a project; discussing what was read; preparing a weekly class newspaper; interviewing various people to obtain information for projects; making books of various kinds (riddle books, *what if* books, books about pets); listening to recordings or viewing high quality films of children's books; being read at least one high quality book or part of a book each day by adults or older children; using the school library and the library area of the classroom regularly. Some children read aloud daily to the teacher, another child, or a small group of children, while others do so weekly. Subskills such as learning letters, phonics, and word recognition are taught as needed to individual children and small groups through enjoyable games and activities. Teachers use the teacher's edition of the basal reader series as a guide to plan projects and hands-on activities relevant to what is read and to structure learning situa-

tions. Teachers accept children's invented spelling with minimal reliance on teacher-prescribed spelling lists. Teachers also teach literacy as the need arises when working on science, social studies, and other content areas.

INAPPROPRIATE Practice

The goal of the reading program is for each child to pass the standardized tests given throughout the year at or near grade level. Reading is taught as the acquisition of skills and subskills. Teachers teach reading only as a discrete subject. When teaching other subjects, they do not feel they are teaching reading. A sign of excellent teaching is considered to be silence in the classroom and so conversation is allowed infrequently during select times. Language, writing, and spelling instruction are focused on workbooks. Writing is taught as grammar and penmanship. The focus of the reading program is the basal reader, used only in reading groups, and accompanying workbooks and worksheets. The teacher's role is to prepare and implement the reading lesson in the teacher's guidebook for each group each day and to see that other children have enough seatwork to keep them busy throughout the reading group time. Phonics instruction stresses learning rules rather than developing understanding of systematic relationships between letters and sounds. Children are required to complete worksheets or to complete the basal reader although they are capable of reading at a higher level. Everyone knows which children are in the slowest reading group. Children's writing efforts are rejected if correct spelling and standard English are not used.

From ''Developmentally Appropriate Practice'' (p. 70) by S. Bredekamp (Ed.), 1987, Washington, D.C: National Association for the Education of Young Children. Copyright © by the National Association for the Education of Young Children. Reprinted with permission.

For example, children might be learning about their town. They might visit the class library center and read books or listen to a tape-recorded story about a local hero. At the writing center, they might write letters to the mayor. In a math center they might sort cans into groups of vegetables, soups, and fruits for distribution to an "adopted family." At a cooking center they might use a recipe to make no-bake cookies for an adopted family. These centers of activities and others provide children with opportunities to grow in all areas of development, including cognitive, physical, emotional, social, and aesthetic. They also support children's literacy learning.

This picture of a classroom may seem far from the picture of a typical first or second grade classroom that many of us remember from our own school experiences or that we have recently visited. Yet, professional opinion—supported by theories of child development and learning—suggests that young elementary children can benefit most from learning in environments such as those described here.

LITERACY-RICH CLASSROOMS: WHAT WE CAN LEARN FROM LITERACY-RICH HOMES

Another way to learn more about how to support children's literacy learning is to look closely at the homes of children who have learned to read and write "on their own" before coming to school or who have become successful readers and writers in school. We believe that characteristics of literacy-rich home environments have direct application to literacy-rich classrooms. By identifying the home-related factors that contribute to children's literacy success, we should be better able to provide classroom environments that support literacy learning.

Quantities and Varieties of Reading and Writing Materials

Children in literacy-rich homes own an average of 80 books, which they store in several rooms in their homes (Morrow, 1983). Because they have library cards and visit libraries frequently, they have access to many other books. Their homes contain a variety of reading materials including magazines, catalogs, *TV Guides,* telephone books, cookbooks, reference manuals, church bulletins, and junk mail (Teale, 1978). Children have access to a large variety of materials for writing, and there are appropriate places for writing in these homes, including low tables and chairs. Permission to use either reading or writing materials is usually unnecessary (Hall, Moretz, & Statom, 1976). Materials for reading and writing are often in plain sight and underfoot in rooms where children spend much of their time (Taylor, 1983).

We can conclude that literacy-rich classrooms should have:

1. A variety and quantity of reading and writing materials appropriate to the age and interests of the children. These materials should be available and

accessible to children. Searfoss and Readence (1985) call such a classroom a *print lab*.

2. A physical setting supportive of literacy activities including comfortable reading and writing centers and attractive displays of literacy products and activities. Literacy-rich classrooms should have a comfortable reading center where children can browse through books. There should also be a writing center that is large enough for children to talk and write together.

Functional Use of Reading and Writing

Parents in literacy-rich homes are readers and writers. They report reading more books and doing more writing than parents of children in nonliteracy-rich homes (Hall, Moretz, & Statom, 1976; Morrow, 1983). At least one study reported that most of preschoolers' writing was initiated by parents or older brothers and sisters who were frequent writers (Schickedanz & Sullivan, 1984). Parents are not the only readers and writers in literacy-rich homes. Children in literacy-rich homes, even preschoolers, participate in functional reading and writing experiences (Taylor, 1983). Children write grocery lists and checks along with their parents. They read junk mail as their parents read letters and other correspondence. These activities spill over into play when children write prescriptions as they play doctor and read coupons as they play house. As they progress through elementary school, children continue to participate in family literacy activities and include literacy in their play.

Therefore, literacy-rich classrooms should have:

3. Teachers who read and write and who plan activities involving children reading and writing for everyday purposes and not just for the purpose of learning reading and writing. Teachers in literacy-rich classrooms should be aware that reading and writing are learned *for* a purpose. They should recognize the value of play in supporting children's literacy learning. Reading and writing should be integrated into content study, literature study, and daily classroom routines.

Literacy Routines

Storybook reading is a daily routine in most literacy-rich homes (Durkin, 1966). Other families report routines such as reading the Sunday comics or reading a list of things-to-do (Schickedanz & Sullivan, 1984). Parents in literacy-rich homes routinely use writing as a part of their daily activities (Heath, 1983; Taylor, 1983).

Therefore, literacy-rich classrooms should have:

4. Daily literacy "routines." Teachers in literacy-rich classrooms should read aloud to children daily. They should write with children for routine reasons such as making a list of activities accomplished at the end of the school day.

Children should be given time each day for free choice reading and writing activities.

Written Language Interactions and Talk

As parents in literacy-rich homes read bedtime stories, they ask questions and encourage their children to ask questions related to the book (Yaden & McGee, 1984). Parents and children talk about written language as they write together (Gundlach, McLane, Scott, & McNamee, 1985). Children ask persistent questions about how to spell words, how to form letters, and what their writing might "say."

Therefore, literacy-rich classrooms should have:

5. Children and teachers who interact as they read and write. Teachers in literacy-rich classrooms should know that children need to interact with other children and with their teacher as they read and write. They should know that the questions children ask and the comments children and teachers make during reading and writing activities are important avenues of literacy learning.

Responsibility for Supporting Learning

Many parents believe their children taught themselves how to read. But, parents of successful readers and writers also feel they have a duty to help their children learn (Dunn, 1981; Hess, Holloway, Price, & Dickson, 1982). As their children gain more knowledge and control over literacy activities, parents are more likely to insist that their children complete a task such as retelling a favorite story or writing their name (Baghban, 1984; Snow, 1983).

Therefore, literacy-rich classrooms should have:

6. Teachers who feel responsible for helping children learn about reading and writing and who believe that their children are readers and writers. They should believe that their students can learn about reading and writing, and indeed, that they *are* readers and writers.

Sensitivity to Children's Knowledge

Parents in literacy-rich homes intuitively seem to know how to adapt their reading and sharing of books so that their children find the experience meaningful and enjoyable (Ninio, 1980). They are more accurate in predicting how much their children know and what they can do on literacy tasks than parents from less literacy-rich homes (Adams & Hiebert, 1983). Parents in literacy-rich homes are also willing to accept the level of their children's performances (Baghban, 1984).

Therefore, literacy-rich classrooms should have:

7. Teachers who are knowledgeable about the individual and unique needs of their children and who are willing to accept children's nonconventional read-

ing and writing efforts. Teachers in literacy-rich classrooms should expect children's literacy efforts to be child-like and not adult-like. They should be aware of each student's level of knowledge and respond in appropriate ways to individual children's different approaches to literacy learning.

LITERACY PRACTICES IN CLASSROOMS

So far in this chapter we have described professional opinions about appropriate early childhood literacy practices. We have discussed our beliefs about seven characteristics of literacy-rich home environments that we argue *should* have direct application for literacy-rich classroom environments. Although our beliefs and the opinions of other professionals are based on research of children's homes and on theories of child development, opinions and beliefs are sometimes insufficient. In this section of the chapter we draw upon research that has been conducted in actual school and school-like settings. We will ask three questions: To what extent are the seven characteristics of literacy-rich environments typical in classrooms? Is there research that has shown that children learn better if classrooms have each of the characteristics of literacy-rich environments? and What materials and practices have researchers used to create literacy-rich classroom environments?

In this section of the chapter we will observe classrooms as the researchers found them. Keep in mind that teachers do not always have complete control over what materials are used and what activities take place in their rooms (Shannon, 1983). Administrative and public pressures sometimes influence what teachers do and what materials they use.

In the past, most educational research focused on identifying which of two or more reading programs or instructional techniques seemed to help children learn the most (see, for example, Bond & Dykstra, 1967). Today, more researchers are looking at *teachers in classrooms* to find out what they do that seems to help children learn better (Cochran-Smith, 1984; Duffy, Roehler, & Rackliffe, 1986; Edelsky, Draper, & Smith, 1983). Given this relatively new area of research, we have few studies from which to draw conclusions about typical practice or literacy-rich classrooms. However, we believe it is extremely useful to examine what is happening in real classrooms.

Literacy Materials

The first characteristic of literacy-rich environments is that they are filled with an abundance and variety of literacy materials appropriate to the age and interests of the children.

Typical Classroom Practice

According to one survey, most nursery schools and kindergarten classrooms have a classroom library containing at least several children's books (Morrow, 1982). We were unable to find a survey of the kinds of reading and writing materials that are typical in elementary classrooms. However, at least one survey found that 94 percent of reading instructional practice in elementary classrooms centered on the use of commercial instructional materials (Educational Products Information Exchange, 1977). These materials usually consist of workbooks, ditto sheets, books containing a collection of stories to use in reading instruction (called basal readers), and books used in language arts or writing instruction. Other researchers have examined the quality of commercial materials designed for reading and writing instruction. They found that some commercial materials are not of the best quality, and many reading specialists have called for improvements (Anderson, Hiebert, Scott, & Wilkinson, 1985; Goodman, 1986; Templeton, 1986).

Commercial materials, used effectively, might contribute to children's literacy learning. However, since children seem to spend so much of their class time with commercial materials, they might not have much time to spend with other literacy materials such as children's literature, functional print items, and writing materials.

Research Supporting a Variety and Abundance of Literacy Materials

Three studies provide valuable evidence that having a quantity and variety of writing and reading materials in classrooms improves children's reading achievement and willingness to read and write as free choice activities. Morrow and Weinstein (1982, 1986) demonstrated in two studies that changing a typical library collection (which contains few children's books and no props for storytelling) into an exemplary library collection (which contains many children's books, props for storytelling, and tapes for listening to stories) increased the number of kindergartners and second graders who voluntarily visited the library center. Taylor, Blum, and Logsdon (1986) found that kindergartners in classrooms that had an abundance of functional print (such as directions for cooking and a schedule of daily events), writing materials, and children's literature (and activities for using these materials) performed better on reading achievement tests than kindergartners in classrooms in which there were few of these materials. Based on the research in these classrooms, we can make several suggestions for literacy-rich classrooms.

Practice in Literacy-Rich Classrooms

Literacy-rich preschool and elementary classrooms have classroom libraries containing a variety of children's literature, a collection of functional print items, and a variety of writing materials.

Children's literature.   Literacy-rich classrooms have a large classroom collection of children's literature (Huck, Hepler, & Hickman, 1987). Teachers add eight to ten new books to the collection each month and remove books children no longer show interest in. Many of the books included in the collection are quality picture books, although many seven- and eight-year-olds enjoy longer books with fewer illustrations. The books in the collection include fairy tales, folk tales, realistic fiction, fantasy, poetry, biography, and nonfiction. An important part of the library collection is books written by the teacher and children. Child-authored and teacher-authored literature are often the most popular reading materials in a classroom library.

The books in the library collection of early childhood classrooms will also include: wordless picture books, pattern books, participation books, language play books, and concept books. Many books fit into more than one of these categories. These books are particularly enjoyable to children, and they have features that help children make literacy discoveries.

Wordless picture books. Wordless picture books portray a story through illustrations only; they appeal to a range of ages, even to adults (Abrahamson, 1981). *Pancakes for Breakfast* (dePaola, 1978) appeals to both preschoolers and older children. It illustrates the efforts of a little old woman as she makes pancakes. Young children enjoy the wordless book *Sunshine* (Ormerod, 1981), which illustrates the actions of a young girl as she dresses herself while her parents oversleep. Second and third graders enjoy *Deep in the Woods* (Turkle, 1976), especially when they discover its play on the Goldilocks story.

Children enjoy telling stories again and again to accompany these delightful books. They also enjoy composing stories for wordless books. Many teachers use special notepaper with sticky backs (Post-its®) for writing stories in wordless books. Children stick a Post-it® to each page of the wordless book so that their written text accompanies the pictures.

Children benefit in a number of ways from wordless picture books (Huck, Hepler, & Hickman, 1987). Because the pictures in wordless books are often arranged from left to right on the page, young children can gain a sense of left-to-right organization and can practice handling books. They practice interpreting pictures as an important part of reading a story. A list of wordless picture books is presented in Figure 3.2.

Pattern books. Pattern books contain repeated dialogue or events. For example, the character, Gingerbread Boy, in the pattern book *The Gingerbread Boy* (Galdone, 1975) repeats actions; he runs past a series of characters who chase him. He also repeats dialogue; each time he runs past a character he taunts, "I've run away from a little old woman. I've run away from a little old man. And I can run away from you, I can." Pattern books are often referred to as *predictable books* because children can predict text by remembering repeated dialogue and events.

Pattern books become favorites quickly. Often after only one reading, preschoolers can read them independently by remembering the repeated dialogue and events. These books provide a useful structure for children's own story compositions (Rhodes, 1981; Tompkins & McGee, 1989).

Pattern books are especially useful for helping children learn to read their

Figure 3.2 *Wordless Picture Books*

DeGroat, D. (1977). *Alligator's tooth-ache.* New York: Crown.

de Paola, T. (1978). *Pancakes for breakfast.* San Diego: Harcourt Brace Jovanovich.

Dieter, S. (1987). *Where's my monkey?* New York: Dial.

Euvremer, T. (1987). *Sun's up.* New York: Crown.

Goodall, J. (1973). *The midnight adventures of Kelly, Dot, and Esmeralda.* New York: Atheneum.

Hoban, T. (1972). *Push-pull, empty-full.* New York: Macmillan.

Hoban, T. (1980). *Take another look.* New York: Greenwillow Books.

Krahn, F. (1970). *How Santa Claus had a long and difficult journey delivering his presents.* New York: Delacorte.

Krahn, F. (1976). *Sebastian and the mushroom.* New York: Delacorte.

Krahn, F. (1978). *The biggest Christmas tree on earth.* Boston: Little, Brown.

Krahn, F. (1978). *The great ape.* New York: Viking-Penguin.

Mayer, M. (1974). *Frog goes to dinner.* New York: Dial.

Mayer, M. (1977). *Oops.* New York: Dial.

McCully, E. (1985). *First snow.* New York: Harper and Row.

Spier, P. (1982). *Peter Spier's rain.* New York: Doubleday.

Turkle, B. (1976). *Deep in the forest.* New York: Dutton.

Winter, P. (1976). *The bear and the fly.* New York: Crown.

---

first printed words (Bridge, 1986). As children hear the repeated text of pattern books and see printed words repeated, they have many opportunities to connect printed words with spoken words. Pattern books also encourage children to use active reading strategies such as predicting future story events. Figure 3.3 presents a list of pattern books.

Participation books. Participation books have special devices for involving the reader (Glazer, 1981). Scratch-and-sniff and touch books are examples of books that invite the reader to participate by smelling or feeling. Young children enjoy smelling a rose, strawberry jam, pine needles, a peach, a dill pickle, and a mint cookie with Little Bunny in *Little Bunny Follows His Nose* (Howard, 1971).

Other participation books include the popular movable books (McGee & Charlesworth, 1984). Movable books include pop-up books such as *Dinnertime* (Peinkowski, 1980) and lift-the-flap books such as *Where's Spot?* (Hill, 1980). These books have special appeal because children can imitate actions of characters by manipulating portions of the book. For example, in *Where's Spot?* readers can help mother dog look for Spot by lifting up a bedcover, opening a closet, and peeking in a basket. Elementary children are intrigued by making their own movable books (Abrahamson & Stewart, 1982).

Participation books may help children make the transition from interpreting real actions to interpreting actions portrayed in illustrations (McGee & Charlesworth, 1984). They may be especially useful in developing concepts about natural science (Radencich & Bohning, 1988). As children push and pull parts of

Figure 3.3 Pattern Books

Burningham, J. (1978). *Would you rather . . . ?* New York: Crowell.

Carle, E. (1977). *The grouchy ladybug.* New York: Crowell.

Charlip, R. (1964). *Fortunately.* New York: Parents.

Ets, M. (1973). *Elephant in the well.* New York: Viking.

Flack, M. (1932). *Ask Mr. Bear.* New York: Macmillan.

Fox, M. (1987). *Hattie and the fox.* New York: Bradbury.

Galdone, P. (1968). *Henny Penny.* New York: Scholastic.

Hines, A. G. (1987). *It's just me, Emily.* Boston: Clarion Books.

Hutchins, P. (1982). *Goodnight, owl!* New York: Macmillan.

Keats, E. (1971). *Over in the meadow.* New York: Scholastic.

Kent, J. (1971). *The fat cat.* New York: Scholastic.

Kraus, R. (1970). *Whose mouse are you?* New York: Collier.

Lexau, J. (1969). *Crocodile and hen.* New York: Harper and Row.

Martin, B., Jr. (1983). *Brown bear, brown bear.* New York: Henry Holt.

Sendak, M. (1962). *Chicken soup with rice.* New York: Harper and Row.

Tafuri, N. (1984). *Have you seen my duckling?* New York: Greenwillow.

Tresselt, A. (1964). *The mitten.* New York: Lothrop, Lee, and Shepard.

Van Laan, N. (1987). *The big fat worm.* New York: Knopf.

Vipont, E. (1986). *The elephant and the bad baby.* New York: Coward.

Zemach, M. (1965). *The teeny tiny woman.* New York: Scholastic.

movable books, their manipulations imitate changes that occur in natural life cycles or movements in space. Movable books also encourage children to take an active role in storyreading. Many participation books take the form of question-and-answer books. Children are encouraged to supply answers by manipulating parts of the book. In *Who Does What?* (Hill, 1981), children answer questions such as "Who works in a library?" by lifting a flap to discover a librarian. Figure 3.4 presents a list of participation books.

Language play books. Books with language play feature rhyme and alliteration. Children love listening to the rhythm and rhyme found in *Chicken Soup with Rice* (Sendak, 1962) and to the alliteration in *One Old Oxford Ox* (Bayley, 1977). Dr. Seuss' books such as *Hop on Pop* (Seuss, 1963) are famous for their language play. Although they often require mental operations not appropriate for young elementary students, books that have plays on word meanings and word forms are sometimes appealing to second and third graders. One such favorite is the story *Amelia Bedelia* (Parish, 1963). When Amelia is asked to dust the furniture, she happily complies by putting dusting powder on the sofa and chairs.

Language play books are beneficial in helping children focus on language as something that can be talked about (Geller, 1982). As children practice saying rhyming words, they learn to consider sounds of spoken language apart from the meanings associated with that spoken language. As they discover the humor in misinterpreted word meanings, they learn to manipulate language. Figure 3.5 presents a reference list of books with language play.

Figure 3.4 *Participation Books*

Ahlberg, J. & Ahlberg, S. (1981). *Peek-a-boo.* New York: Viking.

Anga, S. (1981). *Who has the yellow hat?* Los Angeles: Intervisual Communications.

Carle, E. (1981). *The honeybee and the robber.* New York: Philomel.

Carle, E. (1984). *The very busy spider.* New York: Putnam Publishing Group.

Crowther, R. (1977). *The most amazing hide and seek alphabet.* New York: Viking.

Crowther, R. (1981). *The most amazing hide and seek counting book.* New York: Viking.

de Paola, T. (1982). *Georgio's village.* New York: Putnam.

Gerstein, M. (1984). *Roll over.* New York: Crown.

Hill, E. (1981). *Where's Spot?* New York: Putnam.

Hill, E. (1982). *Opposites peek-a-book.* Los Angeles: Price/Stern/Sloan.

Hill, E. (1982). *Who does what?* Los Angeles, CA: Price/Stern/Sloan.

Pienkowski, J. (1980). *Dinnertime.* Los Angeles, CA: Price/Stern/Sloan.

Pienkowski, J. (1981). *Robot.* New York: Delacorte.

Pienkowski, J. (1983). *Gossip.* London: Gallery Five.

Roffey, M. (1983). *Home sweet home.* New York: Putnam Publishing Group.

Roth, H. (1988). *Let's look all around the house.* New York: Grosset & Dunlap.

Tafuri, N. (1983). *Early morning in the barn.* New York: Greenwillow Books.

Tarrant, G. (1982). *Butterflies.* Los Angeles: Intervisual Communications.

Figure 3.5 *Language Play Books*

Ahlberg, J., & Ahlberg, A. (1978). *Each peach pear plum.* New York: Scholastic.

Benjamin, A. (1987). *Rat-a-tat, pitter pat.* New York: Harper/Crowell.

Blos, J. W. (1987). *Old Henry.* New York: Morrow.

Carlstrom, N. W. (1987). *Wild wild sunflower child Anna.* New York: Macmillan.

Demars, J. (1985). *What do you do with a . . . ?* New York: Willowwisp Press.

Komaiko, L. (1987). *Annie Bananie.* New York: Harper and Row.

Lenski, L. (1987). *Sing a song of people.* Boston: Little, Brown.

Mahy, M. (1987). *17 Kings and 42 elephants.* New York: Dial.

Noll, S. (1987). *Jiggle wiggle prance.* New York: Greenwillow.

Perkins, A. (1969). *Hand, hand, fingers, thumb.* New York: Random House.

Seuss, Dr. (Theodore Geisel) (1957). *The cat in the hat.* New York: Random House.

Seuss, Dr. (Theodore Geisel) (1963). *Hop on pop.* New York: Random House.

Silverstein, S. (1964). *A giraffe and a half.* New York: Harper and Row.

Sonneborn, R. A. (1974). *Someone is eating the sun.* New York: Random House.

Watson, C. (1971). *Father Fox's pennyrhymes.* New York: Scholastic.

Wells, R. (1973). *Noisy Nora.* New York: Dial.

Wildsmith, B. (1986). *Goat's trail.* New York: Knopf.

Wood, A. (1987). *Heckedy Peg.* New York: Harcourt, Brace, Jovanovich.

Concept books.   Concept books are designed to help children acquire understandings about colors, shapes, alphabet letters, numbers, and a variety of other everyday concepts. There are many alphabet books that are appropriate for children from preschool through elementary school. *Animal Alphabet* (Kitchen, 1984) is an example of an alphabet book that includes just the letter and a picture for labeling. In contrast, *On Market Street* (Lobel, 1981) is an alphabet book that tells a clever story while illustrating alphabet letters. The benefits of alphabet books include their supporting children's language development and their teaching of letter names.

Counting books are another popular type of concept book. Even older children enjoy counting books such as *Anno's Counting Book* (Anno, 1975). Counting books help children make the transition from manipulating objects to looking at visual representations on a page as they develop mathematical concepts. Counting books are also useful for language development. Figure 3.6 presents a list of two kinds of concept books: alphabet and counting books.

Functional print.   A literacy-rich classroom has many different types of print items for children to read. Functional print includes print that is written by the children and the teacher such as directions and messages. Letters or notes are also functional print items that make useful and enjoyable reading materials. Teachers can facilitate the production and reading of these kinds of print materials by establishing a classroom message center or post office. The message center might simply be a portion of a bulletin board where children and the teacher can post notes. Teachers who post a few notes to children in the message center soon find out how popular this activity can be. Lists kept as a record of information, such as lists of children who have fed the class pet, are also included in this category.

Other kinds of functional print items include telephone books, maps, cookbooks, reference books, *TV Guides,* catalogs, and newspapers. The class daily schedule, calendar, and job chart are also functional print items found in literacy-rich classrooms. A number of magazines, which appeal to a range of ages and interests, are published especially for children. Figure 3.7 presents a list of children's magazines.

Writing materials.   Literacy-rich classrooms contain many types of writing implements and surfaces. Figure 3.8 presents a list of writing materials that are found in literacy-rich classrooms. In addition to these materials, creative teachers will find many unusual writing materials that appeal to children, such as smelly markers, alphabet stamps, and letter cookie-cutters. Children occasionally enjoy using unusual writing surfaces such as magic slates, pebbleboard, and scratch-off paper. Office or art supply stores sell many kinds of exciting writing materials that creative teachers can adapt for classroom use.

Physical Setting Supportive of Literacy Activities

The second characteristic of literacy-rich environments is that they have comfortable places for reading and writing.

Figure 3.6 *Concept Books: Alphabet and Counting Books*

Alphabet Books

Anno, M. (1976). *Anno's alphabet.* New York: Crowell.

Aruego, J. & Dewey, A. (1987). *Alligator arrived with apples, a potluck alphabet feast.* New York: Macmillan.

Baskin, L. (1972). *Hosie's alphabet.* New York: Viking Press.

Bruna, D. (1967). *B is for bear.* New York: Macmillan.

Burningham, J. (1964). *John Burningham's ABC.* London: Jonathan Cape.

Eichenberg, F. (1952). *Ape in cape.* San Diego, CA: Harcourt Brace Jovanovich.

Hoban, T. (1987). *26 letters and 99 cents.* New York: Greenwillow Books.

Ipcar, D. (1964). *I love an anteater with an A.* New York: Alfred A. Knopf.

Isadora, R. (1983). *City seen from A to Z.* New York: Greenwillow Books.

Kellogg, S. (1987). *Aster Aardvark's alphabet adventures.* New York: Morrow.

Lionni, L. (1985). *Letters to talk about.* New York: Pantheon.

Lobel, A. (1981). *On Market Street.* New York: Greenwillow Books.

McMillan, B. (1986). *Counting wildflowers.* New York: Lothrop.

Seuss, Dr. (Theodore Geisel). (1963). *Dr. Seuss's ABC.* New York: Random House.

Tudor, T. (1954). *A is for Annabelle.* New York: Walck.

Wildsmith, B. (1963). *Brian Wildsmith's ABC.* Danbury, CT: Franklin Watts.

Counting Books

Anno, M. (1975). *Anno's counting book.* New York: Crowell.

Bang, M. (1983). *Ten, nine, eight.* New York: Greenwillow Books.

Ernst, L. (1986). *Up to ten and down again.* New York: Lothrop, Lee, & Shepard Books.

Feelings, M., & Feelings, T. (1976). *Moja means one.* New York: Viking.

Hoban, T. (1972). *Count and see.* New York: Macmillan.

Hoban, T. (1985). *1, 2, 3.* New York: Greenwillow Books.

Hughes, S. (1985). *A walk in the park.* New York: Lothrop.

Hutchins, P. (1982). *1 Hunter.* New York: Greenwillow Books.

Kitchen, B. (1987). *Animal numbers.* New York: Dial.

Oxenbury, H. (1968). *Numbers of things.* Danbury, CT: Franklin Watts.

Pearson, S. (1987). *When baby went to bed.* New York: Viking Kestrel.

Tafuri, N. (1986). *Who's counting?* New York: Greenwillow.

Wildsmith, B. (1984). *Brian Wildsmith's one, two, three.* New York: Oxford University Press.

Typical Classroom Practice

Few researchers have examined whether classrooms have special locations for reading and writing, nor have many researchers described what these locations might be like. According to one survey, many preschool and kindergarten classrooms did not have library centers that were especially inviting or comfortable for reading (Morrow, 1982). Few classroom libraries had rugs or comfortable seating. Most of the libraries were not located in a quiet, out-of-the-way nook in the classroom. Therefore, it seems that typical classrooms may not have specific locations for reading that are comfortable and inviting. We know very little about special locations in classrooms for writing.

Figure 3.7 Children's Magazines

Chickadee: The Canadian Magazine for Children. Published by the Young Naturalist Foundation, 56 The Esplanade, Suite 304, Toronto, Ontario, Canada M5E 1A7. (3–9 years).

Children's Digest. * P.O. 10681, Des Moines, IA 50381. (8–10 years).

Cricket. Published by Open Court Publishing Co., P.O. Box 51144, Boulder, CO 80321-1144. (6–12 years).

Happy Times. Published by the Concordia Publishing House, 35585 Jefferson Ave., St. Louis, MO 63118. (3–5 years).

Highlights for Children. * 2300 West Fifth Ave., P.O. Box 269, Columbus, OH 43272. (3–12 years).

Humpty Dumpty's Magazine. P.O. Box 10681, Des Moines, IA 50381. (6–8 years).

Jack and Jill. Published by Children's Better Health Institute, 1100 Waterway Blvd., P.O. Box 567, Indianapolis, IN 46206. (6–8 years).

Lollipops, Ladybugs and Lucky Stars. Published by Good Apple, Box 299 Carthage, IL 62321-0299. (3–5 years).

Ranger Rick's Nature Magazine. * Published by the National Wildlife Federation, 1412 16th St., N.W., Washington, DC 20036. (5–11 years).

Scholastic Let's Find Out. Published by Scholastic Magazines, 1290 Wall St. W., Lyndhurst, NJ 07071. (5 years).

Sesame Street. Published by Children's Television Workshop, P.O. Box 2896, Boulder, CO 80322. (3–8 years).

Stone Soup: The Magazine by Children. * Published by the Children's Art Foundation, P.O. Box 83, Santa Cruz, CA 95063-9990. (6–12 years).

Turtle: Magazine for Preschool Kids. Published by the Children's Better Health Institute, 1100 Waterway Blvd., P.O. Box 567, Indianapolis, IN 46206. (2–5 years).

Your Big Back Yard. Published by the National Wildlife Federation, 1412 16th St., N.W., Washington, DC 20036. (3–5 years).

*Indicates magazine publishes children's art and writing.

Research Supporting Literacy-Rich Physical Settings

Changes in the physical environment of the classroom contribute to children's literacy learning. Morrow and Weinstein (1982, 1986) transformed a typical library center into one that was more supportive of literacy activities. They partitioned off the library center from the rest of the room, added carpet and pillows, and enlarged the space to accommodate at least four or five children. This transition (with the addition of more books and props for storytelling and more story-reading activities) increased the number of kindergartners and second graders who voluntarily visited the library center.

Taylor, Blum, and Logsdon (1986) helped kindergarten teachers transform their classrooms into literacy-rich environments by setting up library centers, writing centers, and print displays. Written language activities were included as part of these centers and in daily classroom routines such as attendance taking and signing up for painting. Kindergartners in the literacy-rich classrooms gained more concepts about print than kindergartners in more typical classrooms.

Figure 3.8 *Writing Materials*

pencils: colored, medium and soft lead, thin and thick, with and without erasers	paper: assorted colors, textures, sizes, shapes (including newsprint, construction paper, typing paper, computer print-out paper, index cards, stationery)
pens: variety of ink colors	
markers: variety of colors, variety of tip widths, all watercolor	file folders
crayons: variety of colors and widths	magic slates
chalk and chalk board	envelopes
alphabet letter stamps and ink pads	hole punch
plastic alphabet letters	scissors
cookie cutter alphabet letters	stapler
alphabet letter blocks	stickers
yarn	glue or paste
clay or Play Doh™	pencil and crayon sharpeners
typewriter	tape
variety of magazines	wallpaper and gift wrapping paper

These studies confirm that well-designed literacy displays, library centers, and writing centers are important in encouraging and enhancing reading and writing. We use insights from this research to suggest physical designs supportive of literacy learning.

Practice in Literacy-Rich Classrooms

Literacy-rich classrooms have large, comfortable library centers and writing centers that are clearly labeled. They also have many displays of written language, including child-authored drawings and writings, teacher-authored messages, and children's dictations.

Library center. Morrow and Weinstein (1982, 1986) made many recommendations about library center designs. They suggested that library centers should be partitioned into small alcoves or "nooks" by arranging shelves or some other furniture to form a partition. Each center should have shelves or a series of boxes in which to store books and other literature materials. Books should be organized in some way, such as by subject (animals, weather, families, or holidays) or alphabetically by author. Children might be invited to suggest organizations for books. Rugs and pillows or other comfortable seating arrangements should be provided.

Library centers should contain several displays and objects that motivate children to visit them and that can be used in literature activities. For example, listening to audio tapes of favorite stories with a tape recorder and earphones is a favorite activity in a library corner.

Each library center should contain several literature props. Literature props are items that call to mind a specific story. For example, three stuffed bears make good literature props for *The Three Bears* (Galdone, 1972). Other literature props might include puppets or masks depicting story characters.

Writing center.   The writing center in literacy-rich classrooms includes a large table and several chairs of comfortable height for children. The table is large enough to accommodate several children and to include displays of greeting cards, messages, signs, and special words that encourage children to write. Shelves or a rolling cart for storing writing materials are nearby. Writing materials are labeled and easily accessible on the shelves. The materials are changed frequently so that children can explore a variety of writing implements and surfaces.

Writing centers include directions and materials for binding books. Children in the primary grades can create their own bound books that contain their dictated or written compositions. Parents or teachers can bind books for younger children's writing and drawing. Figure 3.9 gives directions for binding books.

Displays of written language.   Literacy-rich classrooms contain many displays of written language, including children's drawing and writing. Many of the displays can be placed in activity centers. Children in the math center could make guesses about how many M & M's are in a jar. Each child's name and guess could be displayed. Displays are placed at children's eye level and within their reach; the displays change frequently. Many written language displays have portions requiring children's manipulations. Teachers might display a large bunny with an empty basket. The display might read, "Help Bunny fill the basket. Make an egg. Sign your name when you have made your egg." Children would be encouraged to use many different art materials to make an egg to paste on the basket. They then would sign their name on a special list attached to the bottom of the display to indicate their participation in the activity.

Reading and Writing Are Functional

The third characteristic of literacy-rich environments is that reading and writing are used in a variety of functional ways.

Typical Classroom Practice

There are only a few researchers who have examined the functions that reading and writing serve in school. They have found that reading and writing activities in elementary school rarely serve functions such as communicating to others, creating imaginative stories or poems, or seeking new information (Bridge & Hiebert, 1985; Florio & Clark, 1982). The two most frequent writing activities in first and third grades were handwriting exercises and copying activities (Bridge & Hiebert, 1985). Children spent less than one minute writing to communicate their own ideas.

Research Supporting Functional Use of Reading and Writing

In contrast to studies described in the preceding section, there are other studies showing that some preschool and elementary children use reading and writing for real purposes in play, content study, and literature activities (Cochran-Smith, 1984; Milz, 1985).

Play has long been considered a major avenue of young children's learning, including literacy learning (Fein & Rivkin, 1986; Isenberg & Quisenberry, 1988). In imaginary play, children use reading and writing in many functional ways just as their parents use reading and writing in real life. Research by Pelligrini (1986) suggests that imaginary play supports the development of written-language ways of communicating and the understanding of stories (Pelligrini, 1986).

DeFord (1986) described one classroom which used literature as a basis for planning units of study. Children used reading and writing to complete many meaningful projects such as conducting surveys about pets and recording information about chickens hatching. Children's writing in this classroom was compared to children's writing in classrooms where children primarily read and wrote to demonstrate literacy knowledge. The children in the literature classroom wrote on a greater variety of topics, used a greater range of vocabulary, and knew more spellings of words.

Based on the research in classrooms where reading and writing are used to serve a variety of functions, where play abounds, and where literature serves as a basis for developing units of study, we can make several recommendations for literacy-rich classrooms.

Practice in Literacy-Rich Classrooms

Children in literacy-rich classrooms have many opportunities to explore reading and writing through play. They are involved in meaningful projects that teach them about content area knowledge and let them explore literature (Cullinan, 1987).

Reading and writing in play.   The home center included in most preschool classrooms and many kindergarten classrooms provides children with many play opportunities. It can easily be adapted to encourage reading and writing. Children naturally assume the role of reader when magazines and newspapers are available for reading. They naturally assume the role of writer when notepads and pencils are located near a telephone.

There are many ways that play can be used in the classroom in addition to using the home center. Special dramatic play centers that are related to units or themes under study can be established. For example, a hospital play center can

***Figure 3.9** Directions for Binding Books*

1. Determine how many pages will be used in the story to be placed in the book. Divide this number in half. Add 3 pages to that number (1 page for front and back plates, 1 page for the title page, and 1 page for dedications, acknowledgments, or comments).

2. Select the paper. Since the paper will be folded in half, it must be twice as large as the paper in the finished book.

3. Fold the papers in half and sew (with dental floss) along the fold as shown.

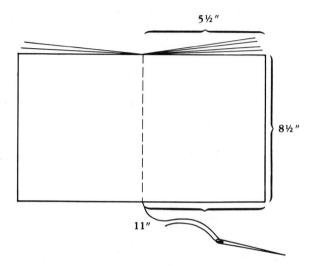

4. Cut 2 pieces of cardboard (mat boards from art supply stores are best) for the covers. Each cardboard piece should be 1″ longer and 1/2″ wider than the paper in the finished book.

5. Place the cardboard pieces side-by-side with about 1/2″ between them. Tape them together as shown.

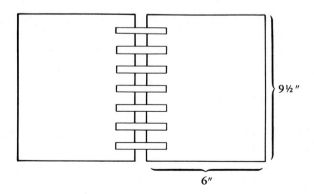

6. Cut contact paper (wallpaper or other attractive paper) so that it is 2″ longer and 2″ wider than the measurement of the two cardboard pieces taped together.

Figure 3.9 *(continued)*

7. Lay the contact paper out and carefully place the two pieces of taped cardboard on it so there is a 1″ overlap on all sides as shown. If you use a paper other than contact paper glue the cardboard in place using rubber cement.

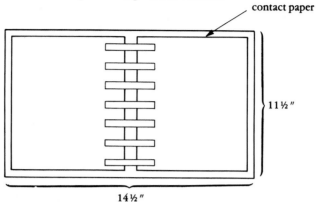

8. Miter the corners of the contact paper and fold paper in as shown. If you use a paper other than contact paper, glue the folded paper in place with rubber cement. This forms the hardcover of the book.

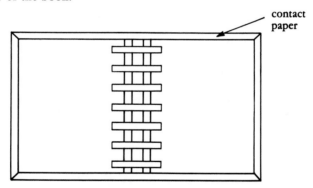

9. Place the hardcover so that the folded part of the contact paper (or other paper) is facing up. Use rubber cement to glue the front and back plates (first and last pages of the sewn book) to the hardcover as shown.

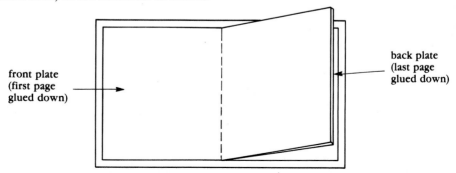

be established as part of a health theme or a café play center can be included as part of a food unit. These play centers offer many opportunities for children to read and write. The hospital play center might have magazines to read in the waiting room, patient charts for doctors and nurses to write, and get-well cards for visitors and patients to read and write.

Reading and writing in study units.

Reading and writing in study units.   In the elementary grades, units of study in content areas or units focusing on children's literature are effective means for encouraging children to use reading and writing for a variety of purposes (Gamberg, Kwak, Hutchings, & Altheim, 1988). For example, second graders might use reading and writing to learn about their town. They might compare a 50-year-old map of their town with a more recent map. They might interview residents who have lived in their town for 50 years or more. They might write to the Chamber of Commerce for literature on economic development in their town. Finally, they might write reports of their findings to share with their classmates.

In addition to planning units around content study, units of study can be focused on literature (Moss, 1984). To plan a literature unit, teachers select a group of books that have a common element. Books selected for a unit might have the same author, focus on a certain kind of character, have a similar literary device, or involve a similar theme. Children could explore this literature by writing to the author, producing a puppet play about one of the literature selections, or keeping a journal as one of the characters in a literature selection.

Literacy Routines

The fourth characteristic of literacy-rich environments is that reading and writing are part of daily routines.

Typical Classroom Practice

Most teachers recognize the importance of reading aloud to children as a routine part of their literacy program. However, research on actual practices of reading aloud to children has shown that many kindergarten and nursery school teachers read aloud to their children only an average of three times a week (Morrow, 1982). Most teachers did not discuss the stories they read aloud with children. Children had few opportunities to respond to these stories through drama, art, or retelling activities.

Another familiar and popular literacy routine many teachers recognize is setting aside a time during the school day for children to read or browse through books. This is a time when children can select books of their choice for pleasurable reading and not be required to complete reading assignments. Daily reading for pleasure is often called *Booktime* (Hong, 1981; Kaisen, 1987), *USSR* (Uninterrupted Sustained Silent Reading), *SSR* (Sustained Silent Reading), or *DEAR* (Drop Everything And Read) (Berglund & Johns, 1983). A similar activity for encouraging children to write is called *SSW* (Sustained Silent Writing) (Bromley, 1985).

Despite the popularity of these strategies for encouraging daily free-choice reading, few teachers in nursery school or kindergarten actually provide time for independent and free-choice reading such as SSR (Morrow, 1982). There is little research on whether free-choice writing is a routine part of children's classroom life. However, one study of the writing practices in elementary classrooms showed that children spend little time in writing activities and that most of these are assigned writing activities involving verbatim copying (Bridge & Hiebert, 1985). Perhaps the stress on "back to basics" has resulted in less attention being given to reading and writing and more attention being paid to learning reading and writing.

Research Supporting Literacy Routines

Many studies have shown that the amount of time children spend reading independently either at home or at school is directly related to their literacy achievement (Anderson, et al., 1985). Reading aloud to children is also a valuable literacy activity. First graders who listened to their teacher read stories every day scored better on reading tests than first graders who spent the same amount of time in teacher-directed reading activities (Feitelson, Kita, & Goldstein, 1986).

Research also confirms the importance of using props (such as a flannel board) to enliven story experiences. Children whose teachers used creative storytelling techniques read more often than children whose teachers did not read frequently and did not use creative storytelling techniques (Morrow & Weinstein, 1982, 1986). Providing time for children to interact with literature through storytelling or drama is also supportive of literacy acquisition (Wagner, 1988). Children who participate in retelling activities remember more about stories and learn more about the organization of stories than children who answer questions about stories (Morrow, 1985). Children who act out stories after hearing them also remember more than children who draw a picture or have a discussion about the story (Galda, 1982).

In summary, there is much research that confirms the value of reading aloud to children, encouraging children to respond to literature in creative ways, and providing time for children to read and write independently. We draw on this research to make suggestions about practice in literacy-rich classrooms.

Practice in Literacy-Rich Classrooms

Teachers in literacy-rich classrooms read literature to children daily, use creative storytelling techniques, provide time for and plan activities that encourage children to respond to literature, and provide time for children to read and write as independent and free-choice activities.

Sharing literature with children.   There are many ways teachers can share literature with children. They can read stories, tell stories, or show films and filmstrips about quality literature. When reading aloud or telling stories to children, teachers should be seated slightly above the children's eye level. The children should be seated so that everyone has a clear view of the teacher and the book.

Sometimes teachers read a book aloud with few interruptions for comments or questions. Some books hold children spellbound by the rhythm of language or by the mood created by the author. Interrupting such stories with questions or comments spoils the effect. At other times, teachers invite many comments and questions as they read and talk about stories.

Teachers plan carefully before sharing literature with children. They keep in mind the age and interests of the children as they select books to read aloud. Books selected for reading have illustrations that are large enough for a group of children to see (Glazer, 1981). Teachers preview books carefully to become familiar with story texts and illustrations and to develop purposes for sharing (we will describe more what these purposes might be in later chapters).

Frequently, teachers tell stories using special props (Cliatt & Shaw, 1988; Ross, 1980). There are many kinds of literature props that teachers can use to tell a story including objects, clothesline props, flannel board props, puppets, and masks. Object props include objects that are selected to represent certain characters and actions. Object props for the story *Where the Wild Things Are* (Sendak, 1963) might include a teddy bear (to represent Max sent to bed with no supper), an oar (to represent his travels to the land where the Wild Things Are), a crown (to represent Max's becoming King of the Wild Things), a drum and horn (to use in the wild rumpus), and a plate and spoon (to represent the smell that brought Max back to his room where he found his dinner).

Clothesline props include pictures drawn to represent important events in the story. These pictures are clothespinned to a clothesline stretched across the classroom as a story is read or told (see Figure 3.10). Clothesline prop pictures that could be used to tell the story *Where the Wild Things Are* might include an illustration of Max yelling at his mother; Max sailing in the boat to the land of the Wild Things; the Wild Things rolling their eyes, gnashing their teeth, and showing their claws; Max becoming King; Max and the Wild Things creating a rumpus; Max sailing back home; and Max finding his dinner at home. Many teachers create clothesline prop illustrations by making simple drawings.

Figure 3.10 Clothesline Props

Puppets make perfect props for storytelling. Finger puppets can be made by drawing characters on paper and carefully cutting them out to include special tabs for fastening around the finger. Stick puppets can be made by coloring characters on stiff paper, cutting them out, and attaching them to soda straws. Figure 3.11 presents a finger puppet and stick puppet that could be used in retelling *Where the Wild Things Are.*

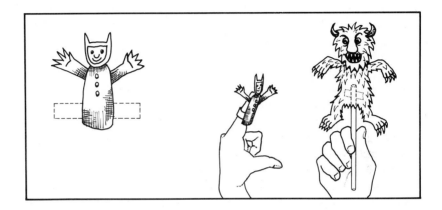

***Figure 3.11** Finger and Stick Puppets*

Flannel board props can be made from velcro, felt, yarn, lace, or other sewing notions. Figure 3.12 shows flannel board props that can be used in telling *Where the Wild Things Are.* Figure 3.13 presents a mask that could also be used in telling this story.

***Figure 3.12** Flannel Board Props*

curls of
paper

paper rolled
into cone

paper

Figure 3.13 *Mask of a "Wild Thing"*

Response-to-literature activities.   Response-to-literature activities encourage children's emotional and intellectual involvement with literature. These
activities can serve many purposes, including helping children explore the language of stories, the themes of literature, the media of illustrations, and the connections between literature experiences and life experiences. Response activities
can support children's imaginative, creative, social, moral, intellectual, and language development (Glazer, 1981). Examples of response activities include
laughing, writing, drawing, retelling, commenting, questioning, rereading, modeling in clay, pantomiming, dramatizing, dancing, singing, cooking, and painting
(Hickman, 1981). Teachers in literacy-rich classrooms plan a variety of these
activities from which children can choose and provide time for children to engage in them.

Retelling as response to literature.   Children enjoy talking about and
retelling favorite stories. One way of encouraging children to retell stories is to
provide them with literature props. Children enjoy making their own props to
retell stories. They also enjoy making illustrations to accompany story retellings.

Another way of retelling stories is to use movement, pantomime, and drama-
tization. Children can enact single events in stories through movement (Stewig,
1983), or teachers can act as narrators to help children enact longer portions of
stories. For example, *Lilly at the Table* (Heller, 1979) involves a girl's fantasy
trip in a refrigerator where she slides down celery, walks a tightrope of spaghetti, and swims in a glass of milk. As the teacher retells this portion of the
story, children can pantomime Lilly's actions. Children can also add dialogue to
their story enactments. Teachers can guide children so they develop their own
dialogue or they can help children remember essential dialogue from the story.
Pattern books that have characters who repeat dialogue are perfect for dramatizations.

Drama as a response to literature.   Drama as a response to literature
usually involves four steps (Heinig & Stillwell, 1981; Stewig, 1983). The first step
is teacher preparation. The teacher selects literature that has plenty of action and
conflict, characters who are active and have striking personalities, and a lot of
dialogue. Portions of the story that are appropriate for movement, pantomime,

or enactments with dialogue are identified. These selections should be easily dramatized in a short time period. Then, questions to use in discussing the story and in planning the enactment with the children are prepared. Second, the teacher reads the story aloud and uses the questions to help the children plan the enactment. Children are then assigned to portray the necessary characters. Third, the teacher directs the enactment either by taking the role of narrator and acting as a side coach or by playing the role of one of the characters. Fourth, the teacher helps children evaluate their drama activity. Children can identify movements or dialogue that were particularly effective. Following evaluation, the teacher selects other children to portray the characters; the second enactment is followed by another evaluation.

Going beyond the story as a response to literature.   There are many kinds of response-to-literature activities that take children beyond the story. Children can write new endings for stories, write a play about a story character, create a collage or a painting based on the mood evoked by the story, compose a poem, dress paper dolls to resemble story characters, or plan a drama around a story character in a new situation. Young children love to bake and decorate gingerbread cookies and practice eating them as a response to *The Gingerbread Boy.* They also enjoy learning about origami after reading *Curious George Rides a Bike* (Rey, 1952).

Interpretation as response to literature.   Experiencing literature means more than understanding or retelling the story as the author wrote it. As children experience literature they enter into a world partially created from their own imaginations and experiences and partially created by the author's text (Iser, 1974). This new story created by the child is an interpretative creation, one which Bruner (1986) called a *possible world.* Children naturally respond to stories by creating their own interpretations. Three-year-old Kristen interpreted *Cinderella* as she insisted on wearing her best dress and shoes so that she could go to the ball. As she dressed, she chatted about why Cinderella needed socks that matched her dress. Four-year-old Lolly looked at an illustration of empty shoes and asked, ''Where did the witch go?'' (Mikkelson, 1985, p. 372). She decided, ''I think she melt, you know, in *The Wizard of Oz* and one of those people throw water at her'' (p. 373). As children interpret, they make connections with their own past experiences and with past literary experiences (Cox & Many, 1989) and they interpret literary themes (Lehr, 1988).

Teachers can support children's interpretative response to literature through literature response groups (Strickland, Dillon, Funkhouser, Glick, & Rogers, 1989). Response groups allow children to explore personal meanings for stories. They encourage children's talk about related real-life events and challenge their thinking. Teachers encourage children to talk together as a way of building an interpretive community (Fish, 1980).

Daily reading and writing.   Children in literacy-rich classrooms have time to read books of their choice and to write on topics of their choice. Many

schools and classrooms use SSR to encourage free-choice reading. Even preschools can establish a daily free-choice Booktime. These are times when children are expected to look at books, use literature props, or listen to story tapes.
Unlike elementary classrooms, preschool and kindergarten Booktime periods are
not likely to be silent. Young children prefer to share books by talking about
pictures, retelling stories, or accompanying story tapes with sound effects.
Figure 3.14 provides directions and suggestions for using Booktime in preschool
and kindergarten classrooms (Hong, 1981; Kaisen, 1987). Figure 3.15 provides
directions and suggestions for using SSR in elementary classrooms (Berglund &
Johns, 1983).

One way to establish a daily writing activity is by having children write in
a journal (Hipple, 1985; Kintisch, 1986). Each child in the classroom is given his
or her own journal. Journals may simply be small books made by stapling paper
together or they may be more elaborate books that children or adults have bound
(see directions for binding books in Figure 3.9). A special time each day is set
aside to write in journals. Children are allowed to write (copy or draw) anything
they wish in their journals. Preschool, kindergarten, and even first grade teachers usually invite a few children each day to dictate to them. Dictations can be

Figure 3.14 *Suggestions for Using Booktime in Preschools*
and Kindergartens

General Guidelines:

1. Booktime should last from 5–10 minutes daily.

2. Booktime should be held in the classroom library center.

3. Teachers and children should look at books, talk about stories, use story props, and
listen to tape-recorded stories during Booktime.

The Teacher's Role:

1. *Gather reading materials.* The classroom library should be equipped with wordless
picture books, pattern books, participation books, and other books that encourage children's active responses.

2. *Promote interest.* Teachers should read aloud to children daily. Books that teachers
read aloud should be available during Booktime. Teachers should use literature props
frequently to read or to tell stories. These props should be available to children during
Booktime.

3. *Form small groups.* Teachers should divide children into small groups for Booktime.
Each small group should have Booktime at the same time each day. The teacher will
accompany each of the small groups during Booktime. The composition of Booktime
groups should change frequently.

Adapted from Hong, L. K. (1981). Modifying SSR for beginning readers. *The Reading Teacher, 34,*
888–891 (Reprinted with permission of the International Reading Association); and Kaisen, J. (1987).
SSR/Booktime: Kindergarten and 1st grade sustained silent reading. *The Reading Teacher, 40,* 532–
536 (Reprinted with permission of Jim Kaisen and the International Reading Association).

Figure 3.15 Suggestions for Using SSR in Elementary Classrooms

General Guidelines:

1. Initially SSR should last from 5 to 15 minutes daily.

2. The amount of time spent for SSR should be gradually lengthened.

3. No reports, discussions, or work is required in connection with SSR.

4. Children should read at their tables or desks (or other agreed upon locations in the classroom).

5. All children and the teacher read silently without interruptions.

The Teacher's Role:

1. *Gather reading materials.* The classroom library should be equipped with children's literature, functional print, magazines, student-authored literature, and teacher-authored literature.

2. *Promote interest.* Teachers should read aloud to children daily. Books that teachers read aloud should be available during SSR. In addition, teachers should hold booktalks several times a week. Booktalks include reading short portions of books aloud, talking about stories, and having students speculate on story outcomes.

3. *Establish simple rules.* Some examples of effective rules are:

   a. Everyone must look at or read something during SSR.

   b. No talking or interruptions, please.

   c. Have reading materials ready.

4. *Determine a routine for selecting reading materials.* Some teachers have SSR early in the day so that children can select their reading materials as they enter the classroom. Other teachers have SSR after lunch so that children can select their materials anytime in the morning when they have free time to do so.

Adapted from Berglund, R. L., & Johns, J. L. (1983). A primer on uninterrupted sustained silent reading. *The Reading Teacher, 36,* p. 534–539. Reprinted with permission of R. Berglund and the International Reading Association.

stimulated simply by asking, "Tell me what you have written" (Hipple, 1985, p. 256). Teachers of elementary children may read journal entries only if children invite them to.

There are many variations on journal writing. For example, dialogue journals are written conversations (Gambrell, 1985). Children converse by writing a question or statement in their journals. The questions or statements are read either by a classmate or by the teacher, who writes an answer or further comment. Dialogue journals capitalize on elementary children's love for passing notes. They may also be a way for children to communicate with teachers in a very private and intimate way.

Another variation of journal writing that can be used in the preschool and kindergarten is the home-school journal (Elliott, Nowosad, & Samuels, 1981).

These journals are prepared around topics such as "Food" or "Toys." Two pages in the journal are devoted to each topic: one page for home and one page for school. Children can dictate to their teacher about "Food at School." They are given opportunities at school to read their dictations. Then they take their journals home to dictate to a parent about "Food at Home."

Interaction during Reading and Writing

The fifth characteristic of literacy-rich environments is that learning occurs as children and adults talk together.

Typical Classroom Practice

Several researchers have examined the kinds of talk found in elementary classrooms. In general, the results of this research suggest that children do very little (official) talking in classrooms other than to answer questions. Teachers do most of the talking in kindergarten and primary grade classrooms, and they control the kinds of talk children engage in (Dillon & Searle, 1981; Steinberg, 1985). Most discussions in language activities can be characterized by three parts (Cazden, 1988; Mehan, 1979): teacher asks a question, student answers, and teacher gives feedback. Teachers use language in only a few ways: mainly to control, direct, and inform children. They rarely use language in more imaginative ways such as in dramatic play or in statements such as "I wonder what would happen if . . ." They rarely provide children with opportunities for using language in ways other than for answering teacher-initiated questions that call for rote information or obedience to implied commands (Dillon & Searle, 1981).

Research Supporting Interaction during Reading and Writing

Research shows that children can learn by talking with other children (Genishi, McCarrier, & Nussbaum, 1988). Group efforts in composing and writing seem to be especially fruitful activities for children to learn through their own talk. In three studies, kindergartners and first graders helped each other read, compose, spell, correct grammar, and clarify information—all activities that are usually reserved for the teacher (Kamii & Randazzo, 1985; Long & Bulgarella, 1985; Piazza & Tomlinson, 1985). Preschoolers' talk is also an important avenue for both their own and their peers' learning. Lamme and Childers (1983, p. 47) described a group of preschoolers as they wrote together with their teacher. When Laurel directed classmate Terry to "Look at my *L*," Terry argued, "It's a *V,* you silly." When Laurel insisted she had written an *L,* Terry replied, "*That* is a *V.*" It is easy to imagine that Laurel discovered that the letter *L* has to be written just right in order not to be mistaken for the letter *V.*

The kind of talk teachers use is also an important component in literacy learning (Linfors, 1988). Certain kinds of talk that parents and teachers use while writing with children are related to more mature written productions. Children produce less mature writing when parents or teachers control their writing by telling them what and how to write (Hoffman, 1987; Hoffman & McCully, 1984). The quality of teachers' talk during instruction in elementary school is also an important variable in how well children learn. Students learn more from teachers who can talk out loud about how they think during reading (Duffy & Roehler, 1987). Teachers' responses to children's writing are important factors in their writing growth (Calkins, 1986; Graves, 1983).

Research suggests that children can learn from each other as they talk together about reading and writing, and that teacher talk affects learning. The kind of teacher talk that is most supportive of children's learning is not typically found in classrooms. Supportive teacher talk explains, asks children to clarify, and helps children solve problems. These findings have implications for the kinds of talk that will be found in literacy-rich classrooms.

Practice in Literacy-Rich Classrooms

Teachers in literacy-rich classrooms provide many opportunities for children to learn from each other. They plan many group activities in which children can interact together as they read and write. Often this means allowing groups of children to work together cooperatively (Rasinski & Natheson-Majia, 1987). Teachers also think carefully about their language and how they use talk in the classroom. They ask questions that do not have one right answer, and they ask students to clarify and explain or to predict and interpret. They respond to students' responses with praise and concern (Hoffman, 1987).

An important part of teachers' talk is to allow children to be in charge of their own learning. We call this *letting the literacy learner maintain ownership* (Calkins, 1986; Hoffman, 1987). Teachers who help children maintain ownership of their own literacy efforts ask children to think of solutions to a problem rather than provide solutions to the problem. Supportive teachers *invite* children to read their own writing even when the writing is nonconventional. When children ask how to spell a word, supportive teachers *suggest* that children say the word slowly and listen for letters they know. Supportive teachers say, "Write it the way you think. I will be able to read it" (Hoffman & McCully, 1984, p. 45).

Responsibility for Supporting Children's Literacy Learning

The sixth characteristic of literacy-rich environments is that adults feel responsible for helping children learn about reading and writing.

Typical Classroom Practice

Visits to many classrooms suggest that teachers in typical elementary classrooms devote large amounts of time to literacy instruction, particularly to reading. The results of large-scale testing programs (National Assessment of Educational Progress) have demonstrated that this instruction is largely successful. Children have made gains in the basic processes involved in reading in the last decade (Anderson, et al., 1985). Teachers spend less time on writing instruction. One study showed that less than 15 percent of the elementary school day was devoted to writing instruction (Bridge & Hiebert, 1985).

Research Supporting Teacher Responsibility for Literacy Learning

Although it seems that teachers typically plan to include literacy instructions in their daily activities, some teachers' instruction is clearly more effective than that of other teachers. There is much research that suggests some teachers are better than other teachers at providing explanations about reading and writing and at getting their students actively involved in reading and writing activities. More effective teachers have students who learn more (Brophy, 1983).

Research on direct instruction, also called *teacher effectiveness research,* has shown that teachers who plan lessons in which they provide explicit instruction on how to accomplish a specific task have students who perform better than teachers whose instruction is neither explicit nor focused on specific tasks (Evans & Carr, 1985; Tharp, 1982). Teachers who hold elementary school children accountable for participating in lessons have students who make greater gains in reading tests of basic skills (Anderson, Evertson, & Brophy, 1979). (Basic skills in reading are the skills that are measured in reading tests such as matching letters and sounds, identifying main ideas, and defining a word's meaning.)

Research clearly shows that elementary children make greater gains on standardized tests of basic literacy skills when they have teachers who provide effective instruction. These findings suggest that teachers in literacy-rich classrooms should not only plan reading and writing activities, but also should work to develop effective instructional abilities.

Practice in Literacy-Rich Classrooms

Teachers in literacy-rich elementary classrooms expect children to be actively engaged in reading and writing activities, and they plan effective lessons that help children acquire new literacy knowledge. Teachers plan instruction so that students are actively involved. The amount of time students are actively involved in learning is called *time on task, engaged time,* or *academic learning time* (Duffy, 1981). Children in literacy-rich classrooms have great amounts of engaged time when they are actively involved with reading and writing learning (Fisher, et al., 1978).

So far, most research on the effects of time on task and direct instruction has been conducted in elementary classrooms. The notion that children must be engaged in an activity in order to learn about the activity is still an important one in the preschool. Children who do not read or write during their preschool day have no opportunity to gain greater knowledge about reading and writing. *However, the notion of direct instruction—that teachers must control instruction and focus on skills—does not apply to preschool.* We would be hard pressed to list "basic skills" of reading and writing which would apply to three- and four-year-olds. Certainly children this age might be learning to recognize alphabet letters and to write their names, but we know they are learning a great deal more than this. The way young children learn to recognize the alphabet and to write their names seems to be through participating in reading and writing and not through "drill and skill" activities.

The research on direct instruction and teacher effectiveness seems to conflict with studies suggesting that children can direct their own learning and research on the kinds of talk most supportive of young children's writing growth. On the one hand, teachers who are the most directive, who do most of the talking, and who control the kinds of talk and activities of children, seem to produce the most gains in reading and writing. On the other hand, teachers who allow children to talk and to direct their own activities seem to have children who learn on their own. One answer to this dilemma might be related to what it is children are supposed to learn. Direct instruction research has been based on basic skills. Research on children's own learning has focused primarily on quality of writing, a more global phenomenon that is harder to test. Reading and writing do not consist only of basic skills. We cannot completely break reading and writing into tasks that are easy to test or to teach. Our opinion is that some aspects of reading and writing can be taught very well through direct instruction; these include easily tested behaviors such as knowing when to double a final consonant when adding a suffix to a word. Other aspects of reading and writing can be learned through interaction with others; these include learning to understand stories that are read aloud and developing a sense of audience in writing.

Recognition of Children's Individual Needs

The seventh characteristic of literacy-rich environments is that adults know a great deal about children's knowledges and approaches to literacy learning. They provide support for literacy learning that is compatible with children's level of knowledge.

Typical Classroom Practice

The idea that students should perform tasks compatible with their current level of knowledge has had a long tradition in literacy instruction (Smith, 1965). The traditional way that elementary teachers have provided students with instruction that matches their level of knowledge is by dividing children into small groups. Each small group receives instruction that best meets the needs of the children included in the group. Most teachers can make accurate judgments about the reading abilities of their children (Stern & Shavelson, 1983), and they use these judgments to group children for reading instruction. Writing groups are also becoming popular.

Although grouping children according to ability for reading and writing instruction is a good thing in theory (it allows teachers to meet individual needs and insures success), it has not proven to be beneficial in practice, particularly for students in lower ability groups. Teachers seem to spend more time teaching children about decoding and other skills in lower ability groups than they do in higher ability groups (Hiebert, 1983). This means that students in lower ability groups spend less time on the more important activity in reading—exploring what stories mean (comprehension). Higher ability groups read as much as ten times more material in a school year than lower ability groups (Allington, 1984; Gambrell, 1984). That means higher ability groups get more practice reading than lower ability groups.

Research Supporting Recognition of Individual Needs

There is much research that suggests providing instruction that is within children's level of knowledge affects how well they learn. Preschool teachers who used information about their children's literacy knowledge to plan instruction were more effective than preschool teachers who did not (Mason & McCormick, 1981). Teachers who learned to listen to students, assess misunderstandings, and provide instruction to clear up misunderstandings had students who made greater gains in reading achievement than teachers who were not so successful in these activities (Duffy & Roehler, 1987).

Teachers who are able to gauge what their students know and can thus provide activities that children can complete successfully, have children who learn better. These findings suggest that teachers in literacy-rich classrooms should spend time carefully observing children. They should plan activities in which each child can be successful.

Practice in Literacy-Rich Classrooms

Instruction and activities in literacy-rich classrooms is planned with a child's knowledge in mind. We believe it is crucial for teachers to be knowledgeable of their children's literacy knowledge. The next seven chapters in this book are devoted to helping teachers learn more about different kinds of literacy knowledge that children can be expected to have as they grow into more accomplished readers and writers.

The notion of success is an important one in literacy learning. When teachers plan instruction that is congruent with their children's level of literacy knowledge, children are successful. Children who are successful feel confident and are able to move more quickly through the material to be learned. Moving more rapidly in learning means more material is covered and students have more opportunities to learn.

One way teachers in literacy-rich classrooms meet the needs of their children and insure success is to plan many activities that are open-ended. *Open-ended activities* allow children at many different levels of literacy knowledge to participate successfully. They alleviate many of the problems associated with grouping children for instruction. Journal writing is an excellent example of an open-ended writing activity. Three-year-olds can write in journals as well as eight-year-olds when teachers accept their efforts. An example of an open-ended reading activity is retelling a favorite story. Three-year-olds may only retell a few actions of the story and use simple language not related to the story text. Eight-year-olds may remember almost all of the story in detail and may even repeat much of the text. Both responses are successful and both provide children with valuable learning experiences.

Chapter Summary

Literacy-rich classrooms meet professional guidelines for appropriate practice. Two important statements about appropriate literacy practice include the National Association for the Education of Young Children's *Developmentally Appropriate Practice* and the joint statement of *Literacy Development and Pre-First Grade* made by several professional organizations. These statements stipulate that children in their early childhood years (from birth to age eight) learn best when they have many opportunities to explore materials directly, to make choices about learning activities, and to engage in play.

Literacy-rich classrooms are similar to literacy-rich homes in seven ways. Children in literacy-rich homes and classrooms have: (1) a variety and quantity of reading and writing materials; (2) a physical setting supportive of literacy activities; (3) parents and teachers who read and write and who include children in reading and writing for functional purposes; (4) daily literacy routines; (5) parents, teachers, and children who interact as they read and write; (6) parents and teachers who feel responsible for helping children learn and who believe that children are capable readers and writers; and (7) parents and teachers who are knowledgeable about children as individuals and who are willing to accept children's reading and writing efforts even when they are unconventional.

Teachers in literacy-rich classrooms establish reading and writing centers that are amply supplied with children's literature, functional print, child-authored print, and teacher-authored print. Literacy-rich classrooms have a large classroom literature collection with a variety of types of children's literature but especially including wordless picture books, pattern books, participation books, language play books, and concept books. Literacy is used for authentic reasons in such activities as play and study units. Literacy routines including sharing literature through reading, storytelling, and response-to-literature activities frequently occur. Children read and write daily in sustained silent reading and journal writing. Teachers are aware of the importance of their talk; they model using talk to meet several kinds of functions. They offer children opportunities to learn through their own talk. They plan instruction, and they include many open-ended activities to meet the needs of children operating with many different literacy knowledges.

Literacy-rich classrooms are not typical classrooms. Many practices that make classrooms literacy-rich are not found in the typical classroom. Typical classrooms have few functional reading and writing activities; instead, over 90 percent of elementary children's reading and writing is spent working with commercial materials designed to teach reading and writing. Many teachers do not read aloud to children daily, do not provide children time to interact with literature or to write on topics of their choice, and do not encourage children's own talk as a way of learning. However, research justifies taking time in order to complete these and other activities suggested in this chapter.

We caution that our descriptions of typical classrooms are based on relatively few research studies, and many studies included only a few classrooms. We also caution that early childhood educators have not asked the same questions that we have asked about classrooms. We know very little about the typical literacy activities and materials in pre-elementary school settings.

Given the millions of classrooms and teachers, it is nearly impossible to define typical classroom practice. The more important point is that, despite what we know about what should go on in classrooms, it sometimes does not occur. However, when teachers are knowledgeable about effective and appropriate classroom practice, children learn better.

All teachers need to strive to create literacy-rich classrooms. We acknowledge that not all teachers will be able to or will want to use all of the activities and practices suggested in this chapter. Each teacher needs to set realistic goals for enriching the literacy environment and learning opportunities in his or her own classroom.

Applying the Information

A description of Mrs. E's kindergarten classroom and literacy activities follows. Use the seven characteristics of a literacy-rich classroom to think about the literacy environment in Mrs. E's classroom. Also use the recommendations on developmentally appropriate literacy practices (Figure 3.1 and Appendix A) to think about the literacy environment in Mrs. E's classroom. Discuss how Mrs. E's classroom illustrates each of the seven literacy-rich characteristics. We believe Mrs. E's classroom is very supportive of literacy learning, but Mrs. E. is always looking for ways to improve her literacy program. What suggestions might you make?

Mrs. E has twenty-two kindergartners in a relatively small room. Nearly all of the children who attend this school receive free lunch (their families fall below the poverty limit established by the federal government). A map of the classroom is presented in Figure 3.16. This map illustrates that Mrs. E's room is equipped with twenty-eight desks and one table. The entire room is carpeted.

Each morning Mrs. E reads at least one selection of children's literature to the entire class. The children gather around her on the rug in the large-group area. Next, Mrs. E has experience time. During this time she might demonstrate a science experiment, have a guest speaker, or read nonfiction. Each of these daily experiences is related to a topic of study. For example, one unit of study focused on insects. A man who keeps bees visited the classroom and brought his equipment to the class. The children kept ants in an ant farm. Mrs. E read many books that had insects as characters as well as informational books about insects.

After experience time, the children usually dictate and read accounts of what they learned that day or dictate

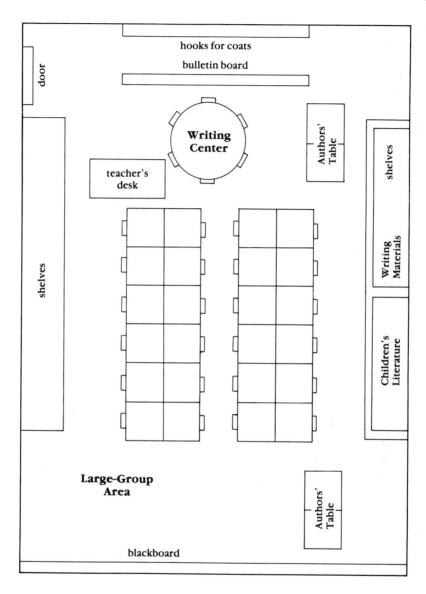

Figure 3.16 *Mrs. E's Classroom*

and read retellings of stories Mrs. E. has read to them. Sometimes Mrs. E prepares her own accounts of the previous day's experience for the children to read with her. She also frequently writes short stories or poems using the content of the children's study unit and a pattern from a pattern book she had earlier shared with the children. One day she wrote:

Caterpillar, caterpillar what do you see?
I see a beetle looking at me.

using the pattern from *Brown Bear, Brown Bear* (Martin, 1983) as a part of the insect unit.

Next, children are encouraged to write. Mrs. E usually holds a five to ten minute lesson or discussion designed to motivate the children to write. During the insect unit children were encouraged to write poems, stories, and pattern stories about insects. One of the lessons Mrs. E taught was to show the children a poster she had made about the letters *b* and *c*. On the poster were several pictures of objects with names beginning with these letters (*boat, bat, beaver, cat, candy, cookie*). Mrs. E reminded the children that as they listened to words they wanted to write, they might hear some sounds like those in the words *boat,* or *cat.* They could use the letters *b* and *c.*

After the lesson, the children write at their desks. Mrs. E circulates around the room asking questions, making comments, and answering children's questions. As the children finish their writing, they read their writing to each other, select books from the library center, or read child-authored poems, stories, and books that are kept on the authors' tables.

Last, Mrs. E holds author's chair. (A special chair is placed in the group area on the rug for a child to sit in as he or she reads his or her writing.) Many children have opportunities to read their writing. The children know that they may choose to "talk about their writing" or "read what they wrote." They feel very comfortable as the other children make comments and offer praise. Mrs. E always comments on some aspect of the content of the writing, "I didn't know there were ants called carpenters. We will need to read more about them. Will you help me find out about them?"

Going Beyond the Text

Visit a preschool or elementary school classroom and observe literacy instruction and activities. Look carefully at the literacy materials that are available in the room. Note how often children interact with these literacy materials. Observe the children and their teacher as they interact during literacy instruction and as the children work on literacy projects. Use the seven characteristics of literacy-rich classrooms as a guide for discussing your observations. Finally, use the recommendations on developmentally appropriate literacy instruction to evaluate what you observed.

References

ADAMS, C. S., & HIEBERT, E. H. (1983, April). *Fathers' and mothers' perceptions of their preschool children's print awareness.* Paper presented at American Educational Research Association, Montreal.

ABRAHAMSON, R. F. (1981). An update on wordless picture books with an annotated bibliography. *The Reading Teacher, 34,* 417–421.

ABRAHAMSON, R. F., & STEWART, R. (1982). Movable books—a new Golden age. *Language Arts, 59,* 342–347.

ALLINGTON, R. (1984). Content coverage and contextual reading in reading groups. *Journal of Reading Behavior, 16,* 85–96.

ANDERSON, L. M., EVERTSON, C. M., & BROPHY, J. E. (1979). An experimental study of effective teaching in first-grade reading groups. *The Elementary School Journal, 79,* 193–223.

ANDERSON, R. C., HIEBERT, E. H., SCOTT, J. A.,

& WILKINSON, I. A. G. (1985). *Becoming a nation of readers: The report of the commission on reading.* Washington, D.C.: The National Institute of Education.

ANDERSON, R. C., OSBORN, J., & TIERNEY, R. J. (Eds.). (1984). *Learning to read in American schools: Basal readers and content texts.* Hillsdale, NY: Erlbaum.

ANNO, M. (1975). *Anno's counting book.* New York: Harper & Row.

BAGHBAN, M. (1984). *Our daughter learns to read and write.* Newark, DE: International Reading Association.

BAYLEY, N. (1977). *One old Oxford ox.* New York: Atheneum.

BERGLUND, R. L., & JOHNS, J. L. (1983). A primer on uninterrupted sustained silent reading. *The Reading Teacher, 36,* 534–539.

BOND, G. L., & DYKSTRA, R. (1967). The cooperative research program in first-grade reading instruction [Entire issue]. *Reading Research Quarterly, 2.*

BREDEKAMP, S. (Ed.). (1987). *Developmentally appropriate practice* (Extended Ed.). Washington, D.C.: National Association for the Education of Young Children.

BRIDGE, C. (1986). Predictable books for beginning readers and writers. In M. R. Sampson (Ed.). *The pursuit of literacy: Early reading and writing* (pp. 81–96). Dubuque, IA: Kendall/Hunt.

BRIDGE, C. A., & HIEBERT, E. H. (1985). A comparison of classroom writing practices, teachers' perceptions of their writing instruction, and textbook recommendations on writing practices. *The Elementary School Journal, 86,* 155–172.

BROMLEY, K. D. (1985). SSW: Sustained spontaneous writing. *Childhood Education, 62,* 23–29.

BROPHY, J. E. (1983). Classroom organization and management. *The Elementary School Journal, 83,* 265–285.

BRUNER, J. (1986). *Actual minds, possible worlds.* Cambridge, MA: Harvard University Press.

CALKINS, L. M. (1986). *The art of teaching writing.* Portsmouth, NH: Heinemann.

CARLE, E. (1969). *The very hungry caterpillar.* New York: Philomel.

CAZDEN, C. (1988). *Classroom discourse.* Portsmouth, NH: Heinemann.

CLIATT, M. & SHAW, J. (1988). The storytime exchange: Ways to enhance it. *Childhood Education, 64,* 293–298.

COCHRAN-SMITH, M. (1984). *The making of a reader.* Norwood, NJ: Ablex Publishing Corporation.

COX, C., & MANY, J. (1989). Worlds of possibilities in a child's response to literature, film, and life. *Language Arts, 66,* 287–294.

CULLINAN, B. E. (Ed.). (1987). *Children's literature in the reading program.* Neward, DE: International Reading Association.

DEFORD, D. E. (1986). Classroom contexts for literacy learning. In T. E. Raphael & R. E. Reynolds (Eds.), *The contexts of school-based learning* (pp. 163–190). New York: Random House.

dePAOLA, T. (1978). *Pancakes for breakfast.* New York: Harcourt Brace Jovanovich.

DILLON, D., & SEARLES, D. (1981). The role of language in one first grade classroom. *Research in the Teaching of English, 15,* 311–328.

DUFFY, G. G. (1981). Teacher effectiveness research: Implications for the reading professional. In M. L. Kamil (Ed.), *Directions in reading, research, and instruction* (pp. 113–139). Washington, D.C.: National Reading Conference.

DUFFY, G. G., & ROEHLER, L. R. (1987). Improving reading instruction through the use of responsive elaboration. *The Reading Teacher, 40,* 514–520.

DUFFY, G. G., ROEHLER, L. R., & RACKLIFFE, G. (1986). How teachers' instructional talk influences students' understanding of lesson content. *The Elementary School Journal, 87,* 3–16.

DUNN, N. E. (1981). Children's achievement at school-entry as a function of mothers' and fathers' teaching sets. *Elementary School Journal, 81,* 245–253.

DURKIN, D. (1966). *Children who read early.* New York: Teachers College Press.

EDELSKY, C., DRAPER, K., & SMITH, K. (1983). Hooking 'em in at the start of school in a "Whole Language" classroom. *Anthropology and Educational Quarterly, 14,* 24–32.

EDELSKY, C., & SMITH, K. (1984). Is that writing—or are those marks just a figment of your curriculum? *Language Arts, 61,* 24–32.

EDUCATIONAL PRODUCTS INFORMATION EXCHANGE. (1977). *Report on a national study of the quality of instructional materials most used by teachers and learners* (Technical Report No 76). New York: EPIE Institute.

ELLIOTT, S., NOWOSAD, J., & SAMUELS, P. (1981). "Me at School," "Me at Home": Using journals with preschoolers. *Language Arts, 58,* 688–691.

EVANS, M. A., & CARR, T. H. (1985). Cognitive abilities, conditions of learning, and the early development of reading skill. *Reading Research Quarterly, 20,* 327–350.

FEIN, G., & RIVKIN, M. (Eds.). (1986). *The young child at play.* Washington, D.C.: National Association for the Education of Young Children.

FEITELSON, D., & GOLDSTEIN, Z. (1986). Patterns of book ownership and reading to children in Israeli school-oriented and nonschool-oriented families. *The Reading Teacher, 39,* 924–930.

FISH, S. (1980). *Is there a text in this class?* Cambridge, MA: Harvard University Press.

FISHER, C. W., BERLINER, D., FILBY, N., MARLIARE, R., COHEN, L., DISHAW, M., & MOORE, J. (1978). *Teaching and learning in elementary schools: A summary of the beginning teacher evaluation study.* San Francisco, CA: Far West Regional Laboratory for Educational Research and Development.

FLORIO, S., & CLARK, C. (1982). The functions of writing in an elementary classroom. *Research in the Teaching of English, 16,* 115–129.

GALDA, L. (1982). Playing about a story: Its impact on comprehension. *The Reading Teacher, 35,* 52–55.

GALDONE, P. (1972). *The three bears.* New York: Scholastic Books.

GALDONE, P. (1975). *The gingerbread boy.* New York: Clarion Books.

GAMBERG, R., KWAK, W., HUTCHINGS, M., & ALTHEIM, J. (1988). *Learning and loving it.* Portsmouth, NH: Heinemann.

GAMBRELL, L. B. (1984). How much time do children spend reading during teacher-directed reading instruction? In J. A. Niles, & L. A. Harris (Eds.), *Changing perspectives on research in reading language processing and instruction* (pp. 193–198). Rochester, NY: The National Reading Conference.

GAMBRELL, L. B. (1985). Dialogue journals:

Reading-writing interaction. *The Reading Teacher, 38,* 512–515.

GENISHI, C., McCARRIER, A., & NUSSBAUM, N. R. (1988). Research currents: Dialogue as a context for teaching and learning. *Language Arts, 65,* 182–191.

GLAZER, J. I. (1981). *Literature for young children.* Columbus, OH: Charles E. Merrill.

GOODMAN, K. S. (1986). Basal readers: A call to action. *Language Arts, 63,* 358–368.

GRAVES, D. H. (1983). Teacher intervention in children's writing: A response to Myra Barrs. *Language Arts, 10,* 841–846.

GUNDLACH, R., McLANE, J. B., SCOTT, F. M., & McNAMEE, G. D. (1985). The social foundations of children's early writing development. In M. Farr (Ed.), *Advances in writing research: Vol. 1. Children's early writing development* (pp. 1–58). Norwood, NJ: Ablex.

HEATH, S. B. (1983). *Ways with words: Language, life, and work in communities and classrooms.* New York: Cambridge University Press.

HEINIG, R. B., & STILLWELL, L. (1981). *Creative drama for the classroom teacher* (2nd ed.). Englewood Cliffs, NJ: Prentice-Hall.

HELLER, L. (1979). *Lilly at the table.* New York: Macmillan.

HESS, R. D., HOLLOWAY, S., PRICE, G. G., & DICKSON, W. (1979). Family environments and the acquisition of reading skills. In L. Laosa & I. Siegel (Eds.), *Families as learning environments for children* (pp. 87–113). New York: Plenum Press.

HICKMAN, J. (1981). A new perspective on response to literature: Research in an elementary school setting. *Research in the Teaching of English, 15,* 343–354.

HIEBERT, E. H. (1983). An examination of ability grouping for reading instruction. *Reading Research Quarterly, 18,* 231–255.

HILL, E. (1980). *Where's Spot?* New York: Putnam's Sons.

HIPPLE, M. L. (1985). Journal writing in kindergarten. *Language Arts, 62,* 255–261.

HOFFMAN, S. (1987). The language of teaching: Responses to children's developing literacy. *Childhood Education, 63,* 356–361.

HOFFMAN, S., & McCULLY, B. (1984). Oral language functions in transaction with children's writing. *Language Arts, 61,* 41–50.

HONG, L. K. (1981). Modifying SSR for beginning readers. *The Reading Teacher, 34,* 888–891.

HOWARD, K. (1971). *Little bunny follows his nose.* Racine, WI: Western Publishing Company.

HUCK, C. S., HEPLER, S., & HICKMAN, J. (1987). *Children's literature in the elementary school* (4th Ed.). New York: Holt, Rinehart & Winston.

INTERNATIONAL READING ASSOCIATION. (1986). Literacy development and pre-first grade: A joint statement of concerns about present practices in pre-first grade reading instruction and recommendation for improvement. (ACEI, ASCD, IRA, NAEYC, NAESP, NCTE) (1986). Newark, DE: Author.

ISENBERG, J., & QUISENBERRY, L. (1988). Play: A necessity for all children. *Childhood Education, 64,* 138–145.

ISER, W. (1974). *The implied reader.* Baltimore: Johns Hopkins University Press.

KAISEN, J. (1987). SSR Booktime: Kindergarten and 1st grade sustained silent reading. *The Reading Teacher, 40,* 532–536.

KAMII, C., & RANDAZZO, M. (1985). Social interaction and invented spelling. *Language Arts, 62,* 124–133.

KINTISCH, L. S. (1986). Journal writing: Stages of development. *The Reading Teacher, 40,* 168–172.

KITCHEN, B. (1984). *Animal alphabet.* New York: Dial.

LAMME, L. L., & CHILDERS, N. M. (1983). The composing processes of three young children. *Research in the Teaching of English, 17,* 33–50.

LEHR, S. (1988). The child's developing sense of theme as a response to literature. *Reading Research Quarterly, 23,* 337–357.

LINFORS, J. W. (1988). From ''talking together'' to ''being together in talk''. *Language Arts, 65,* 135–141.

LOBEL, A. (1981). *On Market Street.* New York: Greenwillow.

LONG, R., & BULGARELLA, L. (1985). Social interaction and the writing process. *Language Arts, 62,* 166–172.

MARTIN, B. (1983). *Brown bear, brown bear.* New York: Holt.

MASON, J. M. & McCORMICK, C. (1981). *An investigation of prereading instruction: A developmental perspective* (Technical Report No. 224). Urbana, IL: University of Illinois, Center for the Study of Reading.

MAYER, M. (1968). *There's a nightmare in my closet.* New York: Dial Press.

McGEE, L. M., & CHARLESWORTH, R. (1984). Movable books: More than novelties. *The Reading Teacher, 37,* 853–859.

MEHAN, H. (1979). *Learning lessons.* Cambridge, MA: Harvard University Press.

MIKKELSEN, N. (1985). Sendak, *Snow White,* and the child as literary critic. *Language Arts, 62,* 363–373.

MILZ, V. (1985). First graders' uses for writing. In A. Jaggar & M. T. Smith-Burke (Eds.), *Observing the language learner* (pp. 173–189). Newark, DE: International Reading Association.

MORROW, L. M. (1982). Relationships between literature programs, library corner designs, and children's use of literature. *Journal of Educational Research, 75,* 339–344.

MORROW, L. M. (1983). Home and school correlates of early interest in literature. *Journal of Educational Research, 76,* 221–230.

MORROW, L. M. (1985). Reading and retelling stories: Strategies for emergent readers. *The Reading Teacher, 38,* 870–875.

MORROW, L. M. & WEINSTEIN, C. S. (1982). Increasing children's use of literature through program and physical design changes. *The Elementary School Journal, 83,* 131–137.

MORROW, L. M., & WEINSTEIN, C. S. (1986). Encouraging voluntary reading: The impact of a literature program on children's use of library centers. *Reading Research Quarterly, 21,* 330–346.

MOSS, J. F. (1984). *Focus units in literature.* Urbana, IL: National Council of Teachers of English.

MOYER, J., EGERTSON, H., & ISENBERG, J. (1987). The child centered kindergarten. *Childhood Education, 63,* 235–245.

NINIO, A. (1980). Picture book reading in mother infant dyads belonging to two subgroups in Israel. *Child Development, 51,* 587–590.

ORMEROD, J. (1981). *Sunshine.* New York: Lothrop.

OSBORN, J. (1981). *The purposes, uses, and contents of workbooks and some guidelines for teachers and publishers* (Reading Education Report No. 27). Urbana, IL: University of Illinois, Center for the Study of Reading.

PARISH, P. (1963). *Amelia Bedelia.* New York: Harper & Row.

PEINKOWSKI, J. (1980). *Dinnertime.* New York: Price/Stern/Sloan.

PELLIGRINI, A. D. (1986). Communicating in and about play: The effect of play centers on preschoolers' explicit language. In G. Fein & M. Rivkin (Eds.), *The young child at play* (pp. 79–91). Washington, D.C.: National Association for the Education of Young Children.

PIAZZA, C. L., & TOMLINSON, C. M. (1985). A concert of writers. *Language Arts, 62,* 150–158.

RADENCICH, M., & BOHNING, G. (1988). Pop-up, pull down, push in, slide out. *Childhood Education, 64,* 157–160.

RASINSKI, T. V., & NATHESON-MAJIA, S. (1987). Learning to read, learning community: Considerations of the social contexts for reading instruction. *The Reading Teacher, 40,* 282–287.

REY, H. A. (1982). *Curious George rides a bike.* Boston: Houghton Mifflin.

RHODES, L. K. (1981). I can read! Predictable books as resources for reading and writing. *The Reading Teacher, 34,* 511–518.

ROSS, R. R. (1980). *Storyteller* (2nd ed.). Columbus, OH: Merrill.

SCHICKEDANZ, J. A., & SULLIVAN, M. (1984). Mom, what does U-F-F spell? *Language Arts, 61,* 7–17.

SEARFOSS, L. W., & READENCE, J. E. (1985). *Helping children learn to read.* Englewood Cliffs, NJ: Prentice-Hall.

SENDAK, M. (1962). *Chicken soup with rice.* New York: Harper & Row.

SENDAK, M. (1963). *Where the wild things are.* New York: Harper & Row.

SEUSS, DR. (THEODORE GEISEL) (1963). *Hop on pop.* New York: Random House.

SHANNON, P. (1983). The use of commercial reading materials in American schools. *Reading Research Quarterly, 19,* 68–85.

SMITH, N. B. (1965). *American reading instruction.* Newark, DE: International Reading Association.

SNOW, C. E. (1983). Literacy and language: Relationships during the preschool years. *Harvard Educational Review, 53,* 165–189.

STEINBERG, N. R. (1985). Turn-taking behavior in a kindergarten classroom. *Language Arts, 62,* 159–165.

STERN, P., & SHAVELSON, R. J. (1983). Reading teachers' judgments, plans, and decision making. *The Reading Teacher, 37,* 280–286.

STEWIG, J. W. (1983). *Informal drama in the elementary language arts program.* New York: Teachers College Press.

STRICKLAND, D. S., DILLON, R. M., FUNKHOUSE, L., GLICK, L., & ROGERS, C. (1989). Research currents: Classroom dialogue in literature response groups. *Language Arts, 66,* 192–205.

TAYLOR, D. (1983). *Family literacy.* Exeter, NH: Heinemann.

TAYLOR, N. E., BLUM, I. H., & LOGSDON, D. M. (1986). The development of written language awareness: Environmental aspects and program characteristics. *Reading Research Quarterly, 21,* 132–149.

TEALE, W. (1978). Positive environments for learning to read: What studies of early readers tell us. *Language Arts, 55,* 922–932.

TEMPLETON, S. (1986). Literacy, readiness, and basals. *The Reading Teacher,* Vol. 39, 403–409.

THARP, R. (1982). The effective instruction of comprehension: Results and description of Kamehameha Early Education Program. *Reading Research Quarterly, 17,* 503–527.

TOMPKINS, G. E., & McGEE, L. M. (1989). Teaching repetition as a story structure. In D. M. Glynn (Ed.), *Children's comprehension of text.* (59–78). Newark, DE: International Reading Association.

TURKLE, B. (1976). *Deep in the forest.* New York: E. P. Dutton.

WAGNER, B. J. (1988). Research currents: Does classroom drama affect the arts of language? *Language Arts, 65,* 46–55.

WELLS, G. (1986). *The meaning makers.* Portsmouth, NH: Heinemann.

YADEN, D. B., JR., & McGEE, L. M. (1984). Reading as a meaning seeking activity: What children's questions reveal. In J. Niles (Ed.), *Thirty-third yearbook of the National Reading Conference* (pp. 101–109). Rochester, NY: National Reading Conference.

Appendix A Literacy Development and Pre-First Grade: A Joint Statement of Concerns About Present Practices in Pre-First Grade Reading Instruction and Recommendations for Improvement

Association for Childhood Education International

Association for Supervision and Curriculum Development

International Reading Association

National Association for the Education of Young Children

National Association of Elementary School Principals

National Council of Teachers of English

OBJECTIVES FOR A PRE-FIRST GRADE READING PROGRAM

Literacy learning begins in infancy. Reading and writing experiences at school should permit children to build upon their already existing knowledge of oral and written language. Learning should take place in a supportive environment where children can build a positive attitude toward themselves and toward language and literacy. For optimal learning teachers should involve children actively in many meaningful, functional language experiences, including *speaking, listening, writing,* and *reading.* Teachers of young children should be prepared in ways that acknowledge differences in language and cultural backgrounds and emphasize reading as an integral part of the language arts as well as of the total curriculum.

WHAT YOUNG CHILDREN KNOW ABOUT ORAL AND WRITTEN LANGUAGE BEFORE THEY COME TO SCHOOL

1. Children have had many experiences from which they are building their ideas about the functions and uses of oral language and written language.

2. Children have a command of language, have internalized many of its rules, and have conceptualized processes for learning and using language.

3. Many children can differentiate between drawing and writing.

*Prepared by the Early Childhood and Literacy Development Committee of the International Reading Association

Reprinted with permission from the International Reading Association.

4. Many children are reading environmental print, such as road signs, grocery labels, and fast food signs.

5. Many children associate books with reading.

6. Children's knowledge about language and communication systems is influenced by their social and cultural backgrounds.

7. Many children expect that reading and writing will be sense-making activities.

Concerns

1. Many pre-first grade children are subjected to rigid, formal pre-reading programs with inappropriate expectations and experiences for their levels of development.

2. Little attention is given to individual development or individual learning styles.

3. The pressures of accelerated programs do not allow children to be risk-takers as they experiment with language and internalize concepts about how language operates.

4. Too much attention is focused upon isolated skill development or abstract parts of the reading process, rather than upon the integration of oral language, writing and listening with reading.

5. Too little attention is placed upon reading for pleasure; therefore, children often do not associate reading with enjoyment.

6. Decisions related to reading programs are often based on political and economic considerations rather than on knowledge of how young children learn.

7. The pressure to achieve high scores on standardized tests that frequently are not appropriate for the kindergarten child has resulted in changes in the content of programs. Program content often does not attend to the child's social, emotional and intellectual development. Consequently, inappropriate activities that deny curiosity, critical thinking and creative expression occur all too frequently. Such activities foster negative attitudes toward communication skill activities.

8. As a result of declining enrollments and reduction in staff, individuals who have little or no knowledge of early childhood education are sometimes assigned to teach young children. Such teachers often select inappropriate methodologies.

9. Teachers of pre-first graders who are conducting individualized programs without depending upon commercial readers and workbooks need to articulate for parents and other members of the public what they are doing and why.

Recommendations

1. Build instruction on what the child already knows about oral language, reading and writing. Focus on meaningful experiences and meaningful language rather than merely on isolated skill development.

2. Respect the language the child brings to school, and use it as a base for language and literacy activities.

3. Ensure feelings of success for all children, helping them see themselves as people who can enjoy exploring oral and written language.

4. Provide reading experiences as an integrated part of the broader communication process, which includes speaking, listening and writing, as well as other communication systems such as art, math and music.

5. Encourage children's first attempts at writing without concern for the proper formation of letters or correct conventional spelling.

6. Encourage risk-taking in first attempts at reading and writing and accept what appear to be errors as part of children's natural patterns of growth and development.

7. Use materials for instruction that are familiar, such as well-known stories, because they provide the child with a sense of control and confidence.

8. Present a model for students to emulate. In the classroom, teachers should use language appropriately, listen and respond to children's talk, and engage in their own reading and writing.

9. Take time regularly to read to children from a wide variety of poetry, fiction and non-fiction.

10. Provide time regularly for children's independent reading and writing.

11. Foster children's affective and cognitive development by providing opportunities to communicate what they know, think and feel.

12. Use evaluative procedures that are developmentally and culturally appropriate for the children being assessed. The selection of evaluative measures should be based on the objectives of the instructional program and should consider each child's total development and its effect on reading performance.

13. Make parents aware of the reasons for a total language program at school and provide them with ideas for activities to carry out at home.

14. Alert parents to the limitations of formal assessments and standardized tests of pre-first graders' reading and writing skills.

15. Encourage children to be active participants in the learning process rather than passive recipients of knowledge, by using activities that allow for experimentation with talking, listening, writing and reading.

Part 2

Exploring the First Steps

Part 2 describes children as they first begin to explore literacy. This is the first of three parts that will examine in detail what children know about literacy and will present ideas for supporting children's learning. Chapter 4, "Infants, Toddlers, and Twos Learning about Literacy," describes what these very young children learn about literacy. Infants, toddlers, and two-year-olds learn much about written language as they share books, draw, and talk about familiar print with their parents or other caring adults. Chapter 5, "Threes, Fours, and Fives Becoming Novice Readers and Writers," describes what preschoolers and kindergartners learn about written language. Novice readers can read print on familiar signs and labels. Novice writers make marks that look like recognizable objects and people. They can also make letter-like symbols and lines of cursive-like writing. Chapter 6, "Classroom Support for Novice Readers and Writers," describes characteristics of classrooms and activities that support the literacy learning of novice readers and writers. It focuses on activities that include reading, writing, talking, drawing, and playing as part of meaningful activities.

Infants, Toddlers, and Twos Learning about Literacy

Chapter 4 describes what infants, toddlers, and two-year-olds learn as they are involved in their first literacy experiences. These children are *literacy beginners*. Literacy begins when parents read aloud to their babies. Infants learn much from these interactions with their parents, with books, and with language. Some parents may not begin reading to their children at such early ages, but children see much print in their homes—on bills, advertisements, telephone books, coupons, newspapers, and even on television. Parents take their children to print-filled places such as grocery stores, drug stores, department stores, and fast-food restaurants. They read print in their homes and in other places. They talk to their children about what they read. These children, too, learn much from their interactions with their parents, with print, and with language.

Toddlers are insatiably curious. They grab and explore and manipulate anything they can. Pencils, pens, markers, and crayons hold as much fascination for children as do keys, cookies, and coins. Toddlers bang and scribble away when given crayons or markers. They learn both from their interactions with paper and marking tools, and from their parents' reactions to these activities. It is these early interactions with people, print, and language that form young children's foundations for reading and writing.

Chapter 4 begins with a description of one young child's literacy experiences as she interacts with her parents and with books, print in her environment, and crayons and markers. We begin with a description of Kristen's literacy experiences with books and other familiar print; next, we describe Kristen's literacy experiences with crayons and markers. Each description is followed by our inferences about what she and other children who have similar experiences learn from these beginning experiences. We then describe an important aspect of Kristen's learning during these beginning years of life—her ability to make and use symbols and to construct meaning from literacy experiences. Following this, we

123

…e in detail how parents interact with their young children in bookreading …ences. Finally, we describe how parents and other adults, especially in …care settings, can support the literacy learning of infants, toddlers, and …year-olds.

ONE CHILD'S BEGINNING LITERACY EXPERIENCES

Kristen is an only child. Her parents like to read, and both write frequently. Kristen and her parents own many books. Their home includes many kinds of paper, crayons, markers, pens, and pencils. By the time Kristen was two and one-half years old, she had many literate behaviors. She included characters and words from stories in her make-believe play with her "babies" and she invited the neighborhood children to draw and write "their abc's" with her.

"Let's Read, Daddy": Experiences with Books and Other Familiar Print

Kristen received her first books when she was just a few months old. Most of her books were sturdy cardboard ones such as *A Goodnight Hug* (Roth, 1986). They were kept in her toy basket along with her rattles. Her mother and father read to her while she sat in their laps. When just a few months old, Kristen began to grab for rattles and soon she could pick them up and hold them. She also began grabbing her books, picking them up, and holding them. Kristen did not look at the pictures in her books; instead, she made insistent attempts to turn the pages. Her mother and father found reading the texts in the books frustrating as Kristen became proficient at turning the pages. Her parents would only have time to make short statements such as "Look at the baby " or "Oh, there's a ball " before she would turn the page.

Some months before her first birthday, Kristen began gazing at the pictures in her books. She learned to recognize books by their names. Her father would say, "Let's read the Humpty Dumpty book." Kristen would crawl to the book basket and select her "Humpty Dumpty book" (*The Real Mother Goose,* Wright, 1916). She would turn to the page that had the Humpty Dumpty rhyme and sway her body as her father recited the rhyme. Kristen participated in bookreading in other ways as well. She received a copy of *Pat the Bunny* (Kunhardt, 1940) and learned to play peek-a-boo and wave "bye-bye" upon turning to the appropriate pages.

At the time of her first birthday, Kristen would often sit alone, spending many moments looking at her favorite books. She would hold a book right-side-up and turn the pages from front to back. Sometimes she smiled and patted the pictures or turned pages over from one side to the next, intently checking the pictures on each side of the page. Kristen also liked to look at the coupon section of the Sunday paper; she would turn the pages quickly, looking for a familiar animal such as a dog or cat. Then she would look up at her father and laugh.

Kristen also enjoyed looking at catalogs and magazines with her mother. She would point to objects and her mother would name them as Kristen turned the pages.

A few months after her first birthday, Kristen began to point to things around her, saying "dat?" with a rising intonation. She would also point to and ask "dat?" about animals and people pictured in her books. Her mother or father would obligingly name the animals and people. Kristen's mother often requested that she locate animals or people in her books. She would ask, "Where's the kitten?" and Kristen would point to it. At this time Kristen could say a few words. She would say "bah" and point to the picture of a ball in her book.

When Kristen was about sixteen months old, she began interrupting book-reading by jumping off her father's lap to seek a toy or object in the house. She did this only when she saw certain pictures in her books. Each time Kristen saw a picture of crayons in one of her books, she would get up and find *her* crayons.

At eighteen months of age, Kristen would sit by herself and look at her books, saying the names of some of the objects in the pictures while pointing at them. Kristen had several ABC books in which she was particularly interested at this time. She noticed the alphabet letters on the endpapers of *Dr. Seuss's ABC Book* (Seuss, 1963a). One day, while she was looking at the letters, her mother sang the ABC song to her and pointed to each letter as she sang. Whenever Kristen read this book, she would turn to the endpapers and repeatedly point at the letters saying "A-A-A" in her singing voice. She pointed to letters in other locations—even on manhole covers. Each time, she would point at the letters repeatedly, look at her mother, and say "A-A-A" in a singing voice.

At two years of age, Kristen was able to capture some of the text meaning in her own words. In *Hop on Pop* (Seuss, 1963b), Kristen said, "No. No. No sit " after her mother read "No, Pat, No. Don't sit on that." As her father read the text of *Goodnight Moon* (Brown, 1947), he would pause for Kristen to fill in part of the rhyme. He would read, "Goodnight cow jumping over the . . ." and Kristen would say, "Moon" (Brown, 1947, unpaged). Also at two years, Kristen began recognizing McDonald's and Burger King signs. She would say, "DeDonald's" or "Bugar King" each time she saw the signs. Kristen also pointed to her favorite cereals and cookies in the grocery store, saying, "Aisin Ban" and "Oeos."

At two and one-half years of age, Kristen participated in book and familiar print reading in many ways. She made comments about characters and actions depicted in her books. Pointing to the picture of the wolf in *Walt Disney's Peter and the Wolf* (Disney Productions, 1974), she said, "He needs to be good." She commented about the predicament of Wully-Wully in *Babar and the Wully-Wully* (de Brunhoff, 1975), saying "He's in the cage" and "He got out" as she pointed to the pictures of Wully-Wully captured and rescued. She asked questions. She asked, "What's that?" as she pointed to one of the characters in the Babar book. She answered questions. Her father asked, "What's she going to do?" referring to the little girl who takes the bear home in *Corduroy* (Freeman, 1968). Kristen replied, "Give him a hug."

What Kristen Learned

From the first few months of her life, Kristen learned many things about books, print, and reading. She enjoyed interacting with her parents as they shared books and other familiar print together. She discovered that books were entertaining, both when she looked at them alone and when she interacted with her parents and books. Kristen learned to locate and name objects in familiar print and in the pictures in her books, and she began to anticipate some of the language her parents used as they shared books with her. She learned to find meaning in her books and in other print. All young children learn these things as they interact with print, books, and other people in literacy events.

Books Are Pleasurable

Perhaps one of the most important aspects children can learn at the beginning of their literacy experiences is that reading is a pleasurable activity. When children are read to beginning early in their lives, they play with books as a preferred and frequent activity (Doake, 1986). Bookreading is one of the closest activities parents and children share. Children nestle in Dad's lap or lean over Mom's arm while they take part in this activity. The special feelings generated from this closeness of parents and children is associated with books. It is no wonder that some children will sit alone and look at books far longer than they will sit with their other toys.

Books Are Handled in Particular Ways

Another literacy-related knowledge that is developed in this beginning period is *bookhandling*. There are many aspects of bookhandling. Kristen learned how to hold books right-side-up and how to turn pages. She also discovered that books are for viewing and reading and not just for turning pages (Snow & Ninio, 1986). In addition, she learned to focus her attention where her mother or father directed it (Lamme & Packer, 1986), and later she learned to name objects that her parents pointed to in pictures.

Sharing Books Involves Certain Routines

The development of *booksharing routines* is another literacy-related knowledge. Kristen learned how to initiate and participate in bookreading sessions. She did not always wait for her bedtime story. Rather, she frequently selected a book and backed into a lap. She clearly signaled she wanted to share a book. Once her mother or father began sharing a book, she helped turn pages, located characters when asked to do so, and solicited comments from her mother or father by pointing to something in the picture or making comments and asking questions. She learned to answer questions. Gradually, she learned to listen to more of the story her mother or father read. Kristen discovered that, just like her mother and father, she also had certain roles to play in the bookreading (Ninio & Bruner, 1978).

Pictures in Books Are Symbols

Another aspect of literacy learning involves discovering that the shapes and colors in pictures represent things. Children learn that pictures are symbols for objects and actions. Kristen showed that she had discovered this when she found her crayons after she saw a picture of crayons in a favorite book. She was discovering that pictures are not only interesting to look at, but they are also representations of real things. Children learn that pictures in books are not things; rather, they represent things (Snow & Ninio, 1986). Kristen learned that she was not patting real objects when she patted the pictures in her books; they were only symbols for real things that she could pat.

Books and Print Communicate Meaning

At this time, children learn another important literacy-related knowledge that is used later on in reading. It is the ability to construct meaning from written language. Learning how to construct meaning is not new to children. They have been busy since birth trying to make sense of their environment. Learning to construct meaning from written language makes use of children's natural inclination to understand the actions and people around them. It begins as children look at pictures in books and other familiar print. Kristen learned to make sense of the pictures in her books, in magazines, in catalogs, and even on her cereal boxes. Learning that pictures are symbols is only one aspect of learning how to construct meaning. Children also learn to make sense of stories that are read aloud to them. Kristen was learning to find meaning in the pictures of her storybooks by relating things in the pictures to things in her experience. She was also beginning to link things she heard in stories with things in her experience. Kristen commented about "the old lady who whispers 'hush'" in *Goodnight Moon,* that she's "just like Mommy." Later in this chapter, we will devote more attention to children's learning to make meaning from books.

"Look at All These Raindrops": Experiences with Crayons and Markers

Kristen received crayons as a Christmas present when she was fifteen months old. Her first attempts at drawing were rapid back-and-forth swipes at paper (see Figure 4.1). She would quickly make a few marks and push the paper on the floor, indicating she wanted another sheet of paper. Kristen would try to write whenever her mother or father were writing. She grabbed pencils and pens from her father's hands as he tried to grade exams or write lectures.

At eighteen months of age, Kristen continued to make back-and-forth lines. At that time, she enjoyed selecting and using different colors of crayons. She would layer color after color on her pictures, saying "Look. Look." When she was twenty-one months old, Kristen began making round-and-round lines and dots. Her mother and father began drawing to entertain her. They drew people, houses, flowers, cats, dogs, and other familiar objects.

When Kristen was two years old, she began making jagged lines and single

Figure 4.1 *Back-and-Forth Lines*

straight lines. She often labeled her pictures "dots." At that time, Kristen often commanded that her parents draw "a little girl," "a little boy" or any other object she could think of. She also asked them to write, "Kristen," "Mommy," "Daddy," and the names of all the people she knew.

At twenty-seven months of age, Kristen made concentrated efforts to control her marks. She would slowly draw a continuous line all around the edges of her paper. It seemed as if she were pushing the crayon around the paper and watching its progress. She began making circular shapes of just a single line or a few lines (see Figure 4.2). One day she drew the picture presented in Figure 4.3. Her mother asked her, "What did you write?" and Kristen replied, "abc's." This was a rare occurrence. At this time, Kristen did not often choose to use her markers or crayons to draw. Rather, she insisted that her mother or father draw

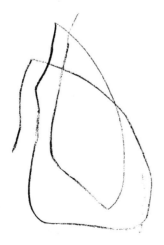

Figure 4.2 *Circular Shapes*   ***Figure 4.3*** *"ABC's"*

or write. She also frequently refused to answer when her mother asked, "What did you draw?"

Once, when Kristen was two and one-half years old, her mother began drawing a face. She stopped after drawing the shape of the head, and she asked Kristen to point to where the eyes, nose, mouth, and hair should go. Kristen pointed to where each feature belonged. Her mother coaxed her to draw some eyes. Kristen tried to put eyes on the face, but became frustrated. She announced, "I can't draw that." One morning, Kristen's mother convinced her to draw by saying, "Just do some lines and dots and circles." Kristen selected a blue marker and make several quick line strokes down her page (see Figure 4.4). After making several of these marks, she cried, "Look at the rain." She made several more marks, saying, "More rain. Look at the rain, Mommy." Then she began making dots, saying, "Look at all these raindrops."

Figure 4.4 *"Rain" and "Raindrops"*

A few days later, Kristen was encouraged to make a picture for her aunt. She made a single line down her page and said, "B" (see Figure 4.5). She made another line and said, "C." She continued making lines and naming letters. As she gave her picture to her aunt, she said, "Look at the ABC's."

What Kristen Learned

Kristen learned many things related to drawing and writing. She enjoyed interacting with her parents and with other adults as she made marks with crayons and markers. She learned that her parents would draw and write at her command, and she learned to label her drawings. All young children learn these things as they interact with crayons, paper, and other people in literacy events.

Figure 4.5 *"ABC's" Again*

Drawing and Writing Are Pleasurable

When children begin scribbling under the watchful eyes of an appreciative audience, they naturally want to scribble again and again. Children learn that one sure way of getting attention is to find their paper and crayons and ask someone to draw or write for them. They use drawing and writing as a way to interact with special others (Baghban, 1984). Sometimes Kristen was willing to draw at her parent's suggestion; at other times, she wanted her parents to draw for her.

Movements Are Controlled

Children learn motor "schemes" for drawing shapes and lines (Gardner, 1980). *Motor schemes* allow children to control their movements so they can make intentional shapes and lines. In order to be able to put circles and dots on a page where they intend them to go, children must learn how to control their movements. Kristen showed that she was learning to control her movements when she intently watched the progress of her crayons as she drew. Just as Kristen did, children's earliest developing motor schemes seem to be how to make back-and-forth marks, round-and-round lines, dots, and jagged lines. Later, they make circle-like shapes and single lines (Gardner, 1980). Eventually, children learn to make as many as twenty basic scribbles, which become the building blocks of art as well as writing (Kellogg, 1969).

Drawing and Writing Involve Certain Routines

For toddlers and two-year-olds, drawing and writing are likely to involve others. Young children draw both to engage their parents' attention and to engage other children in play. Kristen quickly learned many routines that initiated drawing and writing as social interactions. She would say to her friends, "Let's make ABC's," or to her father, "Let's draw. You draw. Draw a little girl." When her father suggested that she draw (because he suspected she needed a new activity), Kristen replied, "No, you draw." Kristen, like other young children with willing parents, engaged in "command-a-picture" or "command-a-word" routines (Lass, 1982). In these routines, children name a word, letter, or object, and parents write or draw it.

Drawing and Writing Can Be Named

Children learn to label their lines and shapes. Howard Gardner (1980) reported that he often drew things for his son. One time he drew a bird and, while drawing, repeatedly talked about birds. Later, his son drew round-and-round lines, which did not resemble a bird in the least, and called his picture "bird." Gardner called this *romancing*. Many children "romance" both drawings and writing. They draw with no seeming intention to create something specific or meaningful, and when they finish, they label their creation as Gardner's son did. Kristen romanced writing the "ABC's" (Figures 4.3 and 4.5). Such drawings are not really *representational* drawings or symbols because they do not objectively resemble the object labeled. However, romancing pictures and drawings—not planning what a written mark will be or even intending it to be meaningful, but rather labeling it or assigning meaning to it after the mark is completed—is a step in the direction of creating symbols in representational drawing. Children are led in this direction when their parents treat even their unintentional drawings as if they were intentionally representational. They ask children to "tell me about your picture." This is an example of how ascribing intentionality moves children onward (see Chapter 2).

Drawings Are Symbols

Sometime between the ages of two and five years old, children begin to plan their drawings, and these drawings begin to resemble recognizable objects. When children's drawings begin to look to an objective viewer like what children label them, they are called *representational drawings*. Their drawings become recognizable symbols. Children learn that they not only can name their drawings, but that their drawings can also become representations of things. Kristen demonstrated the beginning of this knowledge as she drew her "Rain" picture. She drew lines and noticed that they looked like rain. Then she made dots that she called "raindrops." Kristen learned that she could not only make lines and dots, but she could also make "rain" and "raindrops." She used her lines and dots as symbols.

Children's early representational drawings or symbols depict humans. Most children's early representational drawings of people consist of a circle with two vertical lines reaching downward. These drawings are called *tadpoles* (see Figure 4.6).

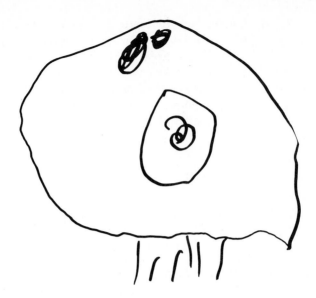

Figure 4.6 *Tadpole*

We have already indicated that one of children's most important learnings, that of constructing meaning from written language, starts when children look at pictures either in books or in other places. In the next section we discuss more about what children learn as they begin to construct meaning from the written language they hear.

MEANING CONSTRUCTION

Learning to "mean" (Halliday, 1975) is involved in nearly every activity, not just literacy activities. It is the great undertaking of life—we constantly try to understand the messages that bombard us and to send messages to others. We use many cues to help us understand others and to help others understand us. We use the situation we are in and its clues to meaning (characteristics of the location or clothing of people), as well as spoken language and its clues to meaning (words, stress, and intonation). Because our society is a literate one, another powerful set of clues to meaning is written language. Written language, too, is used along with situation (getting out a checkbook at the grocery store), with spoken language ("That will be $81.47"), and with written symbols (81.47 printed on the computer display of the cash register).

Children learn to use these cues, including the written language ones, to make meaning. We are not implying that infants are looking at print and trying to read it like an adult does. However, when an adult reads print aloud, tells a story, or talks about pictures in a magazine, infants and toddlers try to make sense of what is going on. They attempt to understand the situation, the talk they hear, and the visual symbols they see.

Many young children learn to construct meaning from books that are read aloud to them. This ability to make sense of stories is more than learning to listen and more than learning to understand words. We will spend considerable time describing children's experiences with constructing meaning from books because research is emerging which suggests that children's experiences with written language in books is particularly important for their literacy learning throughout school (Wells, 1986). We caution that not all young infants, toddlers, and two-year-olds have experiences reading books with their parents or other adults.

Constructing Meaning in Stories

Three bookreading episodes follow which illustrate the development of children's meaning construction during the early years. The first episode describes an interaction between Kristen and her mother which occurred before Kristen was two years old. The second episode describes an interaction between Elizabeth, a two-year-old, and her mother. The final episode describes Elizabeth's retelling of a favorite story. We call these bookreading episodes *booksharing* interactions because the mothers in these episodes are very skillful in encouraging their children to participate in the book episode.

Kristen and Her Mother Share *Billy Goats Gruff*

Figure 4.7 presents a portion of the dialogue between Kristen and her mother as they shared *Billy Goats Gruff* (Hellard, 1986). Kristen was seventeen months old at the time of this interaction. The dialogue demonstrates that Kristen already knew much about meaning construction; she knew how to get to something in books that made sense to her. When her mother began talking about the three goats, Kristen quickly moved to another page—a page on which she found something that was meaningful to her. Kristen also sought information: she repeated "tee" each time, looking at her mother as if for confirmation of her meaning and label. Kristen seemed to monitor her meaning making by observing her mother's reaction.

Kristen's mother hugged and shook Kristen and used her voice to attract Kristen's attention to a central character, the Troll. This technique was effective because when Kristen saw the Troll on another page, she imitated her mother's action, showing that she knew how to use her mother's language and actions as cues to meaning.

It is noteworthy that none of the story text was read in this bookreading episode. Kristen's mother knew that Kristen found her talk, not reading of the text, most meaningful. Although Kristen contributed very little language in the interaction, she was actively participating. She turned pages, used gestures and movements, gazed at her mother, and said words.

Elizabeth and Her Mother Share *Where's Spot?*

A portion of the interaction between Elizabeth (twenty-six months) and her mother as they shared *Where's Spot?* (Hill, 1980) is presented in Figure 4.8. In

Figure 4.7 *Kristen and Her Mother Share* Billy Goats Gruff
(Hellard, 1986)

Brackets indicate portions of the dialogue that occurred simultaneously.

Kristen: (brings *Billy Goats Gruff* to her mother,
         sits on her mother's lap, holds book, and
         turns book with cover facing up)

Mother: Three billy goats gruff. (points to each goat on the cover)
     ⎡ Look, a little one (points to small goat). A middle-size—
     ⎣K: (opens book and turns 2 pages, gazes at picture, and
         points to a picture of a tree) tee
         (looks up at her mother)

M: Yes, it's a tree.

K: (points to another tree) tee
   (looks up at mother again)

M: Hm, um

K: (points to another tree) tee

M: (points to picture of troll, puts her arm around Kristen,
   and shakes them both)
   (changes voice to deeper tone) Look at the Trolllllll.
   I'm going to eat you up.

K: (laughs, turns page)
⎡M: Look. The first Billy Goat—
⎣K: (shakes her head, points at troll)

M: Oh, yes, I see (lowers voice) the Trolllll

K: (laughs, turns page, points to tree) tee

---

this interaction, Elizabeth followed both the story and the story text much more closely than Kristen did. In addition, Elizabeth contributed more language to the reading episode. However, her mother still contributed the majority of talk.

Elizabeth's mother encompassed her reading of the story text with much context for understanding its meaning. She repeatedly reminded Elizabeth that the mother dog was looking for her puppy as a context for understanding why the dog was looking behind doors and under beds. She was skillful in interweaving the story text with her talk (Altwerger, Diehl-Faxon, & Dockstader-Anderson, 1985). The story text seemed to be included as part of a conversation she was having with her daughter about the story. She helped Elizabeth find meaning from the words of the text by using her explanations of the pictures and conversational style as a support for meaning construction.

Elizabeth's mother was also skillful in inviting and encouraging, even demanding, that her child actively participate in the meaning construction. She asked questions and made requests for Elizabeth to tell what she saw in the pic-

Figure 4.8 *Elizabeth and Her Mother Share* Where's Spot?
(Hill, 1980)

Paraphrased text is underlined. Brackets indicate portions of the dialogue that occurred simultaneously.

⌐Mother: We are looking for Spot. Let's turn the page.
│   He's a little tiny puppy. Can you see if you can find him
└   <u>behind the door.</u> Is he there?

  E: (turns to next page)

  M: No?—What's inside the clock? Is he in there?

  E: He's in there.

  M: That's a snake. That's not a little dog.

  E: Let me read it.

  M: Ok

  E: It's a snake

⌐M: Turn the page. Where's Spot? Let's see if we can find the puppy. Is he—
└ E: (turns back to look at snake again)

  M: Let's see what's behind the next page. We need to find Spot.
     Is he in there? (points to piano)

  E: There's a doggy there (points to Mother Dog, Sally)

  M: He's looking for another doggy. Spot's not there.

  E: There? (points to Sally on next page)

  M: Yes. That's a doggy. He's looking for another doggy, a puppy.
     Is there a puppy <u>in the piano?</u>

  E: No.

  M: What's in the piano?

  E: A, a

  M: What is that?

  E: What is that?

⌐M: It's a bird.
└ E: Let's close it up. (closes flap on piano)

  M: Let's see if we can find that puppy <u>under the stairs.</u>
     Is he in there?

  E: Uh uh

  M: No puppy in there.
     He's looking for the puppy <u>in the closet.</u>
     Is he in there?

  E: No puppy in there. He's upstairs.

tures. Elizabeth also asked questions as a means of constructing meaning about the story. She knew that her mother was a valuable source of meaning about stories.

In addition to learning how to use her mother's dialogue, text reading, and the pictures as cues to meaning, Elizabeth learned much about stories and the particular kinds of meanings important in stories. Elizabeth's mother carefully established a reason for looking under beds and in closets—she pointed out that Mother Dog must find her puppy. She helped Elizabeth understand something about character motivations. She highlighted that certain aspects of stories are important. She helped her daughter to learn characteristics of stories, that is, to develop a concept of story. We will discuss story concepts more later in this chapter.

Elizabeth Retells *Where's Spot?*

In the next interaction, Elizabeth attempted to retell *Where's Spot?* to her mother. Her mother asked some questions and made some comments. A portion of this interaction is presented in Figure 4.9.

Elizabeth used very little language in retelling the story. If the pictures were not there and if the story text were not available, we would not be able to under-

Figure 4.9 *Elizabeth Retells* Where's Spot? *(Hill, 1980)*

Elizabeth: (opens book to page with door) Hind the door? He's hind the door.	Illustration: Mother dog peeking behind a door (bear inside door)
Mother: What's behind the door?	
E: A bear. He's peeking out there. Hind the door.	
M: No puppy there.	
E: (skips several pages) There? (lifts flap)	Illustration: Mother dog peeking in a closet (monkey inside closet)
M: Here's Sally. No Spot in there.	
E: No No Spot in there There's the monkey, Mom. See the monkey.	
M: Yes	
E: He's peeking out. (turns back to page with stairs and lifts flap) No Spot in there.	Illustration: Mother dog peeking under the stairs (lion under stairs)

stand Elizabeth's story. Elizabeth, like Kristen, used details in the pictures to cue her meaning. On the first page, Elizabeth repeated some of the text, but on the succeeding pages she relied on her actions of opening each flap (*Where's Spot?* is a lift-up-the-flap book) to represent the story text. Still, with the help of the pictures and prompts from her mother, Elizabeth was able to retell the story so that it included some characters, objects, and actions in the story sequence. In particular, her retelling of the last two pages by saying "No Spot in there" captured much of the meaning of the story.

Meaning-Making Strategies

The preceding bookreading episodes illustrate that children learn many strategies for making sense of stories they share with their parents or other readers. One meaning-making strategy children learn is that things in pictures have names and are labeled (Snow & Ninio, 1986). Things and actions in pictures can be talked about by naming them. Later, they can be talked about by describing them and comparing them to other experiences or people.

A second meaning-making strategy children learn is to draw on their own experiences as a basis for making meaning. Children make sense of actions depicted in stories because they know that while pictures do not move, they can depict familiar actions (Snow & Ninio, 1986). Children connect actions in pictures to their own experiences. They draw on their "scripts" of daily activities—their knowledge of what goes on, for example, at bedtime (McCartney & Nelson, 1981)—to link pictures of these activities with meaning.

A third meaning-making strategy children acquire is to draw on information provided in their mothers' or other adults' talk about pictures and text. They learn to listen to what their mothers say about the story as a way of constructing meaning. This is the first step toward learning that the words they hear in the story text provide the meaning cues they will later use exclusively as they move away from reading picture books.

A fourth meaning-making strategy children learn is to ask questions. Children actively seek more information. Sometimes they seek information as a way of monitoring their understanding of the pictures and story. At other times, they are curious about new activities or persons and about why characters act as they do.

A fifth meaning-making strategy children use is to pay attention to particular components of stories which they have learned must be considered in order to construct a story's meaning. Children learn to use what they know about stories (their concept of stories) to understand stories. In the next section we describe children's developing concepts of stories.

Concept of Story

Many young children's early experiences with written language are with stories—the stories their parents read to them. Children also become familiar with stories by watching television or by listening to their older brothers or sisters tell narratives about their days' activities. Through these experiences children begin to build a concept or schema of what a story is. A story concept or schema is a mental conception of what is in a story and how it might proceed.

Story Schema

Before we describe a child's story schema and how it changes, we need to describe an adult's story schema. We know that adults know a great deal about stories. In its simplest form, a story contains at the onset a state of equilibrium followed by a disruption of that equilibrium. Then, a character recognizes the disruption, and an action aimed at repairing the disruption ensues. The story ends with a reinstatement of the initial equilibrium (Leondar, 1977, p. 176).

Cognitive psychologists used the notion that all stories have a basic structure to create *story grammars* (Mandler & Johnson, 1977; Thorndyke, 1977). Story grammars are sets of rules which are intended to represent the kinds of content people think are included in stories and how that content is organized. Figure 4.10 presents a story grammar and a sample story (McGee & Tompkins, 1981, based on Stein & Glenn, 1978).

Children's Concept of Story

Of course, young children have not yet acquired the same concept or schema of a story as adults. However, their concept of story is very important in learning to construct meaning from stories. Children give hints about what their concept of story might be like in the kinds of stories they tell (Botvin & Sutton-Smith, 1977). Applebee (1978) examined many stories told by children to find out what their concept of story might be like. He found children's stories to be very different from what adults might expect. He also found that children's concept of story changes. Applebee discovered at least six increasingly complex concepts of stories. The most complex concept is very similar to the story schema presented in Figure 4.10. Children gradually acquire a concept of story or story schema like an adult's schema of story. They come to know that stories have characters and settings, that some action triggers the character to form a goal, that the character performs actions to try to achieve the goal, and that the story ends with the character's obtaining (or not obtaining) the goal.

We will use Applebee's work (1978, pp. 55–66) to describe six increasingly complex story concepts. We believe they are useful as a starting point for observing what children know about stories. However, we caution that children's behaviors with stories rarely fit neatly into any one category. Their behaviors with stories frequently fall into one category in one context, such as in booksharing with a parent, and fall into another category in another context, such as in their retelling a story.

Figure 4.11 presents six increasingly complex categories of story concepts from least complex to most complex. We use our own names for the categories. Toddlers and two-year-olds who are literacy beginners are likely to have concepts of stories that resemble the least complex of these categories. Later in this

Figure 4.10 Story Grammar

Story Components	Story Example *The Old Woman and Her Curious Cat* (by Lea M. McGee)
Main characters (animals or people)	There once was an old woman and a very curious cat
Setting (description of location)	who lived together on a tiny farm.
Action or event (introduction of problem)	One day the cat overheard his friends the blackbirds talking on the roof of the barn. He got so curious about what they were saying that he climbed to the very top of the roof. Once he got up there he realized that getting back down was not going to be easy.
Goal (formulation a goal)	The cat decided to ask the blackbirds to fly down and tell the old woman of his predicament.
Attempt (actions that solve problem)	The blackbirds agreed to help if he promised to have the old woman set out bread crumbs for them during the winter. The cat promised, so the black-birds flew down on the shoulder of the old woman and told her where her cat was.
Resolution (outcome of actions)	The old woman quickly got a ladder and climbed up to rescue her cat. The cat kept his promise and had the old woman set out bread crumbs for the blackbirds that winter.
Reaction (character's feelings about goal attainment)	And as for the cat, he never climbed to the barn roof again.

Adapted from McGee, L. M., & Tompkins, G. E. (1981). The videotape answer to independent reading comprehension activities. *The Reading Teacher, 34,* p. 428. Reprinted with permission of the International Reading Association.

book, we describe children producing stories in ways that show they have an understanding of the more complex categories of story knowledge shown in Figure 4.11.

Importance of Concept of Story

Children's concept of story, in part, influences how they understand stories, retell favorite stories, tell original stories, and ask questions about stories. For example, when toddlers or two-year-olds retell stories (as Elizabeth did in Figure 4.9), they may only label objects in pictures (Sulzby, 1985). The objects

Figure 4.11 *Increasingly Complex Concepts about Stories*

Collections

A collection of ideas arranged and selected on an arbitrary basis. (Often the ideas are related to items within the child's view at the time of telling.)
Applebee called these stories *heaps*.

Example Stories:

This boy named David. This girl name Lisa. And Casey and Wynell and William. And this boy named Travis.

Tina and a boy and a dog. The grandmother was dancing. They made music. Bunny seen a grandmother and her gave her a flower.

Patterns

Actions or characters repeated to form a pattern. Applebee called these stories *sequences*.

Example Stories:

There once was a little boy. He went to the store and bought potato chips. He went to the store and bought some milk. He went to the store and bought some junk food. He went to the store and bought apple juice.

The girl going home. The boy going to sleep. The sister eating. The mama taking a bath. The daddy reading a book.

Scripts

Ideas that occur in predictable everyday events. (Actions are usually grouped into short sequences as they habitually occur in children's lives.)
Applebee called these stories *primitive narratives*.

Example Stories:

An elephant climbed up and he fell and bumped his head. The gorilla kissed his head.

Once upon a time there was a little girl. Her mama spanked her and then she cried. Then she went to her room.

Chains

Characters who act seemingly at random within a common "story world."
Applebee called these stories *unfocused chains*.

Example Stories:

One day the girl went out to the town for to go and get her mama. And the ghost was not in the house. But the man wasn't afraid of the ghost. The girl was scared and the daddy had to get the ghost.

Once there was a little fish and he couldn't swim. A big shark came and then another little fish came. The little fish swallowed the bigger fish. The shark swam and swam.

Figure 4.11 (continued)

Sequences or Descriptions

Ideas centered on one character. [The ideas in the story either describe the character or relate events that happen to the character. These stories often tell ''All About'' a character or chronicle the events of a character from ''Bed to Bed'' (Calkins, 1986).]
Applebee called these stories *focused chains.*

Example Stories:

A lady went in the castle. Then she walked around. Then she took some jewelry. She put it on and went home. She wore it to bed.

There was teacher. She had shoes and pants. She had a skirt and she was nice. She let us play.

Narratives

Ideas centered on one character who overcomes some trouble. (These stories have a main character, an event suggesting a problem, actions toward overcoming the problem, and a resolution.)
Applebee called these stories *narratives.*

Example Stories:

There was a little boy and he saw a balloon and climbed up the light to get it. Then he was walking fast because he knew the other boys were going to pop it. So he went home.

Once there was a little boy. He lives in a tent. Then the little boy went up a beanstalk. There was a big giant. He ate the little boy. Then the boy went down the beanstalk and got home. The giant fell down and was dead.

---

they select to label may have little or nothing to do with the story. Kristen (in Figure 4.7) did this when she labeled the trees in the story *Billy Goat's Gruff.* Retelling a story in this way would be expected if a child's concept of story were like the simplest of the concepts of stories described in Figure 4.11, collections. This concept of stories is also reflected in the kinds of questions children ask about stories. Toddlers' and two-year-olds' first questions about stories are usually requests for names of objects in pictures (Yaden & McGee, 1984).

Constructing Meaning
in Environmental Print

Environmental print items play an important part in the beginning literacy experiences of toddlers and two-year-olds. Many children have more experience with environmental print items—toy packages, street signs, and food labels—than they have with books. Yetta Goodman (1980) argued that children learn to recognize meaning in environmental print by being immersed in daily activities involving items which include print. As children eat breakfast they see a box of

Rice Krispies, and they hear talk about eating the Rice Krispies. They observe and listen in the grocery store as their mothers look for Rice Krispies. As children acquire language, they learn to talk about "Rice Krispies" just as they learn to talk about "ball" or "baby" or "car." Just as children learn that things in pictures have names and can be labeled, they learn that things like cereal boxes and cookie packages can be named as well.

Many toddlers and two-year-olds do not notice or pay much attention to the print on their cereal boxes or cookie packages; nonetheless, the print is there. The print on the packages becomes part of what children know about those objects. Later children will recognize just the print and stylized picture or logo without the object being there.

In the next section we discuss how young children learn about literacy. Chapter 2 listed several strategies that describe young children's literacy learning in a general way. Examples in this chapter describe more specifically what parents or other adults naturally seem to do to help infants, toddlers, and two-year-olds learn.

SUPPORTING THE LITERACY LEARNING OF INFANTS, TODDLERS, AND TWO-YEAR-OLDS

Parents and other adults play many important roles in children's literacy learning. They supply the materials; they clearly signal that these activities are important by engaging their children in them; they provide reinforcement for attempts, however approximate they may be; they say, "Yes, that's the bunny" when their children point to a bunny and say, "Buh" and they clap at every mark written by their children. However, parents and other adults provide more than moral support and materials.

Researchers have listened carefully to parents and their children as they read together (Altwerger et al., 1985; Snow, 1983). They have also observed parents and their children as they draw and write (Baghban, 1984; Gardner, 1980). They found that many parents were naturally and intuitively skillful in helping their children acquire literacy knowledge.

Parents' Support for Drawing

How did Kristen learn to make her first written symbol—her "rain?" No one knows for sure, but we have some good guesses. Kristen's parents played an important role in her transition into a symbol maker by providing her with crayons, markers, pencils, and paper. Kristen knew where these materials were, and she was encouraged to seek them when she wanted to draw. Her parents often modeled reading and writing. They wrote as part of their daily activities, and they drew pictures at Kristen's request. They provided examples of what adults produce when they write and draw.

Parents do something more subtle which helps their children become symbol makers. Recall from Chapter 2 that one of the most important things parents do is to act as if their children are doing something before their children can actually do it. Kristen's parents often did this when Kristen made lines, dots, and circles. They acted as if her lines were really a representational drawing. While Kristen was drawing, she often sat with her father and mother. They would say to her, "What are you *drawing?*" It is clear that Kristen's parents expected that she would make drawings and name them.

Parents' Support for Story Meaning Making

Kristen's and Elizabeth's mothers played crucial roles in their learning to understand stories. First, they provided materials—they made sure their children had plenty of books that were appropriate for young children. They also established daily routine times for reading, usually at bedtime. While they read, they often provided information about bookhandling and reading (Chapman, 1986). Kristen's mother often asked Kristen to "turn just one page" or "move your hand—I can't see the words." Kristen's mother also encouraged her to act like a reader. She praised Kristen for choosing to read on her own and often encouraged her to do so: "Would you like to read your books?" She would often say, "I really like how you read your books." In this, Kristen was getting the message that she was a reader and that her mother expected her to be one.

Most important, Elizabeth's and Kristen's parents developed strategies for the way in which they shared books with their children (Ninio, 1980; Panofsky, 1986). These strategies allowed their children to participate in booksharing by pointing, gesturing, talking, commenting, questioning, and supplying text words. The strategies changed over time as their children became more skillful at participating in bookreading (Altwerger, et al., 1985).

Parents' Booksharing Strategies

Parents seem naturally to encourage their children's active responses to books. Before infants learn to talk, parents elicit babbling, pointing, and gestures. As infants approach their first birthday, parents encourage their children to respond with utterances that sound more and more like words—they expect their children to label pictures. Parents do the pointing, gesturing, and naming. They show their children how to point and gesture appropriately by taking their babies' arms and waving "bye bye." Similarly, parents praise any gesture a child makes with a book, such as patting it, and treat the gesture as if their child had spoken about the book. They say, "Yes, you see that kitten," as the child slaps at the book over the picture of a kitten. Gradually, a routine emerges. Parents ask a question, baby responds with a gesture or sound, and parents reinforce the response by answering back as if the child responded in exactly the manner the parents intended. These routines provide a scaffold (see Chapter 2) for the child's successful participation in bookreading (Snow, 1983).

Ninio (1980) found three kinds of routines in bookreading. The first routine is called the *Name Routine.* Parents point to part of a picture, call their children's attention to the picture, and provide the name of the object: "Oh, look at the bird.'' Then, to whatever response the child gives (pointing, laughing, looking), the parents give positive feedback: ''Yes. That's the bird.'' The second routine is called the *Where Routine.* Parents ask a *where* question: ''Where is the bird?'' Either the child points to the bird and the parent provides positive feedback or the child points to the wrong object and the parent provides information about the name of the object the child pointed to. The third routine is called the *What Routine.* Here parents ask, ''What's this?'' When the child supplies the correct name, the parent provides positive feedback and often new information about the named object ''Yes, that's the kitten. Look, he's eating.'' Besides eliciting the names of objects, What Routines are also used to elicit responses about attributes of objects (Heath, 1982). Parents ask, ''What's this?'' while pointing at the *tail* of the kitten. The What Routine also expands into the *Who Routine:* ''Who is this?'' (Chapman, 1986). The object of this routine is for the child to provide the names of specific characters.

When children begin listening to parts of texts read aloud, parents use other routines that are still intended to elicit responses from their children. One routine parents use is the *Pause-for-Repeat Routine* (Altwerger, et al., 1985; Chapman, 1986). In this routine, parents might read a short text segment and then use a rising intonation followed by a pause to invite the child to join in. At first, parents reread the text, but gradually they expect their children to repeat the text fragment. A similar routine is the *Fill-in-the-Blank Routine* (Chapman, 1986). In this routine, parents read a short, familiar text phrase and pause before saying the final word. They expect the child to supply the word.

These bookreading routines are derived from observations of parents and children as they interact with books. Most parents would be surprised to know that they use them. What parents think is important during bookreading is to help their children respond to and enjoy the bookreading experience, not to engage their child in a routine.

Changes in Parents' Booksharing Strategies

Parents' booksharing strategies change to meet the growing needs of their children. One way parents change how they read is by moving from only talking about pictures to including text reading (Altwerger et al., 1985). At first, the story text may be included as part of the parents' talk about the pictures, as Elizabeth's mother demonstrated when she shared *Where's Spot?* This shift from talking only about pictures and text to reading text involves more than a change from conversation to text reading. It means a shift from describing pictures as if they were not necessarily related to a story to focusing on story meaning. Parents gradually draw attention to aspects of the pictures that are salient to understanding the story. In effect, they signal to children that there is a relationship between what is in the pictures and what is going on in the story (Panofsky, 1986). We will describe more of this shift from pictures-as-separate to pictures-as-part-of-story in Chapters 5 and 6.

A second way parents change how they read is by holding their children accountable for aspects of the story (Snow, 1983). Parents expect their children to display knowledge during bookreading. When parents know their toddlers can say certain words, they expect them to say those words in response to questions during bookreading. At first, parents accept that their children will quickly tire of a book. Later, when they know their children are familiar with a book and have examined it for long periods of time in previous bookreading episodes, parents expect their children to sustain their interest for longer periods of time. After extensive experience with a familiar book, parents expect their children to be able to tell much of the story by themselves.

A Caution about Booksharing and Drawing

So far, we have described infants, toddlers, and two-year-olds whose parents have surrounded them with books and writing materials. We have described parents who encourage their children to participate in reading and writing activities. However, just as children are individuals, so are parents. Not all parents use the booksharing strategies we have previously described (Heath, 1982). There is no *single* correct method of booksharing. Some parents do not read books to their preschoolers. Other parents, even well-intentioned ones, believe reading and writing are the responsibility of schools. There is a wide variety in the amount of reading and writing materials available to children, in the frequency of reading and writing events, and even in the value given to reading and writing in different homes. Some parents do not view reading to young children as appropriate early experiences. Other parents may not know how to engage their young children in bookreading interactions (Heath with Thomas, 1984). However, after they have acquired children's books and some knowledge of booksharing strategies, many parents enjoy sharing books with their young children (Edwards, forthcoming).

We also know that children who have book experiences earlier and more frequently than other children gain much from these experiences (Teale, 1984). They are more likely to become early readers (Clark, 1976) and to be more successful academically (Wells, 1986) than children who have fewer booksharing experiences. At least one researcher (Snow, 1983) argues that booksharing experiences provide children with essential knowledge about written language that they cannot acquire in other types of activities with other types of written language. Therefore, it is important that teachers of young children provide experiences with bookreading much like those of children from literacy-oriented families. The next section describes how teachers of young children can provide literacy experiences for infants, toddlers, and two-year-olds.

Implications for Child Care and Nursery School

Soon after they are born, many children spend much of their waking hours in the care of adults at child care and nursery school centers. We do not believe that infants, toddlers, and two-year-olds ought to have structured literacy activities. However, teachers in these situations can take advantage of what we know about how parents support literacy learning to provide appropriate opportunities for young children to explore literacy.

Literacy Materials

Teachers must provide literacy materials even for very young children. Books should not be on top shelves for display, but rather in easy-to-reach locations. They should be placed within reach of infants who can sit up, but not yet crawl. We recommend that nursery schools and child care centers have at least one "book nook" set up in an out-of-the-way place in each room (Schickedanz, 1986). Some teachers of toddlers prefer to keep books in large baskets that they can bring out during booksharing time.

Paper, crayons, and markers should be made available on a daily basis. Toddlers have a hard time holding the paper still while they draw. One way to solve this problem is to use large rolls of paper that will cover toddler-sized tables. This paper can drape over the table, or it can be taped to it. Toddlers and two-year-olds enjoy trying out new kinds of pencils, markers, and crayons. They also enjoy using new colors and writing on new textures.

Environmental print items can be used in a housekeeping center or they can be brought in as part of other activities. One teacher of toddlers kept a bag of familiar environmental print items (such as a McDonald's bag, cereal boxes, and candy wrappers) to use during "talk time." Talk time is a special time during the day when she invites one child at a time to sit on her lap in a rocking chair and to talk with her. The environmental print items are one of the things the children might select to talk about.

Children's Literature

Teachers need to be sensitive to the kinds of books that are most appropriate for the children they work with. Infants enjoy books made with cardboard pages because the pages are easier to turn and the books are more durable. Cloth books are frustrating—the pages are extremely difficult for infants to manipulate (Butler, 1980). Figure 4.12 presents a list of cardboard books that are appropriate for infants and toddlers. These books feature photographs or realistic illustrations on uncluttered backgrounds, and the content is within the experiences of young children (Dinsmore, 1988). Experts on children's literature also recommend Mother Goose and rhyme books for infants and toddlers (Huck, Hepler, & Hickman, 1987). A list of appropriate Mother Goose and rhyme books for young children is presented in Figure 4.13.

Concept books capitalize on toddlers' growing language abilities (Huck, Hepler, & Hickman, 1987). They encourage children to label pictures. Simple ABC and counting books with few objects per page are especially appropriate for naming. Figure 3.6 in Chapter 3 presents several ABC and counting books that can be used with infants and toddlers. Older toddlers and two-year-olds enjoy simple-to-manipulate participation books. Infants especially enjoy *Pat the Bunny* (Kunhardt, 1940). Figure 3.4 in Chapter 3 includes participation books

Figure 4.12 *Cardboard Books for Infants and Toddlers*

Bialosky, P., & Bialosky, A. (1984). *Bialosky stays home*. Racine, WI: Western Publishing Company. (See also *Bialosky goes out*.)

Heyduck-Huth, H. (1973). *The Christmas story*. London: Burke Publishing Company.

Hoban, T. (1985). *1,2,3*. New York: Greenwillow. (See also *Red, blue, yellow shoe*, and *What is it?*.)

Leoni, L. (1983). *What?* New York: Pantheon.

Omerod, J. (1984). *Messy baby*. New York: Lothrop, Lee & Shepard.

Oxenbury, H. (1981). *Dressing*. New York: Wanderer. (See also *Family, Friends, Playing*, and *Working*.)

Ricklen, N. (1988). *Grandma and me*. New York: Simon & Schuster. (See also *Baby's clothes, Baby's toys, Baby's friends, Baby's home, Daddy and me, Mommy and me*, and *Grandpa and me*.)

Roth, H. (1986). *A goodnight hug*. New York: Grosset & Dunlap. (See also *Nursery school*.)

Slier, D. (1985). *What do babies do?* New York: Random House. (See also *What do toddlers do?* and *Whose baby are you?*)

Szekeres, C. (1986). *Sammy's special day*. Racine, WI: Western Publishing Company.

Wright, B. (1916, 1955, 1984). *The real Mother Goose green husky book*. New York: Rand McNally & Co. (See also other color books of Mother Goose.)

Ziefert, J., & Ernst, L. (1988). *Bye bye Daddy*. New York: Viking Kestrel. (See also *Let's get dressed*.)

that are appropriate for the very young child. Older toddlers and two-year-olds can be introduced to simple stories (Friedberg, 1989), many of which include repetition or patterns such as *The Runaway Bunny* (Brown, 1942) and *The Gingerbread Boy* (Galdone, 1975). Figure 4.14 presents a list of suggested storybooks for toddlers and two-year-olds.

Responding to Children's Literacy Activities

We believe children should see teachers read and write and they should be invited (not required) to read and write daily. Exemplary nursery school teachers do not try to read aloud to whole class groups of children who are younger than

Figure 4.13 *Books with Mother Goose Rhymes for Infants, Toddlers, and Two-Year-Olds*

Ahlberg, J., & Ahlberg, A. (1979). *Each pair each plum*. New York: Viking.

Cauley, L. (1982). *The three little kittens*. New York: Putnam.

Chorao, K. (1977). *The baby's lap book*. New York: E. P. Dutton.

de Paola, T. (1985). *Tomie de Paola's Mother Goose*. New York: Putnam.

Galdone, P. (1985). *Cat goes fiddle-i-fee*. New York: Clarion.

Galdone, P. (1986). *Three little kittens*. New York: Clarion.

Hill, E. (1982). *The nursery rhyme peek-a-book*. New York: Price/Stern/Sloan.

Marshall, J. (1979). *James Marshall's Mother Goose*. New York: Farrar.

Wright, B. F. (Illustrator) (1916). *The real Mother Goose*. New York: Rand McNally.

Figure 4.14 *First Storybooks for Toddlers and Two-Year-Olds*

Brown, M. (1947). *Goodnight moon.* New York: Harper.

Brown, M. (1942). *The runaway bunny.* New York: Harper.

Burningham, J. (1971). *Mr. Grumpy's outing.* New York: Holt.

*Carroll, R. (1932). *What Whiskers did.* New York: Walck.

*Carroll, R. (1970). *The Christmas kitten.* New York: Walck.

Clifton, L. (1977). *Amifika.* New York: E. P. Dutton.

Crews, D. (1978). *Freight train.* New York: Greenwillow.

Freeman, D. (1968). *Corduroy.* New York: Viking.

Galdone, P. (1973). *The little red hen.* New York: Scholastic.

Galdone, P. (1973). *The three bears.* New York: Scholastic.

Hill, E. (1980). *Where's Spot?* New York: Putnam.

Hughes, S. (1985). *Bathwater's hot.* New York: Lothrop, Lee & Shepard.

Hutchins, P. (1971). *Rosie's walk.* New York: Macmillan.

*Keats, E. (1974). *Kitten for a day.* Danbury, CT: Franklin Watts.

Kuskin, K. (1959). *Which horse is William?* New York: Harper and Row.

*Ormerod, J. (1981). *Sunshine.* New York: Puffin.

*Oxenbury, H. (1982). *Good night, good morning.* New York: Dial.

Rice, E. (1981). *Benny bakes a cake.* New York: Greenwillow.

Slobodkina, E. (1947). *Caps for sale.* New York: Addison.

Tolstoy, A. (1968). *The great big enormous turnip.* Danbury, CT: Franklin Watts.

*Wordless books

two or three years old. Rather, teachers can keep notes on children with whom they have read. Some nursery schools have a policy of having the teacher read individually with each child at least three times a week. Either a child is invited to read with the teacher (and the teacher only reads if the child is interested) or the teacher takes her cue from the child's own reading and joins the child. These sessions only last as long as a child desires and they center on books selected by the child. Figure 4.15 presents a list of effective booksharing behaviors that teachers can use to guide their reading with infants and toddlers (Resnick, et. al., 1987).

Two-year-olds sometimes enjoy sharing books in groups of two or three children. This number of children allows teachers to sit close to the children just as parents do in one-on-one booksharing. Teachers can use the same strategies and routines in sharing books with children that parents do. Many of the suggestions offered in Figure 4.15 are still appropriate for sharing books with two-year-olds. In addition, teachers can use the Where, What, Who, Pause-for-Repeat, and Fill-in-the-Blank routines. Effective teachers are very willing to share favorite books again and again. They are more likely to talk about the story than to read the text. They invite children to participate by asking questions and making comments. Effective teachers use gestures and intonation to enrich the story meaning, and they tell how pictures and story actions are related to children's real life experiences.

Figure 4.15 *Effective Booksharing Strategies*

Body Management (positional arrangements)

Effective Behaviors	*Ineffective Behaviors*
clears immediate area	pinches, pulls, or pushes child
places child on lap	restricts child's movements
partially encircles child	
places child between legs	
lies or reclines with child	
maintains physical contact	

Book Management (handling and control of book)

Effective Behaviors	*Ineffective Behaviors*
issues invitation	resists child turning pages
starts at front of book	interrupts reading to talk to someone or other distraction
allows child to hold book	becomes absorbed in book and ignores child
allows child to turn pages	continues to read after child loses interest
permits child to explore book	
points to pictures or words	
asks child to identify objects in pictures	
varies voice	
acts out (makes noises, gestures)	
comments on book's content	
links content of book to child's experiences	
removes distractors	
ends reading when child loses interest	

Language (reader's talk and encouragement of child's talk)

Effective Behaviors	*Ineffective Behaviors*
uses multiple word sentences	insists child listen only
labels objects in pictures	
describes pictures	
repeats child's vocalization	
elaborates child's vocalization	
gives words to child's vocalization	

Attention to Affect (emotional reaction to child's actions)

Effective Behaviors	*Ineffective Behaviors*
pauses for child's response	reprimands child
whispers and coos	makes negative comments about child's participation
inspects child's face	
comments positively about child's participation	
makes approving gestures	

Adapted from Resnick, M. B., et al. (1987). Mothers reading to infants: A new observational tool. *The Reading Teacher, 40,* 892. Reprinted with permission of M. B. Resnick and the International Reading Association.

Chapter Summary

Very young children begin their literacy learning when they interact with their parents and other caring adults as they share books or other kinds of print items. Young children who have opportunities to draw and to talk about their drawing are also on their way to knowing about literacy. Infants, toddlers, and two-year-olds are not yet literate (as we describe *literate* in the preface of this book), but they do have many literacy behaviors and they do know something about literacy. They enjoy reading and writing activities and engage in them frequently; they know how books are handled; and they know roles for participating in bookreading and writing routines. Young children can control their arms, hands, and fingers so they can create shapes they have in mind, and they know that the shapes they draw and the pictures they view can be named, are symbols or representations of real objects and actions, and communicate meaning.

One way children learn meaning-making strategies that will be useful in later literacy activities in schools is by participating in booksharing interactions with parents or other adults. Five meaning-making strategies that young children learn include knowing how to: (1) name and talk about pictures, (2) draw on their own experiences as a basis for making meaning, (3) use information provided in their mothers' or other adults' talk about pictures and text, (4) seek additional information through asking questions and seeking confirmation, and (5) pay attention to particular components of stories. As children gain experience with stories, they acquire knowledge of what stories are like; they begin to develop a concept of stories. Children's concepts of stories are not like those of adults. Children's concepts undergo changes and become more complex as they have more experiences with stories.

Another way children learn meaning-making strategies is by interacting with environmental print items such as magazines or food boxes. Toddlers and two-year-olds begin recognizing and naming objects that have print as a prominent feature.

Parents play an active role in their children's literacy learning. They model reading and writing and respond to their children's drawing in ways that signal that these drawings are meaningful. Many parents intuitively share books with their children in ways that support their children's literacy learning. They use Name, Where, What, Pause-for-Repeat, and Fill-in-the-Blank Routines that encourage children's active participation, and they provide literacy materials for their children's exploration. Teachers can also play an important role in the literacy beginnings of young children. They can make literacy materials available and offer literacy experiences. They can also select literature for children and respond appropriately to young children's literacy experiences.

Applying the Information

Two examples of Steven's literacy activities follow. The first event involves the retelling of a favorite story and the sec-ond event involves writing and talking with his sitter. Discuss what each of these literacy events reveals about Stev-

Figure 4.16 *Steven Retells* Bears in the Night *(Berenstain & Berenstain, 1971)*

Story: Bears investigate a sound in the night by creeping out of bed, down a tree, and up a hill.

Steven: (points to moon)
     moon
     (points to lantern)
     i-eet

TEXT: IN BED
Illustration: Seven bears in bed. Open
     window with a crescent moon. A
     lighted lantern hangs on the wall.

(turns page,
points to moon)
moon
(points to lantern)
i-eet

Illustration: One bear out of bed,
     otherwise similar to previous page.

(turns several pages rapidly,
gazes at picture for several
seconds)

Illustration: Bear going up hill with
     lantern in hand. Moon in sky. Owl
     at the top of hill.

(turns page)

Illustration: The word "WHOOOOO,"
     an owl, and four frightened bears
     jumping up.

(shakes head, points at owl)
OOOOOOOOOOO

---

en's literacy knowledge and behaviors. Describe how Steven's sitter (and parents) supported his literacy learning.

When Steven was nineteen months old, he retold *Bears in the Night* (Berenstain & Berenstain, 1971). He turned the book so that the cover faced him right-side-up. He turned past the first page (title page) quickly. Figure 4.16 presents Steven's retelling.

When Steven was twenty-five months old, he enjoyed drawing with his babysitter. She would encourage him to get his crayons, and he would color while she folded clothes or cleaned. He often made nonsense sounds as he colored. His sitter would talk to him as she worked. She would imitate his sounds and he would imitate hers. Sometimes

Steven would sing songs he knew as he colored. Figure 4.17 presents one of Steven's pictures.

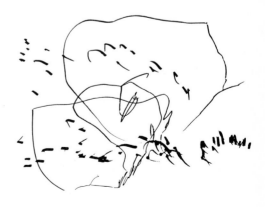

Figure 4.17 *Steven's Drawing*

Going Beyond the Text _____

Visit a child care center and take note of the literacy materials and activities in the infant, toddler, and two-year-old rooms. What books are available? How often and how do care givers read with children? How frequently do children draw? Take at least three books to share with a small group of toddlers or two-year-olds. Describe their booksharing strategies. Join the children as they draw. Describe their drawing behaviors and make inferences about their literacy knowledge. Interview at least one care giver. What does he or she believe about reading and writing for infants, toddlers, and two-year-olds?

References _____

ALTWERGER, B., DIEHL-FAXON, J., & DOCK-STADER-ANDERSON, K. (1985). Read aloud events as meaning construction. *Language Arts, 62,* 476–484.

APPLEBEE, A. N. (1978). *The child's concept of story.* Chicago, IL: University of Chicago Press.

BAGHBAN, M. (1984). *Our daughter learns to read and write.* Newark, DE: International Reading Association.

BERENSTAIN, S., & BERENSTAIN, J. (1971). *Bears in the night.* New York: Random House.

BOTVIN, G. J., & SUTTON-SMITH, B. (1977). The development of structural complexity in children's fantasy narratives. *Developmental Psychology, 13,* 377–388.

BROWN, M. W. (1942). *The runaway bunny.* New York: Harper and Row.

BROWN, M. W. (1947). *Goodnight moon.* New York: Harper and Row.

BUTLER, D. (1980). *Babies need books.* New York: Atheneum.

CHAPMAN, D. L. (1986). Let's read another one. In D. R. Tovey & J. E. Kerber (Eds.), *Roles in literacy learning* (pp. 10–25). Newark, DE: International Reading Association.

CLARK, M. M. (1976). *Young fluent readers.* London: Heinemann Educational Books.

de BRUNHOFF, L. (1975). *Babar and the Wully-Wully.* New York: Random House.

DINSMORE, K. E. (1988). Baby's first books. *Childhood Education, 64,* 215–219.

DISNEY (WALT) PRODUCTIONS. (1974). *Walt Disney's Peter and the wolf.* New York: Random House.

DOAKE, D. B. (1986). Learning to read: It starts in the home. In D. R. Tovey & J. E. Kerber (Eds.), *Roles in literacy learning* (pp. 2–9). Newark, DE: International Reading Association.

EDWARDS, P. A. (forthcoming). Supporting lower SES mothers' attempts to provide scaffolding for bookreading. In J. Allen & J. Mason (Eds.), *Reducing the risks for young learners: Literacy practices and policies.* Portsmouth, NH: Heinemann.

FREEMAN, D. (1968). *Corduroy.* New York: Viking.

FRIEDBERG, J. (1989). Helping today's toddlers become tomorrow's readers. *Young Children, 44,* 13–16.

GALDONE, P. (1975). *The gingerbread boy.* New York: Clarion Books.

GARDNER, H. (1980). *Artful scribbles.* New York: Basic Books.

GOODMAN, Y. (1980). The roots of literacy. In M. Douglass (Ed.), *Claremont reading conference* (44th Yearbook) (pp. 1–32). Claremont, CA: Claremont Graduate School.

HALL, N. (1987). *The emergence of literacy.* Portsmouth, NH: Heinemann.

HALLIDAY, M. A. K. (1975). *Learning how to mean: Explorations in the function of langauge.* London: Edward Arnold.

HEATH, S. B. (1982). What no bedtime story means: Narrative skills at home and school. *Langue in Society, 2,* 49–76.

HEATH, S. B., with THOMAS, C. (1984). The achievement of preschool literacy for mother and child. In H. Goelman, A. Oberg, & F. Smith (Eds.), *Awakening to literacy,* (pp. 51–72) Exeter, NH: Heinemann.

HELLARD, S. (1986). *Billy goats gruff.* New York: Putnam's.

HILL, E. (1980). *Where's Spot?* New York: Putnam.

HUCK, C. S., HEPLER, S., & HICKMAN, J. (1987). *Children's literature in the elementary school.* New York: Holt, Rinehart and Winston.

KELLOGG, R. (1969). *Analyzing children's art.* Palo Alto, CA: National Press Books.

KUNHARDT, D. (1940). *Pat the bunny.* New York: Western Publishing.

LAMME, L. L., & PACKER, A. B. (1986). Book-reading behaviors of infants. *The Reading Teacher, 39,* 504–509.

LASS, B. (1982). Portrait of my son as an early reader. *The Reading Teacher, 36,* 20–28.

LEONDAR, B. (1977). Hatching plots: Genesis of story making. In D. Perkins & B. Leondar (Eds.), *The arts and cognition* (pp. 172–191). Baltimore, MD: Johns Hopkins.

MANDLER, L., & JOHNSON, N. (1977). Remembrance of things parsed: Story structure and recall. *Cognitive Psychology, 9,* 11–51.

McCARTNEY, K. A., & NELSON, K. (1981). Children's use of scripts in story recall. *Discourse Processes, 4,* 59–70.

McGEE, L. M., & TOMPKINS, G. E. (1981). The videotape answer to independent reading comprehension activities. *The Reading Teacher, 34,* 427–433.

NINIO, A. (1980). Picture-book reading in mother-infant dyads belonging to two subgroups in Israel. *Child Development, 51,* 587–790.

NINIO, A., & BRUNER, J. (1978). Antecedents of the achievements of labeling. *Journal of Child Language, 5,* 1–15.

PANOFSKY, C. P. (1986). Parent-child reading interactions: The importance of nonverbal behavior. In J. A. Niles & R. V. Lalik (Eds.), *Solving problems in literacy learners, teachers and researchers* (pp. 250–258). Rochester, NY: The National Reading Conference.

RESNICK, M. B., ROTH, J., AARON, P. A., SCOTT, J., WOLKING, W. D., LARSEN, J. J., & PACKER, A. B. (1987). Mothers reading to infants: A new observational tool. *The Reading Teacher, 40,* 888–894.

ROTH, H. (1986). *A goodnight hug.* New York: Grosset & Dunlap.

SCHICKEDANZ, J. A. (1986). *More than the ABCs.* Washington, DC: National Association for the Education of Young Children.

SEUSS, DR. (THEODORE GEISEL) (1963a). *Dr. Seuss's ABC Book.* New York: Random House.

SEUSS, DR. (THEODORE GEISEL) (1963b). *Hop on pop.* New York: Random House.

SNOW, C. E. (1983). Literacy and language: Relationships during the preschool years. *Harvard Educational Review, 53,* 165–189.

SNOW, C. E., & NINIO, A. (1986). The contracts of literacy: What children learn from learning to read books. In W. H. Teale & E. Sulby (Eds.), *Emergent literacy: Writing and reading* (pp. 116–138). Exeter, NH: Heinemann.

STEIN, N., & GLENN, C. (1979). An analysis of story comprehension in elementary children. In R. Freedle (Ed.), *Advances in discourse processes (Vol II): New directions in discourse processing* (pp. 53–120). Norwood, NJ: Ablex.

SULZBY, E. (1985). Children's emergent reading of favorite storybooks: A developmental study. *Reading Research Quarterly, 20,* 458–481.

TEALE, W. H. (1984). Reading to young children: Its significance for literacy development. In H. Goelman, A. Oberg, & F. Smith (Eds.), *Awakening to literacy* (pp. 110–121). Exeter, NH: Heinemann.

THORNDYKE, P. (1977). Cognitive structures in comprehension and memory of narrative discourse. *Cognitive Psychology, 9,* 77–110.

WELLS, G. (1986). *The meaning makers.* Portsmouth, NH: Heinemann.

WRIGHT, B. F. (illustrator) (1916). *The real Mother Goose.* New York: Rand McNally.

YADEN, D. B. JR., & McGEE, L. M. (1984). Reading as a meaning-seeking activity: What children's questions reveal. In J. Niles (Ed.), *Thirty-third yearbook of the National Reading Conference* (pp. 101–109). Rochester, NY: National Reading Conference.

CHAPTER 5

Threes, Fours, and Fives Becoming Novice Readers and Writers

The preschool years are an exciting time. Children's worlds expand beyond home, family, and children in the immediate neighborhood to encompass new playmates and experiences, including literacy experiences. They learn a great deal about reading and writing.

Around the age of two or three, some children recognize a McDonald's sign or a toy logo, even when the sign or logo is not located at a McDonald's restaurant or on a toy. Around the age of three or four, some children write shapes and lines to communicate meaning in dramatic play or as they participate in reading and writing events with their parents or other readers and writers. Young children who use written language in these new ways are *novice readers and writers*. In the first portion of Chapter 5 we will describe these new behaviors and knowledges and define novice reading and writing.

In the remainder of Chapter 5, we will outline what novice readers and writers learn in the four domains of written language knowledge: meaning, form, meaning-form links, and functions. Children who are three, four, and five years old continue to refine meaning-making strategies that they began using when they were toddlers and two-year-olds. Many three-, four-, and five-year-olds begin paying attention to written language forms and learn a great deal about three written language units: alphabet letters, their names, and texts. Preschoolers begin to use context to link meaning with written forms. They use the contexts in which written signs and labels are found to discover meaning in those signs and labels. Finally, three-, four-, and five-year-olds are motivated to learn about and use written language by being included in literacy events. As they participate in literacy events with their families and with other children, they acquire knowledge of how written language functions.

WHO ARE NOVICE READERS AND WRITERS?

In this chapter, we examine the literacy learning of many preschoolers, kinder-gartners, and even some first graders whom we call *novice readers and writers.* Our choice of words to describe these children's reading and writing is inten-tional: in everyday usage, the words *novice* and *beginner* are nearly synony-mous. Our decision to use the word *novice* in this chapter and the word *begin-ner* in Chapter 4 signifies that although we describe a change in literacy behaviors, we recognize that there are overlaps and interactions between our two concepts of beginning literacy and novice-like literacy.

Learning about written language is a gradual process. Children's literacy de-velopment is a matter of their taking small steps and making minor adjustments in their perspectives. Children form new hypotheses in response to the discov-ered inadequacies of past strategies. Thus, we will not be able to identify a single criterion of novice literacy. A child may act like a literacy beginner in one literacy event and like a novice reader or writer in another event. Still, careful observers will notice that in some literacy events children begin using written language in ways that signal new insights about literacy. In this chapter, we will describe the many indications that show children have constructed new understandings about literacy.

New Insights about Communicating with Written Language

Preschoolers sometimes use written language in ways different from those we described beginners as using. They go beyond labeling their written marks as be-ginners do (in Chapter 4 Kristen called her written lines and shapes "ABC's"). *Nov-ices intentionally create written symbols that they use to communicate a message.* Carrie's writing in the "Ted's Delight" literacy event in Chapter 1 is a good example of a novice's writing that is intended to communicate a message. Carrie wrote a check (Figure 1.3) as a part of restaurant play with her brother and father. Although her writing is not conventional, her behavior as she handed the check to her father indicated she intended her writing to mean something like "pay for your food."

Another way children indicate their new written language insight is by re-sponding to the written symbols they find in the environment. Many children respond to printed symbols such as written words and logos that are associated with familiar signs, labels, and packages. Novices go beyond simple recognition of meaning in familiar items or contexts that happen to include printed symbols and words. *Novices react to the meaning communicated in printed signs and labels even when they are not located on the items they represent or in the context in which they are usually found.* They construct meaning from the sym-bol of the printed words and logos; they recognize the Raisin Bran and McDon-ald's logos even when the actual object (the box of cereal) is not present or when the familiar context (the restaurant building) is not available.

Examples of Novices

Three literacy events involving Quentin, Kristen, and Courtney follow. These children have had many experiences sharing books with their parents and nursery school teachers.

Quentin is three and one-half years old. He frequently draws with his older sister as she does her homework. Sometimes she will draw pictures and write words or letters at Quentin's request. One day, while his sister was doing her spelling homework, Quentin drew a large circle with one line radiating down from it. He pointed to this primitive *Q* and said, "Quentin." Later, when his mother was checking his sister's spelling words, he gave her his paper and said, "I wrote mine."

Kristen is thirty-two months old. One day, while she was riding in the car with her mother, she said, "Pizza man." Her mother looked and finally spotted a Domino's pizza sign. This sign consists of two domino shapes in red, white, and blue and the word *Domino's*. Kristen's family frequently has a Domino's pizza delivered to their home. Kristen had never been to a Domino's pizza place because Domino's only delivers pizzas—it is not a restaurant.

Courtney is twenty-nine months old. She frequently requests that her mother or father write the letters *o* and *e*. Courtney's mother encourages her interest in writing. When she writes in her calendar, takes notes for classes she is attending, signs birthday cards, or makes lists, she gives Courtney paper and pens or crayons and suggests that Courtney write, too. One day, as her mother was writing a letter to accompany a birthday card, Courtney said, "I write 'Happy Birthday to you'" (see Figure 5.1). Courtney's mother suggested that they send her letter, too.

Figure 5.1 *"Happy Birthday to You"*

What They Are Learning

Quentin's, Kristen's, and Courtney's behaviors and talk indicate that they intend for their written symbols to communicate messages and that they recognize messages can be communicated in written symbols. It is important to note that these children saw or made written symbols, in the form of scribbles, letters, words, and logos, and that they found these symbols meaningful. Previous to these three episodes, these children had frequently experienced meaning in written language *that was read aloud to them from their books.* What is significant about these events is that Quentin, Kristen, and Courtney constructed meaning from *written symbols that they constructed or noticed on their own.*

Kristen constructed the meaning "pizza man" from a printed sign and logo without the clues of an actual pizza, a delivery man, or a familiar location associated with eating pizza. Her behavior indicated a new understanding that printed symbols communicate messages: she knew that written marks in environmental print are significant. Quentin constructed the meaning "Quentin" by printing something like a letter *Q*, and Courtney constructed the meaning "Happy birthday to you" by writing round-and-round and jagged lines. Their behavior, too, indicated their awareness that printed symbols communicate messages. It is significant that the messages Quentin and Courtney constructed were part of a larger activity involving writing to communicate. Quentin joined his sister as she practiced her spelling words and Courtney joined her mother as she wrote a birthday message.

Are They Reading and Writing?

This is an important question, which has been at the center of controversy in the past few years. We discussed in Chapter 1 that traditionalists define reading as the ability to identify words printed in isolation or in simple stories. Similarly, they define *writing* as the ability to write identifiable words in isolation or in simple stories. After careful observation of children like Quentin, Kristen,and Courtney, some educators have argued that we need a new definition of reading and writing (Baghban, 1984; Goodman, 1980; Harste, Woodward, & Burke, 1984).

We believe that *children are novice readers when they intend to get meaning from written symbols* even when those symbols are highly familiar signs, labels, and logos. Kristen did not say that the Domino's pizza sign said "Domino's"; rather, she indicated it meant "pizza man." Obviously, Kristen was not reading the words on a sign as an accomplished reader would; nevertheless, she constructed meaning from the sign. Even when signs and labels appear in situational context, novice readers frequently respond to the written symbols rather than merely to the context. Three weeks after Kristen identified the pizza sign, she asked "What does that *name say*?" about a familiar sign on the Baskin Robbins ice cream store. For months Kristen had said, "I want ice cream" as she passed the store. Because a picture of an ice cream cone is prominently displayed on the front of the store, we might conclude that Kristen is merely interpreting a picture (of an ice cream cone) or recognizing a familiar context (an ice cream store) when she said, "I want *ice cream.*" However, Kristen's later request that her mother tell her what the *name said* demonstrated her awareness of the written sign and its power to communicate.

We believe *children are novice writers when they intentionally convey meaning with written marks.* Quentin communicated meaning when he made his printed symbol *Q*. It is important to notice that Quentin's writing was not yet conventional; he did not write his full name *Quentin*, nor did he form the letter *Q* perfectly. Still, he intended to write something that was meaningful—a symbol for his name. Courtney communicated meaning when she made her jagged and round-and-round lines. She did not include any letters or words in her writing at all, but she intended her writing to convey the message "Happy birthday to you."

Repertoire of Knowledges

Some researchers have described developmental sequences of children's literacy acquisition (for example, Ferreiro & Teberosky, 1982). We included some of these ideas in Chapters 2 and 4 (see the discussion about Piaget in Chapter 2 and Applebee in Chapter 4). Because we distinguish between literacy beginners and novice readers and writers, it may seem as if we favor a developmental approach to literacy learning. We believe that children's *knowledge* grows and changes as they have more and different literacy experiences. However, we also believe that the *strategies* children use to acquire literacy for themselves are similar for infants, preschoolers, and young elementary school children (see Chapter 2).

Some researchers have noted that children seem to display a repertoire of literacy knowledges as they engage in different kinds of literacy activities (Dyson, 1985; Sulzby, 1985). That is, when performing one kind of literacy task, children might display one level of literacy knowledge and when performing another task, they might display another level of literacy knowledge. We have observed many children who display different kinds of literacy knowledges in different literacy events. At the time Kristen's mother noted her new awareness of printed symbols in some environmental signs, she also noted that Kristen was not responding to all environmental signs, nor was she using her written marks to communicate messages. After Courtney wrote her birthday message, she spent several months writing lines and shapes that she labeled as letters or words, but that she did not intend to be messages.

We believe that children draw upon a variety of understandings about literacy as they participate in literacy events. Although we use the words *literacy beginner, novice reader and writer* (and later will use the words *experimenting reader and writer* and *accomplished reader and writer*) as useful devices for describing children's literacy behaviors and understandings, we do not intend that these words be used as labels for young children. Rather, we believe our descriptions of beginning literacy and novice reading and writing will provide teachers with useful guides for carefully observing what children do with reading and writing in specific literacy events.

We add several cautions. First, it is very difficult to make inferences about young children's knowledge. Because young children are still novices at talking, it is quite possible that what they say while writing or reading may not accurately convey what they are thinking. Second, when children are given different *directions* for tasks, they may perform very differently. DeFord (1980) told children to "draw a picture and write your name." She found that children differentiated between drawing and writing as early as two years of age. In contrast,

Dyson (1984) simply observed children as they wrote and drew without giving them any directions. She found that children's conceptions of writing and drawing were undifferentiated. Finally, very few researchers have considered children's own intentions when they were writing. Dyson (1985) found that children wrote for varied purposes and their apparent concepts about written language differed according to their purposes for writing. She found that one child, Tracy, seemed to be interested in constructing; her writing was filled with conventionally spelled names. In contrast, another child, Rachel, was interested in narrating; her writing consisted of stories written in unconventional letter-like shapes.

KNOWLEDGE ABOUT WRITTEN LANGUAGE MEANINGS

Novice readers and writers learn to construct meaning from an ever-increasing variety of texts such as menus, *TV Guides,* telephone books, grocery lists, coupons, and especially stories. Novice writers make meaning by creating an increasing variety of written symbols.

Constructing Meaning from Environmental Print

By the age of two and one-half or three years old, many young children find some environmental print symbols meaningful (Goodman & Altwerger, 1981; Hiebert, 1978). It is not accidental that environmental print symbols are the first written symbols that most children find meaningful. Environmental print symbols share many characteristics with oral language. In oral language events, young children make sense of what their parents are saying by looking at what is being pointed at or by paying attention to the context in which the talk takes place. Context is particularly important for young children's making sense of oral language.

Children's first experiences with environmental print also occur in contexts that make the meaning of the printed symbol obvious. A McDonald's sign is located in front of the place where children get hamburgers. The McDonald's logo is on the bag that holds the hamburgers and on the paper in which the hamburger is wrapped. This kind of print is *contextualized written language.* It appears in a context or situation that usually helps cue the meaning; it is similar to contextualized oral language. Children naturally apply their oral-language strategy of paying attention to the context as a way of constructing meaning from environmental print.

Eventually, children no longer need the actual physical context to signal meaning. When children are familiar with printed symbols such as the McDonald's logo, the context of the building or hamburger is not necessary to cue its meaning. Children find the printed symbol itself meaningful. They operate with the knowledge that written language symbols communicate meaning. Many children begin to ask "What does that say?" about environmental signs. They know that the signs they see will communicate some message that might be interesting to know about.

Constructing Meaning from Stories and Other Literature

The strategy of paying attention to context pays off in children's interactions with print in the environment, but it does not help with all written language. Children cannot look around the room in which a story is being read (the context) in order to find clues to the story's meaning. In order to construct the meaning of a story being read to them, children must listen to the words of the story. Of course, most books for children include pictures that provide salient contextual cues for understanding stories. Eventually, however, children must learn to rely only on the text and not on picture context to construct meaning from stories that they will read. These strategies of finding meaning from the text-bound language of stories (see Chapter 1) are particularly important for later success in reading (Dickinson & Snow, 1987).

Strategies for Constructing Meaning

Novices expand their meaning-making strategies by being able to understand more story text as it is real aloud. Some preschoolers enjoy listening to stories for many minutes without interruption as their parents read aloud to them (Magee & Sutton-Smith, 1983). At other times, children make comments and ask many questions about stories. Figure 5.2 presents a portion of an interaction between three-year-old Jon-Marc and his father as they read *The Story of Ferdinand* (Leaf, 1936) together (Yaden, 1984). The way Jon-Marc's father shared this story is similar to the way a teacher would share it. He read the text rather than interweaving it in his conversation (see Chapter 4, Figure 4.8 for an example of how a parent interweaves text reading with talk about a story). It is obvious that Jon-Marc was having some difficulties understanding the story and text; however, his questions clearly indicate he was actively attempting to make sense of the story (Altwerger, Diehl-Faxon, & Dockstader-Anderson, 1985).

One strategy Jon-Marc used to make sense of the story was to ask questions about words in the story text that he did not understand. He asked, "What does *drid* (Madrid) mean?" Another strategy Jon-Marc used to construct meaning was to ask questions related to reasons for story events and actions. He asked, "Why (did they have to take Ferdinand home)?" Jon-Marc's question probed the causes of an event. His father's answer repeated information provided in text that he had already read, but also made explicit the chain of causally related events: Ferdinand liked flowers; he didn't like to fight; the men wanted him to fight; when he wouldn't fight, they took him home. Jon-Marc's struggle to understand this sequence of related events illustrates his growing concern about linking several story events into a meaningful whole. Jon-Marc was learning to understand more than just a single event; he was learning to make sense of an event *in relation to other events as they formed a story-as-a-whole.*

Figure 5.2 *Jon-Marc and His Father Share* The Story of Ferdinand
(Leaf, 1936)

Text is presented in all capital letters.

Illustration: Ferdinand (very large bull) jumping around after having been stung by a bee. Five men are jumping with joy in the background.

Father: HERE WAS THE LARGEST AND FIERCEST BULL OF ALL. JUST THE ONE FOR THE BULL FIGHTS IN MADRID.

Jon-Marc: What does drid mean?

Father: Madrid. That's the name of a city. Ma–drid, that's the name of a city, a city in Spain.

Father: (reads several more pages of text)

Illustration: Ferdinand in a small cart going over the mountain. A bull ring is the background.

Father: SO THEY HAD TO TAKE FERDINAND HOME.

Jon-Marc: Why?

Father: Because he wouldn't fight. He just wouldn't fight. He didn't like to fight. He just wanted to smell the flowers. (Note, this is a paraphrase of the text that had just been read on the previous pages.)

Jon-Marc: Is that why they wanted to . . . to . . . to fight in the drid?

Father: In Madrid? Yeah, they wanted . . . they wanted him to fight in Madrid. Madrid's the name of a city. They wanted him to fight the Matador. But he didn't. He just wanted to go home and smell the flowers.

Jon-Marc: And . . . and . . . and love her mother cow?

Father: Yeah, and . . . and love his mother.

Jon-Marc: Where's her mother cow?

Father: Well, she's back in the book a little bit.

A third strategy Jon-Marc used to make meaning was to apply his understanding of events in the real world to make inferences about story events. Jon-Marc asked if Ferdinand would (go home) "And . . . and . . . and love her mother cow?" This question reveals that Jon-Marc used inferences to predict story events (after going home, Ferdinand would love his mother). It also illustrates that he used his own life as a frame of reference for understanding the story. Jon-Marc probably went home to love his mother so he inferred that Ferdinand would be going home to love his mother.

Constructing Story Meanings in Groups

Most children's early experiences with constructing story meanings take place as they share stories with a parent or other adult. These sessions are highly personalized; they capitalize on children's experiences with particular stories. As children approach school age—preschool or kindergarten—their storybook experiences will be in many-to-one situations. Teachers are likely to share books with groups of children rather than with one child at a time. In group story sharing situations, children are not as close to the pictures as they are in one-to-one story sharing situations. Thus, they have to rely more on the words of the text to construct story meaning than on extensive viewing of pictures.

Effective preschool and kindergarten teachers are skilled in capturing each child's attention as they share books with small groups of children. Still, young children must learn to pay attention not only to what the teacher is doing and saying (showing pictures, asking questions, making comments, and reading text), but also to what their classmates are doing and saying.

Cochran-Smith (1984) observed over 100 bookreading episodes in a preschool classroom with three- and four-year olds. Her most important observation was that storyreading in this classroom was similar to the interactive booksharing episodes that we describe in both Chapter 4 and this chapter. The meaning that emerged from these preschool booksharing events evolved from both the teacher's and children's comments and from the text that the teacher read.

Mrs. Jones is a preschool teacher who is skillful in sharing books with her class of four-year-olds. Figure 5.3 presents a portion of the interaction among 9 four-year-olds and Mrs. Jones as she shared *There's a Nightmare in my Closet* (Mayer, 1968).

Children's meaning-making strategies.   The children's comments and questions demonstrate that they understood much of the literal meaning of the story. Obviously the children understood there was a nightmare in the closet; they knew the character needed protection. Their comments and questions demonstrate that they also made many inferences about implied meanings in the story. They made inferences about motivations for the character's actions (he shut the door "Cause he doesn't want the nightmare to come out"); about the character's traits ("He's a scaredy cat"); and about reasons for the character's feelings (he was afraid "cause the wind blow"). The children also made predictions about upcoming story events. Just before Mrs. Jones turned to the last page of the story, which contains an illustration of a second nightmare peeking out of the closet, one child predicted, "There's gonna be another one."

In addition to making inferences and predictions about sequence and causal relations, the children projected themselves into the story ("My momma take the light off, I'm not scared"). They also evaluated the story meaning based on their knowledge of the real world ("I guess he ain't [getting rid of the nightmare] cause that's not a real gun.")

The children also paid attention to each other's comments. When one child commented about an action of the character ("Cause he's scared"), another one agreed ("He's a scaredy cat"). Similarly, when one child noted that "the wind blow," another child added, "Yeah, the curtain's out."

This short story interaction illustrates that four-year-olds in group story sharing can construct many kinds of meanings (Martinez, 1983). They understand

Figure 5.3 *A Portion of Mrs. Jones and Pre-Kindergartners Sharing*
There's a Nightmare in My Closet *(Mayer, 1968)*

Brackets indicate portions of the dialogue that occurred simultaneously.

Mrs. J: (shows cover of book, invites children to talk about nightmares, reads title and author, and reads first page of text stating the character's belief that a nightmare once lived inside his bedroom closet)

Child 1: He got toys and a gun on his bed.

Mrs. J: Umm, I wonder why?

Child 2: So he can protect him.

Mrs. J: Protect him. Umm. (reads text about closing the door to the closet)

Child 1: Cause he's scared.

⌈Child 3: He's a scaredy cat.
⌊Child 1: My momma take the light off, I'm not scared.

Child 4: He might lock it.

Mrs. J: Why would he lock it?

Child 4: Cause he doesn't want the nightmare to come out.

Mrs. J: (reads text about character being afraid to even look in the closet)

Child 1: Cause the wind blow.

Mrs. J: The wind blows?

⌈Child 3: Yeah, the curtain's out.
⌊Child 2: It's blowing.

Mrs. J: It must have been a dark, windy night. (continues reading text, making comments, and asking questions)

Children: (continue making comments and asking questions)

Mrs. J: (reads text about character deciding to get rid of the nightmare)

Child 1: I guess he ain't cause that's not a real gun.

Mrs. J: (turns page to illustration of the nightmare coming out of the closet and walking toward the boy in the bed)

⌈Child 1: There he is.
⌊Child 5: Why he's awake?

Mrs. J: Well what did it say? He was going to try to get rid of his nightmare, so he stayed awake waiting for his nightmare.

---

what the author says—the literal meaning. They understand what the author implies—inferential meaning. They make judgments about what the author says—evaluative meaning.

Teachers' support for meaning-making. Mrs. Jones played an important role in the children's meaning making. When one child commented about items in the picture, "He got toys and a gun on his bed" she asked, "Why?" Her question prompted the children to consider the items in the picture as *part of an event in a story.* Mrs. Jones frequently asked questions that required children to make inferences about relations between events.

Mrs. Jones also helped children apply their real-world understandings to understanding the story. One child asked, "Why he's awake?" This question suggests that the child was making inferences based on real-world knowledge—the room was dark and so the character should be asleep. But when Mrs. Jones reminded the child, "Well what did it say?" she implied that readers must pay attention to what the text says. She reminded the child that the text said, "He was going to try to get rid of his nightmare." Then she made explicit the inference that should have been made to interpret the story meaning, "So he stayed awake waiting for his nightmare."

Constructing Meaning in Writing

As we described the new literacy insights that signal a child is becoming a novice writer, we discussed childen's new interest in participating in the sending of the message and not just in the activity of writing. Much of novice writers' message making is a part of playful activity. They imitate their parents' or siblings' sending messages in their dramatic play. One day, when Giti and her mother had returned from having a snack at the Big Wheel Restaurant, Giti walked around with a pencil and paper and stood in front of her mother with the pencil held over the pad just as she had seen the waitress at the restaurant do. She said, "You want?" Her mother dictated, "Hot dog" and Giti wrote a jagged line. Then her mother said, "French fries" and Giti wrote again. After several minutes of this game, Giti said, "Ready?" just as her mother had when she was ready to leave the restaurant (Baghban, 1984, pp. 61–62). Giti's behaviors indicate her intention to write something meaningful. She wrote the food orders that her mother dictated.

Much of children's meaning making in writing is dependent upon their experiences with functional uses of reading and writing. Giti would not have used writing to create a food order if she had not observed orders for food being written and read. This illustrates the interrelatedness of our four knowledges of written language. In this case, Giti's knowledge of written language functions served her meaning making in writing.

KNOWLEDGE ABOUT WRITTEN
LANGUAGE FORMS

At the same time novices construct meaning from written symbols, they also gain knowledge of written language forms. Novice writers create symbols that have many features of letters or texts. Some novice writers place jagged lines in horizontal rows; this indicates an awareness of the feature of linearity in texts. Other novice writers produce symbols that have many letter features called *mock letters*. Figure 5.4 presents a story and a grocery list written by a four-year-

Figure 5.4 *A Story and a Grocery List*

old novice writer. Although the writing is unconventional, it is easy to distinguish the story from the list simply by how each looks. The writing in Figure
5.4 also illustrates an awareness of letter features. There are a few conventionally formed letters in the story and list; however, most of the letters are mock
letters composed of different letter features.

Novice readers also pay attention to details of written language forms, especially in environmental print. Giti is a novice reader who recognized many environmental print signs. One day, she pointed to the letter *K* in Special K cereal
and said, "K Mart" (Baghban, 1984, p. 30). In order to have made this response,
Giti must have noticed the particular shape we call *K* in the words *K Mart* and
in the words *Special K*.

A third written language form that many novice readers and writers learn
about is their names. Parents frequently write their children's names as part of
command-a-word games (see Chapter 4). Because novice readers and writers are
still so egocentric, there is particular appeal in learning to read and write special
words that symbolize them, their signature.

Alphabet Letters

One of the most obvious knowledges that novice readers and writers acquire
about written language forms is the ability to name and write alphabet letters.
Although the ability to name and write letters is important, it is not the only
thing that children learn about alphabet letters.

Knowledge of Letter Names and Formations

As preschoolers, some children learn the names of many letters and acquire the
ability to write several recognizable alphabet letters. By the age of three, some
children can name as many as ten alphabet letters (Hiebert, 1981; Lomax &
McGee, 1987). By age four, some children can write some recognizable letters,
especially those in their names (Hildreth, 1936). It takes some time for even

these early letter learners to acquire the names of all the alphabet letters. Even precocious youngsters who become accomplished readers and writers prior to entering kindergarten take about six months to learn all the letter names (Anabar, 1986; Lass, 1982). A child may take as long as two or three years to perfect writing his or her name (Hildreth, 1936). Of course, in this aspect, as in all literacy learning, there is a wide variation in the age at which children acquire certain knowledges (Morgan, 1987). There are many children entering kindergarten who do not recognize any alphabet letters and cannot write their names.

Knowledge Prior to Learning to Name
or Write Alphabet Letters

Before they learn to name any alphabet letters or to write recognizable letter formations, children learn a great deal about alphabet letters and written language. One thing young children learn is to recognize that alphabet letters are a special category of visual graphics that can be named. Lass (1982) reported that alphabet books were among her son's favorite books. She noticed that her son began calling each of the letters in his alphabet books or in environmental print signs *B* or *D* when he was still a toddler. It seemed as if Jed had learned to recognize the special category we call letters. He called all of the visual graphics (letters) in his category *B* or *D*. Kristen also recognized the category of letters. Like Jed, she did not know the name associated with any single letter. (Even though Jed called all the letters *B* and *D*, he did not recognize the letters *B* or *D* by name.) Kristen found alphabet letters everywhere—on her father's t-shirts, on her mother's books, and even on man-hole covers. She said, "That has letters on it."

Children associate letters with meaningful contexts prior to learning their first alphabet letter names. Baghban (1984) noted that the letter *M* was the first alphabet letter to which her daughter responded. At two years, Giti pointed to the letter *M* in the words *K Mart* and said, "McDonald's." She also commented about the letter *Z* on one of her blocks, "Look, like in zoo" (Baghban, 1984, pp. 29–30). Giti wrote circle-like shapes something like the letter *G* which she called "Giti," "Grandma," and "Grandpa" (Baghban, 1984, pp. 52, 56).

Giti and Jed are special. Both children learned to name the alphabet letters early in their preschool years and became accomplished readers and writers before going to kindergarten. Still, we can draw an important generalization about alphabet learning from their example. Alphabet letter learning seems to be dependent upon much experience with highly meaningful written language. Giti distinguished *M* and *G* by associating them with important places and people. Jed indicated his attention to letters in the context of favorite books and meaningful environmental print signs. This generalization has important implications for supporting children's alphabet letter learning. It suggests that children do not learn alphabet letter names in any particular order or by isolating letters from meaningful written language (see Chapter 6 for appropriate alphabet letter learning activities).

Other Knowledge Acquired Along with Letter Names and Formations

As children learn to name alphabet letters and to write recognizable letter formations, they also learn that letters have features. Learning letter features allows children to both distinguish among letters (such as between the letters *A* and *H*) and write letters. Learning some letter features and being willing to experiment means that children can discover new letter features and letters (see Chapter 2). Suppose a child named Erin did not make all the crosslines on her *E*; through the comments of a helpful friend or adult, she might discover the letter *F*. Or suppose a child named Carl turned his *C* on its side; he might discover the letter *U*. Children frequently discover letters in their own writing. Figure 5.5 presents Ashley's writing. She wanted her aunt to play with her, but her aunt was busy writing her thesis. Ashley decided to write the thesis for her aunt. Ashley said as she wrote, ''Aunt Linda helps people learn to read. She is a good teacher. The End.'' As she said ''The End '' she pointed to the letter that looks like a backwards *N* on the bottom left of her paper. She said, ''Hey, I wrote an *N*.'' This literacy episode illustrates that sometimes novice writers discover letters after they write.

Figure 5.5 *Ashley's Thesis*

A second concept children discover as they learn alphabet letter names and formations is that some features related to letters must be ignored. Children learn that any of the 26 letters can appear in many different contexts, sizes, and colors and still be the same letter. They learn that features of color or size or special stylized type are not important for naming and writing letters.

Children's comments about letters they find in their reading and writing indicate a third concept about written language that they learn as they name and write letters. One child commented about a friend's writing, ''You turned *R* into a *V*'' and another child said, ''Look—I made a *W*. A Crooked *W*'' (Lamme & Childers, 1983, pp. 30, 40). These comments show that children treat letters as objects that they not only can name, but also can talk about in other ways. This is the beginning of children's ability to talk about written language as an object of interest and signals children's emerging metalinguistic ability (see Chapter 1).

Children's Concepts about Alphabet Letters

Even when children know the names of several alphabet letters and use mock letters and real letters in their writing, they have unadult-like concepts of what those letters are. Many children do not think of letters as units of written language that are parts of words and related to sounds; rather, they think of letters as belonging to or symbolizing something meaningful.

Anders told his mother that the letter *a* in *Safeway* was "one of mine" (Goodman, 1980, p. 28). Santiago said about the letter *S*, "That's Santiago's." When asked, "Does it say Santiago?" he replied, "No, it's Santiago's" (Ferreiro, 1986, p. 19). Dexter said "*N* spell my grandmama." His grandmother's name is Hele*n* (Dyson, 1984, p. 262). These children's comments about letters show that they did not have the same concepts about letters that more accomplished readers have. Santiago did not think of *S* as a letter, as representing the sound of the letter *S*, or even as part of his name. Instead, he thought of the letter *S* as belonging to him.

Signatures

Just as children learn to name and write alphabet letters and acquire concepts about what alphabet letters are, they also learn to write their names and acquire concepts about what written names are.

Writing Signatures

Children's abilities to write recognizable signatures develop along fairly recognized patterns (Hildreth, 1936). This ability depends on children's growing motor control, their awareness of letter features, and their knowledge of letters as discrete units. Figure 5.6 presents Robert's name writing attempts over a nine-month period while he was in a pre-kindergarten program for four-year-olds. The first example of his signature, produced in early September, was a jagged line. Like Robert's early signatures, many children's initial attempts at writing their names contain no letters at all; they are frequently a single line or shape. Such signatures may reflect that children are relatively unaware that the letters in their names are discrete units.

As children gain practice writing their names and begin to notice written language in environmental print or in their parents' writing, they begin to produce a number of discrete letter-like symbols as a part of their signatures. In the second example of Robert's signature, produced in October, there are five letter-like shapes. These shapes do not include many letter features. In contrast, in the third example of Robert's signature, produced in December, there are again five shapes, but they include many letter features. In fact, this signature has a recog-

Figure 5.6 *Robert's Signatures*

nizable *R* and *o*. Eventually, children include more conventional formations for all the letters in their signatures. They begin to place the letters in order and to include every letter, although at first the letters are likely to be scattered around the page or in scrambled order.

The fourth example of Robert's signature, produced in February, includes a symbol for each letter of his name; the letters are recognizable but not conventionally formed. The letters are in order and written linearly. The fifth and sixth examples, produced in March and May, show his growing control over writing. The letters are conventionally formed, and by May, the writing indicates Robert's growing control over letter size and proportion.

Children's Concepts about Signatures

As children learn to recognize and write their names, their notions about signatures are quite different from those of adults. Ferreiro (1986) described two children's concepts about signatures. One of the children, Santiago, had seen his parents write his name and had heard them read it as ''Santiago'' many times. However, when asked, ''What does it say here?'' about his name, he pointed to the letter *S* and replied, ''This is Santiago's.'' When asked, ''What does it say here'' about the remaining letters, he replied, ''Santiago and daddy has gone to work. Mommy and daddy'' (Ferreiro, 1986, p. 19). As he said this, he ran his finger under the letters in his name. Santiago's comments suggest that he considered only the letter *S* as his signature and that he thought the other letters must be about other people.

The second child Ferreiro described, Mariana, claimed that she could write her name. She wrote five capital letters (*PSQIA*) as she said ''Mariana'' several times. When asked, ''What does it say here?'' about the letters *PS*, she replied, ''Two Mariana.'' When asked, ''What does it say here?'' about the letters *QIA*, she replied, ''Three Mariana'' (Ferreiro, 1986, p. 37). Mariana's comments about her signature reflect that she believed each letter she wrote would say her name.

Santiago's and Mariana's comments about their names illustrate that children do not conceive of signatures as words composed of letters that represent sounds. Their ideas about signatures are interwoven with their concepts of alphabet letters.

Texts

Novice readers and writers learn a great deal about different kinds of texts, and they use this knowledge to create a variety of different texts. In particular, children acquire more knowledge about story texts.

Creating Texts

Novice writers produce many different text forms. Carrie wrote a restaurant check (Chapter 1, Figure 1.3), Ashley wrote a thesis (Figure 5.5), Christopher wrote a story and a grocery list (Figure 5.4), and Courtney wrote a birthday message (Figure 5.1). Later in this chapter we will describe Johanna's birthday list (Figure 5.12) and Jeremy's ''Book of Poems.'' Much of these children's texts is included in their talk as they wrote and in the contexts in which the texts were produced. When we look only at Courtney's writing, it does not appear to be a text. It is apparent that it is a text when we pay attention to her talk, to her actions (she put her writing in an envelope), and to the context (she and her mother were writing birthday cards). It is interesting to note that function plays an important role in novices' creation of texts. Courtney created a birthday message as she participated in the functional activity of sending birthday greetings.

Knowledge about Stories

As novice readers and writers gain more experience with stories, their concept of story changes and becomes more complex. We described several ways that children's concepts of stories become more complex in chapter 4 (see Figure 4.11). One of the most important ways that novices' concepts of stories change is that they begin to understand that events must be related to one another in particular ways in order to form a story. Novices learn two important organizational structures that can be used to link events together in stories: sequence and causal relationships. Novices learn that events in stories occur in sequence and that some events in stories cause other events to occur. They discover that the event of a character falling down while skating is related to the event of scraping a knee—falling down caused the character's knee to become scraped.

When children grasp sequence and causal relations and center their stories around a main character, their concept of stories is similar to an adult's story schema (see the story grammar presented in Chapter 4, Figure 4.10). As children use their understandings of sequence and causal relations to link story events together, they are able to perceive of stories-as-wholes. They seem to be able to recreate a story world in their imagination in which they can consider events "before" and events "after." They consider stories from the perspective of "there and then" (Genishi & Dyson, 1984). Younger children who label objects or actions in each individual picture seem unable to move away from the concrete single event captured in each illustration. They consider stories from the perspective of "here and now." Applebee (1978) called children's ability to step back and view story events as part of a larger whole their assuming the *spectator stance.* They begin to take on the role of a spectator in a story world they create as they share stories with their parents or other adults.

As children gain experience with stories, they begin exploring the imaginary world created by the interaction of a story's reading, other children's responses, and their teacher's talk (Rosenblatt, 1978). Children learn the particular ways that language is used in stories (literary language), the kinds of characters found in stories, and the characteristics of specific kinds of characters (Crago & Crago, 1983; Meek, 1982). Children's awareness of literary language and their ability to enter a story's world is frequently observed in their imaginary play. Three-year-old Nat demonstrated this ability when he called his cereal "porridge" and said, "We are the three bears. My chair's broken" (Voss, 1988, p. 275). Another three-year-old invited her mother to enter her story world soon after they had shared *Three Little Kittens* (Galdone, 1986). Kristen was "cooking" on her play stove. As she slipped on her hot pad mitten, she said, "Oh, Mother dear, Mother dear. My mitten, my mitten here. Hey Mommy, you be the mother."

The Importance of Knowledge about Stories

As children gain more experience with stories, their questions about stories begin to change. Children start asking questions about characters' actions and their motivations. This is illustrated in Figure 5.3. (Martinez, 1983; Yaden & McGee, 1984). These questions would be expected if children's concepts about stories included knowledge of causation.

Children's retellings of stories also begin to change. Novices retell stories by telling a story to accompany the pictures. Their stories may not have much relation to the story text, but they do form a story (Magee & Sutton-Smith, 1983; Sulzby, 1985). However, retellings are not always easy to predict. When children retell favorite stories, they can make use of what was developed over many occasions with the help of a more story-concept-wise adult reader, especially if that reader has an interactive reading style. Figure 5.7 presents a four-year-old's re-

Figure 5.7 *Retelling of* The Very Hungry Caterpillar
(Carle, 1969)

Once upon a time there was a little egg on a leaf. It popped and out came a little caterpillar. One day he was hungry and he ate one apple. He was still hungry. At Sunday he
had two pears. He was still hungry. At Saturday he ate three pineapples and he still hungry. Then he ate four strawberries. He was still hungry so he ate a chocolate piece of
cake, a piece of pear, some sausages, and then he was fat. He made a cocoon and he
pushed his way out. And he became a beautiful butterfly. That's the story.

Figure 5.8 *Ben Tells* Deep in the Forest (Turkle, 1976)

Bear. Bear. Bench. Oh oh. He's eating it. Broke chair. Jumping on the bed. The people.
Crying. Bear. She found him. She chased that bear. Find his mother.

telling of a favorite story *The Very Hungry Caterpillar* (Carle, 1969). This retelling captures much of the story's meanings. However, when children must tell
stories from unfamiliar books, they cannot call on remembered story meaning.
Figure 5.8 presents a four-year-old's story to accompany an unfamiliar wordless
picture book *Deep in the Forest* (Turkle, 1976). Not only was the story unfamiliar, but Ben also told the story to an unfamiliar person. His storytelling consisted
of labeling items and describing actions in each individual illustration. He made
no effort to tie objects or actions into a story-as-a-whole. However, Ben's mother
reported that Ben often told complex stories that were similar to the story text
when he shared books with his younger sister. Ben seemed to use a simpler concept of story to accomplish the difficult task of telling an unfamiliar story
(Hough, Nurss, & Wood, 1987).

While children draw on their concept of story to retell a story, they also
draw on their knowledge of literary language and worlds to create stories (King
& McKenzie, 1988). As children play, draw, write, and sing, they weave characters and events in and out of their familiar story settings. They create their own
stories by changing events and characters or mixing in events and characters
from several different stories. Children's emerging storymaking ability is rooted
in their many experiences with literature.

KNOWLEDGE ABOUT MEANING-FORM LINKS

Novice readers and writers do not make the connection between written language (letters) and oral language (sounds); however, they do explore several
ways that meaning might be linked with written forms. Much of what novice
readers and writers do when they read and write is unconventional; it is not
what more accomplished readers and writers seem to do. We have already discussed some of novice readers' and writers' unconventional ideas about
meaning-form links. We described novices' ideas that alphabet letters directly
symbolize meaning, that only one letter in a signature represents them, or that
each letter in a signature represents their name. Although novice readers' and

writers' concepts about the link between meaning and written form may be un-conventional, their concepts are systematic (DeGoes & Martlew, 1983; Ferreiro & Teberosky, 1982). Novice readers and writers rely on context to link written forms with meaning. This link between meaning and form is called *contextual dependency.*

Contextual Dependency

Clay (1975) called children's dependency on context to link meaning and form the *sign concept.* The sign concept is evident when children use the context of play to construct meaning in their writing and reading. As children pretend to be teacher, they write homework on the chalkboard. While the homework may consist of only jagged lines of writing, still it is intended to be a sign that means something like ''learn your lessons.''

We have shown that novice readers find printed symbols in environmental print meaningful. However, if novice readers were shown words from meaning-ful environmental print symbols written on a card, they would not be able to bring meaning to that print. What novices notice about environmental print is not the printed words by themselves, but rather the colors, styles and shapes of letters, special logo designs, and pictures as a whole. The entire sign or label acts as a symbol or sign that means, for example, *McDonald's* or *pizza man.* First, the sign or label assumes meaning because of the actual context in which it is found. Then, the entire sign or label itself becomes a context that signals mean-ing. Children depend on the whole context of a sign or label and not just the words on the sign or label in order to link a meaning to it.

Another indication of this aspect of children's contextual dependency is re-lated to their name reading (Goodman, 1980). Many parents teach their children to write their names in capital letters. Jerome was taught that *JEROME* was the way his name was written and that it said ''Jerome.'' Later, when his preschool teacher showed him his name printed in upper- and lower-case letters on a card above his cubby (*Jerome*), he denied that *Jerome* was his name. He insisted that his teacher write his name as his mother did. Jerome's actions indicate that he did not realize that the letters in his name could be printed in many different forms and still have the meaning ''Jerome.'' To him, *JEROME* was a unique sym-bol signaling the meaning ''Jerome.''

Novice writers also use the context of a situation to link meanings with their written forms. Jeremy's writing is an example of writing that takes on meaning through the context (Gundlach, McLaney, Scott, & McNamee, 1985, p. 8). One day Jeremy decided to play ''police.'' He enlisted his mother to be the police girl and he was the police chief. She joined in the play by pretending to answer the telephone and take a call about an escaped canary. Jeremy said, ''I'd better write this down.'' He wrote *OE* on his paper. His *OE* became a message some-thing like ''there is an escaped canary'' within the context of taking a telephone call about a missing canary. Jeremy used the context of the canary telephone call to link meaning with his writing.

Moving Beyond Contextual Dependency

Although novice readers and writers primarily depend on the context in which their writing is produced and in which written symbols are found to link meaning and form, some use more than context to link meaning and form. Many researchers have explored children's concepts about the links between meaning and print (Dyson, 1982, 1985; Ferreiro & Teberosky, 1982; Sulzby, 1985). What they found is that not all children's concepts about the relations between meaning and form are alike, that many children's concepts about the relations between meaning and form change as they gain experience using written language, and that children's knowledge of meaning-form links is very complex (Ferreiro, 1986).

Using More Than Context to Link
Meaning and Form in Reading

We will describe three children's responses to a reading task designed to illustrate their concepts about meaning-form links. The task involves asking several questions about a written sentence, *The dog is sitting by his house,* which is accompanied by a picture of a dog sitting by a doghouse. (This task is similar to ones used by Ferreiro & Teberosky, 1982, pp. 53–99.) The sentence is written on two lines (*The dog is sitting* on the first line and *by his house* on the second line).

When Wynell was shown the picture and sentence and asked, "Show me where there's something to read" he pointed to the picture. When asked, "What does it say?" he replied "A dog." When asked, "Where does it say 'A dog'?" he pointed to the sentence. Wynell's responses indicate that he believed both the picture and the printed sentence could convey meaning; in this case they both conveyed the meaning *a dog.* Wynell's responses indicate he was using context alone to link meaning and form; the meaning he found in both the picture and the sentence was related to the context of the picture.

Clay responded to this task in the same way as Wynell, with one important difference. He pointed to the written sentence when asked both "Show me where there's something to read" and "Where does it say 'dog'?" Clay seems to have learned an important new concept about the link between meaning and form; the meaning he found was related to the context of the picture (he thought the sentence said 'dog'), *but he knew that print is what is read.*

Matthew's response to this task illustrates that he is moving even farther away from using context alone to link meaning and form. When asked, "Show me where there's something to read" Matthew pointed to the printed sentence. When asked, "What does it say?" he pointed to the first line and said "dog" and pointed to the second line and said "house." Matthew's response indicates he was still using the context of the picture to determine the meaning of the written sentence, but he was trying to match parts of his orally spoken meaning with parts of the written sentence. He pointed to one part of the sentence and said one word (dog), and pointed to the second part of the sentence and said the second word (house). Matthew's response indicates that he noticed two segments of the written text and realized that the orally spoken meaning must relate to those two segments of written text. (Later, Matthew might notice words as segments or units of text and try to match orally spoken words with word units.)

What is important to note about our descriptions of Wynell, Clay, and Matthew is that novice readers try several links between meaning and form, none of which involves the link expert readers use (the link between letters and sounds).

Using More Than Context to Link Meaning and Form in Writing

We will describe four children's responses to a writing task; their responses illustrate children's knowledge of links between meaning and form in their writing. The task involves asking children to write a story and then read it (Sulzby, 1985).

Figure 5.9 presents Patrick's response. He drew a picture and told his story. His response suggests that he believed drawing could convey meaning in ways similar to writing. His response is similar to Wynell's insistence that both a picture and a sentence can be read. Patrick is probably not confusing drawing with writing. Rather, he may be using context alone to link meaning and form. His picture provides a context for meaning.

This is my house.
My sister and D'Shay
and Marie and Troy
and Rufus and Patrick
live in the house.

Figure 5.9 *Patrick's Story*

Figure 5.10 presents John's response. He wrote three lines of mock cursive writing and then read his story. Figure 5.11 presents Constance's response; she wrote her story entirely in mock letters. John's and Constance's responses indicate they may have concepts about meaning-form links that are similar to Clay's.

I have a dog.
He is big.
He is my best friend.

Figure 5.10 *John's Story*

I like you to visit me.
You are nice.

Figure 5.11 *Constance's Story*

Clay indicated that he knew only print could be read. John's and Constance's stories are conveyed in written form without pictures.

Figure 5.12 presents Johanna's response. This response is remarkable for many reasons. First, Johanna chose not to tell a story, but rather to write a list. Her birthday was a few days away and she wrote a list of things she wanted.

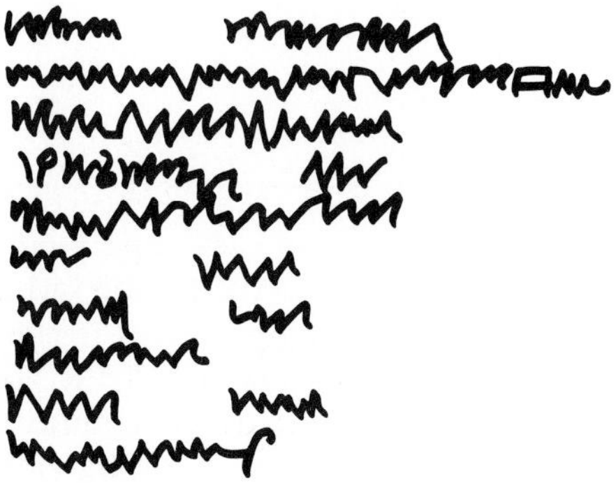

Hoola Hoop
Wishbow kids with a bed
more Mapletown animals
Prince Strongheart
horse for Prince Strongheart
a baby
baby bottles
bonnet
baby clothes
slide

Figure 5.12 *Johanna's Birthday List*

While her list is composed entirely of jagged lines, matching what Johanna said with her jagged lines reveals that Johanna matched one continuous jagged line with one spoken word. Johanna's concept about the meaning-form link is similar to Matthew's; she realized that the written forms she wrote should match with the spoken meaning she intended.

Drawing and Writing

Most novices' written texts are not just composed of drawings without writing (as was Patrick's story) or of writing without drawings (as were Johanna's list and Constance's and John's stories). Instead, their written texts frequently include both drawing and writing. Dyson (1982; pp. 365–366) found that children combined drawing and writing in several ways in their texts. Sherrilynn's text (Figure 5.13) includes a cup of coffee, some houses, a wheel, a golf tee, and the letters *A*, *B*, and *g*. As she wrote, she said, "I wrote some houses, your coffee, an *A* and a *B*, and some other stuff." Her text illustrates that some children draw and write about unrelated things are they create texts.

Figure 5.13 *Sherrilynn's Text*

Lorena's text is presented in Figure 5.14. She said, "This is a dresser" as she pointed to her drawing, and, "This is dresser, too" as she pointed to her writing. Her text illustrates that some children use both drawing and writing to communicate the same meaning. Lorena used her writing to label her drawing.

Andrew drew a picture of himself in a T shirt (Figure 5.15). He said, "I drew the writing on my shirt." Andrew was not trying to communicate a meaning in his writing. Rather, the writing in his text was part of the drawing. He drew the letters on his shirt. Many children draw letters that they see with no intention of using those letters to communicate a meaning.

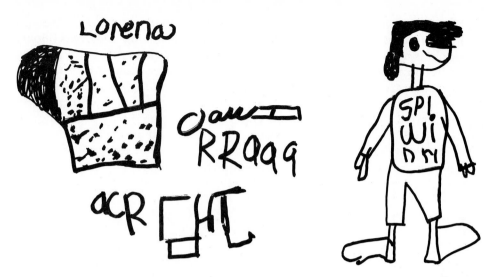

Figure 5.14 *Lorena's Text*   **Figure 5.15** *Andrew's Picture*

Figure 5.16 presents Johanna's picture and story. First, she labeled the objects in her picture, "This is Miss Sharon, Elise, and Mr. K." Then she went on to tell a story, "They have a new baby, Emily. I hope we will babysit Emily. I love Emily Grace." Johanna's writing was more than a label for her drawing; it was a story about the people represented in the drawing.

Given that children so often include drawings with writing and that they read pictures in the same ways that they read print, researchers have wondered whether children differentiate between the two symbolic systems, drawing and

Figure 5.16 *Johanna's Story*

writing. We might suspect that they do not differentiate between drawing and writing. However, the relation between drawing and writing is complex. Some researchers have noticed that children's lines and shapes that they call pictures are different from the lines and shapes that they call writing (DeFord, 1980; Harste, Burke, & Woodward, 1981). This suggest that children notice differences between drawings and writing and that their own drawing and writing reflect these differences. Figure 5.17 presents three-year-old Ryan Patrick's drawing and writing. Careful observation of Ryan Patrick's product suggests that he differentiates between drawing and writing, even though the drawing is not yet representational and the writing is not conventional.

Figure 5.17 *Ryan Patrick's Drawing and Writing*

There are three important characteristics of children's use of drawing and writing. First, it is clear that children's drawings are an important part of their written communications, and teachers can use them to encourage children's writing. Second, the talk that surrounds both drawing and writing is crucial for understanding what children intend to communicate. Third, the talk provides useful information for finding out what children know about written language and how they learn to link meaning and written forms.

Discovering Sounds in Oral Language

Although novice readers and writers do not make the connection between sounds and letters, they do learn something important about oral language which, at a later time, will help them to discover letter–sound relations. Novice readers and writers learn to pay attention to the sounds in oral language. This may sound strange—oral language is composed of sounds. Young children who speak and understand oral language must produce and perceive the sounds of their language. However, they do so without paying much attention to the sounds themselves. They are concerned with the meanings and functions of their speech and not with the sounds used to convey meanings.

Children must be able to hear sounds in words in order to discover the relation between letters and sounds. To write the word *happy*, children must be able to isolate the word *happy* from a stream of oral speech, such as "happy birthday." Then children must be able to isolate sounds within the word *happy*. The ability to isolate the individual sounds in the word *happy* is beyond the abilities of novices. Still, there is one way that some novice readers and writers show that they are learning about spoken sounds; they make up rhyming words.

The ability of novice readers and writers to create rhyming words emerges from their earlier experiences with nursery rhymes and other books with language play. The rhythm created in nursery rhymes highlights and segments speech sounds in a way that conversation does not (Geller, 1983). The syllables *PE ter PE ter PUMP kin EAT er* are naturally separated by the stress in the rhyme. This natural play with language sounds invites children to enjoy the music of language. Children who have listened to nursery rhymes and other books with language play soon begin to play with speech sounds themselves. While four-year-old James was playing with blocks in his preschool room, he muttered "James, Fames, Wames" to himself. James did not know it, but he was attending to the sounds in oral language. This ability will serve him later when he begins to notice that certain letters appear at the same time that certain sounds of language are heard.

In the next section, we will describe what children learn about the functions of written language. Function is the key to novice readers' and writers' literacy learning. Children's involvement in activities that use written language in functional ways provides the base for literacy growth.

KNOWLEDGE ABOUT WRITTEN
LANGUAGE FUNCTIONS

One characteristic of young children is that they want to do whatever they see someone else doing. If Dad is sweeping the porch, his son wants a broom to sweep, too. We find these actions charming. But this willingness, even insistence, on joining in family activities forms a strong foundation for literacy learning. When Dad writes checks to pay bills, at first his son will want a pen and paper so he can join in the activity of writing. Later, his son will want to join in the activity of writing checks to pay bills. Children not only observe adults' reading and writing, but they also participate in using written language, especially in their play. They play "policeman" as Jeremy did, and pretend to write a message about an escaped canary. They play grocery and declare, ". . . the list. Take the list" (Jacob, 1984, p. 81).

Many children from literacy-rich homes go beyond using literacy in their play as Jeremy did in his police play. They use literacy as themes for play. One day Jeremy announced that he was going to make a book (Gundlach, 1985, p. 13). His father suggested that he use some index cards and write his book on the typewriter. After Jeremy had finished typing his cards, he and his father stapled the cards together to make the book. When his father asked him what was in his book, Jeremy replied, "A surprise" (p.13). The next day, Jeremy's father invited him to listen to a radio program of children reading their poetry. After the program, Jeremy asked his mother and father to come into the living room to listen to him read his "Book of Poems." He opened the book he had made the previous day and said, "Page 1." Then he recited a poem that he knew. As he read "Page 2," he could not seem to remember any more poems, so he made up rhyming words and used sing-song intonation. His mother and father applauded his reading.

Jeremy's poetry reading is an example of play using literacy as a theme. Jeremy read by acting out a poetry reading. His parents had an important role in his play; they were willing participants in his enactment (they assumed the role of audience). Because much of what children learn about the functions of written language is supported within the context of family activities, researchers have examined the uses families and communities make of written language. Next, we will discuss the functions of written language in different families and communities.

Family- and Community-Specific Written Language Functions

Children learn what to do with written language as they function as a part of a family that uses written language in particular ways. Naturally, what children know about the functions of written language reflects how written language has been used in their families. In middle-class families, reading and writing are used as a part of daily living. Children in these families participate in these activities as well as observe them. Children communicate among family members and establish friendships through written language (Taylor, 1983). They write and read notes and greeting cards. They write lists of friends to include in clubs.

Lower-class families use print in many of the same ways that middle-class families do. They use reading and writing in daily living routines: for entertainment, for school-related activities, for work and religious obligations, for communication, and for bedtime storyreading events (Anderson & Stokes, 1984). However, there may be differences between the experiences of middle- and lower-class children. Some research shows that middle-class children are more likely to have daily bedtime story routines; lower-class children have fewer of these routines (Anderson & Stokes, 1984). Working-class children are more likely to observe rather than to participate in written language activities (Teale, 1986).

We advise caution about inferring that all children from middle-class families have bedtime story routines or that all children from working-class homes merely observe literacy events. Children have a wide range of literacy experiences in both middle-class and working-class families (Taylor & Dorsey-Gaines, 1987). Most important, we should be careful not to make judgments about what kinds of literacy experiences are best.

The way written language functions within different communities also influences what children learn about reading and writing. Researchers have found that written language functions in different ways in different communities (Heath, 1983; Schieffelin & Cochran-Smith, 1984). In some communities, print is primarily used as a tool for daily living. Written language serves the practical functions of paying bills, providing information about guarantees, and affirming religious beliefs. In other communities, print is also used for recreation and entertainment; people are likely to read for pleasure. Print serves even wider functions in other communities; it provides a means of critically analyzing political, economic, or social issues. It is easy to see that children growing up in these different communities would have different concepts of the functions served by reading and writing.

Because teachers are members of communities that use reading and writing in certain ways, they hold views about why children should be taught to read and write that are influenced by their community's literacy values and beliefs. Most teachers come from professional communities where literacy behaviors are taken for granted. In these communities, written language is viewed as an important source of mental stimulation, learning, and enjoyment (Schieffelin & Cochran-Smith, 1984). Print is viewed as authority; books and other printed materials are used to legitimize experiences and verify information gained through other means. Teachers often unknowingly create classrooms in which such beliefs about written language prevail. Because teachers have their own values and beliefs about literacy, they must be careful not to take them for granted and not to use them to judge others' beliefs and values.

Novices learn how reading and writing are used because they are observers of and participants in reading and writing activities. They learn how reading and writing function within their families and communities. Depending on their experiences, they may learn that reading and writing are used to complete practical daily living tasks like paying the bills. Or, they may learn that reading and writing are important sources of information and authority. The kinds of reading and writing activities in which children participate may vary and what children learn about written language functions may differ accordingly.

Chapter Summary

Novice readers and writers find environmental print meaningful. The contextualized nature of this type of print initially supports children's meaning-making efforts, but novice readers respond to environmental print even when it is not in contexts that clue its meaning. Novice readers make strides in understanding the decontextualized print in stories that are read aloud to them. They learn to construct stories-as-wholes. They learn that stories are more than individual pictures; stories are formed by a causally related series of events. They learn to make inferences and evaluations about characters and events. Novice writers intend for their written symbols to communicate meaning. They often become writers as a part of imaginary play.

Novices learn to recognize, name, and write alphabet letters. They learn that letters can be named, and that letters have features that can be talked about. Novices' concepts of what letters are differ from those of adults. Novice writers learn to write their signatures, but their concepts about signatures are not like those of adults.

Novice readers and writers also learn features of texts. Their writing reflects knowledge of what different kinds of texts look like and their talk about texts reflects an awareness of the content associated with the different kinds of texts. In particular, novice readers and writers develop more complex understandings of the content, language, and organization of stories.

There is one important characteristic of children's early concepts about the link between what they intend to communicate and what they write, and between what they see in print and the meaning they associate with it. Children think written language directly represents meaning through context. This is the concept of contextual dependency. This means that children are dependent on written symbols appearing exactly as they do in context, complete with logo, stylized print, and color in order to link meaning with the written symbol. Children think that pictures and their writing can both represent meaning in the same way. They use the context of their play or an event to link meaning with their writing.

Children gradually begin to focus on written language as conveying meaning differently from drawings or pictures.

They eventually learn that written language can have different forms and still have the same meaning, such as when their name is written in different ways. They eventually learn that the same written language form can have many meanings, such as when they learn that a letter can appear in many names. Learning these concepts moves children along to more complex understandings about the link between meaning and form.

Novices learn how reading and writing are used because they are observers of and participants in reading and writing activities. They learn how reading and writing function within their families and communities. Depending on their experiences, they may learn that reading and writing are used to complete practical daily living tasks like paying the bills; or, they may learn that reading and writing are sources of information and authority. The kinds of reading and writing activities in which children participate may vary, and what children learn about written language functions may differ accordingly.

We add three cautions to our discussion of novice readers and writers. First, we have noted the ages of several of the children we described as novice readers and writers. We believe that many children become novice readers and writers between the ages of two or three. However, children may display knowledge like that of novice readers and writers in one literacy event and knowledge like that of literacy beginners in other events. Many children display novice reading and writing literacy knowledge throughout their preschool years. Many kindergartners and first graders seem to operate with novice reading and writing knowledge. We caution that not all three-, four-, or five-year-olds will be novice readers or writers and that novice reading and writing often does not end at age five.

Second, much of the knowledge we have of young preschoolers' literacy comes from research involving middle-class families. The ages at which many of these youngsters display novice reading and writing may be deceptive; these children have had early and frequent experiences of the kind that would be expected to support early literacy learning. When preschoolers who have not had many literacy experiences gain access to those experiences, they quickly acquire literacy concepts (Mimms, 1988; Morgan, 1987).

Finally, we caution against expecting all children to focus on reading and writing tasks in the same ways (Bussis, Chittenden, Amarel, & Klausner, 1985; Dyson, 1985). Some children seem to be *process-oriented* in their approach to writing (Dyson, 1985). They focus on discovering how written language works. Other children might be *communication-oriented*.

Young children's literacy purposes, interests, and knowledges vary. We believe that one of the most important roles of teachers is their careful observation of children. As three-, four-, and five-year-olds become novice readers and writers, teachers will notice that they acquire an enormous amount of literacy knowledge. Teachers may observe that novice readers and writers:

1. Move from wanting to draw because they observe their parents writing to wanting to write a message because they observe their parents composing. Their talk reflects this, and it changes from, "I draw, too" to "Happy Father's Day. Daddy will like this."

2. Progress from recognizing few environmental signs and labels when they are not in their usual context to recognizing many signs and labels.

3. Change from asking and talking about characters, objects, and actions in illustrations to asking and talking about characters' motives, sequences of events, and causal connections between events in stories. Their spoken language begins to include literary language.

4. Move from not recognizing or writing any alphabet letters to recognizing and writing nearly all alphabet letters.

5. Progress from making marks and lines that have few features to suggest that they are texts to creating a variety of different texts.

6. Move from using only objects as props in their dramatic play (a doctor kit with a flashlight and stethoscope) to using literacy props for reading and writing (reading patient charts and writing prescriptions).

Applying the Information _____

Two literacy events follow. The first event involves two children, Ryan and Rachel, as they talk and write in the writing center of their preschool classroom. The second event involves a four-year-old, David, and his father sharing a bedtime story. Discuss what each child knows about literacy. Describe each child's knowledge of written language meanings, forms, meaning-form links, and functions. Finally, describe how the father supports David's meaning making.

Ryan and Rachel were sitting at the writing table. Ryan began drawing a picture of a little girl (see Figure 5.18). He said, "This is you, Rachel." Then he wrote the word *Rachel* and said, "This is you, too." He wrote the letters *S* and *t* and said, "This is Serita and this is a *t*." He wrote *Rachel* again, "Look, I wrote you again. Now I'm going to write *Marcus*." (He wrote the letter *M*).

Rachel wrote her name (see Figure 5.19) and drew a picture saying, "This is my house and this is me." She wrote the number *4* twice saying, "This is my house number." She wrote the letters *R*, *b*, *u*, and the word *DO*. Then Rachel said, "I want to write to Mrs. Miller" (their teacher). She wrote *I love* on her paper as she looked at the words printed on the big Valentine card displayed on the writing table. Just then, Serita called to her from the block center. Rachel left her writing and went over to the blocks.

David and his father were sharing *Peter and the Wolf* (Prokofiev, 1982). Before his father began reading the story, David asked, "What do you think those are?" as he pointed to the tulip-bulb-like domes commonly seen on Russian buildings that were depicted in the first illustration. His father replied, "Well, I don't know. I think that they're . . . kind of a mosque . . . rooftop. I don't know the name of them exactly." David listened quietly as his father read much of the story. He interrupted his father several times to ask questions such as "Dad, what does shrugged mean?" "What does firmly mean?" and "What does displeasure mean?" Figure 5.20 presents a portion of their interaction near the end of the story.

Figure 5.18 *Ryan's Writing*

Figure 5.19 *Rachel's Writing*

Figure 5.20 *A Portion of David and his Father Sharing* Peter and the Wolf *(Prokofiev, 1982)*

Text is presented in all capital letters.

Illustration:	Three hunters are pulling a wolf on a rope. The wolf seems to be digging his feet in as he is being led along. A grandfather and cat are following behind the wolf.
Father:	There's the old wolf
David:	How could they pull . . . and and he wouldn't eat them?
Father:	You would think that he wouldn't just kind of walk along behind like that. I guess there were just too many of them for him to eat, so he's just walking along.
David:	I think he's trying to pull away
Father:	Yeah, he is, he's kind of dragging because his feet are against the ground
Illustration:	Left page shows the wolf in a cage surrounded by a crowd of people. The right page shows Peter and his Grandfather walking away.
Father:	. . . IF YOU LISTEN VERY CAREFULLY, YOU WILL HEAR THE DUCK QUACKING IN THE WOLF'S STOMACH. FOR THE WOLF IN HIS HASTE HAD SWALLOWED THE DUCK LIVE. quack, quack
David:	Why is she quacking?
Father:	Well, I guess she probably wants to get out
David:	Is it dark in there?
Father:	I think so. Do you remember how dark it was when ah when Burt Dow [referring to the book *Burt Dow: Deep Water Man* (McCloskey, 1963)] was in the whale's stomach?
David:	Yeah
Father:	Probably at least that dark in there . . . in the wolf's stomach.

Going Beyond the Text

Arrange to visit with a family that has a preschooler or visit a preschool or kindergarten. Take a book to share with the preschooler or kindergartner and be prepared to tape record your interaction as you share the story together. Take some paper and markers or crayons and invite the child to draw and write about the story. Record what the child says as he or she draws and writes. Ask the child to write his or her name and everything else he or she can. Invite the child to read what he or she has written. Describe the child's knowledge of written language meanings, forms, meaning-form links, and functions.

References

ALTWERGER, B., DIEHL-FAXON, J., & DOCKSTADER-ANDERSON, K. (1985). Read aloud events as meaning construction. *Language Arts, 62,* 476–484.

ANBAR, A. (1986). Reading acquisition of pre-school children without systematic instruction. *Early Childhood Research Quarterly, 1,* 69–83.

ANDERSON, A. B., & STOKES, S. J. (1984). Social and institutional influences on the development and practices of literacy. In H. Goelman, A. Oberg, & F. Smith (Eds.), *Awakening to literacy* (pp. 24–37). Exeter, NH: Heinemann.

APPLEBEE, A. N. (1978). *The child's concept of story.* Chicago, IL: University of Chicago Press.

BAGHBAN, M. (1984). *Our daughter learns to read and write.* Newark, DE: International Reading Association.

BUSSIS, A. M., CHITTENDEN, E. A., AMAREL, M., & KLAUSNER, E. (1985). *Inquiry into meaning.* Hillsdale, NJ: Erlbaum.

CARLE, E. (1969). *The very hungry caterpillar.* New York: Philomel.

CLAY, M. M. (1975). *What did I write?* Auckland: Heinemann.

COCHRAN-SMITH, M. (1984). *The making of a reader.* Norwood, NJ: Ablex.

CRAGO, M., & CRAGO, H. (1983). *Prelude to literacy: A preschool child's encounter with picture and story.* Carbondale, IL: Southern Illinois University Press.

DeFORD, D. E. (1980). Young children and their writing. *Theory into Practice, 19,* 157–162.

DeGOES, C., & MARTLEW, M. (1983). Young children's approach to literacy. In M. Martlew, (Ed.), *The psychology of written language* (pp. 217–236). New York: John Wiley & Sons.

DICKINSON, D. K., & SNOW, C. E., (1987). Interrelationships among prereading skills in kindergartners from two social classes. *Early Childhood Research Quarterly, 2,* 1–25.

DYSON, A. H. (1982). The emergence of visible language: Interrelationships between drawing and early writing. *Visible language, 16,* 360–381.

DYSON, A. H. (1984). Emerging alphabetic literacy in school contexts: Toward defining the gap between school curriculum and child mind. *Written Communication, 1,* 5–55.

DYSON, A. H. (1985). Individual differences in emerging writing. In M. Farr (Ed.), *Advance in writing research: Vol. 1. Children's early writing development* (pp. 59–125). Norwood, NJ: Ablex.

FERREIRO, E. (1986). The interplay between information and assimilation in beginning literacy. In W. H. Teale & E. Sulzby (Eds.), *Emergent literacy: Writing and reading* (pp. 15–49). Norwood, NJ: Ablex.

FERREIRO, E., & TEBEROSKY, A. (1982). *Literacy before schooling.* Exeter, NH: Heinemann Educational Books.

GALDONE, P. (1986). *Three little kittens.* New York: Clarion.

GELLER, L. G. (1983). Children's rhymes and literacy learning: Making connections. *Language Arts, 60,* 184–193.

GENISHI, C., & DYSON, A. H. (1984). *Language assessment in the early years.* Norwood, NJ: Ablex.

GOODMAN, Y. (1980). The roots of literacy. In M. Douglass (Ed.), *Claremont reading conference* (44th Yearbook) (pp. 1–32). Claremont, CA: Claremont Graduate School.

GOODMAN, Y., & ALTWEGER, B. (1981). *Print awareness in preschool children: A study of the development of literacy in preschool children* (Occasional Paper No. 4). Tucson, AZ: Arizona Center for Research and Development, College of Education, University of Arizona.

GUNDLACH, R., McLANE, J. B., SCOTT, F. M., & McNAMEE, G. D. (1985). The social foundations of children's early writing development. In M. Farr (Ed.), *Advances in writing research: Vol. 1. Children's early writing development* (pp. 1–58). Norwood, NJ: Ablex.

HARSTE, J. C., BURKE, C. L., & WOODWARD, V. A. (1981). *Children, their language and world: Initial encounters with print* (Final Report NIE-G-79-0132). Bloomington, IN: Indiana University, Language Education Department.

HARSTE, J. C., WOODWARD, V. A., & BURKE, C. L. (1984). *Language stories and literacy lessons.* Portsmouth, NH: Heinemann.

HEATH, S. B. (1983). *Ways with words: Language, life, and work in communities and classrooms.* New York: Cambridge University Press.

HIEBERT, E. H. (1978). Preschool children's understanding of written language.

Child Development, 49, 1231–1234.

HIEBERT, E. H. (1981). Developmental patterns and interrelationships of preschool children's point awareness. *Reading Research Quarterly, 16,* 236–260.

HILDRETH, G. (1936). Developmental sequences in name writing. *Child Development, 7,* 291–302.

HOUGH, R. A., NURSS, J. R., & WOOD, D. (1987). Tell me a story: Making opportunities for elaborated language in early childhood classrooms. *Young Children, 43,* 6–12.

JACOB, E. (1984). Learning literacy through play: Puerto Rican kindergarten children. *Research in the Teaching of English, 17,* 73–83.

KING, M. L., McKENZIE, M. G. (1988). Research currents: Literary discourse from a child's point of view. *Language Arts, 65,* 304–314.

LAMME, L. L., & CHILDERS, N. M. (1983). The composing processes of three young children. *Research in the Teaching of English, 17,* 33–50.

LASS, B. (1982). Portrait of my son as an early reader. *The Reading Teacher, 36,* 20–28.

LEAF, M. (1936). *The story of Ferdinand.* New York: Viking Press.

LOMAX, R. G., & McGEE, L. M. (1987). Young children's concepts about print and reading: Toward a model of word reading acquisition. *Reading Research Quarterly, 22,* 219–256.

MAGEE, M. A., & SUTTON-SMITH, B. (1983). The art of story-telling: How do children learn it? *Young Children, 38,* 4–12.

MARTINEZ, M. (1983). Exploring young children's comprehension during story time talk. *Language Arts, 60,* 202–209.

MAYER, M. (1968). *There's a nightmare in my closet.* New York: Dial Press.

McCLOSKEY, R. (1963). *Burt Dow: Deep water man.* New York: Viking Press.

MEEK, M. (1982). *Learning to read.* Portsmouth, NH: Heinemann.

MIMMS, H. (1988). Teacher inquiry in the classroom: "Read it to me now." *Language Arts, 65,* 403–409.

MORGAN, A. L. (1987). The development of written language awareness in Black preschool children. *Journal of Reading Behavior, 19,* 49–67.

PROKOFIEV, S. (1982). *Peter and the wolf* (Trans, M. Calson), New York: Viking Press.

ROSENBLATT, L. M. (1978). *The reader, the text, the poem: The transactional theory of the literary work.* Carbondale, IL: Southern Illinois University Press.

SCHIEFFELIN, B. B., & COCHRAN-SMITH, M. (1984). Learning to read culturally: Literacy before schooling. In H. Goelman, A. Oberg, & F. Smith (Eds.), *Awakening to literacy.* (pp. 3–23). Exeter, NH: Heinemann.

SULZBY, E. (1985). Kindergartners as readers and writers. In M. Farr (Ed.), *Advances in Writing Research Vol. 1: Children's Early Writing Development* (pp. 127–199). Norwood, NJ: Ablex.

TAYLOR, D. (1983). *Family literacy.* Exeter, NH: Heinemann Educational Books.

TAYLOR, D., & DORSEY-GAINES, C. (1987). *Growing up literate: Learning from inner-city families.* Portsmouth, NH: Heinemann.

TEALE, W. H. (1986). Home background and young children's literacy development. In W. H. Teale & E. Sulzby (Eds.), *Emergent literacy: Writing and reading* (pp. 173–206). Norwood, NJ: Ablex.

TURKLE, B. (1976). *Deep in the forest.* New York: E. P Dutton.

VOSS, M. M. (1988). "Make way for applesauce": The literate world of a three year old. *Language Arts, 65,* 272–278.

YADEN, D. B., Jr. (1984). *David's and Jon-Marc's questions about books.* Unpublished manuscript. Atlanta, GA: Emory University.

YADEN, D. B., Jr., & McGEE, L. M. (1984). Reading as a meaning-seeking activity: What children's questions reveal. In J. Niles (Ed.), *Thirty-third yearbook of the National Reading Conference.* Rochester, NY: National Reading Conference, 101–109.

CHAPTER 6

Classroom Support for Novice Readers and Writers

This chapter provides general instructional principles and specific activities that support the literacy learning of novice readers and writers. The activities are designed to encourage children's exploration of written language—its meanings, its forms, its meaning-form links, and its functions. Because we expect that many (but not all) novice readers and writers are preschoolers, the activities are appropriate for nursery school, child care, and preschool settings. They are also appropriate in kindergarten programs and can be adapted for beginning first graders.

The chapter begins with a description of a group of three-year-olds and their teacher, Miss Leslie, as they share books together. A section on general principles about booksharing with young children follows, along with a listing of some booksharing strategies and some activities that might accompany booksharing. Next, we describe a classroom of four-year-olds who have many opportunities to interact with environmental and functional print. A section listing general principles of using environmental and functional print to support children's literacy learning follows. Finally, we highlight the writing activities that occur in these two classrooms, and suggest ways to encourage and support novice writers.

BOOKSHARING AS SUPPORT FOR LITERACY LEARNING

Children learn a great deal from sharing books; they learn strategies for getting the meaning from written language. This section describes using books as part of a literacy-rich classroom.

BOOKSHARING IN MISS LESLIE'S CLASSROOM

Miss Leslie and 6 three-year-olds are gathered for storytime on the rug in their classroom. The children are sitting in a square area bordered by tape on the rug. As she announces storytime, Miss Leslie points to a sign entitled "Storytime" that has a picture of a mother reading to two children. On the sign are clothes-pinned cards with each of the children's names who are to come to storytime: Cory, Echo, Leah, Paul, Laura, and Evan. Miss Leslie points to the names on the chart as she calls each child and reminds them to come to the rug for storytime. As the children approach the rug, she begins to sing one of the children's favorite songs, *Twinkle Twinkle Little Star.*

After she and the children are settled on the rug, Miss Leslie holds up the book *The Little Rabbit Who Wanted Red Wings* (Bailey, 1931). She reads the title, pointing to each word. She reminds the children that she has read this book to them before. The book is about a little rabbit who is not happy with himself and wishes he had what other animals have. The children ask questions and make comments during the booksharing. Miss Leslie reads the text, talks about the illustrations, and asks questions. Figure 6.1 presents a segment of their booksharing.

Figure 6.1 *Miss Leslie and Three-Year-Olds Share* The Little Rabbit Who Wanted Red Wings *(Bailey, 1931)*

Text is presented in all capital letters. Brackets indicate portions of the dialogue that occurred simultaneously.

The illustration depicts a porcupine who is wearing glasses standing under a tree. Little Rabbit is sitting in a large hole in the tree looking at the porcupine.

Miss L: Now who does Little Rabbit see? (points to porcupine)

⌐Child 1: um um its . . .

⊢Child 2: Mr. Beaver

└Child 3: Mr. Porcupine

⌐ Miss L: It does look a little like a beaver. This is Mr. Porcupine.

└ Child 2: (reaches up and touches the picture of the porcupine) Ouch

Miss L: Ooh, I wouldn't want to touch that.

⌐Child 1: Me either

└Child 4: Oh, oh

Miss L: His bristles would stick me. They would stick like a needle.

⌐Child 3: Not me

└Child 2: He sticks you? If you touch him like this? (puts her finger on the picture of the porcupine and pulls it off as if she were stuck)

Miss L: Yes, he might. Those bristles are special. Now I wonder what Little Rabbit likes about Mr. Porcupine?

Figure 6.1 *(continued)*

Child 5: Glasses (porcupine has on glasses)

Child 1: Needles

Child 2: I wouldn't want to touch Porcupine

Miss L: I wouldn't want to touch him either. But what about Little Rabbit? What do you think *he* thinks about those bristles? What do you think Little Rabbit likes?

Child 3: um, um

Child 4: Glasses

Child 1: Needles

Miss L: Do you think *he* wants those bristles? or maybe those glasses? (Laughs, and smiles at Child 1)

Child 1: Yea

Miss L: What would *you* like to have like Mr. Porcupine?

Child 2: I want glasses

Child 5: Bristles

Child 1: I want needles

Miss L: Let's see. (looks at book) WHEN MR. PORCUPINE PASSED BY, THE LITTLE RABBIT WOULD SAY TO HIS MOMMY, (looks at children as if inviting them to join in) "MOMMY, I WISH I HAD (looks back at print) A BACK FULL OF BRISTLES LIKE MR. PORCUPINE'S."

Child 1: Mommy, I want those needles.

Child 5: I wish I had those bristles.

Child 4: I want some bristles.

Child 2: Mommy, . . .

Then Miss Leslie takes a paper bag from beneath her chair. She tells the children that it contains pictures of each of the animals Little Rabbit met in the story. She asks the children to guess what they are. As the children guess, she pulls out a construction paper picture of the animal and asks, "What did Little Rabbit like about this animal?" She clothespins each animal picture to a clothesline hung a few feet off the floor behind her chair. She tells the children they might want to use the animal pictures to retell the story to a friend during center time. She also suggests that they might want to draw pictures and write about the animals or Little Rabbit in the writing center. She shows the children paper cut in the shape of a rabbit's head and tells them that the rabbit-shape paper will be in the writing center for them to use during center time. All the children are then free to select center activities.

Some children go to the block center. One goes to the housekeeping center to join 3 four-year-olds who have been playing there during storytime. The other three children sit down with the animal pictures on the clothesline. They take the construction paper animals and clip each one on the line. As they do this they talk about the story.

Miss Leslie goes to the writing center and announces that she is going to write. Echo and Cory join her, along with three of the four-year-olds who were not participants in the storytime. She says, "I think I'll draw a picture about Little Rabbit. I want to draw his red wings." The children comment on what they might draw, "I'm going to do Mrs. Puddleduck" and "I like trucks." As the children draw and talk, Miss Leslie comments that she is going to write. "I think I'll write that Little Rabbit didn't like the red wings." Cory says, "I'm gonna write, too. I'll write about her feet." Echo says, "I don't want to write." Miss Leslie and the children continue to talk about their pictures and writing. Then Miss Leslie invites the children to read their stories and talk about their pictures.

General Principles of Booksharing

Miss Leslie planned her booksharing with four general principles in mind. They include: (1) knowing and using techniques that encourage interactions during booksharing; (2) recognizing and allowing for individual responses during reading and book activities; (3) planning for children's independent responses and exploration of books and stories; and (4) having a focus for booksharing. The next sections describe these principles in more detail.

Principle 1: Knowing and Using Techniques that Encourage Book Interactions

The first principle of booksharing is that *effective teachers know and use techniques that encourage children's interactions during booksharing.* Miss Leslie clearly demonstrates she is a master story reader. She knows that sharing books with children involves more than reading the text. She has acquired several techniques for encouraging children to be active participants in booksharing. She encourages children to identify characters (she asks, "Now who does Little Rabbit see?" while pointing to the porcupine in the illustration) and to make predictions ("Now I wonder what Little Rabbit likes about Mr. Porcupine?"). She also encourages children to participate by accepting and extending their comments and questions (when Leah touched the picture of the porcupine and said, "Ouch" Miss Leslie commented, "Ooh, I wouldn't want to touch that. His bristles would stick me. They would stick like a needle"). She uses questions that are intended to help children identify with story characters ("What would you like to have like Mr. Porcupine?"). She also provides information that will help children understand words used in the story. (Miss Leslie commented that the porcupine's bristles "would stick like a *needle*" to clarify the meaning of the word *bristles* used in the story text.) She also recognizes all of the children's responses—even when they deviate from the story text. Miss Leslie acknowledged the prediction that Little Rabbit wanted Mr. Porcupine's glasses even though that was not a part of the story.

Miss Leslie uses gestures to help children understand the story. She points to characters and objects in the illustrations as she talks about them or reads text related to them. She uses her voice to help children understand the story. She looks at the children frequently and uses facial expressions to heighten interest in the story. Figure 6.2 summarizes these booksharing techniques, which are an extension of techniques presented in Chapter 4 in Figure 4.15. One way teachers can fine tune their booksharing techniques is to tape record and analyze a booksharing event with their children. They can use the suggestions presented in this chapter and in Figure 6.2 as a guide for self-reflection about booksharing.

An important technique used in booksharing is encouraging children to predict events and outcomes. As children listen to the story text and examine illustrations, they will learn to monitor their predicting efforts by evaluating or confirming their predictions. Tompkins and Webeler (1983) suggest following a three-step cycle of sampling, predicting, and confirming as an effective booksharing technique. Teachers can encourage children to participate in this cycle by talking about the illustrations and text (sampling), asking, ''What do you think will happen now?'' (predicting), and then asking, ''Did we make a good guess?'' (confirming). This cycle is analogous to the Directed Listening-Thinking Activity (modeled after the Directed Reading-Thinking Activity; Stauffer, 1980).

Effective teachers adapt their booksharing techniques to meet the needs of their children. Some young novice readers and writers have had few booksharing experiences; therefore, teachers will spend more time telling the story and talking about the illustrations than they will reading the story text. Other novices have had extensive booksharing experiences; therefore, teachers will spend

Figure 6.2 Guidelines for Booksharing

The Teacher:

Interweaves text reading with asking questions and making comments.
Asks children questions about characters and objects in pictures.
Asks children to predict.
Asks questions that help children identify with characters and actions in the story
 (''What would YOU do . . .'').
Makes comments about characters and actions in pictures and story.
Explains text words and concepts.
Makes comments about relations between the story and real life.
Predicts actions and outcomes.
Makes statements about personal reactions to the story.
Uses gestures.
Points to objects and characters in pictures.
Varies voice to indicate character dialogue.
Answers children's questions.
Acknowledges children's comments by commenting or further questioning.
Extends children's questions and comments by providing additional information.

more time reading and commenting on the story's text. Although all teachers will want to take time to comment on and discuss the language of stories, they do not need to simplify text language as they read books to children. Fox (1985) found that even three-year-olds tolerate uncertainty about the meaning of unfamiliar words in stories they particularly enjoy. As they learn the meanings of words through repeated booksharing opportunities, children will begin to use the language of stories as they retell the stories, tell original stories, and later write stories (Fox, 1985; McConaghy, 1985).

Principle 2: Allowing for Individuality

The second principle of booksharing is that *effective teachers acknowledge children's different literacy needs and responses to literature by planning small group activities and allowing children to choose from among a variety of activities.* Miss Leslie did not read to all of the children in her classroom as a large group activity, although she may do this at times. She has found that the six children she called together will comment more about stories when they are in smaller groups. She also has included two children in the group whose oral language is more mature than the other children's. Miss Leslie believes children learn much from interacting with other children whose abilities are slightly more mature than their own.

In addition to planning activities that she believes fit the needs of children, Miss Leslie also allows the children in her preschool class freedom of choice. She knows that children have individual preferences for and responses to books and activities. She knows which books her children enjoy and she reads them frequently. When she discovers a book she has selected is uninteresting to the children (they wiggle right off the rug), she does not insist that they sit still and listen. Rather, she substitutes an old favorite and tries another book the following day. Children are allowed free choice of center activites. She entices children to join in activities they may be reluctant to select on their own. Miss Leslie encourages some children to write by going to the writing center herself and offering an open invitation to the children to join her there. She welcomes children who were not in the story sharing group to the writing center.

Principle 3: Planning for Independent Booksharing

The third principle of booksharing is that *effective teachers encourage children's independent interactions with books through literature response activities and daily Booktime.* Miss Leslie provides children with these opportunities by having a library center (see Chapter 3 for a description of library centers) well stocked with books and literature props. She uses literature props during booksharing and encourages children to use these props during center time.

Miss Leslie places special literature props in boxes to stimulate children's dramatic response to literature through play. These *literary prop boxes* include

props designed to encourage children's becoming characters from favorite stories. In the *Little Rabbit Who Wanted Red Wings* literary prop box, Miss Leslie
gathered several pairs of rabbit ears (made from headbands and construction
paper), acorns, glasses, several pairs of rubber boots, a mirror, a pair of red wings
(made from construction paper attached to an old vest), several head scarves, a
toothbrush, a bowl and spoon, and two fur vests. She placed an extra copy of
the book in the prop box along with the other props. Children are encouraged
to use the props to act out the story or create their own stories.

Miss Leslie uses Booktime as a way of encouraging independent interaction
with books. (Chapter 3, Figure 3.14 provides suggestions for using Booktime
with preschoolers and kindergartners.)

Principle 4: Having a Booksharing Focus

The fourth principle of booksharing is that *effective teachers have a focus for
their booksharing which includes enjoyment as well as learning about written
language meanings, learning about written language forms, learning about
links between meaning and form, and learning about written language functions.* The first and most important focus for booksharing is enjoyment (Holdaway, 1979). The focus of simply enjoying stories should never be sacrificed in
a rush to help children learn other aspects about reading and writing. A similar
focus is to allow and encourage children's responses to books and stories (Hickman, 1981). Children's responses to literature include laughing, empathizing
with a character's emotions, and rejecting stories (Tchudi, 1985). Children's responses to stories emerge in their art and play. Teachers can acknowledge all of
these responses.

Teachers can plan for other focuses in booksharing as well. The segment of
booksharing presented in Figure 6.1 illustrates that Miss Leslie planned to focus
on at least two additional aspects of written language that she wants her students
to learn. First, she focuses on meaning. She wants the children to notice that
certain features of each of the animals in the book are particularly important.
Second, she focuses on the language of text and on the text itself. She expects
that because the story *The Little Rabbit Who Wanted Red Wings* is a favorite
story, some of the children might remember parts of the text.

Miss Leslie signals her focus on meaning—learning about relevant animal features—with comments and gestures during the booksharing. She encourages
much discussion about the porcupine's bristles. She also has planned the story
clothesline activity. This activity requires children to recall which animals are
included in the story and to name one of their features (for example, "bristles").

The second focus on text and text language is evident in the children's responses; some of the children repeat the text as Miss Leslie reads it. Another way
Miss Leslie helps the children focus on text is through the writing center activity.
She writes and she invites children to write and read their writing. Miss Leslie
knows that as the children watch her write and as they write on their own, they
will discover much about written language.

Developing a Booksharing Focus

One way to plan a focus for booksharing is to use the four written language knowleges—meaning, form, meaning-form links, and function. The first and most important focus for sharing books with children is that they enjoy the experience and have many opportunities to respond personally to literature. But because children will ask for books to be read again and again, there will be many opportunities to help children learn about written language.

Focus on Meaning

One way meaning is created is through talk about illustrations. Discussing what is pictured in the illustrations helps children understand story meanings and learn about the world. Miss Leslie used illustrations as one way of enriching her children's knowledge of porcupines and their bristles. She pointed to the bristles in the illustrations and used the details of the illustrations to help explain porcupine quills.

Another way meanings are expanded is by talking about words in the story text. Children's literature is a rich source of interesting new vocabulary. Miss Leslie's children spent considerable time talking about the word "rubbers" as they looked at the illustration of Little Rabbit talking to Mrs. Puddleduck, who is pictured wearing rubbers.

Sometimes the dialogue might seem to get off track. During a sharing of *The Little Rabbit Who Wanted Red Wings,* one of the children noticed that the porcupine was wearing glasses. Later, this led to a long discussion about whether animals really wear glasses and why Mr. Porcupine was wearing glasses. This feature of the procupine was not the one that Little Rabbit admired about Mr. Porcupine, but discussing it broadened the children's understandings of things that can happen in stories and things that can happen in real life.

Sharing several books which have a common theme can often enrich meanings more effectively than single books. A mixture of fiction and informational books deepens children's understandings. Real experiences that are linked to book experiences also enhance meaning making. Soon after reading the Little Rabbit story, Miss Leslie introduced *The Tale of Peter Rabbit* (Potter, 1902). Leah's grandfather brought in two baby rabbits to show the children. The class enjoyed learning about different kinds of rabbits by sharing *The Bunny Book* (Scarry, 1965). Then Echo brought one of her books, *Little Bunny Follows His Nose* (Howard, 1971).

All books provide opportunities for children to explore story meaning and to expand their knowledge of the world, but wordless picture books are particularly effective for expanding children's meaning making (see Chapter 3, Figure 3.2 for a list of wordless picture books). Because the illustrations in these books are so detailed, they naturally encourage much discussion. Children enjoy telling and retelling their own stories to accompany wordless books.

Focus on Form

There are at least two kinds of focus on form. One concentrates on the story form. Children are helped to develop a more complex concept of story. The other focus on form centers on developing children's knowledge about written language itself—that text is read, that text is composed of words, that words are formed from letters, that letters have names, and so on. This focus helps children develop metalinguistic ability and language to talk about written language.

Focus on concept of story.   Children's concept of story is their knowledge of how stories are organized. Children's experiences listening to and responding to stories help them build these concepts. Novice readers and writers may not have a complex concept of story. Some children may still view each illustration in a story as a separate and interesting picture; they do not connect each illustration's action to the story-as-a-whole. Effective teachers can help children strengthen their concepts of stories by sharing stories so that children focus on the story-as-a-whole. They help children move beyond understanding what is pictured in each illustration to understanding how the events in each illustration are linked. Many of the booksharing strategies discussed in the preceding section (focus on meaning) can be used to help children understand stories-as-wholes. The sampling, predicting, and confirming cycle is particularly effective.

Another way that teachers help children develop more complex concepts about stories is to help them discover aspects that are common to all stories. Teachers can ask questions or make comments that will help children identify *settings,* identify *characters,* discover character *motivations* (why characters act as they do), predict *events,* and think about *causes and effects.* One way teachers might help children learn about story components is to center activities around five story concepts presented in Figure 6.3 (Hoskisson & Tompkins, 1987; McGee & Tompkins, 1981; Tompkins & McGee, 1989). There are many activities that lend themselves to helping children discover these concepts. They involve informal drama, role playing, art, and oral language experiences. Figure 6.3 also presents sample activities for each of the five concepts about stories.

Focus on written forms.   Novice readers and writers begin to notice aspects of the text, such as particular letters (the first letter of names) and aspects of the illustrations, such as details or style of illustrations (Kiefer, 1988). Novices learn features of words, such as that print is read from left to right, top to bottom, and front to back. They learn that the left page is read before the right page, and they learn such concepts as print has "lines" of text. They refine their concepts of words, letters, and story texts.

One of the easiest ways to demonstrate many of these concepts is to read from Big Books (Holdaway, 1979). Big Books are enlarged copies—approximately 20 inches by 30 inches in size—of literature selections. Many publishing companies now sell Big Book versions of some of their popular books. Both the illustrations and print are large. As they read aloud to children, teachers can

Figure 6.3 *Activities for Developing Concepts about Stories*

Story Concept	Example Activities
1. Characters are the animals and people in the story.	a. Have children draw, paint, or make characters in clay. b. Make a three-page book by having children draw and dictate what character looks like, does, and says. c. Make a book of ''Story Characters I Know.'' Have children draw and dictate characters' names.
2. Stories take place in different places, times, and types of weather, called settings (Lukens, 1986).	a. Have children identify different places characters go in the story. b. Have children identify changes in weather in the story. c. Have children decide whether settings are real or make-believe. d. Make a list of ''Story Places I Have Visited.''
3. Characters in stories have problems; they do many things to try and solve their problems.	a. Compose a ''Problem Book'' by listing the problems of story characters and children characters. b. Act out the story using story props. c. Have children suggest other methods of solving the character's problem. d. Use a story line to retell the story. e. Use a flannel board to tell the story. f. Play a guessing game where teacher describes a problem and children guess the name of the character.
4. Some events in stories happen over and over and some words in stories are said again and again (Tompkins & McGee, 1989).	a. Use story line to retell the story, emphasizing repeating words. b. Act out story emphasizing repeating events and words. c. Make a list of repeated events. d. Make a ''Big Book'' of the story. e. Compose a story using the structure but adding new content (Tompkins & McGee, 1989).
5. Stories have a beginning that tells about characters, a middle that tells what characters do to solve problems, and an ending that tells the problem's solution (Hoskisson & Tompkins, 1987).	a. Make a four-page booklet with one page each for title, beginning, middle, and end; children should draw pictures and dictate story. b. Make a ''The End'' book. Children can dictate endings to favorite stories. c. Use three shoe boxes to make a story train as shown here. Make pictures of

Figure 6.3 *(continued)*

Story Concept	Example Activities
	the event in the beginning, middle, and end of the story. Have children put pictures in the train and tell about the story.

Adapted from McGee, L. M., & Tompkins, G. E. (1981). The videotape answer to independent reading comprehension activities. *The Reading Teacher, 34,* 430–431. Reprinted with permission of the International Reading Association.

naturally draw attention to the print and demonstrate concepts about print as they underline text. (Combs, 1987; Heald-Taylor, 1987). Because a group of children can easily see the printed text, they can talk about letters and words. As they hear the text and see the text, children will also notice the link between the text and what teachers read.

Holdaway (1979) has long recognized the value of Big Books and has recommended that teachers (and older children) make their own Big Books of favorite stories. The method of binding books described in Chapter 3 can easily be adapted to making hardbound copies of large-sized books. Teachers who make their own Big Books will want to select stories that children frequently request. The story should be short with only a few lines of text per page. Examples of books appropriate for teacher-made Big Books are *Brown Bear, Brown Bear* (Martin, 1983), and *It Didn't Frighten Me* (Goss & Harste, 1981). These are favorites of young children, they have few words to a page, and illustrations are easily made to accompany the text. Pattern books make excellent Big Books. (See Chapter 3, Figure 3.3 for a list of pattern books).

To make a Big Book, copy the text so that each page in the Big Book matches each page in the original book. Use paint, chalk, markers, crayons, or any other media to illustrate the book. It is not important that the illustrations in the Big Book be exact duplicates of those in the original story. Creative teachers produce illustrations that their young children enjoy as much as the original illustrations. Once Big Books are made, they should frequently be included in booksharing activities.

Focus on Meaning-Form Links

Novice readers and writers know that written language is related to meaning, but they have not yet discovered that written language is related to spoken language. Providing activities that clearly link written and spoken language helps children move in this direction. There are three kinds of activities that support children's discoveries of the link between spoken and written language: rhyming-word activities, memorizing text activities, and alphabet book activities.

Rhyming-word activities.   Playing with language and its sounds is fun for everyone. Teachers can initiate play with language sounds in many ways. They can make up nicknames for children through rhyming (''James Fames'' or ''Sue Blue'') or they can recite nursery rhymes or poems. There are many books that feature rhyming as an important feature (see Chapter 3, Figure 3.5). These books naturally draw children's attention to the sounds of language. We do not recommend that teachers read these books and then ask children to recall rhyming words; rather, we suggest that teachers read these books with an ear to enjoying the play on language. *The Hungry Thing* (Slepian & Seidler, 1967) lends itself nicely to language play. In this story, a monster-like creature comes to town wearing a sign that says ''Feed me.'' The townspeople do not know what to feed it when it asks for ''schmancakes.'' A little boy saves the day by thinking that ''schmancakes sound like fancakes sound like pancakes.'' Children can dramatize this story by taking turns being the monster, the townspeople, and the little boy. They can make up lists of funny things the monster says he will eat and things he really wants to eat.

Memorized-text activities.   One way that children begin to discover the link between spoken and written language is by memorizing books (Hoskisson, 1975; Schickedanz, 1978). Once children know the text of a story, they can begin exploring print. They begin to connect what they are saying as they tell the story with the printed text. Although most novices do not go that far, they can begin by memorizing some of the text language of favorite stories they have shared repeatedly. Pattern books are often the first books children memorize (Bridge, 1986; Rhodes, 1981).

Fortunately, children love to hear favorite stories again and again (Yaden, 1988). Teachers are not surprised when their children ask for a favorite book to be read every day for a week. Children should have many opportunities to hear favorite books frequently. For older preschoolers and kindergartners, teachers can plan daily booksharing events where more than one book is shared. Holdaway (1979) suggested that teachers begin a lesson by sharing a favorite story. This can be done with a Big Book version of the story. Often these Big Books will be pattern stories. Since the children will be familiar with the story, teachers can help them focus on written language form by pointing to the text as they read. To keep interest high, children can act out the story or retell the story using story props. After sharing a favorite book, teachers can share a second book, a new story. Here the focus would be on meaning and on enjoying the story.

Alphabet book activities.   Reading alphabet books provides much information for children's learning about letters and sounds (see Chapter 3, Figure 3.6 for a list of alphabet books). Because most alphabet books show several words demonstrating a letter's sound, much information about the link between letters and sounds is presented without direct instruction about letter sounds. Although novice readers and writers are not yet ready to have direct instruction in phonics, they can benefit from experiences that demonstrate letter–sound relationships.

Children can make their own alphabet books by paying attention to print, rather than to sounds. They can cut familiar words such as logos for Coke, McDonald's, or Pampers from magazines and group them on the pages of an alphabet book by initial letters. Then, as the teacher reads class-composed alphabet books, children will hear the letter sounds. Children who are ready to learn the letter–sound link will discover it for themselves.

Focus on Function

There are many kinds of books that children also enjoy, such as concept books, informational books, biographies, autobiographics, and diaries. There are many other reference books including cookbooks, how-to-do-it books, atlases, and almanacs of interest to children. Teachers include these books in booksharing activities to illustrate the many different uses for reading. The fact that these books are often needed to provide information for other classroom activities illustrates that written language can provide information. As part of an "All about Me" unit, children can bring family photo albums to share. These albums illustrate how books communicate over time and distance. As part of a cooking activity, teachers can read a recipe from a cookbook; reading recipes demonstrates how written language can aid memory.

USING ENVIRONMENTAL AND FUNCTIONAL PRINT TO SUPPORT LITERACY LEARNING

Using environmental and functional print in preschool classrooms offers many opportunities for supporting children's literacy learning (McGee, 1986; Roskos, 1988).

A description of the environmental and functional print activities that take place in Mrs. Miller's preschool classroom follows. Then, we discuss five general principles for using environmental and functional print with novice readers and writers.

Environmental and Functional Print in Mrs. Miller's Classroom

Mrs. Miller's classroom is organized around several centers of activities. One large area is sectioned off with several bookshelves. This area is next to a bulletin board and is used for whole group activities. In the middle of the room is the writing table with a rolling cart nearby that holds materials for the center. There are two other tables in the room; each is partitioned by shelves or other furniture. One table is the game center and the other is the art center. There are several other small areas created by the arrangement of shelves and furniture. Inside three of these small centers are rugs and pillows, and books focusing on a theme ("Books about Three," "Bear Books," and "ABC Books"). There is also a home center, a McDonald's Center, and a science and math discovery center.

By midmorning, children are working and playing at nearly every center. Two children are on the rug in one of the book centers. They are looking at several books together, commenting about the pictures, and talking about the stories. Then they take a paper bag that has their name written on it from a display box on the nearby shelves. They look at the coupons, paper bags, and fronts cut from food boxes that they have taken from their bags. One child gets a doll from the home center, puts it in her lap, and points to each of the items. She reads to her doll by saying a word or two for each item.

Four children are at the McDonald's center. The center is made from a puppet theater to which Mrs. Miller has attached a sign and menu. Inside the theater are empty containers for hamburgers and French fries. Two children are behind the counter in the center. Both have on hats worn by employees at McDonald's. One child is writing on an order pad and the other is pretending to put a McDLT® in a container. Two children are standing in front of the counter. One is dressed in a hat and heels from the home center. She is "mama." She asks "baby" what he wants to eat and then orders. The child taking orders announces, "That will be 10 dollars." "Mama" looks in her purse for money and pays her bill.

Two children are at the writing center. A number of menus and placemats from local restaurants are displayed at the center. Also displayed are several menus composed by children. Some menus have pictures cut from magazines; some have children's mock letters or mock cursive writing; some have words children have copied from menus or newspapers; and others were written and drawn by parent volunteers. One of the menus on display was composed by Mrs. Miller. It is titled "Miller's Meals" and consists of a drawing of people eating, cut-out pictures of food from the food section of the newspaper, and words. One of the children at the center is drawing and writing a menu. She announces, "I'm going to have ice cream" and draws a picture of a double dip cone. The other child comments, "I like ice cream, too. Maybe I'd better write ice cream. People might want ice cream on their cake."

Two children are in the game center. They play for several minutes with Legos® and other small manipulative toys in the center. Then they remove two puzzles from the game shelf. The puzzles consist of boxes of brownie and cake mixes. Inside each box are pieces cut from the fronts of identical boxes. The children spread the cut-up puzzle pieces on the table. They put the puzzles together by looking at the pieces and then placing them on top of the boxes where they match. They talk together as they complete the puzzles, "I like chocolate. I could eat a whole box of these."

Two other children come to the game center and sit on the floor near two large cardboard boxes. A large alphabet letter is painted on the front of each of the boxes (*L* on one and *K* on the other). Attached to one of the boxes is a plastic bag containing several *L*'s and *K*'s that have been cut from construction paper and laminated. The two children sort the letters by placing them inside the large cardboard boxes. As they sort the letters, they say, "I'll be the *L* and you be the *K*. I know whose letter *K* is—Kelita's."

Tammy and Jonathan are painting at easels in the art center. Two index cards are clothespinned to the top of each easel; one card is on top of the other. Tammy's and Jonathan's names are on the top index cards on their easels. When they finish painting, they will unclip their name cards and take them to the bulletin board in the whole group area where a small poster says "I painted today." They will clip their name cards to the poster. When their name cards are removed from the easels, the two bottom cards will tell who can paint text.

One child is in the science and math discovery center. Included in this center is a chart divided into two segments, which are entitled "No TV Last Night" and "TV Last Night." The first title is accompanied by a picture of a TV with a big X over it. The second title is accompanied by a picture of a TV. Under each title some squares of paper have been pasted. Many squares have children's names written on them. Most of the squares are pasted under the "TV Last Night" title. Jermain writes his name on a square of paper and pastes it under the "TV Last Night" title. Displayed on the bulletin board in the center is a similar chart that the children completed the day before. Under this chart are two sentences, "Two children saw no TV Monday night. Ten children saw TV Monday night."

Three children are in the home center. Two children decide to cook a meal for their babies using empty food containers and plastic food in the center. One child says, "I think I'll cook some chicken. Let me look up a good recipe." She opens a cookbook on one of the shelves in the center and begins looking through the pages. Another child is sitting in a rocking chair looking at magazines. Nearby, Mrs. Miller steps into a telephone booth made from a large box. She looks up a number in the telephone book (class telephone book with each child's name and telephone number). She says, "Ring. Ring. Is Melody home?" The child in the rocking chair says, "I'll get that " and answers a toy phone in the center. She says, "Melody is not here. Can I take a message?" She writes on a tablet near the phone and then says, "I'll give her the message. Bye-bye."

General Principles of Using Environmental and Functional Print

The focus in Mrs. Miller's classroom is not on learning to read specific words from environmental and functional print; it is on using print in functional ways. Children are readers and writers in this classroom; they use environmental and functional print to find meaning in reading and to bring meaning to writing. Environmental and functional print are used as tools for helping children discover knowledge about written language.

The environmental and functional print activities in Mrs. Miller's classroom were carefully planned so that children could discover more about the uses of written language, the kinds of meanings found in different types of print items, and the forms of written language found on familiar print. In the following sections, we will describe the activities planned to help children discover more about each kind of knowledge about written language. Our discussion will be organized around five principles for using environmental and functional print to support novice readers' and writers' literacy learning. The first two principles highlight children's learning about written language functions. The next two principles highlight children's learning about written language meanings. The last principle highlights children's learning about written language forms.

Principle 1: Integrating Environmental and Functional Print into Classroom Activities and Routines

The first principle is that *effective teachers integrate reading and writing of environmental and functional print into classroom activities and routines* (Taylor, Blum, & Logsdon, 1986). Mrs. Miller plans many experiences that involve print use, provides many opportunities for children to write their names in functional ways, and uses functional print in classroom routines.

Integrating print and experience. Many of the activities that preschoolers, kindergartners, and first graders engage in naturally can involve written language. Cooking is a favorite activity of all children. Hot plates, toaster ovens, or frying pans can be used (with close adult supervision) in most classrooms. Reading and writing are a natural part of cooking activities. Children can consult cookbooks for recipes, compose grocery lists to make sure the proper ingredients will be on hand, read labels to make sure correct sizes and quantities are selected, and read recipes as the dish is prepared. Some teachers write recipes on large chart paper and use a chart stand for a class cookbook. Snapshots of the children taken as they prepare and eat their dish can add to the pleasure of cooking activities. These pictures, along with captions dictated by the children, can be attached to recipe charts.

Field trips offer numerous opportunities for functional reading and writing. A trip to the zoo suggests using a map to mark the route the class will follow. The class can consult a *TV Guide* to see if any shows will feature zoo animals. They can locate the telephone number of the zoo in the telephone book (the teacher will want to call the zoo and check on the hours and days the zoo is open). Children can dictate letters inviting parents to accompany the class and the replies can be read aloud. Children can also dictate thank you letters to the zoo tour guide.

Written language can be integrated into nearly any activity (Taylor, Blum, & Logsdon, 1986). If the pet goldfish dies, the class can read and write obituaries. When a classmate has a new brother or sister, the class can compose congratulatory cards or birth announcements. Teachers need only to react to everyday occurrences with a literacy activity to show the power of written language.

Using name writing in functional ways. When children are allowed access to favorite activities by seeing their names in print, they quickly learn that print conveys important information. Mrs. Miller notifies children that they may paint by posting their names on the easel. She also keeps track of who has painted and who still needs a turn with her "I have painted" poster. Name writing is used as a record of many kinds of activities. When one child brought a pet hamster to school for a week, the children signed a list titled "I visited Sammy and observed him." Figure 6.4 presents a list that Mrs. Miller's children signed indicating that they had been class leader. Although many of the signatures are not yet conventional, the list served an important function in the classroom.

Figure 6.4 *"I Have Been Leader"*

Using print in classroom routines. There are many kinds of charts that are routinely used in classrooms. Many teachers use an attendance chart, a chart assigning classroom jobs, or a chart of the daily schedule. Teachers need to plan carefully so that children will use these charts purposefully. Instead of assigning classroom jobs on a weekly basis, teachers can change the job chart daily (Schickedanz, 1986). In this way, children must pay attention to the print on the chart each day in order to know when their names will appear.

Another routine that takes place in many early childhood classrooms involves using the calendar. Mrs. Miller combines calendar and name-reading activities in her opening exercises. Figure 6.5 shows the bulletin board where she keeps her "name tree" and calendar. Each month Mrs. Miller writes the children's names on specially shaped cut-outs. (In September she uses a school-house shape and in October she uses a pumpkin shape.) The calendar is a large sheet of paper with squares ruled for each day of the month.

To begin the name and calendar activities, Mrs. Miller brings out a basket in

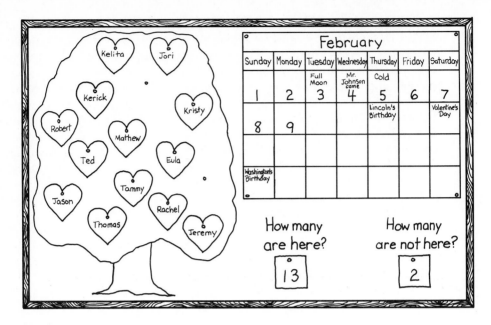

Figure 6.5 Mrs. Miller's Name Tree and Calendar

which she places all the shapes with the children's names. She shows each shape, reads the name, and asks that child to hang the shape on the tree. Later in the year, Mrs. Miller shows the name and the children read it. Still later, Mrs. Miller spells the names and has the children guess the names.

When all the children's names are hung on the tree, they count "how many are here." They count "how many are not here" by counting the names left in the basket. Next, the children count the number of days in the month and one child is selected to write the number of the date. Mrs. Miller always marks special days such as holidays or field trips at the beginning of the month, and the children count the number of days until a special date. Although counting days until special events and naming the days of the week are a part of Mrs. Miller's activities, she realizes that the calendar's real purpose is to help children learn time concepts (Schickedanz, 1986). Therefore, Mrs. Miller also gathers her children at the calendar for closing activities. She frequently writes a message on the calendar, such as "We made chocolate cookies" or "Mr. Howard visited" or "Disney movie on TV tonight." Children are often invited to dictate messages for the calendar. At the end of the month, the children review the month's activities by reading calendar records.

Labeling objects is another frequent practice in preschool and kindergarten rooms. This practice began as a way of helping children notice the link between spoken and written language, but because the labels are not used by the children for any real purpose, their value is often questionable. One way to make labeling classroom objects and toys more effective is to have tickets for play (Raver & Dwyer, 1986). Children who want to go to the block center during center time need to get a ticket with the word *blocks* written on it. They can identify words on a ticket by matching the word on a ticket with the word on the center label.

Principle 2: Encouraging Dramatic Play as a Way of Learning Written Language

The second principle is that *effective teachers use dramatic play to provide children with experiences using reading and writing functionally*. Mrs. Miller realizes that children get ready to take on important adult roles as they try out being "mama" or "doctor" in dramatic play. They can also try out roles in which they read and write environmental and functional print in dramatic play (Roskos, 1988). Mrs. Miller plans her dramatic play centers so that they will support reading and writing.

The home center is one area of dramatic play in Mrs. Miller's classroom. In it she places not only pots and pans, dolls and clothes, and table and chairs, but also food boxes, a telephone book, magazines, and newspapers. Later on, the home center will also include several file boxes filled with coupons and a box of notepaper and pencils. Mrs. Miller calls these specially prepared dramatic play centers *dramatic-play-with-print* centers.

Dramatic-play-with-print centers. Mrs. Miller plans to set up many dramatic-play-with-print centers such as the McDonald's center that will change throughout the year depending on her instructional themes. She begins with centers she knows children are familiar with. Most children have gone to fast-food restaurants and to grocery stores, so these are her first dramatic-play-with-print centers.

There are many dramatic-play-with-print centers teachers can make (Schickedanz, 1986; Roskos, 1988). Figure 6.6 describes dramatic play and print props that can be used to create several of these centers. If classrooms are not large enough to permit a dramatic-play-with-print center, teachers can place the props in boxes. Children can take the boxes and set up their play in any open space in a classroom.

Using dramatic-play-with-print centers. Mrs. Miller carefully prepares her children for these centers. On the day that she introduces a center, she uses whole group time to orient the children to the center. They discuss what happens, for example, at McDonald's. She shows the children the dramatic play and print props and they discuss how the props might be used. Mrs. Miller and two or three children role play with the center props. Several children have opportunities to play with Mrs. Miller. Later, while the children play in the center during center time, Mrs. Miller occasionally joins in. She realizes that children will think of many ingenious ways to use props in their dramatic play and that they should have plenty of opportunities to create their own unique imaginary worlds. However, she also knows that her play can help expand the children's language and increase the complexity of their play.

Some of the dramatic-play-with-print centers are introduced by guests that

Figure 6.6 *Dramatic-Play-with-Print Centers*

	Dramatic Props	**Print Props**
Shopping Mall Center	1. standing racks for drying clothes 2. hangers and play clothes (hang on racks) 3. cash registers 4. hats, purses, wallets 5. play baby strollers 6. dolls	1. check books and play money 2. signs such as names of departments, sale signs 3. sales slips 4. pads to write "shopping lists" 5. tags to make price tags 6. paper bags with store logos 7. credit cards 8. credit application forms
Doctor Center	1. play doctor kit with stethoscope, light, nurse hat, etc. 2. blanket for examining table 3. dolls for sick babies 4. white shirt for doctor	1. patient charts 2. prescription pads 3. sign-in sheet 4. bill forms 5. check books 6. magazines for waiting room
Drug Store Center	1. boxes for counters 2. cash register 3. empty bottles, boxes of various sizes for medicine 4. play shopping carts	1. magazines and books 2. play money 3. check books 4. prescriptions 5. paper bags for prescriptions 6. labels for prescription bottles
Beauty and Barber Shop Center	1. chairs 2. towels 3. play barber kit with scissors, combs 4. telephone 5. hair clips, curlers 6. empty bottles of cologne	1. appointment book 2. check books and play money 3. magazines for waiting room 4. bills

Mrs. Miller invites to the classroom. One of the favorite centers is the TV Weatherperson dramatic-play-with-print center. This center consists of a map on a chart stand, other maps and instruments, a cardboard TV camera, and a large poster with a weather "script." Mrs. Miller invites a weatherperson from a local TV station to speak to the class about weather forecasting. The weatherperson always brings a script used in a recent broadcast, several weather maps, and computer print-outs of weather information. After the visit, many children want to play in the center, so Mrs. Miller posts a schedule of "on-the-air" casts.

Principle 3: Accepting Children's Reading and Writing

The third principle is that *effective teachers accept children's reading and writing and recognize that they will often be unconventional.* Most novice readers' and writers' reading and writing in dramatic play and other environmental and functional print activities are not conventional. Figure 6.7 presents a chart Matthew filled out as a part of the medical center. As Matthew wrote on this chart he said, ''Your eyes look good. Your throat is red.'' Then he wrote the prescription appearing in Figure 6.8. He said, ''Take these pills 10 times.'' Two of the orders written as part of the McDonald's play are presented in Figure 6.9. The children said as they wrote, ''Two McDLT's and a coke'' and ''Three cheeseburgers and a chocolate shake.'' The telephone message for Melody that was taken in the housekeeping center is presented in Figure 6.10. These examples of children's reading and writing demonstrate that novice readers and writers intend to communicate meaning even when their efforts are unconventional. Mrs. Miller accepts these efforts and treats them as meaningful reading and writing.

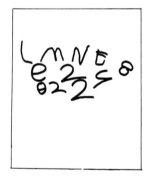

Figure 6.8 *Prescription*

Figure 6.7 *Doctor's Chart*

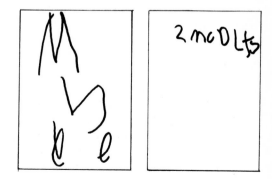

Figure 6.9 *McDonald's Orders*

Figure 6.10 *Telephone Message*

Principle 4: Connecting Reading and Writing at Home and School

The fourth principle is that *effective teachers connect the kinds of reading and writing children do at home with the kinds of reading and writing they do at school.* Children are interested in the environmental print in their homes. Mrs. Miller writes a letter to the parents describing all the different kinds of print that to the children and to their parents that the children are already readers. Mrs. Miller writes a letter to the parent describing all the different kinds of print that children can already read and she explains that she will be using much of this print in her classroom. She includes a list of things that she would like the children to bring to school, such as empty food boxes, bottles, and cans; coupons, old newspapers; magazines; and telephone directories. She tells the parents about a bag of "Things I Can Read" that each child will soon begin to fill. She asks parents to cut the fronts off cereal boxes, to save the wrappers from candy bars, and to tear the labels from canned goods, explaining that these are examples of items that will go into their children's reading bags. Mrs. Miller cautions parents that children should decide what items to keep for their reading bags. She provides parents with many examples of how their children might read, such as when they say "French fries" for a McDonald's bag or "chocolate candy" for an M & M wrapper. Mrs. Miller assures the parents that these responses are quite acceptable because they are meaningful.

Soon the children begin bringing in environmental print items, they read them to the class, and place them in their reading bags. As the children read their environmental print items, Mrs. Miller accepts their responses rather than stressing "reading the right words." When Melody says "red soup" for tomato soup, Mrs. Miller accepts this interpretation and offers her own comments while she points to the words in the print, "Look. This is Campbell's soup and it is 25 cents off. I think it is tomato soup."

Materials in children's reading bags are used for many activities throughout the year. At Halloween, the children compose a list of "Favorite Trick or Treat

Candy" by pasting candy labels on a long sheet of shelf paper. In December, they compose a "Stores We Know" list.

Principle 5: Using Environmental and Functional Print to Focus on Form

The fifth principle is that *effective teachers realize that children need support in moving from merely attending to the meaning of familiar print to attending to written language forms and meanings.* Case studies of the literacy learning of preschoolers have shown that children begin to learn the names of letters in meaningful environmental print words and in familiar persons' names (Baghban, 1984; Lass, 1982). This suggests that the familiar words in environmental print and the names of children in the classroom may be the most powerful resources for helping children learn about letters and other written language forms.

Mrs. Miller uses the writing of words from environmental and functional print as opportunities for focusing on written language form. As part of their unit on foods, Mrs. Miller's class reads many menus and placemats. These are put in the writing center to stimulate children's writing. Mrs. Miller uses group time to compose environmental and functional print such as the menu "Miller's Meals." As Mrs. Miller writes, she points out features of written language such as specific letters, long or short words, or words that are repeated.

Mrs. Miller frequently sits in the writing center so that she can call attention to written language features in the children's writing. In one activity, Mrs. Miller encouraged some children to dictate a "Trash Can Book." The children pasted environmental print items into books made from paper cut in the shape of trash cans. Serita made three pages in her book. She dictated, "I saved Rice Krispies from the trash. I saved Cabbage Patch from the trash. I saved potato chips from the trash." Mrs. Miller drew attention to the words *Rice Krispies, Cabbage Patch,* and *potato chips* written on the environmental print and in the words that she wrote in the book. She asked Serita to talk about how the words were alike and different in the two contexts. Seeing familiar and meaningful words in more than one context helps children begin to move beyond context-dependent reading and writing (Hiebert, 1986). As children focus on form within the meaningful context of the environment, they begin to make connections between written forms (letters and words) and spoken forms (sounds and meaning).

USING WRITING TO SUPPORT LITERACY LEARNING

We have already described many writing activities in Miss Leslie's and Mrs. Miller's classrooms. In this section we will review those writing activities, and discuss some general principles of using writing with novice readers and writers. Finally, we will discuss using a writing center with novice readers and writers and taking dictation from small groups of preschoolers.

Writing in Miss Leslie's and Mrs. Miller's Classrooms

The children in both Miss Leslie's and Mrs. Miller's classrooms wrote as part of many classroom activities. In their dramatic-play-with-print activities they took orders at the McDonald's center, wrote telephone messages in the home center, and wrote grocery lists at the grocery store center. Children also wrote as part of other activities: they wrote their names as a record of who had watched TV and who had not in the science and math center; they wrote menus as part of a food unit; and they dictated thank you letters after a trip to the zoo. In the writing centers they composed menus, "Trash Can Books," and books about rabbits. In these classrooms, the teachers wrote frequently.

General Principles of Writing

There are three principles of writing with novice readers and writers. These include (1) using activities that involve children and teachers writing in a variety of ways; (2) allowing children freedom to choose whether or not to write; and (3) being sensitive to novice readers' and writers' written language knowledges and responding to them appropriately.

Principle 1: Using Writing in a Variety of Ways

The first principle of writing is that *effective teachers plan for a variety of kinds of writing—some involving the teacher's writing for children and some involving children's writing for themselves.* Some writing activities are more controlled by the teacher and others are controlled by the child. In group activities, the teacher writes for children as he or she records what several children say as a part of an activity; in these activities, teachers have more control over writing. Children have a chance to contribute to the composition, but the topic and purpose of the writing activity is usually decided by the teacher. Some activities involve the teacher recording what a single child says, such as when the teacher records a message about a picture that the child has drawn. Children in these activities have more control over writing, especially when they decide the topic and purpose of their drawing and writing.

Some activities involve children writing. When children visit the writing center to write a note to a classmate, they initiate the writing, and they choose the topic. Other activities originate in children's play. As children play house, they may decide to write a phone message. Children have most control over writing when they write for purposes of their own and on topics of their choice. It is important for children to have writing experiences where they are more in control so they can try out their written language knowledge.

Principle 2: Providing Freedom to Write

The second principle of writing is that *effective teachers allow children freedom of choice about writing—children should be free at times to select topics to write about and to determine whether to write at all.* We believe preschoolers should not be required to go to the writing center to complete a particular project. Rather, they should be invited, encouraged, and enticed to go to writing centers and other writing activities. We have similar beliefs about other literacy activities for preschoolers.

Teachers who know what motivates and interests young children in their classrooms can entice many seemingly reluctant readers and writers into participating in activities that lead to reading and writing. Such children may visit a writing center to use the typewriter or letter stamps, or to engage in fingerpainting or pudding writing activities. They may be willing to tell an adult or teacher about a picture that they have drawn, especially if that person is genuinely interested in the drawing. However, teachers must always be able to accept "no" and wait for children to be ready.

Principle 3: Being Sensitive to Written Language Knowledges

The third principle of writing is that *effective teachers are sensitive to the particular knowledges about written language displayed by their children and they make informed responses to children's writing.* One important characteristic of novice readers and writers is that they often intend to convey messages in their writing even though their writing is not conventional. Although the messages may not have observable relationships with what the children write, the context in which novice writers compose will provide valuable clues to their writing's meaning. (See the writing presented in Figures 6.7, 6.8, 6.9, and 6.10.) Teachers must be sensitive to what children intend to communicate in their writing so that they can respond appropriately. They can say, "Tell me about your writing." Better yet, teachers can be present when children write, listen as they talk, and interact with them.

Another important characteristic of novice readers and writers is that their interest is often focused on meaning, letters, or texts. Teachers' talk about written language should reflect their focus. Children learn much by listening to their teacher's comments such as, "Look. John made a *J* just like his name." Because novice readers and writers do not yet understand about the relationship between letters and sounds, teacher's talk about this relationship would probably only be confusing. Such talk about letter–sound relationships is most meaningful when children have learned nearly all the letter names.

Teachers can encourage children to "read your story" or "tell what your writing says" as the children are writing or soon after they are finished. Even then, some novice readers may be reluctant to read or they may not remember much of what the teacher recorded. Sensitive teachers will not insist that children read their stories if they do not want to. These teachers will read what they have recorded for children and accept children's readings.

Using the Writing Center with Novices

The writing center should be a busy place in every classroom, including classrooms of young novice readers and writers. Novice readers and writers can draw, write, experiment with using letter stamps, or make shaving cream designs. Teachers frequently place special materials and displays in the writing center to encourage children to participate in specific writing activities. Children also use the writing center to "Sign In."

Writing Center Activities

There are many activities that can be placed in the writing center for novice readers and writers. Young children enjoy making letter shapes in clay or writing in jello granules on a cookie sheet (Tompkins, 1981). Making greeting cards is always a favorite writing activity; holidays present numerous opportunities for children to write cards (Beardsley & Mareck- Zeman, 1987). Literature is another important stimulus for writing; teachers can record children's retellings of stories. Children enjoy writing on paper cut into shapes suggested by characters or themes of literature. Another favorite writing activity is to have children compose their own functional print items such as menus, grocery lists, catalogs, and *TV Guides.*

Writing center activities should be carefully planned so that they encourage children's literacy growth. When children write on topics of their own choosing and for real-world purposes such as a birthday greeting, they are more likely to use more mature writing strategies (Martinez & Teale, 1987). Having an exciting activity before writing such as cooking also seems to enhance children's writing.

Interacting with children during writing center activities also influences children's writing. Mrs. Miller introduces new writing center activities during group time and follows a routine as she interacts with the children in the center. In December, Mrs. Miller plans several activities related to writing letters to Santa. First, she plans a whole group activity in which she writes a letter to Santa using suggestions from the children. She places stationery cut from green construction paper and envelopes in the writing center. She also displays words such as *Santa, Dear,* and *Love.* Then she places a "Santa Letter" sign up sheet in the writing center; this is a piece of paper with "I will write to Santa today" written at the top and space for four children to sign at the bottom. The children know to sign up as they enter the classroom in the morning if they want to have Mrs. Miller record their letters to Santa.

Using the Sign In Procedure

Novice readers and writers who realize that written marks can communicate messages are ready for the "Sign In" procedure. In this procedure, each child writes his or her name each day on an attendance sign-up sheet (Harste, Burke, & Woodward, 1981). This procedure is a functional one; it should actually serve as the attendance record of the classroom. With young three-year-olds, the procedure may consist of having children place a card with their name on it in a box or on a chart. Later, they may place their name card and a slip of paper (the same size as the name card) on which they have written their names in the attendance box. Eventually, children will sign in by writing their signature on an attendance sheet. Naturally, three- and four-year-olds' signatures will not be conventional when they first begin the Sign In procedure (recall Robert's early signatures presented in Figure 5.6 in Chapter 5). However, by signing in daily, children gradually refine their signatures into readable names.

Mrs. Miller uses the Sign In procedure for two reasons. First, many of the children who come to her classroom have had few writing experiences prior to beginning preschool. Many children do not have crayons and paper in their homes. Before she began the Sign In procedure, few children voluntarily visited the writing center. The Sign In procedure gave the children an opportunity to write each day. As they became comfortable with that very brief writing experience, they gained confidence and began visiting the writing center for more lengthy writing experiences. The children also observed that their writing was useful; Mrs. Miller used the Sign In list to comment on children's absences.

Recording Children's Dictation in Group Settings

Recording what children say and then helping them read their dictation has long been a part of reading and writing instruction. Taking children's dictation is part of the Language Experience Approach to teaching reading (Hall, 1981; Stauffer, 1980). What the teacher records or writes, usually on a large chart for group dictations or on paper for individual dictations, is called the *experience chart* or *experience story.*

The Language Experience Approach usually follows a certain sequence. First, the teacher plans an experience such as making chocolate pudding that will stimulate the children's interest and provide a topic of discussion. After the experience, the teacher tells the children they will write about their experience and invites each child to contribute. The teacher records what each child says and reads it aloud. After all the children have contributed to the experience story, the teacher and children read and reread it several times.

Teachers of young preschoolers often find this procedure frustrating (Cunningham, 1979). Young children take time to think of what to say for an experience chart, and teachers need time to record lengthy sentences. Therefore, it is not surprising that many four-year-olds lose interest in dictation activities. One way to avoid this problem is to take dictation with only one child at a time. In this way, the child has plenty of time to think, the teacher has plenty of time to record, and the experience is tailored to each child's interest and needs. Children should have frequent opportunities to dictate one-on-one with their teacher. However, children learn much from other children—including in dictation experiences. There are two ways that teachers can make dictation experiences more effective for small groups of young children: to have children contribute to pattern writing and to make use of list making.

Using Pattern Writing

Group dictation can be facilitated by using literature patterns as a stimulus for writing. Several books have language that is used in predictable patterns. (See

Chapter 3, Figure 3.3, for a list of pattern books.) After sharing books with predictable patterns, children can dictate the pattern in the book or create new content for the pattern (Bridge, 1986; Heald-Taylor, 1987). Teachers and children can also create their own patterns for writing. Mrs. Miller and her children used a pattern to create their Trash Can Books. They used the pattern "I saved the _____ from the trash can." Patterns for writing can be integrated into any unit or theme. Mrs. Miller's children used the pattern "I hate _____ , but _____ is my favorite food," as another part of their unit on foods.

Pattern writing usually allows children to be more successful in contributing to dictation stories. It is important to keep in mind that the purpose of using pattern writing is to help children become more fluent and creative, rather than to make them conform to an expected pattern (Wason-Ellam, 1988). Often the most creative contribution to a pattern writing activity will be a response that breaks the pattern.

Using Lists

Using lists is another way to solve the problems related to group dictation with small children. List making is effective with young children because each child can contribute several times. Lists can be made quickly since it only takes a few seconds to write a word in the list. Miss Leslie and Mrs. Miller regularly write lists with their children as part of booksharing and environmental print reading. Miss Leslie wrote several lists with her children related to the book *The Little Rabbit Who Wanted Red Wings*. The children dictated a list of animals included in the book, a list of animal features they would like to have, and a list of wishes. Figure 6.11 presents several books and examples of lists that can be written before or after their sharing.

Sometimes young children have difficulty knowing what to say when they are asked to add to a list. Some children may show their confusion by repeating what someone else dictated. We suggest that teachers write what each child contributes even when he or she repeats someone else's responses. Repeated responses provide children with opportunities for paying attention to written language forms. As the teacher and children read and reread their list, they will discover that some words are repeated and that the repeated words look the same.

Learning about Form, Meaning, Meaning-Form Links, and Function through Writing Activities

Children learn much about written language from the kinds of comments that teachers and other children make. In fact, one of the most powerful literacy learning techniques that teachers can use is to talk about written language as it is being written. This kind of talk is called *written language talk*. Effective teachers use their careful observation of children in literacy events to make decisions about what kinds of written language talk might be most useful.

Figure 6.11 *Making Lists with Literature*

Literature Selection	Suggestions for Lists
Brown, M. (1947). *Goodnight moon.* Harper & Row.	1. "Things in the green room" 2. "Things in my room" 3. "Before I go to bed, I"
Carle, E. (1974). *The very hungry caterpillar.* New York: Philomel.	1. "Things the catepillar ate" 2. "I was so hungry I ate"
Goss, J., & Harste, J. (1981). *It didn't frighten me.* School Book Fairs.	1. "Outside my window was" 2. "I'm not afraid of" 3. "Fantastic Creatures"
Pienkowski, J. (1980). *Dinnertime.* Los Angelos, CA: Price/Stern/Sloan	1. "Animals having dinner" 2. "Things for dinner"
Viorst, J. (1977). *Alexander and the terrible, horrible, no good, very bad day.* New York: Atheneum.	1. "Alexander's bad things" 2. "Our bad things" 3. "Wonderful, marvelous, good things"

Written language talk can help children learn about written language forms. As Mrs. Miller wrote her letter to Santa with her children, she told the children she would begin her letter by writing "Dear Santa Claus." At the end of her letter, she wrote, "Love, Mrs. Miller." She explained that letters always begin with the word *Dear* and often end with the word *Love.* From this written language talk, the children learned about the text form of a letter.

Mrs. Miller also talked about alphabet letters as she wrote her Santa letter. She made comments such as, "Look, Santa begins with the same letter as Serita, '*S*'." From this written language talk about alphabet letters, the children learned letter names, features, and perhaps information about sounds associated with letters.

Written language talk can also help children learn about meanings. As Mrs. Miler wrote her Santa letter, she explained that the letter would start with a sentence about her good behavior in the last year. She reminded the children that Santa would want to know that in order to bring what she wanted for Christmas. Through her talk about meaning, the children learned about the kinds of language found in letters. They also learned the kinds of information that are appropriate to include in a letter to Santa.

Written language talk also helps children learn about meaning-form links. As Mrs. Miller wrote, she said each word. As she read her letter, she underlined the text with her hands. The children had many opportunities to connect what they heard Mrs. Miller read with the print she was highlighting. Mrs. Miller's talk about letters provided children with information for discovering letter–sound relationships. Some of the children in her class have begun making some of these discoveries. When Mrs. Miller was writing that she wanted a new sewing machine, Serita commented, "I know what letter sewing has, an '*S*'." Mrs. Miller knew that Serita only made these letter–sound comments about *S* words. Still, Serita was beginning to display some letter–sound relationship awareness. We will talk more about this knowledge in Chapter 7.

Written language talk helps children learn about function. Mrs. Miller talked about taking the letter to the post office and mailing it. She reminded the children that Santa could keep her letter to remember what she wanted for Christmas. She commented that it is a good thing that Santa will have her letter because he will be getting many, many requests for gifts. She did not want him to forget what she wanted.

Children also use written language talk as they watch their teacher write and as they write. Mrs. Miller encourages children to use this kind of talk and always takes time to respond to a child who makes a written language comment. She knows that children's comments provide information about written language that all the children can use to learn about reading and writing.

SOME CAUTIONS ABOUT SUPPORTING NOVICE READERS' AND WRITERS' LITERACY LEARNING

We end this chapter with two cautions about supporting the literacy learning of novice readers and writers. First, it may seem as if the classrooms we described had only novice readers and writers. Although we focused on activities for novices in this chapter, it is unlikely that any classroom will have only novices. Second, there are many commercial materials that are designed for preschool and elementary school classrooms; teachers must make intelligent decisions about these materials.

More than Novices

Even in classrooms with only three-year-olds, it is possible that one or two of the children will operate more like experimenters with written language in some aspects of written language knowledge. (Experimenters will be described in Chapter 7.) In kindergarten and first grade classrooms, there are likely to be not only novice readers and writers, but also experimenters and accomplished readers and writers. (Accomplished readers and writers will be described in Chapter 9.) However, because many of the activities that are useful for novice readers' and writers' learning are open-ended, experimenters and accomplished readers and writers can engage in them, too. What they do may be different, but no more important than what novice readers and writers do.

Because of pressures from school administrators or system policies, it may be difficult to offer first grade novice readers and writers the kind of literacy activities we have described in this chapter. We believe that novice readers and writers, even when they are in first grade, need to explore reading and writing in activities such as those we have described in this chapter before beginning formal reading and writing programs. Creative first grade teachers will find innovative ways to weave many of the activities described in this chapter into their first grade literacy program. (See Chapter 11 for a description of such a teacher.)

A Word about Commercial Programs

There are many commercially available kits, games, and activities designed to help get young children "ready" to read and write. Many are designed to help children develop *visual discrimination,* which is the ability to detect likenesses and differences in visual displays. Visual discrimination activities include having children find two letters that are the same or find a letter that is different from other letters. In order to complete these activities, children do not need to know letter names. They need only to be able to see if two letter shapes are alike or different. Despite the popularity of such activities, most young children do not need them. Research has shown that even three-year-olds have developed the ability to discriminate among letters (Hiebert, 1981; Lomax & McGee, 1987). Children develop these abilities in the kinds of meaningful literacy activities that we have described in this chapter. We do not recommend that children be given these activities in isolation in worksheets or workbooks.

Another kind of pre-reading or "readiness" activity often found in kindergarten and preschool literacy programs is *auditory discrimination.* This activity usually requires children to match pictures that represent rhyming words such as a *bee* and a *tree* or that have the same beginning sounds such as a *bee* and a *bat.* Much practice in listening to letter sounds in isolation accompanies these activities. However, research suggests that visual attention to print develops before attention to sounds, and that being able to look at words in print may actually help children discover that letters have a relationship to sounds (Templeton, 1986). Moreover, this research suggests that children are not ready to match rhyming words until they have experience with written forms of language. That is why we have recommended sharing rhyming books with children for enjoyment and not for teaching rhyming words.

Another questionable practice that is often included as part of readiness programs is helping children learn letter sounds. The objective of many of these programs is to teach children to say sounds associated with letters in isolation and to blend words by sounding individual letter sounds. Most novice readers and writers do not benefit from such activities. These children usually have not grasped the fact that letters can represent sounds. Teaching them sounds associated with letters (which they will mimic) does not seem to lead to the discovery that letters are representatives of sounds any faster than activities we have described in this chapter. Experts in reading and writing warn that teaching letters and sounds in isolation may be detrimental to children who have not developed their own concepts of letter–sound relationships (Goodman, 1986; Harste, Woodward, & Burke, 1984). Knowing about and using information related to letters and sounds are important ingredients in accomplished reading and writing. We will discuss more about helping children discover these concepts in the next few chapters.

Teachers need to examine all commercial materials carefully in light of research and the children they will be teaching (Collins, 1986; Weir, 1989). This means that even kindergarten teachers who are expected to use the readiness materials in the commercial reading program of their school system (basal materials) must carefully consider the teaching suggestions and activities that are recommended in these materials. The principles of using booksharing, environmental and functional print, and writing described in this chapter should help teachers make wise and informed curriculum decisions. We urge all teachers to take charge of their literacy curriculum, to examine commercial materials carefully, and not to depend on a commercial program as the primary determinant of their literacy program.

Chapter Summary

Booksharing, environmental and functional print reading, and writing are three supports for the literacy learning of novice readers and writers. The most important component of a successful literacy program is meaning. Children should be invited to participate in a variety of enjoyable and meaningful reading and writing activities in which they use written language. The talk about written language meanings, forms, meaning-form links, and functions that surrounds interesting literacy activities provides an important avenue for literacy learning.

Sharing books with young children is an important component of literacy-rich classrooms. There are four principles of booksharing: (1) knowing and using techniques that encourage book interactions, (2) allowing for individuality, (3) planning for independent booksharing, and (4) having a booksharing focus. The first and most important focus for booksharing is enjoyment. Because children enjoy having books read again and again, teachers can use books as a way of helping children focus on written language meaning, form, meaning-form links, and functions. Booksharing activities that focus on meaning include talking about illustrations, sharing books with common themes, and using wordless picture books. Activities that focus on form include activities focusing on concepts about stories and using Big Books. Activities that focus on

meaning-form links include reading rhyming word and other language play books, helping children memorize the text of familiar pattern books, and creating alphabet books. Activities that focus on function include sharing informational books and other functional print items.

Environmental and functional print are an important part of children's early literacy activities in classrooms. Five principles guide teachers' use of these kinds of print. (1) Print can be integrated into almost every classroom activity including using name writing in functional ways and using print in classroom routines. (2) Children can practice using print in their dramatic play by using dramatic-play-with-print kits and other dramatic play opportunities. (3) Children's reading and writing of environmental and functional print should be accepted as an important part of their learning even when their reading and writing is unconventional. (4) Parents can be important resources for their children's learning; they can help connect reading and writing at home and school. (5) Children need guidance in focusing attention on the written forms in environmental print and in seeing familiar environmental words in many contexts.

Writing may present a unique opportunity for learning about written language in classrooms. Seeing a teacher write provides information for children to try out as they write; children acquire more information as their friends and teacher comment about their writing. Teachers are guided by three principles of using writing in the classroom: (1) planning a variety of kinds of writing, (2) offering freedom of choice about writing, and (3) being sensitive to individual needs. They can encourage children's exploration of writing by having interesting writing center activities, using the sign in procedure, and using effective dictation procedures.

Descriptions of Miss Leslie's and Mrs. Miller's classrooms showed that the literacy activities they planned were appropriate for the development of their children. Miss Leslie and Mrs. Miller are knowledgable about written language learning and about their children. They are master teachers who have several years of experience. They have gathered many materials and have the benefit of their trial-and-error experiences from previous years in planning effective activities. Not all teachers will have as much equipment, materials, or experience. Teachers are learners just as children are learners. However, we believe that all teachers should strive to become careful observers of children and to become knowledgeable about written language learning. Teachers are the key to any successful literacy program.

Applying the Information

Mrs. Jones is a new kindergarten teacher (or, if you prefer learning about pre-schoolers, imagine she is a new teacher of the three- and four-year-old class). She believes that many of her children are novice readers and writers. Mrs. Jones decides to use booksharing as her primary approach of supporting her children's literacy learning. Although she realizes that she needs to encourage interaction during booksharing and to plan a creative follow-up to her sharing, she is not sure how to begin. How can she plan a week's lesson that will help her children learn about written language forms, meanings, and functions? How can she integrate her writing center with her booksharing activities?

Help Mrs. Jones plan her booksharing activities. Visit the children's section of your local or university library. Select several books that meet Mrs. Jones's needs. Plan five days of teacher-directed activities for a small group of novices. Also plan a classroom, describing centers and activities in which children will engage during center or free choice time. Plan at least one environmental print activity and one writing center activity that can be integrated into the theme suggested by the books. Be sure to include several activities in which the teacher writes. Make sure the activities you plan meet the general principles of booksharing, using environmental and functional print, and writing with novice readers and writers.

Going Beyond the Text

Visit a preschool or kindergarten classroom. Observe several literacy activities, taking careful note of the interactions among children as they participate in literacy experiences. Also note the teacher's talk with the children in these experiences. Make a list of the kinds of literacy materials available in the classroom. Talk with the teacher about the kinds of literacy activities she uses. Follow the general principles of booksharing, using environmental and

functional print, and writing to evaluate the literacy program in the classroom you visit. Make suggestions on ways to improve the program.

References

BAILEY, C. (1987). *The little rabbit who wanted red wings.* New York: Platt & Munk.

BEARDSLEY, L. V., & MARECK-ZEMAN, M. (1987). Making connections: Facilitating literacy in young children. *Childhood Education, 63,* 159–166.

BRIDGE, C. (1986). Predictable books for beginning readers and writers. In M. R. Sampson (Ed.), *The pursuit of literacy: Early reading and writing* (pp. 81–96). Dubuque, IA: Kendall/Hunt.

COLLINS, C. (1986). Is the cart before the horse? Effects of preschool reading instruction on 4 year olds. *The Reading Teacher, 40,* 332–339.

COMBS, M. (1987). Modeling the reading process with enlarged texts. *The Reading Teacher, 40,* 422–426.

CUNNINGHAM, P. (1979). Beginning reading without readiness: Structured language experience. *Reading Horizons, 19,* 222–227.

FOX, C. (1985). The book that talks. *Language Arts, 62,* 374–384.

GOODMAN, K. (1986). Basal readers: A call for action. *Language Arts, 63,* 358–363.

GOSS, J. L., & HARSTE, J. C. (1981). *It didn't frighten me.* School Book Fairs.

HALL, M. A. (1981). *Teaching reading as a language experience* (3rd ed.). Columbus, OH: Merrill.

HARSTE, J. C., BURKE, C. L., & WOODWARD, V. A. (1981). *Children, their language and world: Initial encounters with print.* (Final Report NIE-G-79-0132). Bloomington, IN: Indiana University, Language Education Department.

HARSTE, J. C., WOODWARD, V. A., & BURKE, C. L. (1984). *Language stories and literacy lessons.* Portsmouth, NH: Heinemann.

HEALD-TAYLOR, G. (1987). How to use predictable books for K-2 language arts instruction. *The Reading Teacher, 40,* 656–661.

HICKMAN, J. (1981). A new perspective on response to literature: Research in an elementary school setting. *Research in the Teaching of English, 15,* 343–354.

HIEBERT, E. H. (1981). Developmental patterns and interrelationships of preschool children's print awareness. *Reading Research Quarterly, 16,* 236–260.

HIEBERT, E. H. (1986). Using environmental print in beginning reading instruction. In M. R. Sampson (Ed.), *The pursuit of literacy: Early reading and writing,* (pp. 73–80). Dubuque, IA: Kendall/Hunt.

HOLDAWAY, D. (1979). *Foundations of literacy.* Sydney, Australia: Ashton Scholastic.

HOSKISSON, K. (1975). Successive approximation and beginning reading. *Elementary School Journal, 75,* 442–451.

HOSKISSON, K., & TOMPKINS, G. E. (1987). *Language arts: Content and teaching strategies.* Columbus, OH: Merrill.

HOWARD, K. (1971). *Little bunny follows his nose.* Racine, WI: Western Publishing.

KIEFER, B. (1988). Picture books as contexts for literary, aesthetic, and real world understandings. *Language Arts, 65,* 260–271.

LAMME, L. L., & CHILDERS, N. M. (1983). The composing processes of three young children. *Research in the Teaching of English, 17,* 33–50.

LASS, B. (1982). Portrait of my son as an early reader. *The Reading Teacher, 36,* 20–28.

LOMAX, R. G., & McGEE, L. M. (1987). Young children's concepts about print and reading: Toward a model of word reading acquisition. *Reading Research Quarterly, 22,* 219–256.

LUKENS, R. L. (1986). *A critical handbook of children's literature* (3rd ed.). Glenview, IL: Scott Foresman.

MARTIN, B. (1983). *Brown bear, brown bear.* New York: Holt.

MARTINEZ, M., & TEALE W. H. (1987). The ins and outs of a kindergarten writing program. *The Reading Teacher, 40,* 444–451.

McCONAGHY, J. (1985). Once upon a time and me. *Language Arts, 62,* 349–354.

McGEE, L. M. (1986). Young children's environmental print reading. *Childhood Education, 63,* 118–125.

McGEE, L. M., & TOMPKINS, G. E. (1981). The videotape answer to independent reading comprehension activities. *The Reading Teacher, 34,* 427–433.

POTTER, B. (1902). *The tale of Peter Rabbit.* New York: Frederick Warne.

RAVER, S. A., & DWYER, R. C. (1986). Teaching handicapped preschoolers to sight read using language training procedures. *The Reading Teacher,* 314–321.

RHODES, L. K. (1981). I can read! Predictable books as resources for reading and writing. *The Reading Teacher, 34,* 511–518.

ROSKOS, K. (1988). Literacy at work in play. *The Reading Teacher, 41,* 562–566.

SCARRY, R. (1965). *The bunny book.* Racine, WI: Western Publishing.

SCHICKEDANZ, J. A. (1978). Please read that story again! Exploring relationships between story reading and learning to read. *Young Children, 33,* (5).

SCHICKEDANZ, J. A. (1986). *More than the ABCs.* Washington, DC: National Association for the Education of Young Children.

SLEPIAN, J., & SEIDLER, A. (1967). *The hungry thing.* New York: Scholastic.

STAUFFER, R. (1980). *The language experience approach to teaching reading* (2nd ed.). New York: Harper and Row.

TAYLOR, N. E., BLUM, I. H., & LOGSDON, D. M. (1986). The development of written language awareness: Environmental aspects and program characteristics. *Reading Research Quarterly, 21,* 132–149.

TCHUDI, S. (1985). The roots of response to literature. *Language Arts, 62,* 463–468.

TEMPLETON, S. (1986). Literacy, readiness, and basals. *The Reading Teacher,* 403–409.

TOMPKINS, G. E. (1981). Writing without a pencil. *Language Arts, 58,* 823–833.

TOMPKINS, G. E., & McGEE, L. M. (1989). Teaching repetition as a story structure. In D. M. Glynn (Ed.), *Children's comprehension of text* (59–78). Newark, DE: International Reading Association.

TOMPKINS, G. E., & WEBELER, M. B. (1983). What will happen next? Using predictable books with young children. *The Reading Teacher, 36,* 498–502.

WASON-ELLAM, L. (1988). Using literary patterns: Who's in control of the authorship? *Language Arts, 65,* 291–301.

WEIR, B. (1989). A research base for prekindergarten literacy programs. *The Reading Teacher, 42,* 456–468.

YADEN, D. (1988). Understanding stories through repeated read-alouds: How many does it take? *The Reading Teacher, 41,* 556–560.

Part 3

Making the Transition with Fives and Sixes

Part 3 describes children who are making the transition between reading and writing as novices (described in Part 2) and becoming accomplished readers and writers (described in Part 4). We call these children *experimenters*. Chapter 7, "Experimenting Readers and Writers," discusses what experimenters learn about literacy. Although they do not yet read and write in fully conventional ways, experimenters make several fundamental discoveries. They learn that to be writers and readers they must make systematic use of symbols. With their storybook retellings and their invented spellings, experimenters show that they are engaged in constructing their own symbol systems. Thus, they lay the groundwork for—and truly are in transition toward—eventually learning the conventional symbol systems used by accomplished readers and writers. Chapter 8, "Classroom Support for Experimenting Readers and Writers," describes a school environment and activities that support experimentation with literacy. Included are approaches based on booksharing, writing, functional print, memorized texts, and invented spelling.

CHAPTER 7

Experimenting Readers and Writers

This chapter looks at young experimenters with written language, children who are in transition between being novices and becoming accomplished readers and writers. It is not possible to say that any single characteristic or accomplishment qualifies a young child as an experimenter. We believe, however, that children who show several of the following sets of behaviors will benefit from their teachers' considering them to be experimenters:

1. They know that they do not know how to read and write in the same way as adults.

2. They are aware of the *work* involved in reading and writing. They often devote large amounts of energy to a literacy task, even when the task is a small, concentrated part of the whole process of reading and writing.

3. They attempt literacy tasks that are not necessarily a part of playing a game or a role. They *sometimes* respond to adults' or more knowledgeable peers' efforts to enlist them as writers or readers.

4. They have complete or nearly complete alphabet knowledge and are beyond concentrating on individual letters in their reading and writing efforts.

5. They have a baseline of writing ability that is not conventional writing, but it does include many conventional features such as some conventional letter combinations and words, especially their own names.

6. They *spell*—they work at using letters to write words, usually inventively. Their approach is systematic but not conventional.

7. When they read and write, they use language that is like the language in

books and unlike the language of conversation. They are influenced by the print in their reading.

WHO ARE EXPERIMENTERS?

Learning about written language is a gradual process, and it is not possible to identify absolute milestones. There is no single, great accomplishment that divides beginners and novices from the experimenters described in this chapter. A child may act like an experimenter one day and then go back to the ways of a novice for a while. He or she may experiment in storyreading, but not yet in spelling. Good observers notice a combination of changes that together suggest a child is dealing with written language in a new, experimental manner.

Experimenters' New Awareness

One of the most important changes in children as they become experimenters takes place in their *attitude*. Over a period of time, a careful observer can notice a new attitude that might be described as being more *aware, thoughtful, tentative, testing,* and *vulnerable.*

Awareness may be the key. Experimenters are aware that there is a system to be learned and that they do not yet know it all. They are much more likely than novices to say, "But I don't know how to do that yet." They are more prone to frustration and feelings of inadequacy; they are more likely to say, "I can't write" or "I don't want to read." Experimenters need understanding, support, and patience.

If experimenters have adults' support, however, another aspect of their new attitude may appear; it is *concentration* or *engagement.* Many young children show that they are experimenters by the intensity with which they work at reading and writing. Once they are helped to avoid the potential frustration of knowing that there is much that they do not know, they seem to dig in and work at one small part at a time. Sulzby (1985b) discovered that kindergartners were aware that writing requires much effort. Yet Sulzby also learned that most children are willing to make that effort. They will work intensely when invited to read and write, especially if they know that they can request help and that they need not do a perfect, complete job. Children's appearance of working hard is the result of the careful analysis, the concentrated thinking, and the reasoned "trying out" that is the essence of experimentation and invention. If it is true that what they are doing at this stage is "inventing literacy for themselves" (Goodman, 1980), then it is no wonder that such hard work is involved.

Working intensely does not usually mean working long. Experimenters tire easily and often stop before they complete a task. That is why they need support regardless of the incompleteness of a product. That is why they may work at only small pieces at one time. They may work at how to represent the sounds in a single word they wish to write, or they may work at reading a favorite storybook by concentrating on pictures and print and on their memory of what adults have read on a single page.

Experimenters may on one occasion labor at getting a list, a letter, a story, or a sign to look right or to have the right form. In the process of doing this, they may seem to regress from an ability to form letters or to spell words that was displayed on an earlier occasion.

The important thing to remember is that experimenters are trying out many pieces of the literacy puzzle, and are experimenting with each one. It is an exciting process for both the children and those who support them (Hilliker, 1988; Matthews, 1988). In this process, they gain important literacy knowledge that will be used later when they will be better able to put the pieces together.

Examples: Novices versus Experimenters

Which of these children are experimenters with written language?

Thirty-three-month-old Giti is writing a letter to her grandmother. She announces "For Grandma" and makes several lines of zig-zag scribbles on a paper and underlines them. Part of what she writes is clearly intended to be her grandmother's name and another part her own name. These parts are primitive, but recognizable capital *G*'s. She pretends to mail these letters (Baghban, 1984).

Stevie is confident that he can read. Sometimes he likes to read *to* his mother or father. He holds a favorite book, turns the pages, talks about the pictures, and even tells the story he has heard his mother or father read so often from that book.

Five-year-old Ted has been sent to his room for misbehaving. He either does not remember or does not understand why he was sent there. With pencil and paper, he writes the message shown in Figure 7.1. He dashes out of his

Figure 7.1 *Ted's Protest: "Mom, why are you punishing me? Ted"*

room, tosses this written query or protest on the floor before his mother and runs back into his room.

Julie reads a favorite book to her uncle. She has memorized large parts of it. She will not attempt to read parts she has not memorized. She knows when she has made a mistake (turned two pages, turned too soon, or forgotten a section) and will ask, "How's that go?" But she still is not a conventional reader—she cannot read other books.

Giti and Stevie are novices. As with many children at that stage, their literacy behaviors are charming. Part of the charm lies in what they do *not* know. They do not know how inexpert their products are; thus, they confidently act like readers and writers. Giti knew some functions and benefits of written language (that you can use it to communicate to someone who is not present), but she did not mind that what she produced is not a readable letter. As we indicated in Chapter 2, it is important that adults support that confidence and encourage novices' plunging into reading and writing as if they were indeed readers and writers. When Giti insisted on mailing her letters, her parents took their cue from her. They punched holes in the corners of the envelopes and tied string to them as she asked, so that she could drag them around like the mailman she had seen dragging his sack by its strap (Baghban, 1984).

There is an element of pretending in novices' literacy behavior. Children at this stage pretend they are readers and writers with the same intensity and confidence that is characteristic of their other pretend play. They believe that they *are* what they pretend to be (Chiseri-Strater, 1988).

However, sooner or later children approach written language not with a daring plunge, but with careful experimentation. This can be seen in Ted's and Julie's behaviors. What Ted produced was a record not just of his query or protest, but also of his analysis of English words and their component sounds. Ted knew that he did not know the adult way to spell. He often consulted an authority. However, when he was left to his own devices, he knew that he could get his words on paper if he thought about letter names and sounds in words. Ted sometimes worked intensely, especially when a message was as important to him as this one was. Ted's query appears unfinished; he wrote nothing for the word *me*. It is unlikely that he knowingly wrote an incomplete message; perhaps the effort required for this writing task distracted him so much that he did not realize he had omitted a word. After all, he did continue writing—he signed his name at the very end, and the word *me* would not have been too difficult for someone who had just spelled *punishing*. Julie acted on her theory that she may only say certain words when she reads a story. She had discovered that memorizing was one way to get them right.

Ted's and Julie's efforts were deliberate, experimental, and concentrated on small parts—on specific words of a written query and on specific pages from one favorite book. Their efforts were based on much that they had already learned as novices, but they reflected an understanding that they did not yet know what was required for real reading and writing. Thus, Ted and Julie need adults' support—even more than novices. Without support they might easily feel overwhelmed or frustrated.

Ted and Julie were experimenting in four areas: (1) with meaning (in Ted's case, with expressing his frustration, and in Julie's case, with retrieving her favorite book's message); (2) with form (in Ted's case, with what a word is, and in Julie's case, with what a story sounds like); (3) with meaning-form links (in Ted's case, with how letters and sounds go together, and in Julie's case, with how the page that she is on determines which memorized texts to recite); and (4) with functions of written language (in Ted's case, with making his protest unignorable, and in Julie's case, with entertaining herself and her uncle). The next four sections of this chapter describe experimenters' knowledges in these areas.

EXPERIMENTING WITH MEANING

It is no accident that the list of experimenters' new behaviors at the beginning of this chapter lacks explicit statements about constructing meaning. The meaning making of experimenters is not much different from that of novices. Novices and experimenters share a basic orientation toward written language that is one of novices' greatest achievements. Both write in order to represent a message, and both engage in interactive storybook reading using sophisticated strategies for constructing meaning (see Chapter 5). Experimenters continue to use the meaning-making strategies they devised as novices (Yaden, 1988).

The most striking new achievements of experimenters are related to their greater control over form. However, we do not want teachers, in the midst of their students' striking achievements with form, to lose sight of the important fact that children do not experiment with form in a vacuum. Solving problems of form is not an exercise for its own sake. The meaning making learned as novices is the basis of all that experimenters do.

Although we treat form, meaning-form links, and functions of written language separately, we urge readers to consider this chapter as a whole. One way to do this is always to look (as we did in the examples of Ted and Julie) for evidence of experimenters' continued understanding of the basic communicative nature of written language. Another way is to be aware of the overlaps among all four areas. For example, form often *serves* function, and insights about form often help children to understand the way meaning and form are linked. Finally, it is helpful to remember the connection between reading and writing that was emphasized in Chapter 1.

EXPERIMENTING WITH FORM

Experimenters develop knowledge of what a word is and why that unit is important; they also come to know what the larger organizational units, or formats, of written language are (such as lists, letters, stories, signs, and poems), and to know what wording is typically used in these formats.

Beyond Letters

In Chapter 5, we discussed novices' developing abilities to recognize and to form letters of the alphabet. Experimenters already have sufficient letter knowledge to be able to operate with letters. They know most of the upper-case letters by name, they can recite the alphabet, and—most importantly—they are able to use letters as subcomponents in larger schemes. Letters of the alphabet are not just a set of funny shapes with names from the ABC song. An experimenter can manipulate letters mentally, think about their properties, and talk about them. Knowing that each letter has a name and a unique appearance, experimenters can call on it when they want it to serve a purpose in a literacy task. They can think about what its name sounds like when they start to experiment with sounds in words, and they can try it out in combination with other letters and ask, "Do they look like a word? What do they spell?"

Thus, experimenters move beyond knowing letters to becoming fixated with words. Often the first word a child writes is his or her name. As they experiment, children realize that there are combinations of letters other than their names and that those combinations matter more than individual letters in written language.

Carrie's Discovery of Words

Carrie played with written language as part of her role as waitress in Ted and Carrie's restaurant (see Chapter 1). She could not yet write real letters; she used individual mock letters to write her restaurant check (see Figure 1.3). Five months later, Carrie was still playing with letters when she drew, but an important change had occurred in the way she used letters. Figure 7.2 shows one of

Figure 7.2 *Carrie's Drawing with Combinations of Letters as Signs*

Carrie's drawings. It includes not only many letter-like forms, but also some real letters. Some of the real letters are included in groups or composites of letters such as the composite "CAE" from her name and the composites "Hi" and "iH," two versions of the word *hi* that her brother taught her. Carrie was beginning to use *combinations* of letters as signs instead of using letters themselves as signs. Carrie was focusing on what expert readers and writers call *words.*

We do not know for sure why Carrie turned her attention from letters to words. It may be that there was nothing left for her to know about letters. Having mastered letter identification, she might have been struck by the novelty of different letter combinations [after one runs out of new letters, there are always new *combinations* of letters—see Chapter 2 about Clay's flexibility principle and generating principle (1975)].

Another explanation is suggested by the fact that Carrie included letters from her name in the piece shown in Figure 7.2, and that names were important in other literacy events involving Carrie. At the same time that she produced Figure 7.2, Carrie was very curious about which letters were in her name. She began signing her name to her drawings. Figure 7.3 shows not only her attempt at spelling her own name, but also two of the letters from her older brother, Ted's, name. One day, her father was silently reading a typewritten letter. Carrie climbed into his lap, pointed to a word in the letter that began with the letter *C*, and asked what it was. When told that the word was *concern*, she replied, "Oh. It has a C like my name." Carrie had noted that the word *concern* was something like her name. Both were composites of letters and both began with a *C*. Carries then asked, "What's that word?" about several other words in the letter. Learning about names is a powerful literacy tool that allows children to discover words and their link with meaning.

Carrie's literacy behaviors over the two months that followed her producing Figures 7.2 and 7.3 included other indications that she was experimenting with words. She remained fixated on words. One day, her mother observed her trac-

Figure 7.3 *Carrie's Self-Portrait with Signature*

ing with her finger the colorful capital letters that fill the front of the jacket of the "FREE TO BE YOU AND ME" album. Twice Carrie stopped her father in the middle of a non-literacy activity and said, "Wait. I want to spell that word." Once she traced the letters on a product label (AQUA PATIO). Another time, she pointed to and named all the letters on a store's sign (COSMETICS) in reverse order. Both the tracing and the pointing were followed by the question, "What does that spell?" During this time she also frequently asked her parents, "What does _____ spell?" as she named a combination of seemingly random letters. Sometimes she only named the letters of her made-up word. At other times, she both displayed the letters using her magnetic alphabet set and named them.

This form-related change from playing with letter forms to using letters in order to make and ask questions about words shows Carrie's change from being a novice to being an experimenter. This does not mean that she was an experimenter in all aspects of her literacy behavior. In fact, we will see later that this was not the case. Nor does it mean that her word knowledge was as complete or as sophisticated as an older experimenter's might be. There is still much that she must explore about wordness. However, she showed a concentration on this aspect of literacy and a development from the letter level to the word level that is characteristic of an experimenter. Researchers have noted similar development in other children.

Paul as Word Writer

Bissex's (1980) description of her son Paul's learning to write and read provides another example. At first, like many children, Paul enjoyed just forming letters of the alphabet. Later, he used letters to write messages, but they were messages in which the letters themselves seemed to be the only unit of form. Still later, he used the letters in combinations to make what we would call *words*. As we will see, however, Paul's spellings and his idea of which combinations of letters counted as single words differed from an accomplished writer's.

To explain the difference between writing in which letters are the only unit of form and writing in which letters are used in combinations so that there are word-like units, we will describe two of Paul's written products. The first was composed several months before his fifth birthday; it was a message he wrote to cheer up his mother. The message consisted of five green letters—two *t*'s, an *A,* and *H,* and an *l*—scattered over a page (Bissex, 1980, p. 4). Bissex did not see a word or words in this.

The second of Paul's messages we wish to consider here was a record he typed when he was five years and one month old; it was a record of his own phone number, 4547781 PAULSTLEFNMBR (Bissex, 1980, p. 7). With this stringing of letters together, Paul demonstrated that he had shifted his attention to words. He knew that letters did not directly convey a message; rather, they contributed to a larger unit, a composite of letters, called a *word.* Interestingly, Paul also showed that he understood that a telephone *number* is really a composite of numbers.

Starting at the time that Paul recorded and labeled his phone number, he began paying attention to words in books and to the role that letters play in those words. He tried to figure out what individual words were. On one occasion, he explained that he could identify the word *circus* in a list of book titles he had copied because it ended with an S (Bissex, 1980, p. 5). These few literacy events, which are taken from many similar events that Bissex describes, indicate a change in Paul's perception of what written language is. For Paul, writing had become no longer a matter of just making letters, but of combining them to make words. However, where one word stopped and another started was not yet clear to this young experimenter.

Concept of Word and Word Boundaries

A concept of word develops gradually. In order to understand what children think a word is, we must distinguish: (1) between awareness of words as units of speech and awareness of words as units of written language, and (2) between mastery of the concept and experimentation with the concept. Most children at this point do not show awareness of words as units of *speech*. They have not yet mastered the concept of wordness in written language. What matters is that they begin to use the word *word* and to operate with units that are combinations of letters.

There is considerable evidence that children do not have (and apparently do not need to have) clear awareness of words as units before they begin to experiment with *written* language. The important unit in spoken language is the phrase, not the word (Garvey, 1984). What we choose to designate as a word becomes important only when we read and write. Thus, it is not surprising that most young children fail a variety of experimental tests of spoken word perception, such as tapping a separate poker chip for each word they hear in an utterance (Downing & Oliver, 1973–1974; Huttenlocher, 1964). Even at the end of first grade, many children cannot accurately divide *written* sentences into words. Similarly, they do not perform perfectly when asked whether or not a letter string is a word (Lavine, 1977; Pick, Unze, Brownell, Drozdal, & Hopman, 1978).

The best indications of what young experimenters know about word units in written language come from watching them in their everyday reading and writing attempts at home and in school. We have already noted that Bissex's (1980) son Paul treated PAULSTLEFNMBR (Paul's telephone number) as one word, not three. On the same occasion that Paul wrote and labeled his telephone number, he also wrote a label for his buzzer, PAULSBZR (p. 7). Although he ran the words together in each of these examples and thus treated each label as a single word, he treated the two labels as separate words. He did not run PAULSTLEFNMBR together with PAULSBZR. In fact, he typed the two on separate sheets of paper. Bissex calls this "a first step in segmentation" (p. 7).

The processes of having a concept of word and having a means for showing word boundaries appear together. As Paul began to have a more finely tuned concept of which combinations of letters he should treat as separate words, he discovered ways of showing word boundaries that were less physical than using a separate sheet of paper for each word. When he typed, he sometimes used the space bar efficiently. When he wrote by hand, he began to use dots, as in this sign: PAULZ·HOS·PLANF·ELD·VRMAT (Paul's house, Plainfield, Vermont) (Bissex, 1980, p. 22). It is important to note that Paul was not merely placing his dots where we would put commas because we pause when reading. He placed them between the possessive form of his name and the noun it modified (unlike in PAULSBZR). He placed a dot between parts of *Plainfield* even though he did not place it precisely between the two syllables or the two component words of the compound word *Plain + field*. The spelling VRMAT showed that, although he divided some words, he did not divide them all. At another time, Paul experimented with dots between the actual syllables of *telephone* (this time spelled TAL·A·FON) and between the component words of the compound *afternoon* (spelled AFTR·NUN) (p. 23).

Some children use Paul's strategy of separating words with dots (Temple, Nathan, Burris, & Temple, 1988). Others circle words, put them in vertical arrangements, or even separate them with carefully drawn and blackened squares (Harste, Burke, & Woodward, 1983). In Chapter 1, we described the writing of a boy named Michael; he distinguished one word from another by writing them in different colors. When Carrie was three years old, her eight-year-old brother Ted wanted her to separate the words of a letter she was writing (she had asked for his help with spelling). He advised her to use a vertical arrangement, apparently thinking that it would be easiest for her (see Figure 7.4). When Carrie began experimenting by herself with the concept of word and how to show it, she chose to circle words (see Figure 7.5). She seemed to have a very physical sense of wordness, and explained that the little bump on the top of each circle was a handle "for if somebody wants to pick the letters up."

Figure 7.4 *Carrie's Letter to Keely, Tom, and Holly*

Figure 7.5 *Carrie's Letter to Jade*

Text Forms

Another question of form that young children try to answer during the experimenting stage is, "How do whole written language products look?" They are concerned not only with such components of written language products as words and collections of words, but also with the overall organizational features of different kinds of writing.

Even novices are aware of several text formats when they play with writing in different contexts for various purposes. In Chapter 5, there were several examples of novices' greeting cards, lists, and stories. Experimenters continue to be interested in a variety of text forms.

Variety and Recognizability

Experimenters provide greater recognizability with the variety of text forms they use. Unlike novices' writings, experimenters' writings do not have to be byproducts of a larger activity, such as a pretend game. We can call a novice's letter a letter because the child shows an intention that it be treated as such—as Giti did when she said, "For Grandma" and pretended to mail her letter. However, we do not need these suggestions when we see the letter that a young experimenter writes; it includes composites of real letters of the alphabet (or words) and it is likely to resemble an adult's letter in both choice and arrangement of those words. Figure 7.1 showed Ted's written query/protest. Figures 7.6, 7.7, and 7.8 show a game, a label, and a list Ted wrote when he was five years old. These examples show how an experimenter's written products more closely resemble those of adults than those of novices. Ted asked for help spelling the words in Figures 7.7 and 7.8.

Figure 7.6 *Ted's Homemade Game*

Figure 7.7 *Ted's Picture with Label*

Figure 7.8 *A Job List Ted Made for His Family*

There are two reasons for this recognizability. The first reason is that experimenters have better control over the smaller units of form than novices do. They can form most of the letters of the alphabet and they know that composites of letters (words) are more important than individual letters. The second reason is that experimenters can sometimes use the appropriate language for various kinds of texts, such as "Once upon a time" for stories.

In the next section, we will concentrate on two text forms, the story and the letter.

Story Writing

Suppose we asked some novices and some experimenters to write stories (Sulzby, 1985b). In Chapter 4, we learned that some children might draw their stories, others might scribble their stories, and still others might make stories consisting of mock letters. These are ways in which we would expect novices to compose. The facts that such children are willing to begin a storywriting task and that they can tell a story indicate that they have some notion of what a story is.

Informed refusals.   What would we expect experimenters to do? Although it sounds paradoxical (because even novices are willing to write stories), one thing we would expect some experimenters to do is refuse at first to write a story. Sulzby (1985b) has argued that those who refuse are comparing easy writing tasks that they can do well such as writing their names with the more difficult task of writing a story, and they are saying in effect, "I can't do *that*!" This kind of refusal implies some knowledge of what *that* entails. It is not the outright refusal of a beginner. It is an *informed refusal*. These experimenters know that there are requirements for storywriting and they feel unable to satisfy them.

Informed refusal is typical of the experimenters' behavior of being aware of what they do not know (recall the first behavior set at the beginning of this chapter). It is not that experimenters do not know what a story is; even novices have begun to develop a concept of story, as we saw in Chapter 5. Rather, experimenters know that stories have many more words than they could hope to produce.

Eventually, most experimenters can be encouraged to *try* writing a story, especially if they know that adults will be satisfied with less than a complete story. This willingness to write is what we described in the third behavior set at the beginning of this chapter. When they do comply, it is *not* a case of our calling their writings *stories* after the fact as we often do for novices. Rather, experimenters are willing to write something with the understood *prior* requirement that it be a story; that is a brave undertaking.

Many ways to write a story.   Once experimenters are willing to try writing a story, it is interesting to note the variety of ways they deal with their awareness of their production limitations. Some children who can write words in other contexts such as in making a list remain overwhelmed by this difficult task. They revert to novice-like behaviors such as drawing their stories, producing lines of scribble (as Cody did when she wrote a bedtime story with three wavy lines even though she was able to write both her name and her friend's name with letters—see Chapter 2), or producing combinations of known letter forms and known words. However, if one asks these children to read their stories, they reveal that they know a great deal about how a story sounds; they know what kind of language this text form requires.

Figure 7.9 shows a story written by a first grader named Justin. Immediately after writing, he read it to his teacher: "A little boy. He's little. And he went across the street to do some . . . and somebody picked him up and somebody took . . . and he went with him." When he later volunteered to read his story to his classmates, it was basically unchanged: "There was a little boy. He went across the street. He went to the grocery store and somebody picked him up."

Figure 7.9 *Justin's Story*

Because many experimenters know what kind of language is required in a story, one way to encourage their storywriting is to explain that they can write a story by telling it to another person for that person to write down. Dictating is, in fact, a kind of writing.

Figure 7.10 shows a story that four-year-old Carrie told to her mother during lunch, knowing that her mother would write it down on the blank pages of a little book for Carrie to illustrate. Carrie knew what to do in order to tell a story. She knew she must create a character and keep telling about him or her long enough to fill a book. Her story has some unity in that it is about events in the day of a single character ("a chip"). There is some temporal ordering of those events (school in the morning, lunch, Mother's arrival, and Mother's lunch), but only a few events are necessarily connected. Going to school, being at school, thinking about going home, the bell ringing, and going home form a connected

Figure 7.10 Carrie's Dictated Story

The Chip Goes to School

A chip went to school. When he was at school, he thought, "Oh dear, maybe I need to go home." Then the teacher ringed her bell and said, "It's time to go home." Then he goes home. He looks out the window and sees his friend. He sits on his deck and thinks a little bit. He climbs on his tree and picks some apples. He eats his lunch. He washes his dishes. He sees his mommy driving her car in the garage. He goes in the dining room with his mother, Mrs. Chip. She holds him in her lap. Then they go in the living room and play. The mother has her lunch. Then they read a story. The end.

subset of events that make sense only in relation to each other; eating lunch and washing dishes form another.

The most revealing thing about this early story, which was only the second one Carrie dictated to someone else, is that so much of it was tied to Carrie's immediate experience. The main character was a chip; Carrie was eating chips for lunch. This made a novel character, but there was no follow-up, nothing to suggest how the life of a chip would be different from Carrie's own. After the school episode, which reflected Carrie's own nursery school experience, she depended on immediately available props in order to invent additional events. She included the deck and the apple tree as soon as she noticed them outside the window from the table where she was having lunch. The story ended with what Carrie actually wanted her mother to do with her after lunch (play and read a story).

Some experimenters may call upon their word writing knowledge and produce rows or columns of words using unconventional spelling (a process that will be treated in detail later in this chapter). As we have seen, these experimenters' treatments of word boundaries are also likely to be unconventional. Paul was such a child. A few days after making his PAULSBZR and PAULSTLEFN-MBR labels, which we have already described, he wrote a story. Paul used invented spellings; for example, he spelled "Once upon a time" WANS APNA TM (Bissex, 1980, p. 8). He divided his one-sentence text ("Once upon a time there was a bear and that bear went away and he never came back again") evenly among five pages, sometimes dividing words and sentences unconventionally. Each page contained three rows of print, but what we call a *word* might have been combined with another word or continued from one line to the next or from one page to the next.

Other experimenters might write a story by asking a parent, a teacher, or a more knowledgeable child how to spell the needed words. Figure 7.11 shows a story that a kindergartner wrote by copying the words his teacher had written as he dictated the story.

Whether these stories are dictated, written with invented spellings, or read from the child's non-conventional print, the writer's choice of words can show such story features as sequence of events, past tense, and storywriting expressions. In some cases the arrangement of words may be book-like (as with Paul's use of separate pages).

The detective dog is looking for two things. A pot of gold and a broken toy.

Figure 7.11 A Kindergartner's Story Copied from His Dictation

Three cautions.   At this point, we must present three related cautions. The first is that it is important to look at more than the product when considering a young child's knowledge of text form. You must also observe the child's processes; that is, you must look and listen during and after the child's composing. It is easy to infer that a writer has some knowledge of story text form when he or she produces something that starts with ''Once upon a time'' (even if it is spelled WANS APNA TM), but it is important to recognize that a child who *says* ''Once upon a time'' while scribbling or rereading a ''story'' displays similar knowledge.

Our second caution follows from these examples. It is a reminder that there is considerable variety from child to child and, even for one child, from task to task. Children who revert to novice-like means for writing a story because they know that a story has many more words than they could attempt with real letters may still, with other tasks such as storybook reading or dictating a story, show experimenter-like knowledge of how a story *sounds*.

The third caution is that story knowledge is a very complex set of concepts. With the story text form, it is quite possible for children to experiment with the language of storytelling and to gloss over or put off paying attention to physically representing their stories on a piece of paper. This may be explained by the fact that children can acquire knowledge of story language and of storytelling conventions from a variety of experiences including some—like telling and being told stories—that are divorced from print.

Letter Writing

A simpler example of text form knowledge, which is inseparably tied to print, is knowledge of letter writing. The way the product looks is a more salient aspect of writing a letter (for example, to a friend) than of writing a story.

This time we ask, "How would a novice write a letter and how would an experimenter write a letter?" We have already shown examples of both. Giti is the novice whose letters we described earlier. She wrote letters by scribbling and using the important letter *G*, which is in both her name and her grandmother's. Carrie is the experimenter whose letter writing is shown in Figures 7.4 and 7.5. Carrie's letters to her cousins and uncle include an experimentation with words and written language phrases that Giti's letters lack. Carrie used the strategy of asking her brother or parents how to spell each word.

Two Observations about Text Forms

Two final positive observations about young experimenters' knowledge of text forms must be emphasized: (1) young experimenters are aware that written language products are not all alike, and (2) young experimenters use some of the conventions that accomplished writers use. The first observation is not surprising; we saw its beginnings even in novices' writings. It is an expected result of children's seeing so many kinds of print around them and having so many purposes for writing. The second observation *is* surprising. We tend to think of children at this stage as not yet being very knowledgeable about written language. Even when we are accepting and supportive, what usually catches our attention in children's experimental products are their mistakes. It is important to remember that there is much that is correct in their products, even by conventional standards.

EXPERIMENTING WITH MEANING-FORM LINKS

In order to become literate, children must learn that writing demands special kinds of language and special care with language. Written language uses more complex sentence structures than spoken language. It also uses more specialized vocabulary and many conventional or formulaic expressions such as "Once upon a time" and "Dear _____." In addition, written language is permanent. Unlike spoken language, it can be examined and re-examined; it can be read by people at different times and in locations different from that of the author. Carrie understood this when she wrote to her uncle who lived in a distant state (Figure 7.5). Other ways in which meaning and form are linked have to do with the fact that English orthography (spelling) is alphabetic; that is, letters represent sounds in words. Some of the earlier examples of Paul's writings illustrate his working out the spoken sound/written symbol relation.

Rule One: Sound Literate

One rule that children gradually acquire about the relation between spoken language and written language might be stated: "Use special words and special combinations of words when you write or read. Everyday conversational talk will not do." Acquiring this special talk is related to the experimentation with text form previously discussed. Examples of special talk include children's use of "Once upon at time" and their use of past tense in stories they told or wrote.

Sounding Literate in Reading

Experimenters have opportunities to sound literate when they read books (although they are not "really reading" by conventional standards) and when they dictate stories to an adult scribe. Sulzby (1985a) has developed and tested a classification scheme (Figure 7.12) for young children's retellings of their favorite storybooks. The first step in this scale involves retelling stories by labeling pictures and the second step involves retelling stories using oral or conversation-like language. Novices follow these two steps (see Chapter 4).

A major step along Sulzby's scale is the transition from story retellings' being oral-language-like to their being written-language-like. The intonation of written-language-like retellings is different from the intonation of conversational speech. By slowing their rate of speech and using stress expressively, children sound as if they are reading. Even though its wording may not be verbatim, a written-language-like retelling may use some unusual expressions from the text; it often includes the more formal, more complex sentence structure that the child has come to expect from books (Sulzby, 1985a).

Figure 7.12 *Elizabeth Sulzby's Classification Scheme for Emergent Reading of Favorite Storybooks*

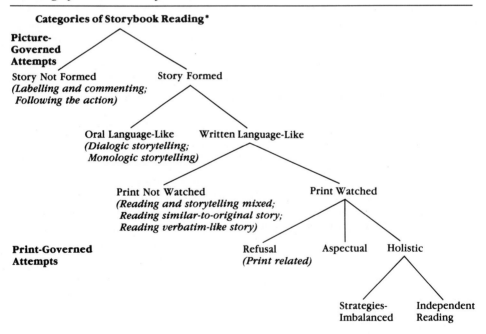

*This figure includes independent reading attempts only: the child is making the reading attempts without dependence upon turn-taking reading or interrogation by the adult.

From Sulzby, E. (1985). Children's emergent reading of favorite storybooks: A developmental study. *Reading Research Quarterly, 20,* p. 464. Reprinted with permission of the International Reading Association.

Four-year-old Carrie had often listened to her parents and older brother read *The Three Bears* (1952). It was one of her favorite books. When her father asked her to read it to him, she knew the story of Goldilocks and the three bears very well, but she could not reproduce it exactly as it was written; she could neither read the words of the text nor depend upon a verbatim memorization. But she *could* use appropriate intonation and she did include expressions and verb tenses from the text that would not occur in her everyday talk.

Carrie retold the entire story of Goldilocks and the three bears. In addition to the traditional content, however, she included elements that are unique to her book's version of the the story. Figure 7.13 shows a portion of Carrie's retelling of *The Three Bears* in which she included descriptions of Papa Bear's repairing the roof, Mama Bear's watering flowers, and Baby Bear's doing tricks on the lawn. Although her book includes illustrations of the three bears doing just those things, an important quality in Carrie's retelling of the story is that she did not merely give a present-tense description of those pictures. Before the pause in the first excerpt shown in Figure 7.13, she was not talking about something in her world. That is, she was not talking about the illustration in the book that she and her father were holding. Rather, she was talking about what had happened in

Figure 7.13 *Selections from Carrie's Retelling of The Three Bears* (1952)

Text:	Reading:
. . .	. . .
(From second and third pages. The illustration shows Mama Bear and Baby Bear in the foreground. She is watering tulips. He and a rabbit are doing handstands while a little bird watches. In the background Papa Bear is on a ladder repairing the roof of their house.)	(In an even voice, at a steady pace, until the end, when her voice rises)
Papa Bear pounded nails in the roof. Mama Bear watered the flowers. Baby Bear did tricks on the lawn.	"And Papa nailed the roof. Mama—Mama watered the flowers. And Baby Bear did tricks on the lawn."
	(Short pause. Laughter. Then in higher pitch, with rising and falling intonation, and faster pace)
	"The bird's just watching!"
. . .	. . .
(From twenty-first page)	(In a very high-pitched voice)
"Someone has broken my tiny chair all to pieces!"	"'And she's broken it all to pieces!'"
. . .	. . .

the different world, the make-believe world of her story, a world that her book's pictures happen to illustrate.

The proof of this is what happened after the pause, when Carried actually shifted out of a story-reading mode into a picture-describing mode. When Carrie said "The bird's just watching " she was commenting about the little bird in the book's illustration that is sitting on the lawn next to Baby Bear as he does his tricks. For this one sentence, Carrie's intonation changed from the official story-teller's steady pace and even voice to the rising and falling voice and quicker pace one uses in conversation. With her comment about the bird, Carrie was back in the present world talking *about* her favorite book to her father, whom she assumed shared her appreciation of the book's charms. Another indication of this shift is the change in Carrie's verb tenses, from past tense (*nailed, watered, did tricks*) when reading the book, to present progressive tense (The bird*'s just watching*) when talking about the book.

Carrie also used language that was peculiar to the text of her very familiar book. She recreated the book's odd description of Papa Bear's behavior. Both the book and Carrie described him not as repairing the roof or fixing the roof, but as pounding nails in the roof!

Throughout Carrie's retelling of *The Three Bears,* she clearly indicated who was talking, at first with dialogue markers such as "Papa said" and "Mama said " and later by using a loud, deep voice for Papa Bear, a high voice for Mama Bear, and a very high voice for Baby Bear.

There were other ways that Carrie's retelling was parallel to, but not a perfect replication of the text. She frequently used the book's verb tenses in her recreation of the characters' speech. For example, in the second excerpt shown in Figure 7.13, she did not have Baby Bear say—as a four-year-old might—that someone "broke" his chair; rather she repeated the book's *has broken* in her "she*'s broken.*" Her retelling also included the book's attempt at a happy ending, with the three bears calling to Goldilocks as she ran away, "Come back! We want to be friends!"

Sounding Literate in Writing

Children who are acquiring Rule One ("Sound Literate") also use special written-language-like talk when they dictate stories. Sulzby (1985b) has described written-language-aware children as being able, in effect, to take charge and dictate a story without asides or inserted questions. They know that dictating a story is different from telling a story. They are aware that they are authors. They do not speak in order to communicate with or to entertain their scribe. Instead, they communicate with unknown, non-present future readers. This awareness of the scribe's true role is related to a notion of faithfulness to print, which is the focus of Rule Two.

Rule Two: Be Precise

A second rule about the relation between spoken and written language might be stated: "Be precise about which words you (or your scribe) write and about which words you read back from your writing (or from someone else's). Only the words that the author formulated while writing may be read when the author or someone else reads what was written.'' In other words, reading is different from telling. There are some corollaries to this rule. One is that you must *not* read if you do not know the very words of the text; only a verbatim rendition counts as reading. Another corollary is that written products must be able to stand alone; they must be decontextualized. Your written product cannot depend on context because the reader will have only the written words with which to build understanding. Still another corollary is that you must have a sense of audience; you must consider whether the wording of your message will be effective for your expected readers. Finally, if someone is writing for you, you must dictate slowly in order to give that scribe time to get every word.

Being Precise in Reading

At the beginning of this chapter, we described the literacy behaviors of Julie, who had memorized large parts of her favorite storybook. She was being precise. Her preoccupation with precision was so great that she would not attempt to read the parts of the story that she had not memorized. This preoccupation stays with some children for a long time—they become ''glued to print'' (Chall, 1983). Sometimes, unlike mature readers (Goodman, 1967), children are so concerned with correct word identification that they neglect to attend to the meaning of text.

As these examples show, Rule Two takes an experimenter beyond the story retelling behaviors that followed from Rule One. It is not enough to use any literate-sounding talk when retelling a story. This kind of precision is part of the later stages of Sulzby's (1985b) scale of retellings of favorite storybooks (Figure 7.12). Sulzby has found that once children begin using written-language-sounding talk, their reading progresses from a mixture of reading and storytelling, through reading with verbatim memorized chunks of story, to several kinds of print-governed attempts at reading. Sulzby makes the important point that children's performances at this stage should not be dismissed as ''just memorization.'' Their effort to retrieve the actual story shows a new sophistication about how written language works.

An example of a child's reading being governed by preoccupation with precision is Sulzby's subject Daniel's reenactment of *My Cat Likes to Hide in Boxes* (Sutton, 1974). He quickly recited the parts that he knew verbatim, but hesitated and used verbal fillers when he was having trouble retrieving the actual words of the story:

> [Quickly] And the cat in Norway—got stuck in the doorway.
>
> [Slowly] And, um, uh, the cat, oh, and the cat in /Spain-liked-to/ drive an airplane.
>
> [Quickly again] But my cat likes to hide in boxes (Sulzby, 1985b, p. 470).

He also asked the researcher to read what he had not memorized: "And read this page—cause I forget that" (Sulzby, 1985b, p. 470).

We have already emphasized that young experimenters can be aware that they do not know all there is to know about writing and reading. When they are also preoccupied with precision, the result can be one of two behaviors that Sulzby classifies under "print-governed attempts." One is their refusing to even attempt to read ("print-related refusals"). The other is their reading only what they are sure of ("aspectual reading"). When Carrie was almost five years old, she refused to pretend to read favorite books. She had heard many of them as often as she had heard *The Three Bears*. It is safe to assume that she could have read them as well or better. But she began saying, "No, I can't read yet. I'm not old enough." One of Sulzby's aspectual readers recited "*Grandma, the, and, the a, and*" (Sulzby, 1985a, pp. 471–472) for page after page because those were the only words she was sure of. She could identify them wherever she saw them. Words that a child can identify on sight, without using any sounding out or context strategies are called *sight words.*

There is one more step on Sulzby's (1985a) scale—holistic reading. This behavior heralds a still higher level of knowledge and it marks the beginning of the accomplished reading and writing that will be discussed in Chapter 9.

Being Precise in Writing

The previous examples were from children's attempts at reading. As with Rule One, we can find other examples of Rule Two in young experimenters' writing. Children who are able to use dictation to write stories are aware that the scribe must record their words precisely (Sulzby, 1985b). They pause to allow the scribe to catch up and use "voice continuant intonation," in which the voice does not fall before a pause, thus letting the listener—in this case, the scribe—know that there is more to come, that the pause should not be taken to be a conversational pause which would signal that the listener may take a turn at talking.

It is helpful, by way of contrast, to look also at those of Sulzby's subjects who were not yet acting by Rule Two. They displayed their inability to use the dictation process in two ways: either they interpreted the task as making conversation (they invited the scribe to speak by inserting comments and questions) or they failed to initiate any talk (the only way the scribe could get something from them to write down was by continually asking them questions).

Invented Spelling

When Carrie wrote the letters in Figures 7.4 and 7.5, she was not a speller. Whenever she wanted to write something other than a few very familiar words such as her own name, *Hi*, and *Mom*, she asked someone to show her how to spell the words or she drew pictures for the words. Carrie did not try to spell a word on her own, even when encouraged to "spell it the way you think it should be" or "see if you can figure out how it goes." She was unaware that there could be a systematic way of doing so. She did not know that there is a reason why certain letters are used for certain words. She did not know that it might be possible to figure out which letters are appropriate—or at least more appropriate than other, randomly chosen letters—for a given word. Each word was a mystery. She would ask "What does _____ spell?" about the letters in a sign or about her random arrangement of plastic magnetic letters, but she never had a clue about what the letters might spell. In previous sections, you have seen evidence that Paul could figure out some of these things. What did Paul know that Carrie did not know?

A Nonconventional System

In order to spell, writers need a system; they need a rather precise, analytic understanding of the relation between spoken and written language; they need the ability to examine words one sound unit at a time; and they need an awareness of letter–sound relations. These relations can be based on a letter's name. For example, the long *e* sound is also the name for the letter *e* and the *j* sound is in the name for the letter *j* and in the name for the letter *g*. Relations between letters and sounds can also be based on learned associations. A child might learn that *apple* is an *a* word and that the short *a* sound goes with the letter *a*.

Even an elementary school child knows much of this. Even before they are in elementary school, however, many young experimenters realize how to use letter–sound relations. Reseachers have called what they do "invented spelling." Read (1971) discovered invented spelling while investigating preschool children's knowledge of English phonology.

Read (1971) began by arguing that it is obvious that even young children know much about the sound system of their language. They *must* have such knowledge in order to speak and understand spoken language. English-speaking children, for example, use two *p* sounds without giving the matter any thought. One is the *p* sound in the word *pit* and the other is the *p* sound in the word *spit*. For the first *p* sound one uses a puff of breath, and for the second sound, one does not. Even young children can say and understand *pit* and *spit*. They use the two different *p* sounds quite well, even though no one has to pay attention to that difference in English words (there is no pair of English words that differs only by one's having one kind of *p* sound and the other's having the other kind of *p* sound).

There are other sound differences that are no greater than the difference between the two *p* sounds, but which *do* distinguish pairs of English words. Even young children handle those quite well too. An example is the difference between the *t* sound and the *d* sound. The only difference between these two sounds is that one is voiced (*d*) and the other is unvoiced, that is, made without using the voice (*t*). However, unlike the difference between the two *p* sounds, the *t*/*d* difference gives information about meanings. For example, that difference alone signals the difference in meaning between the members of the word pairs *tin* and *din, tame* and *dame*, and *tuck* and *duck.*

Even young speakers of English know these things and act accordingly, but they know them unconsciously. *They know without knowing that they know.* Read's research was important in that it demonstrated that such knowledge can be made conscious; it is *accessible* even to young children. He found that many young children, even before they began school, could use their spoken-language knowledge for non-spoken-language tasks. When asked to label their drawings, Read's (1971) preschool subjects, who had not been taught reading or writing or spelling skills, could attend to sound units in words and associate letters with those units in a systematic though unconventional way.

Read's subjects used letter names when deciding what letters to include in their spellings of words. They used the letter *R* in STRT to spell the *ar* segment of *start.* They used sounds in letter names. For example, they paid attention to the *d* sound in the name of the letter *D*, the *k* sound in the name of the letter *K*, and the *m* sound in the name of the letter *M* when writing DA for the word *day* and KAM for the word *came.* They even used similarities in place and manner of articulation. They noted the similarity between the ways the short *i* sound and the name of the letter *e* are pronounced and wrote FLEPR for *flipper* and FES for *fish.* These were not just random mistakes or carelessness; Read found consistencies from child to child. What they did was really spelling.

Read's subjects did not use the standard system that adults have arrived at by convention, but it was just as systematic. Both standard spelling and invented spelling are abstract. That means that they both ignore some sounds in words— not because they are not fully pronounced or not heard, but because they are judged to take care of themselves when the written word is read. But the standard system and invented spelling do not ignore the same things. Standard spelling ignores the affrication in *tr* and *dr* blends. *Affrication* is the burst of air that occurs in the pronunciation of the *tr* and *dr* blends. That sound is not represented in conventional spellings of words that begin with those blends. This is true even though that same burst of air *is* spelled with a *j* or a *ch* in other contexts, such as in *juice* and *chain.* Read (1971) found that inventive spellers repeatedly chose to represent that burst of air in the *dr* and *tr* blends. Children spelled the affrication in *try* with a *ch* (CHRIE) and in *dragon* with a *j* (JRAGIN). On the other hand, invented spelling ignores nasals before consonants (NUBRS for *numbers,* AD for *and,* PLAT for *plant,* and GOWEG for *going*), while standard spelling represents them.

Spelling Development

Read's (1971) work has influenced both classroom practice (e.g., Chomsky, 1971; Lancaster, Nelson, & Morris, 1982; Paul, 1976; Sowers, 1988) and research (Burns & Richgels, 1989; Vukelich & Edwards, 1988). One finding from this research is that inventive spellers progress through stages that culminate with conventional spelling (Gentry, 1982; Morris, 1981). This is reassuring to skeptical parents and teachers, and it is also not surprising. We have just described what inventive spellers know as being a system; their spellings are not haphazard. The fact that their spelling system is not the conventional one adults use is not as important as the fact that it *is* a system. Inventive spellers know what spelling is supposed to accomplish. They must only progress to knowing how to accomplish it in the conventional systematic way rather than in their invented systematic way.

Figure 7.14 shows five stages in that progression. These stages are intended to clarify the direction of change in children's spelling development. Children often show spelling behaviors from more than one stage in a single piece of writing. What is important is that over time their spellings resemble later stages more than earlier stages.

Figure 7.14 is based on similar schemes described by Gentry (1982) and Morris (1981), who based their stages on Read's (1975) and Henderson and Beers' (1980) work. The five stages are labeled *Non-Spelling* (because it is random, not systematic), *Early Invented Spelling, Purely Phonetic Spelling, Mixed Spelling,* and *Fully Conventional Spelling.* Spelling behaviors that are typical of young experimenters are included in the Early Invented Spelling and Purely Phonetic Spelling stages.

The Non-Spelling stage describes novices' fixation with letters. This stage is characterized primarily by a lack of awareness of letter–sound correspondences. Non-Spellers choose letters randomly, as Paul did in his ''cheering up'' message to his mother, described earlier in this chapter (Bissex, 1980). Because they seem to believe in some power of the letters themselves to communicate, Non-Spellers can also be characterized as lacking a concept of word. Individual letters in their writing are not even representative of beginning sounds in the words of their intended message.

There are two stages of spelling development that we do not believe most experimenters reach, Mixed Spelling and Fully Conventional Spelling. Accomplished writers (described in Part 4) move through those stages.

We can use the Early Invented Spelling and Purely Phonetic Spelling stages to make several generalizations about the invented spelling behaviors one can expect to find in many young experimenters' writing. Young experimenters use letters to make words based on analyses of sound units in words and knowledge of letter–sound correspondences. They progress from only partial to nearly complete encoding of word sounds, and from representing only consonant sounds to representing consonants and vowels. At the end of this experimenting time, they may begin incorporating some English spelling conventions for frequently occurring word parts (such as *-ed*). However, the primary characteristic of experimenters is spelling without regard for standard conventions. Instead, they systematically use letter–sound correspondences.

Although experimenters do not spell most words conventionally, Richgels (1986) found that they do know a lot about letter–sound correspondences. First graders at the beginning of the year spelled whole words conventionally only 14 percent of the time, but represented 93 percent of initial consonant sounds, 76 percent of final consonant sounds, and 70 percent of vowel sounds in a manner consistent with the invented spelling strategies described by Read (1971).

***Figure* 7.14** *Stages of Spelling Development*

Non-Spelling

Some alphabet knowledge

No letter–sound knowledge

Random stringing together of letters of the alphabet

No concept of word

Example: Paul's "cheering up" message (Bissex, 1980)

Early Invented Spelling

Nearly complete alphabet knowledge

Knowledge that sounds can be associated with letters

Letter-name strategy

Frequent omission of vowels (especially non-long vowel sounds, for which a letter-name
   strategy does not work)

Encoding of only some parts of a word

Emergence of concept of word (some segmentation of word strings at word boundaries)

Examples: N for *nose*, BD for *bird*, SWM for *swim*

Purely Phonetic Spelling

Based strictly on letter–sound correspondences

Encoding of all parts of a word

Letter-name strategy for long vowels

Use of similarity of articulation for short vowels

Omission of "unheard" vowels and nasals before consonants

Segmentation of letter strings at most word boundaries

Examples: KRI for *cry*, BRD for *bird*, BREJ for *bridge*, PLAT for *plant*

Mixed (Phonetic and Visual) Spelling

Going beyond one-to-one encoding of sounds with letters

Attention to familiar visual configurations of letters and to such word parts as prefixes
   and suffixes

Knowledge of several conventions for encoding a single sound (but not always using the
   correct convention for a given word, and not always remembering the correct order
   of letters in the conventional spelling)

Frequently correct spelling of short vowels

Awareness of basic conventions of English spelling, such as placing a vowel in every
   syllable

Examples: THAY for *they*, ALLSO for *also*, KITTON for *kitten*, BRID for *bird*

Figure 7.14 (continued)

Fully Conventional Spelling

Knowledge of the basic rules of the conventional English spelling system

Recognition of one's own spelling errors

A large repertoire of learned words

Stages are based on Gentry (1982) and Morris (1981). Examples of Early Invented Spelling, Purely Phonetic Spelling, and Mixed Spelling are from research conducted by the authors.

EXPERIMENTING WITH THE FUNCTIONS OF WRITTEN LANGUAGE

We have already presented much information about children's experimentation with the functions of written language. Young experimenters continue what they began as novices. They continue to use written language to communicate for a variety of purposes. Carrie's letter writing demonstrates use of written language for such general purposes as to communicate over distances and for such specific purposes as to thank someone ("Thanks for all the presents"), and even just to be sociable ("How is the weather?"). We have seen writing to tell stories, to voice a protest, to make a game, to label a picture, and to keep a list.

Three Higher Functions of Written Language

What remains in this section is to emphasize three points about all this experimentation with function. One is that children at this stage of literacy development often work with an additional purpose, which is simply to experiment. Young experimenters devote large amounts of energy to literacy tasks; it seems that they realize that one purpose for reading and writing is to learn to read and write. They appear to know that you learn it by doing it. Young experimenters read and write in order to try out their theories of what reading and writing are. We can see this in Carrie's questions about words. She asked what S-C-I-T-E-M-S-O-C (*cosmetics* spelled backwards) spelled and wanted to know "*Now* what does it spell?" about her random combinations of plastic letters. We can also see it in Paul's various attempts to spell and to show boundaries between words. He wrote PAULSTLEFNMBR one time and TAL·A·FON another (Bissex, 1980).

A second point is that experimenters may engage in literacy tasks with the purpose of pleasing others; adults ask them to and sometimes they comply. Experimenters may write and read because they know that showing interest in and an ability for literacy tasks usually wins recognition and applause, just as other achievements such as walking and talking did at earlier ages. Reading and writing serve the function of identifying children as being interested in membership in the elite community of literates. They continue to play at adult roles that include literacy behaviors just as they did when they were novices. Experimenters may continue pretending to be waitresses, doctors, or receptionists, but they also work intensely at "really reading" and "really writing." They do so in ways that experts can more easily accept.

The third point about experimentation with functions has to do with our Rule Two (Be Precise) and Clay's (1975) Message Concept, which is the realization that the message one speaks can be written down. The most significant function-related conceptual change of the experimental stage is the discovery that written language can preserve a writer's message exactly or precisely. Children discover that they can use written language to communicate exactly what they want to say to their cousin or uncle, to keep precise records of important messages, or to tell stories exactly as they want someone else to read them. Of course, even written language is open to various interpretations by others, as was illustrated with the THANK YOU FOR NOT SMOKING example in Chapter 2. However, this can be overlooked by children when they first discover the Message Concept or when they become preoccupied with precision. This gives a unique quality to written language, one that spoken language lacks.

BEYOND THEORY:
AN EXPERIMENTER AT WORK

This chapter has described young children's experimentation with meaning making, with forms of written language, with meaning-form links, and with functions of written language. We will use a case study of Carrie's letter writing as a basis for reviewing many of this chapter's observations about experimenters. This case study also demonstrates how vital it is to observe very carefully what children do when they write and read, how they call for and use support from adults or older children, and their reasons for reading and writing.

Carrie's Letter Writing

During the two months following Carrie's drawing of the composite of letters and pictures shown in Figure 7.2, several factors set off a flurry of letter writing. At the same time that she was very interested in name writing and picture drawing (Figure 7.3), there were several occasions that called for letter writing and many examples for her to imitate of letter writing by her parents and by her eight-year-old brother, Ted.

Five of Carrie's Letters

The first occasion was writing to Santa Claus before Christmas. Carrie's brother encouraged her to write such a letter, but she refused any help from him. Her letter was just her name, spelled iCAiERR, and one other stray mark on a piece of paper that she folded several times and placed in a plain envelope for mailing.

The second occasion occurred within a week of her writing to Santa; her grandfather was in the hospital. Carrie was in her father's office, where she had on past occasions played with the typewriter. She asked her father, "Can I write a letter to Grandpa at the doctor's?'' When he asked why, she replied, ''Cause I want him to feel better.'' Her father agreed to help her write a letter. She told what she wanted to say; he wrote each word on a piece of paper as she needed it; and she copied each word by finding the right keys on the keyboard. The resulting letter (see Figure 7.15) included such conventions as starting with ''Dear _____ and ending with ''Love, _____,'' which Carrie probably learned from having letters read to her.

DEARGRANDPA,

I HOPE YOU REA FEELING BETTER.

LOVE, cAiEPIR

Figure 7.15 *Carrie's Get Well Letter to Her Grandfather*

The sophisticated format of this letter resulted from Carrie's father's showing her the space bar before writing a new word for her to copy and his pushing the return button for each new line. (In her later handwritten letters, she would retain some of these characteristics and abandon others.) Each time she typed a word, Carrie said, ''Wow!'' Her father asked her to sign her name and draw a picture. As she did so, she explained, ''I draw the whole family. I'll draw me first 'cause I wrote the letter.'' Her father addressed an envelope on the typewriter and together they took the letter to the mailbox. On Carrie's next visit to her grandparents, after her grandfather's return from the hospital, she saw her letter displayed on their refrigerator.

The next opportunity for letter writing occurred three weeks later, after Christmas. For two weeks, Carrie's parents talked about and wrote letters they owed people to thank them for Christmas hospitality and Christmas presents and to answer letters received in Christmas cards. They also required that Ted write thank you letters to relatives who had given him Christmas presents.

One day, Carrie wrote three letters. One was a letter that said, "SANTA THANKYOU CARRIE." Carrie included a self-portrait like the one in Figure 7.4, other drawings, and she circled her name. She asked for help with the plastic letters for spelling *Santa* and *Thankyou*. She put the thank you letter in an envelope, taped it shut, and drew another picture of herself on the outside.

Five days later, Carrie wrote another letter to Santa, again with help (which she always requested) using the plastic letters (see Figure 7.16). This letter was all words. On a separate sheet of paper, she also drew a house, wrote *Santa*, and wrote her name. She put both pages in an envelope with SANTA written on the front and CARRIE on the back.

Figure 7.16 *Carrie's Third Letter to Santa Claus*

A final example of Carrie's letter writing was composed a few days later. This letter is Figure 7.5. Carrie announced that she was going to write to her uncle Jade, asked if he had given the family any presents, and asked how to spell *Jade, Thank you,* and *How is the weather?* Each part that Carrie circled in Figure 7.5 was set out separately, using the plastic letters for her to copy. When she said that she was finished, her father asked, "How is Jade going to know who that letter is from?" She answered, "O.K. I'll write 'Carrie.'" She said the name of each letter in her name as she wrote it, made two mistakes, erased them, and corrected them. Then she drew a picture of herself on the back of the paper and said, "Jade's going to be so pleased with the letter." She folded it and asked that her father put it in an envelope.

What Carrie's Letters Show

What does Carrie's letter writing over two months in the middle of her fourth year show? One way to answer this question is to consider the seven behavior sets with which we began this chapter. Those behaviors were children's (1) knowing that they do not know how to read as adults do, (2) being willing to work at reading and writing when it is meaningful to them, (3) responding to someone else's enlisting them to write or read at their level, (4) attending to larger units than individual letters of the alphabet, (5) knowing some conventional features of writing, (6) being systematic spellers, and (7) using written-language-like language. With her letter writing, Carrie demonstrated all of these behaviors, with the exception of spelling. As we noted earlier, she did not have a system for spelling; she used a few words that she knew from memory and depended on others to show her how to spell new words. Carrie's asking for help with spelling showed her awareness that she did not know all that one needs to know to be able to write (Behavior Set One). She worked intensely at her letters, even writing three in one day, and she was willing to take her parents' or Ted's suggestions when there were few and they were offered without criticism (Behavior Sets Two and Three).

Carrie's ability to produce letters of the alphabet was quite sophisticated. She could form any capital letter (Behavior Set Four). One can see a progression in her ability to make an *R*. Her *R*'s in Figure 7.16 look more conventional than those made earlier in Figure 7.15. Carrie was working on more than one level of form at a time; she was working at alphabet letter formation and at letters as a text form.

Carrie's baseline of writing ability included her own name (Behavior Set Five). At first, she did not spell it correctly (see Figure 7.15), but by the last letter in the sequence (Figure 7.5), she not only produced a correct spelling, but also came to it quite conscientiously (saying the letters' names aloud as she wrote, erasing and correcting mistakes).

Finally, Carrie's letters were full of letter-writing language (Behavior Set Seven). From the beginning, she knew that for her products to qualify as letters, they must include a name or names (always either her name or the name of the person she was writing to, often both) even though they also might be composed partly of pictures. Before long, her concept of the letter as text form included certain formulaic expressions, such as "Thank you for all the presents" and "How is the weather?"

The importance of names in letters might have made the letter a particularly attractive text form for a recent novice. Novices' own names are often the only words in their writings. Carrie's first letter was composed of only her name. Her rapid move to include her addressee's name was supported by her family's suggestions and by her own widening interest in names. She was interested in other people's names even outside of her letter writing. Besides her name as signature or label to accompany her self-portrait, Figure 7.3 included an *E* and a *t*, which were two of the letters in her brother Ted's name. Two of the first words (other than her own name) that she learned to spell from memory were *MOM* and *DAD*.

Very soon, Carrie's letters (with their circles around words) and the questions she asked as she composed them (about words and how to spell them) showed that she was fixated on words in general, and not just on names. Her choice of words showed her desire to sound literate and her insistence that her family display spellings for her showed her precision.

Carrie's letter writing exploited several unique functions of written language. She used letters to make communications that she could not make in person and that she wished to be permanent. (Both aspects were epitomized by her letter to her grandfather, which not only was mailed a long distance, but also was preserved and posted on his refrigerator.) Perhaps most striking of all, Carrie wanted to write letters in order to be part of the community of letter writers in which she found herself.

The example of Carrie's letter writing shows the importance of meaning making even while a child experiments with form, meaning-form links, and functions of written language. The messages that Carrie intended to convey were always present in the literacy events we have described. The fact that she wanted to say "Thank you" or "I hope you are feeling better" was never obscured by her experimenting with alphabet letter formation or with the letter text form.

Beyond Carrie's Case

Although not every child writes letters as Carrie did, most children progress from name writing to word writing using the text forms that other people and events in their lives happen to make functional and attractive to them. It just so happened that Carrie found a reason for using names and words in the letter text form at the same time that she was concerned with how letters of the alphabet could be combined to make her name, then other people's names, and then other words. The reason came from serendipitous occasions and from the support and examples given to her by her family.

It is also important to note that there is much room for differences among readers and writers *who are at the same stage of development.* Even an individual child's writing shows the use of different strategies for different tasks (Barnhart, 1988).

Not all experimenters learn in the same ways. These differences can be seen in Carrie and Paul. Although she was an experimenter, Carrie was not a speller like Paul was. These differences may be due in part to cognitive development and in part to opportunity. Spelling as a system may have been beyond three-year-old Carrie's cognitive abilities, while being perfectly congruent with five-year-old Paul's. There was almost always someone available to answer Carrie's requests to display the magnetic letters that would spell a word she wanted. Besides her interested parents, she had an older brother who was sometimes cooperative and was a natural literacy authority for Carrie. In contrast, Paul was an only child.

It is also important to note that both Carrie and Paul were growing up in homes where reading and writing were valued activities. Their parents not only encouraged, but also intuitively expected their children to be readers and writers.

Dyson (1985) noted the importance of another factor that contributes to individual differences in writing and reading development—personality. Some children more readily exhibit one or another of the seven behavior sets with which we began this chapter or they are more likely to be motivated in one of the ways we discussed at the end of this chapter's section about functions of written language—because that is the way they are. Independent children, for example, may not care particularly whether or not they belong to the elite group of literates, but they may be especially driven by intellectual curiosity to work out the spelling of new words using letter–sound correspondences.

We return to the statement with which we began this chapter: There is no single behavior or even profile of behaviors that describes an experimenter. *Some* of the descriptions in this chapter are often sufficient to signal that a child is an experimenter. This time of transition includes much knowledge and many related behaviors in the areas of meaning making, form, meaning-form links, and functions of written language. It is not surprising that no child covers all that territory at once or in the same manner as another child (Fueyo, 1989).

Two Cautions

We hope that this chapter does not lead readers to two misconceptions. The first has to do with ages; they are not the important part of any description of children as experimenters. The children in our examples have been various ages. We have told their ages only to accurately present the facts of the real-life examples we used. As we illustrated in our discussion of Carrie's not being a speller and Paul's being a speller, age may indicate such developmental factors as cognitive ability. However, as Carrie's and Paul's cases also illustrate, age is only *one* pertinent fact in any literacy event. Although Carrie began writing with words when she was three, many three-year-olds do not. Paul was five years old when he began the experimentation with writing and reading that Bissex (1980) describes.

The ages we have given do not set norms against which to compare other children. Many children come to kindergarten and even to first grade not acting as experimenters. We have no reason to believe that they will fail to learn to read or write or even that they will fall behind. Of much greater value than age is the behavior one can observe in a literacy event; what the child knows or learns in the event; and how adults support that behavior, knowledge, and discovery. From this information, we can gain insights that will guide our approaches to other children with whom we share similar literacy events, regardless of their ages.

The second misconception has to do with identification of children as experimenters. *Identification is not important for its own sake.* It does not really matter whether Carrie or Paul or any other child is called an experimenter. What matters is that teachers know what literacy behaviors children are willing and able to engage in. Then teachers will understand and support children in the provision of resources, in actions, and in talk. We know that some children's literacy behaviors fall in some manner—however imprecisely—within the broad territory described as the experimenter's. We hope that when teachers recognize such children, they will know how to support the children's continued development as writers and readers.

Chapter Summary

Experimenters are aware that there is a system of written language that they only partly understand. Still, they are up to the adventure of exploring the unknown territory. They respond to adults' encouragment with short, deliberate, focused episodes of reading and writing.

The meaning making that experimenters do is similar to what they did as novices. They continue writing in order to represent a message, and continue using sophisticated strategies for interacting with books.

Some of the most striking new achievements of experimenters have to do with their greater control over form. They make letters of the alphabet that are recognizable by conventional standards. They acquire a concept of word, and they devise means for showing word boundaries in their writing. Besides knowing what physical arrangements (formats) are appropriate for different text forms, they also know what language (choice of words) is appropriate.

Typically, experimenters can conventionally spell their names and a few other words. Many experimenters go farther and demonstrate their exploration of the relation between spoken lan-

guage and written language by invented spelling. They carefully analyze speech sounds in almost any word they want to write, and match those sounds with letters. Another way experimenters show new knowledge of meaning-form links is by using special written-language-like-talk in literacy events. Often they are aware that written language is more precise than spoken language, and that what readers say depends on what writers write.

As with novices, written language serves a variety of functions for experimenters. A new purpose for their reading and writing is simply to experiment. They sometimes engage in literacy events with the additional purposes of pleasing others and being exact.

Carrie's case study demonstrated the importance of careful observation of young children's experimentation with written language. Each child discovers his or her own path through the intricacies of meaning making, form, meaning-form links, and functions of written language described in this chapter. It is essential that teachers be attentive to how children ask for and use support for that experimentation.

Applying the Information

A case study of a literacy event involving five-year-old Ben and his mother fol-

lows. While there is not as much detail as was presented earlier on Carrie's letter writing, there is sufficient information for you to reach some conclusions about what Ben knows about literacy. How is Ben experimenting with written language? What does he know about meaning making, form, meaning-form links, and functions of written language? Try to organize your observations in the same manner as our observations about Carrie's letter writing.

Ben complained that he had nothing to do. His mother suggested that he write a story. He had never written one

before, but to his mothers surprise, he took up the challenge. He returned in a few minutes with these three lines of letters:

WNSAPNATMTEWDKDRWOTOTNTE
BOSAD HEDKD
FEH

He read them as, "Once upon a time the woodcutter went out in the boat and he did catch fish." Ben's mother understood why Ben ended the story as he did. Ben had been unsuccessful on a recent fishing excursion.

Going Beyond the Text

Visit a kindergarten classroom. Join the children who are writing. Notice what their writing activities are. What experimenting behaviors do you observe? What text forms are the children using? How many of them are spellers? Begin your own writing activity (writing a letter, a story, a list of some kind, a reminder to yourself, or a poem). Talk about it with the children. How many of them take up your activity and attempt similar pieces? Does the character

of their writing change from what it was for their own activities? Is there more or less invented spelling, more or less word writing, and more or less scribbling?

Ask the teacher if children have favorite storybooks. If so, invite children to read their favorites to you. How do they interpret that invitation? If they would rather you read to them, how willing are they to supply parts of the reading? What parts do they know best? What parts do they like best?

References

BAGHBAN, M. (1984). *Our daughter learns to read and write: A case study from birth to three.* Newark, DE: International Reading Association.

BARNHART, J. E. (1988). The relationship between graphic form and the child's underlying conceptualization of writing. In J. E. Readence & R. S. Baldwin (Eds.), *Dialogues in literacy research, thirty-seventh yearbook of the National Reading Conference* (pp. 297–306). Chicago, IL: National Reading Conference.

BISSEX, G. L. (1980). *GNYS AT WRK: A child learns to write and read.* Cambridge, MA: Harvard University Press.

BURNS, J., RICHGELS, D. J. (1989) An investigation of abilities associated with the "invented spelling" ability of four-year-olds of above average intelligence. *Journal of Reading Behavior 21,* 1–14.

CHALL, J. S. (1983). *Stages of reading development.* New York: McGraw-Hill.

CHISERI-STRATER, E. (1988). Reading to Mr. Bear. In T. Newkirk & N. Atwell (Eds.),

Understanding writing: Ways of observing, learning, and teaching (2nd ed.) (pp. 31–39). Portsmouth, NH: Heinemann.

CHOMSKY, C. (1971). Invented spelling in the open classroom, *Word, 27,* 499–518.

CLAY, M. M. (1975). *What did I write? Beginning writing behavior.* Exeter, NH: Heinemann.

DOWNING, J., & OLIVER, P. (1973–1974). The child's conception of a word. *Reading Research Quarterly, 9,* 568–582.

DYSON, A. H. (1985). Individual differences in emerging writing. In M. F. Farr (Ed.), *Advances in writing research, volume one: Children's early writing development* (pp. 59–125). Norwood, NJ: Ablex.

FUEYO, J. (1989). One child moves into meaning—his way. *Langauge Arts, 66,* 137–146.

GARVEY, C. (1984). *Children's talk.* Cambridge, MA: Harvard University Press.

GENTRY, J. R. (1982). An analysis of developmental spelling in GNYS AT WRK. *The Reading Teacher, 36,* 192–200.

GOODMAN, K. (1967). Reading: A psycholinguistic guessing game. *Journal of the Reading Specialist, 4,* 126–135.

GOODMAN, Y. M. (1980). The roots of literacy. In M. P. Douglas (Ed.), *Claremont Reading Conference, 44th Yearbook* (pp. 1–32). Claremont, CA: Claremont Reading Conference.

HARSTE, J. C., BURKE, C. L., & WOODWARD, V. A. (1983). *Young child as writer-reader, and informant* (Final Report Project NIE-G-80-0121). Bloomington, IN: Language Education Departments, Indiana University.

HENDERSON, E. H., & BEERS, J. W. (Eds.). (1980). *Developmental and cognitive aspects of learning to spell.* Newark, DE: International Reading Association.

HILLIKER, J. (1988). Labeling to beginning narrative: Four kindergarten children learn to write. In T. Newkirk & N. Atwell (Eds.), *Understanding writing: Ways of observing, learning, and teaching* (2nd ed.) (pp. 14–22). Portsmouth, NH: Heinemann.

HUTTENLOCHER, J. (1964). Children's language: Word-phrase relationship. *Science, 143,* 264–265.

LANCASTER, W., NELSON, L., & MORRIS, D.

(1982). Invented spellings in Room 112: A writing program for low-reading second graders. *The Reading Teacher, 35,* 906–911.

LAVINE, L. O. (1977). Differentiation of letter-like forms in pre-reading children. *Developmental Psychology, 13,* 89–94.

MATTHEWS, K. (1988). A child composes. In T. Newkirk & N. Atwell (Eds.), *Understanding writing: Ways of observing, learning, and teaching* (2nd ed.) (pp. 9–13). Portsmouth, NH: Heinemann.

MORRIS, D. (1981). Concept of word: A developmental phenomenon in the beginning reading and writing processes. *Language Arts, 58,* 659–668.

PAUL, R. (1976). Invented spelling in kindergarten. *Young Children, 31,* 195–200.

PICK, A. D., UNZE, M. G., BROWNELL, C. A., DROZDAL, L. G., & HOPMAN, M. R. (1978). Young children's knowledge of word structure. *Child Development, 49,* 669–680.

READ, C. (1971). Pre-school children's knowledge of English phonology. *Harvard Educational Review, 41,* 1–34.

READ, C. (1975). *Children's categorizations of speech sounds in English.* Urbana, IL: National Council of Teachers of English.

RICHGELS, D. J. (1986). Beginning first graders' "invented spelling" ability and their performance in functional classroom writing activities. *Early Childhood Research Quarterly, 1,* 85–97.

SOWERS, S. (1988). Six questions teachers ask about invented spelling. In T. Newkirk & N. Atwell (Eds.), *Understanding writing: Ways of observing, learning, and teaching* (2nd ed.) (pp. 130–141). Portsmouth, NH: Heinemann.

SULZBY, E. (1985a). Children's emergent reading of favorite storybooks: A developmental study. *Reading Research Quarterly, 20,* 458–481.

SULZBY, E. (1985b). Kindergartners as writers and readers. In M. F. Farr (Ed.), *Advances in writing research, volume one: Children's early writing development* (pp. 127–199). Norwood, NJ: Ablex.

SUTTON, E. (1974). *My cat likes to hide in boxes.* New York: Parents Magazine.

TEMPLE, C., NATHAN, R., BURRIS, N., & TEM-

PLE, F. (1988). *The beginnings of writing* (2nd ed.). Boston, MA: Allyn and Bacon.

THE THREE BEARS. (1952). Racine, WI: Western Publishing Co.

VUKELICH, C., & EDWARDS, N. (1988). The role of context and as-written orthography in kindergarteners' word recognition. In J. E. Readence & R. S. Baldwin (Eds.), *Dialogues in literacy research* (Thirty-seventh yearbook of the National Reading Conference) (pp. 85–93). Chicago, IL: National Reading Conference.

YADEN, D. (1988). Understanding stories through repeated read-alouds. *The Reading Teacher, 41,* 556–560.

CHAPTER 8

Classroom Support for Experimenting Readers and Writers

This chapter discusses ways that teachers can support the literacy learning of children who are experimenters. It includes a description of a classroom environment and several techniques or methods of instruction that are particularly appropriate for experimenters.

The chapter begins with a description of Ms. Harper's kindergarten classroom and its many centers, which are an important component of her literacy program. Note that the experimenters whose literacy learning is supported in this classroom might also be found in preschools and in first, second, and even third grade classrooms. Not all children in any kindergarten are experimenters and not all experimenters are kindergartners.

In the next section, some principles of literacy instruction for experimenters and some principles of a center-organized classroom are presented. The chapter concludes with a section describing techniques for early literacy instruction that we have chosen from the professional literature. Teachers in any kind of classroom will find these techniques particularly suited to experimenters and to the kinds of literacy knowledge they are constructing.

MS. HARPER'S KINDERGARTEN

The following kindergarten classroom is a composite of several very good classrooms we have observed. We will call the teacher in this classroom Ms. Harper.

Ms. Harper's classroom is a busy place. There is a great deal going on; some of it is directly focused on literacy instruction, most of it is indirectly supportive of literacy learning, and some of it is not even indirectly literacy-oriented. Ms. Harper believes in explicitly teaching many things to her children, only some of which have to do with reading and writing. She also believes in supporting children's discoveries of many truths about themselves, their world, how to get along with each other, and how to communicate with each other and with others who are not part of their classroom community (including by writing and reading).

One of the ways that Ms. Harper's beliefs are realized is by her organizing her class schedule in order to insure one-to-one, teacher-to-child time with each child; small-group experiences both with and without the teacher for each child; and some whole-group activities. Another way is by Ms. Harper's organizing her classroom around several centers.

Ms. Harper's centers are the backbone of her delivery system for instruction, and we feel they are especially appropriate for much of the experimenting that experimenters do. However, not all teachers who have experimenters use a center approach. Some preschool and kindergarten teachers choose to depend less on children's visiting centers and more on their participating in large-group and whole-group activities planned for traditional subject areas. Many first, second, and third grade teachers have to use more traditional approaches because the curriculum for those grades is often quite prescriptive; that is, the expected learning outcomes are very specific. Yet all of these teachers have students who are experimenters. Our hope is that all teachers will include some centers in their classrooms; writing centers and library centers are particularly important for supporting experimentation with written language.

Ms. Harper's room is very large. She has the luxury of much space for classroom centers. However, even teachers who have small rooms can include centers by carefully planning their use of space and by rotating some centers. We know a teacher whose room is smaller than average, but who always has five or six centers in corners, on cupboard tops, behind screens, and wherever else she can fit them.

The Setting:
A Center-Organized Classroom

Figure 8.1 presents a diagram of Ms. Harper's classroom. There is a large, open, carpeted area next to the piano and in front of a blackboard and bulletin board. Ms. Harper has made a large semicircle on the floor with masking tape, and she calls this area "the circle." She holds most of her whole-class activities in "the circle." The children sit on chairs drawn up to this circle at the beginning of each school day. Routine business such as announcements and collection of notes is taken care of during "circle time."

Centers occupy most of the rest of the space in Ms. Harper's room. There are the usual kindergarten centers such as a home center, a block center, an art center, a math center, and a make-believe play center. In addition, there are several centers that we will describe in some detail because of the ways they can be used to support experimenters' literacy learning. These literacy support centers include a writing center, a storybook center, a listening station, a recording station, a sharing center, two unit centers, a "centers center," and a "reading and writing lessons center."

Ms. Harper's *writing center* looks much like the one in the preschool class-

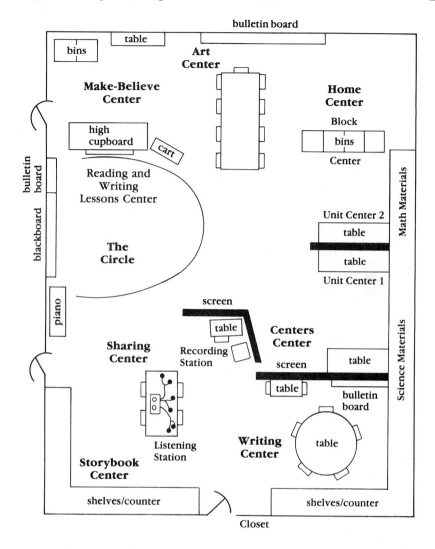

***Figure 8.1** Ms. Harper's Classroom*

rooms described in Chapter 6. Many kinds of writing tools and paper are available. There is a large round table where children, and often Ms. Harper, sit; at this table, children are able to see each other's work and to share their own work. There is also a smaller table where one or two people can sit and write without interruption or distraction. On a low cupboard there are a picture dictionary; a set of plastic magnetic letters; three sets of manuscript letters printed on cardboard and covered with clear contact paper, which are kept together in alphabetical order on a big plastic ring; and a word bank that includes words children have written on cards and saved for future reference (some are illustrated).

Ms. Harper's room has a *storybook center*. Children's storybooks stand on low, deep shelves and lie on low cupboard tops where they are easily accessible. Within the storybook center, there is a *listening station* set up on a table that has four chairs around it. The listening station is a tape recorder with four headsets. Also in the storybook center, set off from the rest of the room with standing screens, is the recording station. This station is on a small table where a tape recorder is kept; next to the table is a bin of audio tapes, one for each child, with his or her name on its plastic container. In the storybook center, there are also soft cushions on which the children (and sometimes Ms. Harper) make themselves comfortable while they read. By quickly rearranging these cushions, the listening station, and the screens that set the storybook center off from the rest of the classroom, Ms. Harper can create a *sharing center*.

Ms. Harper always has two *unit centers* in her classroom. One is the current center in which she places materials to examine, touch, taste, and smell after she has talked about them in the formal circle as part of her ongoing science, social studies, or current events unit of the week. The center also contains visuals such as posters, books, photographs, and postcards, many of which include written language.

The second unit center in Ms. Harper's room is always the center from the previous week. The children like going to a center even after the class has moved on to another unit. They remember what was discussed about items in the display and they use them over and over again. This helps children to unconsciously consolidate and demonstrate to themselves what they have learned; some of what they have learned is about the unit's topic and some—because of the necessary and often deliberately planned inclusion of writing—is about written language.

Ms. Harper's room also contains a *centers center*. This is where children may make their own centers after receiving Ms. Harper's permission. Sometimes Ms. Harper invites children who have not yet done so to make a center. The children then bring items from home, share them with their classmates in an extended show-and-tell session, and put them on display.

The *reading and writing lessons center* in Ms. Harper's classroom is adjacent to the "circle." A small blackboard is fastened to the back of a room-dividing storage cupboard. The center includes a pocket chart on a stand, a chair for Ms. Harper, and a rolling book cart. Small groups of children sit on the floor for instruction.

The purpose of this center is simply to have a special place for Ms. Harper and small groups of children to go for mini-lessons about reading and writing. These lessons clarify or consolidate children's learning about some aspect of literacy that they have discovered. With this center, Ms. Harper and her students acknowledge that sometimes learning about literacy requires focused attention and intense work. Ms. Harper commits herself to giving specific help to those children who have given that kind of attention and are themselves committed to doing that kind of work.

Like all of Ms. Harper's centers, this one is labeled. There is a poster with the words "We have reading and writing lessons here" and photographs of children listening to Ms. Harper and watching her illustrate on the blackboard, of a pair of children categorizing words by sorting student-made flash cards on the floor, and of a child writing on a worksheet.

The rolling book cart in the reading and writing lessons center contains Ms. Harper's instructional materials. These include books she has chosen to illustrate a point, word cards to use in the pocket chart, posters, and workbooks from which she tears appropriate pages for those children who sometimes like follow-up exercises of the workbook variety. Of course, the reading and writing lessons center can actually be a generic center and can have labels or posters showing how it is used for mini-lessons in math, art, or science as well.

The Action: School Literacy Events for Experimenters

The centers just described were not all designed for experimenters' literacy learning. Some of the centers were planned primarily to teach particular content or for enjoyment. Most were intended for all of Ms. Harper's students, many of whom are not experimenters. This section discusses ways that teachers can use centers and experimenters' experiences in these centers to support the specific kinds of literacy learning associated with experimenters.

Using the Writing Center

Ms. Harper knows that there are experimenters in her class who are interested in corresponding with others by writing letters. The writing center includes a mail box for sending messages to others in the classroom. Writing paper and envelopes are available and encourage children to participate in message and letter experimenting.

Ms. Harper also provides for experimenters who are able to work intensely and for long periods on a writing project. She knows that over a span of a few days, children may come back to a piece several times. They like to share finished pieces, and look at them again and again later on. Therefore, she has a "Still Working" box in the writing center for unfinished projects to which writers may or may not return. Ms. Harper puts the contents of this box in children's writing folders at the end of each day. The folders are located in each child's cubby; the children know to bring the folder to the writing center when they first visit the center on a given day. The center has two other boxes for writing: a "Finished for Sharing" box and a "Finished for Myself" box. The center also has a big waste basket.

Ms. Harper knows that experimenters are individuals. They have a variety of writing styles and need a variety of supports for their writing efforts. She tries to help children feel good about their various approaches to writing. There is a poster on the wall over the writing table that says "This is writing:" and it includes several examples of writing. The displays change often; they may include a letter the class has received, a special message Ms. Harper has written to the class, a handwritten illustrated poem, a short handwritten story, an item of environmental print (a store label on a paper bag) or of functional print (a page from *People* magazine), a piece of writing a child has already shared with the class, or a pamplet or other piece of writing retired from a recent unit center. Some children copy these pieces of writing when they are at the writing center, some ignore them, and others make their own versions. Sometimes Ms. Harper helps a child to make a personal version rather than copy what is on the poster. Most children who go to the writing center have something in mind to write, but sometimes they go with friends or are invited there by Ms. Harper. If they cannot think of something to write, Ms. Harper says, "How about something like what is on the 'This is writing' poster?"

Some children in the class know writing communicates specific messages; others are developing a concept of word or are experimenting with invented spelling. When Ms. Harper joins these children at the writing center, she often asks questions that help them to frame their messages or to invent spellings (Calkins, 1986). She may say, "What *one* thing would you like to say about your picture?" or "What one *word* would you like to write? Say it slowly. What sounds do you hear? What letters do you need?"

Ms. Harper sometimes gives the group suggestions for what to do if they choose to go to the writing center. She may suggest that they make a get-well card for their music teacher who is in the hospital, or that they write a book (or a page for a book) like the one she just read to the class. On Friday, she may suggest that they write a list of all the centers they have been to this week to take home and share with their parents (all the classroom's centers are clearly labeled so that children can copy the names of the centers they have been to); she may also suggest that the children illustrate their lists so they remember to tell their parents what they did at the centers.

Sometimes Ms. Harper makes and reads to the children a sample of what they may do when they go to the writing center. She is not very specific about how to form letters or spell words; all her students, experimenters and non-experimenters alike, know that she considers them to be writers and that precision in matching her work is not expected.

Using the Storybook Center

Ms. Harper knows the importance of modeling reading and giving experimenters frequent exposure to favorite storybooks, as well as opportunities to share the products of their own literacy efforts. On one shelf of the storybook center, Ms. Harper keeps books that *she* likes to read (lately her favorites are Dick Francis mysteries). Sometimes she goes to the storybook center and makes herself comfortable with one of her books. The children may read her books if they wish, but, as with all books, they must return them when finished.

Sometimes Ms. Harper puts out a set of four books and a professionally recorded tape of the book in the listening station. At other times, there is just one book for as many as four children to share as they listen to a recording she has made of the book. Occasionally, she sets out a book a child has made, along with the child's tape recording of the book. There is something new at the listening station two or three times per week.

Children use the recording station to make tape recordings of themselves retelling and reading their favorite storybooks from the storybook center. They also use it to record themselves reading their writings.

Sometimes small groups or even the whole class may come to the sharing center, sit on the cushions and on the floor, and listen to one child read his or her favorite storybook. (This pretend reading may or may not correspond to the written text.) At other times, children read their writing to the group. Ms. Harper could use the formal circle where her class sits at the beginning and ending of each day for these readings, but she wants these times to be both special and comfortable. She has found that children are more comfortable reading to their classmates in the sharing center, which is part of the storybook center, and that more choose to do so when the activity is held there.

Sometimes Ms. Harper reads to small groups or to the whole class in the sharing center. More often she reads to them in the "circle" or even in a unit center. It depends both on the purpose for the reading and on how much structure the children need on a given occasion.

Ms. Harper knows that children are able to learn how stories work by hearing all kinds of stories, not just written stories, so she sometimes uses the sharing center for story*telling* (Hoskisson & Tompkins, 1987, pp. 143–146; Nelson, 1989; Roney, 1989). She prepares ahead of time so that she can tell the children a story rather than read it. Some children like to make up stories, or retell fairy tales or other favorite stories (sometimes the one that Ms. Harper has very effectively told recently). They also use the sharing center for storytelling. Everyday sharing of the show-and-tell variety and Ms. Harper's daily announcements and other class business take place in the "circle," not in the special sharing center.

Using Unit Centers

Unit centers are planned primarily to teach content, such as information about science, social studies, or current events. However, Ms. Harper knows that she can plan her unit lessons and centers so that children are also able to learn about written language. Experimenters are interested in letters and sounds and words, in written language formats, and in purposes for reading and writing. Ms. Harper fosters and uses that interest; she exploits the written language that occurs as part of content subject lessons, even in kindergarten.

One week Ms. Harper did a unit about birds. After she read *Birds* (Wonder Books, 1973) and *Flap Your Wings* (Eastman, 1969) to the class, she left the books in the bird center. Also in the center were several posters picturing different kinds of birds.

Ms. Harper and her class made their own poster on a large piece of posterboard. Ms. Harper wrote two headings at the top that said "All birds . . ." and "Some birds . . ." Two subheadings under "Some birds . . ." read, "do" and "don't." Using three inch by five inch cardboard cards with bird pictures and name labels from a wildlife playing card set similar to Old Maid as examples and as discussion-starters, she helped the class discover that all birds have feathers, lay eggs, and have two feet, but that some birds fly and eat worms while other birds do not. She wrote that information below the appropriate headings and got children to tape some of the cards under those headings as examples. Penguin, Eagle, Bluejay, and Robin cards were all at the bottom of the "All birds . . ." column because they all have feathers, lay eggs, and have two feet. But the matching Penguin card was next to "don't fly," the matching Bluejay card was next to "don't eat worms," the matching Eagle card was next to "do fly," and the matching Robin card was next to "do eat worms." This poster was placed in the bird unit center along with an empty robin's nest that Ms. Harper found one year, some wildlife postage stamps picturing and naming birds (cancelled and still on their envelopes) that some of Ms. Harper's students brought to school, a Life nature series book about birds that a student brought to school, and the rest of the "Wildlife 'Old Maid'" card game, along with some more bird cards and cards for many other kinds of animals.

During its holdover, second week in Ms. Harper's classroom, many of her children continued to use the bird center. Groups of two or three used the "All birds/Some birds" poster to reenact the class's creation of it. They took turns acting as teacher and calling on other children to read the poster. Their reading was experimental in different ways. Some children pointed to and read the words exactly as they appeared—"All birds have feathers"; some read words and pictures—"Robins and bluejays and penguins and eagles all have feathers!"; some read labels—pointing to the word *Eagle* on one of the Eagle cards and saying "Eagle!" Some children, who were looking at the postage stamps, identified the birds and read the birds' names; often they misidentified a bird, but still pretended to read its name; sometimes they also tried to read other writing on the envelope, especially those who had brought the envelopes in (for example, "That's my last name—'Peterson'!").

Using the Centers Center

Most children contribute to the centers center from time to time, either individually, in pairs, or in groups of three. All are encouraged to include some writing in their centers. For experimenters, that writing may include inventively spelled words.

One child's center center was a Beatrix Potter collection; it included several of the little storybooks by Beatrix Potter, a ceramic Jemima Puddle-duck statue/musicbox, a place setting of Peter Rabbit dishes, a pop-up version of *Jemima Puddle-duck,* and a Peter Rabbit stuffed animal. Another child brought a display of He-Man figures, two He-Man posters, the box his Castle Grayskull had come in (with a detailed picture on the front), and two issues of He-Man magazine, to which he subscribed. With all the writing on the posters, the box, and the magazine, this child did not have to label his center, but he wanted to. He copied the He-Man insignia fairly accurately and wrote his own name.

Some centers do need labels. In that case, Ms. Harper or an aide helps the child to make a sign, with at least the child's name and a one- or two-word label, such as "Chrissy, Stuffed Animals." Some children make signs ahead of time at home to identify their center or components of the center. Ms. Harper tries to have two or three children's centers in the centers center at all times.

Using the Reading and Writing Lessons Center

Ms. Harper and her children use the reading and writing lessons center for the very specific purpose of following up on and consolidating knowledges about reading and writing that were discovered at the writing center, at the storybook center, or at a unit center. This is the place for the mini-lessons for which children demonstrate a need in their writing and their reading in other places and in other activities. For example, some children may show an interest in the envelopes with bird stamps that are displayed in the bird center. Others may be writing letters in the writing center. Ms. Harper can use the reading and writing lessons center to teach these children how addresses on envelopes work and how to read and write such addresses.

Lessons from Ms. Harper's Classroom

One thing that is especially striking about Ms. Harper's classroom is that it is a literacy-oriented environment. Although Ms. Harper does little formal teaching of reading and writing, she has planned for the occurrence of literacy events in almost all of her centers. Reading and writing are expected parts or necessary consequences of most of her students' daily experiences.

Another striking feature of Ms. Harper's classroom is the independence of her students. They make choices and have opportunities to pursue their own interests and to satisfy personal curiosity. Many of Ms. Harper's students did not at first show this independence. As part of creating a center-organized environment, Ms. Harper had to plan activities that would encourage and reward independence. She had to teach students how to rely on themselves.

Principles of Literacy Learning for Experimenters

Seven principles guided Ms. Harper's literacy instruction for experimenters. The first principle is that *literacy instruction for experimenters must be functional;* that is, it must come from naturally occurring reasons for using written language. Literacy instruction must continue to be based on frequent exposure to environmental print and, especially, to books children like to read and to have read to them. It must be based on writing when there is a reason to communicate with someone. Experimenters, like novices, can best learn about written language from real materials and natural activities, not from contrived kits and workbooks.

Often teachers are very comfortable with functional instruction as long as children are novices. Reading books to children is a large part of what teachers do to support novices' learning about reading. Parents and teachers are increasingly becoming aware of children's ability to read environmental print. However, when children begin to act like experimenters, adults' attitudes sometimes change.

Experimenters may show in their invented spellings or in their efforts to sound out individual words they notice around them that they know something about letter–sound correspondences. Because that is what phonics instruction is traditionally all about, parents are tempted to stop buying storybooks for their children and to start buying supermarket phonics workbooks. Teachers are often tempted to step in and begin teaching phonics in a very traditional way, using phonics kits and workbooks and bulletin boards.

Teachers must resist this temptation. We believe that informal, functional methods are still best. Children still need to be read to often. It is especially important at this point to read to them individually; they need to sit in the reader's lap, so that they can see the print while hearing the story and can ask and receive answers to all their questions.

The chances are good that children will continue to ask about individual words in the books that are read to them ("Is that the word 'mouse'?" pointing to a word that starts with *m*). They are likely to use their knowledge of letter–sound correspondences, along with their understanding of contextual clues, to unlock more and more of the words they come across in the environment and in their storybooks, especially in very familiar storybooks that they may even have memorized at an earlier time.

Another, perhaps even more important, reason for continuing to surround experimenters with children's literature is that they continue to enjoy it (Ellermeyer, 1988). Showing ability to learn more and more about how written language works is no indication that a child wants to or should abandon reading for its own sake.

A second principle of literacy learning for experimenters is that *instruction about written language should be integrated with all the other instruction that children receive.* We have used a kindergarten classroom as our example for this chapter, and many kindergartners are experimenters. But there will be many experimenters in preschool and primary-grade classrooms as well. Whenever children are showing themselves to be experimenters with written language, they are likely also to be experimenters with other subjects. If properly planned, centers whose main focus is not literacy learning can nonetheless be supportive of literacy learning. Ms. Harper's bird center is an example of this. As she and her students used the bird center, they read the "All birds/Some birds" poster, they read the labels on the bird pictures, and they even read the writing on the front of the envelopes. Direct experiences such as a field trip or a hands-on experiment can also lead to reading and writing.

A third principle of literacy learning for experimenters is that *as often as possible, learning should be self-directed.* Of course, there are many times when the teacher delivers explicit literacy instruction: during formal circle times, in unit centers, and in the reading and writing lessons center.

Still, experimenting with literacy learning is by its very nature a self-directed business. There are many times when children's exploration and discovery of literacy must take place without the teacher's being immediately present to ask, explain, or direct.

One way to insure that children's learning is as self-directed as possible is to ensure that center activities are not so complicated or difficult that children are unable to determine how to do them. There must also be choices within a center. Teachers must communicate the expectation that children *can* function on their own. At the same time, teachers must be supportive, giving full descriptions of the activities children will find in centers and watching for occasions when children truly need help. This allows children to learn from play, from talk, and from interactions with the environment and with each other. It prevents them from learning the restricting, negative notion that in order to learn, they must be taught.

A fourth principle of literacy learning for experimenters is that *teachers must expect the unexpected;* that is, they should be prepared for outcomes that are not always what they planned or predicted. This is to be expected with young children whose concepts about reading and writing are different from those of adults.

For example, a teacher may prepare a writing center for making valentines. The center might be well-stocked with red and pink and white paper, and two sample valentines might be displayed. But Henry may decide to create a Great Red and Pink Monster and write a story about it, or he may decide to make another Santa Claus with his pink and red paper like the one for which he received so much praise the week before Christmas. If Henry writes "Santa" on his creation, or "Toys" on Santa's bag, so much the better. If he does not, that is all right.

Sometimes unexpected learnings coincide with a teacher's goals for a center and sometimes they do not. If Henry is reinforced in his learning that he is a good Santa-Claus-maker, that may be just as important *for him* as learning how to make a valentine. Of course, if Henry never wants to make anything but Santas, that would be a different story. This time, though, the teacher thinks it was just the pink and red paper that reminded him of and gave him an opportunity to relive a moment of glory from the past. So she goes along.

We presented another example of accommodating unexpected learning in our account of what happened in Ms. Harper's bird center. Obviously, she wanted her students to learn about birds there. She may have wanted them to learn to read bird names on the pictures and wildlife postage stamps in the center, or even to read some of the other writing on the envelopes containing the postage stamps. But she was not disappointed when several children got especially interested instead in stamps in general. One child even brought in his own stamp collection for the centers center. Ms. Harper has taught him that learning can follow many possible routes, that learning is often based on what you already know and on your interests, and that learning can involve sharing with and learning from others.

A fifth principle of literacy instruction for experimenters may seem at first to contradict the third and fourth. It is that *literacy instruction for experi-*

menters will include some planned lessons. These may be mini-lessons for individuals or small groups of students. They may take place in a writing center, at the teacher's desk, at the formal circle, or in a reading and writing lessons center. Teachers can plan, for example, to teach about letter–sound corespondences or about different text formats when children demonstrate that they can use such knowledge.

A teacher might use words on candy wrappers, coupons, and cereal boxes which children have collected (and which they may have used earlier for other literacy purposes) to teach a short phonics lesson about the sound of the letter *M* at the beginning of a word (*Mars Bars, Milky Way, mustard, macaroni,* and *Malto Meal*). Or the teacher might use the writing of a list of favorite toys to teach several beginning consonants' sounds. As the teacher writes the list, he might call attention to and ask questions about letters and sounds. He will be sure to emphasize the usefulness of such knowledge. All the while, it is clear that the candy bar wrappers are functional; they help the children to identify a favorite food and they once helped them to be able to act as readers ("Look how many of these I can read!"). Likewise, the list-making is functional; it clarifies for the children, as well as for others, what their favorite toys are.

We believe that planned literacy activities using real print objects are better vehicles for new literacy learning than published workbooks and kits. The key to being consistent with the principles of literacy instruction we have described is to make sure that the materials used in planned lessons are naturally occurring and that the purposes for reading and writing in these planned lessons are meaningful to the students.

A sixth principle of literacy learning for experimenters is that *the teacher's emphasis should be more on affective aspects of activities than on cognitive aspects.* Teachers should plan for literacy events that will be positive experiences for their children. One way to insure this is to plan for learning by playing. Another way is one we have often mentioned; it is to treat children as if they *can* write and read. The child who reads her story about feeding birds at her grandparents' house to the whole class in the sharing center and then sees it posted in the bird center (even though it is incomplete, does not include exactly what she said while reading to the class, and includes many invented spellings) knows that she is a writer and a reader. She has communicated through her writing; she likes to write; and she will write more.

A seventh principle of literacy learning for experimenters is that *classroom environments and activities need not be markedly different from those for novices.* A visitor to both Ms. Harper's and Mrs. Miller's (see Chapter 6) classrooms would be more impressed by their similarities than by their differences. Both have many literacy-oriented centers. Both contain many functional print items. This is partly because both teachers' classes include many novices, but there is another reason for the similarities. What Ms. Harper has to do differently for her experimenters is not to create several new centers. Instead, she includes in her centers—which are for all her children—additional options for the experimenters, and she takes time to guide experimenters in the exercise of those options.

Ms. Harper would not have included a "Still Working" box in her writing center if she had no experimenters in her class. With this small addition, Ms. Harper has recognized her experimenters' sometimes persistent and hard-working approach to writing. All of her children use the writing center, but it is most often the experimenters who use the "Still Working" box.

Similarly, Ms. Harper would not have included a sharing center option in the design of her storybook center if she had no experimenters in her class. It is experimenters who sometimes memorize a whole book or who willingly pre-tend to read aloud a book they have had read to them, using written-language-like phrases. The sharing center is a recognition of their willingness to try their reading before others.

Principles of a Center-Organized Classroom

Three principles guide a center-organized classroom. The first principle is that *a center-organized classroom depends upon routine.* This does not mean that everything proceeds by lock-step and that the teacher and students are not open to special opportunities for impromptu teaching and learning ("expecting the unexpected").

Young children need to know what to expect; by being relieved of the effort, if not the anxiety, of having to understand constantly new situations, they can devote their attention and their intellectual energy to their play, their learning, and their exploration. When children know that every morning will begin with a formal circle time, most of them will come to the circle ready to listen. When they know that circle time will be followed by center time, they will be ready for center time and have some idea of which centers they want to go to and what they want to do in them.

Some teachers are more prescriptive than others. Some find it helpful to include in their routines an assigned-center time, during which children must go to a specific center or to one of two or three centers. At other times, children are free to go to whatever centers they wish. Either way, it is important to give children an easy way of knowing what to do—one that causes the least disrup-tion of the entire room.

We know a teacher who lets children choose their own centers most of the time, but she has an assigned-center day a few times a week. When she an-nounces an assigned-center day at circle time, the children know what to expect: they will look for their name cards on little posts (dowels kept upright in wooden bases) by the centers. In fact, most children already know when it is an assigned-center day because during the free time when they are first arriving in the classroom, they noticed the name cards on the posts. Because the children must sign their names to the center's roll whenever they use a center, the teacher is aware of which centers each child has chosen over the past several days. She uses this information in deciding where to assign each child. Sometimes she as-signs children to their favorite centers, where she knows they have wanted to stay or to return recently, but could not because of time constraints. Sometimes she assigns children to centers they have avoided or just missed out on; then she makes sure that either she or an aide is there to help them get started.

Many teachers have rules about how many children can attend a center at one time, and the children know to look for that number on a card in the center. Sometimes a teacher asks everyone to change centers at a signal (although one must be careful that the signal is not interrupting a child in the middle of an important project—and that is often difficult to avoid). Many teachers invite particular children to join them at a center, even when the other children are free to choose a center.

All of the children do not need to be at centers (or doing any other activity, for that matter) at the same time of the day. Group membership is part of many teachers' routines. They assign each child to one of three or four groups. The children know what their group is going to do for the first post-circle-time part of the morning by consulting an activity wheel. The activity wheel is made from two posterboard circles that are held together by a brad through their centers (see Figure 8.2). The teacher can change groups' assigned activities at the beginning of a new period by turning the outside wheel. The teacher can change the activities on the smaller circle by taping different descriptions or pictures in the wedges or by replacing one circle with another one. Because these groups exist only for classroom management purposes (they are a convenient way to be sure

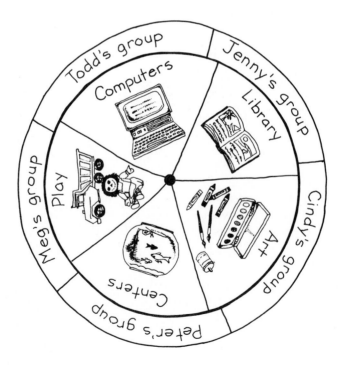

Figure 8.2 An Activity Wheel

that more than one kind of activity can be going on at the same time and that all children have an opportunity for all activities), we feel that they should be heterogeneous and that their composition should be changed frequently.

A second principle for a center-organized classroom is that *teachers should make use of many human resources.* Children can learn from their teacher and from one another. They also learn from older children and from adults other than the teacher. A center-organized classroom has flexible groups and includes many people.

Children sometimes work and play entirely on their own. In a classroom, one might find a child curled up by himself with a favorite book in the storybook center, a child at the listening station by herself, and a child writing on his own at the writing table. Another child might be at her favorite unit center by herself because the teacher allowed her just one more visit there before the center is taken down to make way for another.

At other times, children learn in small groups. Often two or three are at a unit center, at a play center, or at the storybook center, reading to each other. Sometimes the teacher is part of such a small group, when she joins a threesome at the writing center or when she teaches a mini-lesson in the reading and writing lessons center to those who seem ready for that lesson or show a particular need for it.

Children also learn in whole-class groups when the teacher introduces, models, explains, or entertains in the formal circle as Ms. Harper did when first using the "All Birds/Some Birds" poster. Whole-class groups can also benefit from listening to others read a book, read something they wrote, or tell a story in the sharing center. Children learn in a whole-class group when they are an audience to a special guest.

The teacher of a center-organized classroom knows that there are many valuable resource people in her school and in the community. There are parents and community volunteers (as in "adopt a grandparent" programs), as well as workers (secretaries, custodians, the principal, and the librarian) and older children in elementary schools (Potter, 1989). These helpers may share special knowledge with the whole class (as the weatherperson did in Mrs. Miller's classroom in Chapter 6) or they may work with children at centers (listening to them read their favorite storybooks, taking their dictation, helping them operate the tape recorder, overseeing an art project, reading to them, or writing with them).

The third principle of a center-organized classroom is simple to state, but difficult to follow. It is that *the teacher must be an especially good teacher.* This is sometimes easy to overlook when one observes most of the children seemingly doing what they want in a center-organized classroom.

A good teacher is a good *observer.* A good teacher knows which children are ready for or need a mini-lesson about the beginning *P* sound because she has seen them trying to sound out words by paying attention to the beginning letters and the sounds in those letters' names as they appear in classroom labels, in other children's names, and in functional print items. She knows which children should be assigned to a unit center because they never seem to get enough time there and are always able to use their time there well, or because they never go there but might be able to benefit from the center today while there is a volunteer helper stationed there. She knows which children are ready to be invited to read a storybook to her because she has observed them listening to the same book over and over at the listening station and frequently reading that book to themselves or a friend in the storybook center. She knows to invite Sara to the writing center with her today because Sara seldom goes there by herself, but she wrote a very nice list the last time she was invited there.

A good teacher is also a good *model.* Modeling can involve detailed explanation and description, as when a teacher shows how to make the bird feeders that all the children will make during their turn in the art center this week. Modeling can be very specific, as when a teacher shows how to form a lower case *f* so that others can read it. It can also be more subtle, as when a teacher sits down at the writing center and writes a letter to a friend, thereby inspiring letter writing by some of the children at the center. Modeling can be ongoing, as when Ms. Harper includes a shelf of her own favorite books in the storybook center and often goes there to read one of them to herself.

A good teacher *respects* children and what they know, especially when the teacher is intervening to instruct or to help. Good teachers always ask themselves, "What does this child already know?" and they build on that even when it does not match conventional knowledge. Teachers will have answers to that question if they are the good observers we have suggested they be. They will accept and respect nonconventional answers if they understand children's development.

We believe that some of the principles of a center-oriented classroom can be principles of any classroom. All teachers can and should be good observers; all teachers can use many resources to support their students' learning; and all teachers can provide the security of routine while giving their students variety and choice (Rasinsky, 1988). The centered delivery system for instruction merely emphasizes these principles, and in many cases makes it easier to follow them.

Learning about Meaning Making, Form, Meaning-Form Links, and Functions of Written Language

The experimenters in Ms. Harper's classroom learn much about written language's meanings, forms, meaning-form links, and functions.

Meaning making. With the abundance of written language in Ms. Harper's room, her children have frequent opportunities to create meanings from what others have written and to make their own meanings in what they put in writing. Meaning making in reading and writing is particularly appropriate to kindergarten.

We object to the current trend toward making kindergarten too academic, in the sense of introducing formal instruction and graded materials in reading and math and even in such other subjects as science and social studies. Ms. Harper's unit center is an example of something that is academic in a different and better sense of the word. By selecting a topic for her students' meaning making and directing their attention to it, she gave them something that can best be given by schools. She created a unique, in-school opportunity to use written language. Her students learned a new kind of meaning making—not just meaning making in a general sense, but in the academic sense of creating meanings from written language as a source of new knowledge.

It is quite likely that Ms. Harper's students have obtained new knowledge from written language on other occasions, outside of school. But in Ms. Harper's bird center, they are doing so because Ms. Harper meant for them to do so. This is the beginning of a kind of meaning making that will be central to their experience of schools for years to come—learning through literacy.

Form.   Ms. Harper knows that many of her students are experimenting in a variety of ways with form. They are learning that words, not letters, are the important unit of form in written language. In order to support this discovery, Ms. Harper makes sure that her classroom is full of written words, from the labels on every center (even on children's centers in the centers center) to the bird names on the posters and wildlife cards and even postage stamps in the bird center.

There are many opportunities in a typical day in Ms. Harper's room for her merely to comment on words and thus informally to support children's growing awareness of words. She may say, "See how I am leaving spaces between my words" as she writes something at the writing center, especially if she notices that her fellow writers there are working at keeping words separate. Or, as she makes a poster with the class for a unit center, she may comment about the words she is writing. When a child shares a piece of writing with Ms. Harper at her desk, at the writing center, or at the reading and writing lessons center, she may say, "I like the way you kept your words separate with those circles." Ms. Harper may make the same comment in the third person before the whole class. When Karen reads and displays her piece in the sharing center, donates it to the listening station, or allows Ms. Harper to include it in the "This is writing" poster, Ms. Harper may say, "I like the way Karen kept her words separate with those circles."

Another aspect of form knowledge that many of Ms. Harper's students discover is knowledge of text formats. She supports this discovery by modeling writing in a variety of text formats. Her "All birds/Some birds" poster is really a variation on a list. Her children already know about lists from their weekly listing of centers that they have attended, from the lists of their names telling who may use a center on an assigned-center day, and from the "This is writing" poster in the writing center. They are learning about story format from their many experiences with storybooks and with stories they write for each other. Those who are interested in the letter text form can write and send letters to each other via the mailbox in the writing center. Ms. Harper comments about these different kinds of writing and displays them in the writing center. She also comments on different kinds of texts and stories as she reads them at the unit center and at story time.

Meaning-form links.   Ms. Harper is aware that many of her students who are experimenters show their developing understanding of meaning-form links in their invented spellings. She expects invented spelling and encourages it. Most importantly, she looks for opportunities to make comments and to ask questions about letter–sound correspondences in a nonjudgmental, non-evaluative manner. Her questions help experimenters to articulate and thus to consolidate their new discoveries. When a child is pretend-reading a favorite storybook and says, "I know where it says *bear*" and points to a word (correctly or not—it might be the word *briar*), Ms. Harper says, "That is great. You can read! How did you know that?" The child answers, "Because it starts with a *B* and ends with an *R*." She also teaches phonics lessons that are planned, but are not structured around a phonics or basal reader or reading readiness workbook. (An example is the lesson using candy wrappers, coupons, and cereal boxes described earlier.)

Ms. Harper knows about Sulzby's (1985) descriptions of stages in children's pretend readings of favorite storybooks (see Figure 7.12). When a child's storybook sharing includes written-language-like words and phrases, Ms. Harper says, "My, you really sound like a reader!" When children refuse to read because they know there is more to the task than they have learned, Ms. Harper says, "That's o.k. Let's look at the pictures. You can tell me what's happening and then I'll read your favorite part *to you*."

Functions of written language.   Ms. Harper's students know that written language serves a variety of functions. In her classroom, both she and her students use written language to label, to help people to remember, to entertain, to teach and learn content (in unit centers), and to teach processes (in the reading and writing lessons center).

A rich example is provided by something that happens weekly in Ms. Harper's class, even with children who are unable to identify many written words in isolation or to spell many words independently (even using invented spelling). Many children make lists of the centers they have attended during the week. They copy the centers' names from the signs identifying each center. By making the list, they organize knowledge and even create knowledge—perhaps they would not otherwise realize how many centers they had been to—as they make a permanent record that they will be able to share with their parents at a later time and place. As they make their lists and again as they share them with their parents, they are reminded of the fun and learning they experienced at one or more of the centers. As they copy the words from each center's sign, they learn about how to form the letters. Thus, written language is being used for several functions in just this one example of literacy in use in Ms. Harper's class; they are the functions of labeling, listing, recording, sharing information, reminding, and learning about written language.

APPROACHES THAT SUPPORT EXPERIMENTERS' LITERACY LEARNING

We do not want to suggest that good support for experimenters is impossible without centers. This section will describe additional approaches to literacy instruction for experimenters, some of which depend on using a writing center or a storybook center, but most of which can be used within or without a center framework. This section includes descriptions of several methods or approaches that professionals have devised to support the literacy learning of experimenters. This is by no means an exhaustive list. Many more activities are described in professional reading education, language arts, and early childhood education journals. In addition, creative teachers devise their own activities that are as effective or more so because each teacher knows his or her students best. The following activities are presented to give examples of the kind of planned instruction we feel is appropriate for experimenters.

Approaches Based on Booksharing

The character of child-to-adult and child-to-book interactions does not stay the same as children progress through the stages of learning about literacy described in this book. Experimenters are interested in and capable of doing different things with books during booksharing than novices do during booksharing

Parents and teachers should involve all children in bookreading and not wait until the children show an interest in books (some children will not, perhaps *because* no one has yet involved them with books in meaningful, pleasant ways); they should surely not wait until the children are experimenters! However, the techniques presented here for involving children in booksharing can be used with particular effectiveness to support the experimenting that experimenters do. The techniques involve using Big Books, pattern books, and little books.

Using Big Books

In Chapter 6 we described using Big Books with novices. Big Books can also be effective in extending experimenters' literacy knowledge, especially in helping them to appreciate written language forms, to understand the relations between what a reader says and what is written in a book, and to become increasingly influenced by a book's text in their pretend reading. Big Books make text especially accessible to children who are taking these steps (Martinez & Teale, 1988; Trachtenberg & Feruggia, 1989).

Teachers can use Big Books to model reading. Experimenters then use their teacher's modeling as a support for their own reading attempts (Combs, 1987). To introduce a Big Book, the teacher first asks the children what they already know about the book's topic or about an experience that will be described in the Big Book. Then the teacher asks the children to use what they know in order to guess what the characters in the story will do.

During the storyreading, while displaying and reading from the Big Book, the teacher asks the children to confirm or disconfirm their guesses. They stop at predictable parts to allow the children to continue making predictions. Most importantly for experimenters, the teacher demonstrates using *the text* to find out about how the story develops. The teacher points to specific sentences and underlines the text as he or she reads.

After reading, the teacher asks the children to tell what they consider the most important parts of the story and why. During this post-reading discussion, the teacher often returns to the book and shows the children that the text holds the answers to many of their questions. Together they read from the text to find the evidence that supports correct guesses about the story's plot, to provide clues about how incorrect guesses can be modified, and to note what parts stimulated their imaginations.

The teacher then invites children to select a page to read from the Big Books. Often children who at first say that they cannot read are willing to read a Big Book page after the group reading and discussion just described. They become enthusiastic about the Big Books and want to return to them again and again (Combs, 1987).

A teacher who uses this technique with small groups is doing what anyone would do with an individual child sitting in his or her lap; that is, the teacher is responding to the child's developing awareness of story form and of the role of the text in the storyreading. Teachers who are likely to have experimenters in their audience for Big Book sessions should be especially sensitive to children's questions about words, about letter–sound correspondences, and about plot. A child may ask, ''Where does it say *donkey*?'' just after the teacher has read a sentence ending with the word *donkey*. This is a sign that the child is aware of written words and, especially, of the need for a print-to-speech match in reading. The teacher should stop reading to answer the child's question and then may casually ask, ''Do you see the word *donkey* anywhere else on this page?''

Similarly, when a child says, ''He's going to break the pole, isn't he?'' the teacher can praise the child for his or her involvement in the story's unfolding meaning. The teacher can then ask, in a non-interrogating manner, ''What made you think that?''

This type of informal talking with children about what people do when they read can be very helpful to experimenters. Big Books merely make that kind of talk available for more than one child at a time. Thus, they are especially effective in classroom situations in which teachers cannot do one-to-one lap reading as often as they would like.

Using Pattern Books

In Chapter 6 we described using pattern books with novices. Pattern books are also enjoyable and effective for experimenters. Many characteristics of pattern books emphasize the very features of written language with which experimenters are often experimenting. Pattern books have repetitive patterns, good text-to-picture matches, familiar concepts and stories, and they may have cumulative patterns (as in *This is the House That Jack Built,* Rhodes, 1981). For an experimenter, a pattern book may be any book in which elements of plot and dialogue are repeated often. Thus, a folk tale such as *The Gingerbread Boy* qualifies, as well as a shorter language-play book such as *Brown Bear, Brown Bear* (Martin, 1970).

These books are useful for calling children's attention to words, for supporting children's developing letter–sound knowledge, for helping children acquire some sight words, and for expanding children's concept of story. When the picture matches the text and the text is of a familiar, often-repeated refrain, children who are ready to pay attention to graphic details are given the best possible opportunity to notice printed words and to speculate about how they are related to spoken words.

Repeating episodes and finally bringing the repetition to a stop constitute a very common storymaking strategy. Repetition carries a story along and provides a mechanism for its unfolding, but the repetition cannot continue forever. The repetitive story needs a device for coming to an end. In especially repetitive stories, that device can be a twist on the usually repeated action or usually repeated words. Many folk stories end with such a twist. In *The Little Red Hen,* for example, the twist on the hen's repeated invitations to her friends to help her in the steps of making bread (none of which is accepted) is her declining to invite them to join her in the last step, the eating, and her turning them away when they expect to be included. Many experimenters find the clever-twist ending particularly appealing.

During first readings, children are encouraged to become involved with the story and to comment on it. Many children will join in reading the repetitive sentences. Rhodes (1981) uses the example of *The Bus Ride* (Scott, Foresman, 1971), which tells the story of a bus stopping for several characters, one at a time, and then continuing on its way ("Then the bus went fast") until a bee gets on, whereupon all the other characters get off. Each one's exit is told in a separate predictable sentence, and the story ends with "Then they all ran fast!" Even during the first reading, most children will join in reading the sentence "Then the bus went fast."

In the second step of using pattern books with experimenters, the teacher uses subsequent readings of the story to move from whole to part, to notice individual words and even letter–sound correspondences. The teacher points to the text and reads no louder than the children who are reading along. The teacher can help children who are having difficulty. In *The Bus Ride,* children may be unable to tell a rhinoceros from a hippopotamus. The teacher writes those animals' names on the board and elicits the children's observation that they could use the beginning letters to distinguish the words. The teacher may also list children's names that begin with *R* and with *H* (Rhodes, 1981).

The third step is to allow the children opportunities to read the pattern book on their own. The teacher might leave several copies of *The Bus Ride* out for the children to experiment with. She might invite them all to be readers by asking them to think of various ways to read the book. She would observe their ways of reading. Some children might depend entirely on the pictures to know how to adapt the patterns they have learned to their reading of specific pages. In an example Rhodes shares, one boy whom we would call an experimenter told the teacher that his name, Frank, begins with the same letter as *fox*, another character in the story.

It is important to continue to use books with which children have become very familiar. Favorite storybooks are the material for the storybook reenactments, or repeated pretend readings, which we have already seen experimenters using to become more familiar with the form of stories and with read-aloud conventions (Sulzby, 1985). Familiar pattern books can be the resource materials for children's writing. Experimenters are likely to use them to find words and phrases they want to write, even when their written products are not directly modeled on the pattern book. For example, Kara used her favorite pattern book, *Brown Bear, Brown Bear* (Martin, 1970) to find the color words she needed to label the colors in her picture of a rainbow. ''To copy 'purple,' for example, she located the purple cat in the illustrations, said 'purple' out loud several times to determine what letter it began with, found the 'p' word in the text next to the illustration, and copied 'purple' letter for letter'' (Rhodes, 1981, p. 515).

Pattern books can be copied as Big Books. With experimenters, construction of a big pattern book can be a class project (Heald-Taylor, 1987). Children illustrate 12 inch by 18 inch pages of heavy paper, each with one or two sentences of text printed at the top ahead of time by the teacher. When the illustrations are completed, the children can sequence the pages, using memories of the story prompted by the pictures and the predictable text or by another reading of the original book. They may enjoy having the pages arranged along the blackboard or hung from a clothes line for several days. The pages can be bound, with a laminated cover and an information page that names the illustrators, gives a publication date, and even declares what name the class wishes to go by as publisher. Heald-Taylor (1987) suggests binding two or three extra pages at the back of the Big Book on which future readers can write their comments about the book. If the teacher makes a Big Book stand from a podium or an easel, each new book can be displayed for group or individual readings.

Big pattern books can be enjoyed in many ways. If the story has a refrain, the teacher can read the story and the students can say the refrain. The teacher can read one line of the story at a time and give the students a turn to repeat each line. With the cloze technique, the teacher reads most of each sentence, but pauses occasionally for the students to supply a word or phrase. The unison technique calls for the children to read the whole text in unison, with or without the teacher's accompaniment. Students may also read single pages or whole books with a partner or individually (Heald-Taylor, 1987).

Reimer (1983) suggests a use of pattern books that is consistent with the Language Experience Approach to teaching reading and writing. Teachers need not go on a field trip in order to write a language experience story. They can plan an experience with language such as a storytelling session, a puppet show, or the reading of a pattern book. Then they can follow that experience of language with writing and sharing activities based on what was told, what was presented in the puppet performance, or what was read from the pattern book

(Franklin, 1988). Reading a pattern book, then, can be an experience of language, and the writing that follows (the langauge experience story) can be making a copy of the pattern book, making a variation on it, or even reflecting about what it was like to read it (for example, after reading *The Bus Ride,* the teacher can write "Bobby liked best the part when the bee got on the bus").

Using Little Books

Little books are specially written to involve children in book reading. They are designed so that even children who have had little interaction with parents over books and who show little interest in books will read (Mason, McCormick, & Bhavnagri, 1986). They seem to be just the right length and size. Little books have appeal and they work with experimenters. In particular, they are effective in helping experimenters learn some sight words. *Sight words* are words a reader knows without hesitation, "on sight." Experimenters usually know only a few words this way (often proper names).

Figure 8.3 presents a little book, *Balloons,* written by preschool teacher

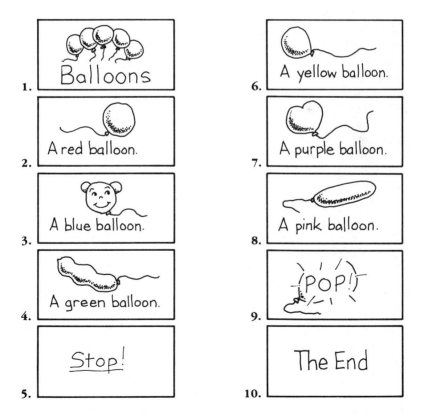

1. Balloons
2. A red balloon.
3. A blue balloon.
4. A green balloon.
5. Stop!
6. A yellow balloon.
7. A purple balloon.
8. A pink balloon.
9. (POP!)
10. The End

Figure 8.3 *A Little Book,* Balloons

Nancy Miller. Little books use few words, some of which children may already have experienced in other contexts. In *Balloons,* they are the often-familiar color words and the word *stop,* which many children know from seeing stop signs. Little books use repetition and are written to be fun and meaningful. *Balloons* conveys a message children can relate to, that balloons are colorful and they usually end up being popped.

In order to prepare for a little book lesson, teachers should compose their own little books, make copies for each child, color the books if color is essential to meaning (otherwise children can color them later as a follow-up), and arrange a small group of children so that their copies of the book are directly in front of them. To begin, the children and the teacher talk about experiences they have had with the topic that is suggested by the cover and the title of the book. They make predictions about what the book will say about that topic.

Next the teacher reads the book aloud, pointing to the words. He encourages and responds to children's questions and comments. Then he rereads the book, encouraging children to read along. At that point, children read on their own. To begin with, each child can read a page or two so that each has a turn and the story is quickly completed. The teacher should accept a child's insertions of words that are not in the text and deletions of words that are in the text, and he should supply words when a child hesitates. Tryouts continue as long as the children want to read or until they know the book well.

To close, the teacher congratulates the children on reading a book! Children elaborate on the story and their experience. They keep their books, read them at school, perhaps color them, and take them home to read to their families.

A classroom copy of each little book (perhaps more durably bound than the children's copies) should be available in the storybook center for children to read on their own even after they have taken their copies home. Some children will want to read little books to the class as a sharing activity. Others will want to write their own little books. Follow-up for experimenters can include the teacher's using the clear tie between printed words and meaning in little books to teach sight words and to teach about letters and sounds.

Approaches Based on Writing

This section includes descriptions of some classroom methods that begin as support for young children's experimentation with writing.

Opportunities to Write and Teacher Talk

Dobson (1985) describes what she calls a practical program for teaching reluctant readers to read by writing. The key elements of her approach are students' daily spontaneous writing, careful teacher observation, teacher talk that gives responsibility to students and responds to meaning, and student-to-student interactions about their writings.

The children in Dobson's examples had gone through half of the first grade without catching on to traditional methods of reading instruction. In her description of what the children knew, Dobson said they could print and read their names and they were familiar with a few sight words, most letter names, and some letter–sound correspondences. In other words, what they knew matches many of the knowledges listed in Chapter 7 for experimenters. We feel that her method would work well with any experimenters.

Sometimes the best method or approach to teaching is not so much to find specialized materials and make specific plans for expected behaviors as it is to find the right attitude and to choose what you say to be consistent with that attitude.

Dobson supplied the writing center with notebooks, pencils, and felt-tipped pens. The first direction she gave the children was simply to draw their own pictures on the pages of the notebooks and write their own stories underneath. When a child asked for help with spelling, she said, ''Notice how your mouth is moving when you say that word. [Pause] Now put down what you know about it.'' (p. 31) She was supportive, encouraging of risk taking, and responsive to meaning rather than to form.

Dobson encouraged children to use each other as resources and to compare notes about how to represent sounds with letters. In one example, three children worked out an invented spelling, ''hoke,'' of the word *hockey*. They were experimenting together because the teacher modeled support for experimentation. When teachers frequently make supportive comments such as ''You are a good writer—I can read that!'' it is not surprising for one student to ask another student, rather than the teacher, ''How do you spell hockey?'' (Dobson, p. 31).

Dyson (1986) provides another example of an approach to writing instruction for experimenters that includes talk, especially children's talk. In this approach kindergarten children were encouraged to choose a journal writing activity at least twice a week. This took place in the classroom writing center during the opening, language arts/free-choice hour of the school day. They drew pictures, dictated stories to go with the pictures, and copied part of the dictation. Their products were bound together to make individual journals. Most important, the children were free to talk to themselves as they drew.

Dyson found that relations between what the children said and what they drew, and between what they drew and what they dictated, copied, and read were complex. Self-expression in this seemingly simple operation varied considerably from one symbolic medium to another and from child to child. Although imaginative talk, drawing, and writing create different kinds of worlds, talk is very often supportive of children's composing. Talking to themselves and with others helps children to experiment with literate ways of making meaning. Thus, encouraging children to talk is essential to both Dyson's (1986) and Dobson's (1985) methods.

Writing Is Writing Even If Others Can't Read It

Martinez and Teale (1987) described a writing program that has been used successfully in several kindergartens. Children in these kindergartens are invited to use the writing center daily, beginning on the first day of school. An important part of this program is that the teacher demonstrates that others' being able to read what you write is not essential to writing. The teacher writes a message on the board and when the students cannot read it, the teacher explains that it is nonetheless writing and that he can read it to the students, just as the students will be able to read their own messages to others. "So from the first day the teachers encourage the students to view themselves as writers" (p. 445).

Martinez and Teale (1987) also give useful suggestions about how to get reluctant children to begin writing. They suggest asking children to "write your own way" or telling children "It doesn't have to be like grown-up writing. Write it the way 5 year olds write." (p. 446).

The roles of teachers and volunteer helpers in the classroom include providing before-writing experiences, helping children during writing by encouraging them to work out their problems, and being an audience for children after they write. It is important for every child to have an opportunity to read what he or she wrote on the same day it was written. After responding to content, the helper or teacher may also give feedback about the form of writing, saying, for example, "I see that you put a space between these two words." Finally, the teacher or helper records on a separate sheet of paper how a child reads his or her writing. These records are kept in folders in order to keep track of children's literacy progress.

Teachers and other adults are not the only sources of support for children's writing. In one of the classrooms Martinez and Teale (1987) describe, two children abandoned scribbling and began writing with invented spellings for the first time after closely observing their friends' inventively spelled writings.

Children can use writing opportunities to exchange mail with one another, to have pen pals in other classes, to have turns at being featured as author of the week, and even to write outside the classroom (in Martinez and Teale's example of this, a boy was invited to write a postscript to a letter his principal had written to his parents, praising him for the good work he had done that week).

None of the writing-based approaches we have described amounts to a fully developed process approach or writers' workshop approach to writing instruction, such as Graves (1983), Calkins (1986), and others describe. We believe that such an approach is better suited to children who are accomplished readers and writers (Chapter 9). We will describe that approach in Chapters 10 and 11.

Specialized Approaches

Two kinds of learning have traditionally been part of children's kindergarten and early first-grade literacy experiences. Both are compatible with our conception of experimenters. They are: (1) learning which sounds to associate with letters (part of what is called "phonics" in traditional instruction) and (2) learning to instantly recognize some printed words (called "having sight words" in traditional instruction). We do not advocate teaching phonics or teaching sight words in kindergarten in the ways they are traditionally taught in formal reading programs. Nor do we suggest that learning letter–sound associations and sight words is more important than other aspects of literacy learning. However, experimenters *will* learn and use letter–sound associations and some sight words within meaningful and functional literacy experiences such as those described here (Hall, 1985; Hall & Hall, 1984).

We have already seen examples in storybook reading and in writing activities of support for children's learning about words and letter–sound correspondences. Children who read the pattern book, *The Bus Ride,* learned to distinguish the words *hippopotamus* and *rhinoceros* by using their beginning letters (Rhodes, 1981). Children at a writing center experimented with sounds and letters in order to spell the word *hockey* (Dobson, 1985). This section presents other opportunities that are specialized, in that teachers purposely provide them as supports for experimenters' learning of letter–sound associations and learning of sight words.

Using Functional Print

We showed in Chapter 6 that novices are able to use environmental print to learn about written language. We use the term *functional print* (McGee, 1986) to describe environmental print that is integral to everyday activities in children's lives. At their stage of literacy development, experimenters are often interested in and attentive to the graphic details (letters and words) in environmental print items, especially very functional environmental print items. This may be so even when those items have few logo-like features (that is, few distinctively printed words like *McDonald's* with the *M* made to resemble the golden arches or *Coca-Cola* with its characteristic red-and-white, curly-cue lettering).

Experimenters can be supported in their discovery of how written language works when teachers provide such functional print items and encourage students to bring their own examples to school. Teachers can teach a unit about "Everyday Things You and Your Family Read" or can provide a place for a permanent collection of these items.

These activities provide occasions for teachers to be opportunistic, to take advantage of everyday materials and of observed student interests. Teachers can emphasize the importance of function by first asking function-related questions. Teachers can support children's attention to graphic detail in the items by asking the children what they can read in the item, noting the degree of correspondence between how the child reads and what is printed on the item, and even asking, "How did you know that?"

Consider, for example, a scenario of a child's reading a *TV Guide* that is opened to a page that includes an advertisement for "The Cosby Show." The teacher asks, "What are you going to watch tonight?" (recognizing that *TV Guide* serves the function of helping one decide what programs to watch). When the child answers, "Cosby!" the teacher asks, "How did you know that was on?" The child turns the magazine so that the teacher can see the picture of Bill Cosby and his television family. The teacher says, "Oh does it say 'Cosby' there?" When the child answers "Yes" and points to the word *Cosby*, the teacher can ask, "How did you know that said 'Cosby'?" If the child says, "Because it starts with a C,'' the teacher can ask where else that word can be found and can help the child locate the entry for "The Cosby Show" under its time in the text of the guide. That can lead to noting how the guide works and to finding other shows' names using beginning letters, even shows that are not featured in big, illustrated advertisements. The child's answering, "Because it starts with a C" can lead to finding other words that start with the letter C in the *TV Guide*, in other functional print, and in other print displayed in the classroom.

Other children may become interested in this functional reading activity. Children can make posters of their favorite television programs and teachers can make posters to announce programs they would like the children to watch. The posters may be illustrated with pictures cut from *TV Guide* or from other entertainment or celebrity magazines, but they must always include the show's name and viewing time, which the poster-maker finds by referring to the *TV Guide*. Children may even produce their own programs in a television play center (either with a cardboard television camera, toy microphones, and a pretend television set made by cutting a "screen" out of the front of a big carton, or with real videotape recording and playing equipment—see McGee and Ratliff, 1987) and write their own guide to the programs.

We have already seen another example of functional print in the classroom and how it led to further learning about written language. The stamped envelopes in Ms. Harper's bird center prompted children's reading bird names on the stamps and the names of addressees. Follow-up included a child's bringing a stamp center for the centers center. With sufficient interest and incentive (possibly in connection with a class pen pal project or with Valentine's Day), the follow-up might also have included lessons about how envelopes are addressed, how the mail carrier knows to whom the letter goes, and how you know who sent you a letter. The teacher can arrange to have some interesting letters mailed directly to the classroom, or can plan a field trip to the post office where children can mail letters that they have written to their parents.

Using Memorized Texts

A technique for supporting experimenters' developing a concept of word and acquiring a small number of sight words is called "fingerpoint reading" of memorized texts (Morris, 1981). The technique is simple. The teacher first teaches the children a familiar rhyme, poem, or song, such as "Twinkle, Twinkle, Little Star," by reciting it or singing it a few times with them. Next, she writes the rhyme on the blackboard or on a large sheet of paper. Then she models fingerpoint reading by reading and pointing to each word as it occurs. It is important to preserve the rhythm of the rhyme. The teacher must be careful not to let her pointing become so emphatic that the pointing, rather than the rhythm of the rhyme, determines the pace of the reading. Next, the teacher and the students perform several choral readings of the rhyme, with the teacher always pointing to the words so that the children can easily see them. Finally, individual children take turns fingerpoint reading.

With careful observation of fingerpoint reading, teachers can determine whether or not children have a concept of word (Morris, 1981). The first question to ask is, "Do children correctly point to each word as it occurs?" It is important to realize that pointing correctly does not require ability to identify the words. What it does require—and this is no small accomplishment—is that children have an understanding of what a spoken word is and what a written word is. As they say one word and then the next, they know to point to one written word and then the next.

The second thing to watch for is whether children know when they have made a mistake, or "gotten off the track" in their fingerpoint reading. If they do, are they able to self-correct without the teacher's help? Usually children first become aware of being "off the track" at an end point. Either they get to the end of their recitation, but are not yet at the end of the written text, or they run out of written text to point to, but are still reciting.

Children can acquire a concept of word by fingerpoint reading or by such informal means as observing text while being read to and paying attention to environmental and functional print. Once they have a concept of word and are able to fingerpoint read successfully, children can use the text and the procedure to learn sight words. Teachers can demonstrate how to begin pointing to and saying a memorized text until the target word is located.

This is an excellent opportunity for experimenters who are already interested in words and letters and sounds. They can use how the target word looks and what they know about sounds in letters' names to make and confirm generalizations about letter–sound correspondences. It is not surprising, then, that there is a connection between fingerpoint reading and invented spelling, a literacy activity that involves knowledge of letter–sound correspondences. Children who demonstrate by fingerpoint reading that they have a concept of word are very likely to be inventive spellers (Morris, 1983).

There are other sources of memorized texts besides familiar rhymes. Many children memorize a familiar storybook which they have asked to have read to them over and over. As we pointed out earlier in this chapter, children can easily memorize little books (Mason, McCormick, & Bhavnagri, 1986). Memorized Big Books, or parts of them, can also be a basis of their learning sight words and letter–sound correspondences.

Using Invented Spelling

Once children begin showing some of the invented spelling behaviors described in Chapter 7, teachers can use their interest in and knowledge about words, letters, and sounds to support their learning more about reading and writing. A technique for doing this in meaningful contexts is called Experimental Reading with Invented Spelling (ERIS) (Richgels, 1987).

The rationale for ERIS is that learning about letter–sound correspondences is most productive when children at the same time use that knowledge in functional reading and writing activities. The method has three components: (1) using *purpose talk* whenever letter–sound correspondences are discussed, (2) providing many opportunities for writing, and (3) reading both conventionally and nonconventionally spelled materials.

As in other approaches presented in this chapter, "teacher talk" is very important in ERIS. When the teacher gives a mini-lesson about the sound of the letter *b* to those children who have been experimenting with sounds and letters, she must remind them that the reason for such learning is to be able to use their knowledge in their writing. The teacher might say, "You are learning the sound at the beginning of *bug* so that you can use the letter *b* when you want to write" or "You may want to write the word *butterfly*—what are some letters you would need?" or "When I wrote the word *bird* on the unit poster about birds, I knew to start with /b/—*b*!"

There are many ways to provide classroom opportunities for writing. The following ways are included in Richgels' (1987) description of ERIS because they support using invented spelling. Teachers can ask children to help with the creation of a poster or a label or some other written display for the classroom ("What letter should I write first for this picture of a panda?"). Teachers can ask a child about the picture he or she is drawing and say, "You can write about that—what letters do you need?" and afterwards ask, "Can you read this to me?" or say, "I can read that!"

Finally, as part of ERIS, teachers make use of, and call attention to, letter–sound knowledge in functional sources of readings. These include language experience stories, students' writings, and stories teachers have written in which they have highlighted those letters whose sounds are easy to discern and easy to use.

Language experience stories will include some words that start with a letter whose sound has been discussed recently. While reading a language experience story, the teacher might say, "Look! We used *b* here to write *basketball*. It's a good thing we learned that *b* stands for /b/, like at the beginning of *basketball*!"

Teachers can model making use of the variety of clues that students provide in their writings. While reading Jonathan's label for his rocket picture, for example, the teacher might say, "Look at Jonathan's picture of a rocket. I know why he wrote an *r* by it. Look—*r*—/r/—rocket! This *r* is for rocket, isn't it Jonathan?" Or while displaying George's monster picture and his label for it (MNSTR), the teacher may only have to say, "Who can read what George wrote under his picture?"

Teacher-written stories with highlighting should include familiar content (see Figure 8.4); they should use the same sentence structures that teachers normally use when speaking with their children, and they should provide many contextual clues such as illustrations and repetition of important words so that children do not have to rely entirely on letter–sound knowledge. Teachers should explain that they have highlighted some parts of words. They can say, "When I wrote these words, I used a red marker for sounds I thought you might know."

Figure 8.4 A Story for a Kindergarten Class about Their Classmate's Birthday. (Highlighting is of familiar words and letters for which some children know sound associations.)

Eddie is 6 **years old.**
Yesterday was his birthday.
He got a Tonka digger for his birthday.
and he brought it to school.
We can use his digger at the **sand table.**

From "Experimental Reading with Invented Spelling (ERIS): A Preschool and Kindergarten Method" by Donald J. Richgels, 1987, *The Reading Teacher, 40,* p. 527. Copyright by the International Reading Association. Reprinted with the permission of Donald J. Richgels and the International Reading Association.

Planning to Use Approaches

One of the principles we drew from Ms. Harper's example was that literacy instruction for experimenters will include some planned lessons. The way she used her unit centers, her reading and writing lessons center, and even her writing and storybook centers depended on her being a good planner. All of the approaches to literacy instruction included in this section also require systematic planning. This does not mean that the teacher is no longer open to unexpected outcomes nor that the resulting literacy program is not child-centered. It means that teachers should become very familiar with the approaches described and other original approaches or other approaches described in the professional literature. Then they should be sure that they have prepared the necessary materials so that they can offer these approaches to children when needs arise.

Once teachers observe that some of their students are experimenters, they should systematically plan activities and lessons to guarantee that those experimenters are supported in their developing knowledge in all four areas of written language competence. Teachers should periodically take stock of their students by asking "Which children are often using written language in experimenter-like ways lately?" and "What experiences am I making available to them so that they have the best chance of discovering experimenters' ways of constructing meanings, the form knowledge that is typical of experimenters, the knowledge of meaning-form links, and the knowledge of functions?"

It is important to realize that teachers may use a technique to increase children's knowledge of one area, such as the relation between spoken language and written language, but that technique will also involve knowledge about the other areas such as meaning making and the form and the functions of written language. This is because the techniques we have chosen for this section use written language samples as integrated wholes; they do not dissect language into isolated, meaningless fragments.

Thus, a teacher may plan to make a point about letter–sound correspondences (the relation between spoken language and written language) with a story he has written highlighting certain letters (as in the ERIS method). But if the story is a good one, it will demonstrate other aspects of literacy: it will be relevant to children's experiences (meaningful); it will be a model of story form (form knowledge); and its purpose will be apparent to the children (function knowledge). (For example, the story in Figure 8.4 has the obvious purpose of memorializing the class's observation of Eddie's birthday.)

Chapter Summary _____

The example of Ms. Harper's kindergarten demonstrated both the cognitive and affective benefits for experimenters of literacy instruction that is functional and integrated with the many other kinds of play and learning that can take place in schools. The physical arrangement of Ms. Harper's room and her provision of many and varied activities within a secure routine required much planning. Careful planning, however, does not imply that the teacher must be an intrusive, dominant force in the classroom. Ms. Harper's teaching included her quiet modeling and her sometimes being out of the way of her students' self-directed learning.

Experimenters are able to discover new information about how written language works by interacting in new, intense ways with books. Big Books support such interaction by making it possible for group reading to be like one-to-one lap reading. Pattern books give experimenters the best possible opportunity to notice the regularities in text upon which reading as a nonrandom act depends. In addition, their repetitiveness makes them very suitable sources for learning about a key story structure characteristic, that is, repeated episodes. Little books are inviting and easy to memorize. They make meaningful book experiences possible for almost all children, and their memorized text can be a resource for teaching sight words.

Experimenters need many opportunities and much support for writing. They may dictate or do their own writing about pictures they draw. They may write in a journal, or join in a planned writing activity that is modeled by an adult at the writing center. They must be free to talk to themselves, with one another, and with adults before, during, and after their writing. They must be given the positive messages that they can write, that there is an audience for their work, and that helpful strategies exist for working on those aspects of writing that they find most difficult, from using the space on the page to finding matches between letters and sounds in words.

Many specialized approaches exist for helping young children experiment with writing and reading. One approach exploits children's appreciation of the usefulness of print in their environment (the functional print approach). Another approach makes use of children's ability to memorize familiar rhymes, favorite storybooks, Big Books, or little books; fingerpoint reading of these texts supports children's developing concept of word, their acquisition of sight words, and their exploration of letter–sound correspondences. A third approach (ERIS) makes use of experimenters' interests in words, letters, and sounds to support their reading and writing in meaningful contexts. These are just a few instructional approaches that can be found in professional journals for teachers of young children.

Applying the Information

Our presentation of Ms. Harper's kindergarten classroom was an extended case study. Choose one of the examples of Ms. Harper's using her centers. (Consider, for example, the way she planned, introduced, and sustained interest in a bird unit for her unit center.) What opportunities did she create through that center for children to experiment with written language? How did the center's activities highlight meaning making, forms of written language, meaning-form links, and functions of written language? Recall from Chapter 7 the literacy behaviors that are characteristic of experimenters. How would you expect children who usually act as experimenters to make use of Ms. Harper's centers? How would their use of the centers differ from that of children who usually act as novices?

Going Beyond the Text

We suggest three possible ways for you to go beyond the text of this chapter.

Plan a unit for Ms. Harper's unit center. Collect or make necessary materials. Imagine a child has come to that center for the first time. How would you help him or her to become acquainted with its resources and its purposes? How would you insure that his or her first experience there is successful and enjoyable? Make sure your unit has "staying power," that it will continue to attract and involve children in the topic and in experimentation with written language even into its second, hold-over week in Ms. Harper's class. Try your unit in a kindergarten class.

Choose one of the approaches to supporting experimenters' literacy learning described in the last half of Chapter 8 (using Big Books, pattern books, little books, various kinds of writing, functional print, or memorized texts). Observe and participate in routine literacy events in a kindergarten class. Which children act as experimenters in those events, especially the events that pertain to your chosen approach? Use the approach with those children. Evaluate its effectiveness. Did the approach help the children make use of the knowledge they had revealed in the routine literacy events? Did it support their continued experimentation?

Near the end of this chapter we discussed systematic planning. Spend some time in a child care center over a period of several weeks. Observe and help care for the three- to five-year-olds. Then ask yourself the "taking stock" questions on page 297. What are the signs that the children are responding as experimenters to literature or to writing opportunities? Where can you find information about the best experiences to make available to those children? Discuss these questions with the center's director and other teachers.

References

CALKINS, L. M. (1986). *The art of teaching writing.* Portsmouth, NH: Heinemann.

COMBS, M. (1987). Modeling the reading process with enlarged texts. *The Reading Teacher, 40,* 422–426.

DOBSON, L. N. (1985). Learning to read by writing: A practical program for reluctant readers. *Teaching Exceptional Children, 17,* 30–36.

DYSON, A. H. (1986, April). *Symbol weaving: Interrelationships between the drawing, talking, and dictating of young children.* Paper presented at the annual convention of the American Educational Research Association, San Francisco.

EASTMAN, P. D. (1969). *Flap your wings.* New York: Random House.

ELLERMEYER, D. (1988). Kindergarten reading programs to grow on. *The Reading Teacher, 41,* 402–405.

FRANKLIN, E. A. (1988). Reading and writing stories: Children creating meaning. *The Reading Teacher, 42,* 184–190.

GRAVES, D. H. (1983). *Writing: Teachers and children at work.* Portsmouth, NH: Heinemann.

HALL, S. (1985). OAD MAHR GOS and writing with young children. *Language Arts, 62,* 262–265.

HALL, S., & HALL, C. (1984). It takes a lot of letters to spell "Erz." *Language Arts, 61,* 822–827.

HEALD-TAYLOR, G. (1987). How to use predictable books for K–2 language arts instruction. *The Reading Teacher, 40,* 656–661.

HOSKISSON, K., & TOMPKINS, G. E. (1987). *Language arts: Content and teaching strategies.* Columbus, OH: Merrill.

MARTIN, B. (1970). *Brown bear, brown bear.* New York: Holt, Rinehart, and Winston.

MARTINEZ, M., & TEALE, W. H. (1987). The ins and outs of a kindergarten writing program. *The Reading Teacher, 40,* 444–451.

MARTINEZ, M., & TEALE, W. H. (1988). Reading in a kindergarten classroom library. *The Reading Teacher, 41,* 568–572.

MASON, J. M., McCORMICK, C., & BHAVNAGRI, N. (1986). How are you going to help me learn? Lesson negotiations between a teacher and preschool children. In

D. B. Yaden, Jr. & S. Templeton (Eds.), *Metalinguistic awareness and beginning literacy: Conceptualizing what it means to read and write* (pp. 159–172). Portsmouth, NH: Heinemann.

McGEE, L. M. (1986). Young children's environmental print reading. *Childhood Education, 63,* 118–125.

McGEE, L. M., & RATLIFF, J. L. (1987). Using the VCR in the language arts. In C. R. Personke & D. D. Johnson (Eds.), *Language arts instruction and the beginning teacher: A practical guide* (pp. 208–216). Englewood Cliffs, NJ: Prentice-Hall.

MORRIS, D. (1981). Concept of word: A developmental phenomenon in beginning reading and writing processes, *Language Arts, 58,* 659–668.

MORRIS, D. (1983). Concept of word and phoneme awareness in the beginning reader. *Research in the Teaching of English, 17,* 359–373.

NELSON, O. (1989). Storytelling: Language experience for meaning making. *The Reading Teacher, 42,* 386–391.

POTTER, G. (1989). Parent participation in the language arts program. *Language Arts, 66,* 21–28.

RASINSKY, T. (1988). The role of interest, purpose, and choice in early literacy. *The Reading Teacher, 41,* 396–400.

REIMER, B. L. (1983). Recipes for language experience stories. *The Reading Teacher, 36,* 396–401.

RHODES, L. K. (1981). I can read! Predictable books as resources for reading and writing instruction. *The Reading Teacher, 34,* 511–517.

RICHGELS, D. J. (1987). Experimental reading with invented spelling (ERIS): A preschool and kindergarten method. *The Reading Teacher, 40,* 522–529.

RONEY, R. C. (1989). Back to the basics with storytelling. *The Reading Teacher, 42,* 520–523.

SULZBY, E. (1985). Children's emergent reading of favorite story books. *Reading Research Quarterly, 20,* 458–481.

TRACHTENBERG, P., & FERRUGGIA, A. (1989). Big books from little voices: Reaching high risk beginning readers. *The Reading Teacher, 42,* 284–289.

Part 4

Moving into Formal Instruction with Sixes, Sevens and Eights

Part 4 describes children who are able to write and read in accomplished, easily recognizable ways. They read fluently, using thousands of sight words and several meaning-making strategies. These children continue to write for their own purposes, but they have an awareness of both their text's autonomy and their audience's needs. They owe this accomplishment partly to their elementary school experience. However, these children also have had years of experience with written language and countless personal experiments with different versions of what it means to be literate. Their accomplishment is the capstone to the experiences and experiments described in the earlier units of this book. Chapter 9, "Accomplished Readers and Writers," describes what accomplished readers and writers learn. Chapter 10, "Classroom Support for Accomplished Readers and Writers," describes what teachers can do to promote such learning. In Chapter 11, "Five Teachers of Accomplished Readers and Writers," five scenarios are presented. The five teachers surmount difficult, but not uncommon obstacles. Their cases show that there is much that teachers can do to support young readers and writers, even after the children have attained a level of conventional competence.

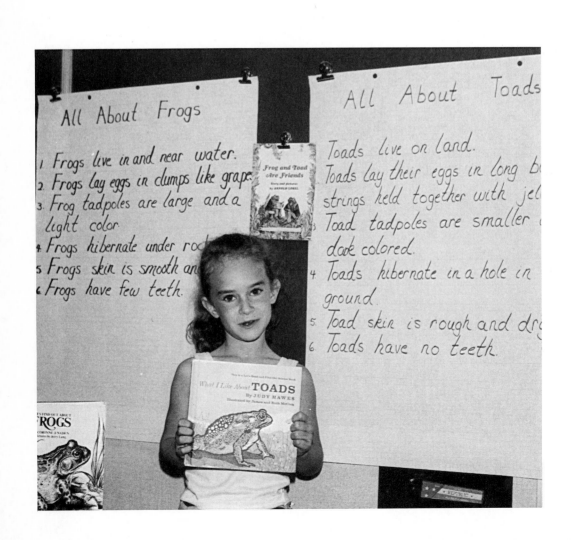

All About Frogs

1. Frogs live in and near water.
2. Frogs lay eggs in clumps like grapes.
3. Frog tadpoles are large and a light color.
4. Frogs hibernate under rocks.
5. Frogs skin is smooth and
6. Frogs have few teeth.

All About Toads

Toads live on land.
Toads lay their eggs in long b[...]
strings held together with jel[...]
Toad tadpoles are smaller [...]
dark colored.
4. Toads hibernate in a hole in [...]
ground.
5. Toad skin is rough and dr[...]
6. Toads have no teeth.

CHAPTER 9

Accomplished Readers and Writers

Most children are capable of becoming accomplished readers and writers by the time they finish third grade. They acquire the skills and strategies needed to read a variety of written materials and to write for many purposes in many genres or text forms. This accomplishment is partly the result of the formal instruction that usually begins in first grade, and it is partly the result of children's individual discoveries, inventions, and experiments with literacy, which were described in the preceding parts of this book and which can continue into the primary school.

This chapter discusses what children know and what their typical literacy behaviors are as they progress from experimenting with parts of the literacy puzzle to becoming accomplished readers and writers. While they are not mature readers and writers as adults are, most elementary children make much progress in reading and writing in their first three years of school. That progress may include the following developments:

1. Accomplished readers and writers are able to give more attention to larger, whole-text meanings because they can pay less attention to surface features of text such as specific letter combinations and the sounds that letters represent.

2. Children's merely performing literacy tasks gives way to their being aware of their reading and writing performances. They acquire metaknowledge.

3. Children progress from sometimes creating meanings only for themselves to knowing that all meaning making is communicative. They learn that as writers, they must have someone in mind who will read their work. They learn

that when they read, they must try to understand what readers an author had in mind.

4. They progress from having rather vague impressions of form to having fairly deliberate control over various well-structured forms. They learn how to write a story that includes necessary elements, and they know that their audience of readers will expect and need those elements. They learn when not to use the story form; they know that some topics require a different form, exposition.

5. They move from experimenting with aspects of reading and writing to processing their own and others' texts strategically. As children acquire some clearly defined strategies, they are able to perform in the same way with similar materials from one literacy event to another.

Our description of accomplished readers' and writers' literacy learning is organized into four categories: meaning making, the form of written language, meaning-form links, and the functions of written language. In addition, we look in greater depth at what children are able to do with their writing during this period of development. Finally, we will make connections between the psycho-sociolinguistic perspective that we have used throughout this book and the traditional perspective underlying most commercial materials and methods for reading and writing instruction in the primary grades.

WHAT ACCOMPLISHED READERS AND WRITERS KNOW ABOUT MEANING CONSTRUCTION

Meaning making is not new to the accomplished reader and writer. As novices and experimenters, children are already able to make meaning during literacy events. They can derive the literal meanings of what is read to them, and they can even make evaluative comments (remarking, for example, "What a silly bear!" or "That's a silly thing to do, isn't it?" when hearing a story about a bear who eats pizza for breakfast).

As accomplished readers and writers who have mastered literacy skills, the children described in this chapter are able to transfer their earlier meaning-making strategies to what they do on their own with books and paper and pencils. In other words, they are able to construct meaning from what they read by themselves (What did the author intend?) and in what they write for someone else (How can I convey for others what I intend?). They are even more aware than novices and experimenters that written language is a communication process.

Accomplished readers have the skills and strategies to attend to salient features of a written text and to use what they know about langauge and about the world. By using these skills and strategies, accomplished readers are able to construct a message that resembles the message the author intended the reader to receive. Although they have been really reading for a long time in the way that novices and experimenters read, they are now really reading in a way that "the person on the street corner" would recognize as reading (Sulzby, 1985b).

What accomplished readers do is more complete than what novices and experimenters do. We do not mean that the children we call accomplished readers and writers have finished with their literacy learning, nor that beginners, novices, and experimenters do not accomplish a great deal. We do mean that accomplished readers and writers are better at putting together the pieces of the literacy puzzle. They know much about letter–sound correspondences (as do experimenters when they spell inventively), they know much about story structure (as do experimenters when they tell stories), and they know much about audience (as do experimenters when they read and write for each other). But, unlike experimenters, they combine all of that knowledge and more in single literacy events.

As an accomplished reader reads a story aloud for her father, for example, she may sound out new and difficult words (using knowledge of letter–sound correspondences), make predictions about characters and events in the story (using knowledge of story structure), and talk about those predictions with her father (showing her awareness of audience). At one point in the story she may labor over the word *porridge,* using all that she knows about phonics (including that the *g* is soft because it is followed by an *e*) because it is not a word she uses in speech. At another point, she may interrupt her reading to say to her father, "What do you think Goldilocks will do next? *I* know!" Still later, she may stop to say "If I were that girl, I'd never be able to sleep in a stranger's bed—especially if I saw that picture of a bear family in clothes hanging on the wall!"

The same is true for writing. Experimenters can write with an audience in mind (as Carrie's letters in Chapter 7 clearly demonstrate), but accomplished writers know better than experimenters the conventions that must be followed in both the mechanics and the logic of their writing if they are to communicate optimally with that audience.

Suppose a boy who is an accomplished writer says of the story he is writing, "I can't write that Kyalee is afraid of the shadows the moon is making. If I do, someone will remind me that I started out by describing him as a brave and fearless hunter." This demonstrates the boy's knowledge that his classmates will demand the consistency in characterization that their teacher has discussed with them.

In some contexts, accomplished writers may use some of their old novice and experimenter skills and strategies, such as invented spelling or early knowledge of text forms. In other contexts, accomplished writers will use new, improved versions of those skills and strategies. What distinguishes accomplished writers is the fact that they are motivated not only to get their ideas on paper, but also to insure that someone else (a reader) is able to understand their ideas and to reconstruct their meanings.

Accomplished readers and writers have a new awareness of the importance of meaning. They know that it is they, whether as authors or as readers, who are responsible for meaning making.

WHAT ACCOMPLISHED READERS
AND WRITERS KNOW ABOUT THE FORM
OF WRITTEN LANGUAGE

As they become accomplished readers and writers, children refine much of what they learned as experimenters about the form of written language. First, as they learn how to identify a growing number of words, they may pay close attention to identifying individual words in their reading. Chall (1983) calls this being "glued to print" (p. 18). Because of their close attention to the written text, they gain knowledge of the fine points of form at the word level in English writing. Children's writing begins to show their achievement of a fully conventional concept of word. Second, they start to use narrative form in their writing. Most children already know a great deal about narrative form and they use it to tell stories. During this period, they begin to use it, as well, to write stories on their own. Third, their knowledge of a different category of text form, *exposition*, grows and they begin to develop strategies for reading and writing expository texts.

Concept of Word

Accomplished readers and writers learn the difference between syllables and words. Bissex's (1980) son Paul demonstrated this new knowledge. When he was five and one-half years old, he wrote *telephone* as three words, TAL·A·FON (p. 23). When he was almost seven, he wrote I HATE GETTING IN TRUBLE and I HATE LOSEING MARBLE GAMES (p. 57). In a year and a half he had learned what a word is, how to signal a word with spaces, and some English spelling conventions.

Accomplished readers and writers learn how *morphemes* work in written language. The morpheme is the smallest unit of meaning in a language. If one divides a morpheme into smaller parts, it is no longer meaningful in its context. For example, *water* is one morpheme; if *water* were divided into *wat* and *er,* neither part would have meaning (although *er* is a morpheme in other contexts, such as in *taller*). On the other hand, *watered* is two morphemes, *water* and *ed;* the *ed* in *watered* adds the meaning "past tense" (although *ed* in other contexts, such as in *red,* is not a morpheme).

Accomplished readers and writers learn that morphemes may be written as individual words, such as the articles *a, an,* and *the;* or they may be written as word parts, such as *-ed, -ing,* and *-s.* At age six and one-half, Paul Bissex used *A* as a morpheme that is part of a word (in *awake* and *asleep*) and *A* as a morpheme that is a separate word (the article in *a owl*). He wrote, "I AM AWACK AT NITE ASLEP IN THE DAY / BUT I AM NOT A OWL" (Bissex, 1980, p. 57).

Accomplished readers and writers know that concepts may appear in different ways in written language. Ideas may be written as separate words, such as *ball* and *snow* in *Sam lost his white ball in the snow,* or they may be parts of single compound words, such as *snowball* in *Sam threw the snowball at the house.*

Finally, accomplished readers and writers know more about the English conventions for showing word boundaries, as well as other rules of punctuation. An experimenter's dots and squares between words, or circles around words give way to spaces between words. Periods and even commas, question marks, and exclamation marks appear in their writing.

Story Form

Many children have had a great deal of experience with stories long before they enter elementary school. They may have had stories read to them from infancy. Many children can tell stories quite well. To write their own stories, however, children need to experience writing processes such as rehearsing, revising, and editing and to know about the mechanics and logic of writing. Acquiring such experience and knowledge is part of becoming an accomplished writer. Accomplished writers are able to write stories because they have learned to spell words conventionally, or almost conventionally; because they can write texts composed of complete sentences; and because their texts are cohesive.

Telling Stories

Story structures were discussed in Chapters 4, 5, and 7. Compared to younger children, school-age children are very likely to be able to tell stories that are well organized. Applebee (1978) found that 70 percent of the stories five-year-olds told him were in the two highest (most organized) of his six categories (see Figure 4.11).

Ted told the story presented in Figure 9.1 when he was five and one-half years old. It shows the sophisticated knowledge of story structure and the control of literary devices that young children can acquire as they tell more and more stories.

Ted told this story to his mother, knowing that she would write it on the blank pages of a book for him to illustrate. He had been telling stories this way for over a year. In Ted's story, there is a clear progression from introduction and description of the main character ("Once upon a time there was a giant," "He

Figure 9.1 *Ted's Dictated Story.*

The Green Man and the Giant

Once upon a time there was a giant. He was so big that spears felt like a shot, and bullets were so little they got worn out by the time they went through his shoe. A big sea looked like a little stream. His neck stretched up into space. He could breathe up in space without a helmet and an air tank. He stomped around on planets and played ball with the earth. He thought it was good for the earth, and he laughed. A green man came up to him and said, "You're destroying buildings. Your fingers are like saws that cut down buildings. And you eat people for your pills in the morning." And then he went away. The green man was the god. The end.

---

was so big . . .''), to consequences of the character's attributes and actions (''A big sea looked like a little stream,'' ''You're destroying buildings''), to some finality (''And then he went away'') and explanation (''The green man was a god''). No event is unrelated to the story as a whole. Although we are left not knowing how the giant will respond to the god's complaint, Ted has given evidence to support alternative hypotheses (a giant who laughs about playing ball with the earth may just laugh at the god's complaints; on the other hand, a giant who thought that such treatment was good for the earth may be more considerate now that he has been informed about the consequences of his actions, especially since his informant is a god).

Learning Story Structure

Even when elementary school children show that they know about story form, their knowledge about stories is not complete. A simple story like the one in Figure 9.2 was read to second graders, and then, after they had spent a minute doing something unrelated to the story, such as solving math problems, they were asked to tell what they had heard. They recalled an average of five of the twelve ideas in the story. Then the researchers reordered the twelve ideas so that they no longer occurred in sequence in the story. In effect, the story was no longer a story. Now second graders recalled only an average of three ideas from this scrambled story. However, they are like sixth graders and adults in this respect; that is, scrambling a story made it harder for anyone to recall (Buss, Yussen, Mathews, Miller, & Rembold, 1983).

Suppose, however, that when the second graders, sixth graders, and adults were asked to recall the scrambled story, they were told specifically to do so in a way that made it a good story. Following such directions, sixth graders and adults made well-ordered stories from their memories of the scrambled stories, but second graders did not. When trying to make sense of a poorly ordered story, second graders have more to learn than older children or adults. Yet, after a very brief training in sequencing a story's ideas, second graders recalled a scrambled story in nearly perfect story order (Buss et al., 1983). Some second graders, therefore, seem to benefit from instruction in story form.

Even some third graders have poorly developed knowledge of story structure and have difficulty recalling simple stories. In one study, over one-third of

Figure 9.2 *A Simple Story with Twelve Idea Units*
(after Stein and Glenn, 1979)

---

(1) Once upon a time there was a little green Martian (2) who circled the earth in his flying saucer. (3) One day as he looked down at the earth, (4) he saw a man working in a garden and a little child waving up at him. (5) ''That child looks friendly,'' the Martian thought, and (6) he decided to swoop down for a visit. (7) So he landed his saucer and (8) popped its hatch. (9) The popping surprised the man. (10) He threw his shovel at the Martian, and ran off with the child under his arm. (11) The Martian was disappointed and (12) decided never again to approach a child earthling when a grown-up was nearby.

---

the third graders participating recalled less than half of the story ideas of a simple story like the one presented in Figure 9.2 (Buss, Ratliff, & Irion, 1985). Some of these story-unaware third graders were taught about story forms using activities like those suggested in Chapter 6 (Figure 6.3). After that instruction, their story structure knowledge and story comprehension improved.

It may be that these children learned about story form so easily because they already had some knowledge about stories—they already had a concept of story although it may not have been very complex. This knowledge may have come from growing up in environments that included much storytelling and bookreading (Atwell, 1989). Capacity to interpret and think critically about narratives is enhanced by repeated exposures to the same story, including exposures in more than one medium, such as in print and in video (Trousdale, 1989).

Writing Stories

We have seen that children's telling of stories and their listening to stories show what they know about story structure. What about their writing of stories? Note that the distinction between telling and writing is not always clear. Telling a story for someone else to write down (as Carrie and Ted did for Figures 7.10 and 9.1) is, in fact, a kind of writing. Many early elementary grade students have opportunities to write in that way, but eventually they are expected to compose on their own. In such composition, the child's knowledge of story structure is not always apparent.

Calkins (1986) has observed two characteristics of beginning writers that are related to knowledge of story form. One is that they have difficulty remembering what they want their stories to say when they are attending to the difficulties of writing. Young writers solve this problem by drawing and talking. If they first draw pictures of their stories, they are able to return later to the pictures for reminders of how their stories should go. For example, if the hard work of spelling the word *elephant* (LFNT) took all of first grader Claire's attention, she might forget what more she wanted to write. Then looking at the zoo picture she drew before writing could remind her that she wanted to write that the elephant was eating apples.

Talk also helps young writers sustain their writing. When they talk about their stories with others while writing, they receive a much-needed kind of feedback. Suppose that a first grade boy stops writing after the single sentence "I got a new bike." It may be that his experience with and expertise at conversation has accustomed him to expect someone else's immediate input as a prompt for his next sentence. Suppose then that someone reads his first sentence and says, "Oh really! What kind?" This enables him to get on to saying and then writing something more, such as "It's red and it's a dirt bike." Drawing a picture or talking with a friend helps children write stories that have better narrative form.

A second observation that Calkins (1986) made is that young authors' stories often barely qualify as stories. Beginning writers seem to avoid the story form altogether. Another way of saying this is that they do not use in their writing all the story structure knowledge that they exhibit during storytelling. Many first written "stories" are not stories; rather, they are "all I know about something" pieces. They are more like inventories of information—and misinformation. Figure 9.3 shows such a piece written by a first grader.

Figure 9.3 *Jeanne's "All About" Book*

A typical "all about" piece lacks story form, a precise sequence of events, and a real end. It may be a book composed of several pages, each with a picture and a caption that tells about some part of the subject the child has chosen. The captions may contain pronouns that refer back to earlier mentions of the subject. Except for such pronoun usage, however, most pages could stand on their own; they have no direct link with what went before or what comes after.

Teachers' talking with young authors helps them to become better writers (Calkins, 1986). When teachers ask questions that help children to discover their own intentions, and that have no right or wrong answers, the children are helped to write better defined pieces. Suppose a girl in first grade has written several "all about" pieces. Her latest piece is about a dinosaur, and it begins "This is Dexter the Dinosaur." The remainder of the text tells only that Dexter is a brontosaurus, that brontosauruses were the biggest creatures on earth, and that they ate only plants. In order to help this young writer move her "all about" piece closer to being a narrative piece, her teacher might ask, "Do you want to write a story like one of your favorite books, *Danny and the Dinosaur* (Hoff, 1958)?'' The teacher can even take another step in supporting the child's writing a narrative by asking, ''What happens to Dexter?'' ''What does Dexter want?'' or ''What problem may Dexter have—being that he is so big and only eats plants—and how might he solve that problem?''

Figure 9.4 shows a story that Ted wrote as a first grader. It is clearly founded in fact. Ted knew a lot about rocket launchings; he might have written many pages ''all about'' rockets. Instead, he wrote a true narrative. His piece tells a story; there are goals, action, danger, problems, and a sequence of events.

Not all children want help turning ''all about'' pieces into true narratives. Their ''all about'' pieces may represent their attempts at another text form, exposition. A child may truly want to write a report rather than a story. Suppose that the teacher of our first-grade dinosaur devotee had reminded her of another of her favorite dinosaur books, one that gives information and does not really tell a story. The teacher might have asked, ''Do you want to write a book like *Dinosaur Time* (Parish, 1974)?'' If the answer were ''Yes,'' then the young author's ''all about'' list could serve as a good beginning, and the teacher could talk about how to write exposition.

Most first graders have much more to learn about expository writing than about narrative writing (Cudd & Roberts, 1989). There is evidence that by third grade, children are able to use knowledge of story structure in their writing. In fact, third graders' written stories have been found to differ very little in form from those of sixth graders and ninth graders (Langer, 1986). However, the same cannot be said of third graders' non-story writing. In the next section, we will look more closely at research about beginning writers' expository writing.

Expository Text Structure

Not all texts are stories. Some texts inform or explain, rather than relate a story; they are called *expositions.* Much non-fiction is exposition.

Even in third grade, children know relatively little about expository text form—that is, about how authors organize ideas in order to best convey the information they want readers to know. Third graders' knowledge of expository text form is especially undeveloped when compared to their knowledge of narrative text form. Langer (1986) found that, unlike storywriting, third graders still had much to learn about report writing. From third to sixth grades, and again from sixth to ninth grades, children's reports were longer, contained more content, and were more highly structured. Langer speculated that children have a head start with story structure compared to expository text structure and that they have earlier, more frequent exposure in the mainstream North American culture'' (p. 42) to fully developed stories.

But what about beginning writers' expository writing? Teachers need to know more than the fact that expository writing has its roots in ''all about'' pieces, and that even third graders have much to learn about exposition. Newkirk (1987) studied the expository writings of 100 first, second, and third graders. He found several ways children organized the expository texts they wrote. His

Figure 9.4 *Ted's Space Trip Story*

The rakit is dlasting of! Thay are
going tho 100 galakses! Peple are
climing a ladr to see them.it has a spashl
shedd all a rond it. In cas there is a atak on
the rakit. Becase you never no. thay are
on TV allso.

The rocket is blasting off! They are going through 100 galaxies! People
are climbing a ladder to see them. It has a special shield all around it.
In case there is an attack on the rocket. Because you never know. They
are on TV also.

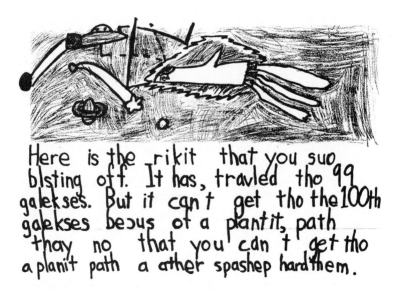

Here is the rikit that you suo
blsting off. It has, travled tho 99
galekses. But it can't get tho the 100th
galekses besus of a plantit, path
thay no that you can't get tho
a planit path a ather spashep hard them.

Here is the rocket that you saw blasting off. It has traveled through
99 galaxies. But it can't get through the 100th galaxy because of a
planet path. They know that you can't get through a planet path.
Another spaceship heard them.

findings are similar to Applebee's (1978) about the structure of children's stories. Children's first expository texts seem to have very little structure or form. Their later expositions have more complex structures involving several elements of form. We use descriptions of some of the expository forms Newkirk identified because they give much insight into the possible origins of children's knowledge of expository text form.

There are two important points about the origins of children's expository writing. The first point is that exposition for young writers is primarily improvisation on listing. The second point is that listing, unlike narrative, is an exclusively written-language form.

Early Expository Writing as List Making

Figures 9.5 and 9.6 show expository texts that are examples of Newkirk's least organized structure. They are both collections of labels, that is, one-word identifications of a picture. Children have a fascination with such lists as inventories of all that they know about something (Bissex, 1980; Clay, 1975). We have already seen that novices sometimes make lists of letters or numbers or even mock-letters in order to inventory all that they can write. Accomplished writers extend this idea by writing lists of facts in the "all about" lists mentioned earlier.

Figure 9.5 *Ted's Collection of Halloween Labels*

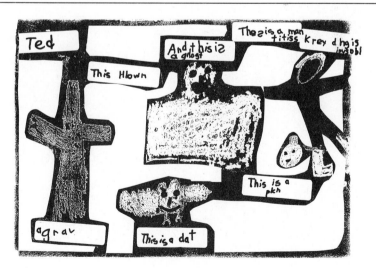

Ted. This is Halloween. And this is a ghost. This is a man. It is gray because he is invisible. A grave. This is a bat. This is a pumpkin.

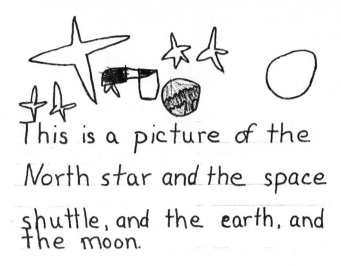

This is a picture of the North star and the space shuttle, and the earth, and the moon.

Figure 9.6 *An Exposition That Is a Label for a Space Drawing*

Ted's expository text, written in first grade and shown in Figure 9.7, is an example of one of the more organized forms that Newkirk (1987) found. It is an *attribute list,* that is, a collection of descriptions or comments about a topic. Although Ted has not attempted to relate one description to another, his descriptions are all related to the topic.

Figure 9.7 *An Exposition That Is An Attribute List about the Solar System*

This is a pacher of spas. We live on Eath. It is th only plan it with E calrs. The hotast planit we no is the sun. The saken Hotast one is very clos to the sun. ploto is tin.

This is a picture of space. We live on Earth. It is the only planet with 3 colors. The hottest planet we know is the sun. The second hottest one is very close to the sun. Pluto is tiny.

Early Expository Writing as a Form
That is Unique to Written Language

We have seen that, from very early ages, children are able to use what they learn about narrative form to tell and then to write stories. In other words, narrative form has its roots in spoken language. This is true historically as well as developmentally. Humans had rich narrative traditions long before they invented written language.

The same cannot be said, however, about expositions. List making is a decidedly written-language activity. It is true that many children have experiences with lists at an early age, just as they have experiences with stories. They see their parents write lists (Heath, 1983), and they are willing to try to read lists (McGee, Lomax, & Head, 1988), but they do not tell lists like they tell stories. In fact, if the expression we just used, "tell lists," sounds wrong, there is a good reason. Listing has a different function than "storying." Listing allows the list maker not only to search memory, but also to sort and categorize in a way "that is almost impossible in speech" (Newkirk, 1987, p. 132).

Newkirk (1987) cites Goody's (1977) historical explanation that early alphabetic writing systems were used mainly to keep administrative lists and that these lists were the first steps toward domesticating or ordering knowledge. Children who begin to use expository form are discovering this unique power of written language just as the first inventors of written langauge did thousands of years ago. "The child who writes a list is not writing down talk; he or she is doing something which talk cannot do" (Newkirk, 1987, p. 141). Thus, children who learn expository text structure are not just learning to write what they could previously tell quite well. They are learning a new, exclusively written language form, with an appropriate written language function.

Narrative and Exposition Together: Early
Expository Writing That Uses Storytelling

One way that children learn to use the new form of exposition is to rely on another, more familiar form—narrative. Some young children's reports have a strong narrative thread. It is not, as some (e.g., Moffett, 1968) have argued, that children must make do with the narrative form because they are ignorant of any other; rather, children are using what they know best in order to take their early steps toward a new form. In some cases, in fact, we can see a strong interplay between listing and storying.

This is not really surprising. The storying ability that Wells (1986) has found in children from literate homes can be a very powerful way of ordering the world of experience. Temple and Gillet (1989) report a charming vignette from Chukovsky (1968) about the robustness of Soviet children's storying ability. After the Russian Revolution, Russian schoolbooks were rewritten with only expositions, and no narratives. The children were given some selections that were informational pieces about the uses of machines for manufacturing. However, the children retold those pieces as *stories* about machines!

Ted wrote the solar system report in Figure 9.7 to accompany the space trip story he had written a few days earlier (see Figure 9.4). Together they make a *hybrid story-report.*

Hybrid story-reports are not just stories. They spring from a different purpose than storywriting; they are written primarily to convey or to preserve information. We will look at another exposition by Ted in order to examine further the interplay between two forms, exposition and narrative.

When Ted was in second grade, he saw Halley's comet. He might have documented his experience simply by writing a collection of factual observations, but the event was too dramatic; it called for storytelling as a means of preserving important information. Ted supplemented his story-report with a drawing. Figure 9.8 shows his report and Figure 9.9 shows his drawing.Ted blended two

Figure 9.8 Ted's Narrative Report about Viewing Halley's Comet

---

THE COMET

In the middle of the night my dad woke me up. It reminded me of when my mom had my baby sister. I thought we were going to have another baby. But Dad said, "Do you want to see the comet?" so I got up, changed my clothes and got in the car with Dad. It was 4:00 a.m. when we left. It took us about a half an hour to get there. We came to an open field and before we got our binoculars out, somebody told us that the baseball field had a better view of the comet. So we went there in our car. It took us about one minute. There was a big group of people looking through binoculars because the people with the telescopes had not come yet. Dad asked one of the people where the comet was. The person told him, "Look for one short pole and one long pole. It would be above the long pole." So he took out his binoculars and looked for the comet, and then he saw it. He let me see. I had seen many pictures of the comet, but this one looked different. But my dad told me it was Halley's Comet. It looked like a big fuzzy blob with a big fuzzy tail.

Then after looking at it for two minutes, we got in line to look through a telescope. When I got to look through the telescope, the comet did not look at all like it did in the binoculars. It was a very bright object, and I couldn't see the tail. Then I let my dad have a turn looking through the telescope. Then after he looked the comet had moved. Now it was over a tree and to the left.

After looking at it through the binoculars again, we got in line for another telescope. And then we met some old ladies who had seen the comet the last time it came. One of the old ladies was eight when she saw it in 1910. One of the ladies said that when it last came, it was higher in the sky and brighter.

Then after we looked in the telescope and had our last look at it with the binoculars, we drove home. It was 5:15. We changed back into our pyjamas and went to sleep again.

by

Ted H. Richgels

March 16, 1986

Figure 9.9 *Ted's Drawing of Viewing Halley's Comet*

kinds of expository form: description ("It looked like a big fuzzy blob with a big fuzzy tail," "It was a very bright object, and I couldn't see the tail") and comparison/contrast ("I had seen many pictures of the comet, but this one looked different," "When I got to look through the telescope, the comet did not look at all like it did in the binoculars," "when it last came, it was higher in the sky and brighter"). He also used such narrative elements as time sequence and dialogue. Finally, he used dramatic inventions. He wrote, "I thought we were going to have another baby." Yet Ted (who had been awakened in the night once before, for his sister's birth) knew that his mother was not expecting a baby, and he did not really expect such a development overnight!

Perhaps the fact that Ted dictated this report contributed to his telling it like a story. In contrast, his very accurate drawing with its labels and objective data such as date and time is more exposition-like than narrative-like. Yet even the drawing has narrative elements. Ted drew posts and trees that figure prominently in his narrative-report, but that would be unnecessary to a merely factual, descriptive record of the comet's appearance.

Later Expository Text Structure Knowledge

What do children know about expository text structure at the stage of becoming accomplished readers and writers? We have seen that although they may spontaneously write "all about" pieces (Calkins, 1986) and although they discover the unique list-making power of written language (Bissex, 1980; Clay, 1975; Newkirk, 1987), their knowledge of non-narrative text form is undeveloped compared to their knowledge of narrative text form (Langer, 1986). The expository texts (reports) that Langer's (1986) third graders wrote often used one of two fairly simple ways of relating one idea to another, *descriptions* and *evaluations.* For example, eight-year-old Mark's report was a collection of four descriptions that elaborated on his title ("How to Be a Good Goaly") and on his closing sentence ("and that's how to be a good goaly") (Langer, 1986, p. 58). Their evaluations were simple commentaries, such as, "I like humming birds" or "Swimming is a fun sport" (Langer, 1986, p. 56).

The most organized of the expository forms Newkirk (1987) identified is a list of *ordered paragraphs.* Each paragraph contains at least three statements that are related to a single topic and that are logically connected to each other. Even accomplished writers seldom write such highly organized expositions. Almost half of the first-grade expositions Newkirk analyzed did not even follow the attribute list form; they were merely labels. By third grade, however, he found most children used at least attribute list forms and some even used the most organized kind of list, the ordered paragraph.

Figure 9.10 *An Exposition That Uses Cause-and-Effect Logic*

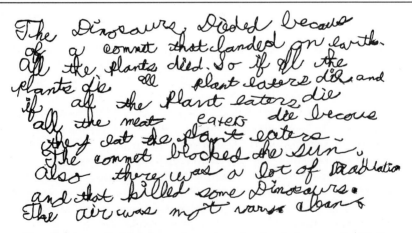

The dinosaurs died because of a comet that landed on earth. All the plants died. So if all the plants die, all plant eaters die, and if all the plant eaters die, all the meat eaters die because they eat the plant eaters. The comet blocked the sun. Also there was a lot of radiation and that killed some dinosaurs. The air was not very clean.

Some accomplished writers begin learning various ways to connect ideas logically, such as time order, cause-and-effect, and compare-and-contrast. An elementary student wrote the paragraph shown in Figure 9.10. This student is beginning to understand how to use cause-and-effect logic to organize ideas in writing.

One of the last steps in learning exposition is knowing that, to present a topic well, one must find the best way to organize its content. This depends on having a repertoire of expository text structures to chose from, such as compare-contrast and cause-and-effect. This knowledge is also part of learning a subject thoroughly. A complete understanding of crocodiles requires knowing how crocodiles are both different from and similar to alligators. A report about crocodiles and alligators could be well organized if the author used a compare-contrast text structure. Similarly, a complete understanding of the age of glaciers requires knowing what effects the glaciers had on plant and animal life and on the topography of the continents. A report about glaciers could be well organized if the author used cause-and-effect text structure. Bruner (1960) called this "the mastery of the structure of the subject matter" (p. 18). Most accomplished readers and writers are only beginning to acquire this sophisticated knowledge.

WHAT ACCOMPLISHED READERS AND WRITERS KNOW ABOUT MEANING-FORM LINKS

Young experimenters with written language already know a great deal about meaning-form links (see Chapter 7). As they come to understand that the language of written text is different from the langauge of everyday conversation and that readers are limited in what they say by the words an author has put on a page, they try to sound literate and be precise. Their invented spellings show an awareness of letter–sound correspondences and an ability to use that awareness to put words in writing.

An important difference between experimenters and accomplished readers and writers is that the latter group uses more literacy strategies. We can better understand this change if we first distinguish between two kinds of literacy strategies. *Discovery strategies* are strategies for finding out how reading and writing work. "Pay attention to such salient features of literacy experiences as letters, letters' names, and sounds in words" is a discovery strategy that leads to experimenters' becoming inventive spellers, and thus to their knowing one way in which spelling works. *Performance strategies* are strategies for successfully accomplishing an act of reading or writing. Although "Be precise" and "Sound literate" are experimenters' performance strategies, most other strategies that experimenters use are discovery strategies. For accomplished readers and writers, however, performance strategies dominate.

Many performance strategies involve knowledge children already have—*prior knowledge*. Prior knowledge can be knowing the content of reading or writing, facts and concepts related to the subject matter. Prior knowledge also can be knowing reading and writing processes, such as knowing how to spell words, how to sound out words, how to organize a report, or what to include in a story. An increase in the latter kind of prior knowledge, which is usually learned in elementary school, contributes significantly to most children's becoming accomplished readers and writers.

Children become accomplished readers and writers as they learn better performance strategies. This entails further development of understandings about meaning-form links in spelling, oral reading, and silent reading.

Spelling

Accomplished writers have learned to spell many words conventionally, in ways "the person on the street corner" would recognize as correct. They may have spelled the word *height* as HIT at an earlier stage and as HITE or even as HEYET at an intermediate stage, but now they know *height* and many other words as sight words, and they have learned rules for spelling a great many others. They have learned this as a result of paying attention to spelling regularities in the context of words.

As the *height* examples suggest, this learning of spelling regularities is best seen as another step in the developmental invented spelling behavior first described in Chapter 7. While invented spelling is perhaps the hallmark of the young experimenter, it is not just a passing phase to be put aside or forgotten either by students at the stage of becoming accomplished or by their teachers. The early drafts of accomplished writers' work often include invented spellings.

Learning Spelling Regularities: Context

One of the most persistent popular misconceptions about English spelling is that it is arbitrary and inconsistent. Many people believe that there are so many exceptions to English spelling rules that the only path to becoming a good speller is rote memorization. Fortunately for all writers and especially for primary grade students and their teachers, this is not really the case. We do not have to memorize the spelling of each word. This explains why most people, even most third graders, can spell a large number of words correctly. They can spell many more words than the twenty words per week presented for study in their spelling books.

Although there are many glaring irregularities in English spelling, there are also many spelling regularities. Two useful strategies for learning spelling regularities are (1) to notice the possible ways of spelling a sound and (2) to pay attention to the contexts in which different spellings of the same sound can occur. For example, one spelling regularity is that the *f* sound (/f/) is spelled only four ways in English: *f, ff, ph,* and *gh.* It is true that there is no apparent reason for spelling /f/ at the end of *laugh* and *half* differently. Still, there is some regularity in ways letters for the *f* sound are used: /f/ is never spelled with *gh* or with *ff* at the *beginning* of an English word; and *ph* is used only with a special class of words, such as those that are built from *phon-* (meaning "sound") and *-graph* (meaning "write"). So, knowing the spelling regularity of the *f* sound suggests that the spellings of /f/ in *telephone,* or even *phone,* and *phonics* and *geography* and *paragraph* are to be expected; but spellings such as *phunny* or *ghunny* or even *ffunny* are not to be expected.

Children's errors reveal their growing awareness that certain spellings can only occur in certain words and in certain parts of words. A child's writing *laff* (for *laugh*) is consistent with our observations about the usual context of *ff* (at the end of words) and so it is less wrong than writing *ghish* for *fish*. *Laff* is not as great a violation of our expectations as *ghish*. *Laff* is wrong in a way that shows a child is learning about English spelling conventions. Expectations about where alternate spellings of the same sound occur are automatic with mature readers and spellers. Still, acquiring such expectations is a big job and an important one for children. It is an important part of their becoming accomplished writers and readers.

Ted's space trip story (Figure 9.4) provides an example of a spelling error that shows that the speller knows something about alternatives and contexts in English spelling. Ted wrote *Thay* for *They*. Although this is incorrect, it shows that Ted understood that *ay* is an alternative to the letter-name spelling for the long *a* sound (he used that letter-name spelling in the same story in *cas* for *case* and *spashep* for *spaceship*). Furthermore, Ted's spelling shows that he knew that the end of a single-syllable word is a likely place for using the *-ay* alternative; after all, *ay* is correct for the long *a* sound in *way, day, say, pay,* and *stay* and many other English words.

Learning Spelling Regularities: Word Families

Most children know a handful of sight words when they are still experimenters. Carrie, for example, knew her own name and *Mom* and *Dad* and *Ted* (her brother's name) as sight words (see Chapter 7).

As they become more accomplished readers and writers, children's sight-word repertoires greatly expand. Again, however, this does not mean that all progress depends upon memorization. Children can use a strategy of noticing *word families,* words that have similar sounds and appearances. For example, a child may know *Dad* as a sight word and know a number of consonant letter–sound correspondences. That child, then, has the prerequisite knowledge to be able to spell a number of words in the ''*-ad* family'' by substituting one beginning consonant for another. Therefore, spellings of words such as *had, bad, mad, fad, pad,* and *sad* do not have to be memorized. If a child also has the ability to attend to individual sounds in words (invented spelling is a sign of such ability) and can blend individual sounds together to read or say the newly constructed word, then he or she can also read several new words.

Having similar sound patterns is not the only way that words can be related. Another regularity in spelling is that many words are spelled similarly because of their similar meanings (Chomsky, 1971). This is often true even when the words have different pronunciations. For example, the second vowel in *precedent* is pronounced ''uh'' but spelled with an *e* to be consistent with the spelling of the second vowel in *precede.*

Learning Spelling Regularities: Letter–Sound Relations and Conventional Spellings

Turn back to Figure 7.14 on page 254. Accomplished writers' stages of spelling are shown in the *Mixed Spelling* and *Fully Conventional Spelling* sections of this figure. Accomplished readers and writers still spell many words non-conventionally, but they come to realize that English spelling is more complex than simply matching single letters with single sounds. One thing they learn is that every syllable must contain a vowel. So they spell *jar* as JAR rather than JR. A related discovery is that letters often work in combination. This leads, for example, to spelling *tail* as TAILL or TALLE (using *A* in combination with *I* or *E* to spell the long *a* sound) rather than TAL.

Another thing accomplished readers and writers notice is that some letters stand for more than one sound. They learn that there are long and short values for each vowel letter. The short value may have nothing to do with the way the vowel's name is pronounced; the letter *a* can be used for the vowel sound in both *Kate* and *cat*.

A third new understanding is that some sounds are represented in more than one way. The letter combinations *ai, a_e,* and even *eigh,* for example, can be used to spell the long *a* sound, and it is sometimes difficult to know which is correct in a given word. Bissex (1980) noted that in first grade Paul used four spellings for the long *a* sound (*ai, a_e, ay,* and the old letter-name spelling using just *a*), four for the long *e* sound (*ea, e_e, ee,* and *e*), four for the long *o* sound (*oa, o_e, ow,* and *o*), and three for the long *i* sound (*y, i_e,* and *i*) (Bissex, 1980, pp. 48–49).

Children learn about letters that seem to have no sound, or that are difficult to hear. In the earlier stages of invented spelling, they simply omitted such letters. Again, context is important; it can help them to know when to include those letters, and it can explain why a letter's sound is sometimes hard to hear. The letters *m* and *n*, for example, belong in the obvious places such as at the beginning of *map* and the end of *fun* and even in the middle of *pencil* and *hamster*, but they must also sometimes be included before a consonant that takes over so quickly that the *m* or *n* sound is eclipsed, as in *pant* and *lamp*. At five and one-half, Paul Bissex wrote VRMAT for *Vermont,* but in first grade, he wrote MINT, PAINT, RESTERANT for *restaurant*, MIND, ORING for *orange,* and AB-SINT for *absent* (Bissex, 1980, pp. 22, 53, and 55).

Finally, children learn that meaning and visual configuration are important in spelling. The regular past tense morpheme, for example, is always spelled with the same two letters, *-ed*. Even though there is no single pronunciation for *-ed*, (compare *wanted, played,* and *walked*), accomplished readers and writers know that it is simply a convenient visual sign that means "past." It is used to spell the past tense of *all* regular English verbs and it never sounds like the *ed* in *red*.

With all these understandings, accomplished readers and writers are able to show an increased flexibility, an ability to choose from several different spelling strategies depending on context. Unlike spellers at the early stages of invented spelling, accomplished spellers are not extremely analytic—in a one-to-one, one-unit-at-a-time way. They are newly *aware* that there is sublety to the spelling process and they are able to consider more than one thing at a time.

Oral Reading

At first, experimenters read orally by memorizing stories. Their oral reading changes when they become aware of print. Some children suddenly refuse to read because they are newly aware that reading in an adult way involves using the print. Other children go through a stage of being glued to the print (Chall, 1983). As they acquire some sight words and some skills for decoding individual words, they read only the isolated words that they are sure of (Sulzby, 1985a).

The new step that children take as they become accomplished readers is also related to their awareness of print. As with the accomplished stages of invented spelling, accomplished readers are able to diversify strategies. In this case, that means that they have more at their disposal than just memorization of specific sight words or of chunks of text such as familiar parts of pattern books. Sulzby (1985a) captures this notion in her name for this stage: "holistic" reading. When asked to read a familiar storybook, children at this stage are able to sound out some of the words, using their developing knowledge of letter–sound correspondences. They are willing to substitute words of their own for words they do not recognize, based on visual similarities, especially identical initial letters (for example, saying "sad" for *sorry*). They correct substitutions that turn out not to make sense (for example, "sunny" for *sorry*). Children at this stage even substitute fillers (such as "You know" or "whatever") for words they do not recognize, but which they decide they can omit as they construct the essential meaning of the text. They understand that their predictions of what the text will be and their memories for what they have heard read to them are legitimate clues, along with the written words themselves, for what to say. They are less "glued to the print." They know that paying attention to print is necessary, but they are also increasingly more attuned to the unfolding meaning of the text.

As they read *The Gingerbread Boy* aloud, for example, they may use their memories to read the Gingerbread Boy's repeated taunt "I've run away from the Little Old Woman and the Little Old Man. I've run away from the cow. I've run away from . . . And I can run away from you, too!" They may carefully sound out the words leading up to that taunt, but while reading the taunt, they know that they get a break from careful attention to the print.

One of the consequences of these developments is that accomplished reading does not necessarily entail word perfect reading. Some of the more interesting examples of independent reading by accomplished readers are those in which the reader makes substitutions, corrections (though not for all substitutions), and comments that reveal an understanding of the given text and of the reading process. Talking with one's audience about the sense of a story can be more important than a straight-out reading of the text. For example, when a girl comments, "That's not so smart," about the Gingerbread Boy's hopping up on the fox's back, she shows an understanding that reading can be a dialogue with an author. She also shows that, for her, reading is not just an oral performance; she is aware of making meaning for others (in this case her listener), not just for herself.

In addition to moving away from being "glued to print," another sign of children's becoming accomplished readers in the primary grades is their ability to read silently as well as aloud. In fact, the two changes go hand in hand. Both reflect a new use of multiple strategies for reading and a devotion to meaning making.

Silent Reading

Knowing that written language can be read silently and that silent reading is different from oral reading are important insights about how spoken language and written language differ. Comprehending such differences is part of understanding how the two modes are related. Acquiring strategies for silent reading is an important step in becoming an accomplished reader.

Accomplished readers distinguish between reading aloud and reading silently. They realize that the two kinds of reading serve different purposes; reading aloud is a performance for an audience, and reading silently is construction of personal meanings from a text. Along with the different purposes go different strategies. Oral reading must be rehearsed and may require a greater fidelity to the print; oral readers may need to prepare by becoming, in a sense, "reglued" to the print. By the time they are ready to perform, they can allow themselves few substitutions, corrections, or repetitions. As with adults, not all children are able to meet this standard. Even those who can meet it find silent reading much easier.

Accomplished readers' silent reading is a flexible, strategy-based, aware interaction with a text. They begin reading with an awareness of their purposes for reading, which vary depending on the nature of the text (narrative or expository, recreational or assigned). As they read, they acquire knowledge of the content of the text. They also use a *metaknowledge* or awareness of how successfully they are accomplishing their purpose. Thus, they pay attention both to what (content) they are reading and to how (process) they are reading.

Children develop strategies for fixing up problems they become aware of while reading (Brown, 1980). Accomplished readers may reread a portion of a story when they realize that something does not make sense or that they have missed one of the elements of story form that they know to expect. They may skip a word they do not know if they are aware that they are still able to understand the story. Sophisticated readers may adjust their pace or change their level of engagement, looking for main ideas and a developing "gist," or noting finer details. They may skim, look for repeated key words, use titles and headings, use past knowledge of the topic and of how texts like the ones they are reading typically are organized, pay closer attention to the exact wording of the text, reread sections, and use pictures and other graphics.

These are sophisticated reading behaviors. They require a level of cognitive development, which might be described as Piaget's stage of formal operational thought, that many children are only approaching during the late primary grades. They are a long way from the "being glued to print" that usually characterizes the beginning of the period described in this chapter. Not all young children, perhaps not even many, will get there. Certainly there is much that even accomplished readers have yet to learn in the upper elementary grades.

Still, many accomplished readers do take important first steps toward aware, flexible, and strategic reading. With skillful teaching, they can acquire and begin to use conscious strategies for using context (the surrounding text), for using letter–sound correspondences, and for using common word parts such as *-ing, -ed, un-,* and *re-* in order to identify unfamiliar words in their reading. Accomplished readers can become aware of and make use of the fact that most words have many meanings; that a word has a particular meaning in relation to other words; and that they can discover the right meaning of a word in a particular text from the network of associations that has been activated by what they already have read in preceding paragraphs and have remembered from past experience.

WHAT ACCOMPLISHED READERS AND WRITERS KNOW ABOUT THE FUNCTIONS OF WRITTEN LANGUAGE

Nowhere are both the continuities and changes involved in children's becoming accomplished readers and writers more evident than in their learning more about the functions of written language. Children continue to read and write for their own purposes, but they also learn another set of purposes for reading and writing—school-related purposes. In schools, reading and writing often entail considering the purposes the teacher has set, the special purposes the textbook authors have for writing, and the unique criteria by which classmates will judge one's writing.

In classrooms, students do not always read and write because they need to enter imaginary worlds, to gain information about their own expanding real world, to discover for themselves how written language works, or to create a permanent record of their ideas and wants. They also read in basal readers in order to learn reading, and they complete writing assignments—whether filling in blanks in handwriting books and in reading skills workbooks or completing assigned essays—in order to learn writing. They have a new purpose for reading and writing: completing assignments and satisfying their teachers.

Successful elementary school teachers make sure that the assignments they give are congruent with children's own urges to write and read. They support children's ideas of the purposes of reading and writing. Children's reading and writing must continue to serve their own purposes even when teachers make use of it for instruction.

Another classroom reality that shapes literacy learning in elementary school is that learning to read and write is a high priority of nearly everyone involved. The teachers are expected to, and in fact required to, teach reading and writing. Given the way that schools in the United States operate, all students must be engaged in reading and writing learning tasks. Students expect this too; if there is one thing that all first graders believe about school, it is that they will learn to read and to write in first grade.

The positive side of the classroom realities just described is the potential those realities create for a special sense of community. The elementary school and its formal reading and writing curriculum can add the sense of a community of a highly literacy-focused group to the young child's purpose-driven learning.

We do not mean to imply by this that preschoolers are not aware of each other's writing and reading efforts, nor that experimenters lack a sense of audience. Some of the most interesting observations of literacy events in preschools are of children's interactions with each other and their teachers at the writing table or at other literacy centers (see Rowe, 1987). Children talk with one another about how written language works and about the meanings they are making.

However, accomplished readers and writers have a keener awareness of audience than experimenters do. They have a more constant and pervasive realization that literacy involves creating meaning with someone else in mind, whether it is the author whose book they are reading, the intended reader of their writing, or the listener to whom they are reading. They understand that such meaning making is the *sine qua non* of reading and writing.

All of this can contribute to the creative hum of a classroom in which children still proceed from their own purposes, but in which teachers create more specifically reading-directed and writing-directed institutions than they do in preschools. These institutions can include explicit lessons, the writing workshop, the conference, the reading circle, the author's chair, assignments, rules and expectations, and even formal assessment procedures (see Chapters 10 and 11).

Students benefit from other students' input and from teachers' inputs, whether they are overt contributions in conferences and lessons or the covert creation of and planning for those institutions. They benefit from such aspects of community as sharing the same long-term goals, being at the same stage of acquisition of literacy knowledge as some others in their classroom, and being a particularly tuned-in audience for each other's reading and writing.

Students who are becoming accomplished readers and writers carry on with those purposes for reading and writing that they learned as novices and experimenters. They also discover new school-related purposes for reading and writing. Written language can serve two new *social* functions. It can make the reader/writer a participating member of the classroom community, and, within that context, it can facilitate a more intense or intimate interaction between authors and audiences than that which occurs before this stage.

WRITING: COMPETENCE AND AWARENESS

At the beginning of this chapter, five changes that may characterize children's becoming accomplished readers and writers were listed. This section uses the writing process as a final illustration of those changes. Those changes include the transitions from (1) being "glued to print" to being aware of the developing gist or global meaning of a text; (2) from being mere performers to having meta-knowledge or self-awareness of their performance; (3) from often focusing on themselves to focusing on others; (4) from having rudimentary notions of form to being able to use narrative structure in writing and discovering expository structure; and (5) from experimenting with aspects of reading and writing to having processing strategies.

Even after a period as experimenters, children are still easily distracted during their writing by the mechanics of getting words down on paper (they are "glued to print" in their writing just as word-calling readers are "glued to print" in their reading). They need the help of the pictures they have drawn or of a conversation with a classmate or teacher in order to get back to writing more. By the time children are accomplished writers, their metaknowledge—their ability to think about their own writing—eliminates the distractions. Their inner voice takes the place of the picture or the outside person; they are able to be their own other person (Calkins, 1986). Furthermore, they have specific strategies for keeping on track and communicating their message. They know not only what they want to say (content), but also something of the processes that are required. This is important because metaknowledge is useless without a repertoire of fix-it strategies from which to draw when the "other person" inside you tells you that you are not communicating.

Some self-monitoring questions and follow-up strategies are purpose related ("For whom is this piece of writing? Maybe I should provide more background information for that person. Maybe for this audience I need a better lead, more focus. If I don't, Jeff is sure to say, 'I didn't know where you were coming from—you just plopped me in the middle of your story.' He always says that about people's stories."). Some self-monitoring questions and follow-up strategies are form-related ("Am I trying to tell a story or give information? I'd better get that straight. This is an information piece about several kinds of card games, not a story about my friend Alex, the card shark. In fact, it could actually be a description. What do I know about writing a description?").

These examples are of rather sophisticated end-point behaviors. Still, something like these self-aware, purpose-related and form-related strategies can be operating earlier, in simpler matters. Children are on their way to this kind of awareness when they are aware that their stories should contain more than one sentence or more than what they would say in a first turn in conversation ("Now that I read my piece, I can see it doesn't tell the whole story. Maybe I should write it like I would tell a whole story and not wait for my partner to ask, 'What's next?'"). They show it when they know how to organize their ideas so that one main point is made ("Now that I look at my piece, I can see that these ideas aren't all the same. Some are details, but this one is the main idea. I should put it first.").

THE TRADITIONAL END-POINTS: READING AND WORD IDENTIFICATION, VOCABULARY, AND COMPREHENSION

We have not used traditional terms to describe what children learn about reading during the early elementary grades. Reading educators traditionally describe the *what* of reading learning in terms of *word identification skills, vocabulary knowledge* and *comprehension ability.* Those terms emphasize the view that, in order to become readers, children must do three things. They must learn to identify new words they encounter in print by sounding them out using phonics knowledge, by recognizing known word parts, and by using the context in which the words occur. They must know the meanings of, and know related words for many of the words that they will encounter in their reading. They must be able to understand what they read (for example, by knowing how the complex sentences they are likely to encounter are constructed and by knowing how main ideas in a passage are supported by details). We agree with this description of what able readers must do. The following discussion is intended to show that the terms we have used cover the same ground, and they were used for sound reasons.

Although the descriptions *word identification, vocabulary development,* and *comprehension* sound very unlike what was used in this chapter, there are similarities. It is not the case that the traditional perspective defines an entirely different phenomenon from the writing and reading processes described from our psycho-sociolinguistic perspective. The difference is in emphasis. The traditional terms emphasize an end-point. Our terms emphasize development. By using the same categories and terms in this chapter that were used in the first eight chapters of this book (*meaning making, knowledge of the form of written language, knowledge of meaning-form links,* and *knowledge of functions of written language*), we have tried to call attention to the origins of accomplished reading and writing, not just what they are. Our terms assumed a long period of development in which children truly are readers and writers even though "the person on the street corner" would not think so. This is a period in which children derive important literacy knowledge that is the basis for their eventual accomplished reading and writing, especially when we acknowledge their accomplishments along the way.

By the end of the period described in this chapter, children are accomplished readers and writers; the traditional terms of description work quite well. We can demonstrate this by casting two of the descriptions given in this chapter in traditional terms. The recasting for the sake of demonstration involves what we have called meaning making; we could have called the end-point of development of meaning making "comprehension." We have said that accomplished readers are able to construct many kinds of meanings, such as literal and evaluative meanings, from what they read; this is reading comprehension.

We have also said, however, that accomplished writers are able to write for an intended audience. They can comprehend for an audience as they write by rereading their writing. This is a kind of writing comprehension that is absent in traditional uses of the term *comprehension*. We believe that this comprehension ability is not an automatic product of teacher-directed comprehension lessons in most reading programs. Children are able to construct literal and evaluative meanings from what they read because they did so when they were read to and because they were encouraged to do so when they engaged in pretend reading long before they neared the end-points described in this chapter. Similarly, children do not write for an intended audience merely because a teacher reminds them to do so; this behavior follows from earlier episodes in which they were treated as authors, as if they intended to communicate, even as they merely scribbled or wrote mock letters.

Our end-point and the traditional reading behaviors are both comprehension. Before that end-point, however, there were important literacy-related knowledges and behaviors for which we found it necessary and helpful to use our more descriptive term, *meaning making*.

Second, we could have also used the traditional term *phonics* as a label for the end-point of one of children's developing knowledges about meaning-form links. Instead, we continued to describe the invented spelling behaviors that first appeared during the experimental period described in Chapter 7, hoping to emphasize that children experiment with letter–sound correspondences long before they are accomplished readers or writers. They use "phonics" in writing as well as in reading; in fact, they use phonics in writing even before they use it in reading.

This is neither a matter of semantics, nor an effort to confuse our readers who come to this book with a traditional perspective. By maintaining the categories and terms we used throughout this book, we show the importance of respecting children's early developing knowledges and allowing children to use them in their own ways for their own purposes. Invented spelling provides just one example of this. Letting children experiment early with invented spelling, and talking with them about their spellings may eliminate the need for many isolated phonics lessons later, in the primary grades. If so, the same end-point is achieved: children are able to use phonics knowledge efficiently for the word-identification and spelling purposes that make sense to accomplished readers and writers.

Chapter Summary

Accomplished readers and writers achieve a new independence in their reading and writing, but they are never alone. They are aware of the author who wrote what they read and of the audience that will read what they write. Thus, they show a keen awareness that written language is a communication process.

Accomplished readers and writers are able to maintain several processes and to juggle several communication strategies in extended episodes of writing or reading. They are aware of how well or how poorly the juggling act is going; they have fix-up strategies for when it goes poorly.

Accomplished readers and writers know the fine points of form at the word level in English; they have a conventional concept of word. They acquire greater knowledge of text structure than they had as experimenters, especially knowledge of expository text structure. They learn to apply their already well-developed knowledge of story structure to both understanding and producing stories, and to both telling and writing stories.

Accomplished readers and writers

have many new performance strategies. They build on their previous understandings of what spelling is all about by adding multiple strategies for representing words in print, some using their earlier knowledge of letter–sound correspondences, and some using visual, contextual, and semantic information in new ways. They are holistic readers, capable of meeting the many demands of a given text and of a given oral reading performance. They are able to read silently, and their silent reading is guided by metaknowledge.

Accomplished readers and writers have new, school-related purposes for reading and writing. Written language can make them participating members of a literate classroom community and can facilitate a more intense or intimate interaction between authors and audiences than was possible before they became accomplished readers and writers.

Applying the Information

The following case presents two literacy events you might encounter in a third-grade classroom. In what ways are Alice and Tom accomplished readers and writers? What evidence suggests that they are making the five kinds of progress listed at the beginning of this chapter?

At the teacher's desk, Alice is rehearsing to read aloud to the class a two-page section of her current reading book. As she rehearses, her teacher, Ms. Lynch, notices that she makes substitutions for several words. She reads "hurried" for *hustled,* "surprised" for *suggested,* and "bunched" for *bundled.* Alice reads with great expression, especially when the main character, an

eight-year-old girl, finally learns to windsurf. Ms. Lynch waits until Alice has read the two pages. She compliments Alice for picking such an important and exciting part of the story to read and tells Alice how exciting she has made it sound. They talk about what they imagine it would feel like to be windsurfing. Then Ms. Lynch points out that "surprised" does not make sense where Alice misread *suggested.* She suggests that Alice practice the two pages with a classmate a few more times and then schedule a time to read for the whole class. "I think you are almost ready, and we will enjoy this selection," she says.

In the writing corner, Tom is working on a report about race cars. His plan for his report is a list of several facts he knows about the NASCAR circuit, the names of several famous drivers, and the model names of some race cars. Several words are crossed out, and some are misspelled or abbreviated. The fact that he has started to classify what he knows is apparent from a circle around the model names and arrows connecting some drivers' names with some of the NASCAR events. The student teacher, Ms. Evans, sees that Tom has stopped writing and sits down beside him. "What are you writing about these days?" she asks.

"Cars," he says, "but I'm stuck."

"May I see?" she asks. "It looks like this is about *race* cars. I don't know much about race cars, but I can see that *you* do."

They begin to talk about Tom's list. Ms. Evans points out the groupings Tom has indicated with his circles and arrows. "Oh yah," Tom says. "I didn't even notice that."

Tom tells Ms. Evans who his favorite driver is and what that driver has earned already this year. Ms. Evans paraphrases what Tom has told her: "So he has won $64,500 in three races already." She continues, "That's a great start, Tom. It seems to me you could write about auto racing by writing about your favorite driver and the events he has raced in. How about trying that?"

Tom agrees and has a two-page draft to read with his writing partner the next day.

Going Beyond the Text

Visit a third grade classroom. Observe the class during a time devoted to reading or writing. Try to identify two children whose behaviors suggest accomplished reading or writing. Interview them. How aware are they of their own literacy knowledge and processes? Ask them what they do when they begin a new writing piece. How do they know when a piece is going well? What do they do to make a piece better? Ask how they choose a book to read for enjoyment. What is leisure reading like when it is going well? What makes them see what the author imagined when he or she wrote the book? How do they begin a reading assignment for social studies or science class? What do they do to be sure that they are learning from it what their teacher expects? Ask them if they would be willing to show you something they have written lately. Ask if they would read part of a book or tell about part of a book they are reading.

Do your interview subjects talk easily about reading and writing? Are they aware of what they know about literacy? Are they aware of audience in both reading and writing?

References

APPLEBEE, A. N. (1978). *The child's concept of story*. Chicago: The University of Chicago Press.

ATWELL, N. (1989). Bringing it all back home. *The New Advocate, 2,* 21–35.

BISSEX, G. L. (1980). *GNYS AT WRK: A child learns to write and read.* Cambridge, MA: Harvard University Press.

BROWN, A. (1980). Metacognitive development and reading. In R. J. Spiro, B. C. Bruce, & W. F. Brewer (Eds.), *Theoretical issues in reading comprehension* (pp. 453–481). Hillsdale, NJ: Erlbaum.

BRUNER, J. (1960). *The process of education.* Cambridge, MA: Harvard University Press.

BUSS, R. R., RATLIFF, J. L., & IRION, J. C. (1985). Effects of instruction on the use of story structure in comprehension of narrative discourse. In J. A. Niles & R. V. Lalik (Eds.), *Issues in literacy: A research perspective* (Thirty-fourth yearbook of the National Reading Conference) (pp. 55–58). Rochester, NY: The National Reading Conference.

BUSS, R. R., YUSSEN, S. R., MATHEWS, S. R., MILLER, G. E., & REMBOLD, K. L. (1983). Development of children's use of story schema to retrieve information. *Developmental Psychology, 19,* 22–28.

CALKINS, L. M. (1986). *The art of teaching writing.* Portsmouth, NH: Heinemann.

CHALL, J. S. (1983). *Stages of reading development.* New York: McGraw-Hill.

CHOMSKY, C. (1971). Reading, writing, and phonology. *Harvard Educational Review, 40,* 287–309.

CHUKOVSKY, K. (1968). *From Two to Five.* Berkeley, CA: University of California Press.

CLAY, M. (1975). *What did I write?* Portsmouth, NH: Heinemann.

CUDD, E. T., & ROBERTS, L. (1989). Using writing to enhance content area learning in the primary grades. *The Reading Teacher, 42,* 392–404.

GOODY, J. (1977). *The domestication of the savage mind.* Cambridge, England: Cambridge University Press.

HEATH, S. B. (1983). *Ways with words: Language, life, and work in communities and classrooms.* New York: Cambridge University Press.

HOFF, S. (1958). *Danny and the dinosaur.* New York: Harper.

LANGER, J. A. (1986). *Children reading and writing: Structures and strategies.* Norwood, NJ: Ablex.

McGEE, L., LOMAX, R., & HEAD, M. (1988). Young children's written language knowledge: What environmental and functional print reading reveals. *Journal of Reading Behavior, 20,* 99–118.

MOFFETT, J. (1968). *Teaching the universe of discourse.* Boston: Houghton Mifflin.

NEWKIRK, T. (1987). The non-narrative writing of young children. *Research in the Teaching of English, 21,* 121–144.

PARISH, P. (1974). *Dinosaur time.* New York: Harper and Row.

ROWE, D. W. (1987, December). The classroom as a community of authors: The role of social context in literacy learning. Paper presented at the 37th annual meeting of the National Reading Conference, St. Petersburg Beach, FL.

STEIN, N. L., & GLENN, C. G. (1979). An analysis of story comprehension in elementary school children. In R. O. Freedle (Ed.), *New directions in discourse processing. Vol. 2* (pp. 53–120). Norwood, NJ: Ablex.

SULZBY, E. (1985a). Children's emergent reading of favorite storybooks: A developmental study. *Reading Research Quarterly, 20,* 458–481

SULZBY, E. (1985b). Kindergarteners as writers and readers. In M. F. Farr (Ed.), *Advances in writing research, volume one: Children's early writing development* (pp. 127–199). Norwood, NJ: Ablex.

TEMPLE, C., & GILLET, J. W. (1989). *Language arts: Learning processes and teaching practices* (2nd ed.). Glenview, IL: Scott, Foresman.

TROUSDALE, A. M. (1989). Let the children tell us: The meanings of fairy tales for children. *The New Advocate, 2,* 37–48.

WELLS, G. (1986). *The meaning makers: Children learning language and using language to learn.* Portsmouth, NH: Heinemann.

Classroom Support for Accomplished Readers and Writers

There is an enormous volume of professional literature about teaching reading and writing to elementary school accomplished readers and writers. Because of this volume of information, Chapters 10 and 11 are devoted to discussing classroom support for accomplished readers and writers, including many literacy instructional practices and terms that teachers in elementary schools will be expected to know. Chapter 10 introduces basic practices, materials, and terminology related to reading and writing in the early elementary grades. Chapter 11 shows how several teachers use some of these basic components in creative ways in their own unique literacy programs.

This chapter begins with a description of the literacy program in Mrs. Robb's first grade classroom. We discuss the many decisions upon which Mrs. Robb's reading and writing activities are based; these decisions reflect her knowledge of the various materials and approaches to supporting reading and writing usually found in the elementary school, and they reflect her beliefs about literacy learning. The remainder of the chapter provides more information about teachers' beliefs or theoretical orientations toward literacy learning, approaches to literacy learning, and specific suggestions for literacy instruction.

ONE TEACHER'S DECISIONS
ABOUT LITERACY INSTRUCTION

Mrs. Robb teaches a class of twenty-five first graders. It is early March, and the children have settled into a comfortable routine. They can find materials, and they can read charts telling them which literacy tasks to work on and which centers they may use. Mrs. Robb is an experienced teacher, and the school she teaches in is well known for its excellence. The classrooms are large and well equipped. The children attending this school come from primarily middle-income families. Most of the children are accomplished readers and writers by early March, although most of the children were not when they entered Mrs. Robb's class in the fall. The children read and write many kinds of texts. They use reading and writing to perform classroom routines, to communicate among themselves and with Mrs. Robb, and to entertain and inform themselves. They enjoy responding to literature and talking about what they have learned from reading books, interacting with functional print materials, and investigating their current writing topics.

Classroom Environment and Materials

Mrs. Robb's classroom includes a library center, an art center, a math center, a collections center, a typing and computer center, a listening center, a small-group instruction area, and a whole-group instruction area. The classroom contains many materials for art, mathematics, music, science, social studies, and physical activities. It also includes many kinds of literacy materials.

Room Arrangement and Center Materials

Figure 10.1 presents a diagram of Mrs. Robb's classroom. The centers are arranged around the perimeter of the room. The *library center* is formed by several bookcases that are arranged so they create a small nook. This center includes two child-sized rocking chairs, pillows, flannel board props for the "Three Billy Goats Gruff," a display bulletin board about reading different versions of books, and six books with different versions of the story "The Three Billy Goats Gruff." The shelves on the bookcases are labeled and contain nearly 250 books. In another section of the library center, there are over 80 child-authored books, which are in the form of hard-bound books, stapled paper books, or photo album books. These books have been authored both by the current children in the class and by children who have previously been in this first grade room.

The *art center* is located on a large table in the back of the room. The makings of an American flag are laid out on the table. The flag is made of long strips of red and white cloth that have been sewn together; more strips of red and white cloth are displayed. Also displayed are needles that have been threaded, scissors, a book about Betsy Ross, and a sign-up sheet. The children have already sewn white stars onto a blue square of cloth to complete their flag; this is displayed on the table as well.

The *math center* is located on another large table and in a nearby closet that is in the back of the classroom. A large dishpan filled with small rocks and gravel is at one end of the math center table. Over twenty tubs, jars, and other containers are also on the table. Measuring implements are arranged together on three pieces of construction paper labeled "gallon," "quart," and "cup." In the center of the table on a cardboard stand is a construction paper label that reads "Measuring," along with the words "We can measure volume in gallons, quarts, and cups." Inside the closet is a large box filled with "junk" such as spoons, pieces of yarn, dolls, toy trucks, and wooden dowels. Beside the box are several

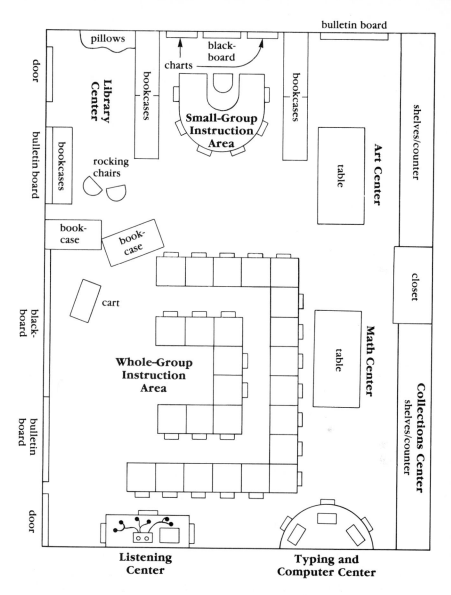

Figure 10.1 *Mrs. Robb's Classroom*

kinds of measuring implements including rulers, yardsticks, and measuring tapes. There is another label for the center that reads "We can measure length in inches, feet, and yards."

The *collections center* is located on top of the counter that runs along the back of the classroom. The first display in this center is a collection of handkerchiefs, which is accompanied by the sign "Mrs. Robb's Handkerchief Collection." Also displayed is a story Mrs. Robb wrote about her collection. Other collections on display include dolls, books, shells, dinosaurs, kaleidoscopes, and records. Each collection has a sign and story accompanying it.

The *listening center* and *typing and computer center* are located on tables pushed against the classroom wall. The listening center includes seats for three children and a box filled with books and tapes in plastic bags. The two type-writers and computer are on another table.

The *whole-group instruction area* is the largest area of the classroom. This area is defined by twenty-five desks arranged to form two U-shapes. The desks face the blackboard and bulletin board on the front wall of the classroom. The *small-group instruction area,* located off to one side of the classroom, in-cludes a horseshoe-shaped table placed in a small alcove created by shelves. A small blackboard and two charts are hung on the wall in this area.

Literacy Materials

Mrs. Robb's classroom includes many kinds of literacy materials. There are child- and teacher-authored books, child- and teacher-created displays in the collec-tions center, sign-up sheets in each center, bulletin boards, children's literature, functional print, and magazines. There are many writing materials stored on spe-cially labeled shelves and on a rolling cart in the large-group instruction area. There are also many commercial literacy materials in Mrs. Robb's classroom.

Commercial literacy materials. All of the commercial literacy mate-rials in Mrs. Robb's room are provided by the school system. Most of these mate-rials are related to the Houghton Mifflin basal reading program. (The school sys-tem in which Mrs. Robb teaches requires that at least a portion of each teacher's reading program be based on one of the two commercial basal reading programs adopted by the school system.) Houghton Mifflin is one of the many companies that publish reading programs [the top five publishing companies sell their pro-grams to over 70 percent of the school systems in the United States (Anderson, Hiebert, Scott, & Wilkinson, 1985)]. Mrs. Robb has over thirty Houghton Mifflin basal readers (collections of stories, poems, and nonfiction selections) in her small-group instruction area. These basal readers are not all the same. Mrs. Robb has ten or twelve copies of each of the three different levels of Houghton Mifflin basal readers that are intended for first grade. (Each publisher prepares basals on several levels that are intended to help children become more proficient readers.)

Mrs. Robb has a teacher's manual for each of the basal readers she uses in her classroom. These manuals include several kinds of information about how to use the stories in the basal reader. They provide lists of skills to be taught in conjunction with each story, suggest sample activities to use in teaching skills, and refer teachers to pages in a workbook that reinforce skills.

Other literacy materials. A rolling cart is kept in the front of the whole-group instruction area. This cart has a variety of writing materials and supplies including pots full of markers, colored pencils, pens, and pencils. The cart also has lined and unlined paper (including special large story paper on which the top half is unlined and the bottom half is lined). There are boxes for scissors, several tape dispensers, a stapler, and erasers. The materials on this cart are frequently changed. In the back of the room on a special shelf are note pads of various sizes, colored paper in different shapes and sizes, and envelopes. There is also a supply of magazines, catalogs, and newspapers. Also located on a shelf in the back of the room is a large box of literature props that Mrs. Robb has used on previous occasions when she has shared literature with the children.

Mrs. Robb has several copies of some selections of children's literature that she keeps in the small-group instruction area. A few of these include *Rosie's Walk* (Hutchins, 1968), *Have You Seen My Duckling?* (Tafuri, 1984), and *Cat Goes Fiddle-i-fee* (Galdone, 1985). Copies of each of these books are also in the library center. Mrs. Robb also keeps several Big Books that she has purchased in her small-group instruction area. Other Big Books are kept in the library center, as are the regular-sized versions of all the Big Books.

Mrs. Robb and Her Children: The Daily Schedule

Mrs. Robb and her children use literacy throughout the day. The children meet with Mrs. Robb in whole-group and small-group literacy lessons. They work independently on literacy projects. They also work together in pairs or in small groups helping each other with literacy projects or completing cooperative activities.

Mrs. Robb's Day

Mrs. Robb presents several whole-group and small-group literacy lessons each day. In addition, she uses literacy activities in her content instruction.

Literacy instruction. Figure 10.2 is Mrs. Robb's schedule. Every morning Mrs. Robb participates in SSR (Sustained Silent Reading) with the children. The children take one or two books each from the library center to their desks as they enter the classroom. At 8:30 Mrs. Robb sets a kitchen timer to ring at 8:42. During this time the children and Mrs. Robb read books or other materials of their choice. At 8:42, two library leaders collect the books and return them to the library center.

At 8:45 Mrs. Robb conducts a writers' workshop. This is a whole-group lesson. Mrs. Robb uses the process approach to writing in her classroom (Calkins, 1986; Graves, 1983). She wants the children to learn how to write by using many of the same processes that professional writers seem to use. Mrs. Robb wants the children to learn to think and gather ideas before writing; to write many drafts; to revise their drafts by adding more ideas or rearranging sentences; and to edit their own writing for capitalization, punctuation, and spelling conventions. To help her children learn these things, she conducts a mini-lesson in writing each morning (Calkins, 1986). Some of her mini-lessons have focused on

Figure 10.2 Mrs. Robb's Daily Schedule

8:15	Children arrive, sign in, sign the lunch list			
8:30	Sustained Silent Reading (Mrs. Robb and whole class)			
8:45	Writers' Workshop (whole class)			
9:00	Concentrated Writing Time (Mrs. Robb and whole class)			
9:15	Transition Time (Mrs. Robbs circulates for five minutes) Reading Group (small group)			
9:45	Transition time Reading Group (small group)			
10:15	Recess			
10:30	Transition Time Reading Group (small group)			
11:00	Individual Conferences, Writers' Conference Groups, Author's Chair:			

	Monday	**Tuesday**	**Wednesday**	**Thursday**	**Friday**
11:00	Group A	Author's Chair	Group C	Group B	Author's Chair
11:20	Group B		Group A	Group C	

11:45	Lunch
12:30	Literature Sharing (Mrs. Robb shares with whole class)
12:45	Mathematics (whole class)
1:00	Mathematics (small groups)
1:30	PE (Tuesday and Thursday) Music (Monday)
2:00	Social Studies and Science Block (Wednesday and Friday begins at 1:30) Art (Thursday every other week)
2:50	Clean up
3:00	Dismissal

showing children how to find topics to write about, how to brainstorm ideas, and how to conduct peer conferences. During some mini-lessons, Mrs. Robb provided a brief experience that stimulated a class collaborated composition. The children brainstormed and dictated ideas. They read and reread their compositions and made revisions together (Karnowski, 1989). Some mini-lessons focused on editing compositions for periods and capital letters. Mrs. Robb often uses the writers' workshop to read to the children a special book that can be used as a model for their writing. In one writers' workshop, she shared *Would You Rather* . . . (Burningham, 1978). She discussed the pattern found in this book and suggested that it might be a pattern that the children could use in their writing.

At 9:00 the writing folder leaders pass writing folders to each student. Mrs. Robb and the children begin writing. They may talk to a friend about what they might write, reread previous drafts they have written, or revise. After she writes for several minutes, Mrs. Robb circulates among the children and stops to make a comment or two to several children about their writing.

At 9:15 Mrs. Robb calls a group of children to the small-group instruction area for reading instruction. She calls a second group to the small-group area at 9:45. At 10:15 the children have a fifteen-minute recess. When they return at 10:30, Mrs. Robb calls the last group.

Mrs. Robb does many things in the short thirty minutes she meets with each small group. She and the children read every day; sometimes they read stories from their basal reader and other times they read children's literature. For example, she and the children have read *Shoes* (Winthrop, 1986) during reading group time. Sometimes she shares children's literature by having the children read a Big Book. She and the children frequently write together as part of reading group time. They sometimes write retellings of the stories or poems they have read, make their own Big Books of a story or poem, or compose original stories or poems (Trachtenburg & Ferruggia, 1989; Wicklund, 1989).

Mrs. Robb also provides information about reading and written language during reading group time. She often demonstrates how to use a reading strategy as she reads or writes, or she has the children describe strategies that they use in their reading. The children discuss alternative strategies for what to do when they are reading and something does not make sense. The group talks about using the letter–sound correspondence knowledge that they use to spell words to figure out unknown words in their reading. They discuss children's different interpretations of a story. They talk about the different meanings that words have in different sentences and different stories.

Mrs. Robb uses her previous observations of the children as they read and write to determine what knowledge or strategy might be most useful to the children (Johnson, 1987). She also consults the teachers' manual of her basal readers to check that the children are learning information related to the skills identified in the basal reading program. (The children must take an end-of-the-year competency-based test in reading that reflects many of the skills in the basal reading series.)

At 11:00 and 11:20 Mrs. Robb has writing conferences or "Author's Chair" (Graves & Hansen, 1983). Sometimes Mrs. Robb plans to use the entire time to meet with individual children in conferences about their writing. Sometimes she forms special writers' conference groups consisting of children who have similar writing needs or who want to explore a common writing theme together. These children meet with her during writers' conference time. Mrs. Robb uses writing conference groups to present language, handwriting, and spelling lessons as they apply to the children's writing. She teaches these lessons as part of children's editing of their writing.

When Mrs. Robb has writers' conference groups, she calls one of her three writing groups at 11:00 and a second group at 11:20. Each group meets two or three times a week; the schedule is posted each week and children know to check the conference schedule for their group's meeting times. On Tuesdays and Fridays Mrs. Robb has "Author's Chair." This is a whole-group activity in which children who have indicated they are ready to share their writing sit in a special chair to read their writing to the class. Occasionally Mrs. Robb takes the Author's Chair to share some of her writing.

Right after lunch (11:45) and recess, Mrs. Robb shares literature. She reads at least one book every day and sometimes two. Mrs. Robb occasionally rereads a favorite story. About twice a week Mrs. Robb uses story props such as story clotheslines, object props, and flannel board props to accompany her storyreading. After reading a book, Mrs. Robb places it on top of the library center shelf in a prominent place. She also places the literature props in the library center (and later in the literature props box). Mrs. Robb encourages children to select these books to read during self-selection time in the morning. She suggests literature response activities that children may also wish to complete during self-selection time. Many times Mrs. Robb asks the children to suggest response activities. She lists these suggestions on poster board and displays the poster along with the book in the library center.

Literacy integrated in content study.   Mrs. Robb uses a unit approach in her science and social studies program. In addition to providing many discovery experiences related to the unit of study, Mrs. Robb reads aloud and invites children to read and write in many different kinds of activities. One example of this approach is Mrs. Robb's potato unit. She and her children grew potatoes in a school garden and donated them to the food bank. As a part of the project, her children read seed catalogs, almanacs, and how-to-garden books. They measured the growth of the plants and made charts of days of sunshine, rain, and growth. The children drew pictures, wrote stories, and invited guest speakers to class. They read fictional and nonfictional accounts related to growth and plants. They also wrote and read language experience stories about their experiences and about the books they had read.

The Children's Day

While Mrs. Robb is teaching small-group lessons in reading or writing, the other children in the classroom are occupied with activities at their seats and at centers. A special assignment chart informs the children of what centers they may visit each day. The assignment chart also informs the children of any assigned literacy activities they must complete during the day. Some children may be assigned to illustrate a Big Book that they composed in a previous reading group lesson, or to prepare a final draft of a story to be published in a class book. In addition to completing assigned activities and visiting centers, children may write or confer with a writing partner; they may write notes or messages to their friends inside or outside the classroom (or to Mrs. Robb). Children may select books from the library center to read at their desks or other locations. The children may use the paper, crayons, markers, glue, or other art materials located near the art center to respond to a story they have read. Children may also use this time to work on their projects related to the science or social studies unit under study.

Figure 10.3 presents Rachel's schedule for the morning. She has a large block

Figure 10.3 ***Rachel's Literacy Schedule***

8:15 Arrival, sign in, sign lunch list

8:30 SSR

8:45 Writers' Workshop

9:00 Concentrated Writing Time

9:15 Reading Group

9:45 Self-Selection and Literacy Assignments (workbook assignments, centers, writing, response-to-literature activities)

10:15 Recess

10:30 Self-Selection and Literacy Assignments Continued

11:00 Individual conference with Mrs. Robb, Writers' Conference Group, or Author's Chair
(Some days her group meets at 11:20)

11:45 Lunch

---

of time in which to complete her assigned literacy activities and centers, and to select additional literacy activities. For example, Rachel has from 9:45 until 11:00 or 11:45 to engage in assigned and selected literacy activities, depending on Author's Chair activities (with a fifteen-minute recess and twenty minutes in writers' conference group two days a week). This is in addition to the time she spends with Mrs. Robb in small-group activities and in SSR and concentrated writing.

Mrs. Robb's Literacy Program

Mrs. Robb's literacy program has changed over the years. There are changes she would still like to make in the program. Mrs. Robb's program is a compromise between what she believes about literacy learning and what she perceives to be her school's policy about literacy instruction.

The Evolution of Mrs. Robb's Literacy Program

When Mrs. Robb first began teaching, her literacy program was quite different from the program she now has established. At first, she closely followed the basal reading program being used in her school. The children read from the basal reader every day and she taught several of the skills suggested in the teachers' manual. Each child was assigned several pages of workbook and ditto activities as independent seatwork. Mrs. Robb thought that she needed these workbooks and dittos in order to provide the children with practice learning skills, and to keep them occupied while she taught reading groups. She only allowed children to complete workbooks, dittos, or other assigned activities such as copying from the board during reading group time. She had a reading and writing center, but children could only go to those centers if they had finished their other work.

Mrs. Robb remembers her structured literacy program. "I followed the basal reading program carefully. I did not attempt to use every activity in the teacher's manual, but I was careful to cover each of the skills listed in the scope and sequence chart (a list of all the skills taught in conjunction with each basal reader in the order in which they are to be presented)."

There were many aspects of this literacy program that concerned her. She noticed that many of the children's written compositions were trivial; in contrast, the same children frequently shared exciting and original stories with their friends. Mrs. Robb also noticed that the children often misspelled words that they had learned as a part of their spelling program when they used them in their social studies projects and creative writing.

It seemed that many of the skills in the basal reading program were really more applicable to writing than to reading. One skill taught in first grade is that in order to add a suffix to words that end in "magic *e*" (words such as *make* where the first vowel takes its long sound and the second vowel—*e*—has no sound), the "magic *e*" is dropped before adding the suffix. Knowing this rule, of course, helps readers recognize that the word *making* is related to the word *make*; if you know how to read *make,* you can read the word *making*. However, knowing how to add the suffix by dropping the *e* and adding -*ing* is at least as relevant to writing as it is to reading.

Mrs. Robb thought reading was overemphasized, as compared to writing. She noted that in spite of her desire for children to write as a part of her social studies and science units, the children had little time for writing. The bulk of their writing consisted of completing assigned workbook pages and writing a single-draft story during the once-a-week creative writing period. She knew that she needed to provide more time for writing, and that the time needed to be sustained throughout the week rather than only on one day if the children were going to use the process approach.

Another of her concerns was the separation of literacy activities into reading, spelling, handwriting, language, and writing. In Mrs. Robb's early literacy program, she had separate times in her schedule in which she taught reading, creative writing, spelling, language, and handwriting.

Mrs. Robb did not like the fact that the children had so little time to read real literature. They only seemed to read during reading groups, and then they read in their basals. She wanted children to have more experiences with quality literature.

Finally, Mrs. Robb was concerned with the overly formal approach to reading and writing she was using by having children sit in their seats all morning to complete workbooks and dittos. Her principal wanted all the teachers to use workbooks, but Mrs. Robb felt that workbooks did not really help children apply their literacy knowledge. Mrs. Robb worried, "My children were only six and seven years old. They were having to spend nearly two hours every day sitting in their seats working with paper and pencil activities. I knew this was inappropriate."

Mrs. Robb discussed many of her concerns with her principal. She described the program that she envisioned would be more successful in supporting her children's literacy learning. Mrs. Robb decided to combine some of the ideas and activities from her science and social studies program with some of the ideas and activities from her formal basal instructional program. She explained that she would use more center activities as alternatives to workbook and ditto exercises, read more children's literature as alternatives to some basal stories, and initiate more social studies and science projects as ways to provide children with real reading and writing experiences. She described using the writing process approach and integrating spelling, language, and handwriting instruction and practice with her writing program. Mrs. Robb's principal was enthusiastic and supportive of her changes. Her principal believed that Mrs. Robb was a knowledgeable teacher who was sensitive to children's needs as well as capable of helping her children perform successfully on the competency-based skills test that was administered to all children in the school system.

Gradually Mrs. Robb changed her literacy program. She began using some literature in place of some of the basal stories. She rearranged her schedule to include time for mini-lessons in writing and time for children to write daily. She included reading aloud to children as a part of her writing program. She rearranged her room and gradually added more centers. She expanded her science and social studies units and encouraged children to work on projects related to their units during their morning literacy periods. She carefully examined the skills in her basal and considered how her children might use the knowledge related to the skills in their reading and writing. She tried to approach teaching the skills through talking aloud to the children about when they might use the information to solve a reading or writing problem. She discovered that her children had good ideas about how to use literacy information.

Now Mrs. Robb teaches some skills in reading and writing groups and sometimes has children read from basal readers. In these more structured and formal activities, small groups of children work on the same materials and complete tasks at the same times. However, she often allows children to choose topics to write about, to use centers with hands-on activities, to select activities and times to complete tasks, to respond to literature they have read, and to use writing to communicate with her and other children in the room. In these less structured and more informal activities, children can select their own activities, take away their own learnings, use different materials, and complete tasks at different times.

She is less attached to the teachers' manual in the basal series. She skips several stories, does not directly teach lessons for many of the skills, and usually does not follow the guidelines on how to teach skills. She tries to use a reasoning approach in her teaching, and she invites children to describe how they might use literacy information related to the skills in their reading and writing.

Reading and Writing Combined

Mrs. Robb's literacy program involves both reading and writing. There are many ways that they are combined in her program. Mrs. Robb encourages children to respond to their reading by writing. She reads to the children and suggests that they use in their writing some of the strategies used by the authors of the books she shares. The children's stories and other writings become part of the classroom library.

Mrs. Robb works hard at integrating reading and writing. She tries to give as much attention to helping children become better writers as she does to helping them become better readers (Shanahan, 1988). She teaches language, spelling, and handwriting as tools for writing. She tries not to plan the focus of writers' conference groups too far ahead. She analyzes the children's writing to determine their needs. Still, she is responsible for teaching certain language skills mandated by her state's curriculum guide. She has discovered that children easily learn many of these skills as a part of her writing, reading, and content study projects.

Mrs. Robb struggles with how to integrate reading group instruction with her writing program. She tries to allow children freedom to select their own topics for writing, but also frequently limits topics. She often has children write about topics that are related to social studies or science units they are studying so that writing can carry over into the afternoon. She also uses many of her science and social studies projects as part of morning literacy activities. When her children study the four food groups, they set up a health food store and cafe, and they write menus, advertisements, and displays for the cafe and store. The children also write stories using the store or cafe as settings. Mrs. Robb uses the writers' workshop to talk about menus and menu formats.

Mrs. Robb realizes that her integration of reading and writing is not perfect. When the children come to reading group, their basal stories have little relation to their unit reading and writing projects. Mrs. Robb laments, "I know the reading and writing should be tied together, but I still have to base at least part of my program on the basal reading program. I always have my eye open for good literature that I could use in reading group which would tie into the unit projects."

Mrs. Robb's Decisions about Literacy Instruction

All teachers face decisions that determine the kind of support children will have for their literacy learning. There are many influences on their decisions. One influence is statements from professional organizations, such as those described in Chapter 3, which outline appropriate classroom practices. Another influence is their knowledge both of the children they have to teach and of literacy learning. Yet another influence on teachers' decisions is their school system's policies and mandates from their state about reading and writing. All of these factors are reflected in Mrs. Robb's decisions about her literacy program. She realized she must use her basal readers in some way in her literacy program and teach many of the skills identified in that series. She knew that she must also provide a room environment compatible with her children's development and recommended by early childhood organizations. Finally, she realized that she needed to modify her literacy program to fit the needs of her individual students.

Mrs. Robb describes her approach to literacy instruction as a combination of formal and informal instruction. Her room environment reflects this combination of approaches. There are many places for children to explore on their own, and they have free access to many literacy materials. There are also times when children are expected to sit alone at a desk and complete an assigned task. Some of Mrs. Robb's instruction is direct, content-centered, skills-based, and determined in part by the skills identified in the commercial reading, spelling, handwriting, and language programs (Slaughter, 1988). However, there are numerous opportunities for children's own exploration, discovery, and use of literacy. Much of her instruction is indirect, more child-centered. It is based on the children's writing, their interpretation of literature, and their dictations.

Mrs. Robb's beliefs about literacy learning can be inferred from her decisions. All teachers must make decisions about the kinds of literacy materials, activities, and instruction that they will use. Their decisions will reflect their beliefs—conscious or unconscious—about how children learn literacy. These beliefs are formed from teachers' theoretical orientations toward literacy learning. We explore theoretical orientations in more detail in the next section.

THEORETICAL ORIENTATIONS
TOWARD LITERACY LEARNING

Currently, there are two prominent beliefs or theoretical orientations about literacy learning and instruction: the skills-based orientation and the whole-language orientation. A third orientation is beginning to emerge: literacy as strategic use of cognitive and language processes.

Skills-based Orientation

A skills-based orientation toward literacy learning is founded on the belief that literacy is most easily learned when the skills of literacy—its component parts or behaviors—are identified and taught in a systematic way. This orientation has a long history and a strong hold on American literacy instruction.

Where Did It Come From?

The skills-based orientation can be traced back to several sources. The orientations of important reading educators in the 1920s are at least in part responsible for the skills-based movement (Paris, Scott, Wixson, & Palincsar, 1986). In 1925, a committee of renowned reading educators noted that essentials of reading instruction included developing effective skills. While the committee admitted that a complete classification of skills had not been made, they did list several skills that they believed had emerged from research and were important for guiding instruction. Every basal reading series published after this date included this list of skills as the objective of its reading program (Paris, Scott, Wixson, & Palincsar, 1986).

Another source from which the skills-based orientation to literacy learning arose was the behaviorist theory of learning that dominated the field of psychology for much of the first half of this century. This was a period characterized by the stimulus-response theory of learning. According to this theory, teaching involves demonstrating a behavior and supplying learners with immediate feedback on how well they performed the behavior. Reading programs were adapted to fit this method of learning by including tests for determining whether learners knew skills teachers had taught. These tests were called *criterion-referenced* or *competency-based* tests. Reading programs consisted of identifying skills, testing learners to find out which skills they did not know, providing learners with materials for learning skills, and retesting learners to see if skills were learned.

Most reading skills programs were organized around four or more major skill areas: word identification (decoding), vocabulary, comprehension, and study skills. Because the behaviorist orientation required that skills be simple and easily demonstrated, the skill areas were broken into smaller components. Word identification skills encompassed a large number of skills for decoding words, including knowing how to sound out words by relating sounds to letters (*phonics*). Another set of word identification skills involved recognizing and using prefixes and suffixes (*structural analysis*). Still another set of word identification skills involved being able to use context or the surrounding words in a text to understand an unknown word in the text (*contextual analysis*). Vocabulary skills included being able to read a large store of words without having to sound them out (*sight vocabulary*). Other vocabulary skills involved learning meanings for vocabulary words. Comprehension was taught in terms of many skills for understanding and remembering what the author says, *literal comprehension;* inferring what the author implies but does not directly state, *inferential comprehension*; and using the author's ideas and determining whether or not they are relevant, biased, or logical, *critical comprehension.* Studying meant applying several skills for self-learning such as using a table of contents or dictionary. The skills-based orientation was organized around lists of skills in each of the four major reading skill areas. (Figure 10.4 is an example of such a skills list.)

Many basal reading programs have adopted much of the skills approach. They have lists of skills (called a scope and sequence chart) and criterion-referenced or competency-based tests. Nearly all school systems adopt a basal reading program, and teachers and other school officials believe that the contents of basal programs are professionally sound (Shannon, 1983). Over 95 percent of the children in this country have participated in basal reading programs.

The skills-based orientation has been applied to other language activities. State departments and school systems often have curriculum guides that are lists of skills in language arts. Figure 10.5 is a sample list of handwriting, spelling, capitalization and punctuation, and written expression skills similar to those that might appear in a skills-oriented language arts curriculum guide.

Reason To Be Cautious

In order to be a reader, one must do many things skillfully. A number of these things can be separately described or labeled. However, there are many negative

Figure 10.4 Some Reading Skills

Word Identification

Identifies rhyming words

Identifies sounds of initial and final consonants, blends, and diagraphs

Identifies long and short vowels

Forms new words by substituting initial and final letters

Forms new words by adding -ing, -ed, -s

Recognizes contractions (I'm, shouldn't)

Recognizes and uses prefixes and suffixes

Vocabulary

Describes pictures

Classifies objects

Identifies and understands concrete nouns (dog, cat, man, horse)

Identifies and understands pronouns (it, she, he, they, us, we)

Identifies synonyms, antonyms, and homonyms

Identifies descriptive words

Identifies and understands abstract words (love, honesty)

Comprehension

Recalls and sequences story details

Recognizes main idea and supporting details

Predicts outcomes

Makes inferences

Draws conclusions

Distinguishes fact and fantasy, fact and opinion

Describes character traits

Study Skills

Alphabetizes

Uses table of contents and index

Previews using titles and subtitles

Uses dictionary to locate spellings

Interprets graphs and charts

Figure 10.5 *Some Language Arts Skills*

Handwriting

Writes manuscript letters

Uses correct word and letter spacing

Writes cursive letters

Uses correct connections between cursive letters

Meets standards of legibility

Spelling

Writes words demonstrating silent *e* pattern (*hate*)

Spells verbs in which final *e* is dropped (*write-writing*)

Spells verbs in which final consonant is doubled (*hit-hitting*)

Spells words in which final *y* is changed to *i* (*cry-cried*)

Capitalization

Capitalizes first letter of proper nouns, first word in sentence, the pronoun I, abbreviations, and titles

Capitalizes heading, salutation, and closing of letters

Punctuation

Uses periods at the end of sentences

Uses commas with words in series, between month and year, and after greetings in letters

Uses quotation marks to indicate words of speaker

features to the skills approach. Reading is more than the sum of several separate parts. Readers know many things related to reading that cannot be described as skills and that cannot be taught by stimulus–response techniques. Readers use cognitive and language processes. Chomsky (1968) has demonstrated that language is not a behavior and that behaviorist learning theory is woefully inadequate for describing how children learn language.

Lists of skills are seductive. They imply that literacy can be reduced to a set of behaviors that can be identified, sequenced, and learned. If learners master the list of skills, they are literate. Lists of skills seem to make it easier for school systems to be accountable; that is, they seem to allow the public to determine whether or not they are getting what they are paying for. However, skills-based instruction is deprofessionalizing. If teachers must teach skills, then their job is not one of thoughtful consideration, but rather one of technique. Within the skills-based approach taken by most basal reading programs there is an implication that teachers should not think about what literacy really is. Their job is to be technicians; they should deliver a product that comes as close to predetermined specifications as possible.

There are some positive features about the theory of the skills-based orientation. Many learners need a systematic approach and explicit directions for some literacy learning (Baumann & Schmitt (1986). The notion that there are many things to learn about reading and writing that should be identified and carefully considered *by teachers* is also important. Teachers *certainly* would not be effective if they did not know about literacy or how to respond to children's literacy efforts in ways that would increase children's literacy learning. The problem with the skills-based approach is that the lists of skills we currently have focus on very small, disconnected bits of knowledge, and not how to use knowledge while reading and writing.

Whole-language Orientation

The heart of the whole-langauge orientation is that children use reading and writing to communicate meaning (Altwerger, Edelsky, & Flores, 1987; Goodman, 1986). Whole-language advocates argue that children learn to read and write by reading and writing, and not by learning skills. Children learn because they use reading and writing to accomplish real tasks.

The idea that literacy learning takes place as learners interact with reading and writing in meaningful activities is not a new one. Even in the 1920s when the skills-based orientation was in its infancy, many schools were using an activities approach to teaching reading and writing. Similarly, the language experience approach was founded on the belief that children's natural capacities for learning oral langauge could be used to help them learn written language (Lee & Allen, 1963; Stauffer, 1980).

Teachers who believe in the tenets of whole language also use study of content such as science or social studies, or study of literature as the major component of their literacy program. What gives a literacy program a whole-language orientation is the teacher's beliefs about literacy and literacy learning (Newman, 1985).

Beliefs about Literacy Learning

Newman (1985, p. 1) described whole language as a philosophical stance. Whole-language advocates are united by a common set of assumptions about language, learning, teaching, and children. They believe that the literacy and language curriculum is not a set of literacy materials (basal readers), nor a set of predetermined skills (a scope and sequence chart). Rather, the literacy and language curriculum is the unique literacy learnings constructed by learners. Therefore, learners and not skills or materials are the heart of the whole-language orientation. Children are viewed as active learners capable of selecting information and constructing knowledge for themselves. Whole-language advocates believe that children can lead the way. Children not only can acquire knowledge on their own, but they also can inform observant teachers about what they might need to learn.

At least three other beliefs form the foundation of the whole-language orientation (Newman, 1985). First, whole-language advocates believe that children learn by participating in demonstrations of literacy. They believe that there are many kinds of knowledges presented in a literacy demonstration and that children select any number of these knowledges to learn. Therefore, rather than selecting a narrow, isolated skill or knowledge as the focus of a lesson, teachers should offer demonstrations of a reading or writing experience that is rich with many potential learning opportunities. One literacy demonstration a teacher might provide is to help children compose a letter to a classmate who has recently moved away. As the teacher and children compose the letter, the teacher would offer comments, ask questions, and invite children to make comments, ask questions, and make suggestions. The children might learn any number of literacy lessons from this demonstration. They might learn about the conventions of letter form, the need to consider the person to whom one is writing when considering what to say in a letter, or how to spell the words *Dear* or *love.*

Another belief of the whole-language orientation is that children should be invited to select literacy activities rather than be assigned particular literacy tasks (Newman, 1985). It follows that if children are viewed as capable learners who can take away many different potential knowledges from a literacy demonstration, then they can select literacy experiences that are personally interesting and offer their own unique potential for literacy learning. Offering children choices and invitations to literacy activities is an important way that teachers empower children as learners.

One way to invite children to participate in literacy activities is to provide open-ended experiences. Open-ended activities allow children with differing kinds of literacy knowledge to work together and to give input toward deciding how activities might be completed (see Chapter 3). For example, children might be studying their state in a social studies unit. The teacher might invite the children to write a special state version of the Goldilocks story reflecting their state's culture and products. Small groups of children might work together to compose versions of the Goldilocks story. There are many possible stories that they might create, any of which would provide a solution to the problem.

Finally, whole-language advocates see reading and writing as a social activity. Reading and writing are viewed as interactive processes involving authors and readers sharing ideas. Children's knowing about and communicating with authors of published books is seen as vital to literacy learning. Whole-language teachers encourage children to write to authors and invite authors to their classrooms to share their work with children. Publishing children's writing and sharing their writing with real audiences is another important part of whole-language programs. These activities stress the communication of meaningful ideas as the goal of reading and writing.

Learning is viewed as a social activity as well. Whole-language advocates believe that children and teachers collaborate and share information, and that learning occurs in situations where children talk together and with their teacher about literacy experiences (Hansen, 1987). Cooperative learning groups, small groups of children who complete projects together, are often a critical component of whole-language programs.

Whole-language advocates believe that children can learn much literacy information and that no single set of materials or practices is synonomous with the whole-language orientation. Gunderson and Shapiro (1988) describe teaching phonics as a part of a writing program. Bridge and her colleagues (Bridge, 1986; Bridge, Winograd, & Haley, 1983) use predictable books in a patterned language approach to teach sight words. Holdaway's (1979) shared book approach using Big Books includes teaching children sight vocabulary, use of context clues, and phonics. What makes these programs whole-language oriented is their belief in children as learners and their use of information gathered from observing children to guide instruction.

Reason To Be Cautious

Recently, Tunnell and Jacobs (1989) reviewed research examining the use of literature-based whole-language programs. They found ten studies where children in whole-language classrooms became better readers and writers than children in traditional basal programs. However, at least one study that compared a program fitting within the skills orientation and a program fitting within the whole-language orientation found that the skills orientation produced more effective readers. Evans and Carr (1985) found that a first-grade reading program with a skills-based orientation and a basal reading series produced greater reading gains than a first-grade reading program with a whole-language orientation and language experience and individualized instruction. Whole-language advocates would see many flaws in this study. First, tests selected to measure reading were more compatible with the skills-based orientation; they measured children's ability to perform small, component parts of reading rather than their ability to gain meaning from reading. It is not surprising that these types of tests would show that skills-based reading programs were superior to whole-language reading programs.

Orientation Based on Strategic Use of Cognitive and Language Processes

A recent orientation toward literacy instruction has emerged from several lines of research. Researchers have discovered that readers and writers use many strategies while they read and write. Readers seem constantly to be aware of whether what they read is making sense. Writers seem to know when they have lost the train of their thoughts and they automatically reread what they have just written. An orientation based on strategic use of cognitive and language processes recognizes the importance of readers and writers being aware of their own reading and writing strategies.

Several research teams have developed approaches that fit within the orientation of strategic use of cognitive and language processes (for example, Brown & Palincsar, 1982; Paris, Cross, & Lipson, 1984). One of the many approaches that fit within the orientation of strategic use of cognitive processes is called *responsive elaboration* (Duffy & Roehler, 1987; Duffy, et al., 1987). Responsive elaboration involves having the teacher inform students of a strategy that is to be learned, when it could be used, and how to do it. Teachers talk out loud and demonstrate their thinking while performing the to-be-learned strategy. Then students practice the strategy, thinking aloud as they do so. Teachers listen carefully to determine how well the students understand the strategy. When students' responses reveal misunderstandings, teachers provide more explanation. Figure 10.6 presents an example of a lesson using responsive elaboration. The teacher is helping a student use a strategy for finding out a word meaning.

Other approaches that fit within the orientation of strategic use of cognitive and language processes emphasize children's natural learning capacities. As chil-

Figure 10.6 *Portion of a Responsive Elaboration Lesson*

A 3rd grade teacher directed her low group students to what to think about when figuring out word meaning rather than just asking for what the word *down* meant in "My pillow is made from the *down* of geese."

T: What word is confusing in there?

S: *Down.*

T: *Down.* Okay, what are you going to do to figure that out?

S: It's like going down, or downstairs.

T: All right. Going downwards. You've already realized that that doesn't make sense. Now, what's next?

S: Look for clues.

T: All right. Are there any clues?

S: Pillow and geese.

T: All right. We looked for clues. Now we've got to think about what those clues tell us. The pillow is made from something of the geese. In your experience, what would a pillow be made of?

S: Feathers.

T: How are you going to know if you're right or wrong, George?

S: Read the sentence with that word in it.

T: All right. Try it, George.

S: My pillow is made from the feathers of the geese.

T: Would that make sense?

S: Yeah.

From "Improving Reading Instruction through the Use of Responsive Elaboration" by G. Duffy and L. Roehler, 1987, *The Reading Teacher, 40,* p. 519. Copyright by the International Reading Association. Reprinted with permission of Gerald G. Duffy and the International Reading Association.

dren read, they paraphrase the meaning in their own words, make predictions, skip things they do not understand, and then come back and reread. As children write, they reread what they have written, say words slowly as they invent spellings, and insert questions to their reader. Teachers capitalize on children's own strategies by having children talk about what they do in reading and writing.

Reason To Be Cautious

While methods of helping children become aware of their own reading and writing strategies are noteworthy, they have primarily been applied to students older than those in the primary grades. This may not be an accident. It may be that six- and seven-year-olds do not have sufficiently developed metacognitive, meta-linguistic, or abstract thinking abilities to use many of the techniques used in strategic approaches. The strategies that may prove most effective for elementary children to use may be ones that focus on their ability to answer questions of different types (Raphael, 1986) and their ability to monitor their understanding of text they are reading. In addition, children are capable of learning several strategies related to writing such as brainstorming with a friend, drawing a picture, or writing a list or cluster as strategies for finding information to write about. (See Calkins, 1986, for a discussion of writing strategies used by children in the primary grades.)

MAJOR APPROACHES TO LITERACY INSTRUCTION

In this section we discuss five approaches to reading and writing instruction that are currently being used in elementary classrooms: the basal reader approach, the language experience approach, the literature-based approach, the integrated language arts approach, and the process approach to writing. An approach to literacy instruction refers to the kinds of literacy materials and lessons that teachers select to include in their literacy program. We also discuss approaches to instruction in spelling, handwriting, and language as a part of the writing process approach.

Basal Approach to Reading Instruction

Basal programs provide a comprehensive approach to reading instruction. They identify skills, suggest methods of teaching skills, and provide materials for reading (basal readers) and practicing skills (workbooks). We have already provided a description of some aspects of a basal approach as it was used in Mrs. Robb's classroom. The following is a more thorough description.

Characteristics of Basal Readers

Basal readers, teachers' manuals, workbooks, and other supplementary materials are written by teams of experts that include reading professionals. Stories and other texts included in most basal readers are written so that children will learn an ever-increasing store of sight words. Children are taught word identification skills (phonics, structural analysis, and contextual analysis) so that they can learn to identify and pronounce sight words on their own. As children read stories and other texts in their basal readers, they practice comprehension skills.

Basal reader stories often have controlled vocabulary. This means that the words in basal stories, particularly for first grade, are selected using criteria such as high frequency of use, adherence to phonics generalizations, and familiarity to children. High-frequency words are those that appear again and again in text; in fact, just a few hundred words comprise nearly 50 percent of the words in any text. Words that adhere to phonics generalizations can be pronounced using knowledge of letter–sound relations and a few rules about letters and sounds (see Figure 10.7 for sample phonics generalizations that might be used in basal reader materials).

Basal Reading Lessons

Basal programs are usually organized around directed reading lessons or activities. *Directed reading lessons* usually have three steps: preparation for reading, directed reading, and follow-up. The preparation phase involves helping children relate their background experiences and interests to the story they will be reading. Teachers introduce vocabulary words in oral discussion, followed by a presentation of a few of the words printed in sentences and in isolation. Word identification skills are often taught in this phase and applied to the new story vocabulary. In the directed reading phase, teachers ask questions to stimulate and guide children's silent reading of the story. The story is usually read in small segments, which are interspersed with questions and discussion. Silent reading is followed by oral reading of particular parts of the story, usually to provide answers to questions. The follow-up phase involves teaching skills that can be applied to further understanding or appreciating the story.

A frequently used alternative to the directed reading portion of the directed reading lesson is the *directed reading-thinking activity* (DRTA) (Stauffer, 1969). In DRTA lessons, the teacher reads the title and shows pictures to the children. The children make predictions about what will happen in the story, which the teacher may record on chart paper. Then the children read a short segment of the story to see which of their predictions are accurate and whether or not their predictions need adjusting. They sometimes refer to their list of predictions and discuss each in relation to the evolving story they have read. Children read portions of the story aloud as they discuss their predictions and they try to prove points related to their predictions. This three-step cycle (predict, read, prove) is repeated several times throughout the story (Davidson & Wilkerson, 1988).

Criticisms of Basal Materials and Lessons

Basal reader materials have been criticized on at least three important points. First, the language used in the stories is not like the language of children nor like

Figure 10.7 Some Phonics Generalizations

1. Each of the consonant letters corresponds to one sound as in the words:

*b*ag	*h*air	*n*est	*t*oe
*d*og	*j*ar	*p*ipe	*v*iolin
*f*an	*k*ite	*q*ueen	*w*ig
	*l*amp	*r*ug	bo*x*
	*m*ilk	*s*un	*z*ebra

2. Consonant clusters are composed of two or three consonant sounds blended together (e.g., bl, cr, dr, fl, gl, pr, sm, st, scr, str, thr, nt)

3. The consonant digraphs correspond to the sounds in the words:
       *ch*urch   *sh*oe   *ph*one   *th*umb   *wh*istle

4. The vowel letters take several sounds such as:

long	**short**	**r-controlled**	**l-controlled**
*a*pe	*a*pple	h*er*	h*all*
*ea*gle	*e*gg	s*ir*	t*alk*
*i*ce	*i*gloo	f*or*	
*o*boe	*o*ctopus	f*ur*	
*u*nicorn	*u*mbrella		
tr*y*			

5. When a word has a VCe pattern, the V usually takes the long sound (*like*).

6. When a word has a CVC pattern, the V usually takes the short sound (*sat*).

7. When the letter *g* is followed by the letters *e, i,* or *y*, the *g* usually takes the soft sound as in the letter *j* (*gym*). Otherwise it takes the hard sound as in the letter *g* (*gum*).

8. When the letter *c* is followed by the letters *e, i,* or y, the *c* usually takes the soft sound as in the letter *s* (*cycle*). Otherwise it takes the hard sound as in the letter *k* (*cake*).

the language in other "real" literature (Goodman, 1988). Children comprehend stories better when the stories conform to their language patterns (Wilkinson & Brown, 1983). More recently published basals have more natural sounding language that resembles other literature.

Second, the stories included in basal readers are often not well structured or well written (Beck, McKeown, Omanson, & Pople, 1984). Many stories found in basal readers do not include all of the components of a well-structured story as outlined in story grammars (see Chapter 4, Figure 4.10). Some stories do not follow time sequences closely and make only vague references to character goals, motiations, feelings, and plans (Bruce, 1984). When stories are not well structured, children have a more difficult time understanding them.

Third, there is little connection between the phonics generalizations taught in connection with particular basal reader stories and the stories themselves (Anderson, Hiebert, Scott, & Wilkinson, 1985). Most basal stories have very few words that illustrate generalizations that have been taught and children have few opportunities to practice using those generalizations in the context of reading meaningful text (Beck, 1981).

Other criticisms of basal materials center on the suggestions for teaching provided in teachers' manuals. Most teacher's manuals provide little information about how to teach comprehension (Durkin, 1981). Instead, the manuals provide many questions that teachers can ask. Strategies that children can use to gain meaning are not evident in teachers' manuals at present, although these might be included in basal materials published in the future.

Professionals suggest that time given to teaching skills (especially when basal reading programs have so many skills) takes time away from what the programs are designed to do—help children read. One study estimated that primary grade children spend less than seven minutes reading daily and that 70 percent of their time in reading activities consists of completing workbooks and other ditto materials (Fisher, et al., 1978).

In defense of basal materials, many of the criticisms we have described can be ascribed to political and economic factors beyond the control of the authors of the basal series. Most basal reader series are authored by professionals who are well versed in current theory and research and who are acutely aware of the criticisms against basal materials. Basal reading programs were never intended to be the entire reading program in a classroom. Reading professionals who author these programs believe that children should also be encouraged to read literature and functional print and to engage in developmentally appropriate activities. They do not recommend rigid adherence to a basal series as the only component to a reading program, exclusive use of workbooks as the only independent reading activities, or the practice of requiring a child to master every skill in a basal reader as a prerequiste to moving forward in a program.

Language Experience Approach to Reading Instruction

There are many versions of the language experience approach (for example, Allen & Allen, 1982; Hall, 1981; Stauffer, 1980). Some teachers use portions of the language experience approach very informally. We have already described how teachers with preschoolers (Chapter 6) and kindergartners (Chapter 8) might use this approach. Other teachers use the language experience approach in a more systematic and formal way to teach reading to accomplished readers.

Two kinds of lessons are usually associated with the language experience approach. Dictation lessons involve stimulating children to talk about an experience, framing their talk into a written "story," and reading the written "story." Language study lessons involve using the written "story" to develop language knowledge such as building word meanings or applying decoding knowledge.

Dictation and Language Study Lessons

The first step of a dictation lesson is to provide children with an experience that will motivate their expressions. The experience can be concrete, such as popping corn, or it can be more abstract, such as reading a story. One teacher, Mrs. Bellanger, brought in several kinds of animal hearts preserved in alcohol. The children looked at the hearts and listened to their own hearts through a stethoscope.

The second step is to encourage children's expression about the motivating experience. Teachers can contribute to this phase of the language experience lesson by their own expressions. They can interject new vocabulary, make explanations, or provide analogies that will extend children's understanding of the experience. Mrs. Bellanger supplied the children with much information about each of the different hearts. She described the heart as a *pump,* she pointed out the *veins* and *arteries* on each heart, and she informed the children that the heart was a *muscle* like other muscles in their bodies. The children tried to guess which heart belonged to a deer, a chicken, and a dog; they talked about eating chicken hearts; and they tried to make their hearts beat faster by jumping up and down.

The third step is to write what children dictate. Frequently, teachers do the writing, but as children gain more experience with written language, they write parts of their language story. In this step, teachers guide children in writing a narrative or an expository text. They might want to introduce children to different names of texts such as "story," "description," or "explanation." The words that are selected to be included in writing should be the child's own. Sometimes teachers ask children to record only a few words, perhaps in a list or as part of the longer dictation. Dictations are recorded on large chart paper or in Big Books. When individual children dictate, teachers write below children's pictures or on letter-sized paper. Mrs. Bellanger asked the children to think of good descriptive sentences about the human heart. The children dictated:

We have a heart.
Our heart is a muscle that pumps blood.
It is as big as a fist.
Animals have hearts, too.
Hearts are usually found in the chest.

Once the written story is produced, the teacher reads it aloud and invites children to read along. The story is reread several times without undue attention to getting it right. Mrs. Bellanger's children read and reread their story several times; then Mrs. Bellanger placed the chart with the heart story in the science center and invited children to read the story to a friend during center time.

Pattern books are frequently used as stimuli to language experience activities (Bridge, 1986). Because pattern books are easily remembered, children can dictate them for language experience charts or for Big Books. Big Books with their pictures covered become the materials for language study lessons.

Language study lessons begin with teachers' and students' rereading their story. With less experienced children, teachers usually read the story several times and invite children to participate. With more experienced children, teachers usually ask children to begin reading. Several kinds of language activities can follow rereading the story. Children can match sentences and then words that are written on sentence strips or cards to those text segments on their story. Teachers can point to words at random on the story chart or Big Book and ask children to read them. Children might practice reading words from the story in other sentences. A phonics lesson might be taught and the generalization applied to reading some of the words in the story. A comprehension lesson focusing on identifying main ideas and supporting details or on sequencing might be applied to the story. Children might write their own story as part of a language study lesson, or they might use part of their dictated story as a pattern for writing more stories.

Criticisms of the Language Experience Approach

Critics of the language experience approach claim that it is not systematic and children may not learn essential knowledge about reading and writing. If many of the experiences used to stimulate dictations are concrete, children will have only oral language models from which to learn about written language; that is, their own conversation will provide the material for their written stories. While this helps children see the connection between oral and written language, it falsely suggests that written language is oral language written down (see Chapter 1). In short, language experience must be carefully used by a knowledgeable teacher if children are to grow in their literacy knowledge. However, language experience is also viewed as one of the most effective approaches to teaching reading to children who come to school with comparatively few literacy experiences. It helps children bridge from the language they know best (oral language) to the language they will need to learn to read and write (written language).

Literature-based Approaches to Reading Instruction

Traditional literature-based reading programs were called *individualized reading programs.* These programs were designed to capitalize on children's interests and rates of learning (Veach, 1978). Children selected their own books, read them on their own, responded to them by selecting a literature response activity, and met with the teacher individually to talk about their books. They also met in small groups in which the teacher presented a skill lesson based on the children's needs.

The Traditional Individualized Reading Approach

In the traditional individualized approach, children spent considerable time reading materials of their choice and sharing their reading experiences with other children. Sharing took a variety of forms and was often called *celebrating reading.* Children celebrated reading by writing plays, making and producing puppet shows, making posters, producing dramas, making literature props, cooking, creating paintings or clay figures, or writing.

Teachers conferenced with each child once a week. They used individual conferences to listen to children read, to determine their reading progress and needs, and to suggest follow-up activities. Teachers met with several groups of children each day. Children were selected for a small group when they demonstrated a common need for learning or a common interest. In these small groups teachers presented specific skills that they knew children needed to learn or provided children with opportunities to read together in a group.

Individualized reading was often coupled with criterion-referenced management systems. These systems included lists of skill behaviors and suggested methods for helping teachers assess whether or not children had mastered skills.

Literature-based Reading

Recent conceptions of literature-based reading instruction continue to include children selecting some of their own books and some teacher conferencing with individual children. Emphasis is still placed on children's selection of reading materials and activities. However, groups of children sometimes read the same literature selection and share its meaning cooperatively (Henke, 1988; Reardon, 1988). Literature-based reading groups involve talking about the meanings children construct from books, describing authors' craft in selecting the language used in stories, and learning about literary conventions such as structure, mood, or genre (Reardon, 1988). Children also explore word meanings and discuss strategies for reading unknown words.

Literature-based reading programs can take many forms. Some teachers organize their programs around themed literature units (Henke, 1988). Several copies of four or five books that have a common theme form the common reading materials used by children in a group. Children read the common selections and discuss their reading in the group. They read aloud portions of the books to substantiate their opinions and discussions. The teacher reads aloud and stimulates discussion by asking questions such as, "Why did the author repeat the phrase 'Drip drop splash' three times?" or "What surprised you about *Time of Wonder?*" (Reardon, 1988, pp. 55–56). Children also read many individually selected books or other materials such as newspaper or magazine articles that fit within the theme, and they share these books and materials with other children in response groups. Several descriptions of using literature for reading and writing instruction are available (see for example, Johnson & Louis, 1987).

Criticisms of the Individualized and Literature-based Reading Approaches

Because traditional individualized reading programs were so often linked with criterion-referenced management systems, individualized reading was often viewed as another skills-based approach. Research supporting the more recent uses of literature-based reading programs is growing. In a large study including over 1150 second graders, Eldredge and Butterfield (1986) showed that literature-based methods were better in helping children learn to read than basal methods. Tunnell and Jacobs (1989) reported on the success of Reutzel's literature-based reading program for first graders and Tunnell's success with disabled readers.

In 1986 California launched its *Reading Initiative.* This statewide effort at encouraging literature-based curricula included a list of over 1000 key literary works and a document describing the initiative's goals (Honig, 1988). Despite the widespread attention and praise for this initiative, some educators worry about how this worthy goal is being translated into classroom practice (Freeman, 1988). Many school systems implementing literature-based reading programs have limited certain selections of literature to particular grade levels. Some teachers have used commercially prepared activities to accompany the literature selections their children read. Some basal reading companies are advertising their programs as literature-based, when in fact, many of their literature selections are abridged and altered versions of original works (Goodman, 1988).

Integrated Language Arts Approach to Reading and Writing Instruction

The integrated language arts approach is based on the notion that reading, writing, listening, and speaking are all used as tools for learning. Advocates of this approach center learning around activities for finding out about topics in content areas such as science or social studies.

The Unit Approach

In the integrated language arts approach, an area of content is identified as a framework for a unit of study. Children might study immigration, westward movement, life cycles, weather, or community services. Within the unit of study, teachers identify general topics of study and generalizations related to the content that children will learn, as well as a variety of methods that children can use to acquire those concepts and facts. Teachers select reading, writing, speaking, and listening experiences that will increase children's learning about the unit. They identify the literacy and language knowledge that children will need in order to participate in the unit's activities, and they plan lessons accordingly. Teachers also carefully observe children as they read, write, speak, and listen in order to identify other literacy and language knowledge that they need to learn. Figure 10.8 presents a cluster diagram for a unit on Louisiana.

Often the integrated language arts approach is used along with another approach. Teachers may base their reading instruction on a basal series, but use content area study as a way to integrate reading with writing and other language

Reading

Read Louisiana stories such as Mary Fontenot's *Clovis Crawfish and Etienne Escargot* (1977) and *Clovis Crawfish and Big Betail* (1963) or Patricia Powell's *Dulac dat Cajun Cat* (1987).

Authors

Write letters to favorite Louisiana authors. Ask for information about authoring.

Listening

Invite an Acadian still speaking Cajun French to tell family stories in Cajun French and English.

Field Trips

Visit Magnolia Mound Plantation during Plantation Week to observe candlemaking, weaving, and cooking. Visit Atchafalaya bayou to observe wildlife and plants.

Research

Study the culture and history of Acadians in Sue Eakin & Manie Culbertson's *Louisiana: The Land and Its People* (1986) and Dennis Fradin's *Louisiana: In Words and Pictures* (1981).

Writing

Write a timeline describing the Acadian move from Canada to Louisiana. Write a report about one of the birds or animals found in the Louisiana bayous on which the Acadians depended for food.

Historical Fiction

Read Berthe Amos's *The Loup Garou* (1979). Describe differences between Robert's and Louis's lives and life today.

Games

Play John Berry's (1989) Louisiana Trivia Game.

ACADIANS IN LOUISIANA

Cooking

Cook Acadian foods using Theresa Blount's *Cooking from Bayou Courtableau* (1984) or V. Roger's *Roger's Cajun Cookbook* (1987). Invite a chef to discuss differences between Cajun and Creole seasonings.

Word Study

Locate Cajun French words (such as Mais Jamais and Jai chaud) in Louisiana literature. Use context to determine their meaning.

Drama

Dramatize Trosclair's *Cajun Night before Christmas* (1973).

Construction

Build an Acadian settlement with popsicle sticks, Lincoln logs, or clay. Write a story about children who might live in the settlement.

Journals

Keep a journal as an Acadian boy or girl living in the 1790s, who moved from Canada to Louisiana.

Art

View Audubon's prints of birds found in Acadiana. View pictures of Louisiana life by Elton Louvier in *Images of Louisiana* (1988).

Maps

Locate early Acadian settlements on a map of Louisiana from the late 1700s. Compare Louisiana then and now.

Literary Patterns

Listen to Justin Wilson's *Cajun Fables* (1982). Compare his *Petite Rouge Riding Hood* and *Goldilocks and the Three Crawfish* to the traditional versions. Write *The Gingerbread Boy* with a Louisiana setting and characters.

Figure 10.8 A Cluster of Ideas for a Content Study Unit

skills. Content area reading and writing is an important component of literacy programs.

Criticisms of the Integrated Language Arts Approach

The problems associated with this approach are related to the amount of teacher preparation and knowledge that are required to use such an approach. Schools need to have well-stocked libraries or media centers in order to provide sufficient materials for learning. No systematic research exists that compares the effectiveness of this approach with other approaches. There are few guidelines for how to plan and manage such a program (however, see McKenzie, 1985).

Process Approach to Writing Instruction

The process approach to writing has become a strong force in children's literacy instruction (Calkins, 1986; Graves, 1983). Within this approach, the focus of instruction is on supporting children's use of writing processes rather than on making sure children write conventionally correct compositions—hence, the "process approach" label. Spelling, handwriting, grammar, and usage are taught within the writing program.

Writing Processes

There are many descriptions of writing processes (for example, Murray, 1987). In general, the writing processes fall into five categories: rehearsing, drafting, revising, editing, and publishing. However, it is misleading to think of these processes as occurring linearly or sequentially; rather, they are interactive and they often occur simultaneously.

One writing process is called *rehearsing* (Calkins, 1986) or *collecting* (Murray, 1987). This process includes a writer's search for a topic, his or her identification of audience and purpose, and his or her collection of ideas about which to write. Many young children draw pictures as rehearsal for writing. Other children rehearse by talking to a friend or to their teacher, by writing a list of ideas, by role playing an experience, by listening to or reading literature, and by just thinking. The purpose of rehearsing is to generate ideas and formulate plans for writing.

Another writing process is called *drafting* (Calkins, 1986). In this process children commit their ideas to paper. Drafting for young children may consist of as much talking and drawing as it does writing. First drafts of accomplished readers and writers can be short, sometimes consisting of only a few words. More accomplished readers and writers write longer first drafts and more consciously consider the necessity of writing details.

Another writing process is called *revising*; it consists of children's rethinking about what they have written. In revising, children reread their drafts; add or delete words, phrases, or sentences; and move sentences. The focus of these activities is on the content of the writing. In another writing process, *editing*, children focus on misspellings and errors in capitalization, punctuation, and usage. Children gradually learn to edit their own writing. The last writing process, *publishing,* consists of making writing available for a wider audience. Figure 10.9 presents several ideas for publishing children's writing.

The Teacher's Role

Teachers play at least three important roles in the writing process approach. First, they interact with and respond to individual children and their writing. Second, they help children learn strategies for rehearsing, drafting, revising, editing, and publishing their writing. Third, they provide knowledge about written language and literary conventions.

It is particularly important that teachers have time to interact with individual children during the writing program. This implies that there will be time for children to write when the teacher is not busy conducting small group lessons. When teachers are available to observe children as they write, they notice when a child is "stuck" and can help the child to get his or her writing going again. Effective teachers use the information about their children's writing gained through careful observation to plan lessons for extending writing knowledge and abilities.

The second role of teachers is to help children learn effective strategies or procedures (Bereiter & Scardamalia, 1982) for writing. Teachers usually provide this kind of help in short mini-lessons conducted in writers' workshops.

Figure 10.9 Suggestions for Publishing Children's Writing

Draw pictures for children's magazines (*Humpty Dumpty, Turtle*).
Write poems, essays, reports, or stories for children's magazines (*Stone Soup*).
Write class, grade-level, or school newspapers or literary magazines.
Read writing in the Author's Chair.
Post writing on an "Author of the Week" bulletin board.
Read writing on a "Parents Share Fair" once a month.
Write letters to children's authors, public figures, government agencies, or members of the community.
Write greeting cards.
Write poems, essays, reports, or stories to be bound into books. (The books can be composed by a class or individual child and can be kept in the class or school library.)
Bind books for Mother's and Father's Day gifts.
Bind books for a nursing home or the children's ward of a hospital.
Bind books to present to obstetricians or pediatricians for use in their waiting rooms (Temple, et al., 1988).
Make a Class Yearbook (Temple, et al., 1988).
Enter local and state literary contests.

Mini-lessons in writers' workshops.   Mini-lessons on writing strategies are often conducted in writers' workshops as part of whole-group activities (Calkins, 1986). During mini-lessons, teachers might talk about the importance of drawing as rehearsal. For more accomplished writers, teachers might demonstrate writing a list of possible topics about which to write. (See Graves, 1983, for a discussion of helping children choose writing topics.) Teachers might also demonstrate writing a *cluster,* which is ideas related to a topic written in a web-like diagram. Figure 10.10 presents Sarah's cluster of ideas for a story about the mysterious disappearances of her friends on a camp-out.

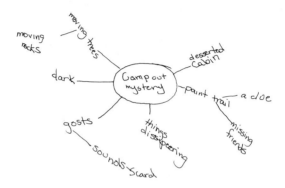

Figure 10.10 *Sarah's Cluster for the Campout Mystery*

Mini-lessons on drafting might include teachers' demonstrations of writing several titles or lead sentences. Mini-lessons related to revising might include role playing peer revision conferences. Children learn to respond in positive ways to writing and to ask writers questions such as "What is the most important thing you are trying to say?" Later, children might be expected to confer with a writing partner as a way of rehearsal and revision. Other mini-lessons on revision might help children provide details with strong images, limit and focus their topics, and try out alternative text forms to communicate information. Mini-lessons related to editing might include learning how to use the dictionary to locate spellings or using an editing checklist. Figure 10.11 presents an editing checklist used in a second grade classroom. Calkins (1986) recommends that a concentrated time in which all children are engaged in writing should follow mini-lessons.

Writers' conferences.   Some teachers form writers' conference groups to serve as collaborative learning groups. Writers' conference groups can be used to provide additional time and support for small groups of children to try out various strategies introduced in mini-lessons. They can also be used to teach children knowledge related to literary and written language conventions such as letter writing, using similes or metaphors, and sequencing of events, as well as proper use of capital letters, periods, commas, quotation marks, and even

Figure 10.11 *Editing checklist*

☐ I have reread my writing to a writing partner.
☐ I have listened for sentences.
☐ I have a capital letter at the beginning of each sentence.
☐ I have a period, question mark, or exclamation mark at the end of each sentence.
☐ I have a capital letter for every time I used the word "I."
☐ I have a capital letter for every person's name.
☐ I have checked spellings of the magic-line words.

---

colons. Many teachers use editing conferences to deal with two additional writing tools—spelling and handwriting.

Spelling

In traditional approaches to spelling, instruction is based primarily on children's learning a list of words specified in a spelling book from a commercial program. Traditional use of spelling books includes beginning the week's spelling activities with a test of the week's words prior to word study. (Children who evaluate their own performance on this pretest usually learn more words—Horn, 1947). Then children study the words, complete spelling activities provided in the spelling book, and take a final test at the end of the week.

Two groups of words appear on spelling word lists. The first group consists of high-frequency words. High-frequency words account for a majority of the words that appear in most texts and that children use to write. Figure 10.12 presents a list of high-frequency words (Hillerich, 1978, p. xiii).

The second group of words appearing in spelling word lists are words that demonstrate orthographic regularity. Orthography is the system of how sounds are mapped onto groups of letters in spelling. For example, the sound of long *i* in the word *bike* can be spelled with several groups of letters including *i* followed by a consonant and *e* as in the word *tide, igh* as in the word *light, ie* as in the word *tie,* and *y* as in the word *try.* Orthography is regular because only a small group of letter combinations is used to spell any sound. Many spelling programs group words together in lists that demonstrate these letter combinations in spellings. Most spelling programs also include words that illustrate rules for adding prefixes and suffixes to words.

The problem with traditional approaches to spelling is that they divorce spelling from writing. Children learn an arbitrary list of words and study them out of the context of any need to know them. Many teachers note that words that children learn to spell correctly for the spelling test are often misspelled when children are at the editing stage of writing.

Spelling in the process approach. Writing process advocates recommend that spelling come from children's writing, and that it be taught as a tool

Figure 10.12 High-Frequency Words for Writing

I	there	to	around
and	with	do	see
the	one	about	think
a	be	some	down
to	so	her	over
was	all	him	by
in	said	could	did
it	were	as	mother
of	then	get	our
my	like	got	don't
he	went	came	school
is	them	time	little
you	she	back	into
that	out	will	who
we	at	can	after
when	are	people	no
they	just	from	am
on	because	saw	well
would	what	now	two
me	if	or	put
for	day	know	man
but	his	your	didn't
have	this	home	us
up	not	house	things
had	very	an	too

From R. L. Hillerich, *A Writing Vocabulary for Elementary Children* (p. xiii) 1978. Courtesy of Charles C Thomas, Publisher, Springfield, Illionis.

to help writers and as a convention used to help readers. This suggests that teachers will not be able to use the predetermined, arbitrary word lists presented in spelling books.

The spelling words accomplished writers should study and learn should be words they have misspelled in their writing, words they need to learn as a part of their content study, and words for which they ask the spellings (Johnson, Langford, & Quorn, 1981). Ideally, lists of words for spelling study should be unique to each child; they should be selected from words misspelled in each child's writing. However, it can be difficult to manage such an individualized approach. As a compromise, teachers might identify some of the words to be included in each child's spelling list and guide children in identifying the remainder of the words from their writing (Hoskisson & Tompkins, 1987). In that way, small groups of children would be learning some words in common and some words that are personal. Teachers can use high-frequency word lists and notes they have taken about spelling problems in children's writing to help them select the words common to all children's spelling lists. Teachers might want to consult Henderson (1985) as a source of information about how children acquire spelling generalizations and of activities that support children's spelling growth.

Spelling in drafting and editing.

An important part of a spelling program is for teachers to convince children that they should not think about spelling words correctly as they draft. Because children will not know the correct spelling of some words, waiting until editing provides the time to locate correct spellings without losing ideas. Therefore, teachers need to demonstrate using strategies to spell words during drafting. This includes listening carefully to words and writing spellings that are not conventional, but that capture many of the words' sounds. Some teachers might worry that allowing and even encouraging misspelling by modeling sounding out words might harm children's later learning the correct spelling. In fact, all children experiment with spellings of words and their experimentation eventually leads them to conventional spelling (Graves, 1983). During seven months in first grade, one child spelled the word *like* as LC, LAT, LOCT, L, LICT, and LIC before spelling it conventionally (Graves, 1983, p. 196).

One way teachers might encourage children's own spellings during drafting is to help children use a "magic line" (Gabriel, 1987). When children come to a word that is difficult to spell, they can draw a short horizontal line on their paper. At editing, teachers should pay close attention to the magic-line words and provide children with their spellings. Discussion of the child's spelling and the word's conventional spelling provides many opportunities for word study and spelling learning. When children ask for help spelling words correctly at the editing stage, teachers need to point out how effective the child's spelling was (Graves, 1983). The teacher's saying, "You really got the beginning and ending of that word. I'd like you to say it again slowly and see if you can hear anything in the middle" will expand children's spelling strategies before providing the correct spelling.

An important part of the writing process is publishing—presenting at least some of each writer's work for an audience wider than the writer, teacher, and a writing partner. Sharing writing with beyond-the-classroom audiences and publishing writing may mean that the teacher will want to perform editorial duties, including making sure that words are correctly spelled. Later, teams of children can perform most of the editorial functions. Making the final draft readable, either through typing or through copying in legible handwriting, is also an important part of publishing.

Handwriting

Handwriting is an important part of composing. When children labor over re-membering how letters are formed, not to mention their labor over listening to sounds they hear in each word, their compositions suffer. The best ideas disap-pear when children focus on pencil and paper instead of the content they are writing. But making children practice letters in isolation, copy letters and words from the board in "their best handwriting," and repeat strokes used in letters again and again will not make compositions better. Children cannot focus on ideas when they are concerned that they write in their best handwriting on the first draft of their paper. Therefore, handwriting instruction must provide chil-dren with both instruction in legibility, for the sake of readers and with opportu-nities for practice where handwriting does not count, for the sake of fluency.

Many traditional kindergarten literacy programs include instruction in form-ing manuscript (printed) letters. Many of these programs consist of having chil-dren trace and copy letters. However, teachers who use writing centers and who write frequently with their children can provide much better handwriting in-struction in those contexts than in formal instruction. Children who are beyond the point of experimenting with letter forms can benefit from having some hand-writing instruction. The instruction should focus on legibility rather than on imitation of examples; it should provide children with language with which to talk about their handwriting and letters, and it should be connected with pub-lishing children's writing.

There are four aspects of legibility that young writers need to learn. First, letters should conform to expected formations as defined by the writing pro-gram. Expected formations, especially of capital letters, differ from one hand-writing program to another. Zaner-Bloser, a publisher of writing programs, is famous for its "ball and stick" manuscript letter formations (Barbe, Wasylyk, Hackney, & Braun, 1984). The D'Nealian handwriting program is known for slanted manuscript letters that are formed with a continuous stroke producing more curved lines (Thurber, 1981). Making expected letter formations does not always mean using the strokes suggested in a handwriting program. Children who begin making the letter *e* by writing it from bottom to top will probably not develop an unbreakable bad habit.

The second aspect of legibility is that letters should be of uniform size, pro-portion, and alignment. Third, letters and words should be evenly spaced. Fourth, letters should have a consistent slant. Most manuscript writing programs show letters written straight up and down (D'Nealian is an exception). Cursive writing, on the other hand, is expected to have a slant. The direction of the slant should be determined by individual children. Legibility does not depend on a slant to the right, but rather on all letters having the same slant.

The time to be concerned about legible handwriting is when writing is for an audience or when accurate and readable notes to oneself need to be taken. Children improve most in their handwriting when teachers are available at the time of writing to comment and provide feedback. Short lessons demonstrating certain problem letter formations, connections between cursive letters, or as-pects of legibility work best. The timing of these direct lessons should be tied to the production of publications in writing. Just prior to binding children's writing into a hardbound book is an opportune time for handwriting instruction. Similarly, preparing to send a letter to the governor will motivate children to polish their handwriting skills.

Criticism of the Process Approach to Writing

The process approach to writing instruction is a relatively new approach. Still, research has shown that certain kinds of process approaches lead to better writing (Hillocks, 1986). Naturalistic classroom observation research has shown that children learn much about the craft of writing and grow significantly as writers within a process approach (for example, Calkins, 1983). Children even seem to learn more about basic writing skills such as punctuation within a process approach (Calkins, 1980).

It is important to note that much of what has become the writing process approach came from observations of older writers in high school (Emig, 1971) and from observations of professional writers (Murray, 1987; however see Graves, 1975). The writing process approach, without a sensitive and observant teacher, might impose adults' writing processes on young children. In addition, much of the writing process approach is based on helping children realize writings' potential for thinking (Murray, 1987). Yet, many groups in the United States view writing more as a tool for daily living than as a tool for self-examination or self-discovery.

So far in this chapter we have described theoretical orientations and general approaches for literacy programs. The next section of the chapter focuses on instruction. It describes four principles of effective literacy instruction for accomplished readers and writers.

EFFECTIVE INSTRUCTION FOR EXTENDING ACCOMPLISHED READERS' AND WRITERS' LITERACY KNOWLEDGE

Accomplished readers and writers develop many effective performance strategies for reading and writing. Many of these strategies are acquired as children read and write to complete meaningful classroom projects, as they talk with their peers about reading and writing, and as they informally share with their teacher. But there are many times when observant teachers note that children might benefit from having additional information about literacy activities or from using a new performance strategy for more effective reading and writing. Children can benefit from effective literacy instruction. We believe that there are three principles which guide literacy instruction: (1) instruction should take place at the time when children can use the instruction to more strategically read or write whole texts, (2) instruction should provide children with more than information about literacy—it should help children understand when and how to use the information strategically, and, (3) instruction should capitalize on a sense of literacy community where the children in the classroom are viewed as valuable supporters of each others' learning.

The first principle emphasizes that instruction cannot be based on an arbitrary list of skills that are taught in a predetermined order. Rather, instruction is based on careful observation of children (Johnson, 1987). Such instruction may take only a few moments as the teacher talks with a child while he or she is reading or writing. Such instruction may also be carefully planned after teachers note that several children could benefit from learning a new strategy. This principle also emphasizes that instruction should extend and enrich children's experiences with reading and writing texts whose purpose is functional and not merely to teach about reading and writing. The second principle emphasizes that teachers and children model using literacy information in reading and writing. Children learn more than facts; they learn how to use facts to approach reading and writing more strategically. The third principle emphasizes that children learn from each other; shared information is a powerful and important learning tool.

In the next section of this chapter, we describe some instruction that helps extend children's knowledge of written language meanings, forms, meaning-form links, and functions, and that follow the three principles of effective literacy instruction.

Extending Knowledge of Meaning Making

Several instructional techniques that extend children's meaning making and meet the three criteria we propose for effective instruction have already been described. The process approach to writing, in particular, focuses on children's meaning-making knowledge. A major thrust of this approach is supporting children's learning of both information about writing processes and strategies for meaning making. Children in the writing process approach learn to read for information, to generate a list of ideas by brainstorming or clustering, and to use talking with a friend as a way of finding ideas. They also learn to use these idea-generating strategies before they write and when they get "stuck" writing. Thus, children know that writing is communicating ideas, they know how to generate some ideas about which to write, and they know when to use their idea-generating strategies.

In traditional reading instruction, the major way teachers helped children extend their meaning making was to ask questions. Questions were supposed to spur children to think carefully about the text and to use higher level thinking. The problem with this approach is that it does not help children develop their own strategies for making meaning while reading.

One of the most important ways that teachers can support children's use of meaning-making strategies is to encourage children to monitor their own meaning as they read and write. Effective readers seem to ask themselves, "Does this make sense? What does this mean to me?" When readers realize that what they are reading does not make sense, they reread and self-correct reading errors to make sense. Effective teachers will foster self-monitoring by frequently asking children, "What does that mean to you?" They will encourage children to skip words that they do not know, to keep reading portions of text that they do not understand, and then to return to reread. Some teachers encourage children to say "blank" when they come to an unknown word as they read aloud.

Another way teachers can support children's meaning making is to encourage children to use their prior knowledge to ask questions before they read (Shanklin & Rhodes, 1989). A similar strategy for using prior knowledge is to have children brainstorm ideas that they think they will read about before reading. Before Mrs. Robb had a group of students read *Your First Garden Book* (Brown, 1981) as part of the potato unit, she suggested that the children think about what they already knew about gardening and growing plants. She made a chart titled "What We Know About Gardening Before Reading" and recorded all the information that the children related on the chart. After reading, the children completed two other lists: "What We Read About Gardening that We Already Knew" and "What We Learned About Gardening from Reading" (Ogle, 1986). Mrs. Robb told the children that thinking about a topic before reading about it is an important before-reading strategy. An after-reading strategy is to think again about what you knew before reading and what you learned by reading. This instruction meets the three criteria for effective literacy instruction: it provides children with information that they can use for reading, it helps children understand when and how to use the information strategically, and it capitalizes on children's shared knowledge.

Extending Knowledge of Written Language Forms

We have described several techniques for extending children's knowledge of written language forms. The process approach to writing offers many opportunities to extend children's form knowledge. Teachers might use mini-lessons to help children learn about story structure (Spiegel & Fitzgerald, 1986), compare-contrast, main idea-detail, cause-effect, and problem-solution expository text forms (McGee & Richgels, 1985); or about other text forms, such as menus, birth announcements, recipes, bumper stickers, post cards, advertisements, or editorials. Figure 10.13 presents a list of text forms teachers may want to integrate into their writing programs or units of study. Children might write advertisements as a part of a unit on the four food groups in which children will set up a cafe and health food store. Teachers might share several examples of advertisements and encourage children to describe advertisement text forms and list their characteristics. They might help children write a class collaboration advertisement. Then students would be invited to write advertisements for the class cafe.

This type of instruction meets the three criteria for effective literacy instruction: it informs children of knowledge they need to know—characteristics of advertisement text forms—when they need it; it informs children how and when they might use that information strategically—to write an advertisement for their class cafe; it extends children's experiences with meaningful text—children write the texts as part of a functional content study unit; and it capitalizes on children's interactions as a way of learning.

Figure 10.13 *Text Forms*

ABC Book	editorial	menu	telephone book
address book	envelope	number book	tickets
advertisement	food package	play	tombstone
advice column	friendly letter	photo album	travel poster
application	grocery list	postcard	trip journal
appointment book	highway sign	prescription	time table
baby book	index	real estate ad	valentine cards
birth announcement	invitation	recipe	weather forecast
bill	joke	record album	will
bumper sticker	junk mail	sign	wish list
classified ad	keepsake book	sports news	yearbook
deposit slip	letter to the editor	song	
diet	map	T-shirt	

Extending Knowledge of Meaning-Form Links

As accomplished readers and writers, children will extend their knowledge of the relations of sounds and letters, of orthography, and of the morphological structure (prefixes, suffixes, and base words) of written language. More importantly, they will learn how to more consciously use this information in their reading and writing. We have already described instruction that extends children's knowledge of letter–sound relations and spelling patterns as a part of their writing program (see the spelling section on using the magic line, for example).

Lessons about letter–sound relation knowledge (phonics) should help children use this information in meaningful reading contexts. Such a lesson might be planned after the teacher notices several children are not combining their meaning-monitoring strategies with their knowledge of letter–sound correspondences. She might prepare several sentences such as, "The *mailman* ran away to join the circus." The word *mailman* is covered by taping a piece of paper over it. The teacher says, "Sometimes when I read I come across a word I don't know, like in this sentence I don't know the word that is covered. I might be reading along and all of a sudden, oops, I don't know a word. I say 'blank' and keep on reading to the end of the sentence. Then I go back and try to figure out what word would make sense." Then the teacher demonstrates reading the sentence saying "blank" for the unknown word. The children offer suggestions for the word and the teacher writes each suggestion in a list under the unknown word. Then the teacher says, "Now, there is a clue I can use to help me decide which of my guesses the word might be. I look at the first letter and see if any of my guesses begin with the sound of that letter." The teacher reveals the letter *m*. The children evaluate their previous guesses and make more guesses using the letter *m*. Then the teacher asks the children to suggest other words that would make sense and that begin with the sound of the letter *m*. Finally, the teacher reminds the children to use the guess-and-look strategy when they come to a word they do not know.

Later, the teacher shows children examples in which the guess-and-look strategy might not work and suggests another strategy. The children might be working with the sentence, "The boy said, 'I dread more homework.'" They are not likely to know the word *dread*. The teacher reads the sentence and stops at the word *dread*, saying, "Oops, I don't know this word. I'll read the rest of the sentence and come back to it." She rereads the sentence, saying "blank" for the word *dread*. Then she says, "Who can suggest a word that would make sense here?" She solicits several suggestions for the word. Then she asks, "Could the word in the sentence be any of the ones we suggested? I want you to look carefully at the word. What letter does it begin with? What sound does that letter make?" It is not likely that any of their guesses begin with the letter *d*. The teacher reminds the children that their strategy of guess and look at the first letter might not always work. Another strategy they might try is guess, look at the end of the word, and then think of a known word that looks like the end of the unknown word (Cunningham, Moore, Cunningham, & Moore, 1983). The teacher says, "I know a word that ends with the letters *ead*. I know the word *head* and the word *dead*. If I put *dr* in front of *head* or *dead*, I get the word *dread*. Hey. That's a new word for me. But, what does it mean? It must mean something like hate since that is a word that makes sense in this sentence." Then, the teacher reminds children to use the guess-look-and-think-of-a-similar-word strategy as they read stories or content materials. This type of instruction meets the criteria for effective literacy instruction: it informs children of useful knowledge about meaning-form links when they need it; it demonstrates how and when to use that knowledge; it promotes children's understanding of whole and meaningful text; and it capitalizes on children's collective thinking. It models reading as a self-aware process with a focus on meaning.

Extending Knowledge of Function

There are many ways that teachers can help children expand their knowledge of written language functions. One of the ways teachers do this is by establishing a classroom environment that calls for children to use written language (Loughlin & Martin, 1987). Mrs. Robb has an announcement board for assigning children to some literacy tasks and has children sign in for attendance and lunch counts. Forgetting to read the announcement board or to sign in has immediate results. Mrs. Robb encourages children to write messages to one another and to her. She always takes time to reply to a message written to her. She also provides opportunities to extend written language functions beyond the classroom; the children learn how to interact with organizations and agencies by writing letters.

Another way teachers extend children's knowledge of written language functions is to use a functional approach to reading and writing. Children learn more about written language functions by using reading and writing in literature and content study (Burchby, 1988). Mrs. Robb's potato growing unit is a good example. Children learn about written language's informative function by reading a how-to-garden book. Mrs. Robb tells children the function of this book and talks about strategies for using the book. She is conscious of extending children's awareness of the usefulness of particular kinds of written text, and she helps children learn when and where to use those kinds of texts. Children learn about written language's recording function by writing notes about the growth of potatoes and about weather conditions. Mrs. Robb tells the children that keeping records can be useful. She brainstorms with the children ways that the notes and records they have written can be used. The children suggest that they leave their record of potato growth in the classroom for next year's children. They suggest that next year's children could use this record as a source of information for their potato growing efforts. Instruction such as this meets the criteria for effective literacy instruction. It informs children; they learn that written language can be used to preserve information. It tells children when the information can be used; they learn that their records can provide other children with information they might need. It applies learning to meaningful reading and writing; children acquire this knowledge as a part of a larger content study unit.

Chapter Summary

Teachers who provide classroom support for accomplished readers and writers either consciously or unconsciously reflect theoretical orientations toward how children learn literacy. They signal their theoretical orientations in the arrangement of their classroom, in their approach to literacy instruction, and in the kinds of activities they plan for children. There are three major theoretical orientations toward literacy learning: (1) skills-based, (2) whole-language, and (3) strategy orientations. Skills-based orientations are reflected in instruction and activities that primarily focus on teaching children knowledge about components of literacy knowledge in a predetermined sequence. Whole-language orientations are reflected in beliefs that children learn by reading and writing in meaningful activities, that children should be in control of their learning, that literacy learning is a social activity, and that learning is best supported by literacy demonstrations. Strategy orien-

tations are reflected in instruction and activities which emphasize helping children articulate strategies that they use in reading and writing and showing children how to use additional knowledge.

There are five major approaches which are used to organize literacy instruction: the basal approach, the language experience approach, the literature-based approach, the integrated language arts approach, and the process approach to writing. The basal approach involves teaching children from a set of basal readers (collections of stories, poems, and nonfiction). Each grade level has a basal reader with a prescribed set of skills to be taught. The language experience approach involves teaching children from their dictated language experience stories. Teachers design language study lessons that extend children's knowledge of written language. Literature-based approaches involve teaching from children's literature selections chosen by both the teacher and the children. Teachers design literacy lessons and children select literature response activities to expand written language knowledge. Integrated language arts approaches emphasize learning about content areas through reading, writing, speaking, and listening. The writing process approach involves children writing daily on topics of either their choice or their teacher's choice. Teachers use mini-lessons, writers' conferences, and author's chair activities to extend children's knowledge of writing processes and literacy conventions. Each of these approaches has strengths and presents reasons for caution. Some of these approaches are closely aligned with a particular theoretical orientation.

Regardless of theoretical orientation or approach, we believe that there are three criteria of effective literacy instruction. (1) Effective literacy instruction should inform children about literacy information when it is useful in helping them to more effectively accomplish functional reading and writing tasks. (2) It should help children understand when, how, and why to use information strategically in their reading and writing. (3) It should capitalize on the power of the literacy community built into each classroom. Effective literacy instruction should expand children's knowledge of written language forms, meanings, meaning-form links, and functions. Teachers should carefully observe their children to determine when children need literacy instruction. Often children's suggestions provide the best basis for literacy learning.

Applying the Information

Select a basal reader, its accompanying teachers' manual, and workbook. Select one story from the reader. Read all the directions for teaching this story and related lessons in the teachers' manual. Read the story in the basal reader and the workbook pages that accompany this story. Analyze the story according to the components of a well-formed story (Chapter 4, Figure 4.10). Look at the structure of the sentences in the story. Decide if the sentence structure would be familiar to a young child who would be expected to read the story. List the "skills" to be taught with the lessons. Read the directions for how to teach the skills. Decide if the directions provide information that would meet the three criteria of effective literacy instruction. Examine the workbook exercises that accompany the story. Decide if the exercises extend children's literacy knowledge of the skills and whether they are appropriate practice activities. Plan instruction that will help children extend their understandings of the story and will help them use the knowledge presented in the skills in their reading and writing. Tell how the instruction meets the three criteria of effective literacy instruction.

Choose a children's literature selection that might be used in place of the basal story. Decide how you would use this children's story in a reading group over three days' instruction. Plan follow-up activities that children could select as independent literacy projects. Plan instruction to extend children's knowledge in each of the four written language domains. Tell how the instruction meets the three criteria of effective literacy instruction. Or plan a language experience that includes a dictation and two language study lessons that extend children's knowledge in each of the four written language domains. Tell how the language study lessons meet the three criteria of effective literacy instruction.

Create a cluster of integrated language arts activity for a unit in science or social studies (see Figure 10.8). Include discovery activities for learning content related to the unit as well as activities involving reading, writing, speaking, and listening.

Going Beyond the Text

Plan to teach a language experience dictation and language study lesson, a minilesson in writing and an author's chair sharing, or a literature-based reading lesson to a small group of young elementary students. Tape record your lesson and collect samples of writing from the children. Transcribe the tape. Use information from the tape recorded lesson and the writing samples to describe what the children know about written language meanings, forms, meaning-form links, and functions. Describe what new literacy information you provided in the lesson or what strategies you helped children to learn. Evaluate your instruction based on the three criteria of effective instruction.

References

ALLEN, R. V., & ALLEN, C. (1982). *Language experience activities* (2nd ed.). Boston, MA: Houghton Mifflin.

ALTWERGER, B., EDELSKY, C., & FLORES, B. M. (1987). Whole language: What's new? *The Reading Teacher, 41,* 144–154.

ANDERSON, R. C., HIEBERT, E. H., SCOTT, J. A., & WILKINSON, I. A. (1985). *Becoming a nation of readers: The report of the commission on reading.* Washington, DC: The National Institute of Education.

BARBE, W. B., WASYLYK, T. M., HACKNEY, C. S., & BRAUN, L. A. (1984). *Zaner-Bloser creative growth in handwriting* (Grades K–8). Columbus, OH: Zaner-Bloser.

BAUMANN, J. F., & SCHMITT, M. C. (1986). The what, why, and when of comprehension instruction. *The Reading Teacher, 39,* 640–646.

BECK, I. L. (1981). Reading problems and instructional practices. In G. E. MacKinnon & T. G. Waller (Eds.). *Reading research: Advances in theory and practice* (Vol. 2, pp. 53–95). New York: Academic Press.

BECK, I. L., McCASLIN, E. S., & McKEOWN, M. G. (1981). Basal readers' purpose for story reading: Smoothly paving the road or setting up a detour? *Elementary School Journal, 81,* 156–161.

BECK, I. L., McKEOWN, M. G., OMANSON, R. C., & POPLE, M. T. (1984). Improving the comprehensibility of stories: The effects of revisions that improve coherence. *Reading Research Quarterly, 19,* 263–277.

BEREITER, C., & SCARDAMALIA, M. (1982). From conversation to composition: The role of instruction in a developmental process. In R. Glaser (Ed.), *Advances in instructional psychology,* Vol. 2 (pp. 1–64). Hillsdale, NJ: Erlbaum.

BIRCHBY, M. (1988). Literature and whole language. *The New Advocate, 1,* 114–123.

BRIDGE, C. A. (1986). Predictable books for beginning readers and writers. In M. R. Sampson (Ed.), *The pursuit of literacy: Early reading and writing.* (pp. 81–96). Dubuque, IA: Kendall/Hunt.

BRIDGE, C. A., WINOGRAD, P. N., & HALEY, D. (1983). Using predictable materials vs. preprimers to teach beginning sight words. *The Reading Teacher, 36,* 884–891.

BROWN, A. L., & PALINSCAR, A. S. (1982). Inducing strategic learning from texts by means of informed, self-control training. *Topics in Learning and Learning Disabilities, 2,* 1–16.

BROWN, M. (1981). *Your first garden book.* Boston, MA: Little Brown.

BRUCE, B. C. (1984). A new point of view of children's stories. In R. C. Anderson, J. Osborn, & R. J. Tierrney (Eds.), *Learning to read in American schools: Basal readers and content texts* (pp. 153–174). Hillsdale, NJ: Erlbaum.

BURNINGHAM, J. (1978). *Would you rather . . .* New York: Harper.

CALKINS, L. M. (1980). When children want to punctuate: Basic skills belong in context. *Language Arts, 57,* 567–573.

CALKINS, L. M. (1983). *Lessons from a child: On the teaching and learning of writing.* Exeter, NH: Heinemann.

CALKINS, L. M. (1986). *The art of teaching writing.* Portsmouth, NH: Heinemann.

CHOMSKY, N. (1968). *Language and mind.* New York: Harcourt, Brace and World.

CUNNINGHAM, P. N., MOORE, S. A., CUNNINGHAM, J. W., & MOORE, D. W. (1983). *Reading in elementary classrooms: Strategies and observations.* New York: Longman.

DAVIDSON, J. L., & WILKERSON, B. C. (1988). *Directed reading-thinking activities.* Monroe, NY: Trillium Press.

DUFFY, G., & ROEHLER, L. R. (1987). Improving reading instruction through the use of responsive elaboration. *The Reading Teacher, 40,* 514–520.

DUFFY, G., ROEHLER, L. R., SIVAN, E., RACKLIFFE, G., BOOK, C., MELOTH, M., VAVRIS, L., WESSELMAN, R., PUTMAN, J., & BASSIRI, D. (1987). The effects of explaining the reasoning associated with using reading strategies. *Reading Research Quarterly, 22,* 347–368.

DURKIN, D. (1981). Reading comprehension instruction in five basal reader series. *Reading Research Quarterly, 16,* 515–544.

ELDREDGE, J. L., & BUTTERFIELD, D. (1986). Alternatives to traditional reading instruction. *The Reading Teacher, 40,* 32–37.

EMIG, J. (1971). *The composing processes of twelfth graders* (NCTE Research Report No. 13). Urbana, IL: National Council of Teachers of English.

EVANS, M. A., & CARR, T. H. (1985). Cognitive abilities, conditions of learning, and the early development of reading skill. *Reading Research Quarterly, 20,* 327–350.

FISHER, C. W., BERLINER, D., FILBY, N., MARLIAVE, R., COHEN, L., DISHAW, M., & MOORE, J. (1978). *Teaching and learning in elementary schools: A summary of the beginning teacher evaluation study.* San Francisco, CA: Far West Regional Laboratory for Educational Research and Development.

FLOOD, J., & LAPP, D. (1989). Reporting reading progress: A comparison portfolio for parents. *The Reading Teacher, 42,* 508–514.

FREEMAN, Y. S. (1988). The California reading initiative: Revolution or merely revision? *The New Advocate, 1,* 241–249.

GABRIEL, D. (1987). *Observations on young children's writing.* Unpublished paper. Sarnia, Ontario.

GALDONE, P. (1985). *Cat goes fiddle-i-fee.* New York: Clarion.

GOODMAN, K. (1986). *What's whole in whole langauge?* Exeter, NH: Heinemann.

GOODMAN, K. (1988). Look what they've done to Judy Blume: The basalization of children's literature. *The New Advocate, 1,* 29–41.

GRAVES, D. H. (1983). *Writing: Teachers and children at work.* Exeter, NH: Heinemann.

GRAVES, D., & HANSEN, J. (1983). The author's chair. *Language Arts, 60,* 176–183.

GUNDERSON, L., & SHAPIRO, J. (1988). Whole language instruction: Writing in the first grade. *The Reading Teacher, 41,* 430–437.

HALL, M. (1981). *Teaching reading as a language experience* (3rd ed.). Columbus, OH: Charles E. Merrill.

HANSEN, J. (1987). *When writers read.* Portsmouth, NH: Heinemann.

HENDERSON, E. H. (1985). *Teaching spelling.* Boston, MA: Houghton Mifflin.

HENKE, L. (1988). Beyond basal reading: A district's commitment to change. *The New Advocate, 1,* 42–51.

HILLERICH, R. L. (1978). *A writing vocabulary for elementary children.* Springfield, IL: Thomas.

HILLOCKS, G. Jr. (1986). *Research on written composition.* Urbana, IL: ERIC Clearinghouse on Reading and Communication Skills and the National Conference on Research in English.

HOLDAWAY, D. (1979). *Foundations of literacy.* Sydney, Australia: Ashton Scholastic.

HONIG, B. (1988). The California reading initiative. *The New Advocate, 1,* 235–240.

HORN, T. D. (1947). The effect of the corrected test on learning to spell. *Elementary School Journal, 47,* 277–285.

HOSKISSON, K., & TOMPKINS, G. E. (1987). *Language arts: Content and teaching.* Columbus, OH: Charles E. Merrill.

HUTCHINS, P. (1968). *Rosie's walk.* New York: Scholastic.

JOHNSON, P. (1987). Teachers as evaluation experts. *The Reading Teacher, 40,* 744–748.

JOHNSON, T. D., LANGFORD, K. G., & QUORN, K. C. (1981). Characteristics of an effective spelling program. *Language Arts, 58,* 581–588.

JOHNSON, T. D., & LOUIS, D. R. (1987). *Literacy through literature.* Portsmouth, NH: Heinemann.

KARNOWSKI, L. (1989). Using LEA with process writing. *The Reading Teacher, 42,* 462–465.

LEE, D. M., & ALLEN, R. B. (1983). *Learning to read through experience.* New York: Appleton-Century-Crofts.

LOUGHLIN, C. E., & MARTIN, M. D. (1987). *Supporting literacy: Developing effective learning environments.* New York: Teachers College Press.

McGEE, L., M., & RICHGELS, D. J. (1985). Teaching expository text structure to elementary students. *The Reading Teacher, 38,* 739–748.

McKENZIE, M. G. (1985). Classroom contexts for language and literacy. In A. Jaggar & M. T. Smith-Burke, (Eds.), *Observing the language learner* (pp. 232–249). Newark, DE: International Reading Association.

MURRAY, D. M. (1987). *Write to learn* (2nd ed.). New York: Holt Rinehart and Winston.

NEWMAN, J. M. (1985). Introduction. In J. Newman (Ed.), *Whole language.* Portsmouth, NH: Heinemann.

OGLE, D. (1986). K-W-L: A teaching model that develops active reading of expository text. *The Reading Teacher, 39,* 564–570.

PARIS, S. G., CROSS, D. R., & LIPSON, M. Y. (1984). Informed strategies for learning: A program to improve children's awareness and comprehension. *Journal of Educational Psychology, 76,* 1239–1252.

PARIS, S. G., SCOTT, G., WIXON, K., & PALINSCAR, A. S. (1986). Instructional approaches to reading comprehension. In E. Z. Rothkopf (Ed.), *Review of research in education* (pp. 91–128). Washington, DC: American Educational Research Association.

RAPHAEL, T. E. (1986). Teaching question answer relationships, revisited. *The Reading Teacher, 39,* 516–522.

REARDON, S. J. (1988). The development of critical readers: A look into the classroom. *The New Advocate, 1,* 52–61.

SHANAHAN, T. (1988). The reading-writing relationship: Seven instructional principles. *The Reading Teacher, 41,* 636–647.

SHANKLIN, N. L., & RHODES, L. K. (1989). Comprehension instruction as sharing and extending. *The Reading Teacher, 42,* 496–511.

SHANNON, P. (1983). The use of commercial reading materials in American schools. *Reading Research Quarterly, 19,* 68–85.

SLAUGHTER, H. B. (1988). Indirect and direct teaching in a whole language program. *The Reading Teacher, 42,* 30–34.

SPIEGEL, D. L., & FITZGERALD, J. (1986). Improving reading comprehension through instruction about story parts. *The Reading Teacher, 39,* 676–682.

STAUFFER, R. G. (1969). *Directing reading maturity as a cognitive process.* New York: Harper & Row.

STAUFFER, R. G. (1980). *The language experience approach to teaching reading* (2nd ed.). New York: Harper & Row.

TAFURI, N. (1984). *Have you seen my duckling?* New York: Greenwillow.

TEMPLE, C., NATHAN, R., BURRIS, N., & TEM-

PLE, F. (1988). *The beginnings of writing* (2nd ed.). Boston, MA: Allyn and Bacon.

THURBER, D. N. (1981). *D'Nealian handwriting. (Grades K-8).* Glenview, IL: Scott, Foresman.

TOMPKINS, G. E., & McGEE, L. M. (1989). Teaching repetition as a story structure. In D. M. Glynn (Ed.), *Children's comprehension of text* (59–78). Newark, DE: International Reading Association.

TRACHTENBURG, D., & FERRUGGIA, A. (1989). Big books from little voices: Reaching high risk beginning readers. *The Reading Teacher, 42,* 284–289.

TUNNELL, M. O., & JACOBS, J. S. (1989). Using "real" books: Research findings on literature based reading instruction. *The Reading Teacher, 42,* 470–477.

VEACH, J. (1978). *Reading in the elementary school* (2nd ed.). New York: John Wiley and Sons.

WICKLUND, L. K. (1989). Shared poetry: A whole language experience adapted for remedial readers. *The Reading Teacher, 42,* 478–481.

WILKINSON, I. A., & BROWN, C. A. (1983). Oral reading strategies of year one children as a function of the level of ability and method of instruction. *Reading Psychology, 4,* 1–9.

WINTHROP, E. (1986). *Shoes.* New York: Harper & Row.

CHAPTER 11

Five Teachers
of Accomplished
Readers and Writers

This chapter presents classroom scenarios involving children who are becoming accomplished readers and writers. We will call the teachers in our five scenarios Miss Acosta, Ms. Bretzler, Mrs. Cousins, Mr. Downing, and Ms. Ervin. They represent grades kindergarten through third grade, and they deal with challenges ranging from the materials-driven curriculum to teacher burn-out. These scenarios were created from common situations and from practices we have observed in exemplary elementary classrooms. Our intention is to illustrate what accomplished readers and writers can do with written language, how they learn more, and how teachers can support them in a variety of classrooms and in several subject areas. There are many kinds of support that teachers can provide for children who are becoming accomplished readers and writers. The supports teachers select depend on many factors that will be illustrated in this chapter.

Readers should consider the five scenarios in this chapter as extensions of Chapter 10. At the end of this chapter, readers will be asked to return to the five scenarios and to apply the information from Chapters 9 and 10.

SCENARIO ONE: A KINDERGARTEN
TEACHER SUPPORTS ACCOMPLISHED
READERS AND WRITERS

In the description of Ms. Harper's kindergarten classroom in Chapter 8, we focused on what she did to support experimenters. We made the point, however, that not all kindergartners are experimenters. In fact, some kindergartners are taking the steps to accomplished reading and writing described in Chapter 9. In this kindergarten classroom scenario, the teacher has carefully provided for the needs of those children who are on their way to becoming accomplished readers and writers.

Changing Views of Kindergarten

Miss Acosta has been a kindergarten teacher for many years. She remembers when kindergarten was meant to be a fun time for children. Children accustomed themselves to going to school, and they acquired important social skills. Almost all children learned the same basic skills in each subject area. They worked on gross motor skills such as skipping and fine motor skills such as cutting with scissors. They learned something about art such as color names and what happens when you combine some colors and something about music such as how to sing a scale. They learned some number skills, including how to count to ten. They had fun with language, and they learned to recite rhymes and to do finger plays. They listened to the teacher read books and they learned to recite the ABCs. But they also had time to play and get to know one another.

In recent years, Miss Acosta has seen many changes in our society and in school curricula. In turn, some of her ideas of what makes a good kindergarten have remained the same and some have changed. Many more of her children have had child care, pre-school, and nursery-school experiences than was the case when she first began teaching. More of her children's parents have read something about children's development and children's learning. Miss Acosta is aware that a number of children already know many of the things that she used to teach to her whole class. Some of what they know is about reading and writing.

Miss Acosta is also aware of considerable pressure nowadays, compared to years ago, to teach academic subjects in kindergarten, to have a reading program and a math program, and even to have children working in workbooks. Miss Acosta is aware of the cautions professional early childhood education organizations have published concerning the use of such formal programs (see Chapter 3). She is happy to have support for resisting those programs and for keeping the play and socialization in kindergarten. Miss Acosta is also aware of experts' recent discoveries about what children can learn on their own about literacy and in other areas; the experts' discoveries confirm what she has observed in her own classroom.

Literacy Support for Accomplished
Readers and Writers
in Miss Acosta's Kindergarten

In response to all of this, Miss Acosta has found ways to support all her children at whatever stage of development of literacy knowledge they may be, without importing the workbooks and ditto sheets to which many of her fellow teachers in the elementary grades seem bound. For her accomplished readers and writers, she includes two non-traditional imports from the elementary grades: an individualized reading program and a process approach to writing. Many elementary teachers prefer these programs for their students; they free the teachers and the students from assigned reading in basals and from lessons in reading workbooks and language books. Miss Acosta has found them to be very appropriate for her students who are becoming accomplished readers and writers (see Chapter 9).

Individualized Reading

A key to an individualized reading program is students' being able to select their own reading materials in topics that interest them. In order to provide for this, a large variety of materials is necessary. The classroom library must include even more interesting books and other printed materials than the storybook center for experimenters described in Chapter 8.

Miss Acosta has a large classroom library for all of her students. It contains many of her own children's books. She is an avid book collector; she buys children's books at professional conferences, at book stores, at garage sales, and from book clubs. Miss Acosta's classroom library also contains some of her children's books from home. She encourages her children to own books, to have personal libraries (she gives them books as gifts and special rewards and makes use of children's book clubs), and to lend some of their books to the classroom (she keeps a careful inventory of those books so that she can return them all). Miss Acosta's classroom library also contains many books that she borrows each week from her school library. The school librarian knows of Miss Acosta's interest in books for young children and she often lends Miss Acosta new books before they go on the library shelves. Miss Acosta's classroom library also contains magazines, pamphlets, newspapers, maps, and brochures—anything that she thinks might interest her children.

This year, Miss Acosta has three students who need support of a different kind than she gives her experimenters. Many of their literacy behaviors match those listed at the beginning of Chapter 9. She noticed these behaviors as children participated in storytelling (they read text from easy-to-read books) and in writing (they wrote texts of several sentences using advanced invented spelling strategies and a few conventionally spelled words—see Figure 11.1).

Miss Acosta does not believe in separating "readers" from "nonreaders." All children in her room know they are readers. She did not group these three separately from the rest of her class; instead, she decided to provide an individualized reading program for them.

Miss Acosta has talked with each child about his or her reading interests; she has made sure that her classroom library contains books in the areas of those interests; and she has previewed some of those books with the children. She asks them to read to her from those books from time to time, makes note of their strengths and weaknesses and their reading styles, and gives them appropriate help. Miss Acosta talks about the story or information in the books, and she asks them to do additional reading before they meet again, so that they will have more to talk about. In these talks, sometimes Miss Acosta and the child work on paper and pencil exercises or blackboard and chalk exercises. These talks are the conferences around which an individualized reading program is usually organized (see Chapter 10). Miss Acosta uses the conferences in order to keep track of the students' progress; to teach specific, needed literacy knowledge; and to share the excitement of books on a personal level. However, with her kindergartners, Miss Acosta does not call these talks "conferences." Although she teaches some skills in the conferences, she does not assign follow-up skills practice for times between conferences.

Figure 11.1 *The Accomplished Writing of a Kindergartner*

April 8, 1988, Adrienne. I like to play outside on Saturday. Do
you? Sometimes we don't because it rained. The End.

Miss Acosta also has talks with other children. In fact, she makes a point of
talking one-to-one with each child at least once a day if only for a minute or two.
Often her talks with other children also focus on a book or a writing activity. But
with the three children who are becoming accomplished readers and writers,
Miss Acosta uses these talks to provide the more focused literacy instruction
about reading skills and strategies that they are capable of receiving. She has
even borrowed from the first- and second-grade teachers in her school a scope
and sequence chart from their basal reader series in order to be aware of what
skills needs these three children may have and in order to know where in the
basal series' teacher's manuals to find suggestions for lessons when she needs to
plan conference activities that target a needed skill or strategy.

Miss Acosta feels that what she is doing for these three is just right for them
and only for them. She realizes that in the course of the year others will begin
to show more and more of the qualities described in Chapter 9; she will then

use the same techniques with them. Her experimenters would be pressured if she taught them in this manner. Miss Acosta decided to use this approach to literacy instruction after careful thinking. She had been given the opportunity to send these three children to a first grade teacher each day "for reading." However, she consulted with their parents and was pleased that all agreed that the children should stay in kindergarten, learn reading at their level through their personal reading and these conferences, and have traditional kindergarten opportunities to play and interact with their peers. Another reason Miss Acosta is pleased to keep these children in her room is that writing is an important component of her literacy instruction. The first grade teacher presents reading as being separate from writing, and Miss Acosta feels strongly that using writing and reading together better supports her kindergartners.

A Process Approach to Writing

Miss Acosta's writing program for her accomplished readers and writers involves them more intensely in the writing processes of rehearsal, drafting, editing, and revising than do the activities she provides for her novices and experimenters. She has imported from the elementary grades a process approach to writing using a writers' workshop.

As we showed in Ms. Harper's room in Chapter 8, it is possible to have a very open-ended writing program in a kindergarten classroom. Children who are becoming accomplished writers, however, are more able to make use of writing processes than experimenters are. Their attention to meaning making, their more deliberate control of various written language formats, their later-stage invented spelling strategies, and their *metaknowledge* about written language (see Chapter 9) all contribute to a new kind of writing that almost *demands* making multiple drafts, revising, and editing. Their more developed literacy knowledge and skill make them able to return to and alter their texts, and their new awareness of meaning and of their own processes make them eager to do so.

In Chapter 8, we described how teachers who interact with children informally as they write provide much support for learning. Children who interact with each other also support each other's learning. What is needed for accomplished writers, in addition to these informal exchanges, is the teacher's looking out for them to see that both she and they take best advantage of opportunities to write. This does not mean that every occasion for writing needs to be turned into a formal lesson. It means that the teacher must establish routines that make it easy for these students to return to already started texts; it should also be easy for the teacher to provide feedback about specific pieces of writing and to give general guidance with rehearsal, revision, and editing.

Miss Acosta often invites those children who are becoming accomplished writers to the writing center together. Her students do not see anything unusual about this; she often invites small groups to the writing center. But with these students, Miss Acosta uses the time to talk about how she or one of them has benefited from a rehearsal step, from drawing or talking about a topic with someone, or from writing a list, a plan, or even just a haphazard record of first thoughts. She sometimes uses this time to talk with each child individually about a previous draft of a story, where it seems to be leading, and where the student wants to take it next. She also uses this time to introduce all three children to new helps for editing [such as dictionaries, word lists, or editing checklists (see Figure 10.11) that contain reminders about punctuation] or to help an individual child edit a piece he or she wants to put in final, publishable form.

Miss Acosta's accomplished writers share their writing products with the rest of the class. These pieces often better resemble adults' writing in form and content than do the writing products of the rest of the class. These accomplished writers have a reputation among their classmates as being "good writers." But the other children are also confident of their own abilities; they too use the sharing center or the recording and listening stations to make their writings available to the whole class. They too receive supportive feedback from the class—because Miss Acosta has modeled giving such feedback and because all her children know that Miss Acosta considers them to be writers.

Principles of Literacy Support: Miss Acosta's Kindergarten

The first principle of literacy support illustrated in Miss Acosta's kindergarten is that *teachers ought to resist labeling and segregating children as readers and nonreaders.* Accomplished readers and writers should not be separated from the other children in a kindergarten classroom. Learning about written language should not be very different for accomplished readers and writers than it is for the other children in a kindergarten classroom.

Miss Acosta was careful to see that her children participated in similar activities. All children used the classroom library; all children had talks with Miss Acosta; all children wrote both with and without their teacher in a variety of forms and for a variety of purposes; and all children shared their writing. Differences in the way accomplished readers and writers were treated came from Miss Acosta's differently planned uses of opportunities that were available for all. The accomplished readers and writers were not given special tests; they were not given a special group name ("the red birds" or worse yet, "the readers"); and they were not shuffled about the room or the school.

Miss Acosta was able to detect what all of her children knew about literacy without testing because all children in her room were given countless opportunities to use literacy knowledge. Sharing and reacting to reading and writing were part of the classroom organization and routine. The children knew that some of their classmates read and wrote very well. But this was viewed as an advantage for all. They would interact with other students—in play, in learning projects (such as unit centers), at the writing center, and in the classroom library or storybook center. Other children would learn about written language from these accomplished writers and readers.

The second principle of literacy learning illustrated in Miss Acosta's kindergarten follows from the first. It is that *accomplished writers and readers have more in common with their classmates than they have differences.* All are learning about themselves, about their world, and about each other. All are using communication skills—in both spoken and written language—to accomplish that learning. There are so many similarities in how novices, experimenters, and accomplished readers and writers perceive written language. Children at all points on our continuum of literacy development deal with issues of meaning, form, meaning-form links, and functions of written language. There is so little precision in our descriptions; we describe novices, experimenters, and accomplished readers and writers only to provide some points of reference along an *unbroken* continuum, not to encourage labeling. There are also many age-related, social, and developmental commonalities among kindergartners.

Miss Acosta provided the accomplished readers and writers with opportunities to enjoy the typical kindergarten experience because she understood that there is much in that experience that is good for all children. There is much that even children who read and write better than most of their age peers still must learn about playing and working together. Finally, we ought not to deprive them of the fun that kindergarten still can be.

SCENARIO TWO: A FIRST GRADE TEACHER SUPPORTS ACCOMPLISHED READERS AND WRITERS AT THE BEGINNING OF THE SCHOOL YEAR

Much of what was just described for accomplished readers and writers in a kindergarten setting is also true at the beginning of first grade. There is not that much time between these two scenarios, and the concern in both is dealing with children who are in the minority—those who are already reading and writing in ways that children usually do not until they have received some amount of formal literacy instruction.

One big difference between these two scenarios, however, has to do with what is typical in kindergartens and first grades. In most first grades, unlike most kindergartens, all children are expected to be in a formal reading program of some kind. They are tested and grouped and given first grade instructional materials.

The Materials-driven Curriculum

Some first grade teachers begin the year by using reading readiness materials (see Chapter 1). Some use these materials only with children who do poorly on a reading readiness test. Other teachers put all children through a readiness program regardless of what understandings of written language they may already have.

However, many of the teachers who make adjustments for children according to their literacy knowledge are constrained to doing so within a very narrow range of options. Teachers may not want to have more than three reading groups, so even the most accomplished readers in beginning first grade must do what the top reading group does. In turn, what the top reading group does is often determined by the structure of the basal reading series.

Many school districts discourage placing any child too far in advance of a grade-level reader in the basal reading series. Thus, first graders can go no higher than the highest of the first grade readers, of which there are usually three in a basal series. When a child gets too great a head start, the placement problems multiply for the next year's teacher and other teachers down the line. Other than these questionable concerns, a good reason not to place a child in a high-level reader that he or she may be able to read is that its stories were probably chosen by the publisher with much older children's interests in mind.

The result of all of this is that in many first grades at the beginning of the year, the most accomplished readers are placed a little above the beginning level of the top group of children; this group may also include many children who know far less about reading than the very accomplished readers. Being grouped with children whose literacy knowledge is less developed is not, of course, a problem in itself. We have advocated planning for interactions among children with varying levels of literacy knowledge because they can learn from each other. The problem is that because the group is formed specifically to use a set of instructional materials—in this case, the first grade basal readers—the children's learning is defined and paced by the materials, and not by their interactions with one another. Children who are accomplished readers and writers will be "taught" what the basal teachers' manual says to teach, even though they may already know it.

This may seem to be only a minor inefficiency. It may seem reasonable to expose children to what they already know, with the notion that "it can't hurt them." Some children seem to enjoy the opportunity to show what they know instead of having always to learn something new. These appearances may, however, mask some real dangers.

If the differences between the very accomplished readers and the other members of their instructional group are small, and if everyone's level of knowledge about literacy leaves some room for growth, then grouping them together is all right. We recognize that there *is* much variety among children who are on their way to becoming accomplished readers and writers; for many, there *will* be room for growth in a "top-first-grade" basal reader.

However, if the difference is so great that children are *never* challenged, then they can become bored and begin to exhibit learning and behavior problems. Most dangerous is the possibility of their feeling that what they have learned on their own is not important, that experimentation, discovery, and self-motivated and self-directed learning do not count. These children can come to feel that the teacher does not value what they know and that there are no opportunities to put their knowledge to use (Searcy, 1988). This must be avoided.

Literacy Support for Accomplished Readers
and Writers in Ms. Bretzler's Classroom

Ms. Bretzler was not always a first grade teacher; she used to teach kindergarten. Two years ago, when she began teaching first grade, she gave much thought to what it meant for her children to be in first grade rather than in kindergarten. She thought about the greater specificity of her school district's curriculum goals for first graders than for kindergartners. She noticed the greater numbers of instructional materials in her first grade room than in her kindergarten room. Now she understood why first graders needed their own desks—for sitting for large parts of the day, completing pages in workbooks! She decided that in order to help her children with these demands, it was her responsibility to put all of them through a sequence of academic first steps. A study of the manuals for all the instructional materials led her to believe that the first steps in reading are visual and auditory discrimination exercises, alphabet practice, elementary phonics drills such as beginning letter–sound activities, texts with only very simple sentence structures, and books written with controlled vocabularies.

In her first year, Ms. Bretzler noticed that most of her children were content to work in the workbooks. Many children needed those academic first steps. Some children even enjoyed the grown-up atmosphere of it all. But Ms. Bretzler also noticed that some children did not really need those first steps. She knew a few of these children from her kindergarten class of the previous year. They had written with invented spellings and had pretended to read using their small store of sight words and their memories for large parts of the texts of their favorite storybooks. They had known how to imitate the language of texts, including its sophisticated and complex sentence structures. They had known about the form of stories. They had taken other first steps of their own that somehow made the discrimination and phonics exercises in the workbooks unnecessary. They were bored and restless going through the very exercises that their fellow students in the top first grade reading group found exciting. Ms. Bretzler decided that during her second year as a first grade teacher she would do something different for these children. She would find a way to avoid having every child go through those academic first steps.

The answer to Ms. Bretzler's problem appears obvious: do not put accomplished readers and writers in a basal reading group. However, it is important to understand the pressures of the classroom and of district curricular guidelines that made it difficult for her to do the obvious thing that first year. Some teachers will say, "My school district requires every child to be in a basal reader" or "Do you mean I have to teach these children separately, when I already have three groups? I don't have time for *four* reading groups!" These are real concerns and we will address them in a later scenario with Mr. Downing. For now, we will look at the alternatives Ms. Bretzler tried in her second year as a first grade teacher. We suggest them for teachers who can avoid a basal placement for all or some children. They will be helpful as well for teachers who must place every child in a basal, but who want activities for some children to replace parts of the basal program that those children do not need. They are good alternatives for any child, but especially for the accomplished reader who really has nothing to gain from being put through all the first steps of the at-grade-level, or only slightly-higher-than-grade-level basal text.

Beyond the Basal

The alternatives Ms. Bretzler devised for her accomplished writers and readers are the same as what Miss Acosta did with her accomplished kindergarten readers and writers, but in a first grade context. Ms. Bretzler decided to begin her second year teaching first grade using an individualized reading program and a process approach to writing with her accomplished readers and writers. She still felt that her other students needed some first steps that could best be provided in the basal reading series. She did not want to try an individualized reading approach based on conferences and student-selected materials with all of her children. But to those whom she knew were beyond her first grade basal materials (at least the preprimers and first primer)—she introduced student-chosen materials and conference-based instruction.

There were four such children at the beginning of the year. Ms. Bretzler included them in the top reading group and they often read and discuss stories in the basal reader along with that group. But rather than complete the top group's workbook and sit in on all their skills lessons, these children have periodic conferences with Ms. Bretzler; they sometimes read and work in pairs; they read books of their choice; and they complete special assignments including some special book reporting, "conference preparation" worksheets (see Figure 11.2), and some skills worksheets.

As the year progresses, Ms. Bretzler is finding that more and more of her students are beyond the first steps. They are able to learn from self-selected reading materials and they enjoy sharing them with her and with their classmates. Ms. Bretzler has decided that she was too quick, even at the beginning of her second year of teaching first grade, to place children in instructional groups and in graded materials. Some of her children may still need the basal materials' presentations of the first steps, but she plans next year to give all her children more time to show what they already know about written language. She plans to include more time for children to write on their own and to write and read language experience stories. She will begin the school year by making her students comfortable with first grade, helping all in her room to get acquainted with one another, and observing her children's abilities in many areas, including literacy knowledge. She anticipates that more of them will begin their formal instruction with a combination of the basal and an individualized reading program.

The Language Experience Approach

Two developments in Ms. Bretzler's second first-grade year led to her plan for her third year to have a program that was more individualized and child-centered. The first was that she began to use a language experience approach to

Figure 11.2 *A Conference Preparation Sheet*

Conference Preparation Sheet

(Fill in 1-7 during or right after a conference)

1. Name _____

2. Date _____

3. Today I read from

_____ (pages _____).
       (book's title)

4. We talked about _____

5. I did very well with _____

6. We worked on _____

7. For next time, _____, I will read
         (date)

_____ / / (Check
                                             when
and do _____ / / done)

(Fill in 8-10 before your next conference)

8. Things I want to tell about next time:_____

9. Parts I want to read next time:_____

10. Things to ask about next time:_____

teaching reading and writing, as a supplement for all children (Karnowski, 1989). At first she used it only after a special activity, such as to write a big thank you letter to the firemen who had come to the classroom during Fire Prevention Week. The entire class had composed a fine letter of thanks that included many memories of their favorite parts of the visit. Many of the children had been able to read what they had dictated. Ms. Bretzler had been able to use the letter (on a big piece of chart paper) to talk with even the low-group readers about aspects of written language they would never have heard about in lessons in their level of the basal reading series, such as how to arrange the parts of a letter and what a comma is.

Ms. Bretzler began using language experience stories in all her reading groups as a way to get away from the basal from time to time, and in her social studies and science classes as a way to sum up lessons, experiments, and other shared experiences. She decided that language experience stories would continue to supplement basal instruction in her third year. They would be an especially good way to teach and to informally assess reading and writing in her class during that time at the beginning of the year when she planned to hold off getting started with basal placements and basal reading groups.

Daily Personal Writing

The second influential development in her second year as a first grade teacher was the success of a writing program for all students. She had wanted to let her accomplished readers and writers do more writing on their own, in addition to reading on their own, but she decided she did not need to treat those four children as a separate group for writing. All her children could write in one way or another.

Ms. Bretzler started using a writing process approach for the whole class. She reasoned that if she were expected to make these six-year-olds write for large periods of the day in workbooks, she might as well use some of that time for daily personal writing time, for writing conferences, and for writing sharing times (Clark, 1989). All of the children could rehearse, draft, revise, and edit in their own ways, and many could learn from each other. Of course, she expected more mature products from the four more accomplished writers, and she expected them to be able to stay at one piece longer. But she also found that in the more grown-up, formal, academic atmosphere of the first grade, all her children—even experimenters and novices—benefited from process writing.

Principles of Literacy Support: Ms. Bretzler's First Grade

The first principle of literacy support illustrated by Ms. Bretzler's example is that *in order to support accomplished writers and readers, the first grade teacher must resist many typical beginning-of-the-year practices.* In a way, the first grade teacher faces the opposite problem from the kindergarten teacher when dealing with accomplished writers and readers. Miss Acosta was careful not to cause her accomplished writers and readers to miss out on the important socializing and play experiences of the typical kindergarten. Ms. Bretzler, on the other hand, learned to be careful not to force her accomplished readers and writers to participate in activities and instruction usually provided at the beginning of first grade. In fact, she gradually learned that many other first graders were also better off not being forced into a rigid materials-driven program. (Compare her plans for her third year with what she did her first year.)

The explanation for accomplished readers' and writers' being able to benefit, along with all their classmates, from many typical kindergarten literacy activities while seeming to be unable to benefit from typical first grade literacy activities is found in the large gap between what is typical in kindergarten and what is typical in first grade. Typical kindergarten literacy programs are informal and child-centered; typical first grade literacy programs are formal, structured, and materials-centered. However, as Ms. Bretzler learned during her first two years as a first grade teacher, first grade literacy programs do not have to be that way; they can be more child-centered.

Ms. Bretzler also discovered that there can be legitimate differences between first grade and kindergarten literacy programs. A second principle that can be derived from Ms. Bretzler's example is that *teachers ought to keep their eyes open to classroom realities; they should keep a wide perspective.* Teachers must be good at knowing when to apply each of these seemingly contradictory principles. Ms. Bretzler's experience illustrates how to accomplish this juggling act. It is something she learned only gradually.

Ms. Bretzler was right to pay attention to the materials she was given when she began teaching first grade and to the district's (and parents') expectations as expressed in curricular goals. She was correct to include plans for some children to take their literacy steps with some of the traditional first helps. There will always be some children who need systematic approaches to learning letter names, some who can benefit from traditional beginning phonics instruction, and some who will first be comfortable and successful reading texts written with simple sentence structures and controlled vocabularies, such as are found in first grade basal readers. We have used traditional materials ourselves and seen others use them successfully to help children who have little self-discovered knowledge about written language to progress on their way to becoming readers and writers.

Ms. Bretzler was also right, however, to look beyond traditional materials— in one way for her accomplished readers and writers (an individualized reading program) and in other ways for her other students (supplementary language experience activities). We contend that children who come to school knowing comparatively little about written language have even more to gain from natural meaning-making opportunities than do their cohorts who have had more frequent pre-school experiences with several varieties of written language. What is important is for teachers not to lose sight of all the options that are part of the reality of any classroom. Most children can learn from parts of many approaches.

The realities of the first grade classroom made it desirable for Ms. Bretzler to plan a period of adjustment, observation, and trial for all her students at the beginning of the year. She will use language experience stories and a writing process approach for all. She will combine, as she did in her second year, individualized reading and basal reading in varying degrees for some children. She will follow most of the basal teacher's manual's directions for other children. She has learned from her first two years of teaching first grade how to find out who needs what. She now has the professional self-confidence to make those choices herself.

The principle of paying attention to classroom realities is most clearly illustrated in Miss Acosta's and Ms. Bretzler's different approaches to their writing programs. Miss Acosta rightly reserved a more structured writing process approach for only her accomplished writers. For the others, that more structured approach would have taken time from the typical kindergarten experience; they did not need a more structured writing program than what they were getting at the writing center. Ms. Bretzler rightly initiated a writing process approach for all her students. They were already spending large amounts of time at their desks writing; they were better off writing for their own purposes and learning what the writing process approach teaches about processes, purposes, and audiences for writing.

SCENARIO THREE: A THIRD GRADE TEACHER SUPPORTS ACCOMPLISHED READERS AND WRITERS

There comes a point in the early elementary years when nearly all of the children in a classroom are accomplished readers and writers (see Chapter 9). We have chosen third grade as an example of such a classroom.

A Classroom Majority of Accomplished Readers and Writers

There might still be one or two experimenters in some third grade classrooms, and sometimes, under special circumstances, one or two novices (although these children will probably be far enough behind grade level expectations that the school system will provide special help for them in and out of the regular classroom). The usual situation, however, is that by the third grade the accomplished readers and writers who were in the minority in our first two scenarios have become the majority.

This presents special challenges and opportunities. With the resource of literacy competence that the majority possesses, the teacher can plan many exciting uses of written language for *all* children in the classroom. Those who are accomplished writers and readers can work with those who are not to do things with literature and writing that were not possible in the classrooms described so far.

Literacy Support in Mrs. Cousins's Classroom

Mrs. Cousins tells anyone who will listen that third grade is the best possible grade to teach. "So many new areas are open to third graders," she says. "So many children already know how to read and write well. I can count on using children's reading and writing abilities for everyone's learning and enjoyment."

Literature Study

The first thing a visitor notices in Mrs. Cousins's classroom is that she and her students love literature. They learn from "real" books, not just from textbooks (Tunnell & Jacobs, 1989). Trade books are everywhere. There is a large classroom library. There are displays of new books, books with a common theme, books by the same author, both fiction and nonfiction books to accompany a unit of study in social studies or science, books a single student has read in the last month and recommends to his or her classmates, books Mrs. Cousins has read and is planning to read to the class, and books Mrs. Cousins has read and is reading for her personal reading.

Book talks.   Two corners of Mrs. Cousins's classroom are carpeted and contain big pillows and bean bag chairs in which children can get comfortable with their books. A small area of Mrs. Cousins's room is set off from the rest of the classroom with bookcases and a tall rolling cupboard. A small blackboard is attached to the back of the cupboard facing this area; there is a small table and six chairs in this area; and a bulletin board is on the wall. Mrs. Cousins usually uses this area to teach small groups, but it is also the "Book Talk Area."

The bulletin board in this area contains the message "Let's talk about books" along with several displays children have made. Some are posters; some are book reports, written by hand or by word processor and mounted on colorful tag-board; and some are reports of surveys children have conducted about their classmates' preferences (their favorite fairy tale, favorite book about kids their age, favorite science fiction book, and favorite character in a book they have all read or heard read to them).

Mrs. Cousins reads to her class daily. Her class also has SSR each day. Many days she ends that time by allowing small groups to go to the "Book Talk Area" and to discuss with each other what they have been reading. At the beginning of the year, she had to be present in order to model talking about books and to ask discussion-starting questions. But after a month, most groups were able to discuss on their own what they had been reading.

From time to time, Mrs. Cousins also invites her students to do more formal "Book Talks" about books of their choice. She modeled giving these oral book reports and gave the students a checklist of things to tell about their book (see Figure 11.3). A child signs up with Mrs. Cousins to do a book talk, and they talk about the book together. Mrs. Cousins helps the child decide what to say about the book and what to read from it. Then, Mrs. Cousins, her aide, or a volunteer helper listens to the child rehearse his or her book talk. Finally, the child gives the book talk several times in the "Book Talk Area" to up to five other children at one time during a seat-work or center activity time.

Authors.   Mrs. Cousins's children have written letters to authors. When an author replies, Mrs. Cousins photocopies the letter so that each child may keep a copy; she displays the original on a bulletin board; and eventually she moves the original to a scrapbook of letters that her class has received over the years.

Mrs. Cousins has a small collection of autographed children's books that she has accumulated from attending authors' talks at professional conferences. She keeps this collection in a special corner of her classroom library. Children especially enjoy borrowing these books, reading the authors' inscriptions (many are addressed to Mrs. Cousins's students), and reading the books.

Mrs. Cousins has sometimes been able to arrange a visit or a telephone interview with a children's book author. The children read all the author's books and

Figure 11.3 A Book Talk Checklist

Book Talk Checklist

Be sure to include:

_____ Title of the Book

_____ Author's name

_____ Illustrator's name (if there is one)

_____ Is your book a story book or information book?

(For story books)

_____ Setting   _____ Characters   _____ Problems

(For information books)

_____ Topic   _____ Way topic is presented   _____ Charts, maps?

You may include:

_____ Sample to share

_____ Reason for chosing the sample

_____ Something your audience might like—or wonder about

_____ Information about the author

_____ A question for the author

_____ This question for your audience: ''What questions do you have about my book?''

plan questions ahead of time. On a few occasions the whole class has gone on a field trip to attend a children's literature conference at a nearby university, where they hear talks given by children's book authors, and attend autograph and visiting sessions. Mrs. Cousins feels that these opportunities not only make a few books more personal, but they also help children to realize that there is a real person behind *every* book. Mrs. Cousins has also noticed that as her students come to think of themselves as authors because of their own classroom writing activities, they especially appreciate these contacts with published authors.

Reading clubs.   Mrs. Cousins's children may belong to reading clubs in the classroom. Any student may join any number of clubs, depending on his or her interests and willingness to keep up with the club's reading (if students cannot read the book themselves, they may have someone else read it to them—a classmate, Mrs. Cousins's aide, a volunteer helper, a brother or sister, or a parent). Clubs begin around a single book. Mrs. Cousins has several copies of many books. She previews one of these books for the class and then signs up a club of children who are interested in that book. They read (or are read) assigned parts between sessions and then they discuss and share favorite parts when the club gets together. Usually Mrs. Cousins or an aide or volunteer meets with the club to participate in and guide the discussion. Mrs. Cousins has found that the only preparation she or another guide needs is to have read the book herself. Often clubs (or some of the members) want to stay together when they finish a book. Sometimes they read another book with a similar theme or topic, or another book by the same author. Other times they become a theme or topic club, and each child reads whatever books he or she wants that come under the theme or topic (for example, fantasy, hobbies, sports, animals, folk tales, mysteries, and biographies).

    Book productions.   Two or three times each year, Mrs. Cousins has a "Book Production Time." During a book production time, which may last from a few weeks to a month, children team up to make some production based on books. One group may choose to dramatize a favorite book. Another may choose to make a video based on a book (Mrs. Cousins's school system has portable video cameras and recorder/players that teachers may sign out for two-week periods). These videos have taken the forms of dramatizations of a book's story and "You Are There" interviews of the characters at crucial points in a story. Another group may choose to write their own book using a similar theme or setting, or the same characters as a book they like. They work together on composition (writing several drafts before producing a well-edited final copy), on illustrations, and on production (typing on a word processor, photocopying several copies, and binding). Another group may produce a literary review, a newspaper-like publication containing children's reviews of books they have read recently. Multiple copies are made for the whole class.

    Mrs. Cousins has found that parents are very willing to help with these productions. In her weekly letter to parents, she announces a book production time several weeks before work begins and lists kinds of help she would like such as video recording and editing assistance, costuming, typing, bookbinding, helping with rehearsals, taking dictation, and assisting with revisions and editing. She always invites parents to attend productions.

    Mrs. Cousins has found that some of these productions last longer than the prescribed time. A drama group or a video group may want to stay together and work on additional productions between book production times. The literary review may go into several editions, on a year-long basis. One year, a parent who published a local shopping newspaper printed the class's literary review on newsprint using his presses. The professional-looking product inspired the participation of most of the class, and several editions were published that year.

Writers' Workshop

Mrs. Cousins's children do a lot of writing. In addition to writing as a response to book reading, the children in Mrs. Cousins's class participate in a fully implemented writers' workshop or process approach to writing.

The writing process approach in third grade can take on a different character than it does in first grade. Mrs. Cousins has more accomplished writers than Ms. Bretzler, and so more of her students are able to and eager to return to a piece several times as they refine their message and make better use of various text formats. Mrs. Cousins's students are able to benefit from peer conferences as well as student-teacher conferences. Students help one another to decide where they want to take their pieces, how they want to make revisions, and what editing they need to do.

Mrs. Cousins feels that her children's collaborative efforts in so many other areas of the curriculum contribute to the smooth operation of the writing process approach. Her students are accustomed to working together, helping one another with difficulties, and recognizing one another's strengths. This atmosphere predisposes children to learn from peer conferences and from Author's Chair sessions, during which constructive criticism is given and received.

Microcomputers.   Mrs. Cousins's school has several portable microcomputers; teachers can sign up to have them in their classrooms. Mrs. Cousins is able to have two or three microcomputers in her room for two-hour periods three times each week. Students may sign up to use the computers during these times.

The computers are mostly used for word processing and for data bases. Mrs. Cousins does *not* use her valuable computer time for the many computer games (or "skill-and-drill software") that are available nowadays to give children opportunities to practice reading skills. She knows that they are fun and attractive to students (at least when they are new), but she considers them to be too expensive and too narrowly focused.

Many of Mrs. Cousin's students do some of their writing on the microcomputers, using a word processing program (her students use *Word Star*). It is not practical for them to do all their writing that way. Her class has a concentrated writing time each day and writers' conferences that can include rehearsing, drafting, revising, editing, conferencing with a peer or teacher, receiving writing mini-lessons, or attending Author's Chair sessions. All students write daily, but there are only two or three computers in the classroom three times per week. In order for Mrs. Cousins's students to do as much writing as they now do using only a word processor, each student would need his or her own computer for half an hour every day.

Most of Mrs. Cousins's students do much of their planning and drafting with paper and pencil, rather than with a word processor. They are quite adept at making revisions with cross-outs, arrows, and brackets and cut-and-paste (see Figure 11.4). Many students sign up for a word processor to do third-, second-to-last, and final drafts, to run spelling checks, and to print final copies of their pieces for publication in the classroom. They appreciate the ease of making changes with the word processor and the clean look of their computer-printed final copies.

Some students never use the word processor because they do not like waiting for a sign-up time or because they lack keyboard skills. Either they are quite

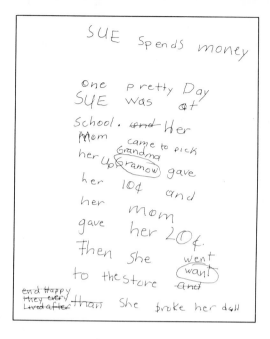
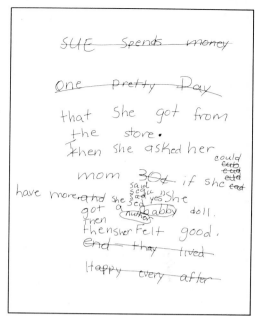

Figure 11.4 Brittney's Draft with Revisions

satisfied with their handwritten products—many of which are very neatly produced—or they can get a classmate or teammate to type their pieces for them.

Data bases are cross-referenced computer files that students create as they are doing research for a subject-area project or report (Strickland, Feeley, & Wepner, 1987). Instead of leaving their notes in notebooks or on 3 inch by 5 inch cards or on scraps of paper, Mrs. Cousins's students have learned to enter them into the computer (see Figure 11.5). It is easier for the children to use these files in their final products, and the files remain available for anyone else in the class.

Mrs. Cousins has heard that her school system's high school subscribes to several data-base services that make information on thousands of topics available to students via computer terminals, telephone lines, and computer printers. She is lobbying to make each elementary school a subscriber to these data bases because she believes her students could make good use of such a service. She volunteered to serve on her school's committee for overseeing computer use. At committee meetings, she argues against spending great amounts of money on skill-and-drill software and advocates subscribing to one or more data bases. She wants her school to use one of its computers and printers as a data-base station in the school's library.

Expository writing.   Mrs. Cousins's students are showing their biggest writing growth in their writing of expository texts (see Chapter 9). They write reports for which they use their classroom data bases and the many printed re-

Figure 11.5 *A Microcomputer Data File*

Data File

Explorer: Ferdinand Magellan

Nationality: Portuguese

Dates: 1480? - 1521

Accomplishments: Organized the first expedition to sail around the world. (Note: People sometimes say he was the first to sail around the word, but he didn't make it all the way himself—he was killed on the way. His sailors did go all the way around.)

Other information: The Strait of Magellan at the south end of S. America (between it and Antarctica) is named for him. So is the Magellanic Cloud—a galaxy you can only see from the southern part of the world (Southern Hemisphere)—and one of the closest galaxies to our galaxy.

Source of information: *World Book Encyclopedia* and the dictionary

Books about this explorer: don't know

File name: Magellan

Cross reference words: Magellan/explorers/Southern Hemisphere/South America/Antarctica/galaxies

This file was created by:
date:

This file was amended by:
date:

This file was used by:
dates:

---

sources in their classroom and school libraries. They use their reading and writing abilities in all areas of the curriculum, especially in social studies and science classes. Students are invited to write reports for many purposes. The writing workshop overlaps the rest of the day when students write current events reports, descriptions of family vacations for which they were excused from school attendance, historical essays for social studies, or descriptions of individual- or team-conducted experiments in science class.

Mrs. Cousins devotes much of her formal instruction about writing (in mini-lessons and in small-group and whole-class writers' conferences) to how to write expository passages. She has used a modified language experience approach to model expository writing (Kinney, 1985) and is experimenting with a method that uses special outlines called "graphic organizers" to teach about different text structures that authors use to write about causes and effects, about problems and solutions, or about contrasts and comparisons (McGee & Richgels, 1985).

Literacy Groups

The descriptions of Mrs. Cousins's class given so far do not include mention of reading groups. With the attention given to children's literature and to writing,

Mrs. Cousins's students certainly learn much about reading. Mrs. Cousins keeps track of her students' literacy learning using a three-group plan for reading instruction (Smith and Johnson, 1980). Each of her students belongs to an instructional group, a recreational group, and an informational group.

Instructional reading groups.   Each student belongs to an instructional reading group. Members of this group have similar abilities and instructional needs. Mrs. Cousins meets with them to teach targeted reading skills and strategies such as how to make inferences while reading expository texts (Carr, Dewitz, & Patberg, 1989). She turns to her school's basal reading series for a list of skills (a scope and sequence chart), and for lessons designed to teach the skills (in the teachers' manuals). She also finds instructional techniques described in professional journals (e.g., Bauman & Schmitt, 1986; Raphael, 1986). Children know that they may not do their most exciting reading while in their instructional reading groups, but that they sometimes do need explicit lessons and, most important, that there are plenty of other times during the school day when they can engage in more exciting, personally motivating reading and writing. Most students stay with the same instructional reading group all year because changes in their reading abilities usually keep pace with those of other members of the group.

Recreational reading groups.   Each student also belongs to a recreational group. The members of such a group merely talk together about their personal reading. We have already mentioned Mrs. Cousins's practice of scheduling SSR for the whole class each day. Sometimes members of a recreational reading group like to sit together in one of the book corners as they read their own books during SSR. Several times each week (usually immediately after a personal reading time), Mrs. Cousins asks recreational reading groups to meet and discuss with one another what they have been reading lately. These are not formal "Book Talks" and they do not follow a prescribed format. The children in each group get along well enough that they can visit briefly about their reading.

Recreational reading groups also may overlap with some of the other activities in Mrs. Cousins's room. As we have mentioned earlier, Mrs. Cousins sometimes designates the "Book Talk Area" for post-personal-reading-time discussions if she knows they will take a long time. Mrs. Cousins changes the composition of recreational reading groups from time to time in order to expose children to more of the reading interests of their classmates. However, if a group wants to remain together when this happens, members may form a book club and belong to it in addition to one of the new recreational reading groups each is assigned to. The children are responsible for the composition of book clubs. Mrs. Cousins determines the composition of recreational reading groups and sees to it that each student always belongs to one.

Informational reading groups.   The informational group is composed of children who share an interest in a topic. They stay together as long as it takes to produce a report or some other production about their topic. The reading and writing abilities of members of this group may vary considerably. They help each other; they use their strengths to compensate for others' weaknesses. A group that is interested in space travel, for example, may create or use the class data bases on space and rockets, as well as resource books in the classroom and school libraries as they prepare a report about space travel. Eventually they make an oral presentation and publish a written report for the rest of the class to read. They may use concentrated writing time and may have conferences with Mrs. Cousins during the time it takes to produce this report. They may or may not use the word processor to produce their report. This group could also work as a team during a "Book Production Time" to make their own book about space travel or a "You Are There" videotape about America's first moon landing based on a book they have read about NASA's Apollo Program.

When the group's product is finished, the group will disband; members will be assigned to other informational reading groups. Some of the members, however, may wish to stay together as a book club that is interested in space travel. Regardless of how these informational groups may overlap with the book clubs and other teams in Mrs. Cousins's classroom, each student always belongs to one informational reading group.

Mrs. Cousins uses the three-group system to keep track of what her students are doing in three very important areas: reading to learn to read, reading for enjoyment, and reading to learn about other things. With the many literacy-related groups and activities in her classroom—many of them student-centered and student-chosen—Mrs. Cousins feels that these groups give the structure she needs. It does not bother her that there are overlaps between these groups and other groups; in fact, she sees this as a strength of the system. Of course, it would be possible to eliminate the overlaps, and only have book clubs and no recreational reading groups, or only have informational reading groups and no book production times. Mrs. Cousins feels, however, that each has its special character and that students enjoy the diversity of activities she provides daily and over the course of the year. She considers the most important benefit of the three-group plan to be that it communicates to children that she values reading for all three of the groups' purposes. She institutionalizes reading for each purpose; that is, she devotes time and other classroom resources to each. Figure 11.6 presents a one-week schedule in Mrs. Cousins's class, including times for each student to meet with his or her instructional, recreational, and informational groups.

Principles of Literacy Support: Mrs. Cousins's Classroom

The first principle of literacy support illustrated in Mrs. Cousins's classroom is that *it is important to give students at this age reading and writing experiences that are beyond even those they would receive in a traditional individualized reading program and a process approach to writing.*

Mrs. Cousins wants her students to feel that they belong in the world of books (Johnson & Louis, 1987). The many book experiences we have seen in

Figure 11.6 *Mrs. Cousins's Weekly Schedule*

8:30– 9:30	**M—F:** Personal silent reading time followed by process writing.
9:30–10:30	**M:** Begin by introducing week's spelling.
	M & Th: Recreational reading groups, small-group book talks, or meetings of reading clubs (or sometimes book production preparations).
	T & F: Instructional reading groups, or mini-lessons (for those who need specific helps in reading and writing).
	W: Whole-class sharing (of finished writing pieces, finished book productions, finished informational reading group presentations) or other whole-class activities (guest presentations, movies, vocabulary development activities, science demonstrations, preparations for field trips or school programs).
10:30–10:45	Recess

[Note: computer in room **T** and **Th** 8:45–10:45]

10:45–11:30	**M–F:** Math
11:30–12:30	lunch
12:30– 1:15	**M–F:** Read to class for first part of this time (number of minutes varies).
	M, W, & F: Music or art (or sometimes book production preparations).
	T & Th: Science and/or informational reading groups and/or more process writing (for those whose pieces are suited to science).
1:15– 1:45	**M—F:** Physical education.
1:45– 2:15	**M, T, & Th:** Whole-class sharing (of finished writing pieces, finished book productions, finished informational reading group presentations).
	W & F: Spelling and instructional reading groups, or mini-lessons (for those who need specific help in reading and writing).
2:15– 3:15	**M, Th, & F:** Social studies and/or informational reading groups and/or process writing (for those whose pieces are suited to social studies).
	T & W: Recreational reading groups, small-group book talks, or meetings of reading clubs (or sometimes book production preparations).

[Note: computer in room **M** 1:15–3:15]

Mrs. Cousins's classroom created an intensity of involvement in reading and writing that is more than the sum of each child's abilities and interests. The children experience an excitement and satisfaction that comes from their realizing the potential of becoming a community of literate people (see Chapter 9). They know books; they know authors; and they are authors. They have the excitement of sharing this knowledge with one another.

The second principle of literacy support illustrated in Mrs. Cousins's classroom is that *a third grade teacher should take full advantage of third graders' developing abilities to work together and their varying, but often considerable literacy abilities.* Not only does Mrs. Cousins have a majority of students who are accomplished readers and writers, but also she has a classroom full of students who are at an age when they can and will work together.

Most of Mrs. Cousins's students can read and write on their own in a variety of text formats and for a variety of purposes; but everyone belongs, everyone learns, everyone has an opportunity to share in the satisfaction and excitement—even students who are not as able. This is because Mrs. Cousins has trusted her students to work in teams. She has taught them how to function in a variety of small instructional groups, how to learn from one another, and how to complement one another (Settle, 1986).

The third principle of literacy support illustrated by Mrs. Cousins is that *teachers ought to support spoken language as well as written language.* Teamwork was emphasized in the second principle. Such teamwork would not be possible without the habit of speaking with sensitivity about one's own and others' work and the ability to use conversation (speaking *and* listening) as a learning tool. Mrs. Cousins teaches her students by model and by precept how to make comments that recognize strengths ("I really like the way you . . ."); that focus on the product, not the person ("This part of your report is not clear to me"); and that suggest alternatives ("What would you think of trying to do _____ with this part?"). These communication skills make possible the smooth operation of peer writing conferences, Author's Chair sessions, groups working on "Book Production Time" projects, informational reading groups, and booksharing sessions. Mrs. Cousins feels that these skills also equip her students for success in later life.

Mrs. Cousins's students have many opportunities to use spoken language skills other than conversational skills. They use spoken language to make formal reports such as when they do a formal Book Talk, when their informational reading group gives an oral report to the class, or when they present a display of books by their favorite author that will stay in the classroom for a week. They learn to speak scripted parts in dramatizations and video programs. Many of these uses of spoken language are tied to book and writing experiences. Mrs. Cousins realizes that abilities to use spoken language and written language are interrelated.

SCENARIO FOUR: A SECOND GRADE TEACHER SUPPORTS ACCOMPLISHED READERS AND WRITERS USING BASAL READERS AND OTHER PUBLISHED MATERIALS

Mr. Downing is a second grade teacher who feels that he must use an array of published instructional materials, and who finds ways to do so that are consistent with the philosophy emphasized in this book. In many ways, Mr. Downing's situation is like Mrs. Robb's (see Chapter 10). Both have found ways to combine traditional materials and new approaches based on recent findings about how children learn to write and read as functional, communicative language processes (Fountas & Hannigan, 1989).

Teacher Burn-Out

Each school in Mr. Downing's school system is stocked with several expensive sets of basal readers and accompanying manuals and support materials published by a well-known company. Each student pays a textbook fee each year, which includes money for whatever basal reading series workbooks he or she will need during the year, one spelling workbook, and a handwriting workbook. In addition, each classroom is provided with a class set of hardcover "language books" and an accompanying teachers' manual. The language books contain lessons about grammar, listening activities, and writing lessons (such as how to write a topic sentence for a paragraph).

Up until a year ago, Mr. Downing used all of these materials. He explained that he felt he was expected to use them. Each student comes to him having completed earlier levels of all these books the year before, and each is expected to be ready to move on to a higher level in third grade. Mr. Downing worried that if students did not finish their workbooks, with every page completed and corrected, parents would not feel they were getting their money's worth from the textbook fee. Mr. Downing's school uses a computer to score unit tests in the basal reading series; print-outs of each student's scores are kept in the student's file in the school office. Mr. Downing felt that if he did not use the basal reader, his students' poor or missing test scores would reflect badly on him.

Mr. Downing liked the security that his workbooks provided. He could point to good test scores as evidence that he was teaching well and that his students were learning. He always knew what to assign his students and they always had something to do during seat-work times.

But all was not well. Mr. Downing's problem is familiar to many experienced teachers. Students could pass tests; they could read and write in readers and workbooks; but they did not seem to enjoy reading and writing. In fact, they did very little reading and writing outside of the instructional materials. More importantly, Mr. Downing was feeling burned-out and bored with teaching.

Beginning with Writing

Two years ago Mr. Downing took a language arts methods course at a nearby university as part of his master's degree program. He heard and read a great deal about using children's literature in the classroom, about integrating the language arts, about teaching writing using a process approach, and about giving children choices and allowing them to work in groups. In effect, he heard about teaching the way Mrs. Cousins teaches. At first, he did not think it was possible in his situation. After all, there were those workbooks, textbook fees, and tests. He felt that his school district, his fellow teachers, and his principal expected him to stick to the traditional program.

The more he read and thought about the new approaches, however, the more Mr. Downing wanted to try them—if only a little bit at a time. The semester after taking that language arts course, Mr. Downing went to his language arts professor and asked her how to get started. His former professor had conducted a small version of the writing process approach to writing in her language arts course. She remembered that Mr. Downing had enjoyed writing and was a good writer. She suggested that Mr. Downing begin with a writing process approach in his classroom. Remembering how much he had enjoyed his professor's writing, mini-lessons, and conferences, Mr. Downing made a commitment to writing. He decided it would be worth giving up some time several days per week from his language arts time blocks. There would still be time left for his students to receive most of the basal lessons, use the basal materials, and continue to take the basal unit tests.

The writing process approach was successful. Mr. Downing's students enjoyed the pieces he wrote and shared with them as part of this approach. They also enjoyed writing about topics of their choice. They became interested in returning to their compositions for revisions and editing, just as Mr. Downing demonstrated with his compositions.

Mr. Downing stopped using his language books. He needed time he would have spent teaching those lessons to spend giving mini-lessons and having conferences. This seemed a safe step; there were no workbooks to accompany the language texts and no unit tests to enter into the school computer. No one seemed to notice that the language books remained on the shelf, and the students certainly did not mind.

More Time for Writing

Two developments led to further changes in Mr. Downing's classroom. The first was that the students and Mr. Downing wanted more time for writing. The current concentrated writing time of twenty minutes per day, which he had formerly devoted to language study, was not enough. Even when he doubled up times by having writing forty minutes every other day, there never seemed to be enough time for students to get involved in rehearsing or drafting their pieces or having conferences about them. He wanted to use some of the spelling period or the reading period, but he still did not want to give up his traditional instruction in those subjects.

Writing Connections

The second development was that his students showed Mr. Downing some connections between writing and other parts of the day. Some students' compositions reflected what they had learned in reading class. Susan wrote a continuation of the excerpt from *The Little House on the Prairie* by Laura Ingalls Wilder that her reading group had read in their basal reader. Pete, who had written *partys* instead of *parties* in an earlier draft of an essay, corrected himself after a basal lesson and workbook practice pages on ''changing the *y* to an *i* and adding *es.''* In a writing conference, Pete told Mr. Downing that he had remembered how to do that from reading class. Wendy, who had signed up to write an extra-credit report for social studies class, asked Mr. Downing if she could use concentrated writing time to work on her report. Mr. Downing could think of no reason to say no.

Another connection involved the neglected language books. During one writing time, two boys were working on a letter to the local television station in which they protested its moving its daily broadcast of the *He-Man* cartoon show from 4:30 P.M. to 6:30 A.M. They had included some convincing arguments and suggested some alternative times. They wanted to mail their letter, but they needed to put it in the correct format for a business letter. Mr. Downing remembered a series of lessons in the language books about writing business letters, so he got the books out and showed the boys how to use the lessons to improve their letter before sending it.

After these incidents, Mr. Downing decided he could justify devoting more time to his writing program if he exploited connections between writing and other subjects in the curriculum. He also decided that he could teach reading skills lessons and even lessons from the language book in response to the needs he saw as he helped children with their writing.

Less Time in Traditional Approaches

Mr. Downing found that he was devoting less time to teaching the lessons that the basal reader prescribed after each story. He kept track of which skills children showed that they already knew by their writing; he did not teach those skills when the basal teachers' manual said to cover them in reading class.

Instead of waiting until students had finished a whole workbook to send it home, Mr. Downing began tearing completed basal reading workbook pages out of the workbooks and sending them home each week. When he had allowed a child to skip a page (usually on the back of a page the child had completed), he merely crossed it out in red or wrote at the top "Already Mastered."

Mr. Downing began teaching selected lessons from the basal as well as from language books when students needed them. He was relieved, but not really surprised, when students still did well on reading tests. He was still using the spelling and handwriting workbooks and most of the basal readers and their workbooks, but he began excusing selected children from doing some pages of their spelling and handwriting books too. (Children who had already learned about dropping *y* and adding *es* in reading class did not need two more pages about that in spelling class, and children who were producing beautifully hand-written final drafts in their writing did not need to do pages of copy work in their handwriting books.) Gradually Mr. Downing began using many of the reading and spelling lessons and workbook pages as resources at the editing table. Children asked for help with them or were referred to them when their editing of their pieces or their preparation for writing final drafts required it.

The most convincing benefit of all these changes was not Mr. Downing's students' test scores. (He began to suspect that many of the high scorers would have done as well all along without any instruction.) It was their original, enter-taining, and sometimes moving pieces of writing.

Involving Parents and the Principal

As Mr. Downing gained confidence in what he was doing, he made a point of including parents. He staged a very successful "Young Authors' Night" at which his students read their best pieces to their guests, autographed bound copies of student-authored books, and shared cookies and punch. He also invited his principal to observe the writing process approach in progress.

On the occasion of one of his principal's visits, he made a point of teaching a mini-lesson to a group of students from the language book. It was clear to the principal that they were not using all the lessons from that book in sequence and that not all students were receiving that day's lesson, but it was also clear that the students were able to apply what they learned. During the principal's visit, Mr. Downing also introduced his class to two new features of their class-room. At the editing table he had placed a collection of laminated lists of words the students had learned so far that year in their spelling series. He called the list the *Spell Checker.* They could refer to the *Spell Checker* when editing and would be expected to spell these words correctly in final drafts of their writing pieces. Also new was a classroom spelling center, in which Mr. Downing had placed a "challenge test" activity (see Figure 11.7). Students could take a challenge test in spelling each week by looking up and learning words that followed the patten of words in that week's spelling test. They would not know ahead of time ex-actly which words would be part of the challenge test, but they would know that the challenge words would follow that week's pattern (Personke, 1987).

Figure 11.7 *A Spelling Challenge Test Activity*

Spelling Challenge

This week's spelling words are:

fight	eight	caught
night	height	though
light	straight	cough
slight	thought	rough
tight	through	ghost

Most of these words have a silent *gh*, but in the last three words, the *gh* sounds like a hard *g* or an *f*.

I challenge you to find more words with a silent *gh* and a *gh* that sounds like an *f* or a hard *g*. Think about it. Pay attention to words while you read. Start keeping a list. Com-pare lists with your classmates. Can you know anything for sure about where a *gh* will be silent or where it will sound like an *f*—or at least where it *won't* sound like an *f*?!

There will be a special challenge test on Friday with words not from this list.

Later Steps Out of a Traditional Approach

After hearing many reports from Mr. Downing about the success of his writing program, his former professor began to encourage him to make children's literature a more integral part of his reading and writing instruction. She suggested some of the activities that were described in Mrs. Cousins's classroom. Mr. Downing followed a few of these suggestions. He adopted Smith and Johnson's (1980) three-group plan, and in that way he maintained a connection with the basal reader in students' instructional reading groups. His students still read most of the selections in their basal readers, and he still taught many of the skills lessons to both accomplished readers and to experimenters. However, they also had time for personal reading in the classroom and for talking about what they read with one another and with Mr. Downing.

Mr. Downing has decided after one year to continue with his new approach. He is working on a proposal to his principal that the school use textbook money to buy only half the number of workbooks it usually buys for his classroom. He calculates that he will only need half the usual number if he can try not to give each child his or her own workbook. Instead, he will keep a pool of workbooks from which he will tear pages for small groups or individual children as they need them. He is proposing to use the money saved in this way to purchase good children's books as a start toward building a quality classroom library. He wants to use works of literature in content classes as well as in reading class (Brozo & Tomlinson, 1986).

Principles of Literacy Support:
Mr. Downing's Classroom

The first principle illustrated in Mr. Downing's classroom is that teachers ought to begin with a simple precept *"Know yourself"* (Newman, 1987). Mr. Downing paid attention to his feelings about teaching (his feeling burned-out because he had forfeited the direction of his teaching to the publishers of his instructional materials) and to his own strengths (his satisfaction with his own writing, which led to his beginning with the writing process approach).

When we described Mrs. Cousins's classroom, we emphasized her love of books and her children's total involvement with children's literature; that love was Mrs. Cousins's strength. Mr. Downing may come to use many of the book-related activities that Mrs. Cousins uses; indeed, he is thinking about building a classroom library. His former professor had taught Mr. Downing about many of those activities, but when Mr. Downing came to her for advice, she did not automatically tell him that he ought to begin with those activities. Instead, she noted that he was a good writer and suggested using that interest and talent. Beginning with that strength, he was able to initiate some significant changes in his classroom, move himself and his students out of a rut, and then gradually discover other changes—natural next steps—which he had not at first anticipated such as going back to the abandoned language books and combining his writing program with social studies.

It is interesting to note that strengths as well as obstacles can be internal. Initial self-examination can suggest best first steps; later self-examination can tell one where powerful old notions may have been mistaken. Mr. Downing discovered many things about his students, their parents, his principal, and himself during his year of experimentation. The most striking discovery was that not all of the restrictions under which he and his students had formerly labored were external; some had come from within himself. He found that parents and administrators and fellow teachers did not ostracize him when he began using prescribed materials in flexible and selective ways. Once he had convinced himself of the possibility of omitting some exercises and using others in nontypical time slots, there was really no one else he needed to convince. The students did not protest and their enthusiasm and the quality of their reading and writing were apparent to everyone else.

The second principle of literacy support illustrated in Mr. Downing's classroom is that *change need not be radical or wholesale.* Mr. Downing began very conservatively, replacing only his traditional language instruction with something new. Even at the end of his first year, he was still using the majority of his classroom's traditional materials. He was using them, however, in sensible, informed ways, and he had come to those new ways gradually. Insights for next steps in his gradual change came from the situation itself and from his students as much as from Mr. Downing and his former professor. Once it was begun, the writing process approach was its own best argument for more nontraditional use of time. Once students began writing, their needs for instruction as well as their existing abilities were obvious.

SCENARIO FIVE: A FIRST GRADE TEACHER SUPPORTS NOVICES AND USES TRADITIONAL MATERIALS

This first grade teacher faces a problem that is opposite from Ms. Bretzler's. Ms. Bretzler is the first grade teacher who learned how to provide for children who were already accomplished readers and writers. Ms. Ervin is concerned about the children in her first grade class who at the beginning of the year are apparently complete novices about written language.

This is Ms. Ervin's first year teaching. She has been informed that she must use the traditional basal materials provided by her school district. The district's reading coordinator was appalled one December to discover that several first grade students were still doing only reading readiness exercises. In the packet of orientation materials Ms. Ervin received in August was a memo from that reading coordinator directing that all first graders must be placed in at least the first preprimer of the district's basal reading series no later than the first week of October. (A preprimer is one of the very first reading books in a basal reading series; it includes big pictures and only a sentence or two on each page, and uses only words from a basic list of 20–30 sight words.)

A Classroom Minority
of Novice Readers and Writers

As a first-year teacher, Ms. Ervin was very excited about teaching her children to write and to read. In her last year of college, she took a course about children's literacy development from birth to age nine. As she began the school year, she anticipated that most of her students would already know a great deal about written language; that is, they would know much of what we have described experimenters as knowing. They would have had many positive experiences with books at home and in kindergarten; they would have been supported in their experimentation with environmental print; they would have had many opportunities to write in many text formats and for many purposes; and they would think of themselves as writers. Their invented spellings would show how much they knew about the relation between spoken language and written language.

Ms. Ervin, however, was very surprised to discover that ten of her twenty-three students did not fit these descriptions. She learned that in her small, rural school district, many of her students had seldom visited a library, few had attended nursery school, and many had never been read to at home. Ms. Ervin visited her school's kindergarten and saw very little evidence of support for literacy development. There were no samples of children's writing on display, and there were few written posters and labels. There was no writing center and no classroom library. The kindergarten teacher did have a set of reading readiness workbooks, but she planned to save them until after Christmas vacation and then have every student work in one. Ms. Ervin began to understand why ten of her students were, in effect, responding to written language as novices.

As the school year got under way, Ms. Ervin found that although she would have to adjust some of her expectations for these ten children, she could still use many of the activities she had learned from her early literacy course. She would just have to start with activities for an earlier point of development than she had expected. Ms. Ervin's ten novices very soon responded to her suggestions that they *could* write (she began much as Mrs. Miller did—see Chapter 6), and they were excited to find that their reading of milk cartons and pencil package labels "counted" as reading.

The problem, however, was that memo about the preprimer. It was almost the first week of October and Ms. Ervin was worried. She did not want to begin her teaching career by violating district policies. She decided that she would have to find ways to place her novices in the basal reading series *and* continue to support their personal discovery of written language.

Meeting the Needs of Novices
in Elementary School

Ms. Ervin did with these 10 children many of the activities described for novices in Chapter 6 while at the same time insuring that they were well prepared for instructional experiences in the preprimer. Ms. Ervin's novices' experiences of the preprimer itself were in fact not much different from their classmates' preprimer experiences. All of her students had preparation and application activities before and after using the preprimer. The preprimer was not any student's total reading program. It was the nature of those pre- and post-activities that differed from novices to experimenters to accomplished readers and writers. We will describe Ms. Ervin's classroom in November of her first year.

Bookreading

Even in her first year of teaching, Ms. Ervin has a good-sized classroom library. She reads to her class every day and she encourages all her students to read books by themselves, to one another, and to her. For her novices, however, Ms. Ervin plans many special novice-oriented booksharing activities like those described in Chapter 6. Her bookreading always has a focus (for example, a focus on form when she emphasizes that the text is composed of words and that words are formed from letters and that the letters have names). She plans for interactions between herself and the small group to which she is reading (sometimes all ten novices, but more often only five of them at one time).

Ms. Ervin's questions and comments help students to construct the meaning of the text, and they invite them to comment about it to one another and to her. She may say, "That was an odd thing to say to his mother, wasn't it? Have you ever said that to *your* mother?" She often uses book props that the students can use in their turn when they read the books. As she completes a bookreading session, Ms. Ervin always suggests ways that the children can later independently use the book she has read. She often says, "Maybe you would like to read this book on your own during personal reading time. You can look at the pictures, remember what I read and what we talked about, and tell the story to yourself or to a friend. I'll leave the book out on this shelf for you."

Environmental and Functional Print

Ms. Ervin uses environmental and functional print items with all of her students. She believes that first grade is not too late for play. She reserves a corner of her room for an activity center that is really a play center. The activity always has to do with the class's current social studies unit and it often includes functional print items. During this first week in November, the unit is about grocery shopping. (Ms. Ervin is leading up to their buying groceries for a Thanksgiving feast that the students will prepare and eat on the day before Thanksgiving.) The activity center is a grocery-store play center stocked with pretend food, much of which is empty food packages that Ms. Ervin and the students have brought from home.

Some children are writing stories about grocery store incidents in their lives (for example, "What It Was Like to Ride in the Grocery Cart When I Was Little"); others are making shopping lists (see Figure 11.8), gathering coupons, collecting the needed items from the play center shelves, and figuring the cost of

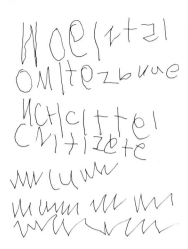

Figure 11.8 *A Novice Writer's Grocery List*

their purchases. Most of the children enjoy "playing store" when there is free time to play during the fifteen minutes before school when children are arriving and during some center activity times.

For her novices, however, Ms. Ervin makes a point of planning environmental print activities in addition to those any student might perform in the activity center. Each novice has a "Words I Can Read" bag like the ones Mrs. Miller's children use for storing environmental print items (see Chapter 6). More often with her novices than with her other students, Ms. Ervin uses functional print items as models of suggested writing projects. For example, she and a group of five novices are making their own coupons. First, she displayed a handful of coupons from the grocery store center and they talked about the typical features of a coupon. Now she is making a coupon good for one free Star Wars sticker after reading a book from the classroom library (she will photocopy this one and give copies to every student in her class) (see Figure 11.9); one student is making

Figure 11.9 *A Classroom Coupon*

a rather faithful copy of a coupon for 5 cents off the cost of a 12-pack of Fudge-bars; and another student is making a coupon to give to her mother, entitling her to a free vacuuming of the living room.

Basal Materials

In spite of her provision of special activities for novices, Ms. Ervin strives to make her novices' experience of first grade as much like the other children's as possible. Often these special activities are preparation for and application of what is done in the basal preprimer. For example, the group might find the new words they were learning for a preprimer story, which are often high-frequency words, such as *the* and *with*, on the environmental print items in their "Words I Can Read" bag. Or they might apply a basal phonics lesson about the sound associated with the letter *B* by sorting their environmental print items by first letters in words and seeing how many of those letters' sounds they know.

Not all children are in preprimers (some are in higher levels), but all are in some level of the same basal reading series. Not all children receive novice-oriented preparations for reading in the basal series, but all receive preparations of some kind. With all groups, Ms. Ervin talks before reading a basal story about the story's topic, about possibly relevant experiences the children have had, and about new words they will encounter in the story. With her whole class, she does concept development or vocabulary development activities that will enrich their background knowledge and thus make any reading comprehension easier (Johnson & Pearson, 1984). Not all children receive the same post-basal-reading application activities as novices do, but in different ways all apply what they learn to reading literature and to doing personal writing.

Reading and Writing Beyond the Basal

Children in all basal groups in Ms. Ervin's class have many literacy experiences outside of their reading groups. Reading from a basal reader or working in a reading workbook is just one literacy event in their school day. The children read and write as part of grocery store play, they read and write functional print, and they read and write books. Ms. Ervin treats all children as writers and readers, and they all see one another as writers and readers, regardless of the level of their literacy knowledge. She is wise to make the special activities she does with the novices as unremarkable as possible. Increasingly frequent occasions of novices' acting like experimenters will not seem surprising, either to Ms. Ervin or to her students.

Principles of Literacy Support: Ms. Ervin's Classroom

The two principles of literacy support we draw from Ms. Ervin's example are repeated from earlier in this chapter. The first is the same as one we drew from Miss Acosta's kindergarten classroom: *teachers ought to resist segregating stu-*

dents. We have seen that Ms. Ervin provided special experiences for her novices, just as Miss Acosta provided special experiences for her accomplished readers and writers. However, both found ways to make those children's experiences in their grade as much like their classmates' as possible, both made it possible for all children to learn from one another, and both saw benefits from appreciating what all their students had in common as young readers and writers.

Because she did not segregate any of her students, Ms. Ervin was able to provide her novices with experiences that may seem to others to be typical of preschools rather than elementary schools. There was no problem in using pre-school activities because doing so did not make the novices stand out from the rest of the class. It did not seem silly to the non-novices that their classmates used "Words I Can Read" bags full of functional print items. This is because Ms. Ervin also provided those non-novices with meaningful experiences with functional print items in play settings.

The second principle of literacy support is derived as easily from Ms. Ervin's classroom as it was from Ms. Bretzler's. It is that *teachers do well to keep a wide perspective.* On the one hand, teachers of novices in elementary school must remain aware of the many resources that are available to them; even the basal reader can be a valuable resource if children are well prepared for their experiences in it and are able to apply its learnings elsewhere.

On the other hand, it is especially important with novices not to go down the very narrow path prescribed by some basal preprimers, which defines literacy knowledge only in terms of decoding skills and sight words. Even though they may not yet have discovered it all on their own, novices in elementary school can come to literacy knowledge in the four areas described in Chapter 5: knowledge about meaning making, knowledge about written language forms, knowledge about the link between form and meaning, and knowledge about written language functions. Teachers must plan literacy activities that focus on those areas. Even more than with their other students, teachers must not let novices' entire reading program consist of the traditional basal materials. Novices should not have to spend more time than their classmates in the basal, in pursuit of a false notion of catching-up.

Chapter Summary

With the five scenarios in this chapter, we have presented solutions we would like teachers to pursue when they face the common problems presented in those scenarios. A common theme in the solutions is sensible, well-grounded change. Ms. Acosta was able to provide some of her children with kinds of literacy support that no child demanded years ago, but at the same time she did not deprive any child of the fun and growth of a full kindergarten experience. Ms. Bretzler negotiated the change from teaching kindergarten to teaching first grade by rediscovering the importance of a child-centered curriculum. Mr. Downing changed from feeling powerless in his own classroom to being a decision-making professional. He discovered he had talents and strengths he did not know about and that many of his anxieties were unfounded. Both Ms.

Bretzler and Mr. Downing took a few years to accomplish big changes. The change in Mrs. Cousins's example is a daily phenomenon. Her students thrive on the variety that follows from her many activities and her devotion to literature (which itself is so many-faceted and variable). But that change too has sensible foundations; Mrs. Cousins organizes it and manages it by means of the many classroom institutions she has built and maintained (from process writing to the three-group literacy pro-

gram; from the sign-up sheet for the rolling computers to the "Book Production Times"). Finally, even a first-year teacher, Ms. Ervin, changed. She changed her preconceived notions of what literacy knowledge to expect of her first graders. Those expectations were based on sound information she received in a college course about emerging literacy, but so were the adjustments she made to accommodate the ten students who were her unexpected novices.

Applying the Information

This chapter has been an extended case study. Use the five scenarios as tests of your ability to apply the concepts discussed in Chapters 9 and 10. For each scenario, determine to what extent the teacher identifies with a skills, strategy, or whole-language orientation to literacy instruction and to what uses the teacher puts the five major approaches to literacy instruction (the basal, language experience, individualized, integrated language, and process writing approaches). For some scenarios, your

answer will depend on your choice of a point of time in the scenario.

We frequently used the scenarios to stress similarities among children and the need to avoid markedly different treatment based on minor differences in literacy knowledge. For each scenario, what features (both literacy-related and nonliteracy-related) would all the students be likely to share? As a teacher, how would you recognize and take advantage of those similarities?

Going Beyond the Text

Observe several early elementary school teachers. Keep in mind the presenting problems in our five scenarios: changing views of the kindergarten curriculum (Miss Acosta's problem), materials-driven grouping and instruction (Ms. Bretzler's problem), teacher burn-out (Mr. Downing's problem), and the equally challenging situations posed by a classroom majority of accomplished readers and writers (Mrs. Cousins's problem) and by a classroom minority

of literacy novices (Ms. Ervin's problem). Do you recognize these problems? How are teachers dealing with them? Interview the teachers. Do they recognize the problems? Are they aware of their ways of dealing with them? What other problems and challenges do you see that we did not present in our five scenarios? What solutions can you suggest that would be consistent with this book's principles of support for literacy learning?

References

BAUMAN, F., & SCHMITT, M. C. (1986). The what, why, how, and when of comprehension instruction. *The Reading Teacher, 39,* 640–646.

BROZO, W. G., & TOMLINSON, C. M. (1986). Literature: The key to lively content courses. *The Reading Teacher, 40,* 288–293.

CARR, E., DEWITZ, P., & PATBERG, J. (1989). Using cloze for inference training with expository text. *The Reading Teacher, 42,* 380–385.

CLARK, A. (1989). Helping primary children write about reality. *The Reading Teacher, 42,* 414–416.

FOUNTAS, I. C., & HANNIGAN, I. L. (1989). Making sense of whole language: The pursuit of informed teaching. *Childhood Education, 65,* 133–137.

JOHNSON, D. D., & PEARSON, P. D. (1984). *Teaching reading vocabulary* (2nd ed.). New York: Holt, Rinehart, and Winston.

JOHNSON, T. D., & LOUIS, D. R. (1987). *Literacy through literature.* Portsmouth, NH: Heinemann.

KARNOWSKI, L. (1989). Using LEA with process writing. *The Reading Teacher, 42,* 462–465.

KINNEY, M. A. (1985). A language experience approach to teaching expository text structure. *The Reading Teacher, 38,* 854–856.

McGEE, L. M., & RICHGELS, D. J. (1985). Teaching expository text structure to elementary students. *The Reading Teacher, 38,* 739–748.

NEWMAN, J. (1987). Learning to teach by uncovering our assumptions. *Language Arts, 64,* 727–737.

PERSONKE, C. R. (1987). Spelling as a language art. In C. R. Personke & D. D. Johnson (Eds.), *Language arts instruction and the beginning teacher: A practical guide* (pp. 75–85). Englewood Cliffs, NJ: Prentice-Hall.

RAPHAEL, T. E. (1986). Teaching question answer relationships, revisited. *The Reading Teacher, 39,* 516–522.

SEARCY, B. (1988). Getting children into the literacy club—and keeping them there. *Childhood Education, 65,* 74–77.

SETTLE, S. (1986). Leading from behind. *Language Arts, 63,* 660–661.

SMITH, R. J., & JOHNSON, D. D. (1980). *Teaching children to read.* Reading, MA: Addison Wesley.

STRICKLAND, D. S., FEELEY, J. T., & WEPNER, S. B. (1987). *Using computers in the teaching of reading.* New York: Teachers College Press.

TUNNELL, M. O., & JACOBS, J. S. (1989). Using "real" books: Research findings on literature based reading instruction. *The Reading Teacher, 42,* 470–477.

Part 5

Meeting Special Needs

Part 5 discusses the literacy learning of children whose patterns of growth and development are different from those of most children. It describes children who present special challenges because the language spoken in their home is not English. In addition, it includes children whose families use language in different ways than those used in school and whose ways of learning are different from those ways of learning teachers are most likely to expect. Chapter 12, "Literacy Learners with Special Needs," describes many techniques that teachers can use to support the literacy learning of special learners. It discusses children's special needs for literacy learning and many of the ways that teachers can meet those needs through reading, writing, talking, drawing, and playing.

Literacy Learners with Special Needs

In this book we have described the literacy learning of young children who follow expected patterns of development. We have stressed that all children are unique. Even so, some children need special help with their literacy learning because of special conditions that make their development and learning different from that of other children. Chapter 12 describes three conditions that call for teachers to provide special help for literacy learning. Children with special needs include children whose developmental or learning patterns are different from those of their peers, whose language is different from the language used in school and by teachers in instruction, whose cultural heritage emphasizes ways of learning that are different from those of middle-class children. We describe each of these conditions and discuss why these children have special needs. Next, we describe several techniques that can be beneficial for all children, but especially for children who have special needs.

WHO ARE CHILDREN WITH SPECIAL NEEDS?

All children are special. They approach tasks, including literacy tasks, with their own special style and unique knowledge. Yet most children develop within a range of expected knowledge and approaches. For young children, this range of expected knowledge and approaches is wide and allows for much individual variation. The children who do not or cannot develop within the range of expected knowledge and approaches are children with special needs.

Children with Developmental or Learning Differences

Some children's special needs arise from physical, neurological, psychological, or learning conditions. These conditions result in different developmental patterns or learning difficulties.

Laws Regarding Children with Developmental or Learning Differences

The Education for All Handicapped Children Act of 1975 (PL 94–142) and a later Act (PL 99–457) assured an equal educational opportunity for children with special needs. These laws require that all school systems provide free evaluation services to families who request them. They also stipulate that special-needs children (from three to twenty-one years old) will have access to an appropriate education. PL 99–457 provides monies for families with a special-needs child under the age of three years old to obtain home-based education, language therapy, medical services and equipment, or other needed services. Special-needs children three years and older are given the right to attend classes with non-special-needs children to the extent appropriate. Many children with special needs can benefit from spending part or all of their school day mainstreamed or integrated with non-special-needs children. However, not all children with special needs will be found in regular preschool and elementary classrooms.

Kinds of Developmental or Learning Differences

There are many types of special-needs children whom preschool and elementary teachers may encounter. Not all of these children may be mainstreamed or integrated into classrooms. Special-needs children who are likely to be identified during their preschool years include children with sensory impairments such as deafness or blindness, children with orthopedic impairments such as spinal bifida, children with severe communication disorders (sometimes referred to as austistic), gifted children, and children with non-categorical impairments (children with impairments not yet categorized, but usually including children who have developmental delays). In elementary school, additional types of special-needs children may be identified: children who show emotional disabilities, learning disabilities, and mental retardation (*Federal Register,* August 23, 1977, pp. 785–786).

While we present descriptions of children with these types of special needs as a way to learn about them, we want to be careful about applying labels to children. The practice of identifying children as learning disabled, in particular, is controversial (McGill-Franzen, 1987). We believe that preschool teachers, child care givers, and elementary teachers can provide valuable insight into children's knowledge, development, and behavior, but only highly trained school psychologists, special educators, and medical personnel should make final judgments that categorize children with special needs.

Why a Special Need?

In general, children who differ from their peers either developmentally or in learning approaches lag behind or are ahead of their classmates in cognitive, language, physical, emotional, or social development. Some special-needs children may need special adaptive equipment or materials to be able to read and write; for example, low-vision special-needs children must have books with very large print. However, most special-needs children can benefit from the same literacy activities that have been described in earlier chapters in this book when they are geared to the particular needs and level of development of the child. Some additional activities that are particularly suited to meeting the special needs of these children are suggested later in this chapter.

Children with Language Differences

Children whose first language is not English and children who speak with a dialect considered to be nonstandard are also identified as special-needs children.

Children with Limited English Proficiency

There are many terms applied to children whose home language is not English: bilingual, English-as-a-second language learners, and children with limited English proficiency. *Bilingual* is probably the best known term for children whose first language is not English. The term *bilingual* implies that children are equally proficient in two (bi) languages (lingual). Most children are not equally proficient in two languages; rather, they are limited in English proficiency and more proficient in their first or home language. Some children show no English proficiency. All of these *limited-English-proficiency* (LEP) children learn English as a second language.

Laws and practices regarding bilingual education.   The number of non-English-speaking children of school age has risen sharply in the last few decades. Many school districts, especially in large urban settings and in the southwestern region of the United States, have large numbers of students whose home language is not English. Congress enacted the Bilingual Education Act of 1978 that stipulates that school-age limited-English-proficiency children must be identified and provided with special instruction, including instruction in English acquisition.

There are many controversies surrounding education for limited-English-proficiency children. One of the controversies centers on whether children should receive instruction only in English or in both English and their home language (Hudelson, 1987). Experts argue that all bilingual children should continue to develop their home language abilities, including the ability to read and write in that language (Ortiz & Engelbrecht, 1986).

Why a special need?   In many child care centers and preschools, there are no special bilingual teachers who teach English. While many limited-English-proficiency children in elementary school will attend special bilingual or English as a second language (ESL) classes, not all of these children will have access to special classes. Even when bilingual or ESL teachers are available, many limited-English-proficiency children spend much of their school day in regular classrooms. The length of time children may receive help learning from special teachers varies. Some schools provide only a few years of support for these students, and children may acquire only very limited English skills before spending most of their time in regular classes. For all of these reasons, much of the challenge of helping children develop their oral and written English skills will rest with regular preschool and elementary school teachers. In fact, almost half of all public school teachers in the United States have or have had a limited-English-proficiency student (*TESOL Newsletter,* 1984, p. 1).

Children with Dialects

The way we speak English varies according to our social class, gender, occupation, locale, and ethnic background. Variations of a language are called *dialects.* All dialects of a language are understandable by all speakers of a language, but they are sufficiently different from one another to be distinctive (Bryen, 1982). Many speakers from New York City have what speakers from other parts of the country consider a dialect, but New Yorkers are easily understood by English speakers from San Francisco, Atlanta, or any other location in the United States.

Dialects are distinguished by differences in pronunciation, word choice, grammatical structure, and communicative style or usage. For example, the words *park* and *car* are pronounced *pahk* and *cah* in Boston or New York and *pawk* and *caw* in New Orleans (Barnitz, 1980). A sandwich on a long roll is called a *hoagie* in Philadelphia and a *Po Boy* in parts of Louisiana. Some people say they must be home by *quarter til 5,* while others say they must be there by *quarter of 5.*

Nonstandard and standard dialects. There is no one form or dialect of English that is "standard." This is a difficult concept to accept. As speakers, we are capable of, and unconsciously make, judgments regarding other people's use of language. When we consider their language use to be standard or nonstandard, we are not applying any consistent criteria. Many speakers would label, "I ain't parkin no car," as nonstandard English. When asked why, they usually say that it violates rules of grammar. Yet they may consider the sentence, "None of the cars were parked" to be standard even though it violates a rule of grammar: the use of a singular subject (none) with a plural verb (were). In other words, although the word *standard* implies otherwise, there are no objective criteria for determining whether a dialect is standard. All speakers have a range of language patterns that they use depending on situation and audience. This is called *code switching* or *register switching.* Again, the point is that "nonstandard" English and "standard" English are not absolute language patterns, but rather they represent a range of language patterns.

Dialects considered nonstandard. There are many dialects frequently considered to be nonstandard by large segments of the population, especially by teachers and other educated groups. Some of these dialects are tied to locale, and others are tied to social class (Labov, 1966). Many researchers have described a dialect referred to as Black English (for example, Smitherman, 1977). Black English as a dialect has perhaps received the most attention and has engendered the largest controversy of any American English dialect (see for example, Turner, 1985). Many Black Americans do not use Black English, and many of the features of Black English are found not only in so-called standard English, but also in many other dialects. However, an important court case, *King Elementary School Students* vs. *The Ann Arbor, Michigan, School District Board* highlighted the need to recognize children's dialects, and in particular the dialect known as Black English, as an important consideration in children's education (Smitherman, 1985). This court ruled that teachers need to be familiar with the home language, in this case Black English, and to become more sensitive to children's special needs.

We will not be able to explore different dialects in detail here. Nevertheless, there are two facts related to dialects that early childhood educators need to know. First, all language systems, including dialects considered to be nonstandard, are rule-bound and the rules describing both nonstandard and standard dialects are often similar. Rule-bound means that the features of the language can be described. Linguists' rules are *descriptive* rather than *prescriptive.* They do not tell speakers what to do and they do not explain why speakers do what they do; they do allow us to predict what speakers of a given dialect will say under certain conditions. For example, many speakers of dialects considered nonstandard pronounce the word *left* as *lef;* that is, they simplify the word by deleting the final consonant sound of the letter *t* (Bryen, 1982). However, when the word *left* precedes a word beginning with a consonant, as in "She left *T*om all her money," even speakers of dialects considered standard do not pronounce the final consonant sound of the letter *t.*

Second, some features of dialects are more stigmatizing than others (Wolfram, 1970). Listeners use just some features of language to label a speaker's dialect. One such feature of a dialect considered by many to be nonstandard is the absence of the copula (a form of the verb *to be*), as in "He good to me." This feature of the dialect is more likely to be used as a labeling criterion than another feature of the same dialect such as embedding of direct questions as in "I wonder, did the package come."

Why a special need? We not only make subjective judgments about whether speakers have standard or nonstandard speech patterns, but we also make other kinds of judgments based on our assessment of their language. Sometimes people unconsciously think that speakers of a different dialect might not be very intelligent or may have a low social status. Such judgments are especially harmful when teachers make them about children. Children who speak dialects their teachers consider to be nonstandard are more likely to be identified as having cognitive lags, needing language therapy, and needing special remedial reading and writing instruction (Bartoli, 1986). They are more likely to be placed in lower ability groups for instruction and to receive lower achievement scores than their peers. This is an injustice. We must understand why it occurs so that we will not perpetuate it.

There are three reasons why children who speak dialects considered to be nonstandard are more likely to be included in remedial or lower ability groups.

The first reason is related to the unconscious practice of using language patterns to judge the worth of a whole person. Teachers are not exempt from the phenomenon of unconsciously deciding on a person's intellectual capacity by virtue of his or her speech. In one study, teachers rated students' potential for academic success after listening to them answer questions on an audiotape. Half of the students spoke in dialects considered by many teachers to be nonstandard and half spoke in dialects considered to be standard. In spite of the fact that all the children's answers were correct, teachers rated the answers of students with nonstandard dialects lower than the answers of students with standard dialects (Crowl & McGinitie, 1974).

The second reason that students who speak dialects considered to be nonstandard are at risk is that tests that assess reading and writing do not use their dialect. While we know that written English is different from anyone's spoken English dialect, there are degrees of difference. When test questions are phrased in syntax that is greatly different from a speaker's dialect, the speaker is penalized. Dialect difference, and not content knowledge or intelligence, is measured.

The third reason that students who speak dialects considered to be nonstandard are at risk is that teachers may spend more time helping them acquire standard English than they do helping them learn to read and write. Some preschool teachers insist that children speak in complete sentences and use what they consider to be standard language when the children talk about stories or answer questions. Some elementary teachers spend considerable time correcting children's reading "errors," insisting that children read, "He is coming home" instead of "He comin home." Time spent achieving dialect conformity takes away from time spent learning reading and writing. We are not saying that children ought never to be taught a dialect that employers and other powerful people in our society will accept as standard. We are saying that teachers of young children are powerful, too. They ought not to postpone children's literacy learning by first requiring them to learn a new dialect.

Children with Cultural Differences

Children whose cultural background differs from that of middle-class children and teachers are a third group of special-needs children. They not only may have limited English, but they also may have different ways of relating to adults, and in particular, to teachers.

Cultural Ways of Learning and Communicating

Speakers use more than words to communicate. Eyes, body stance, gestures, intonation, and timing communicate conscious as well as unconscious messages. In order to interpret those messages, the listener must be aware of the significance of these factors. Speakers and listeners within one cultural group share these understandings; a speaker from one cultural group and a listener from another cultural group often do not. Therefore, a speaker's message communicated through body stance and eye contact may be misinterpreted. A teacher may think that a child who will not look her in the eye is being disrespectful when in fact the opposite may be true.

Some cultural groups have different ways of helping children learn. In some Native American communities children are expected to learn by observing adults as they perform tasks; this implies that little verbal interaction takes place. Children who expect to learn from watching adults may not learn well in writing centers where teachers expect children to learn by talking with each other as they write. In other communities, children learn cooperatively with other children; the emphasis is on developing a group understanding and performance rather than on individual achievement. Children from these communities may have difficulty in reading groups where teachers expect only one child at a time to answer a question.

Why a special need? All communities have ways of teaching children and ways that children are expected to interact with adults. Teachers, too, have cultural expectations that influence their opinions of children and of how learning occurs. Learning proceeds smoothly when teachers' and children's ways of learning and communicating are similar; learning becomes more difficult when their ways of learning and communicating differ.

STRATEGIES FOR SUPPORTING LITERACY LEARNING

There are two priorities in supporting special-needs children's learning. The first priority of meeting the needs of special children is to provide a classroom environment where children with special needs have a strong sense of self-esteem and where non-special-needs children have positive attitudes toward children with special needs. The second priority is to plan activities and instruction that are particularly effective in the literacy learning of special-needs children.

Building Self-Esteem and Positive Attitudes

Children are naturally curious especially about things that are novel and different. Having a special-needs child in the classroom often means that he or she will be the focus of much curiosity. Aoki, an Asian American, reported a childhood incident that illustrates this point (Aoki, 1981). She remembered when her teacher read the story *The Five Chinese Brothers* (Bishop & Wiese, 1938) to her class. (While this book is often considered a classic, it portrays Asians as stereotyped characters.) As her teacher showed the illustrations, a few children darted quick glances at her. Aoki began to sink down in her chair. She recalled that other children taunted her by pulling their eyes so that they slanted. This incident illustrates several points about helping special-needs children, and all children, to develop more positive attitudes and self-esteem. First, unlike Aoki, children with special needs need to feel welcome and safe in their classrooms, and they need to believe in their own worth and abilities. Second, non-special-needs children need to be sensitive to the feelings of children with special needs. This depends on teachers' creating a safe environment where students and teachers can discuss special needs openly.

Children's literature presents excellent opportunities to introduce children to concepts about special needs (Dobo, 1982; Engel, 1980). Good quality literature provides children opportunities to explore their feelings and satisfy their curiosity about special-needs characters. Characters with special needs offer positive models for children with and without special needs. By relating to these characters, non-special-needs children can learn about what it means to have a special need and about the accomplishments of special-needs people. Special-needs children can discover that they are not alone in facing challenges and that it is possible to have high aspirations and to make important contributions. Figure 12.1 presents a list of children's literature that features special-needs children with developmental and learning differences that can be used to develop more positive attitudes.

Children's literature also offers many opportunities to explore both language differences and cultural heritages with children. There are many literature selections about different cultural groups and heritages that present nonstereotyped characters. As teachers read these selections to children, they can help children explore common heritages, customs, and human qualities. If Aoki's teacher had been sensitive to stereotypical portrayals in children's books, she might have instead shared *Umbrella* (Yashima, 1958). The children would have learned to identify with the little girl in the story. Their teacher could have asked them to describe common experiences.

Children should have many opportunities to explore different cultural experiences and heritages, including their own, through literature. Figure 12.2 presents children's literature that features characters from different cultural heritages.

Figure 12.1 *Children's Literature with Characters That Have Developmental and Learning Differences*

Charlip, R. (1987). *Handtalk birthday: A number and story book in sign language.* New York: Four Winds Press. (hearing impaired)

Clifton, L. (1980). *My friend Jacob.* New York: E. P. Dutton. (mentally retarded)

Cohen, M. (1983). *See you tomorrow, Charles.* New York: Greenwillow Books. (visually impaired)

Geller, N. (1985). *Talk to God . . . I'll get message: Black version.* Lewiston, ME: N. Geller Publications. (hearing impaired)

Hirsch, K. (1977). *My sister.* Minneapolis, MN: Carolrhoda Books. (mentally retarded)

Honeyman, A. (1980). *Sam and his cart.* St. Paul, MN: EMC. (cerebral palsy)

Martin, B., & Archambault, J. (1987). *Knots on a counting rope.* New York: Holt. (visually impaired)

Ominsky, E. (1977). *Jon O, a special boy.* Englewood Cliffs, NJ: Prentice Hall. (Down's Syndrome)

Figure 12.2 *Children's Literature with Characters Having Different Cultural Heritages*

Acadians (commonly referred to as Cajuns)

Amoss, B. (1979). *The loup garou.* Gretna, LA: Pelican.

Edler, T. (1979). *The adventures of Crawfish Man.* Baton Rouge, LA: Little Cajun books.

Fontenot, M. A. (1985). *Clovis Crawfish and his friends.* Gretna, LA: Pelican.

Rice, J. (1977). *Gaston goes to Mardi Gras.* Gretna, LA: Pelican

Afro-Americans

Clifton, L. (1973). *Us come cross the water.* New York: Holt, Rinehart and Winston.

Feelings, T. (1974). *Jambo means hello: Swahili alphabet book.* New York: Dial.

Steptoe, J. (1987). *Mufaro's beautiful daughters.* New York: Lothrop, Lee & Shepard.

Thomas, I. (1973). *Aunt Hattie.* New York: Harper and Row.

Asian Americans

Aruego, J. (1972). *A crocodile's tale.* New York: Scribner's.

Coutant, H. (1974). *First snow.* New York: Knopf. (Vietnamese)

Yashima, T. (1965). *Soo Ling finds a way.* Chicago: Children's Press.

Hispanic Americans

Behrens, J. (1978). *Fiesta.* Chicago: Children's Press.

Bolognese, D. (1970). *A new day.* New York: Delacorte Press.

Galbraith, C. K. (1971). *Victor.* Boston: Little, Brown

Todd, B. K. (1972). *Juan Patricio.* New York: G. P. Putnam and Sons.

Native Americans

Hungry Wolf, A., & Hungry Wolf, B. (1987). *Children of the sun: Stories by and about Indian kids.* New York: Morrow.

Martin, B., & Archambault, J. (1987). *Knots on a counting rope.* New York: Holt.

Toye, W. (1980). *The fire stealer.* New York: Oxford University Press.

Robins, R. (1979). *How the first rainbow was made.* New York: Parnassus Press.

Much children's literature is available in languages other than English. Parents or other community members can serve as guest readers. Schon (1985, pp. 668–670) presents a list of children's literature that is available in Spanish. Some children's literature selections include dialect features. Seeing different dialects in print and hearing a teacher use them when reading a story help to communicate that teachers appreciate language variety (Simms, 1982). Figure 12.3 presents a list of children's literature that includes dialect features.

Figure 12.3 Children's Literature with Dialect Features

Clifton, L. (1975). *My brother fine with me.* New York: Holt, Rinehart, and Winston.

Flournoy, V. (1985). *The patchwork quilt.* New York: Dial.

Greenfield, E. (1974). *She come bringing me that little baby girl.* Philadelphia: Lippincott.

Hamilton, V. (1985). *The people could fly.* New York: Knopf.

Mathis, S. B. (1975). *The hundred penny box.* New York: Puffin.

Mayer, M. (1976). *Liza Lou and the Yeller Belly Swamp.* New York: Four Winds Press.

Techniques for Supporting Children with Developmental or Learning Differences

The early childhood classroom is an especially supportive environment for young children with developmental or learning differences. Here, children select activities that promote growth in all areas and levels of development. Because teachers spend little time in whole-group instruction and more time with small groups and individual children, accommodating instruction for the special-needs child is usually not difficult.

Children with developmental or learning differences in elementary school are placed in regular classrooms when special education teachers feel they can benefit from small-group instruction and activities planned for non-special-needs children. With some adjustments, children with special needs can benefit from small-group instruction along with other children in the regular classroom.

All special-needs children from the age of three who have identified developmental or learning differences will have an individualized educational plan (IEP) developed by a team of specialists and the child's parents. Teachers should ask for a copy of the plan and quickly become familiar with it so they can prepare activities that will help the child achieve the goals outlined in the IEP.

Children with Hearing Impairments

There are approximately 70,000 preschool age children in the United States who have hearing impairments (Andrews & Mason, 1986). Most hearing impaired adults communicate through a manual language called *sign language.* There are several forms of sign language that the hearing impaired use. American Sign Language (ASL) is used by most hearing impaired adults. It differs from English in two ways: not all single ASL signs correspond to single words and the syntax of ASL differs from the syntax of English. An alternative version of ASL, Signed English, uses ASL signs to communicate ideas (words or phrases), but substitutes English syntax. In addition, there are signs called finger spellings that correspond to each letter of the alphabet. The way the hand is shaped for fingerspelling letters is similar to the shape of written English letters.

Not all hearing impairments are alike. Some children may be hard of hearing but capable of using residual hearing; other children may be deaf and seem not to hear any sounds (Carlsen, 1985). Some hearing impaired children learn to communicate with ASL; others are also taught to produce and understand spoken language. Some hearing impaired children use FM (frequency modulation) assistive listening devices (special hearing aids that amplify and clarify sounds). Hearing impaired children who use assistive listening devices may be mainstreamed into regular preschool and elementary school classrooms. In these cases, children expand their oral and written language knowledge through talking, listening, reading, and writing just as other children do. Although the regular classroom teacher will not be expected to communicate through sign language, knowledge of sign language can be extremely valuable in supporting hearing impaired children's language growth.

What are their special needs? Hearing impaired children typically have underdeveloped signed and spoken vocabularies (Conrad, 1979). Similarly, they have less mature syntactic knowledge (Champie, 1981) and may have trouble noting relationships between ideas when those ideas are presented in more than one sentence. Figure 12.4 presents a signed interaction between a teacher and a five-year-old hearing impaired child as they shared the story *The Tale of Fancy Nancy* (Koenig, 1977). The child's attempt to retell the story is included as a part of this interaction. This figure demonstrates that the child has few signs for the ideas presented in the story and also has difficulty understanding the story as a whole.

Children who cannot hear any voice sounds cannot develop concepts about the relation between sounds and letters. They cannot use phonics as a decoding or spelling strategy (see however, Hirsh-Pasek, 1987, for a discussion of using finger spellings). Hearing impaired children who can hear some sounds may still have difficulty sorting similar sounds that are associated with different letters. Other hearing impaired children receive extensive training matching sounds and letters as part of their speech instruction (Carlsen, 1985). Teachers must be aware of how well children can hear speech sounds or how well they are able to use place of articulation or vibrations as a method of detecting differences in sounds.

Effective literacy techniques. Preschool teachers will need to plan activities that expand concepts. As hearing impaired children learn new concepts, they will also learn the words (spoken or signed) that label those concepts. Hearing impaired children may not know the vocabulary words for familiar everyday objects and activities that hearing children learn incidentally by hearing language in their everyday experiences. Teachers will need to be explicit about naming objects and activities, and to help hearing impaired children use these words as they participate in experiences. We recommend focusing on concepts and vocabulary words in categories as part of meaningful activities. For example, children can learn names of vegetables, meats, and fruits as a part of a food unit that involves using a class grocery store, cooking foods from different food groups, writing or dictating books about favorite foods, and making a class ABC chart with coupons.

Reading stories aloud (or signing stories) and discussing or commenting on

Figure 12.4 ***Hearing Impaired Child Shares and Retells*** The Tale
of Fancy Nancy *(Koenig, 1977) in Sign Language*

Illustrations: Fancy Nancy (a mouse in a fancy dress) standing beside a series of animals
dressed in suits.

Text: Consists of conversations between Fancy Nancy and a series of male animals who
ask Nancy to marry them. Nancy asks each of her suitors to sing. After listening to each
of them sing, she replies, "OH MY," . . . "I CAN'T MARRY YOU. YOUR VOICE IS TOO
LOUD."

Teacher (signs): What animal do you see?

Child (signs): Sheep

Teacher: (pointing to ram) Will you marry me? (pointing to Nancy) Can you sing?
(pointing to ram) Yes, baa, baa. (pointing to Nancy) No, I will not marry
you. Your voice is too loud.

Teacher: Who is this?

Child: chicken

Teacher: Then a rooster came. (pointing to rooster) Will you marry me? (pointing
to Nancy) Can you sing? (pointing to rooster) Yes, crow crow. (pointing
to Nancy) No, I will not marry you. Your voice is too loud.

Teacher: Who is this?

Child: frog

Teacher: Then a frog came. What do you think the frog said?

Child: don't know

Teacher: (pointing to frog) Will you marry? (pointing to Nancy) Nancy said can
you (paused, looked at child)

Child: sing

Teacher: The frog croaked. Nancy said, No, I will not marry you your voice is
too loud. A mouse came. What do you think the mouse said?

Child: marry

Teacher: What did Nancy say?

Child: sing

Teacher: Nancy said, No, I will not marry you. Your voice is too loud. Who came?

Child: cat

Teacher: What did the cat say?

Child: marry

Teacher: Yes, will you marry me? What did Nancy say?

Child: sing

Teacher: Yes, can you sing? (Nancy agrees to marry the cat)

Teacher: Now you tell the story.

Child: (turns to front of book) mouse (turns page), sheep (turns page), chicken
(turns page), frog marry, can marry, too loud

the story events are effective both for vocabulary development and for helping children relate story ideas to a whole (Manson, 1982). Children's literature provides a rich store of vocabulary. The illustrations provide opportunities to build new meanings of words. Reading the story aloud (or signing) surrounds children with models of English syntax, and discussion and comments provide clues to understanding that syntax. The story unit presented in Chapter 6 could be used to help hearing impaired children learn about story structure.

When beginning more formal reading instruction, books that have closely related pictures and text are especially helpful to hearing impaired children. Little books (see Chapter 8) that have only a few words of predictable text on each page may be especially useful. Teachers report that young children learn many sight vocabulary words from these books as they read them again and again. Having hearing impaired children write their own little books can help them develop a store of known words for writing.

Children with Visual Impairments

Approximately one in every one thousand school-age children is visually impaired (School, 1987). There are two categories of visual impairment: low vision and blindness (Ward & McCormick, 1981). Children with low vision have some sight, although it is limited. Blind children have no useful vision. (They may be able to see differences in light and dark.) Low-vision children may be able to learn through visual experiences, whereas blind children must rely on tactile, auditory, and other sensory experiences for learning. Low-vision children will most likely use reading materials printed in large type and will learn to write as sighted children do. Blind children will use braille reading materials and will learn to use a brailler (a machine like a typewriter) to write. Both large type and braille versions of many basal reading series are available from the American Printing House for the Blind (see Ward & McCormick, 1981).

Braille is an alphabetic writing system that is very similar to the printed English writing system. It consists of characters created by a series of raised dots that the visually impaired read by feeling across the page from left to right. Just as in printed English, braille includes one character representing each letter of the alphabet. Since braille characters are larger than print letters, reading braille can be slow and tedious. A system was devised that uses single letter characters or a combination of a few letter characters to represent whole words; these abbreviated words are called *signs*. The only difference between learning to read and write Braille and learning to read and write print is that visually impaired children must also learn these signs.

What are their special needs?   Low-vision and blind children may have limited background experiences and concepts. An important avenue for all children's learning is active exploration of their environment, including feeling, tasting, and looking. Overprotective parents may not allow visually impaired babies to crawl and explore as they would sighted babies. Toddlers and preschoolers also learn through incidental visual exploration such as looking around the room and accompanying oral explanation. Low-vision and especially blind preschoolers cannot use such visual explorations for learning, but rather must rely on tactile explorations with auditory explanations. It is easy to imagine all of the knowledge that visually impaired youngsters may miss. Therefore, visually impaired children may have fewer concepts and their concepts may be distorted by inadequate information.

Visually impaired children also do not have as many opportunities as sighted children to interact with the print (braille) they will later learn to read and write. Many parents of visually impaired children are likely to read to their children from printed books rather than from braille books. Therefore, visually impaired children will not feel braille while hearing the story text as sighted children see print while hearing the story. Visually impaired children do not have experiences with reading environmental print. Consequently, visually impaired children are likely to have fewer concepts about written language and the relation between written and oral forms of language.

Effective literacy techniques.   Teachers need to plan activities that include a tactile component for visually impaired children. For all children it is important to accompany activities with a rich verbal interaction, and this is particularly important for the visually impaired. For example, Ward and McCormick (1981) describe an effective technique for visiting a farm. They suggest the visually impaired child should be guided in feeling all over animals in a systematic way. All during the time the child is feeling an animal, the teacher is describing the animal. The child should be encouraged to describe what is felt and to compare the animal with other animals.

Most activities designed to help sighted preschoolers to develop concepts about written language may be adapted for visually impaired children (McGee & Tompkins, 1982). For visually impaired children who will learn to read and write braille, brailled words and letters can accompany printed words and letters (a special teacher or community volunteer can produce these materials). For low-vision children who will learn to read and write with large type, words and letters can be printed in unusually large sizes. Dramatic-play-with-print-kits can include large-type and braille materials such as a braille menu. Braille or large-print dictations can be placed on visually impaired children's art. A brailler should be placed in the writing center. Low-vision children should be given felt tip markers in dark colors so their writing will be more obvious (School, 1987). Special interlined books with print between lines of braille (available from the Howe Press of Perkins School for the Blind, Watertown, Massachusetts 02172) can be used to read stories aloud with visually impaired children. The lap method works best—the child sits on the reader's lap and feels the page as it is read. Tactile books are especially effective for the visually impaired. Teachers and children can make tactile books using textured materials, cut-out shapes, and other objects for children to feel as they share the story (McGee, 1985).

Mentally Retarded and Noncategorical Special-Needs Children

Children whose general intellectual abilities and adaptive behaviors lag significantly behind their peers' abilities include preschoolers with noncategorical special needs and mentally retarded elementary children. These children operate cognitively and socially at earlier developmental stages than other children their age. They may also have deficits in adaptive skills, such as self-care, independence, and social responsibility with their peers.

What are their special needs?   Preschoolers with noncategorical special needs and mentally retarded children experience more difficulty with social interaction among children their own age (Burstein, 1986). In groups, particularly in preschools, these children are likely to have difficulty attending to tasks and they spend more time off-task than their peers. Many educators believe that mentally retarded children have difficulty making generalizations.

These three characteristics (fewer social skills, more difficulty staying on task in group situations, and more difficulty making generalizations) have implications for the kinds of activities teachers should plan, as well as the kinds of knowledge that need to be stressed in literacy learning programs. First, we believe that literacy is learned, in a large part, through interactions with others, including other children; therefore, children with noncategorical special needs and mentally retarded youngsters need special help in developing skills for interacting with other children. Second, teachers should present learning opportunities in groups of no more than three or four children. Finally, teachers will need to plan activities and instruction that make explicit how abilities learned in one situation can be applied in other situations.

Effective literacy techniques.   One of the most effective techniques for supporting the literacy learning of children with developmental delays is to provide instruction that is compatible with the child's developmental level, rather than his or her age. A second effective technique is to provide social experiences that involve interacting with other children on similar social developmental levels, rather than with children of similar ages. Many of the techniques we have described for younger novice readers and writers or experimenters with reading and writing are appropriate for older children with developmental delays.

Dramatic-play-with-print centers are effective learning tools for children with developmental delays through the elementary school years. Environmental print reading is also especially effective in helping children with developmental delays learn about written language and reading. Teaching children how to write the names of their friends and family members is another meaningful literacy activity. Both environmental print reading and name writing activities provide opportunities for teachers to help children with these special needs transfer knowledge from one situation to another. As children learn to write the names of many of their special friends and family members, the teacher can point out the names of letters that are found in more than one name. Teachers need to explain how learning to write the letter *B* in Brandi is also like writing the letter *B* in Brad. When children read a Raisin Bran cereal box, the teacher should explain again the connections between the letters found in Brandi, Brad, and Bran.

More formal techniques for teaching children with developmental delays to read and write are similar to techniques that support all children's learning to read and write (Dixon, 1987; Sindelar, 1987). Special educators suggest that if children are to become effective readers, they need to read whole texts (not isolated words); however, children with developmental delays may need more practice and may take a longer time than other children. There are several ways that teachers can help children read whole texts and give them the extra practice that they need to become good readers. Teachers can read stories first as children follow the text. The method of repeated reading provides practice with whole texts (Dowhower, 1989; O'Shea & O'Shea, 1987). In this method children repeatedly read stories (or parts of stories) that are about fifty or one hundred words in length until they can read the selection with only three to six errors. Children begin the repeated readings only when they understand the story.

Learning Disabled Children

Learning disabled children show severe and specific learning difficulties related to language, math, or reasoning. Although these children may be identified in preschool, most are identified when they reach elementary school. They usually are in regular classrooms for some or much of the school day.

What are their special needs?   There are many diagnostic labels and criteria that have been used with learning disabled children (Lerner, 1985). Many characteristics have been associated with learning disabled youngsters. (See McGill-Franzen, 1987, for a discussion about the consequences for literacy instruction of identifying children as learning disabled.) Many of the characteristics associated with learning disabled children are also characteristics of children with other special needs. Children with learning disabilities may have difficulty either starting tasks or completing tasks; they may have difficulty paying attention and understanding directions; they may be easily distracted and are more often off-task than their peers (Lerner, 1985); and they may be more passive learners who do not make inferences suggested by language cues (Ackerman, Anhalt, & Dykman, 1986).

Because of the tendency of many learning disabled children to be easily distracted from completing tasks, teachers have been encouraged to break tasks into smaller or easier-to-complete components and to use tasks that are highly structured. One activity that might seem to make learning to write letters easier is to have children copy only three letters several times. Although learning disabled children might learn to form the three letters from this activity, they will not learn how letters operate within the written language system, which is much more important than merely learning to form a few letters. We recommend that teachers rarely use drill on isolated written language tasks with any child, and especially with children who may have trouble figuring out the complexities of reading and writing.

Effective literacy techniques.   Few learning disabled children are identified in their preschool years. Learning disabled youngsters in elementary school need help in monitoring their own learning behaviors. They need to learn what "paying attention" or "completing a task" and "not paying attention" and "not completing a task" mean in terms of explicit behaviors and products. Teachers can demonstrate what these terms mean by role playing.

Extensive pre-writing activities may be particularly important for structuring writing experiences for the learning disabled child (Tompkins & Friend, 1986). As the children brainstorm ideas, teachers can record their ideas on a chart. Then the teacher can help the children to cluster their ideas into groups. Teachers can demonstrate how to use the cluster by writing a group-collaborated composition that in turn may also be used in reading instruction.

There are many ways that teachers can help children become more actively involved in reading and writing. One way children are active during reading is by making predictions about what they are going to read and drawing conclusions about what they have already read (Norris, 1988). Hoskisson and Tompkins (1987) suggest that pattern books are effective for supporting active reading and writing of learning disabled children. These books have predictable sequences that make it easier for children to draw inferences as they predict what will happen next. Children can easily use the prediction cycle described in Chapter 6.

Emotionally Disabled Children

Children with emotional disabilities are significantly more aggressive or withdrawn than their peers. They may act out their emotions in unacceptable ways or they may not respond at all.

What are their special needs?   Emotionally disabled children need help in learning to express their emotions and to control their expressive behavior. D'Alessandro, a teacher of these children, noted that "Inner turmoil, confusion, anger, and self-hatred make it impossible for them (emotionally disabled children in her classroom) to take control of their actions" (D'Alessandro, 1987, p. 516). Because they are likely to act out or to become withdrawn, these children may be isolated from learning opportunities and have lower achievement levels. They need support in developing more positive images of themselves as persons and learners.

Effective literacy techniques.   The writing process is an effective approach in helping emotionally disabled children successfully communicate their feelings (D'Alessandro, 1987). Daily writing encourages children by implying that they have something meaningful to communicate. A process approach to writing deemphasizes spelling and mechanics, which can be significant stumbling blocks for emotionally disabled children. By focusing on ideas, the writing process supports these children's self-esteem. Emotionally disabled children need to learn that the teacher will help only when asked. This freedom from pressure to "get it right" also supports their need for success. During revision, teachers need to be especially careful because too much revision can frustrate the child into discarding a good composition. The most effective motivation for revision occurs when children discover they have difficulty reading their own compositions as they present their work in the Author's Chair (D'Alessandro, 1987).

Gifted Children

A few gifted children develop certain abilities such as reading, writing, or playing musical instruments at faster rates than their peers. These children may be included in both preschool and elementary classrooms.

What are their special needs?   Gifted children have learning abilities that are associated with much older youngsters. They explore subjects of their own interest to the exclusion of other activities; they sustain interest and attention for long spans of time. Gifted children make inferences easily, and they detect commonalities and connections among events and make generalizations quickly; therefore, they often use abstract and complicated ideas (Gallager, 1986; Maker, 1986). Gifted children need opportunities that will allow them to sustain study on topics of their choice, to proceed to more abstract levels of thinking, and to discover complex principles related to their topics of interest.

Effective literacy techniques.   Literacy is used as a tool for the learning of all children, but gifted children are able to use literacy as a learning tool earlier than other children. They need less formal instruction in literacy abilities and more experiences *using* literacy in content study. Maker (1986) suggests that topics of study for gifted preschoolers should include abstract and general principles that are taught using concrete material and factual information. Children should learn not only the ideas, facts, and generalizations related to a topic, but also about the people recognized as significant to an area of knowledge, the methods of inquiry used to develop information in an area of knowledge, and the attitudes and values associated with the area (Maker, 1986). Reasoning and discovery should be the primary methods of learning, rather than telling or showing.

Inquiry reading (Cassidy, 1981) is an effective method for helping gifted children in elementary school to research and present a topic of interest. Inquiry reading has three requirements: children investigate self-generated questions, they sustain their inquiry and study activities over approximately four weeks, and they produce some product or report that will communicate the results of their inquiry to others. Teachers help children formulate questions, identify sources of information (especially human resources), master methods of notetaking and interviewing, and construct or prepare their products for display and discussion. Gifted children enjoy making movable books (Abrahamson & Stewart, 1982) or films (Cox, 1983) as unusual methods of sharing their inquiry (Hoskisson & Tompkins, 1987). Making video tapes is another method of sharing information either through making documentaries or producing child-authored fiction (McGee & Ratliff, 1987). Of course, these activities should not be restricted to only gifted children; all children enjoy these activities.

Techniques for Supporting Children with Language Differences

Language-different learners include limited-English-proficiency children and children who speak with dialects perceived as nonstandard. The following section describes techniques for supporting both the oral language and literacy learning of these children.

Children with Limited English Proficiency

Children whose home language is not English may speak English fluently, a little, or not at all. When they come to preschool or elementary school, it may be the first time they are expected to speak English, or they may have had many opportunities to speak English prior to their school experiences. One of the first concerns that teachers voice is how to teach children, especially children who speak no English, to speak and to understand English.

Techniques for teaching children to speak English.   In preschool as well as in elementary school, the easiest way to learn to speak English is to participate in meaningful activities (Genishi & Dyson, 1984). The structure provided by familiar objects and activities supports children's language learning. To be effective, the objects must be real and the children must use them in real activities. Just as many toddlers first learn familiar phrases or words associated with repeated activities (called "routines"), so do limited-English-proficiency children first learn familiar phrases and words in English (Urzua, 1980). Many toddlers learn to say "Night night," "go to sleep," and "read books" because these routine phrases are repeated daily as they participate in the activity of getting ready for bed. Preschool limited-English-proficiency children can learn the same phrases as they interact with their teacher and other children in their play with dolls, blankets, beds, and books in the housekeeping center. Many dramatic play activities such as grocery shopping, visiting the dentist, and taking a trip to McDonald's provide rich language-learning experiences. Teachers can join in play and provide models of language. At first many limited-English-proficiency children will be silent in their play as they internalize the sounds of English and discover the actions of routines. They may switch between using English and using their home language (this should not be forbidden—Lara, 1989).

Even in elementary school props and dramatic play can be used as a bridge to English. All children enjoy a pretend trip to McDonald's that includes props such as bags, hamburger containers, drink cups, and hats for the employees. As part of the McDonald's play, children will learn the English words *hamburgers, French fries, Coke, milk, ketchup, salt,* and *money.* They might learn routine phrases such as "Welcome to McDonald's," "May I take your order please?" "I'd like a hamburger," or "Give me a coke." Pictures of familiar activities can also be used to increase limited-English-proficiency children's oral language proficiency (Moustafa & Penrose, 1985).

In elementary school, teachers need to be certain that limited-English-proficiency children learn the names of objects in the classroom and phrases that will be used frequently (Bulos, 1982; Rodrigues & White, 1981). They need to understand and say the words *paper, pencil, crayon,* and *color* as well as the phrases *sit down, line up,* and *come here.* Concept picture books are useful in helping elementary children learn the names of objects and activities as well as for learning specific syntactic English forms (see Moustafa, 1980, for a list of concept books for limited-English-proficiency children). As children learn the names of common objects and actions and become familiar with many routine phrases, teachers can then help them begin to master the complex syntax of English. Pattern books can be used to introduce many syntactic forms of English. Limited-English-proficiency children can practice their oral language skills as they tell stories to accompany wordless picture books. Older children can use wordless picture books as part of content study (Flatley & Rutland, 1986).

Techniques for teaching reading and writing in English.

All children begin learning about reading and writing when they are surrounded by meaningful written language. Written English becomes meaningful to limited-English-proficiency children when spoken English is meaningful. The spoken English word *McDonald's* takes on meaning when children are familiar with eating hamburgers and French fries at McDonald's. The written English word *McDonald's* takes on meaning when children are familiar with the spoken English word *McDonald's.* The experiences and activities that we have described for young novice readers and writers and experimenters with written language are useful for limited-English-proficiency preschoolers. They will benefit from using dramatic-play-kits-with-print, listening and talking about stories, dictating, writing, and reading environmental print as they learn about spoken English.

The more formal reading and writing instruction of limited-English-proficiency children in elementary school should be tied to their oral language experiences. Dialogues that emerge from activities such as the pretend trip to McDonald's provide material for reading and writing (Feeley, 1983). After participating in dramatic play about a visit to McDonald's, children can learn to read and write many words found on the environmental print at McDonald's and associated with going to a McDonald's restaurant, such as *McDonald's, restrooms, men, women,* and *push* (Hudelson & Barrera, 1985). The teacher can prepare a story about the children's activities incorporating English words and phrases used as part of the McDonald's play experience. Children can also dictate or write about their experiences (Moustafa & Penrose, 1985). Photos of the children taken during the activity provide useful supports for reading these stories or writing about the experience (Sinatra, 1981). These language stories can be used to help children develop sight words or practice decoding skills as described in Chapters 10 and 11. Figure 12.5 presents a story dictated by a limited-English-proficiency student in second grade after he made Play Doh.

In addition to language experience materials, limited-English-proficiency children need frequent and early experiences with children's literature both to read and as a support for their writing (Hough, Nurss, & Enright, 1986). Pattern books are particularly effective as first reading materials for all children, including limited-English-proficiency children. Chapter 8 describes how pattern books can be used to encourage children's reading and writing. Wordless picture books are also useful to stimulate dictation and writing.

Allen (1986) described a thematic approach to literacy and language learning for limited-English-proficiency children that begins with a literary experience. Such an experience would begin by sharing a favorite story with children. The best stories have strong illustrations which support meaning making and have repetitive language. The story is read and reread and followed by many extending activities. Such an experience might begin by reading and rereading *Strega Nona* (De Paola, 1975). Then the teacher might share other books containing magic objects [such as Galdone's *The Magic Porridge Pot* (1976)]. The children might discuss the magical possibilities of "magic objects" such as a crystal paper weight or a feathered hat, examine different kinds of pasta (such as rotelle, fettuccini, rigatoni), make spaghetti from a recipe, and invite guests to a class spaghetti luncheon (Allen, 1986, pp. 62–63). These activities include many hands-on activities that bring meaning to language (Moll, 1988) and provide a springboard for children's reading and writing.

Using a class or school postal system may be one way to encourage and support all learners, including limited-English-proficiency learners, in their literacy growth. Children can help make mailboxes and establish a routine for delivering and receiving mail. Teachers can encourage children to write to them, to each other, to school personnel, and to famous people (including favorite children's authors). Writing letters and notes can become part of free time activities or it

Figure 12.5 Limited-English-Proficiency Child's Dictation

Lim Makes Play Doh

I can use two cup flour.
I put one cup salt.
I am mix with spoon.
I am measure with water and flour.
I put spice in bucket.
I put two tablespoon oil in bucket.
We put color in bucket.

can become part of more formal reading and writing lessons. Teachers who have used this system have found that limited-English-proficiency children begin writing in their home language. This practice should be encouraged as a way for children to continue their literacy growth in their home language. Teachers in areas where a majority of children come from families whose first language is not English will welcome this opportunity to demonstrate the value of being literate not only in English, but also in other languages. This cross cultural literacy can be reinforced by including materials written in languages other than English in the classroom, sending notes home to parents in both the language of the home and in English, and posting signs and labels in both the predominant language and English, (Ortiz & Engelbrecht (1986).

Gradually, non-English speaking children begin to write their notes and letters in English to communicate with children who write in English (Greene, 1985). Limited-English-proficiency children may find letter and note writing especially motivating because the emphasis is placed on communicating meaning to friends, rather than on correct conventions. Writing may be a particularly meaningful bridge to literacy in English (Urzua, 1987).

Children with Dialects Considered to be Nonstandard

One of the most hotly debated topics in language education is whether, how, and when children should be taught to speak what is considered standard English. Because language is so closely interwoven with a person's sense of identity and self-worth, using language in a different way can be threatening. However, it is hard to counter the argument that people who speak so-called standard English have more access to educational and economic opportunities.

Teaching children to speak English that is considered standard in their region. Most experts agree that preschoolers should be encouraged to communicate, whether their language is perceived as standard or as nonstandard (Genishi & Dyson, 1984). Teachers need to be more concerned with what children have to say than with how they say it. The practice of requiring children to speak in complete sentences or to "say it right" is not recommended. As all children get older and as they hear a greater variety of language models, they naturally begin to include in their speech more forms considered standard by most people in their region (Padak, 1981). Reading aloud to young children provides a model of written English, which is actually different from any spoken dialect, yet is often the standard against which people compare their so-called standard dialects.

Children in elementary school should have opportunities to use language in many different situations. Role playing activities can provide children with opportunities to try out more formal speech. For example, they may practice interviewing a community leader, a minister, and a senior citizen as preparation for data gathering in a social studies unit. As children role play each of these persons in practice for their actual interviews, they will explore the more formal speech used by these persons. Children in elementary school are capable of discussing how different kinds of language are appropriate in different situations.

Children's literature continues to provide rich models for language growth. Children enjoy hearing and saying many kinds of language found in literature. There are many fine examples of literature in which a dialect considered to be nonstandard contributes to the authenticity and enjoyment of the story (see Figure 12.3). These selections can be used to demonstrate the variety and richness of language. As children explore language variety through literature, they can also explore language that most consider to be standard (Cullinan, Jaggar, & Strickland, 1974). Children naturally use the language of literature as they retell stories, role play story actions, and write stories of their own.

Teaching reading and writing.   No special techniques are necessary to introduce written language to preschoolers who speak with a dialect considered to be nonstandard. All children, whether in preschool or in elementary school, learn about reading and writing when written language is presented in meaningful activities.

In more formal reading and writing programs in the elementary school, teachers need to be knowledgeable of how children's dialects are reflected in their reading and writing. We will give two examples of how dialect is reflected in reading and writing. First, because reading and writing are language activities, children's language will influence how they read aloud and write. Children who speak with a dialect considered to be nonstandard will use that language as they read aloud—they may translate the text into their own speech patterns. Similarly, they may use their language as a basis for writing—what children write may reflect their oral language patterns. Teachers of children who speak with a dialect considered to be nonstandard should recognize when children translate text into their own oral language patterns. Table 12.1 presents a list of contrasts between text language and spoken language of children whose dialects are considered nonstandard. As children read the *text,* they may translate it into their spoken language. These translations from text language to spoken language are expected based on what we know about dialects considered to be nonstandard (Bryen, 1982). Teachers who are sensitive to children's language will recognize dialect translations as positive indications that children comprehend as they read.

Our second example of how dialect is reflected in reading and writing involves homonyms, words that sound alike. Because dialects involve differences in pronunciation of sounds, many word pairs are homonyms in one dialect, but not in another (Barnitz, 1980). Teachers should be aware of these differences. For example, in many dialects considered to be standard, the words *pear* and *pair* are pronounced the same (homonyms), although they have different meanings. On the other hand, in many dialects considered to be nonstandard, the words *toll* and *told* are homonyms because they are pronounced the same (Barnitz, 1980). Not surprisingly, the use of the homonyms *toll* and *told* in phonics lessons and in spelling lessons is confusing when teachers and students do not

Table 12.1 *Language Contrasts: Text Language and Spoken Forms of Dialects Considered Nonstandard*

Text:	Child Reads[1]	Language Feature[2]
The boy took two *pennies.*	The boy took two *penny.*	Plural marker (*s*) deleted
His *feet* got wet.	His *feets* got wet.	Plural marker (*s*) on irregular nouns inserted
The *girl's* coat was red.	The *girl* coat was red.	Possessive marker (*'s*) deleted
She *jumps* high.	She *jump* high.	Third person singular verb marker (*s*) deleted
The man *hopped* over the fence.	The man *hop* over the fence.	Past tense verb marker (*ed*) deleted
I'll see you soon.	*I* see you soon.	Auxiliary verb in contraction deleted
Mary *is* coming, too. (Mary's coming, too)	*Mary* coming, too.	*Is, are* deleted
He did nothing.	He didn't do nothing.	Multiple negation
Who do you think will win?	Who you think will win?	Auxiliary verb deleted in wh-question
He *is* coming home.	He *be* coming home.	Invariant *be* inserted

[1]These are *possible* spoken forms that speakers who have dialects considered to be nonstandard *might* use to read text. Younger children are more likely to use these spoken forms than older children.

[2]These language features are used as contrasts between spoken forms of dialects that are often considered standard versus nonstandard.

have the same perceptions of which words are homonyms. Figure 12.6 presents a list of words that might be homonyms for speakers of a dialect considered to be nonstandard.

One activity that will help elementary children spell homonyms is to help them make a class collaboration book of "Words That Sound Alike." Children could suggest words that they think sound alike and then illustrate the pages. Figure 12.7 presents a page from a nine-year-old's "Words That Sound Alike" book. Although this child's work is remarkable both for its illustrations and word choice (*four* sounds like *foe*), it still shows that children are valuable resources for literacy learning activities.

Teachers need to be careful, however, not to assume that all nonstandard dialects are alike. Not all children's dialects are the same, even when they live in the same neighborhood. Teachers who are familiar with their children's

Figure 12.6 *Possible Homonym Pairs in Dialects Considered Nonstandard*

1. cad	cab		8. poke	pork
2. cat	cap		9. sheath	sheaf
3. hole	hold		10. told	toe
4. leg	led		11. toll	told
5. let	lick		12. web	wed
6. pass	past		13. wreath	reef
7. pat	pack			

Suggested by Barnitz, J. G. (1980), Black English and other dialects: Sociolinguistic implications for reading instruction. *The Reading Teacher, 33,* 779–786; and by Geissal, M. A., & Knafle, J. D. (1977), A linguistic view of auditory discrimination tests and exercises. *The Reading Teacher, 30,* 134–141.

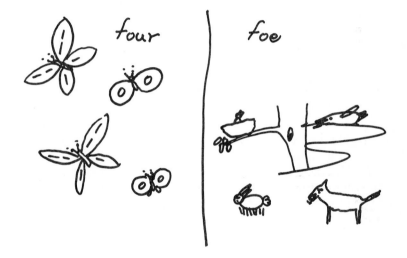

Figure 12.7 Four *and* Foe *from a "Words That Sound Alike" Book*

speech are best able to make instructional decisions such as whether to teach children to notice "sound alike" words.

Children's dialects are also reflected in what and how they write. Figure 12.8 presents a story written by a boy whose dialect is considered nonstandard by many (Meier & Cazden, 1982, p. 507). Even when we are sensitive to Darryl's dialect, we know that he has several problems with writing. His story lacks the details that make writing vivid, although it is certainly startling. He has many misspelled words (over a fourth of the text) and most of the sentences are ineffective. Although teachers do not need to know a great deal about dialects to see Darryl's weaknesses, they may need this knowledge to see his strengths (Meier & Cazden, 1982). For example, Darryl's use of *in* for both the words *in* and *and*

Figure 12.8 Darryl's Story: The Spooky Halloween Night

The Spooky Halloween Night

One there was a mummy named Eddie Mcdevitt he was so dume at he dump his head in the can in then he chod his head off and then he went and to his house and then he went outside and chod his arm off in then the cops came and chase him away and then he tuck some lade and kidl here in then she came alive and chod his bode off and then his spirt comed in kill everybody.

From "Research Update: A Focus on Oral Language and Writing from a Multicultural Perspective" by T. R. Meier and C. Cazden, 1982, *Language Arts, 59,* p. 507. Copyright © 1982 by the National Council of Teachers of English. Reprinted with permission.

may reflect that he says the word *and* like he says the word *in*. Similarly, the deletion of the letters *ed* on some of his past tense verbs reflects that the pronunciation rules of his dialect include simplification of past tense verbs (that is, dropping the pronunciation of the final sounds /t/ or /d/).

There are many more important strengths to this story that reflect both what all children learn, and specifically, what Darryl is learning about good stories. His story has a beginning, complications, and an ending all centered on a single character, Eddie Mcdevitt. Darryl's story also contains features of a "trickster tale" (Smitherman, 1977). This is a special kind of story told by Black Americans that usually involves a black male who triumphs over adversaries through cunning and unusual feats (Meier & Cazden, 1982). Although he lacks a head or a body, Eddie lives on at the end of the tale. Teachers who are sensitive to children's language recognize what children bring to writing and are in a better position to build on children's strengths. Writing may be the most effective way to help children gain control over language considered to be standard.

Dialects and dictation.

Although many teachers are sensitive to their children's language and they view *oral* language diversity as valid, they wonder what to do when writing down children's dictations. Should teachers translate children's speech into standard text or should they write what children say? Figures 12.9 and 12.10 present a kindergartner's dictated story and a first grader's dictated retelling of *There's Something in my Attic* (Mayer, 1988). These child-authored texts include some language many consider to be nonstandard. Many teachers are concerned that parents will object to such a text since it is not regarded as standard English. They wonder if children's reading of such texts will somehow be harmful.

There are at least three arguments for writing what children dictate, although words should be spelled conventionally and not as children pronounce them (Jaggar, 1974). First, the main reason for writing down children's dictations, such as stories about their art work, is so children can realize that what they say is what is written. Children whose dictations are not written as they are dictated may not discover this concept. Second, one of their most valuable reading strategies is children's understanding of what language is like. Therefore,

Figure 12.9 *Natasha's Story*

They was hiding eggs in the grass.
When they went to bed the Easter Bunny come.

Figure 12.10 *Latosha's Retelling*

There was a little girl.
She had a dream about a ghost.
She got off the bed and her dad put her back in the bed.
He say, "Go to sleep."
She got off her bed and went upstairs to her attic.
The little girl tooks a rope and catch the ghost.

teachers will want to write what children say in dictations so that children can use this strategy as a method of reading. Finally, writing what a child says demonstrates acceptance of the child; it suggests that teachers find children's ideas important and they recognize the validity of children's expressions.

One method of helping children build bridges from the oral language patterns they use in dictations to the written language patterns found in texts is to use more than one language story for some dictation experiences (Gillet & Gentry, 1983). In some dictation exercises, the teacher might prepare an experience story that is similar to the children's dictated story, but it will be in language considered to be standard. Figure 12.11 presents a language story dictated by six-year-olds that includes some language considered to be nonstandard. Figure 12.11 also presents a story written by their teacher. This story includes many of the same words used in the children's dictation. The teacher and children read and reread both stories many times. Although the teacher might have drawn attention to the differences between the two stories and used the teacher-authored story to begin teaching some written language English forms, we believe six-year-olds may be too young to benefit from such instruction. Teachers need to use this technique with care so that the children's stories are as valued as their teacher's stories.

Figure 12.11 *"The Holiday Memory Book"*

Children's Dictated Story

The Christmas Tree and Hanukkah Candles

We put seven ball on the Christmas tree.
We puts some lights on the Christmas tree.
We put a lot of candy cane on the Christmas tree.
We lighted candles for Hanukkah.

Teacher's Story

Holiday Celebrations

We celebrated Christmas and Hanukkah. We decorated a Christmas tree. First, we put lights on the tree. Then we put balls and candy canes on the tree. Last, we lit Hanukkah candles. We enjoyed our celebration of Christmas and Hanukkah.

Techniques for Supporting Children with Cultural Differences

How we understand events and people is influenced by how others in our cultural group interpret such events and people. As a result of increased interest in ethnic backgrounds, most preschools and elementary schools make provisions for celebrating and learning about different cultures in multicultural programs (Charlesworth, 1987).

Children's learning is an important part of every society. Every cultural group has beliefs about how children should behave and learn. Teachers who are knowledgeable about the ways the children in their classrooms learn best are better able to support their children's literacy learning. One way that teachers can learn more about the children in their classroom is to visit the children's neighborhood, attend neighborhood celebrations, and meet community leaders.

Children's culturally acquired ways of learning and participating in language activities can either support or interfere with school learning. Many children have more difficulties learning because the ways they behave in learning situations are different from the ways that teachers expect them to act (Ogbu, 1985).

Two Examples of Culturally Compatible Instruction

Following are two examples of how teachers developed instructional strategies that were compatible with the learning styles of their children and at the same time helped their children learn to operate more successfully with the learning styles usually associated with schools. This kind of instruction is called *culturally compatible*. The first example of instruction is from Au and Kawakami's (1985) description of the Kamehameha Early Education Project (KEEP), and the second is from Heath's (1982) description of a project examining children's questions and talk conducted in schools in a southeastern city.

KEEP: The talk story lesson.   Teachers in a special school in Honolulu for children of Polynesian-Hawaiian ancestry studied carefully the kinds of interactions or talk used by Hawaiian children. They researched talk in the community and talk in the classroom. These teachers discovered that their Hawaiian children engaged in interactions resembling "talk stories." In talk stories many speakers participate together, jointly speaking—often at the same time—to create a narrative. There are few times in a talk story when only one child is speaking at a time. Leaders in talk stories are skillful in involving other children, rather than in carrying the conversation alone. This way of interaction is not compatible with interaction that teachers traditionally expect during reading instruction.

Once teachers recognized that children who "spoke out" during reading group time were not being disruptive, they began to consider ways of using this type of interaction to foster reading growth. They decided that they would plan the questions they asked, but allow children freedom in the way they answered questions. They allowed more than one child to respond at a time. The teachers tape recorded reading lessons to examine whether allowing children to talk in what seemed to be a disruptive manner helped children to learn better. They found that 80 percent of the children's responses in "talk story" reading lessons focused on the story. In contrast, only 43 percent of the children's responses in a traditional lesson focused on the story (Au & Kawakami, 1985).

Questioning at school.   An important way that children learn and demonstrate their learning is by answering questions. As teachers, we assume that the kinds of questions we ask make sense to children. Heath (1982) discovered that children from different communities in nearby towns and cities in the southeast were exposed to different kinds of questions from their earliest language experiences. In one community, the kinds of questions toddlers and preschoolers were familiar with were not the kinds of questions that were later used by their teachers. In another community, toddlers and preschoolers were exposed to questions much like those their teachers would use later in elementary school. When children from these two different communities began attending elementary school together, differences in their achievement were noted. When faced with unfamiliar school-like questions, some children seemed unable to learn and were considered less able than other children.

Teachers in these schools were concerned with helping their children achieve success. They worked closely with Heath to identify ways that would help their students, especially the less successful ones, to learn more effectively (Heath, 1982). First, the teachers tape recorded the kinds of questions they asked in their classrooms and compared them to the kinds of questions children were exposed to in their communities. They discovered that the questions they used in the classroom were requests for labels (for example, "What is that?" about an object in an illustration), were veiled attempts to control or direct behavior ("Is someone not following the rules?" which really means, "Someone better sit down and be quiet"), or were requests for display of book-related knowledge or skill ("Where should I begin reading?"). Many of their children seldom heard such questions in their communities. At home children were asked questions that were like analogies ("What is that like?"), questions that started stories ("What happened to Maggie's dog yesterday?"), and questions that accused them of wrongdoing ("What's that all over your face?") (Heath, 1982, p. 116).

Once teachers realized that their questions were not the kind their students were accustomed to answering, they began planning ways to use different kinds of questions in their instruction. They prepared social studies units based on pictures taken in the children's communities. Teachers asked questions that did not require children to label or name objects in the pictures; rather, they asked questions such as "What is going on here?" and "What is this like?" that were similar to the questions children were familiar with. Only later did teachers ask naming and labeling questions. When the teachers tape recorded the lessons, the children enjoyed listening to the questions and their answers. The tape also provided children with valuable practice in listening to new kinds of questions and their answers.

Developing Culturally Compatible Instruction

The KEEP and questioning projects demonstrate how teachers can alter their ways of instruction and help children develop new ways of interacting in the classroom. There were two characteristics that distinguished these projects. First, teachers researched not only their children's community, but also their own way of teaching. They were willing to make changes in how they conducted lessons in order to support their students' learning. Second, teachers sought methods of helping their children make the transition from community ways of learning to school ways of learning. Teachers not only helped children learn, but they also helped children learn how to learn in school. Both projects were fortunate in having the support of anthropologists who supplied much insight into the communities in which the teachers worked. Not all teachers will have the support of such professionals. Yet, tape recording lessons, visiting community activities, and talking to parents can provide all teachers with valuable information about developing culturally compatible learning activities for their children.

Chapter Summary _____

Young children are unique individuals with their own ways of learning about reading and writing. Yet within the broad areas of development, most children by the end of their early childhood years have similar patterns of growth and achievement, including the acquisition of literacy. These patterns of growth and achievement allow for wide ranges of variation. Some children, who do not follow the patterns of growth and devel- opment followed by the majority of children, present special challenges as well as special joys.

There are three kinds of special- needs children: children with develop- mental or learning differences, children with language differences, and children with cultural differences. The reasons that these children present special needs vary. Special needs of children with de- velopmental or learning differences arise from physical, mental, or psychological conditions that make adaptations for teaching necessary. These children include children with sensory impairments, children with orthopedic impairments, children with severe communication disorders, gifted children, children with non-categorical impairments, children with emotional disabilities, children with learning disabilities, and mentally retarded children.

Special needs of children with different languages and heritages arise from sociopolitical conditions that make adaptations for teaching necessary as well. These children include children whose first language is not English, children who speak with a dialect considered to be nonstandard, and children whose ways of learning and communicating are different from those that teachers may expect. These children present two special needs. The language of instruction in most regular classrooms in the United States is English, in spite of the fact that there are many citizens whose first language is not English. Limited-English-proficiency speakers will need special help in learning English. In addition, children who speak with a dialect considered to be nonstandard or whose ways of communicating are different from those of

teachers may be victims of teachers' unconscious judgments about their academic potential and intellectual abilities. These children will need teachers who are especially sensitive to the ways in which the children's communities shape language and learning.

Teachers who have special-needs children have two priorities. First, they need to help all children, including special-needs children, develop healthy and positive attitudes about themselves and their abilities. Children's literature offers many opportunities to build self-esteem and feelings of self-worth. Second, teachers need to be aware of the special needs of children and effective techniques for supporting the literacy learning of special-needs children. All children, including special-needs children, can benefit from the kinds of instructional activities described in the earlier chapters of this book. This chapter has described some techniques that are effective in supporting special-needs children's learning. These techniques for the most part include active, hands-on experiences where language and literacy are used in meaningful and functional ways. Sharing literature and writing are an important part of all young children's literacy learning, but especially for special-needs children.

Applying the Information _____

Miss Fran, a preschool teacher with 10 three- and four-year-olds, has just found out a new child will be entering her classroom. TJ is nearly four years old. He has spinal bifida and wears cable braces. He uses crutches and is almost toilet trained, although he sometimes has accidents. TJ's special teacher has assured Miss Fran that TJ is a happy, energetic child with enthusiasm for learning. Al-

though his motor skills are still at the two-year-old level, his language development is in the normal range for his age. She feels TJ will benefit from interacting with other children his age. She suggests several procedures to adapt to TJ's needs. Special playground equipment and toys will be borrowed from the special-needs educational center. TJ will wear an apron with large pockets for carrying things (Klein & Sheehan, 1987). She hopes that TJ will be mainstreamed into the local kindergarten in a year and a half. She praises Miss Fran for her reputation of providing children with such a successful foundation for entering school. She knows that TJ, too, will gain from being with Miss Fran.

Help Miss Fran plan literacy activities for TJ. In your description, include plans for preparing the other children for TJ's arrival and for TJ's integration into the classroom.

On the first day of school, Mr. Torrence greeted the children as their parents brought them to his second grade classroom. He recognized many of the students from having seen them on the playground last year. One new student, Amer, caught his attention. Amer's father, Mr. Alzaid, told Mr. Torrence that his son had just arrived from Kuwait last week. He was proud that his son could already read and write in Arabic. He told Mr. Torrence that Amer could speak a little English and he was sure Amer would learn quickly. Mr. Alzaid asked Mr. Torrence to be sure to call home when he could answer because his wife spoke no English.

Mr. Torrence found many opportunities to speak to Amer during the school day. He notified his principal, who called the ESL office at the local school board. The next day Mrs. Flores, the ESL teacher, told Mr. Torrence that she would schedule Amer in her morning English class. Amer would return to Mr. Torrence's classroom in the afternoon. She reminded Mr. Torrence that he, too, would be responsible for Amer's reading and writing and language learning. She warned Mr. Torrence that Amer only knew a very limited amount of English—a few phrases such as "hello," "goodbye," and "how are you?"

Help Mr. Torrence plan language and literacy activities for Amer.

Going Beyond the Text

Visit a preschool or elementary school that has special-needs children. Observe the children in their classroom as they interact with the other children and during literacy activities. Take note of ways that the special-needs children are similar to and different from the other children. If possible, talk to a teacher about supporting the literacy learning of special-needs children. Take at least one reading and one writing activity that you can share with a special-needs child. For example, take a children's book and literature props for the child to retell the story, plan a hands-on experience such as popping corn that will stimulate writing, or prepare a special book that you can give to the child for his or her own journal. Carefully observe the child's language and behaviors during these literacy activities. Be ready to discuss what this child knows about literacy.

References

ABRAHAMSON, R. F., & STEWART, R. (1982). Movable books—a new golden age. *Language Arts, 59,* 342–347.

ACKERMAN, P. T., ANHALT, J. M., & DYKMAN, R. A. (1986). Inferential word-decoding weakness in reading disabled children.

Learning Disability Quarterly, 9, 315–324.

ALLEN, V. (1986). Developing contexts to support second language learning. *Language Arts, 63,* 41–66.

ANDREWS, J. F., & MASON, J. M. (1986). Childhood deafness and the acquisition of print concepts. In D. Yaden Jr. and S. Templeton (Eds.), *Metalinguistic awareness and beginning literacy.* (pp. 277–290). Portsmouth, NH: Heinemann.

AOKI, E. (1981). "Are you Chinese? Or are you just a mixed-up kid?" Using Asian American children's literature. *The Reading Teacher, 34,* 382–385.

AU, K. H., & KAWAKAMI, A. J. (1985). Research currents: Talk story and learning to read. *Language Arts, 62,* 406–411.

BARNITZ, J. G. (1980). Black English and other dialects: Sociolinguistic implications for reading instruction. *The Reading Teacher, 33,* 779–786.

BARTOLI, J. S. (1986). Is it really English for everyone? *Language Arts, 63,* 12–22.

BISHOP, C. H., & WIESE, K. (1938). *The five Chinese brothers.* New York: Coward, McCann and Geoghegan.

BRYEN, D. (1982). *Inquiries into child language.* Boston, MA: Allyn and Bacon.

BULOS, A. V. (1982). Teaching a few ESL students in a regular English class. In C. Carter (Ed.), *Non-native and nonstandard dialect students* (pp. 16–19). Urbana, IL: National Council of Teachers of English.

BURSTEIN, N. D. (1986). The effects of classroom organization on mainstream preschool children. *Exceptional Children, 52,* 425–434.

CARLSEN, J. M. (1985). Between the deaf child and reading: The language connection. *The Reading Teacher, 38,* 424–426.

CASSIDY, J. (1981). Inquiry reading for the gifted. *The Reading Teacher, 35,* 17–21.

CHAMPIE, J. (1981). Language development in one preschool child. *Annals of the Deaf, 126,* 43–48.

CHARLESWORTH, R. (1987). *Understanding child development* (2nd ed.). Albany, NY: Delmar.

CONRAD, R. (1979). *The deaf school child: Language and function.* London: Harper and Row.

COX, C. (1983). Young film-makers speak the language of film. *Language Arts, 60,* 292–304, 372.

CROWL, T. K., & MacGINITIE, W. H. (1974). The influence of students' speech characteristics on teachers' evaluation of oral answers. *Journal of Educational Psychology, 66,* 304–308.

CULLINAN, B. E., JAGGAR, A. M., & STRICKLAND, D. S. (1974). Oral language expansion in the primary grades. In B. E. Cullinan (Ed.), *Black dialects and reading* (pp. 43–54). Urbana, IL: National Council of Teachers of English.

D'ALESSANDRO, M. E. (1987). "The ones who always get the blame": Emotionally handicapped children writing. *Language Arts, 64,* 516–522.

De PAOLA, T. (1975). *Strega Nona.* Englewood Cliffs, NJ: Prentice-Hall.

DIXON, R. (1987). Strategies for vocabulary instruction. *Teaching Exceptional Children, 19,* 61–63.

DOBO, P. J. (1982). Using literature to change attitudes toward the handicapped. *The Reading Teacher, 36,* 290–292.

DOWHOWER, S. L. (1989). Repeated reading: Research into practice. *The Reading Teacher, 42,* 502–507.

ENGEL, R. (1980). Understanding the handicapped through literature. *Young Children, 32,* 26–32.

FEDERAL REGISTER (Vol. 42). (1977, August 23). Washington, DC: Department of Health, Education and Welfare.

FEELEY, J. T. (1983). Help for the reading teacher: Dealing with the Limited English Proficient (LEP) child in the elementary classroom. *The Reading Teacher, 36,* 650–655.

FLATLEY, J. K., & RUTLAND, A. D. (1986). Using wordless picture books to teach linguistically/culturally different students. *The Reading Teacher, 40,* 276–281.

GALDONE, P. (1976). *The magic porridge pot.* New York: Seabury Press.

GALLAGER, J. J. (1986). The need for programs for young gifted children. *Topics in Early Childhood Special Education, 6,* 1–8.

GEISSAL, M. A., & KNAFLE, J. D. (1977). A linguistic view of auditory discrimination tests and exercises. *The Reading Teacher, 30,* 134–141.

GENISHI, C., & DYSON, A. H. (1984). *Language assessment in the early years.* Norwood, NJ: Ablex.

GILLET, J. W., & GENTRY, J. R. (1983). Bridges between nonstandard and standard English with extensions of dictated stories. *The Reading Teacher, 36,* 360–364.

GREENE, J. E. (1985). Children's writing in an elementary school postal system. In M. Farr (Ed.), *Advances in writing research, volume one* (pp. 201–296). Norwood, NJ: Ablex.

HEATH, S. B. (1982). Questioning at home and at school: A comparative study. In G. Spindler (Ed.), *Doing the ethnography of schooling: Educational anthropology in action* (pp. 102–131). New York: Holt, Rinehart and Winston.

HIRSH-PASEK, K. (1987). The meta-linguistics of fingerspelling: An alternative way to increase reading vocabulary in congenitally deaf readers. *Reading Research Quarterly, 22,* 455–474.

HOSKISSON, K., & TOMPKINS, G. E. (1987). *Language arts: Content and teaching strategies.* Columbus, OH: Merrill.

HOUGH, R. A., NURSS, J. R., & ENRIGHT, D. S. (1986). Story reading with limited English speaking children in the regular classroom. *The Reading Teacher, 39,* 510–514.

HUDELSON, S. (1987). The role of native language literacy in the education of language minority children. *Language Arts, 64,* 827–841.

HUDELSON, S., & BARRERA, R. (1985). Bilingual/second-language learners and reading. In L. W. Searfoss & J. E. Readence, *Helping children learn to read* (pp. 370–392). Englewood Cliffs, NJ: Prentice-Hall.

JAGGAR, A. M. (1974). Beginning reading: Let's make it a language experience for Black English speakers. In B. E. Cullinan (Ed.), *Black dialects and reading* (pp. 87–98). Urbana, IL: National Council of Teachers of English.

KLEIN, N., & SHEEHAN, R. (1987). Staff development: A key issue in meeting the needs of young handicapped children in day care settings. *Topics in Early Childhood Special Education, 7,* 13–27.

KOENIG, M. (1977). *The tale of fancy Nancy.* London: Catto and Windus.

LABOV, W. A. (1966). *The social stratification of English in New York City.* Washington, DC: Center for Applied Linguistics.

LARA, S. G. M. (1989). Reading placement for code switchers. *The Reading Teacher, 42,* 278–282.

Learning Disabilities: Issues on Definition (1983). *Learning Disability Quarterly, 6,* 42–44.

LERNER, J. (1985). *Learning disabilities: Theories, diagnosis, and teaching strategies* (4th ed). Boston, MA: Houghton Mifflin.

MAKER, C. J. (1986). Suggested principles for gifted preschool curriculum. *Topics in Early Childhood Special Education, 6,* 62–73.

MANSON, M. (1982). Explorations in language arts for preschoolers (who happen to be deaf). *Language Arts, 59,* 33–39, 45.

MAYER, M. (1988). *There's something in my attic.* New York: Dial.

McGEE, L. M. (1985). Techniques for teaching blind children to read. In L. Eldridge (Ed.), *R is for reading* (129–133). Washington, DC: Library Service to Blind and Physically Handicapped Children.

McGEE, L. M., & RATLIFF, J. (1987). Using the VCR in the language arts. In C. R. Personke & D. Johnson (Eds.), *Language arts instruction and the beginning teacher: A practical guide* (pp. 208–216). Englewood Cliffs, NJ: Prentice-Hall.

McGEE, L. M., & TOMPKINS, G. E. (1982). Concepts about print for the young blind child. *Language Arts, 59,* 40–45.

McGILL-FRANZEN, A. (1987). Failure to learn to read: Formulating a policy problem. *Reading Research Quarterly, 22,* 475–490.

MEIER, T. R., & CAZDEN, C. B. (1982). Research update: A focus on oral language and writing from a multicultural perspective. *Language Arts, 59,* 504–512.

MOLL, L. C. (1988). Some key issues in teaching Latino students. *Language Arts, 65,* 465–472.

MOUSTAFA, M. (1980). Picture books for oral language development for non-English speaking children: A bibliography, *The Reading Teacher, 33,* 914–919.

MOUSTAFA, M., & PENROSE, J. (1985). Comprehensible input PLUS, the language experience approach: Reading instruction for limited English speaking students. *The Reading Teacher, 38,* 640–647.

NORRIS, J. A. (1988). Using communication strategies to enhance reading acquisition. *The Reading Teacher, 41,* 668–673.

OGBU, J. U. (1985). Research currents: Culture-ecological influences on minority school learning. *Language Arts, 62,* 860–869.

ORTIZ, L., & ENGELBRECHT, G. (1986). Partners in biliteracy: The school and the community. *Language Arts, 63,* 458–465.

O'SHEA, L., & O'SHEA, D. (1987). Using repeated reading. *Teaching Exceptional Children, 20,* 26–29.

PADAK, N. D. (1981). The language and educational needs of children who speak Black English. *The Reading Teacher, 35,* 144–151.

RODRIGUES, R. I., & WHITE, R. H. (1981). *Mainstreaming the non-English speaking student.* Urbana, IL: ERIC Clearinghouse on Reading and Communication Skills and the National Council of Teachers of English.

SCHON, I. (1985). Remarkable books in Spanish for young readers. *The Reading Teacher, 38,* 668–670.

SCHOOL, G. T. (1987). Appropriate education for visually handicapped students. *Teaching Exceptional Students, 19,* 32–36.

SIMMS, R. (1982). Dialect and reading: Toward redefining the issues. In J. A. Langer & M. T. Smith-Burke (Eds.), *Reader meets author/Bridging the gap* (pp. 222–236). Newark, DE: International Reading Association.

SINATRA, R. (1981). Using visuals to help the second language learner. *The Reading Teacher, 34,* 539–546.

SINDELAR, P. T. (1987). Increasing reading fluency. *Teaching Exceptional Children, 19,* 59–60.

SMITHERMAN, G. (1977). *Talkin and testifying: The language of black America.* Boston. Houghton Mifflin.

SMITHERMAN, G. (1985). "What go round come round": *King* in perspective. In C. K. Brooks (Ed.), *Tapping potential: English and language arts for the black learner* (41–62). Urbana, IL: National Council of Teachers of English.

TESOL NEWSLETTER. (1984). Vol. 18 p. 1.

TOMPKINS, G. E., & FRIEND, M. (1986). On your mark, get set, write! *Teaching Exceptional Children, 18,* 82–89.

TURNER, D. T. (1985). Black students, language, and classroom teachers. In C. K. Brooks (Ed.), *Tapping potential: English and language arts for the black learner* (pp. 30–40). Urbana, IL: National Council of Teachers of English.

URZUA, C. (1980). Doing what comes naturally: Recent research in second language acquisition. In G. S. Pinnell (Ed.), *Discovering language with children* (pp. 33–38). Urbana, IL: National Council of Teachers of English.

URZUA, C. (1987). "You stopped too soon": Second language children composing and revising. *TESOL Quarterly, 21,* 279–304.

WARD, M., & McCORMICK, S. (1981). Reading instruction for blind and low vision children in the regular classroom. *The Reading Teacher, 34,* 434–444.

WOLFRAM, W. A. (1970). Nature of nonstandard dialect divergence. *Elementary English, 41,* 739–748.

YASHIMA, T. (1958). *Umbrella.* New York: Viking.

Name Index

Subject Index